THE BLUE GUIDES

Countries **Austria**
Belgium and Luxembourg
Channel Islands
China
Corsica
Crete
Cyprus
Czech
Denma
Egypt
Englan
France
France: Burgundy
Western Germany
Greece
Holland
Hungary
Ireland
Northern Italy
Southern Italy
Malta and Gozo
Morocco
Portugal
Scotland
Sicily
Spain
Switzerland
Turkey: the Aegean and Mediterranean Coasts
Wales
Yugoslavia

Cities **Athens and Environs**
Barcelona
Boston and Cambridge
Florence
Istanbul
Jerusalem
London
Moscow and Leningrad
New York
Oxford and Cambridge
Paris and Versailles
Rome and Environs
Venice

Themes **Churches and Chapels of Northern England**
Churches and Chapels of Southern England
Gardens of England
Literary Britain and Ireland
Museums and Galleries of London
Victorian Architecture in Britain

Østerlars Church is the best known of the Bornholm round churches. Photo: Lennard

BLUE GUIDE

DENMARK

W. Glyn Jones and Kirsten Gade

Maps and plans by John Flower

A & C Black
London

WW Norton
New York

First edition 1992

Published by A & C Black (Publishers) Limited
35 Bedford Row, London WC1R 4JH

© A & C Black (Publishers) Limited 1992

ISBN 0–7136–3474–X

A CIP catalogue record for this book
is available from the British Library

Published in the United States of America by
WW Norton & Company, Incorporated
500 Fifth Avenue, New York NY 10110

Published simultaneously in Canada by
Penguin Books Canada Limited
2801 John Street, Markham, Ontario L3R 1B4

ISBN 0–393–30839–1   USA

Printed and bound in Great Britain by
William Clowes Limited, Beccles and London

The publishers and the authors have done their best to ensure the accuracy of all the information in Blue Guide Denmark; however, they can accept no responsibility for any loss, injury or inconvenience sustained by any traveller as a result of information or advice contained in the guide.

Please write in with your comments, suggestions and corrections. Writers of the best letters will be awarded a free Blue Guide of their choice.

Kirsten Gade trained as a teacher in Copenhagen and worked for many years for the Greenland Education Service. She has taught Danish language at the universities of Newcastle upon Tyne and East Anglia. Her publications include Danish textbooks, childrens' books, and, with Glyn Jones, *Danish. A Grammar*.

W. Glyn Jones was educated at Cambridge and Århus and has taught at universities in England, Iceland and the Faroe Islands. He is now Professor of European Literature at the University of East Anglia. His publications include, in addition to numerous translations, a series of critical studies: *Johannes Jørgensens modne år*, *Johannes Jørgensen*, *William Heinesen*, *Færø og Kosmos*, *Tove Jansson*, *Denmark. A Modern History*, *Georg Brandes. Selected Letters*, and, with Kirsten Gade, *Danish. A Grammar*.

CONTENTS

Maps and Plans

Atlas *at the back of the book*

Town Plans

Ground Plans

ACKNOWLEDGEMENTS

The authors would like to express their thanks to the many people who have helped in the writing of this book. In particular, we thank the Danish Tourist organisations: the Danish Tourist Board's London office, the members of its headquarters in Copenhagen, and the many representatives of individual tourist offices throughout Denmark, whose help in some cases has been quite outstanding. For photographs we are again indebted to the Danish Tourist Board and to individual Tourist Association offices. We are grateful to the DFDS shipping company for travel facilities, and to representatives of many Danish museums, churches and historical buildings for their courteous assistance. Last, but by no means least, we thank Gemma Davies of A & C Black for her unfailing help, advice, patience—and good humour.

KGJ. WGJ.

A NOTE ON BLUE GUIDES

The Blue Guides series began in 1915 when Muirhead Guide-Books Limited published 'Blue Guide London and its Environs'. Finlay and James Muirhead already had extensive experience of guide-book publishing: before the First World War they had been the editors of the English editions of the German Baedekers, and by 1915 they had acquired the copyright of most of the famous 'Red' handbooks from John Murray.

An agreement made with the French publishing house Hachette et Cie in 1917 led to the translation of Muirhead's London Guide, which became the first 'Guide Bleu'—Hachette had previously published the blue-covered 'Guides Joanne'. Subsequently, Hachette's 'Guide Bleu Paris et ses Environs' was adapted and published in London by Muirhead. The collaboration between the two publishing houses continued until 1933.

In 1931 Ernest Benn took over the Blue Guides, appointing Russell Muirhead, Finlay Muirhead's son, editor in 1934. The Muirheads' connection with Blue Guides ended in 1963 when Stuart Rossiter, who had been working on the Guides since 1954, became house editor, revising and compiling several of the books himself.

The Blue Guides are now published by A & C Black, who acquired Ernest Benn in 1984, so continuing the tradition of guide-book publishing which began in 1826 with 'Black's Economical Tourist of Scotland'. The Blue Guide series continues to grow: there are now more than 40 titles in print with revised editions appearing regularly and many new Blue Guides in preparation.

'Blue Guides' is a registered trade mark.

INTRODUCTION

Denmark consists of the peninsula of Jutland (Jylland) and some 400 islands, of which 97 are inhabited. Some of these islands are very small indeed. The total area of Denmark is c 43,069 sq km, 29,766 of these being in Jutland, the remainder in the islands. The largest island is Sjælland (7015 sq km), then comes Fyn (2984 sq km), Lolland (1234 sq km), Bornholm (588 sq km) and Falster (514 sq km).

The total population of Denmark is now c 5,500,000 of whom some 1.4 million live in the Copenhagen area. Some 250,000 live in Greater Århus, 155,000 in Greater Ålborg and 172,000 in Greater Odense.

Denmark's only land frontier is with Germany and is no more than 68km long. On the other hand, thanks to its many islands, Denmark's coastline is vast in relation to the land mass, covering 7300km in all. This particular geographical nature has had far-reaching historical implications, and these days it provides a host of splendid beaches for the holiday-maker.

The most northerly point is Skagen, at 57° 45′ N, the most southerly at Gedser, 54° 34′ N. Situated in this northerly position, Denmark has days which reach 17½ hours at mid-summer and only 7 hours in mid-winter. In mid-summer there is, in Denmark, no midnight sun, but there are what are known as 'light nights', when there is a bright sheen to the sky, a kind of lucent twilight. The summers are seldom inordinately hot: the mean temperature in July is 16.6°C, and the temperature rarely exceeds 25°C. Winters, on the other hand, are rarely terribly cold, though temperatures can, and do, drop as low as –20°C for short periods. When this happens, the sea freezes, and ice breakers can be needed to keep shipping lanes clear. On rare occasions the temperature has dropped even further; the lowest air temperature recorded was –31°C in 1940, but it must have been at least as low as that when the Great Belt froze over in the 17C sufficient for the Swedes to march an army across it!

By its very position, linked to Germany, but with a Scandinavian culture and language, Denmark forms a natural link between mainland Europe and mainland Scandinavia. Travellers from further north have been known to say that on travelling south they feel that they are 'in Europe' when they come to Copenhagen, and that on going home, they feel they are in Scandinavia when they reach the Danish border. In feel, Denmark is without doubt more 'Continental' than the other Scandinavian countries, more outgoing, some would say more relaxed.

There are no mountains in Denmark, the highest point being some 171m at Møllehøj in Jutland (though the nearby Yding Skovhøj reaches 173m if you include the burial mound at the top). Instead, the countryside is typically glacial moraine deposits, which have provided a rolling countryside, admirably suited for farming. In the south, particularly on the islands of Lolland and Falster, the countryside is very flat indeed. There are no large rivers, but on the other hand there are several sizeable lakes, of which Arresø is 40.6 sq km.

Denmark was once, like all Scandinavia, covered by forest, but this began to disappear at an early stage of settlement, and by now there is little real forest left. However, there are large forests still at Gribskov in North Sjælland, and Rold Skov in Jutland. Jutland, too, is renowned for its heath, and was predominantly moorland a century ago. Now only a few stretches are left, the remainder having come under cultivation. On the other hand West Jutland is characterised by a large number of fir trees, while East Jutland and the islands tend rather to deciduous varieties, in particular the beech, which is almost a national symbol.

Until the mid-twentieth century Denmark was predominantly an agricultural country, and intensive farming obviously still plays an important part in the economy. There are relatively few hedgerows, and fields tend to be open, divided by fences. On the other hand, only about ten per cent of the population are now employed in agriculture, the remainder being in industry or the service sector.

If one were to try to characterise the impression Denmark is likely to make on the visitor, it is probably one of idyll rather than of splendour. Fyn, in particular, is often referred to as the garden of Denmark, with beautiful, well-tended cottages and delightful villages. Jutland, on the other hand, can provide great sweeps of countryside, wide views across forest-lined fjords, while many parts of Sjælland have wooded, rolling countryside of great charm. In general, a friendly, inviting country, easy to get around in whether by public transport or by car, with an endless store of archaeological and historical remains as well as all the facilities demanded by a modern visitor.

BACKGROUND INFORMATION

History

The story of Denmark is that of a territorially small country which, once it was organised as a unity, came to play a dominant role in northern European history. Placed at the crossroads of trade north and south and east and west, and always at least partly in control of the entrance to the Baltic, it is a country which has had an importance far in excess of its size. For a period it led the Kalmar Union, that union of the northern countries which was in fact the largest unified kingdom in Europe, comprising not merely Denmark, Norway and Sweden, but Finland to the east and Iceland and Greenland to the west and north. Even when the Union was dissolved, Denmark retained the whole of Norway and the Swedish Sound Provinces, the southernmost of which, Skåne (Scania), remained loyal to Denmark for centuries. To the south Denmark was long in at least partial control of what is now northern Germany as far south as Hamburg, and the North German coast has also known Danish rule. Yet her undoubted expansionist dreams in the early period brought their reactions, and Denmark had to relinquish her Baltic domains to Sweden and subsequently her southern duchies to Germany, becoming for a period at the end of the 19C even smaller than she is today.

The expansionist dream came with the Vikings. By 878 the Danelaw (those parts of Anglo-Saxon England subject to Danish rule) was established, and by 1033 all England was under the Vikings. The year 911 saw the Viking Rollo in possession of Normandy as the first Duke after his warriors had laid waste to the land around the Seine. Just how many of these Vikings came from Denmark, it is difficult to say, as the English tended to call them all Danes, whether they came from Denmark or Norway, while the French tended to call them all Norsemen. There was little to distinguish them from each other.

Yet these Vikings were strikingly receptive to foreign cultures wherever they established themselves. Celtic influence can be traced in early Norse literature and in the carvings and metalwork of the Viking Age. In England, where they found a people with whom they were distantly related, and with whom they could communicate to a certain extent in their own language, they were gradually assimilated into the population. In Normandy the same assimilation took place, and the military skills of the Vikings were duly responsible for the superiority of the Norman warriors who invaded England in 1066. In religious matters, too, the Vikings were tolerant of a different culture and receptive to it, even if the ancient Norse religion left its mark on popular superstition for centuries after the conversion of the North.

While the Vikings were thus ravaging far and wide, the population at home was gradually fashioning Denmark in the shape she was to have for centuries. The southern frontier with Germany was still vague, but it stretched roughly to the Ejder—a fact that was to have repercussions in the 19C Schleswig-Holstein problem—while the sea formed a natural boundary between Denmark and the other Nordic lands. The people were farmers, and by about 1250 they had settled the entire country and founded the villages which to this day are the basis of Danish rural society.

Independent farmers had either to pay taxes to the king or to provide him with military forces. While the smaller ones chose to pay tax, the wealthier and more powerful preferred to provide the military assistance. Consequently, a new class emerged who expected and received privileges from the king, and on whose support the king could rely to strengthen his own position in the country. This brought about a close relationship between the king and an incipient nobility at a time when the king was trying to centralise power. In time, however, as the nobles themselves sought to consolidate their rights, the resultant split between them and their monarchs was to have far-reaching consequences. It must be remembered in this connection that the kings of Denmark were elective monarchs, and although it was customary to choose the new king from among the sons of the previous one, it was by no means an unbreakable rule.

Another source of increasing power in the 11C was the Church. The first attempt at converting Denmark to Christianity was made by the Anglo-Saxon bishop Willibrordus around the year 700. He went to Denmark and was received by an early king, Angenthjor, whom however he did not succeed in converting. It was then another hundred years before a concerted effort was made to overcome paganism in Denmark. The first step was taken by the Emperor Louis the Pious who sent the Archbishop of Reims, Ebo, to Denmark with the aim of converting the people. In 826 an early King Harald, together with a following of about 400, was baptised, and it looked as though Christianity was about to assert itself over the country of which Harald was king. It was not, however, until the baptism of Harald Bluetooth in 960 that the Church can really be said to have thoroughly established itself on Danish territory, and only then did the pagans begin to lose ground rapidly. The conquest of England in the following century even further strengthened the influence of the Church in Denmark, for it must be remembered that England had long been Christian, and although politically dominated by Denmark, was herself able to exert a significant cultural influence.

Even so, the Church was by no means an established Church. It fell to King Knud (Canute) II (St Knud) and his next successor but one, King Erik Ejegod (Erik the Kind-Hearted), finally to establish it in all its power and independence. Knud, under the influence of Cluniac Christianity and Pope Gregory VII, did much to liberate the Church from the legal authority of the state, and he also sought to introduce tithes and enforce celibacy, but he succeeded in neither of these objectives. His piety stood in some contrast to his treatment of his subjects, and finally, after an attempt to launch a new Viking expedition to England in 1086, the Jutland peasantry rebelled. Knud fled, but was caught and murdered in Odense. Nine years later Erik was elected king, and he succeeded in freeing the Church in the North from the archbishopric of Hamburg. A new archbishopric was created in Lund in Skåne, which was at that time Danish territory, and in 1104 Asser was made Archbishop of Lund and thereby Primate of the North. With his appointment the temporal authorities saw the possibility of greater political independence from the German states. As a further gesture of the close relationship between Church and Crown, the king now managed to introduce a system of tithes which made the Church financially independent and enabled it to increase its influence. A further result of this new and regular influx of wealth to the Church was that it was now possible to build churches in stone instead of wood as hitherto, and so permanent buildings, many of them still at least partially extant, were erected, not least among which were the great cathedrals.

The Age of the Valdemars and Danish Expansion. King Erik had been a strong and determined monarch. He was succeeded by a weaker man, and for a generation the country was plunged into a series of civil wars, as kings fought against pretenders, and the throne became an object of dispute. It was not until 1157 that true stability was brought to the country with the acceptance as king of Valdemar I, and the period of growth and power, known as the Age of the Valdemars, began. It lasted from the accession of Valdemar I, Valdemar the Great, to the death of Valdemar II, Valdemar the Victorious, in 1241, and alongside the kings the central figures in this age of glory were the three archbishops of Lund—Eskil, Absalon (the founder of Copenhagen) and Anders Sunesøn.

When Valdemar I came to the throne, Denmark was weak, ravaged by the civil wars of the past decades, and overshadowed by Germany. Like his predecessors, Valdemar had to acknowledge the Holy Roman Emperor as his overlord, but he began to turn this dependence to his own advantage. During the period of weakness, the Wends, the Slavic peoples of the Baltic, had taken the opportunity of ravaging the Danish coasts and plundering the villages. Valdemar set about putting an end to this. To do so he needed the help of the Saxons, who were also enemies of the Wends. His armies supported theirs and took a small share of the booty, until they were powerful enough to conquer the Wendic stronghold of Rügen on their own.

Denmark was gradually fortified and began to assert herself as a power to be reckoned with both in Scandinavia and in the Baltic as a whole. Yet Valdemar had other plans which were equally ambitious and equally important to the country's internal affairs. So far the monarch had been elective, and the main voice in choosing the new king had been that of the people expressing themselves in *things*—the ancient Nordic gatherings of the people where laws were formulated and recited, and lawsuits heard. Valdemar wanted to strengthen the monarchy and make it independent, and between 1165 and 1170 he succeeded in his aim. In this he had the full support of Archbishop Eskil. No longer was kingship to be the gift of the people; it was to be bestowed by the Church instead. Although in theory the *things* continued to influence the choice of king, in practice hereditary monarchy was introduced. It was still not absolute monarchy, and until the 17C it became the practice for each elected king to sign a charter limiting his powers. But in effect the system was in full flower, the monarchy strong internally as well as externally.

It enjoyed, moreover, the powerful support of the Church. When, as an old man, Eskil was forced to resign his archbishopric, the obvious choice as his successor was Absalon, who had so far been Bishop of Roskilde and Valdemar's right-hand man. Absalon was not merely a zealous churchman, but a first-class organiser and military mind, and he was bent on centralising power in Denmark and diminishing the influence of the various regions. When Valdemar died in 1182 and was succeeded by his son Knud, Absalon was able to continue the policies of Valdemar for the next two decades. It is Absalon who fuses the reigns of the two Valdemars into one glorious age.

His policy was one of expansion, and while Valdemar I, coming to the throne at a time of weakness, was forced to acknowledge the Emperor, Knud refused to do so. This refusal led to war, but Denmark was now strong, and gradually took possession of Mecklenburg and Pomerania as well as the territory as far south as the Elbe, including Lübeck. The most important trade centres in the north of Europe were thus under Danish rule. Only one year after Absalon's death, Knud was succeeded in 1202 by Valdemar II, and the expansionist policy continued. By 1219 Denmark possessed the whole Baltic coast as far as the eastern boundary of Estonia. But Valdemar had gone too far. In 1223 he was taken prisoner by Count Henrik of Schwerin, and before he was released Denmark had to give up most of her Baltic possessions, while the southern boundary was drawn at the Ejder. Even here the seeds of future trouble were already sown, as the population in the area was no longer purely Danish. It contained many Saxons who had moved in from Holstein when Denmark was in possession there, and their presence was to be felt again in the 19C with the Schleswig-Holstein problem.

Instead of external expansion, Valdemar II now worked for internal growth, and his reign saw profound internal changes in the country's administration. The legislative power, which hitherto had been with the *things*, passed more and more into the king's hands, as was made plain by his giving the people the Jutland Law of 1241. It was a law of good government, and it codified what in fact had been traditional law before this time. It is perfectly plain that the country was now unified both administratively and legally, and that a change was taking place from a primitive society to one which was sophisticated for the Middle Ages. A community based on the three estates was emerging, and as a whole it was a community which could equal those of other European countries, with a literature, the ballads, and a culture of its own, a country with the ability to build and to fashion an architecture distinct from that of other countries.

The following period, until c 1300, was one of economic growth. Skåne became a great trade centre, with the resultant appearance of a wealthy merchant class. Towns were established, and with the development of new skills the craft and trade guilds emerged. In the country districts life was less good, and the number of independent farmers fell from about 50 per cent of the total about 1250 to between 10 per cent and 12 per cent around 1400, the remainder having sacrificed their freedom for the protection of the wealthier nobility. By 1350 the system which was to last until the 18C was beginning to take shape.

Politically these were troubled times. Valdemar II made his sons dukes in various parts of the country, and they quarrelled as to the succession and their rights under the new king, Erik Plovpenning (Erik Ploughpenny). Under these conditions Schleswig acquired a degree of independence not enjoyed by any other part of the country. Duke Abel of Schleswig, one of Erik Plovpenning's brothers, fought for the independence of his duchy, and finally, with the support of the counts of Holstein—still completely independent of Denmark—murdered his brother and was made King of Denmark. Two years later he fell in battle, and although he left two sons, the Danes chose another of Valdemar II's sons as Christoffer I. Abel's sons could do little in face of this, but they did manage to secure the semi-independence of Schleswig. Schleswig drifted closer to Holstein, and when in 1460 King Christian I of Denmark was elected Duke of Schleswig and of Holstein against a promise never to divide the duchies, the seeds of the 19C conflict were planted deep.

Meanwhile, after the death of Valdemar II, the Danish nobles saw a chance of increasing their power, and a struggle developed between them and the Crown. The nobles won, but they brought untold trouble to the country as a whole. In order to maintain power, and in an attempt to put down a rebellion in Jutland and Fyn, Christoffer II had to pawn large areas of the country. Holstein was in virtual control of

Jutland, having taken it as a pledge for a sum of money which Christoffer had no hope of raising. Another Holstein count, Johan, was in control of Sjælland and Skåne. For a time it even seemed possible that Denmark might cease to be a unified state, and for eight years after the death of Christoffer II, the country was without a king.

Yet his son, almost symbolically named Valdemar, was to succeed in reuniting the country. In 1340 the Holstein Count Gert was murdered in Jutland. The Danish nobility, disunited as they were, saw their only hope in the re-establishment of a strong monarchy, and negotiations led to the election of the son of the former king, with the task of freeing the country from foreign domination.

No one could have been better suited to this. Valdemar IV was strong and determined, and these qualities he combined with shrewdness and ruthlessness. Within 20 years he had reunited the country and restored its total independence. As had happened before, however, a king went too far. In 1361 Valdemar attacked the Swedish island of Gotland and won it, but this move was to lead to his downfall. Sweden, Holstein, Schleswig and, most important, the Hanseatic League joined forces against him. Peace was bought, but only at a price. The Peace of Stralsund (1370) gave the Hansa a number of outposts in Skåne and the right to trade there for 15 years.

The Kalmar Union. In 1375 Valdemar died and was succeeded by his five-year-old grandson Oluf, the son of his daughter Margrethe. Oluf's father, King Haakon VI of Norway, died five years later, and Oluf automatically succeeded to the Norwegian throne, thus uniting the two kingdoms.

During Oluf's infancy, his mother ruled in his place, and when Oluf died in 1387, she was chosen as queen in her own right. Thanks to internal strife in Sweden, Margrethe was invited to become Queen of Sweden as well, and so by 1389 the whole of Scandinavia was united under her rule. To ensure the continuance of the union, Margrethe had her nephew, Erik of Pomerania, crowned King of the North in 1397, at which time she also executed a formal document of union, known as the Kalmar Union. Despite complaints that Margrethe, herself a Dane, showed too many favours to the Danes, she managed to maintain the union, but Erik of Pomerania was less successful, and finally lost his throne in 1439. This was not, however, before he had carried out important economic reforms within Denmark. In order to increase the wealth of the towns, he insisted that much foreign trade should go through Danish merchants instead of direct from Hanseatic merchants to his subjects. He also introduced a toll on ships passing Helsingør (Elsinore), and thus 1429 saw the start of the Sound Dues which were to be a bone of contention in later centuries.

The Union outlasted King Erik, but it fell apart under Christian II, who sought to crush opposition to his rule in Sweden. In 1520 he had himself crowned in Stockholm, celebrating the occasion by summoning the flower of the Swedish nobility to Stockholm Castle. He arrested them on charges of heresy and had 82 of them executed, after which he carried out a series of bloody reprisals against opponents in the Swedish provinces. The result was a full-scale rebellion which led to the end of the Union.

Christian's policies made him enemies not only in Sweden, but also in Lübeck, while the Danish nobility felt itself threatened. In August 1522 a Lübeck fleet sailed against Denmark, to be joined by ships from Danzig and other Hanseatic cities. This action coincided with unrest in Jutland, where one of the king's sheriffs had been murdered. The king repaid in kind, burning the city of Ålborg where the murder had taken place. By the end of the year a group of Jutlandic noblemen came together in a conspiracy aimed at bringing down Christian, and in January 1523 they renounced their oath of allegiance to him. By 13 April Christian had fled to Holland, and in his place Duke Frederik of Gottorp, who had supported the rebellion, was proclaimed King Frederik I.

There was more, however, to the discontent in the country than mere political oppression. Already in the final years of Christian II's reign, the first signs of the Reformation had appeared in Denmark, and Christian had shown some sympathy for the Lutheran cause. He aimed, however, at reforming the Church from within, not bringing about a break with Rome. When Frederik I came to the throne, he sought to avoid taking sides; a Catholic himself, he made it his aim to be neutral and to allow the Lutherans a certain freedom, even going so far as to give protection to the leading Reformer, Hans Tavsen. In adopting this stance he avoided giving offence to the Emperor at the same time as gaining the favour of the Danes many of whom supported the Lutheran cause.

And popular support was just what he needed, for Christian II was making an attempt at a comeback. He landed an army in Norway, and was now invited to Denmark under safe conduct. He accepted the invitation, was arrested and kept prisoner for the rest of his life, at first in Sønderborg and later in Kalundborg. This was 1532.

Frederik I died in 1533, and his likely successor was the zealous Protestant Duke Christian, to whom there was considerable resistance from the still Catholic nobility. An attempt was now made to reinstate Christian II, with the help of a Lübeck army led by Count Christoffer of Oldenborg, from whom the resultant civil war has received the name of The Count's War. This army occupied Sjælland and Fyn, but was then opposed by the Jutlandic nobility who supported Duke Christian. At the same time, in opposition to him, a peasant revolt was organised in North Jutland under the leadership of Skipper Klement. This was put down with great brutality in 1534 by the Holstein Johan Rantzau, who then proceeded to defeat the Lübeck army at Øksnebjerg in Fyn in 1535. Christian III was finally proclaimed king. He then imprisoned all the Catholic bishops and in 1536 established Lutheranism as the Danish state religion.

Rivalry between Denmark and Sweden. During the following century Denmark became preoccupied with more worldly matters. Trade prospered, and thanks to rising prices and plentiful supplies of money in South Europe, Denmark succeeded in exporting more corn than ever before. Later, under Christian IV, there was to be a period of veritable mercantilism with the establishment of an East Indies Company based on a small colony which Denmark founded in Tranquebar.

Meanwhile, as Skåne still belonged to Denmark, Denmark was in total control of the entrance to the Baltic, deriving considerable profits from the tolls exacted from all ships entering and leaving. Sweden decided to try to put an end to this. The result was a series of wars between the two countries, spread over the greater part of a century. First, there was the Nordic Seven Years' War (1563–70), which led to enormous devastation and brought about little change. Then, Sweden turned on Russia and gradually acquired the entire eastern Baltic, as far as Estonia, gradually extending its dominions until Sweden bordered on Denmark to the south as well as to the north. Christian IV tried to bring this to an end by entering the Thirty Years' War and securing the north coast of Germany. The episode, which lasted from 1625 to 1629, led to a resounding defeat and the occupation of Jutland by Wallenstein's forces, until the Danes made a promise not to take any further part in the war.

It was then Sweden's turn, and Swedish soldiers under Gustav II Adolf joined the Protestant North Germans and helped to decide the outcome of the war in the North. From the Swedish point of view, however, mastery of the Baltic was of paramount importance. Having established themselves there, the Swedes, infuriated by continued Danish opposition, followed Wallenstein's example and occupied Jutland. By the resultant Treaty of Brömsebro in 1645, Sweden acquired some of the Danish provinces in the north of the Sound, and also ensured freedom from Sound Dues both for the Swedish mainland and for all Swedish possessions in the Baltic.

The next stage in the struggle between Denmark and Sweden came in 1657 when Sweden was fighting a nationalist uprising in Poland. Denmark, now under Frederik III, saw the chance of revenge and declared war on the Swedes. The Swedes immediately occupied Jutland, while the Danes withdrew to Fyn, where they appeared to be safe. Then the unforeseeable happened. In the extremely harsh winter of that year the water between Jutland and Fyn and between Fyn and Sjælland, froze over to enable the Swedish army to cross the ice on foot and thus make for Copenhagen. By the terms of the Treaty of Roskilde, Denmark had to give up her possessions north of the Sound, and Sweden acquired the entire coastline south of the Norwegian border. Peace seemed to be restored, and Denmark humiliated, but Sweden did not trust her southern neighbour to keep out of the war still being waged in North Germany, and consequently broke the treaty within months by invading Sjælland without warning, with the object of taking over the whole of the country.

This was too much for the Dutch. Little as they had liked the Danish mastery of the Sound, they did not relish the prospect of Swedish domination either, and they sent a fleet to the relief of Copenhagen, which had withstood a lengthy siege. Sweden was forced to sue for peace. The 1660 Treaty of Copenhagen acknowledged that Sweden had been defeated, but did not give back to Denmark all the provinces that Sweden had taken after the Treaty of Roskilde. In particular, Sweden was allowed to keep the Sound provinces, whereby that country took on something like its present shape.

The Establishment of the Absolute Monarchy. Despite the cost of the many wars, the end of the 17C was one of economic growth, symbolised especially by the architectural glories of the age of Christian IV. Not everyone benefited from the economic changes, and the less affluent rural population became yet less affluent and were subject to exploitation by the increasingly rich and demanding landowners. On the other hand, the towns did benefit, not only directly from improved trade patterns, but also because it became the policy of Christian IV to give state support to trade both at home and abroad. An increasingly influential middle class appeared, and the period saw the emergence of a Copenhagen bourgeoisie which was to play an important part in establishing the absolute monarchy when the final struggle between the Crown and the nobility got under way.

Since the rise of the nobility as a political power, with the privilege of forcing a charter upon each king before allowing him to take the throne, there had been an obvious source of strain between them and the king. In practice the nobles had not been as strong as the theory might suggest, but no king was happy at having his power limited by them. Nevertheless, each king had been to a great extent militarily dependent on the nobility. In times of war he looked to the nobles to provide his armed forces, and in return they were given widespread privileges. Things changed in the 17C. The wider use of firearms made the king less dependent on the foot-soldiers whom the nobles could provide, and at the same time the nobles found themselves less wealthy than they had been. The king's power, on the other hand, was obviously in the ascendant, especially when Frederik III exiled the leaders of the nobility.

His chance to break the power of nobility once and for all came immediately after the siege of Copenhagen. In order to encourage the citizens to hold out, he had promised them special privileges, including that of deciding how much tax they should pay. A meeting of all the estates in 1660 decided that all, including the nobility, should be liable to pay taxes. Sensing their new influence, the Copenhagen citizens then went on to suggest a hereditary monarchy, which would, of course, put an end to the system of charters. After a show of reluctance, the king went along with this. When the new constitution was drawn up in 1661, it was not quite what the citizens had foreseen, as the king was proclaimed not only a hereditary monarch, but also an *absolute* hereditary monarch. Whether Frederik III had actually intended this is not certain, but absolute power in the style of Louis XIV of France was certainly introduced, lasting in differing forms until the middle of the 19C.

The rather exaggerated love of grandeur which has often accompanied absolutism was also felt in late 17C Denmark. It persuaded the kings to build magnificent squares and palaces—Kongens Nytorv in Copenhagen is one example—and it gave rise to the baroque style in architecture and poetry. But the one field in which glory could be won by the absolute kings would be in the recovery of the Swedish provinces, the loss of which had been an enormous blow to national pride. Denmark was allied to Holland, and Sweden to France, and it was obviously impossible for Denmark to wage war on Sweden while Sweden had such an ally. However, in 1675 the pretext and the opportunity came. France, herself at war with Holland, persuaded Sweden to attack Brandenburg, where the Swedes suffered a defeat. Denmark could not resist the opportunity, and after occupying Sweden's small ally to the south, Gottorp, which included parts of Schleswig, the Danes landed an army in Skåne, where it was well received by the local population. Denmark won the war, but once more, the wishes of a major power, France, prevented the return of the old Danish territories. Despite terrible losses, Denmark was allowed to keep nothing of what she had conquered.

However, Denmark was still not prepared to give up the attempt, and a rapprochement with France took place just at the same time as Sweden made a move to improve relations with England and Holland, who had previously supported Denmark. This new constellation was in existence at the beginning of the Great Nordic War, which lasted from 1700 to 1721. The final outcome was that Sweden once and for all lost most of her Baltic possessions, while Russia for the first time came to play a dominant role in the Baltic. Denmark failed to regain the Swedish provinces, however, and merely achieved an end to the Swedish freedom from Sound Dues and the cessation of Swedish support for Gottorp. As a result of this Frederik IV was able to strengthen his own position in Schleswig, while allowing the Duke of Gottorp to keep Holstein. It was hoped thereby to remove the frontier problem both to the north and the south. Peace between Denmark and Sweden now seemed possible.

18C Pietism and Enlightenment. The Lutheranism which came to Denmark with the Reformation in 1536 quickly led to a new orthodoxy and intolerance. However, the close connection existing between the Lutheran State Church and the Crown meant that little could be done to overcome this or to allow new ideas to penetrate into Denmark. It was not until the beginning of the 18C that new developments occurred with the arrival from Germany of the pietist movement. There was no obvious desire to stray from the strictly Lutheran teaching, but merely to intensify the spiritual life, and so it was difficult for the State Church to prevent the spread of pietism. By 1720 Frederik IV himself was sympathetic towards the new movement, and his successor Christian VI was himself a convinced pietist. Under his rule there was a period of intensification of Danish religious life, accompanied by increasing intolerance. Not only were all forms of entertainment forbidden on Sundays, but pietist influence also brought about the closing of Copenhagen's Royal Theatre for a period, just when Ludvig Holberg, the greatest dramatist in the North, was at the height of his creative powers. On the other hand, the pietists laid great stress on charitable acts and help for those in need. Among those in need were children in want of education, and under the pietists an attempt was now made to provide a minimum of schooling for all, an attempt which only met with limited success because of opposition from the landowners who had to finance it, and the farmers who would rather have their sons in the fields than in the classroom.

Nevertheless, the pietists' interest in education can be seen not only as a special aspect of their creed, but as the forerunner of the 18C Enlightenment, which replaced pietism later in the century and led to an increased interest in education generally. At the end of the century schools such as the School for Civic Virtue were founded, a private, liberal experimental school aiming at as broad an education as possible. In effect it was a reaction against the established grammar schools, mainly medieval institutions often attached to the cathedrals, after which they were named—Cathedral Schools. It was the learning by rote associated with these schools that became the object in the 19C of N.F.S. Grundtvig's criticism.

A school commission was set up in 1789, and its report formed the basis of the 1814 Education Act, which really did introduce a new era into Danish education. It provided for free schooling for all, though parents who wished either to teach their children at home or send them to private schools were entitled to do so. The new schools were to be paid for out of taxation. In addition, provision was made for training proper teachers, though it was several decades before the supply was sufficient to satisfy all needs. The 19C benefited from the new Education Act, but it was essentially a result of 18C philanthropy.

On a different level it was also an offshoot of the peasant reforms, one of the major achievements of the late 18C. Stemming from a happy combination of philanthropy, a period of increasing prosperity, an enlightened monarch and perhaps a touch of Rousseauist idealism, the peasant reforms saw a reversal of the trend towards the oppression of the farming community which had been such an obvious characteristic of the past three or four centuries. A commission was set up in 1786 to consider peasant reforms, resulting, the following year, in a radical liberalisation of the status of the poorer rural population.

With this change the landowners lost their grip on their tenant farmers. Now it became common for a farmer to buy back his farm instead of leasing it. The state encouraged this, and by 1814 some 60 per cent of Danish farmers were once more independent. They were not thereby made wealthy, and many had a hard time because of falling prices, but they acquired a self-esteem which they had not had for centuries.

Prosperity, War and Poverty. The agricultural reforms had coincided with a period of increased agricultural and national prosperity. Thanks to the Industrial Revolution, England's population had risen rapidly, and from being a corn-exporting country, England had started importing corn. Denmark had been among those countries which benefited from this turn of events, and such a turn, combined with the introduction of a corn monopoly in Norway (still part of Denmark), meant good news for Danish farmers.

Denmark's economy benefited also at first from the wars between Britain and France at the end of the 18C and from the American War of Independence, in all of which the country declared itself neutral and set about trading with both sides. Copenhagen achieved its old objective of becoming the centre of Baltic trade. By 1784 trade restrictions were abolished, and Denmark was able to enter the 19C in a period of affluence and free trade.

However, none of the belligerent powers was happy to see Denmark trading with its enemies, and in particular Britain sought to stop and search Danish ships and confiscate cargoes whenever there was the slightest excuse. In 1780, therefore, Denmark joined with Russia, Prussia and Sweden in an armed neutrality aimed at safeguarding trading rights in America, and was largely successful in doing so until the end of the War of Independence in 1783. However, when Britain was again embroiled in war with revolutionary France, Denmark was less successful, and the decision to organise a convoy system met with immediate British opposition. Denmark gave in, but went on to join the second Armed Neutrality with Sweden and Russia. After this apparent disrespect for an agreement just made, Britain in 1801 sent a fleet to Copenhagen. The force found the Danish fleet unprepared for it, and so won a resounding victory, despite stubborn resistance. The Danes had to yield and withdraw from the Armed Neutrality.

The difficulties in which Denmark found herself, caught between two major warring powers, were a sign of things to come. In particular the situation became difficult when Napoleon announced the Continental Blockade in 1806, and even more so when Britain set in motion a counter-blockade. Denmark, dependent as always on the sea for communication, both between the islands and between Denmark and Norway, was at the mercy of the British fleet. It was not surprising that the British Government, after the events of 1801, was scarcely sure of the Danish attitude, though in fact Denmark was mainly interested in keeping out of trouble.

After the signing of the peace treaty between France and Russia at Tilsit in 1807, the position became even more difficult. Russia joined in the Continental Blockade, and, although this was not known, the intention was to force Denmark and Sweden to join in, too. Sensing this, Britain started pressing Denmark for an alliance, a provision of which was to be that Denmark should deliver her navy to Britain as a pledge. The Danes were aware that if this happened, France would invade Jutland, with unforeseeable consequences. On the other hand, if an alliance were made with France, the outlook for trade was bleak. In the event, Denmark played for time and tried to work on the fact that while the English were in Copenhagen making demands, the Crown Prince was in Kiel with his army. But they wavered too long, and the British lost patience. In order to force an alliance on the Danes they occupied Sjælland and bombarded Copenhagen for three days, during which they laid waste to parts of the city and killed hundreds of civilians. When at the end of it all the city gave in, the British confiscated the entire Danish fleet and sailed off with it.

Had they played their cards better and been less impatient, it may well be that they would have gained what they wanted, for on the whole the Danes sympathised with their cause. But by behaving in so high-handed a manner, and cowing the city into surrender and then taking the fleet, they made themselves the object of hatred in Denmark for a long time to come. The bombardment of Copenhagen was felt as a national humiliation, and it gave rise to an upsurge of radical nationalism.

In these circumstances an Anglo-Danish alliance was out of the question, and instead the Danes joined Napoleon. But it was too late, and it soon became obvious that they were on the losing side, a side, moreover, that the average Dane did not love. Attempts to break with France and to join the alliance against Napoleon were thwarted by Sweden, where the new king, Carl Johan, himself one of Napoleon's generals who had turned against the Emperor, had been promised Norway once the war was over, provided Denmark was on the losing side. Thus, in 1814, a year after a state bankruptcy had been declared, Denmark had to sign away Norway in the Treaty of Kiel and found herself reduced from a medium-sized but affluent state to a minor and poverty-stricken one.

The period up to 1828 was marked by the struggle to recoup the national finances on the one hand and on the other by the beginnings of the Schleswig-Holstein troubles which were to dog Denmark until 1864. Should Denmark plus the duchies become a unified state, or should Holstein be allowed to join the German Confederation, formed in 1815? In this case, what should become of Schleswig, which was tied to both? The end of the Napoleonic Wars brought about an upsurge of nationalism in all the elements forming the Danish state, and it also brought about a demand for democratic reforms to bring about the end of the absolute monarchy, for whether or not the king was accessible and delighted in being a father to his people, he *was* still an absolute monarch.

In 1831 the king gave in to some of the demands and ordered legislation to establish four consultative assemblies to allow public opinion throughout the country to have a voice—though he made sure that none of them was in Copenhagen. When they met, they consisted of individual delegates only, as no political parties as such existed. However, these delegates soon divided into two broad camps of conservatives and liberals, with the liberals predominating. The movement towards democratic government had begun, but it was not to be completed until 1901.

Nevertheless, this was a period of reform and reconstruction. Agricultural reforms, begun in the 18C, were taken a step further, and efforts were made to improve the lot of the poorer members of the rural community, in particular by means of loans to enable them to buy their own land. Trade within the country, which had hitherto been subject to ancient restrictions, was liberalised, and the Sound Dues were abolished, allowing Copenhagen to compete on equal terms with its great rival Hamburg as a trading centre. By 1844, the first railway line was established, ironically enough running between Altona and Kiel in Holstein, but by 1870 the railway system of today had in essence been laid out.

Meanwhile, the pressure for constitutional reform gathered impetus, and by the 1840s the king, Christian VIII, decided to give in to it and renounce his absolute authority. He ran into trouble, however, when the new written constitution had to take account of Schleswig and Holstein, where different conditions obtained. Christian died before the constitution was signed, but despite hesitations, his successor, Frederik VII, was persuaded to put the proposals into effect in January 1848. It was a notably liberal constitution, but it led to a reaction in the duchies, which sought a common constitution for themselves and demanded permission for Schleswig to join the German Confederation. Danish national feeling was also running high, and the government proved intransigent. Consequently, Danish troops were sent to Flensburg, in Schleswig, where they encountered a force of 30,000, including Prussian soldiers. Ultimately, Denmark appeared to win this war, though it was largely due to pressure on Prussia from abroad, a fact that was lost on many of the Danish politicians. Consequently, when further trouble ensued in 1863, Denmark thought it could repeat the performance, and once more it took on Prussia. This time Denmark was thoroughly beaten, and the border was drawn to the north of the duchies, just south of Kolding.

The king, who still had the prerogative of appointing his government, now brought in new men to lead the country. They were, however, still predominantly wealthy landowners, and there was a period of political stagnation—though a number of much-needed social reforms were carried out. It was at the same time a period of internal conflict, as improved educational standards and a changing social pattern made people unwilling to accept a form of aristocratic, semi-authoritarian government by a group which came to represent a diminishingly small section of the elected parliament, the *Rigsdag*. The last years of the 19C thus became a battleground for parliamentary government, with the king maintaining his conservative cabinet in the face of an increasingly liberal parliament. For a time there was virtually dictatorial rule under the Prime Minister J.B.S. Estrup, but by 1901 the principle of parliamentary government was accepted.

Meanwhile, alongside the parliamentary struggles, Denmark had been making progress in other spheres. The final liberalisation of internal trade in 1862 led to a period of eager industrial activity, and something like 1000 new firms—some of them still in existence—were established within two years. A free harbour was established in Copenhagen, bringing a marked increase in international trade activities. Easier transport meant that industry could develop in the provinces as well as in Copenhagen, and the period saw an increase in the populations of the provincial towns as well as Copenhagen. One result of this move to the towns was the construction of large blocks of cheap flats, particularly in Copenhagen. Another was the emergence of the Social Democrat Party and the incipient trade unions to look after the needs of this new social class.

In the country districts changes were also taking place, not least in the form of intensified farming. Here, too, there was a reaction against the power of the wealthy farmers and their conservative supporters. Perhaps the most striking feature of rural developments was the establishment of the co-operative movement, which to this day is a potent force in Danish life. Inspired by the co-operative movement in Rochdale in England, the first co-operative store was opened in Thisted, but the movement was not limited to small shops. The smaller farmers clubbed together to open co-operative dairies and slaughter-houses, thus providing the foundations for the efficient organisation of the modern Danish meat and dairy industries. This co-operative movement went hand in hand with the Folk High School movement, inspired by the principles of N.F.S. Grundtvig, and aimed at providing a Christian education for the rural population who had been deprived of an academic schooling. These schools, which quickly spread throughout the country, provided relatively short courses to give the rural population an appreciation of Danish culture and history, to fuse a sense of nationhood with Christian virtues and, not least, to teach them an appreciation of traditional crafts. These schools, which are still an important feature of Danish life even if they have changed somewhat in character, are doubtless a product of the National Romantic movement, but they have played an inestimable role in educating and enlightening the broad population of Denmark, and are to be thanked for the widespread appreciation of art, design and culture which is such a striking characteristic of modern Denmark.

The advent of democratic government in 1901 brought calls for a liberal reform of the constitution, and a great deal of time and energy was spent on this. Before this process could be completed, however, World War I broke out, and new preoccupations replaced the subject of constitutional change. As had happened before, Denmark had good relations with both sides in a war, although 1864 had by no means been forgotten, and the government decided to remain neutral if at all possible. It was possible, and Denmark managed to maintain a—sometimes precarious—neutrality, and initially the country's balance of payments went into surplus as a result of an increase in demand for Danish goods abroad. The new conditions brought the different parties in Denmark together, and agreement was now reached on a new constitution, which was signed on the by now traditional constitution day of 5 June in 1915.

The war nevertheless brought shortages and economic problems to Denmark after the initial buoyant months. The national debt grew, and taxes were increased, while profiteering was rife. The workers did not benefit from the new conditions, and became a prey to syndicalists and bolsheviks. These influences continued after the war, and in 1920 there was a confrontation between the king and the workers which, in the eyes of some, was a potentially revolutionary situation. However, the trouble blew over, and once more Denmark sought to stabilise its situation. The most immediate effect of the post-war period was the holding of a referendum in the lost territories of Schleswig and Holstein. This was done on a parish-by-parish basis, and resulted in the present border being drawn, very largely reflecting the cultural boundary between the Danish and German-speaking populations. Minorities there were, and bitterness there was for many years, but of late the problems have disappeared, and the two populations now mix easily and peacefully.

After World War I, Denmark suffered severe economic problems, which in the 1930s were compounded by the world-wide slump. The period to World War II was also, however, one of reform, first of the penal system, which had been in need of modernisation, and then of the social system. K.K. Steincke's Social Reform, as it was known, was thought out in the 1920s and introduced in 1933. It made for wide-ranging improvements in social provisions, introducing the insurance principle for sickness, disablement and old age, as well as for unemployment and accident. It produced, in fact, one of the most advanced social security systems of its day, and formed the basis for Danish social security legislation for the next 50 years. Other practical measures were introduced, and the same egalitarian principles also prompted the government to introduce a new Education Act, the aim of which was to improve the quality of schools and to ensure equal opportunities for all, whether in town or country.

When war in Europe broke out again in 1939, there was no doubt where Danish sympathies lay, but Denmark hoped once more to remain neutral. By April 1940, however, Hitler's troops had invaded. By general standards, Denmark had a 'good' occupation, and its elected politicians were, within limits, allowed to run the country until 1943. Then, under the pressure of increasing opposition, the occupation forces introduced a state of emergency and took over full administrative powers, which they retained until the end of the war.

In many respects the Danes suffered less both nationally and personally from the effects of the war than did the people in other occupied countries. Until August 1943 the regime was tolerable and life could go on in many ways as normal. Thereafter things became more insecure. The fact that the government of the country, together with the police force, had remained in Danish hands, had helped alleviate what could otherwise have been an unpleasant and dangerous situation. In the same way, food had been more plentiful in Denmark than in other occupied countries, and the farming industry had succeeded in maintaining a high level of production despite the difficulty of obtaining fertiliser and fodder.

Since 1945, Denmark has undergone a period of increasing prosperity, despite balance of payments problems caused by huge loans to finance a new infrastructure. After some hesitation, the decision was taken to join NATO, but Denmark otherwise showed a greater tendency to Nordic as opposed to European co-operation. Thus, in the 1960s, there was an attempt at forming a Nordic common market, but it came to nothing, even if Nordic co-operation in other spheres was and still is, intense. Consequently, Denmark joined EFTA, until in 1972 a referendum was held on membership of the European Community. The vote showed a majority of 56.7 per cent in favour, and Denmark became a full member of the EC on 1 January 1973. There was a good deal of opposition to this, as a large proportion of the Danish population felt that their Scandinavian bonds were closer than any ties to Europe at large. As time has passed, however, this opposition has become far less significant.

Today, Denmark stands as a country with a very high standard of living indeed, a country notable for its efficiency and its humanity, and for the respect in which it holds all its citizens. Equality was one of the claims made by the Vikings in their day, and it seems that that instinct has either survived the ages or been revived in the twentieth century.

Brief Chronology

Danish monarchs and the most important events in their reigns.

Gorm den Gamle (Gorm the Old) died c 940
Harald Blåtand (Harald Bluetooth) c 940–86
  Introduction of Christianity
Svend Tveskæg (Svend Forkbeard) 986–1014 (died in Gainsborough;
  buried in Roskilde)

Conquest of England 1013
Harald II 1014–18
Knud I den Store (Canute the Great) 1018–35 (died in Shaftesbury;
    buried in Winchester)
    The Ejder defined as South border of Denmark
    Denmark frequently at war with the Wends from 1022
Hardeknud (Hardicanute) 1035–42 (died in London; buried in
    Winchester)
    The last Danish King of England 1040–42
    Magnus den Gode (Magnus the Good) 1042–47
Svend II Estridsøn 1047–74
    Nephew of Svend Forkbeard, born in England
    Responsible for ecclesiastical organisation of Denmark many
    churches built during his reign
Harald III Hen 1074–80
    Established unified monetary system in Denmark
Knud II den Hellige (St. Canute) 1080–86
    Murdered and buried in Sankt Albani Kirke in Odense
    Canonised
Oluf I Hunger 1086–95
Erik I Ejegod (Erik the Kind-Hearted) 1095–1103
    The first Danish king to undertake a pilgrimage to the Holy Land
Niels 1104–34
Erik II Emune 1134–37
Erik III Lam 1137–46
Oluf II c 1140–43
Svend III Grathe 1146–57
    Killed in the Battle of Grathe Heath by Valdemar I
Knud III 1146–57
    Co-regent with Svend Grathe, by whom he was murdered at a
    banquet in Roskilde
Valdemar I den Store (Valdemar I, The Great) 1157–82
Knud IV 1182–1202
    The first Danish king to be anointed and crowned by the Church
    Assumed the title of 'King of the Wends'
Valdemar II Sejr (Valdemar II, The Victorious) 1202–41
    Made an unsuccessful attempt to establish a Kingdom of the Baltic
Erik IV Plovpenning (Erik IV, Plowpenny) 1241–50
Abel 1250–52
Christoffer I 1252–59
Erik V Glipping (or Klipping) 1259–86
    Murdered by Rane Jonsen in Finderup Barn near Viborg
Erik VI Menved 1286–1319
Christoffer II 1320–26; 1330–32
Valdemar III 1326–30
Valdemar IV Atterdag (Valdemar IV, Another Day) 1340–75
    Concluded peace with the Wends 1365
Oluf III 1375–87
Margrethe 1375–97 (died 1412)
    Kalmar Union 1397
Erik VII af Pommern (Erik VII of Pomerania) 1397–1439
    Øresund Dues introduced 1429
Christoffer III af Bayern (Christoffer III of Bavaria) 1440–48
    Copenhagen created the capital of Denmark
Christian I 1448–81
    Copenhagen University founded
Hans 1481–1513

Defeated in the Ditmarshes 1500
Christian II 1513–23
  Stockholm Bloodbath 1520
  Driven into exile by the nobility 1523
  Union with Sweden breaks down 1523
  Prisoner in Sønderborg Castle 1532–49
  Prisoner in Kalundborg Castle 1549–59
  Frederik I 1523–33
  Governs from Gottorp Castle
Christian III 1534–59
  The Count's War 1534–36
  Last battle against the Wends 1536
  The Reformation proclaimed 1536
  The Government returns to Copenhagen 1539
Frederik II 1559–88
  The Nordic Seven Years War 1563–70
Christian IV 1588–1648
  The architect king, founder of many of Denmark's finest buildings
Frederik III 1648–70
  The Karl-Gustav Wars 1657–60
  Svend Poulsen (Gøngehøvdingen) leads guerilla warfare 1658–1660
  The storming of Copenhagen
  Establishment of Absolute Rule 1660
Christian V 1670–99
  The Scanian War 1675–79
  The Battle of Køge Bay 1677
Frederik IV 1699–1730
  Serfdom abolished 1702
  Great Northern War 1700–21
  240 cavalry schools established
Christian VI 1730–46
Frederik V 1746–66
Christian VII 1766–1808
  Suffered from mental illness
  Coup d'état by Struensee 1771
  The abolition of adscription (the liberation of the peasantry) 1788
  Napoleonic Wars
  The Battle of the Copenhagen Roads 1801
  Bombardment of Copenhagen 1807
Frederik VI 1808–39
  State bankruptcy 1813
  Loss of Norway 1814
  Advisory Provincial Assemblies 1834
Christian VIII 1839–48
  First public State accounts 1841
Frederik VII 1848–63
  End of absolute monarchy 1848
  First Schleswig War 1848–50
  First Constitution June 1849
  End of Sound Dues 1857. The death of Frederik VII marked the end
  of the Oldenburg dynasty, which had ruled through 16 reigns for 415
  years
Christian IX 1863–1906
  Glücksborg dynasty founded. Christian IX elected as a descendant
  of Christian III
  Second Schleswig War 1864
  Schleswig and Holstein surrendered to Germany 1864. Introduction

of parliamentary democracy 1901
Frederik VIII 1906–12
Christian X 1912–47
  World War I 1914–18
  Revision of Constitution 1915, providing for universal suffrage—also
  for women
  Return of South Jutland 1920
  World War II 1939–45
  Occupation of Denmark 1940–45
Frederik IX 1947–72
  Denmark joins NATO 1949
  Revision of Constitution 1953, resulted in: abolition of the Landsting
  (the Upper House); the possibility of female succession to the
  Throne; Greenland becoming an integral and equal part of the
  Kingdom of Denmark
  Danish membership of EFTA 1959
Margrethe II 1972–
  Danish membership of EC after referendum 1973

On Danish Churches

A Benedictine monk, Ansgar (801–865), subsequently canonised as St.
Ansgar, is usually given credit for converting Denmark. He certainly
had a church built in Ribe during his lifetime. The conversion process
was, however, a slow one, and it was c 1000 before it could reasonably
be claimed that Denmark was a Christian kingdom. Adam of Bremen
wrote in 1070 that there were 150 churches in Sjælland and 100 in Fyn,
and there is a view that there were altogether some 500–600 churches
in Denmark as a whole. The period during which church building
blossomed, however, was between 1100 and 1200, when some 1500
churches large and small were built. These have provided the foundations for Danish churches to this day, even when, as has happened in
most cases, the original Romanesque buildings have been extended in
the age of Gothic architecture. They are a unique source of insight into
both architecture and custom, while the frescoes decorating them
provide a lively, sometimes amusing, commentary on beliefs and ways
of life. Some are almost like strip cartoons in the way in which they
portray tiny scenes, often revealing an unspoken criticism of authority
both ecclesiastical and temporal. The names of some of the fresco
artists are known, such as the Elmelunde Master; he is probably the
greatest of them all and was a gifted artist by any standards. Others
are more homespun, some quite primitive. Village churches are often
small, occasionally intimate, and with their corbie-stepped gables and,
often, their whitewashed walls, they are very much a part of the
Danish countryside. They are usually open during daylight hours, and
when they are not, the key can normally be obtained from the verger,
whose address is likely to be shown on the noticeboard outside. Visit
them: they grow on you—they are an inexhaustible source of historical
knowledge, and in their furniture they are often a storehouse of artistic
inspiration.

Glossary

ANTEMENSALE. The decorative panelling in front of an altar

ANTEPENDIUM. Cloth hanging over the front of an altar

AURICULAR. An ornate baroque style, also known as Ohrmuschel style

BAROQUE. Extensively ornamented, decorative style of art and architecture stretching from the late 16C to early 18C. Often bombastic in tone

EPITAPHIUM. Memorial Tablet

GOTHIC. Style of architecture usual between the 12C and 16C, characterised by pointed arches

ROCOCO. Style of architecture and decoration common in the 18C, ornate and intricate, but more graceful than baroque

ROMANESQUE. The earliest style of Danish church architecture, lasting until the 12C, when it was replaced by Gothic. It is characterised by massive, relatively undecorated walls, and rounded arches and windows.

Early Church Artists

One of the delights of the early Danish churches is the wealth of frescoes found in them. Many, if not most, frescoes are by unknown artists, but some of the painters are either known from their signatures or identifiable by their styles, and several of these are referred to in the text. Among other early artists there are some outstanding sculptors, ranging in time from the early Middle Ages to the Reformation period. The following provides brief information on some of the best and most interesting of them.

Berg, Claus: born c 1470, died after 1532. Sculptor and painter centred on Odense. Main works: altarpiece and memorial in the Greyfriars' Church in Odense, now in St. Knud's Cathedral; altarpieces in Nørre Broby, Sanderum, Holmekloster (Fyn), Tirstrup near Randers, Bregninge on Ærø; crucifixes in Vejlby, Skamby, Asperup, Vindinge (Fyn) and Sorø; Ivar Munk's tombstone in Ribe Cathedral.

Brarup Master: active around 1500. Fresco painter. His late Gothic frescoes are characterised by rather primitive figures. Main works: Tågerup, Sædinge (Lolland), Kongsted (South Sjælland), Gjerrild, Hyllested (Djursland).

Elmelunde Master: active c 1480–1500. Fresco painter. Based his work on a book of biblical illustrations with short rhymed texts. Characterised by expressionless faces amidst wealth of decorative invention. Main works: Elmelunde, Fanefjord, Keldby (all on Møn), Nørre Alslev, Tingsted, Åstrup (all on Falster), Bogø.

Goti: early medieval sculptor, probably Swedish, active in Jutland and in Sweden. In the church in Gjøl he not only left his mark, but included a portrait of himself in the Paradise motif which he sculpted. Also responsible for the reliefs in Voldsted.

Helligtrekonger (The Three Kings) Master: active end of 15C. Fresco painter deriving name from exquisite late Gothic frescoes in the Helligtrekonger Chapel in Roskilde Cathedral. Seems to have been influenced by German and Dutch art. Other work: Tyrstrup (Christiansfeld); Vordingborg.

Horder: active c 1200 in the Djursland area of East Jutland, responsible for Romanesque portals in many churches, of which those in Rimsø, Vejlby and Ørsted are the most important. He takes his name from a signature on the Gjesingholm Stone, found near Randers and now in the National Museum.

Isefjord Master: active c 1450. Fresco painter. Lively biblical scenes, of which the best preserved are in Mørkøv. Characterised by figures with rounded cheeks and big eyes, tapestries and rugs with diamond patterning. Main works: Bregninge, Herlev, Kirke Hyllinge, Lynge, Mørkøv, Måløv, Over Dråby, Skamstrup.

Jørgensen, Lorentz: active c 1644–81. Sculptor. His early work is on Langeland, but he later moved to the area around Holbæk and is responsible for work in many Sjælland churches. His main works are the auricular altars in Kalundborg, Køge and Helsingør, and the pulpit in Sankt Peders Kirke, Næstved.

Kolding, Peter Jensen: died c 1670. Sculptor. Main work is the auricular Clausholm Bed. Also altarpieces in Odder, Jannerup, Glud, Saksild, Vor Frue Kirke in Horsens, Ølsted.

Kongsted Master: active c 1430–50. Fresco painter, possibly pupil of Martinus. His faces often have characteristic small chins, and he fills his space with foliage and other decoration. Main works: Kongsted near Fakse, Ballerup and the Slagelse region.

Lily Master: active c 1500 in South Jutland and West Fyn. Fresco painter responsible for some 15 churches, recognisable by the stylised lilies of which he made frequent use. Main works: Janderup, Nørre Løgum.

Martinus Maler: active in early 15C. Fresco painter, responsible for Gothic paintings in Sjælland, some bearing his signature. Characterised by ornamentation based on branches, leaves and shells. Main works: Gimlinge (dated 1409), Kirke Såby, Mogenstrup, Gerlev (his most important), Flakkebjerg, Hjembæk, Nordrup, Sankt Peders Kirke in Næstved, tower chapels in Roskilde Cathedral.

Quellinus, Thomas: (1661–1709). Sculptor. Dutch, but mostly worked in Denmark. Monuments in Copenhagen Cathedral; Tølløse; Hørning; St. Knud's Cathedral, Odense; Sankt Petri Kirke, Copenhagen; Auning; Herlufsholm; Fraugde; Århus Cathedral.

Sødring Master: active end 15C. Fresco painter. Feminine faces are characteristic of his work. Main works: Sødring, Udbyneder and Randers area.

Torum Master: active c 1530. Fresco painter. Late Gothic frescoes in North Jutland. Often filled his pictures with inscriptions and painted several scenes in a single panel. Main works: Grinderslev, Torum, Vester Hornum.

Træskomaleren (The Clog Master): active in East Fyn in 1480s. Named after clog in Ørbæk Church, but also recognisable by his suns and dedication crosses with flames. Main works: Hesselager, Skrøbelev, Vindinge.

Union Master: also known as the Undløse Master. Active 1440–60 in Denmark and Sweden. One of the most important late Gothic artists. Characterised by men's faces with long noses and graceful female figures. Main works in Denmark: Undløse, Nødebo.

Vinderslev Master: active c 1500. Fresco painter. Recognisable by the face he always painted on the Virgin. Main works: Vinderslev, Maria Magdalene, Marved and Ottestrup.

PRACTICAL INFORMATION

The Danish Tourist Board

General information can be obtained from The Danish Tourist Board, Sceptre House, 169–173 Regent St, London W1A 2LT, tel. (071) 734 2637; or, in the USA, 655 Third Avenue, New York, NY 10017, tel. (212) 949-233. A range of useful brochures is available including guides to hotels, inns, youth and family hostels, camping, cycling, ferries, events lists and maps.

Getting to Denmark

By Air. Copenhagen's Kastrup Airport is one of the major European airports, with regular services to all parts of the world, and with frequent connections to Danish provincial airports. Most air traffic to Denmark will take you to Kastrup, though there are a few international services to the provinces, e.g. to Esbjerg, Århus and Billund (for Legoland).

Kastrup Airport is some 12km from Copenhagen centre, and there are frequent SAS buses to the main railway station, Hovedbanegåden. The journey takes about 20 minutes. There are also rather slower—and cheaper—services by ordinary bus (Service 32) to Copenhagen Town Hall Square (Rådhuspladsen).

The following airlines run regular scheduled flights to Denmark from the UK: Scandinavian Airlines, tel. (071) 734 4020; British Airways, tel. (081) 897 4000; Maersk Air, tel. (071) 638 7920; Air Europe, tel. (0345) 444737; Aer Lingus (UK), tel. (0345) 010101; Aer Lingus (Eire), tel. (0001) 377777; Birmingham European Airways, tel. (021) 782 0711; Business Air, tel. (0382) 66345; Muk Air, tel. (0224) 722331; New Air, tel. (0652) 688491. In addition, Star Tours, tel. (071) 706 2520, run a weekly charter service. For scheduled flights from the USA contact: Scandinavian Airlines, tel. (800) 221-2350; TWA, tel. (800) 892-4141; Finnair, tel. (800) 223-5500; Icelandair, tel. (800) 223-5500.

By Rail. There are good rail services connecting with cities throughout Europe. There are daily connections both to and from London, Victoria via Ostende and to London, Liverpool Street via Hook of Holland. The journey takes approximately 24 hours. For information and bookings contact British Rail International Rail Centre, tel. (071) 834 2345/828 0892; Eurotrain, tel. (071) 730 3402. Thomas Cook's European timetable gives details of all rail and ferry services in Europe.

By Coach. Several coach services are available to Denmark. London Coaches, tel. (071) 227 3456, travel to Copenhagen, Funen and Jutland thrice weekly (journey time approximately 26 hours). Roundabout Enterprises, tel. (0923) 835696, run a weekly service to Copenhagen, Odense and Fredericia via France (journey time approximately 25 hours). National Express Eurolines, tel. (071) 730 0202, also run a regular service, via Amsterdam (journey time approximately 26 hours).

By Sea. There are connections most days between London, Liverpool Street and Copenhagen via Harwich and Esbjerg (sailing time 18 hours), Copenhagen–Esbjerg (5 hours); London–Harwich (1½ hours). The ships on this route are operated to a high standard by Scandinavian Seaways, tel. (071) 493 6696. If you are taking your car, this is the obvious way to go, unless you want to drive up through Germany. In the summer, passengers from the North of England can take the Scandinavian Seaways ferry from Newcastle to Esbjerg (19 hours), again with connecting service to Copenhagen (tel. (091) 296 0101).

By Car. The Harwich–Esbjerg route is the easiest. However, you can drive from any of the Channel or North Sea ports by good motorways, usually using the E45 and entering Denmark via Jutland or the E47 via Lübeck and taking the ferry from Puttgarden to Rødbyhavn, from where there is a motorway most of the way to Copenhagen. It is also possible to take the W coast route N of Hamburg via Husum to Tønder, while a ferry operates from Kiel to Bagenkop. There are minor frontier crossings as well, though they are little used except for local traffic.

Customs. For travellers arriving from another EC country checks are minimal, and in general informality is characteristic of customs inspections. If you take the main frontier crossing from Germany via Padborg you may encounter delays in the summer. From Sweden there are very frequent ferries from Hälsingborg to Helsingør and also from Malmö to Copenhagen. Other services: from Limhamn to Dragør, Göteborg to Frederikshavn, Halmstad to Grenå, Hälsingborg to Grenå, Varberg to Grenå, Landskrona to Copenhagen (Tuborg Havn). From Norway there are ferries from Larvik, Oslo, Moss and Frederiksstad to Frederikshavn and from Oslo, Egernsund and Kristiansand to Hirtshals. Larger ferries sail between Bergen and Stavanger and Hirtshals and between Oslo and Copenhagen.

Travel in Denmark

Domestic Ferry Routes. Denmark consists of the peninsula of Jutland and a large number of islands, many of which are connected by bridge. However, ferry connections are common between many of the islands, and at weekends and in the summer holiday months you are advised to book beforehand to avoid waiting for free space. The State Railways, DSB, run many of the ferries, and you can book on these at any railway station. For others you should seek advice in a travel agency or Tourist Information Office. If travelling via Puttgarden–Rødbyhavn, you are similarly advised to book beforehand.

Main roads in Denmark are systematically numbered. Those connected with international routes have a number prefixed by E: E20, E55, and indicated by *green* signs. Next in the hierarchy come other main roads, designated on *yellow* signs by a 2-digit number: 11, 13. In this book we have prefixed these routes with an A: A11, A13. Good secondary roads have 3-digit numbers on *white* signs: 160, 283. In addition there are many unclassified roads, all of high quality. You need never be afraid to use them—and there is often remarkably little traffic on them.

Motorways are provided with *blue* signs indicating places served by the next exit and *green* signs indicating places reached by driving straight on. Exits are all numbered.

Speed Limits. 50kph in built-up areas, 80kph outside urban areas, 100kph on motorways. Built-up areas are indicated by the name of the town/village, together with a sketch of houses and a church. The speed limit is then cancelled by the same sign with a line drawn through it.

Warning Triangles. Motorists are expected to carry warning triangles with them in Denmark.

Headlights. You are required to drive with dipped headlights throughout the day in Denmark. Remember to have them masked for driving on the right.

Parking. Parking meters are not unknown in Denmark, but they are not common. Many car parks are free, but you are limited to time. You are obliged to obtain a parking disc (available in banks, Tourist Information Offices, garages and a host of other places) to attach to your windscreen, indicating your time of arrival. If you fail to use it, you risk a fine.

Road Maps. These are available from petrol stations and Tourist Information Offices. If you want a detailed map of the whole country, we recommend 'Danmark. 1:100 000. Topografisk Atlas' published by Kort- og Matrikelstyrelsen. It is excellent—but expensive.

Travel by Train within Denmark. The railway network (DSB) covers most of the country and is very efficient, clean and reliable. Inter-City trains run between Copenhagen and Jutland every hour, with connections to towns not served directly, and there are the 'Lyntog' (Lightning Trains), which are faster but limited in the main to the busier times. Tickets should be bought in advance, although they can also be bought on board. Fares are calculated on a zonal system, with the cost per km reduced the longer the journey.

There are several fare reductions available, the main ones being: *cheap day tickets.*—These offer a reduction on 2nd class travel when a journey covers at least 13 zones (approx 100km). Between 1 May and 31 October cheap day tickets are available for travel on a Tuesday, Wednesday or Thursday. The rest of the year they can be used on any day except Fridays and Sundays (certain restrictions on bank holidays). *Group reductions* are available when three or more adults travel together 2nd class. The reduction is even greater with a group of seven adults or more, providing reservations have been made by 15.00 at the latest on the day prior to travel. *Child reductions.*—Children under four travel free, and children under 12 at half fare. There is also an additional saving when an adult and child make a journey of at least 13 zones.

Trains are taken on the ferry across Store Bælt, sailing time c 1 hour, and there are cafeterias and restaurants on board. Seat tickets on the train are required if you are crossing Store Bælt by rail.

The public transport system within the Copenhagen area (as far out as Roskilde and Køge) is highly co-ordinated. This means not only good connections, but also that tickets purchased are available for use on all buses or trains within a certain period. You can buy discount tickets valid for varying distances and times, but you must insert them in the yellow machines on the railway stations or on entering buses to have them clipped and time-stamped, and then remember how long they are valid. The Copenhagen area is divided into zones, for which you must have the appropriate number of clips. Bus drivers and station offices will advise you on what is needed. Children under 12 pay approximately half fare.

General Information

Accommodation. Accommodation varies in price and quality. However, the Royal Privilege Inns (*Kongelige priviligerede Kroer*), an almost 800-year-old institution, are scattered throughout the country and offer you comfortable accommodation—and good food—at reasonable cost. There are other good inns (Kroer), too. Remember: *Kro* means *Inn*. The Danish Tourist Board produces a list of hotels, and a booklet that gives details on how to book accommodation in hotels, manor houses, inns, holiday homes and farms.

Banks. Banks are usually open from 9.30 to 16.00. They do not open on Saturdays.

Beaches. Denmark has a vast coastline, over 7000km, and most of the beaches are suitable for bathing or sunbathing. One thinks in particular of Rømø and Fanø, the west coast of Jutland, the north coast of Sjælland, Lolland, parts of Bornholm; but there are many, many more. Some of the best are referred to specifically in this book, but we have not been able to cover them all. The Tourist Information Offices have free maps showing beaches for bathing.

Churches. Many churches are open during daylight hours, but thefts and vandalism over recent years have led to more and more being kept locked. However, when a church is locked it is usually possible to obtain the key from the pastor or verger or churchyard attendant, whose address will usually be displayed at the entrance either to the churchyard or the church.

Copenhagen Canal Trips. There are canal tours throughout the summer, with or without guides, leaving at half-hourly intervals from Gammel Strand and Kongens Nytorv.

Copenhagen Card. Visitors to Copenhagen will be interested in the *Copenhagen Card*, which will give free admission to over 40 museums and sights in and around Copenhagen, and also free travel on buses and trains in the Copenhagen area. You can buy cards valid for 1, 2 or 3 days in all main railway stations and travel bureaux, in many hotels and in Danvisit, H.C. Andersens Boulevard 22. Other large towns are considering introducing similar cards (see below for details of the Odense Fairytale Card).

Copenhagen Sightseeing Buses. Sightseeing buses without guide leave Town Hall Square every half hour from 10.00 to 16.30 in the summer months. Tickets are valid for 24 hours, and you can get on and off as you like at any one of nine designated stops. Half price for holders of Copenhagen Cards.

Copenhagen Tours and Excursions. Longer tours of Copenhagen and North Sjælland are on offer throughout the summer. Details from Danvisit, H.C. Andersens Boulevard 22.

Country Walks. The Danish countryside is less private than, say, in Britain. There are certainly private estates, but you will have access to much more than you might imagine. You are, of course, expected to respect the countryside.

Currency. The main unit is the *krone*, which is divided into 100 *øre*. Foreign currency is freely exchangeable, and the major credit cards are widely accepted, as are Eurocheques.

Cycling is very common in Denmark, and cycle paths are very widespread, both in towns and on the busier country roads. Cycling is, however, prohibited on motorways and on certain major roads called 'motortrafikveje'. You can easily hire a bicycle in Denmark if you wish.

House Numbers. In Denmark house numbers follow the name of the street, and we have decided to adopt the same system in this book. So the address is Jyllandsgade 5, not 5 Jyllandsgade.

Meals. Danish food is very good indeed. Prices vary enormously, but if you are looking for a good two-course meal at a reasonable price you can do worse than find a restaurant advertising the *Dan Menu*. There are plenty of such restaurants all over the country. Alcoholic drinks taken in restaurants are subject to a special restaurant tax, and are thus very expensive. For more information on Danish food see p 36.

Museums. Museum opening times vary greatly, and it has not been possible to give exact opening times for all the museums to which we refer. We have, on the other hand, tried to give some indication. In general, you must be prepared for museums to be closed on Mondays—though this is by no means always the case. When no opening times are given this indicates that the museum is open all year round, but not on Mondays.

Odense Fairytale Card. Valid for 2 days, the *Odense Fairytale Card*, offers free admission to 13 museums in Odense, Brandts Klædefabrik, Odense Zoo and Tivoli, a free boatride on Odense Stream and free admission to five swimming baths and an open air pool. The card can be purchased from a large number of places including the local tourist office, museums, railway stations, campsites and hotels.

Personal Names and Place Names. Without resorting to affectation or artificiality, it has proved impossible to be completely consistent in our treatment of personal names and place names. On the whole, unless there is a totally accepted English equivalent, we have followed the principle of using the Danish form. Hence Fyn and Sjælland, but Jutland, not Jylland. That we use Copenhagen, and not København, goes without saying, but there was a problem with Helsingør/Elsinore. We chose the Danish form—but have given the English form in parenthesis in the chapter heading. Slesvig/Schleswig and Holsten/Holstein gave even greater problems due to the historical meeting of languages and cultures in this area; we decided on Schleswig and Holstein purely because these are the forms normally found in English references to the area.

One personal name proved difficult: Knud or Canute. The king who tried to stop the waves is inevitably Canute to the English reader—but what when we come to his namesakes St. Knud and Knud Lavard? Canute hardly seemed fitting here. The problem is compounded by the fact that the modern Danish, Knud, is in any case not the form they

used! However, we decided that, as the Cathedral in Odense is defi-
nitely Sankt Knuds Kirke, and as street names including the name
Knud cannot be juggled with, we would keep to the Danish form—
though again we have on occasion put the English Canute in brackets,
just to keep you on track.

Pleasure Parks. We have referred to a number of pleasure parks, but
as they are now mushrooming, it is simply not possible to mention all
of them. All over the country you will see 'Sommerland' or 'Ferieland',
both of which indicate pleasure parks of one sort or another. Hygiene
and safety standards are high, and in many there is an entrance fee,
after which all entertainments are free.

Public Holidays. The following are public holidays in Denmark: New
Year's Day, Palm Sunday, Maundy Thursday, Good Friday, Easter
Sunday, Easter Monday, *Store Bededag* (Common Prayer Day: 4th
Friday after Easter), Ascension Day, Whit Sunday, Whit Monday, Con-
stitution Day (5 June: shops shut at noon), Christmas Day, Boxing Day.
(Most shops will shut at midday on Christmas Eve.)

School Holidays. The main school summer holidays are from mid-June
to about 8 August. Autumn holidays are the week including the 3rd
Tuesday in October. Easter holidays last from Palm Sunday to the
Wednesday after Easter, and Christmas holidays about a fortnight,
beginning around 22 December.

Self-Catering. There is a myth that food in Denmark is very expensive.
It is only a myth, though it would be wrong to assert that it is cheap.
However, if you eat as the Danes eat—e.g. rye bread, liver paste,
vegetables, dairy produce—you will find prices quite tolerable. If,
however, you insist on eating the foods which are not common in
Denmark—then you will help perpetuate the myth.

Shopping. Normal shopping hours are from 09.00 to 17.00, but many
bakers are open much earlier—from 07.00 in many cases. Bakers may
well remain open on Saturday afternoons, but *all other shops will close
by 14.00*. Many bakers open at 07.00 too on Sundays—not least because
of the Danish love of fresh bread and rolls for Sunday breakfast. Bakers
usually also sell a limited amount of dairy produce, including cheese
and ice cream, and often have newspapers on a Sunday.

Sightseeing. Information on the wide selection of sightseeing tours can
be obtained from Tourist Information Offices. However, you should be
aware of the *Copenhagen Card* (see above).

Sporting Facilities. It is impossible to give a satisfactory brief summary
of sporting facilities of interest to anglers, golfers, windsurfers, cyclists,
yachtsmen, the disabled, and tourists with children. However, Tourist
Information Offices will often have pamphlets giving you information.

Tipping. Tips are not expected in Denmark, as all indicated prices are
inclusive, whether they be for taxis, meals or hotels. If, on the other
hand, you have found the service outstandingly good, no one is going
to be insulted if you offer a tip.

VAT (Danish: MOMS) can be reclaimed for large purchases. Non-EC
citizens arrange first with the shop concerned and then reclaim the
amount paid at the border crossing on leaving the country. EC citizens
take their receipt to their own customs on arriving home, pay their local

VAT and obtain a receipt. This is then sent to the shop where you purchased the goods, and they will refund the equivalent of the Danish VAT.

Some useful WORDS. Most Danes will speak English, but you might find the following of use as you look around:

Afgang, Departure
Ankomst, Arrival
Apotek, Chemist's Shop
Banegård, Railway Station
Benzin, Petrol
Bil, Car
By, Town/Village
Bælt, Belt
Fare, Danger
Farvel, Goodbye
Færge, Ferry
Gade, Street
Goddag, Hello
Godmorgen, Good Morning
Godnat, Goodnight
Havn, Port/Harbour
Herregård, Mansion
Højre, Right
Ja, Yes
Kirke, Church
Kloster, Convent/Monastery
Landsby, Village

Lufthavn, Airport
Læge, Doctor
Lukket, Closed
Nej, No
Olie, Oil
Politi, Police
Rutebilstation, Bus Station
Skov, Forest
Slot, Castle/Palace
Sø, Lake
Strand, Beach
Stræde, Street
Sund, Sound
Tak, Thank you
Tandlæge, Dentist
Til togene, To the trains
Tog, Train
Torv, Square/Market Square
Vej, Road
Venstre, Left
Å, River
Åben, Open

Numbers

0	Nul	16	Seksten
1	En	17	Sytten
2	To	18	Atten
3	Tre	19	Nitten
4	Fire	20	Tyve
5	Fem	21	Enogtyve
6	Seks	30	Tredive
7	Syv	40	Fyrre
8	Otte	50	Halvtreds
9	Ni	60	Tres
10	Ti	70	Halvfjerds
11	Elleve	80	Firs
12	Tolv	90	Halvfems
13	Tretten	100	Hundrede
14	Fjorten	200	Hundrede
15	Femten	1000	Tusind

Months

Januar, January
Februar, February
Marts, March
April, April
Maj, May
Juni, June

Juli, July
August, August
September, September
Oktober, October
November, November
December, December

Days of the Week	Torsdag, Thursday
Mandag, Monday	Fredag, Friday
Tirsdag, Tuesday	Lørdag, Saturday
Onsdag, Wednesday	Søndag, Sunday

Days of the Week
Mandag, Monday
Tirsdag, Tuesday
Onsdag, Wednesday

Torsdag, Thursday
Fredag, Friday
Lørdag, Saturday
Søndag, Sunday

And a useful sign. You will find this sign very often: ⌘ It indicates a museum or place of historical or cultural interest.

Danish Cuisine

The Danes know how to enjoy their food, and they have a characteristic, though not exotic, list of typical dishes. A one-time British ambassador to Denmark, Robert Molesworth, writing at the end of the 17C, bewailed the lot of the Danes who, as he saw it, failed to cultivate decent wheat and were forced to grow rye instead. Little did he know! Few Danes would do without their rye bread (rugbrød), which they eat mainly at breakfast and lunch. If anything is typical of the Danish taste in food, this must be it. Always cut in much thinner slices than the white bread (which you also find), it is dark brown, firm, but not heavy, and can be made from finely or coarsely ground rye flour. It forms the basis of most of the open sandwiches (smørrebrød) for which Denmark is renowned.

Breakfast. (Morgenmad) is likely to consist of rye bread and white bread (franskbrød) with sliced cheese, jam and possibly salami or some other sliced meat. If you want a rather better selection of bread, you can try one or more of the many kinds of rolls on sale. Traditionally, *rundstykker* (crusty rolls) and *kryddere* (the dictionary translation of rusks gives no idea of these crisp, extra-baked rolls) are the most common, but there are many others, and the traditional ones are nowadays supplemented with 'healthy' rolls made of various kinds of flour. All these rolls are given the generic name of *morgenbrød* ('morning bread'), and many Danes will go out of their way to have them for breakfast on a Sunday. They will also be on offer for your breakfast in hotels. Breakfast cereals such as cornflakes are also eaten, but you will just as often find oatflakes eaten raw with sugar and milk. You may be offered one or other of the soured milk products in the same family as yoghurt or fromage frais; yoghurt itself is among the many on offer, but perhaps the finest is *ymer*. The unimaginatively named A38 is a lighter type. Many of these products are eaten with a mixture of brown sugar and grated ryebread. If they want something sweet, Danes are just as likely to eat jam or honey as orange marmalade. You can drink either tea or coffee to taste. In hotels you will also be offered juice, and it is not at all uncommon to have a glass of milk. You may occasionally see a Dane drinking a bitter snaps (Gammel Dansk) with breakfast, and this is certainly available in hotels and restaurants, but the habit is not common, even if it is very much to be recommended. In hotels you will find Danish pastries (Wienerbrød) on offer. This is an old custom, and many people will still buy it as part of their Sunday morning breakfast.

Lunch (Frokost) is usually eaten between 12.00 and 13.00. A typical family lunch will often be a basic meal consisting of a couple of ryebread open sandwiches, with liver paste, sliced meat, salami, egg, cheese and possibly a little green vegetable (often raw) or fruit. This will be accompanied by milk, beer, tea or coffee. A slightly more elaborate lunch will include more expensive meat slices and some kind of fish, in particular marinated or smoked herring (Bornholm smoked herring is particularly good). The herring will often be washed down with an ice-cold snaps. Some lunches will also include some kind of warm dish, possibly *frikadeller* (rissoles, or meat balls—but much better than these names imply) or some other light meat dish, perhaps a fried breaded fish such as a plaice fillet. At still more expensive lunches there may well be smoked eel or *gravad laks* (salmon treated with herbs), or perhaps shellfish. And there will almost certainly be one of the countless varieties of salads available in Denmark.

Dinner (Middag) is usually eaten between 18.00 and 19.00. An ordinary family meal will often consist simply of a meat or fish dish with potatoes and some kind of salad, supplemented with a little fruit as a second course. Danes do not eat anywhere near as many sweet dishes as are common in England, though there is no lack of splendid desserts for those who want them.

If you eat out, or if you are entertained to dinner, a two- or three-course meal is the norm. The choices are legion, and the following are just a few of the dishes likely to be on offer.

Soups. Many Danes still tend to make their own soups rather than rely on cans. Consequently, their soups are good. In general Danish soups do not differ from those eaten in most other European countries, such as chicken soup, oxtail soup and vegetable soups. However, some differences can be found. You will often find small meat balls, dumplings and vegetables in the soups. You will also often find the meat or chicken on which the soup is based, served together with it, but on a separate plate, often accompanied by (mild) mustard or horseradish sauce. One typical Danish winter soup deserves special mention. This is *gule ærter* (split pea soup). It is made of split peas boiled with pieces of pork, cured gammon, or possibly *medisterpølse* (similar to Cumberland sausage), and containing various vegetables such as carrots, celeriac, leeks, onions and potatoes. At a time when traditional dishes are tending to be replaced by more exotic offerings, this is still very much in vogue and one of the few hot dishes with which a snaps and a beer are considered in good taste.

Main Course. Danish cuisine is these days pretty untraditional, but various specifically Danish dishes are still quite common:
Hakkebøf: a superior kind of burger made from the finest minced beef unmixed with other ingredients. Fried in a frying pan and usually served with fried onions.
Frikadeller: fried minced pork mixed with egg, flour, milk and onion. They are often served with *rødkål*, boiled red cabbage with a sweet-sour taste.
Karbonader are 'burgers' made of minced pork.
Cuts of meat are often different from the English custom, and so you are likely to find other names on your menu. Thus, a *flæskesteg* may well be a leg of pork, but it can equally well be the joint which in England is used for chops—which you will, of course, also find in Denmark. *Mørbradbøffer* are delicious small steaks of tenderloin. You will find the traditional roast of beef, *oksesteg*, but you will just as often find smaller joints known as *culottesteg* or *cuvettesteg*, cut from a leg of beef and—providing they have been well hung—extremely well tasting.

You should also try Danish sausages, which normally are of a very high quality. *Medisterpølse* with red cabbage (rødkål) is another traditional dish, while frankfurters are yet another which you may get in a private home, but which you really ought to try from a *pølsevogn*, one of the stalls selling them everywhere you turn—the Danish equivalent of fish and chips.

Potatoes are not mere filling in Denmark, and Danish potatoes are usually very tasty and much firmer than the usual English varieties. They will be served boiled or, often, baked.

Desserts. The huge variety of cakes in Denmark is usually of a very high quality. You will often find *lagkage* (layer cake) as a dessert, though you should not expect to find it served with extra cream. You are unlikely to need it.

Fromage, made with raw egg and gelatine, is rather similar to the English 'fool', tasting of one of a variety of fruits or spirits.

Budding is not like English 'pudding', but is rather like blancmange or real custard. *Rombudding* (rum pudding) is the traditional flavour, but there are many other varieties.

Ris à l'amande is a special Danish dessert consisting of boiled rice, whipped cream and almonds. It is quite a light dish and is eaten with stewed fruit—or fruit preserved in spirits. It is the traditional Danish Christmas pudding.

Is (ice cream) is a very common dessert—and Danish ice cream is very good indeed, though not so sweet as is common in England.

After a restaurant dinner it is worth asking whether you can have *kransekage* with your coffee. These are small individual cakes based on almonds and eggs. And if you want a short drink with your coffee, this is *not* the time to ask for snaps, which is drunk purely and simply with lunch, and then mainly if accompanying marinated herring! It was, on the other hand, an old Danish custom to have a snaps poured into your (black) coffee, but you will not often find this today.

It is worth noting that alcoholic drinks are very expensive in Danish restaurants due to the high tax placed on them there. Shop prices, on the other hand, are not affected by this tax. Wines tend to be a little cheaper than in the UK, and spirits rather more expensive.

The times indicated above are the traditional Danish meal times—though guests may well find that dinner is served rather later, as in other European countries. One result of the earlier times is that between-meal coffee etc. is also drunk rather earlier: *formiddagskaffe* (morning coffee) between 10.00 and 11.00, and *eftermiddagskaffe* (afternoon coffee) at about 15.00. If you have anything to eat with your morning coffee, it will be a *småkage* (cookie) rather than the English biscuit, which is not common in Denmark (though they are available in shops). In the afternoon you are more likely to have a *konditorkage* (fancy cake, cream cake) or a piece of *wienerbrød* (Danish pastry) of one kind or another. The northern English 'high tea' is unknown in Denmark.

Bibliography

Gorm Benzon: *Vore gamle kirker og klostre*, Lademann, Copenhagen 1973.

Jens Fleischer: *Ture i København*, Politikens Forlag, Copenhagen, 1986.

J. Broby Johansen: *Kunstvejviser over Danmark*, 1–15, Hamlet, Copenhagen, 1978–1986. *Den danske Billedbibel i Kalkmalerier*. Gyldendal, Copenhagen, 1948.

Svend Cedergreen Bech: *Københavns historie gennem 800 år*, P. Haase & Søns Forlag, Copenhagen, 1967.

Svend Cedergreen Bech and Jan Danielsen (eds.): *Danmark*, 1–10, Gyldendal, Copenhagen, 1986–89.

Odd Brochmann: *Seværdige København*, Arkitektens Forlag, Copenhagen, 1968.

Danmark 1:100 000. Topografisk Atlas, 3rd ed., Kort- og Matrikelstyrelsen, Copenhagen, 1989.

Dræbel, Eilstrup, Meyer, Rasmussen: *Danmarks Kongeslotte*, Lademann, Copenhagen.

Fakta. Gyldendals Etbindsleksikon, Gyldendal, Copenhagen 1988.

Lise Gotfredsen & Hans Jørgen Frederiksen: *Troens Billeder. Romansk kunst i Danmark*, Systime, Copenhagen 1988.

Harry Hjortaa: *Naturen Danmark rundt*. Politikens Forlag, Copenhagen, 1979.

Ulla Kjær & Poul Grinder-Hansen: *Kirkerne i Danmark I- II*, Boghandlerforlaget, Copenhagen 1988–89.

Hans Edvard Nørregård-Nielsen: *Dansk Kunst* 1–2, 1983.

Jytte Ortmann: *Guide over Danske Herregårde og Slotte*, Herluf Stokholms Forlag, Copenhagen, 1985.

Niels M. Saxtorph: *Danmarks kalkmalerier*, Politikens Forlag, Copenhagen, 1986.

Poul Svendsen: *Museer og seværdigheder i Danmark* I-II, Branner og Korch, Copenhagen, 1989–1990.

Tourist in Copenhagen and North Zealand, Dansk Bladforlag, Copenhagen, 1990.

J.P. Trap: *Danmark*, 5th ed. 1–31, G.E.C. Gad, Copenhagen, 1953–72.

Further Reading

Bent Rying: *Denmark. History*, Royal Danish Ministry for Foreign Affairs, Copenhagen, 1988.

P.V. Glob: *The Bog People*, Faber & Faber, London, 1971. *Danish Prehistoric Monuments*, Faber & Faber, London, 1971.

W. Glyn Jones: *Denmark. A Modern History*, Croom Helm, London, 1986.

Elisabeth Munksgaard: *Denmark: An Archaeological Guide*, Faber & Faber, London, 1970.

Stewart Oakley: *The Story of Denmark*, Faber & Faber, London, 1972.

Danish Literature in Translation

Works by many of the Danish writers mentioned are available in translation. We refer you to the following:

Hans Christian Andersen: The *Fairy Tales* are available in a host of translations of very varying quality. We suggest those by Reginald Spink og R.P. Keigwin as being the best British versions—though they are now out of print. A good American version in print is Patricia Conroy and Sven Rossel, *Tales and Stories by Hans Christian Andersen*, University of Washington Press, Seattle and London, 1980.

Andersen's autobiography, *The Fairy Tale of My Life*, tr. W. Glyn Jones. Copenhagen 1954; London, New York 1955.

Herman Bang: *Tina*, tr. Paul Christophersen. London, Dover, NH, 1984.
Karen Blixen (Isak Dinesen) is generally available in English, as much of her work was originally published in English.
Steen Steensen Blicher: *Diary of a Parish Clerk*, tr. Alexander Fenton, Herning 1976.
Martin A. Hansen: *The Liar*, tr. John Jepson Egglishaw. London, Melbourne, New York, 1986.
Jens Peter Jacobsen: *Marie Grubbe*, New York, 1952. *Niels Lyhne*, New York, 1967.
Johannes V. Jensen: *The Fall of the King*, tr. Patrick Kirwan, London, 1933.
Johannes Jørgensen: *St. Bridget of Sweden*, tr. Ingeborg Lund, London, 1954.
Søren Kierkegaard: all his works are now available in English.
Henrik Pontoppidan: *The Royal Guest and Other Classical Danish Narrative*, tr. P.M. Mitchell and Kenneth H. Ober, Chicago, London, 1977.

There are two comprehensive bibliographies of Danish literature in English translation:

Elias Bredsdorff: *Danish Literature in English Translation*, Copenhagen, 1950.
Carol L. Schroeder: *A Bibliography of Danish Literature in English Translation 1950–1980*, Copenhagen, 1982.

1   Esbjerg to Odense

Total distance 137km. E20 to (91km) **Lillebælt.**—E20, 161 to (46km) **Odense.**

Esbjerg (71,000 inhab.; Tourist Information: Skolegade 33, Torvet. Railway Station: Jernbanegade. Ferries: DFDS, Englandsterminalen, tel. 75 12 48 00) the main port of entry into Denmark from England, can almost be described as a city without a history. It was founded in 1868 (when there were said to be 20 people living in the area on a couple of windswept farms) with the express intention of its becoming an export centre, and it was given its charter as a market town in 1899. Until then, Hamburg had been an important centre for Danish overseas trade, but with the 1864 war and the subsequent loss of Denmark's other small west coast ports in South Jutland, a new outlet became necessary, not least because of the rapidly growing British market. The establishment of Esbjerg had long been discussed, but the final initiative was taken despite a great deal of scepticism by the much-maligned autocratic prime minister J.B.S. Estrup. Esbjerg is now Denmark's biggest port, not only for overseas trade, but as the home of some 550 fishing boats, and encompassing a large container terminal. It is Denmark's fifth largest town.

In a sense, Esbjerg has represented the modernisation of Denmark, the growing awareness at the end of the 19C that Denmark was what would nowadays be called an under-developed country, living in a grandiose dream of the past. After the 1864 war, which reduced Denmark to the smallest area it had ever known since becoming a united kingdom in the early Middle Ages, the decision was taken that 'what was lost abroad shall be won at home'. There is, then, little point in searching in Esbjerg for the 17C and 18C half-timbered houses for which Denmark is famous. Even the small houses here are brick-built, with an exterior reflecting modest affluence. The streets are intersecting straight lines, in the opinion of some inspired by American town planning, and in the view of others reflecting the influence of Fredericia, in which there are also straight intersecting streets in one of the older districts.

However this may be, Esbjerg is a city representing the new dynamism of an age of internal and external trade, a symbol of expansion. Its energy and ambition are perhaps already demonstrated by the watertower, looking like the remains of a medieval castle, built on the highest point, Baunehøj, dominating the town and visible from far out to sea. And the general architecture in the town centre reflects this: the impressive railway station, with its twin towers looking for all the world like the gateway to another castle, and the Landmandsbank building on the Market Square (Torvet), with its splendidly extravagant corbie-stepped façade. Indeed, the Market Square is in general a fine piece of architecture, one of the more expansive creations in a town otherwise bustling with business activity. The shopping centre is excellent, and the dead-straight pedestrian precinct, *Gågaden* belies its straightness, and has a charm of its own with a spaciousness leaving room for rows of small trees on either side of the main thoroughfare.

Yet there is also, as in most Danish centres, an interest beyond the merely commercial, and Esbjerg is well equipped with museums. At Havnegade 20 an art gallery, the *Esbjerg Kunstforenings Samling*, was opened in 1962—with a 3m-high piece of metal sculpture by Robert Jacobsen entitled *Esbjerg* and representing the brash energy which has gone into the town, adorning the gardens. It contains over 400 paintings by important 20C Danish artists as well as a large collection of lithographs. The *Esbjerg Museum* at Nørregade 25 specialises in local history and archaeology, and contains a fascinating series of reconstructions of façades, shops and dwellings from the early part of the century.

Another museum, the Museum of Printing (**Bogtrykmuseum**) in Borgergade 6, close to the railway station, is unique in Scandinavia. Dedicated to the history of printing and containing a range of old presses, all in working order, it provides a very special experience (open May–September).

In Tarphagevej, reached along the Hertingevej, there is a splendid museum dedicated to fishery and seamanship: **Fiskeriog Søfarts-museum**. It is particularly well arranged, with extensive collections of old equipment as well as models of old fishing boats. It also houses a saltwater aquarium containing most species of fish found in the North Sea, and a sealarium, where the seals can be watched through glass walls. An outdoor area offers reconstructions of a harbour, a stretch of sand dunes, a World War II shelter, a ropewalk and a lifeboat station, in all of which you are free to move about and explore the exhibits. Children will love it.

While many of Denmark's towns and villages can boast of interesting old churches, Esbjerg takes pride in its modern ones, two of which are special interest. On Fyrvej, to the north of the city, there is *Sædden Church*, designed by the architects Inger and Johannes Exner, and incorporated into a large shopping centre. In Kirkegade, rather closer to the centre, there is the Roman Catholic *Sankt Nicolaj Kirke*, designed by Otto von Spreckelsen, who achieved world-wide renown by his design for the monumental Grande Arche in Paris. The massive quadrilateral lines of the church echo those of the arch.

If you do not intend to return to this part of Denmark, you should make a trip 30km to the S of Esbjerg to the ancient city of *Ribe (Rte 15).

EXCURSION FROM ESBJERG TO FANØ. Before leaving Esbjerg, you should take a trip by ferry (20 mins) to *Nordby* (2500 inhab.) on **Fanø**, the low-lying island with 18km of spreading white sandy beaches and a *North Sea Swimming Baths* (*Vesterhavsbad*) opposite the harbour. You have in fact a good view of it to starboard (on the right side) on arrival at Esbjerg and can scarcely fail to note the wind farm on the coast.

This small island, which is now a tourist paradise with excellent sports and camping facilities, has had a mixed history. Originally the King's hunting ground, it was sold to the inhabitants themselves in 1741. These must have been lively people, for in 1685 they had managed to assure themselves the rights to sell their own fish without paying dues on them. After buying the island they made considerable profits from coastal traffic—and smuggling—and they subsequently established no fewer than four shipyards on the island. The income from these, together with the seafaring tradition already existing, led to a period of prolonged prosperity, which is reflected in the well-to-do aspect of the neat thatched houses in *Nordby* and the other small town on Fanø, *Sønderho*, 12km to the S, with its 100–200 old seamen's houses, one of which, *Hannes Hus*, is a museum seeking to recreate the typical Fanø house of former times (open school summer holidays).

Fanø has maintained much of the stubbornness of the island tradition, and both Nordby and Sønderho have succeeded in maintaining much of their old character; they still seek to show their traditions during weekends in July, when the tourist is likely to find people dressed in national costume, dancing traditional dances and even celebrating traditional weddings. Nordby has its Fanø Fair during the first weekend and Sønderho its Sønderho Fair in the third weekend.

Both Nordby and Sønderho have simple small churches with seafaring associations, that in Nordby dating from 1786, that in Sønderho from 1782. The *Fanø Museum* in Nordby has a fine collection of seafaring relics and many examples of the national costume which was long worn on Fanø (open Jun–Aug).

At Herluf Trollesvej 1 there is a toy museum with an array of toys, dolls and models from the past two centuries (open May–Oct).

Sønderho is the home of Denmark's oldest licensed inn, with a licence going back to 1722. The old lifeboat station from 1887, *Sønderho Gamle Rednings-station*, and the windmill from 1895 are now both museums (both open summer school holidays).

There are two very different routes across Jutland from Esbjerg to the **Lillebælt** strait. The direct route (total distance 91km) has very little to offer apart from the lower mileage, while the alternative route (109km) takes you to sights both ancient and modern.

DIRECT ROUTE TO LILLEBÆLT (total distance 91km). The road E of Esbjerg is low-lying, much of it reclaimed from the marsh and moorland which were once the hallmarks of Jutland. On reaching (33km) Holsted, you should drive a further 2km and then turn off right to *Tirslund* (4km), where, in the woods, you will find a huge erratic boulder, 3.5m high and 5.6m in diameter, standing on its own in a clearing, transported there by the ice in a distant past. Legend has it that Harald Bluetooth wanted to use the stone as a memorial to his parents at Jelling (Rte 21), but that when he had got it as far as this he heard that his son was organising a rebellion, and so he took it no further. But this is only legend. Judging by the name (Tirslunde = Tir's Grove), this must once have been a shrine of the god Tyr.

Back on the E20 you pass through the grounds of *Estrup manor* (built 1721) before you arrive at (15km) *Vejen* (Tourist Information: Nørregade 42), where there is a gallery of works by South Jutlandic artists. Standing in front of it there is a striking statue by Niels Hansen Jacobsen, 'Troll Scenting Christian Blood', from 1896. It clearly shows the influence of Rodin, whose work Hansen Jacobsen had become acquainted with during a stay in Paris.

Near the SW outskirts of Vejen lies *Askov*, the site of one of Denmark's great folk high schools.

Askov is inevitably associated with N.F.S. Grundtvig, whose idea of a high school movement to give a non-academic education to the rural population, and to fill them with Christian and patriotic ideals, was first put into practice by C. Flor at *Rødding* just S of Askov. This first *folk high school* was, however, situated on territory that was lost in the 1864 war, and consequently a new start had to be made in 1865. The main building of a disused farm in Askov was then the spot chosen, just N of the Kongeå river (the Danish–German border between 1864 and 1920), and with its views across the lost Danish lands it soon became a place of great emotional significance. Askov Folk High School has since attracted all the great popular Grundtvigian orators of its time, and although the ethos of the folk high schools today is a different one, Askov has retained a central position in the Danish consciousness. An offshoot of 19C National Romanticism, the folk high school movement has now for more than a century fostered a cultural awareness and a sense of a Danish Scandinavian cultural identity which it is perhaps difficult for non-Scandinavians to appreciate.

As a result of the growing importance of this non-academic education, Askov Folk High School has been subjected to various extensions over the years, and few of the original buildings are now left. Visits are possible on application.

A minor road S from Askov will take you to *Skibelund Krat* (3km), a wooded area just N of the old border. This, too, has memories of Grundtvigian patriotism, and was a spot where large popular gatherings were organised in the period up to 1920. There is a large amphitheatre with seating for 4000, and there are monuments to many Danish patriots. There is a wide view across what was then German territory.

Malt Romanesque church just W of Askov is known for having one of the best-preserved Romanesque fonts in Denmark. The motifs on it are in themselves curious: in addition to complex ornamentation, four men are portrayed engaged in combat, while a woman is seen fleeing and carrying a child.

From Vejen you follow the E20 E through increasingly undulating country. At 20km you meet the E45 motorway from Germany. From here the E20 (your route) follows the E45 N for 7km, at which point the two roads divide again and you follow the E20 to (14km) Lillebælt.—If you want to visit Kolding (Rte 13)—and you really ought to—you drive straight ahead where the E20 meets the E45. (For Lillebælt see below.)

ALTERNATIVE ROUTE FROM ESBJERG TO LILLEBÆLT—VIA LEGOLAND (total distance 109km). You leave Esbjerg on the E20, after 11km turning left on to the A30 to (35km) the industrial town of *Grindsted* (8930 inhab.; Tourist Information: Østergade 25). There is a very large church here, sometimes referred to as the Heath Cathedral. In 1921–23 an impressive new nave and tower were added to the original Romanesque church. The old altarpiece and much of the old furniture is now on view in the tower, to which access may be had on application.

You now turn right on to the A28, which takes you direct to (12km) *Billund* (4380 inhab.; Tourist Information: Åstvej 1), now mainly known as the home of **Legoland**. Over 33 million Lego bricks are said to have been used in building this pleasure park, with among other things its miniature reconstructions of buildings from all over the world. You can see eminently recognisable reconstructions of Copenhagen, Amsterdam, London, Stockholm and many other famous cities. Legoland has a huge collection of antique dolls, the oldest being from c 1580, as well as a comprehensive collection of antique toys of all kinds. Then there are dolls' houses, including, as the jewel, *Titania's Palace*, said to be the most elaborate miniature palace in the world, standing 185cm high and covering an area of 230cm x 295cm. There are 18 rooms in it, and over 3000 pieces of furniture and equipment. It took the maker, Sir Neville Wilkinson, 15 years to complete his building, which was bought by Legoland in 1978. Another special feature of Legoland is a collection of 19C toys recently recovered from a ship which sank in 1870. Surmounting the whole site with its Legotrain, Indian Legoredotown, miniboats and Traffic school is a rotating restaurant at the top of the Legotop observation tower. Very much for the children, but acceptable for all ages, being kept in good Danish taste and beautifully laid out.

Here too you will find Museumscenter Billund, containing the motorcar museum, *Danmarks Bilmuseum*; the aircraft museum, *Danmarks Flyvemuseum*; the museum illustrating the history of the Falck Emergency Service, the *Falckmuseum*; and the *Billund Terrarium* (reptile zoo).

Leave Billund on the 176 S, a good and not-too-busy road. In 17km you will pass through *Egtved*.

Egtved parish is known to contain some 260 burial mounds, though only a small number have been preserved. However, on excavation in 1921, one of these revealed one of Denmark's major Early Bronze Age finds, the *Egtved Find*. The mound contained the body of a 20–25-year-old woman, the *Egtved girl*, in a remarkable state of preservation and surrounded by a large collection of grave goods. She was in an oak coffin, lying on cowhide, fully dressed, and furnished with two bracelets and an earring of bronze. The charred remains of a child, possibly a sacrifice, lay close to her. The mound, to the NW of Egtved, is still visible, but the find itself is now on show in the National Museum in Copenhagen. However, a wooden hut on the spot contains photographs demonstrating the excavation and the opening of the coffin, and there is a reproduction of the clothing worn by the Egtved girl.

The Romanesque *church in Egtved is equipped with an octagonal tower added in a fit of zealous restoration in the 1860s. The purist will regret this zeal, but will look with interest at the fresco frieze of the

Dance of Death which was uncovered in 1969. There are two other friezes of this kind in Denmark, one in Nørre Alslev in Falster and one in Jungshoved on Stevns (both Rte 10). This one is nevertheless different in that the heads are missing from all the figures! All three friezes seem to be related to the more famous one of the same kind in Lübeck.

14km further on you reach the 441. Here you turn right, and in another 5km you meet the E20, which by now has become a motorway, but also acts as a sort of glorified ring road to the splendid old town of Kolding (Rte 13) which, time permitting, should be visited. If, however, you decide against a visit, you just join the E20 E to (17km) Lillebælt.

Lillebælt, the sound that separates Jutland from Fyn, is the narrowest of the three stretches of water separating the Kattegat from the Baltic. Whereas *Storebælt* (The Great Belt) and *Øresund* (The Sound) are considered international shipping routes, Lillebælt has much more of a local Danish character. It is about 130km long and at the narrowest point no more than 700m wide. It is only 13m deep at the entrance, and so it is impossible for large ships to sail through.

The stretch along Lillebælt is very beautiful, and both to the N and to the S there are often large numbers of sailing ships to be seen. This is particularly so in July during the annual sailing race around Fyn known as 'Fyn Rundt'. However, Lillebælt has other things to offer—magnificent beaches for bathing, ideal conditions for windsurfing and sailing, and excellent fishing.

There are two bridges across Lillebælt. The *old Lillebælt Bridge* was opened in 1935 and was at that time a tourist attraction for all Danes. It is a combined road and rail bridge. There are two railway tracks, a roadway and a footpath. Its total length is 1178m, 825m of which is over the water.

Building commenced on the new motorway bridge in 1965, and it was opened in 1970. With its 1080m this is the longest suspension bridge in northern Europe. It has two 120m-high towers, and the piers are box caissons in 19m of water, supported on ferro-concrete piles.

From Lillebælt you have the choice of two routes across Fyn to Odense. The fast direct route (total distance 46km) is described first; see below for the slower, winding one (64km). However, Middelfart (Rte 12), 2km S of the motorway is an optional digression on both, but the decision for or against a visit there has got to be taken within 1km after leaving the bridge!

DIRECT ROUTE FROM LILLEBÆLT (total distance 46km). Leave the E20 motorway at (10km) Junction 57 and continue your route on the 161, the old main road across Fyn.

4km ahead you could make a small DETOUR. Follow an unclassified road N to *Brenderup* (4km), where you will find the mansion of *Kærsgård*. The neo-classical house is from 1817 with outbuildings from 1868. It is not generally open, but access to it and the chapel can be arranged on application. A special feature of this estate is the c 60 old carriages and sleighs which have been collected there.

Return to the 161 and drive another 15km to *Vissenbjerg*, where you will find on Roldvej 53 *Fyns Akvarium*, with some 300 species of fish including piranha, surgeon fish and sharks, and at Kirkehelle 5 a large *Terrarium* (reptile zoo).

It is now only 17km to Odense (see below).

ALTERNATIVE ROUTE FROM LILLEBÆLT TO ODENSE—VIA MID-FYN (total distance 64km). This secondary route from Lillebælt to Odense is slower but more idyllic and will take you past two mansions. At

22km (Junction 55 on the motorway) you turn S on the 329 towards
Årup. After c 2km, you will find an estate, *Erholm*, on the left. The
'English' park is open to the public, and you will have a view of the
neo-Gothic mansion dating from 1850. The house is open to parties of
25 or more by arrangement beforehand. The wine cellar, however, is
open 12.00–15.00 on Sat for the tasting and sale of Romanian quality
wines.

4km further S lies the village of *Skydebjerg*, with a curiously stumpy
Gothic church tower which was never quite finished. Another 6km of
this lovely, hilly, wooded countryside will bring you to a minor road on
your left leading you to (5km) *Krengerup*, a glorious, harmonious,
neo-classical mansion from 1772, flanked by a half-timbered home
farm and outbuildings from 1771. The farmyard opens straight on to
the road, giving a fine view of the mansion. There is public access to
the park during daylight hours and there are marked walks. During
the summer public concerts are held in the house.

Drive on now to (2km) Nårup where you turn right, joining the 168
E after 3km to (11km) *Bellinge*. Here there is a Gothic *church containing some of the best of Danish church frescoes, uncovered in 1883
and restored the following year, portraying scenes from the Old and
New Testaments. There is also a painting of St. George and the Dragon,
and in between the principal motifs there are all kinds of small
figures—jugglers, men carrying guns, etc. Most unusually, these
frescoes are signed and dated: Ebbe Olesen and Simon Pedersen, 1496.
The brick-built altar is from 1595 and is surmounted by an altarpiece
from c 1525. From Bellinge the road leads you straight into (9km)
Odense.

ODENSE (137,000 inhab.; Tourist Information: Rådhuset) is the principal town and administrative centre of Fyn. It has been the seat of a
bishop since the 10C and, since being overtaken by *Århus* (Rte 16) in
the 1880s, is now the third largest city in Denmark.

It is the centre of Odense which is particularly interesting, the quite
small area immediately S of the railway station and down to the river.
Here the streets are busy where traffic is permitted, but there are many
pedestrian streets which allow the visitor to savour that mix of old and
new in architecture and manner of life which is one of the hallmarks
of modern Denmark. Old shops and houses stand cheek by jowl with
modern counterparts, and street musicians are likely to be heard
playing music which is scarcely in harmony with the older façades. The
area is architecturally dominated by St. Knud's (St. Canute's) Cathedral,
and it is here, too, that the birthplace and the later home of Hans
Christian Andersen are to be found. The area has been renovated rather
than modernised on the outside, and has something of the fairytale air
of the past which it is intended to invoke. Whether the clean, tidy
exteriors of these old houses today bear much resemblance to what
they were at the time of Andersen, must stand open to question. But a
certain charm cannot be denied. Outside this central area there are
industrial estates and large residential developments of a more stylised
and less individual nature.

The earliest known reference to Odense is found in a document from 988 and,
consequently, the town celebrated its millennium in 1988. It is likely, however,
that, with its central situation, a crossing point of the river, and with river access
to the sea, it is much older, as is suggested by the name itself, almost certainly
meaning 'Odin's shrine'. Attempts have been made to find relics of the heathen
cult, and there are signs of earthen ramparts like those in Trelleborg on
present-day Nonnebakken, S of the river.

In 988 Emperor Otto III issued a letter to the Archbishop of Bremen in which he exempted the town from taxes and declared his support for the creation of a bishopric there. The 11C historian Adam of Bremen talks of Odense as the 'magna civitas' of Fyn, and large numbers of coins were struck there in the reign of Knud I the Great (1000–35) and for successive centuries. Although Knud the Great (King Canute of England 1014–35) was associated with Odense, it was Knud II, St. Knud (1040–86), who came to occupy a central position in the town's history. In his efforts to establish a firm royal and ecclesiastical power, he caused a rebellion in Jutland. He fled to Odense, where he sought refuge in the then wooden church of St. Alban (relics of whom had been brought from England, probably in 1075). There, kneeling before the altar, he was murdered together with his guard. By the end of the century the mood had changed, and in 1101 he was canonised, his body having already been moved in 1095 to a stone-built church for which he himself was responsible. The canonisation of St. Knud led to Odense's becoming a place of pilgrimage, the home of six convents and monasteries, including two of the biggest in the country.

It is uncertain when Odense received its charter, though it may have been under King Valdemar III (1326–30), and from the beginning of the 15C it became the residence of many members of the Pomeranian, and later Danish, aristocracy. This, together with the large number of clerics attached to the See and the monasteries, gave the city its special character. Odense maintained its position as a centre of ecclesiastical affairs around and after the Reformation, when meetings of the aristocracy and of clerics were held to further the cause of the reformers.

In 1529 Odense was devastated by fire, and this was followed by further difficult years of suffering during the Count's War, when it was occupied first by one and then by the other side. By the mid-16C, however, it was on its way up again, and in the following hundred years it benefited greatly from the upsurge in foreign trade. Its position as a centre for great assemblies was re-established by the kings, and it was here the assemblies took the decision to open war on Sweden in 1654 and 1657. In 1658 Odense was occupied by the Swedish army, which stayed for a full two years and imposed crippling taxes on the citizens.

With the establishment of the absolute monarchy in 1661, the city lost its influential position as a meeting place, and a period of poverty ensued, lasting until the 18C. It was King Frederik IV who was largely responsible for improving the position. He and his Queen were fond of Odense, and in 1720–21 he had the old Sankt Hans Monastery transformed into Odense Castle (where he in fact died in 1730). The King's frequent visits to Odense brought back some of the aristocracy, and trade flourished once more. A sugar factory was established in 1751, followed by a soap works two years later and other industries throughout the rest of the century. In 1795 a theatre was opened.

War again put an end to this flourishing time. From 1807 to 1814 Denmark was involved on the French side in the Napoleonic Wars, which led to a period of impoverishment here as elsewhere in the country. Nevertheless, by the mid-19C the gradual move towards present prosperity began, partly as a result of the canal opened in 1804. Linking Odense direct to the Odense Fjord this led to the establishment of a harbour in the city. Moreover, Odense came to enjoy an advantageous position as a meeting point for virtually all the railways in Fyn.

One native of Odense associated with the wealth created in Denmark in the late 19C was Carl Frederik Tietgen, the financier and banker who was Director of Privatbanken in 1857 and who was one of the driving forces behind the estab-lishment of the shipping company DFDS, the Great Northern Telegraph Company, the Danish Sugar Refineries, and the Tuborg Breweries. There is a statue in memory of him in the park, Kongens Have, immediately opposite the railway station.—There, too, is a statue to Christmas Møller, the Conservative politician who during World War II was forced to flee to London, where he became the spokesman for Danes in exile.

To the SE of Kongens Have stands Odense Castle, partially rebuilt on the site of the old St. John's (Sankt Hans) Monastery by Frederik IV, and now, partly as the residence of the Chief Administrative Officer of Fyn, in the possession of the City of Odense. Immediately adjoining, in Nørregade, is *Sankt Hans Kirke*, once the monastery church. It is the only church in Denmark to have an outdoor pulpit. It fell into disrepair after the Reformation, and has been the subject of a good deal of rebuilding and restoration.

Odense is a busy city and was renowned for its traffic problems until the ring road was completed. Now, however, it is possible in parts to

Carl Nielsen Mus.
H.C. Andersen Mus.
Montergården Mus.
Vor Frue Kirke
Skt. Albani
H.C. Andersen Have

THOMAS B.
THRIGES GADE
KOCHSGADE
ENGGADE
ØSTERGADE
ØSTERGADE
RIDEHUSGADE
ØSTERBRO
GRØNLANDSGADE
DANMARKSGADE
PJENTEDAMSGADE
PJENTEDAMSGADE
CLAUS BERGSGADE
HANS
MULES GADE
JØRGENS
GADE
KERTEMINDE
JENSENS STR.
BANGS BODER
SANKT
OVERGADE
NEDERGADE
BROGADE
CHRISTIANSGADE
GEORGSGADE
FREDERIKSGADE
TORVEGADE
ALBANI TORV
ALBANIGADE
TVÆRGADE
LANGEGADE
NYBORGVEJ
NYBORG
RØDEGÅRDSVEJ
KRONPRINSENSGADE
ALBANIGADE
SKT. KNUD GADE
ABSALONSGADE
FREDENSGADE
ALLEGADE
ALLEGADE
GLOTHABSGADE
HJALLESEVEJ
MUNKEBJERSVEJ
REVENTLOWSVEJ
JAGTVEJ

N

ODENSE

0 metres   200

University

forget traffic and to stroll quietly along streets which have stood here
for many years, streets with charming names such as *Filosofgangen*
(Philosopher's Walk), *Vintapperstræde* (Tapster Street) and *Poge-
stræde* (Infant Street).

A walk from the railway station down the busy Jernbanegade will
take you past the impressive *Fyn Art Gallery*, built 1883–84 and
extended in 1897–98. Here there are extensive collections of Danish
art, from the great early figures such as Jens Juel and Christoffer
Wilhelm Eckersberg to major modern figures like Asger Jorn, Richard
Mortensen and Robert Jacobsen. Beyond the heavily restored former
Greyfriars' Monastery, Jernbanegade brings you to the pedestrian
precincts and the older part of the town, and a left turn into *Vestergade*
will soon see you in *Flakhaven*, with the *Town Hall (1883) on one
side. The 57m-long façade facing the square with its statue of Frederik
VII by H.W. Bissen and the large abstract metal sculpture presented
by Robert Jacobsen on the occasion of Odense's millennium, is a
mixture of neo-Gothic and Italian, surmounted by figures representing
the legislative and judicial powers. The internal decorations of the
Town Hall are partly by the Fyn painter Johannes Larsen and can be
seen on conducted tours in the afternoons in summer. The lateral
wings of the original three-winged building were demolished in the
1940s. In 1955 they were replaced, and a fourth wing added to a
design by Helweg Møller. One wing overlooks *Albani Torv* square
with its Roman Catholic Sankt Albani church (built 1906–08) in North
German style and the old Odense *Adelig Jomfrukloster* (residence for
ladies of the aristocracy). Beyond lie two parks, *H.C. Andersen Have*
and the *Klosterhave*.

The *Cathedral** is one of Denmark's major cathedrals, with shrines
to SS. Knud and Alban (or possibly St. Knud and his brother Benedikt)
in the crypt, and with several royal tombs. St. Knud was himself
responsible for the original travertine church, in which he was subsequently buried. After fires in 1157 and 1247 a virtually new building
was commenced under the guidance of Bishop Gisico, resulting after
almost two centuries in the wholly brick-built Gothic cathedral now
standing. The strikingly lofty nave with its elegant arches was finished
by 1300, the chancel being added towards the end of the century. This
chancel is approached by a broad flight of steps—its height is because
the crypt from the original church was left in place, if not entirely
intact. The immediate impression of this cathedral is one of lofty
harmony and space, though the whitewashed walls give it a slightly
severe appearance. This is offset, however, by the *altar, a magnificent
triptych by Claus Berg, almost 5m high, which was originally made in
1521 for the old Greyfriars' Church and installed in its present position
in 1885. Based on a painting from 1515 by Lucas Cranach, it is Claus
Berg's masterpiece, containing almost 300 carved figures and representing the work of redemption. It consists of a huge central panel with
eight smaller panels in the triptych wings and a further panel at the
bottom. In addition to Christ crucified and the Apostles and the Virgin,
there are recognisable portraits of the Church Fathers, of St. Francis of
Assisi and members of the Danish Royal Family. An inordinate amount
of gold has been used on the altarpiece, which stands as one of the
most impressive, perhaps *the* most impressive in Denmark, both for
the splendour of the figures and for the intricacy of the decoration.

The Cathedral's other principal treasures are in the *crypt, where
there are two Romanesque reliquaries, one containing the relics of St.
Knud, the other now generally thought to contain the relics of St.
Knud's brother, but by some thought to be those of St. Alban. These

reliquaries have had a complicated history: probably hidden at the Reformation and found again walled up in 1582, they were finally removed and put in place in the Cathedral in 1833. In 1806 the remains of King Hans, Queen Christine, and their sons Frants and Christian (the later Christian II) were moved to the Cathedral on the closing of the old Greyfriars' Church; they are now in a vault in the E end of the N nave, surmounted by a splendid epitaphium to King Hans by Claus Berg, dated 1513 and thought to be a true likeness of the king. A memorial tablet to Prince Hans, also attributed to Claus Berg's workshop, can be seen near the entrance to the crypt. At the E end of the N aisle is the Valkendorf Chapel, containing a monument by Thomas Quellinus and enclosed in a wrought-iron gate by Christian IV's metalwork artist, Caspar Fincke. Opposite is the Ahlefeldt Chapel, also with a memorial monument by Quellinus.

Adjoining the Cathedral on the S are the former domestic buildings of the Benedictine St. Canute's Monastery, now the Diocesan Library. In the courtyard there is a bust of Thomas Kingo, Bishop of Odense (1634–1703) and one of Denmark's great hymn-writers. A baroque poet of great note, Kingo was given the task of compiling a new hymn book, but the job was taken away from him again when it was discovered that he was filling it with his own hymns. Ultimately, however, the undertaking was returned to him, and he produced what became known as Kingo's Hymn Book, which in some parishes was used into the present century.

On leaving the Cathedral, if you proceed down Sankt Knuds Kirkestræde, you will come to Munkemøllestræde, where at Nos 3–5 there is a relic of a different kind in the house in which *Hans Christian Andersen* lived from the age of two until, at 14, he went to Copenhagen. Serving as an annex to the Hans Christian Andersen Museum proper, this tiny house contains an exhibition seeking to illustrate the author's childhood. There is not room for more.

> The home where I spent my childhood was one single little room where almost all the space was taken up by the workshop, the bed and the settle on which I slept. The walls, however, were covered with pictures; on the chest of drawers there were some pretty cups, glasses and ornaments, and over my father's bench there was a shelf containing books and songs...
> By means of a ladder it was possible to go from the kitchen on to the roof, and there, in the gutters between it and the neighbour's house, stood a box of soil with chives and parsley growing in it;—it was all the garden my mother had, and in my story of 'The Snow Queen' that garden still blooms.

The main **Hans Christian Andersen Museum*, however, is the house in which Andersen was born, in Hans Jensenstræde 37–45. This is most easily reached by retracing your steps to the Town Hall, crossing Vestergade and going up Dansestræde to Gravene, which will lead you under the ring road into Hans Jensenstræde. Here, several houses have been converted into a museum, containing spoken commentaries on the writer's life, rooms containing his furniture, letters, photographs and manuscripts, together with a large collection of Andersen's work in many languages. Andersen was a great traveller, and the museum contains his trunks, his hat case (and hat) and, not least, the length of rope which he always took with him in case of fire. Certainly a museum for the tourist, but the serious Andersen scholar will also find plenty of interest. The central hall is decorated with paintings by Niels Larsen Stevns illustrating episodes in Andersen's life.

Close by, in Claus Bergsgade at the further end of Hans Jensensstræde, is the *Carl Nielsen Museum*, giving a visual and aural presentation of the life and work of the great composer and of his wife, the sculptress Anne Marie Carl Nielsen. This museum makes no concessions to the olde worlde atmosphere of this part of town, and is a modern, purpose-built edifice.

If you walk down to the other end of Claus Bergsgade, you come to Overgade, and a left turn will bring you to the *Møntergården Museum* based on 16C and 17C buildings from Odense, and intended to illustrate the history of the city. There is also a numismatic collection (open Mar–Dec).

A few metres further along Overgade will bring you to *Vor Frue Kirke* (Our Lady's Church), the oldest surviving church in Odense, part Romanesque, part Gothic, though heavily restored in the 19C. Built in brick, it contains remnants of an older, stone-built church on the same spot. It was in this church that Claus Berg's altarpiece was placed before being removed to the Cathedral in 1885; that replacing it is more modest, a painting of the Crucifixion by A. Dorph, 1885. There is a carved wooden font from c 1650 and an impressive baroque pulpit by Anders Mortensen, dated 1639.

Odense is well furnished with museums, most of which are within easy reach of each other. Retrace your steps again and walk down the busy Vestergade until, on your right, you come to Brandts Passage. There at No. 37 you will find *Brandts Klædefabrik*, which houses an art gallery (*Kunsthallen*) with travelling exhibitions, a *Museum of Photographic Art*, unique in Denmark, and *Denmark's Graphic Museum*, an exhibition of graphic processes from the Middle Ages to the present.

Two more museums in the city itself must be mentioned. The *Falck Museum* in Klostervej contains a historical collection of old fire engines and ambulances such as those which have been used by the Falck ambulance and fire service (open May–Oct). And, returning to the station and going beyond it, there is the *Danish Railways Museum*, a large collection of old rolling stock and other relics from the past 140 years (open summer; limited opening winter).

Odense is the home of one of Denmark's modern universities. It is situated about 3km SE of the centre, and can best be approached via Albanigade and Hjallesevej, turning left into Niels Bohrs Allé; the *University then stands a few hundred metres on the right on Campusvej, a large, monumental building from the 1960s, in rust and black.

2km E of the University you will find **Den fynske Landsby** (The Fyn Village), one of the largest of Denmark's open air museums. It contains farms, houses, mills and other buildings such as a toll booth and a prison house, all taken there from different parts of Fyn (open Apr–Oct; limited opening winter). The river *Odense Å* flows nearby, and for those with a will to walk, there is a path all the way along this charming river to the environs of Fyn Village. (In the opposite direction the path follows the river through and well beyond the city of Odense, broken only briefly at Filosofgangen and Klosterbakken, and restarting at Albanitorv.) For those wanting a more leisurely approach to Den fynske Landsby, there are sailings from the central Munke Mose and Filosofgangen to *Fruens Bøge*, from where *Erik Bøghs Sti* leads to the village. These boats call on the way at the *Fyns Tivoli* (fairground) and *Odense Zoo*, both of which also can be reached by car of course, leaving Odense along Søndre Boulevard.

Close to Den fynske Landsby, too, on Dalumvej, lies *Dalum Kloster* (Dalum Convent). The convent and its church were founded around 1200 by Benedictine nuns, many of whom belonged to the nobility, and it developed into one of the richest convents in Fyn, owning a great deal of land. At the Reformation it became Crown property, though the nuns were allowed to remain there until the last died sometime before 1580. Christian IV invested Ellen Marsvin, the mother of his morganatic wife Kirstine Munk, with the freehold of the estate, and his children from that marriage were brought up there. The King himself often visited Dalum Kloster. In 1682 the estate was sold to Didrik Schult and was given the name of Christiansdal, a name which it retained until in 1906 it was bought by the Order of St. Hedvig, who turned it into a rest home. The original convent buildings have all disappeared, apart from the church, *Dalum Kirke*, originally the N wing of the convent, and modified in the 17C. In 1930 the St. Hedvig's Sisters had a new church built for their own use.

At Hestehaven 201, S of the University, lies Hollufgård, a 16C mansion, now in the possession of Odense City Council. It is used as a prehistoric museum, incorporating historical workshops and a Bronze Age milieu.

N of Odense, beyond the airport, there is yet another museum in the Jernalderlandsbyen (Iron Age Village), where archaeologists have sought to recreate an Iron Age atmosphere.

EXCURSION FROM ODENSE TO NORTH FYN AND BOGENSE (total distance c 70km). Take the 303 W from Odense via Korup to (15km) Morud, stopping at (14km) *Langesø Skov*. These woods are a favourite spot for the people of Odense, with three paths for walking clearly indicated, two of them passing close to the elegant 18C neo-classical *Langesø mansion*.

From Morud follow the 335 N to (7km) *Søndersø*, where there is a splendid and largely Romanesque church. The horizontally striped exterior of granite ashlars alternating with whitewashed brick is unusual, while the interior exhibits some outstanding frescoes from c 1500, depicting the Immaculate Conception, the Annunciation, the Birth of Christ and the Adoration of the Magi. There is a Romanesque font, and the N door, from 1483, has an inscription in letters of iron.

Now take the 311 to (15km) *Bogense* (3000 inhab.; Tourist Information: Adelgade 26), passing just S of the town *Harritslevgård*, a mansion from 1606, now used as a residential college. Bogense is the smallest market town in Fyn, with a charter from 1288. It has a fishing harbour, and a modern marina dating from 1976. There are splendid views of Jutland and the tiny island of Æbelø from the harbour and from other vantage points. Perhaps the most striking feature of this small town is the market place, Torvet, which is 'different', an elongated wide road flanked on each side by elm trees, and behind them a row of small neat 19C houses.

At the end of Torvet, on the NW side, stands the church, originally dedicated to St. Nicholas, the patron saint of seafarers. Other old houses are *Den gamle Købmandsgård* in Annagade, and in Østergade *Erik Menveds Kro*, the oldest building in Bogense. In Adelgade there is, surprisingly, a copy of the famous Manneken Pis from Brussels, presented to Bogense in 1943 by Consul Willem Fønns. A dominant position is occupied by the Town Hall and Courthouse (1921) in Østergade. The old railway station in Jernbanegade is now the *North Fyn Museum* (open Jun–Aug; limited opening winter).

The 327 will take you all the way back to Odense. At 3km E you will catch a glimpse to the right of the impressive *Gyldensten mansion*, dating from 1640, standing in the largest estate in North Fyn. 13km further on you reach *Uggerslev*, from where it is a short drive W to *Skamby* (3km). The church here is one of the oldest in Fyn and has a fine crucifix by Claus Berg. Close to Skamby, between *Torup* and *Glavendrup*, you will find the *Glavendrupsten* (The Glavendrup Stone), bearing Denmark's longest runic inscription.

From Uggerslev it is 17km to Odense.

EXCURSION FROM ODENSE TO THE HINDSHOLM PENINSULA, KERTEMINDE AND LADBY (total distance c 78km). This tour takes you to the NE corner of Fyn and back. Leave Odense on the 165 and drive to (15km) *Munkebo*, once a small fishing village, but now dominated by the modern Lindø shipyard. From Munkebo you drive uphill along the Munkebo Bakke hill, providing splendid views towards Hindsholm, across the Odense Fjord and the Kerteminde Fjord. Fork left towards (8km) *Mesinge*, where there is an unusual church with a pre-Reformation copper spire surmounting a corbie-stepped gable, and on to (5km) *Stubberup*, passing the village of *Dalby* and the mansion of *Scheelenborg*, with a history going back to the 13C (not open to the public). At Stubberup you will find a village church—known locally as 'the white virgin'—standing high, with splendid views across the sea.

Legend has it that this is the burial place of the regicide turned national hero, *Marsk Stig*, who died in 1293. As he was outlawed, his funeral had to take place in secret, and the story goes that the local priest was awakened one night and ordered to say a requiem mass for an unnamed dead person. He went to the church, found a grave already open in front of the altar and a coffin lying before it. He was sworn to secrecy after the funeral had taken place, but the maid in the presbytery had seen what had happened, and took the splendid drapings off the coffin in order to make her wedding dress of them. Unwittingly, she told her lover, who declared that she thus knew where his master was buried, and so must die. She was then buried in the cloth she had intended for her wedding dress. Despite the trappings, there is some chance that the main story is founded on fact, though Stubberup is not the only church in Denmark to claim to be the burial place of Marsk Stig.

Finally, driving through *Martofte* you will reach the very tip of *Hindsholm*, at (8km) *Fyns Hoved*, remembering that this peninsula was an island until the early 19C, when a land reclamation programme joined it to mainland Fyn. Fyns Hoved is a cliff 25m above the sea, and there are striking views from it of the North Fyn coast, N up the Belt to the island of Samsø, and even across to Sjælland.

This is also an area with a large number of neolithic and Viking burial sites, and the landscape is dotted with burial mounds. On your way S you should try and visit *Mårhøj*, just N of Martofte and a couple of hundred metres from the road. It is the biggest passage grave in Fyn, dating from c 200 BC. The main chamber, reached through a narrow passage 7m long, is over 10m long and almost high enough to stand up in. It is made up of 18 large upright megaliths surmounted by seven cover stones. Two other passage graves are *Tornehøj* and *Hestehøj*.

Now drive as far S as Mesinge, there turning left and following the minor road to (2km) the delightful village of *Viby*, where there is a restored windmill (limited opening), and an early Gothic church with a half-timbered tower which was added in 1718. Continue S to (6km) Kerteminde, noting the late 18C mansion of *Hverringe* on the way. The present rococo house was built in 1790, but the estate goes back to the days of King Valdemar IV.

Kerteminde (5000 inhab.; Tourist Information: Strandgade 5A) is another of the idyllic small market towns of Fyn, with a charter dating from 1413. There is a market, an old harbour, a large and well-equipped marina and many old buildings, mainly in a simple style, for instance those in Fiskergade. A harbour festival is held the first weekend in August, and every year on Midsummer's Eve, when bonfires are lit all over Denmark, there is a large bonfire on the N beach.

One of the fine old houses, *Farvergården* (The Dyers' House), in Langgade, is now the town museum, with exhibitions covering local history and art, and including a reconstructed interior from the 19C (open Mar–Oct). Also in Langgade there is an alderman's house from 1630, while an old half-timbered house has been adapted as a bank. Close by, in Trollegade, is the *Høker* (Grocer), a 17C house renovated and turned into an olde worlde village store or 'museum shop' (open Jun Aug, and Dec). The old customs house in Strandgade now exhibits the work of local artists, but the local artist par excellence is, of course, Johannes Larsen, whose home on *Møllebakken* is now a *museum dedicated to his work and that of other local painters (open Apr–Oct).

Johannes Larsen, one of the Fyn School, is famous for his bird paintings, combining both accuracy and great artistry, and for his impressionistic recreations of Danish provincial scenes. One of his most famous paintings, 'View across roofs in Kerteminde, early morning in May' from 1896 or 1897 is for many the epitome of Danish provincialism, and Kerteminde seeks to preserve this as its ideal. Others of Johannes Larsen's pictures can be seen in the restaurant Pavillon Pax.

Close to the Johannes Larsen Museum is *Svanemøllen* (The Swan Mill), the only surviving mill of three which once stood on this hill, and named after the weather vane surmounting it. It has been carefully restored, and is open Apr–Oct.

Kerteminde was also the birthplace of the late Romantic poet Frederik Paludan Müller, whose verse novel 'Adam Homo' (1842–49) was a precursor of Danish realism.
Copenhagen has its little mermaid, and Kerteminde has its Amanda, a granite statue, on *Langebro*, of a fisherman's daughter. Amanda's real name was Sofie Krag, and her life as a review actress in Copenhagen was somewhat less idyllic than the statue seems to indicate.

A visit to *Højskolernes Håndarbejde* in Tyrebakken 11 is well worth while. A folk high school with exhibition and shop, this represents the efforts to preserve Danish traditional handicrafts, sewing, embroidery and design, and it is possible to buy a host of tasteful designs and materials to carry on the good work yourself.

On the S outskirts of Kerteminde lies *Lundsgård*, a mansion dating from 1765; and a little further S another one, *Risinge*, from c 1750.

To return to Odense from Kerteminde, you should follow an unclassified road SW, in the first instance as far as to (3km) *Ladby*, from where a minor road NW will take you to one of the major Scandinavian ship burials, found in 1935. The Viking ship used in this 10C burial was 22m long and 3m wide, and the Viking warrior was buried in it together with 11 horses and five hunting dogs. It has been possible to reconstruct the outline of the ship, thanks to nails which were still in place, and the remains of the horses and dogs and some harnesses are still clearly visible. The whole is now a sophisticated *museum housed in what looks like a burial mound. Tickets are available near the parking area in a small house, where you can also buy yourself a cup of coffee.

Now continue SW to (4km) *Hundslev*, where you can take a detour left as well as right. To the right lies *Ulriksholm* (3km), a 17C mansion now an hotel, and to the left the village of **Rynkeby** (2km), the special feature here being the frescoes in the *church. These frescoes were not discovered until the 1960s, and when uncovered they turned out to be quite sensational. Thought to be from between 1562 and 1565, they are unusual both in being post-Reformation, and also because of their subject: they represent a company of 31 angels playing medieval musical instruments, many of which were not otherwise known. A visit to this 'angelic orchestra' is therefore a must for anyone interested in old musical instruments. There are other interesting features in the church, including three Romanesque gravestones.

3km S of Hundslev there is another possible detour to the left, this time to the village of *Birkende* (3km), which is noted as the birthplace of Hans Tavsen (Rte 2).

Back on your route again you will, at 2km, meet the 160 in *Vejrup-lund*, from where it is only 9km back to Odense.

2   Odense to Copenhagen

Total distance 149km. E20 or A160/E20 to (37km) the Storebælt ferry at *Knudshoved*.—(Ferry Knudshoved–Halsskov c 1hr).—E20/150 to (17km) **Slagelse**.—150/E20 to (15km) **Sorø**.—E20 to (15km) **Ringsted**.—A14 to (30km) *Roskilde*. —(35km) **Copenhagen**.

The motorway is by far the quickest way of driving to (37km) the Knudshoved ferry near Nyborg. It can best be reached either by taking the A9 in the direction of Svendborg, joining the motorway after 7km at junction 49, or by taking the 160 in the direction of Nyborg and after 13km following the spur on the right to join the motorway at Langeskov—junction 47. You will, of course, join either of the roads leading E of Odense via the ring road.

There are, however, two alternative, more interesting routes from Odense to Knudshoved. The direct route (total distance 35km) mainly follows the 160 (the old main road), and offers several interesting detours (see below for the alternative route).

DIRECT ROUTE FROM ODENSE TO NYBORG (total distance 35km). 12km from Odense you can visit *Birkende* (1km), where the Gothic church has been subject to extensive alterations. Birkende, however, is most noted as the birthplace of Hans Tavsen, in memory of whom there is a statue by Aksel Hansen in the village.

Hans Tavsen is remembered in Denmark as the dominant figure in the Reforma-tion movement and the translator of the Bible. Originally a monk, he went to study in Wittemberg, where he was powerfully influenced by Luther. On his return to Denmark he began to introduce Luther's ideas and, in these pre-Reformation years, he was protected by the King. His translation of the Bible was later of profound significance for the newly-established Lutheran Church, and its lan-guage played much the same role for Danish as Luther's Bible did for German. In 1541 Hans Tavsen was made Bishop of Ribe, where he remained until his death.

After a further 7km you reach Ullerslev, where the 315 S will take you to *Hindemae* (2km), a splendid neo-classical mansion from 1787 which now houses a permanent exhibition of antiques from the 17C, 18C and 19C. Twelve rooms in the main building are open to the public every day in the main holiday season and on Saturdays and Sundays in the spring and autumn. There is a large selection of antiques for sale, and there are café and restaurant facilities.

Back on the 160 you fork right after 5km in order to join the E20 to (10km) the *Knudshoved ferry harbour*. However, yet another splendid mansion is within easy reach from here. Instead of forking right, you

can first proceed a further 500m and turn left to have a look at
Juelsberg (1km), from 1771. The adjoining park is open to the public,
and paths are marked for walking.

Now there is only one more temptation before the ferry, but that is a
real one, a visit to the old town of **Nyborg**, which is described in Rte
14.

ALTERNATIVE ROUTE FROM ODENSE TO KNUDSHOVED (AND FERRY)—
VIA FRAUGDE (total distance 39km). Take the 301 SE to (8km) **Fraugde**,
where there is an important church. First mentioned in 1239, it was
extended in the early 15C. Some fine murals were discovered and
restored in 1974. In the N Chapel there are the tombs of Admiral
Frederik Christian Kaas and his wife Birgitte Kaas, together with
memorials to members of the Marsvin family.

However, the name of Fraugde is primarily associated with Denmark's great
hymn-writer, Bishop Thomas Kingo. He is buried in the S chapel, together with
his third, much-loved wife Birgitte Balslev. His first wife had died within a year
of marrying. His second marriage, with a woman 16 years his senior, had
presumably been a marriage of convenience, though perhaps it was inconvenient
for Kingo that she lived to be 76. Within seven months, at Christmas 1694, the
now 60-year-old Kingo married the 30-year-old Birgitte Balslev, who had grown
up at nearby *Fraugdegård*. On the death of Birgitte Balslev's father, the mansion
had passed into the hands of her brother, from whom Kingo now bought it. He
and his wife spent much of their time there, and Kingo regularly preached in the
chapel there. As early as five years prior to their marriage, he had been inspired
by Birgitte Balslev to write one of his most beautiful secular poems, 'To Candida',
an amazingly fresh and youthful expression of devotion for a man of his age in
the 17C. The marriage lasted until Kingo's death in 1703. The coffins stand in
front of an epitaphium by Thomas Quellinus, containing a poem written by Kingo
in memory of Birgitte Balslev's parents, and surmounted by a medallion of Kingo
and Birgitte Balslev. The work was done in 1702, and one must assume that Kingo
himself saw it.

Continue now on the 301, turning left after 5km to visit the unspoilt
village of *Davinde* (1km), where there is another interesting, but very
different, church. Although there are inevitably Gothic extensions,
thanks to its low vaulting the Romanesque nave has retained much of
its original character. The village also boasts one of the best preserved
of Danish thingsteads, the place where village meetings were once
held. It dates from the 18C and consists of a circular area surrounded
by 13 large stones with, in the middle, a lime tree growing up through
the central hole of a millstone standing on three stone pillars.

Another 4km brings you to *Ferritslev*, where you turn left towards
Nyborg, driving through (3km) *Ellinge*, where the young Carl Nielsen
worked as a grocer's assistant. When 7km later you meet the A8, you
turn left again and drive as far as (2km) the E20, which will take you
direct E to (9km) *Knudshoved ferry harbour*. However, being as close
to **Nyborg** as you are now, a visit to this historical town is worth
contemplating (see Rte 14).

The ferry crossing from *Knudshoved* on Fyn to *Halsskov* on Sjælland
takes about 1 hour, and there are regular sailings. You can book
beforehand from any railway station, but this is not normally necessary
except at busy holiday weekends.

There are two routes covering the initial stretch on Sjælland, that
between Halsskov and Sorø is the direct route (total distance 32km),
mainly following the E20 and calling at Slagelse. *Korsør*, just S of
Halsskov is incorporated in the alternative route (71km; see below).

DIRECT ROUTE FROM HALSSKOV TO SORØ (total distance 32km). From

Halsskov you follow the E20 as far as (11km) Exit 40, where you turn off to (6km) **Slagelse** (28,500 inhab.; Tourist Information Office: Løvegade 7).

Now one of the more important industrial towns in West Sjælland, Slagelse has a history going back to pagan times, when it is thought to have been a religious centre, with a temple standing on the site of the present *Sankt Mikkels Kirke*. By the 11C coins were being minted here, and a century later there were two churches, one of them, *Sankt Peders*, where the later local saint, Sankt Anders, was a priest.

King Erik Menved granted Slagelse a charter in 1288, and this was renewed and extended in the following centuries. Largely because of the fertile countryside around, the town flourished and grew until the beginning of the 16C, when it suffered both fire (there were 16 major fires between 1515 and 1804!) and Swedish occupation. At the beginning of the 18C it became a garrison town, but otherwise suffered seriously from a nationwide fall in agricultural prices. A new period of growth began at the end of the century, not least thanks to the opening of the main road from Copenhagen to Korsør. The railway came in 1856, ensuring sustained growth, and Slagelse is now a main commercial centre for West Sjælland.

There are relatively few old buildings left (though you can see the restored executioner's house in Fruegade), and Slagelse stands mainly as a thriving modern town.

Sankt Mikkels Kirke, high above the town, was founded in the 11C, and traces of the original structure were found during repair work in 1970. The present church, a pseudo-basilica, dates back in part to 1333, and the interior still bears many traces of the original workmanship. Nearby stands the old Gothic tithe barn, which at various times has served as a hospital, a grammar school and a police station. A marble plaque in the S wall lists famous pupils who attended the school. Hans Christian Andersen's name is among them—though in fact the school was situated elsewhere when he attended it!

Sankt Peders Kirke, in Herrestræde, dates from c 1150 and contains traces of its original Romanesque form; the old N door and some Romanesque windows can still be distinguished, though they are bricked up. The church was considerably extended in later centuries. St. Anders is believed to be buried in the N transept. Nearby, in Bredegade, stand the remains of the old monastery, *Helligåndshuset*, from the late 15C. It was restored in 1935 and contains frescoes by Niels Larsen Stevns. Also on Bredegade you will find Slagelse *Museum of Trade, Handicrafts and Industry*, demonstrating workshops of various kinds (open mid-Jun to end Aug).

One of Denmark's most famous old monasteries, **Antvorskov**, lies on the outskirts of Slagelse. It is reached by going S from the town centre, along Slotsgade and then Slotsallé (past the memorial stone to Hans Tavsen). At the end of Slotsallé you turn right along Hunsballevej, where, on the left, you will find the monastery ruins—at least those which are not covered by the motorway.

Founded in 1165 by Valdemar I, this was the home of the Knights of St. John of Jerusalem, and one of the largest and most influential of Danish monasteries. It was here Hans Tavsen became incensed at what he considered the luxurious manner of life in the monastery. Consequently, on Maundy Thursday 1525, he preached the sermon which is generally considered to have initiated the Danish Reformation movement. Most of the buildings were demolished in the 19C, and only a few ruins now remain. A little of it can, however, still be *heard*: the bell, from 1490, rings every day before morning service in the Cathedral in Copenhagen.

EXCURSION FROM SLAGELSE TO TRELLEBORG. The huge Viking encampment of Trelleborg, dating from c 980, lies about 8km from

Slagelse. To reach it, first drive SW along the 150 for 5km, turning right on a minor road to (3km) **Trelleborg**. It is a circular complex, surrounded by 5m-high ramparts, and with gates at the four points of the compass. The wooden streets linking these gates intersect in the middle of the complex. In each quarter of the circle there are four halls each 29.4m long, forming a square, and 15 similar, but smaller, buildings are placed side by side outside the main ramparts in such a way that their axes all point to the centre of the complex. Close to these is a burial ground. The original ramparts have been restored, and there are now cement piles to show the original position of the halls; a reconstruction of a hall has been built outside the complex.

This was the first of the Viking fortresses to be found; three others are known: Fyrkat, near Hobro (Rte 20), Aggersborg (Rte 19) on the Limfjord and Nonnebakken in Odense. (Aggersborg can hardly be traced by the layman, and Nonnebakkken is totally covered over.) Trelleborg is—like Fyrkat—open Apr–Sept.

Trelleborg, Viking encampment, West Sjælland, with the outlines of the houses clearly visible.
Photo: Dieter Betz

ROUND TRIP SOUTH OF SLAGELSE (total distance 27km). The trip will take you through a typical Sjælland landscape and past a series of churches.

You leave Slagelse S on the 259 turning left after 3km to *Slots Bjergby*. Here, on a rise just S of the old Gallows Hill, stands a large whitewashed church, partly dating back to the Romanesque period. Romanesque windows can still be discerned, and there is some fine Gothic vaulting in the nave. In the E wall in the porch there is a stone known as the *Krummerygsten* (Bent Back Stone) which, according to local tradition, was once used in the punishment of miscreants. The

Gallows Hill (Galgebakken) and Hashøj, just N of the church, are
ancient burial mounds. The Gallows Hill was excavated in 1946 and
revealed plenty of evidence that this prehistoric burial mound had
indeed been used for executions right up to the 19C.

Driving S on the 259, it is only 2km to *Gerlev*, the site of one of W
Sjælland's finest village churches. The nave and chancel are
Romanesque, and both the original doors have survived as have many
other individual features. However, it is the wealth of Gothic frescoes
in the chancel and nave that is most striking, signed by Martin Maler,
Martin the Painter ('Martinus Malera bene fecit') and now splendidly
restored. In the chancel there is a painting of the Day of Judgement
and one of a Last Supper consisting of Danish medieval dishes, while
in the nave there are representations of the Passion and Christ in
Glory. The antemensale of the altar is from 1589, and there is a noble
carved altarpiece by Lorentz Jørgensen, from 1667. The font is
Romanesque.

While in Gerlev you should drive the short distance NE to the small
mansion of *Falkensten* (2km), from 1774, said to be built of material
from Antvorskov Monastery. Most striking in the complex is the
enormous half-timbered *barn from 1862, with a sweeping thatched
roof.

From Gerlev a minor road takes you SE to (3km) *Skørpinge*, where
you turn right and drive a further 3km S to *Flakkebjerg*. Here, there is
a fully preserved Romanesque church of unusual asymmetrical shape.
Here, too, there are some fine frescoes dating from c 1300 (women at
the tomb of Christ) and c 1450 (Christ as Judge of the World). Both are
surrounded by intricate floral patterning.

Yet another 3km—this time to the NE—and you come to a third
church worth visiting, that in *Gimlinge*, also Romanesque. Once more
it is the frescoes which are the great attraction, some painted by Martin
the Painter and dated 1409. Others are from between 1375 and 1400.
Martin has again painted the Day of Judgement and scenes from the
Passion. The antemensale is from c 1600, as is the ornate Renaissance
altarpiece. The pulpit dates from 1594.

From Gimlinge a minor road E takes you to (3km) the A22, where
you turn left, past the mansion of *Gyldenholm*, back to (10km) Slagelse.

Returning to the main route, from the centre of **Slagelse** the 150/E20
leads on to (9km) *Kindertofte*, where the altarpiece in the church is a
painting by Lucie Ingemann, the wife of the Romantic poet and
novelist B.S. Ingemann.

The main road now takes you through lovely wooded terrain to (6km)
Sorø (see below).

ALTERNATIVE ROUTE FROM HALSSKOV TO SORØ—VIA KORSØR AND
SKÆLSKØR (total distance 71km). Leave the motorway at Exit 42 only
2km after joining it in Halsskov and drive across the bascule bridge
into **Korsør** (14,700 inhab.; Tourist Information: Nygade 7), immediately to the S.

There are references to Korsør as early as 1241, but there are signs of much earlier
settlements in *Korsør Nor* (Korsør Cove) and the islands in it. The Cove is
immediately E of the town, and the entrance to it divides Korsør from Halsskov.
The now ruined castle of Tårnborg to the N of the present town was established
here as a defence against the Wends, and after a chequered period it saw a small
settlement, Korsør, develop over the following centuries.
  Korsør received its first charter in 1425. It was a natural port for communications
with Fyn, and in the 17C it was decided that Korsør should become a main port
for foreign trade. It was, however, the opening of the railway across Sjælland in

1856 that gave the impetus for the major expansion. Industry, not least the shipyard, made its home there, and connections by sea were established with Kiel and Århus. With increasing traffic, Korsør has maintained its position as one of the major ferry ports in Denmark, and all railway traffic between Sjælland and Fyn/Jutland still uses it, while most cars now use the nearby Halsskov ferry terminal. Korsør will maintain its central importance when the bridge connecting Sjælland and Fyn is established, the rail link supposedly in 1993 and the motorway in 1996.

The old Korsør castle keep still stands, one of the only two medieval fortress towers remaining in Denmark, the other being in Vordingborg (Rte 9). Standing 25m high, it can clearly be seen from the harbour as the ferry approaches. It now houses a *museum illustrating the history of the town and the ferry connections to Nyborg, and is well worth a visit. Nearby there is a powder store built by Christian IV (not open to the public) and the coastal battery once built to defend Korsør from attack from the sea.

As Korsør developed relatively late—and like so many other towns suffered from fires—there are few very old buildings. On the other hand there are many interesting 18C houses. They are centred on the charming main streets Algade, Slottensgade and Havnegade. Among them is Rasmus Langeland's house from 1761, also known as *Kongsgården* (The King's Residence), so called because this is where royal parties waited for suitable sailing conditions for crossing the Great Belt. It is a long single-storeyed house with a mansard roof. The façade is decorated with inscriptions and reliefs and four statues, while Rasmus Langeland's gravestone is now fixed in the E end. A collection of sculptures by Harald Isenstein (1898–1980) is housed here. Note, too, the small but ornate toll booth from 1785, now used for small exhibitions. On *Havneplads* you will find the statue of the poet Jens Baggesen, who was born in Korsør in 1764. Baggesen is one of the major poets of the late 18C and early 19C, and the only one really to bridge the pre-Romantic and Romantic periods.

Korsør has a good golf course and a first-rate marina, and it also has a busy fishing harbour. For those wanting to fish in the sea, there are plenty of possibilities along the coast, and fishing excursions by boat can also be arranged.

Korsør has another museum, the *Sparekassemuseum* (Savings Bank Museum) c 4km S of the town, close to the house of *Klarskovgård*. This museum illustrates the development of the Danish savings banks since 1810, and shows the vast changes that have taken place over that time in furniture, office equipment—and atmosphere.

You leave Korsør to the S on the 265, making your first stop at (9km) *Boeslunde*. Here, overlooked by a 54m-high mound in which six golden bowls were found at the end of the 19C, and on top of which archaeologists have found the remains of another medieval castle, stands Boeslunde *church, dating back to the 14C, once a place of pilgrimage thanks to a sacred spring, the Holy Cross Spring—which still exists. The altarpiece is by Niels Skovgaard, replacing a very special and ornate medieval folding altarpiece which could be changed according to the calendar—and which is now in the National Museum in Copenhagen.

Continue along the 265 and you will come to (6km) Skælskør.

Skælskør (5800 inhab.; Tourist Information: Algade 1) is a small, out-of-the-way market town which in the distant past was the main ferry link between Sjælland and Fyn, and which received a charter as a market town in 1414. Having lost its former status, it has on the other hand kept a good deal of charm, with colourful houses rising on a hill around the harbour.

At the top stands the church, formerly dedicated to St. Nicholas and though going back in part to the early 13C, mainly Gothic, with a fine Gothic altarpiece from c 1475. The carved pulpit is from 1630. Built into the churchyard wall in *Gammelgade* is a medieval stone-built house which at various times has been a tithe barn, grammar school and almshouse. Most of the other old houses are of modest dimensions, though there is a picturesque half-timbered house in Vestergade and a more imposing example in the same style from c 1600 in Algade.

2km S of Skælskør, reached by a minor road running close to the fjord, stands the striking manor house of *Borreby*, the scene of Hans Christian Andersen's story 'The Wind Tells of Valdemar Daae and His Daughters', and one of the oldest and best preserved of Danish Renaissance castles. It was erected in 1556 by the great chancellor Johan Friis, and stands almost unchanged, surrounded by a moat, part castle, part mansion. In the 17C it came into the hands of Valdemar Daae, the central character in Andersen's story. It is an ironic twist that the steps in the spiral staircase in the tower are made of gravestones taken from the old Carmelite convent in Skælskør. The park and parts of the building (now including an exhibition of Sjælland handicraft) are open to the public. Borreby Marsh is a bird sanctuary.

Leave Skælskør on the 265 E, turning right at (9km) *Bøgelunde* to (3km) **Ørslev**, the site of one of the most famous of Denmark's church murals. This is the mid-14C 'dance frieze', a colourful and lively presentation of a medieval chain dance, the dance now only found in the Faroe Islands. The dancing figures are lifelike in their dress and movement, and provide a striking insight into medieval life. There are other quite unusual frescoes, too, with both religious and secular motifs.—Just S of Ørslev, approached via an embankment, lies the tiny island of *Glænø*, a delightful holiday area.

After your visit to Ørslev you should drive E again, past the mill to (4km) *Holsteinborg*, another magnificent mansion, built between 1598 and 1651, this time with four wings and corner towers. Another of Hans Christian Andersen's favourite places, it was once surrounded by a moat, only part of which remains. The park is open to the public.

From Holsteinborg a minor road takes you N across the 265 to (4km) *Venslev*, the centre of some of the popular religious movements in the early 19C, one of which ultimately became the evangelical wing of the Danish church, Indre Mission (Home Mission). From here you take the road N through the village of Hyllested to (5km) Dalmose, where you turn right into the 157. At (3km) *Ting Jellinge* you will find one of the country's smallest churches, built in the North German style in the 14C, and complete with tower and porch.

Continue now along the 157 to (10km) *Lynge Eskilstrup*, where you will find *Kongskilde Friluftsgård*, an estate of 400 hectares in the midst of the Tystrup-Bavelse Nature Park. The entire park, which contains many prehistoric monuments, is open to the public, and there are facilities for eating and for overnight accommodation. And while you are here you should follow the lakeside road opposite to *Tystrup* village (3km), delightfully situated beside the beautiful *Tystrup Sø* lake. The church here, standing high above the lake, is from c 1370, with extensions from 1450. There are some interesting frescoes of Judgement Day and Christ enthroned, with inscriptions in Danish, as opposed to the customary Latin, and with a clear connection with frescoes in the Three Kings Chapel in Roskilde Cathedral.

From Lynge Eskildstrup it is only a further 8 beautiful km to Sorø.

Sorø (6100 inhab.; Tourist Information: Rolighed 5C), once stood on an

island, and in practice is still three-quarters surrounded by two lakes—
Sorø Sø to the W and S and *Tuelsø* to the NE—and these in turn are
surrounded by forest. There is a certain amount of light industry, but
Sorø owes its renown less to that than to its historical significance.

A monastery was founded here in the 12C by Asser Rig, the father of Bishop
Absalon, the founder of Copenhagen. The island, as it then was, was an out-of-
the-way place, ideal for a monastic foundation. After a period of decline the
monastery developed into a rich institution until it was abolished at the Reformation in 1536. There had already been a school there, laying the foundations for
an academic tradition, and this was allowed to continue. In 1623 Christian IV
decided to develop the school as an academy for the sons of the aristocracy,
thereby founding one of the most distinguished of Danish boarding schools, to
this day known as Sorø Academy. Some of Denmark's leading scholars were
associated with the school, Ludvig Holberg, the 18C dramatist, essayist, historian
and novelist, being perhaps the most famous. In the 19C there were the poets
B.S. Ingemann and Carsten Hauch. By their time the original buildings had been
replaced by Peder Malling's present building.

Sorø Academy, now a State-run co-educational boarding school, is
private, but the area around the buildings and the surrounding park
bordering the lake—corresponding more or less to the former monastery grounds—is open to the public. Lying in the S of the town close to
the market place (*Torvet*), it is approached through the original monastery gate, the only one left in Denmark, and now, as the home of one
of the teachers, the oldest inhabited house in the country. This leads
into an open square where, as well as the Academy buildings, 100m
in front of you to the left is the largest monastery church in Denmark,
dating back to 1201 and, together with Ringsted Church, one of the
two oldest brick-built buildings in the country. Absalon is buried here
behind the high altar, while several members of the Royal Family,
including Valdemar II and Christoffer II, and other ancient and distinguished figures, are buried elsewhere in the church. Ludvig Holberg
lies here, too. Queen Margrethe I was originally buried here, but her
body was subsequently removed to Roskilde Cathedral on the orders
of her Chancellor, Peder Lodehat, who was also Bishop of Roskilde.

This elegant Romanesque church, built in the 1160s to the pattern of
the mother monastery at Fontenay, with its long nave flanked by aisles
on either side, has vaulting from the following century but has otherwise retained much of its original character, despite some 15C alterations. The monks' misericords are still in place, as is the original night
staircase leading up to the dormitory, though most of the furniture is of
later date. The oldest piece is a large wooden crucifix from c 1247, with
the cross and the figure of Christ all carved from a single piece of
timber. Also medieval is the carved reliquary. From a later period there
is the huge 1527 *crucifix by Claus Berg, at 8m in height the biggest
in Denmark. The tall 1654 altarpiece has carved figures by Lorentz
Jørgensen. Below the windows in the nave there are frescoes of the
coats of arms of many of those buried in the church, especially the
ancient Hvide family, to which Asser and Absalon belonged. The
oldest date back to the late 13C, but they were repainted c 1515. The
churchyard dates from the time when the church was built, and is still
in use. The E wall is from the old monastery.

Apart from the Academy and church, Sorø has other areas of interest.
Immediately W of the market square *Søgade* boasts a row of old houses
mainly from the 18C and 19C. Nevertheless, one of them, once used
as residences for the pupils, is from 1650. The Library, in Storgade, was
established by Christian IV. Next to it stands the art gallery, *Vestsjæl-
lands Kunstmuseum*, containing an excellent collection of Danish
paintings from the 18C to the present day, supplemented by another

of fine medieval wooden sculptures gathered from the churches around
Sorø. Also in Storgade there is *Sorø Amtsmuseum*, housed in a beautiful
half-timbered building and offering a comprehensive collection of local
historical exhibits, including a memorial room for the poet B.S. Ingemann (open summer; limited opening winter).

The entire region around Sorø is one of historical interest, whether you look to
the Middle Ages or to more recent times. Of these latter **Tersløsegård** is of
particular interest. Situated near the village of **Tersløse**, 11km NW of Sorø, this
three-winged thatched house was the home of Ludvig Holberg, and is is now a
museum (open Apr–Nov) containing many memories of one of the truly great
figures of Scandinavian literature (see Rte 7).

Leave Sorø on the E20 E. At (4km) *Slaglille*, where there is an unusually
ornate stone-built Romanesque church, you should leave the main
route, turning off left, to *Bjernede* (2km) to visit yet another church,
this time a round one standing by the village pond.

Bjernede church is the only round church on Sjælland, and the most elaborate
of the seven still left in Denmark. A Latin inscription over the entrance says that
it was the work of Sune Ebbesen, a cousin of Absalon, which dates it to before
1186. Over the years, the church has undergone a good deal of rebuilding, and
the present strictly Romanesque exterior is in fact the result of a restoration from
1892. The interior is notable for four massive pillars supporting the vaulting,
surmounted by a further four columns supporting the octagonal tower. Much of
the furniture is either Gothic or Renaissance.

Back on the E20 you continue towards Ringsted. After c 2km you will
come to Fjenneslev, and immediately after that you will see, on your
right, *Kirke Fjenneslev*, with its unusual church with two towers. The
church itself dates from c 1130 and the towers from c 1200 (though they
were reconstructed in the 20C). It was built by Asser Rig, and legend
has it that he had to go to war and leave his pregnant wife behind. He
told her that if the child was a girl she should add a spire to the church,
and if it was a boy, she should build a tower. When he returned, he
saw—two towers. However, this is *only* a legend, as Asser Rig's two
sons Absalon and Esbern were not twins. Besides, Asser Rig and his
wife were both dead by the time the towers were erected. At all events,
this is an impressive Romanesque church with walls that are notably
high in relation to their length. There are some fine frescoes from
1150–1200, mainly on the chancel arch, with two figures which might
possibly represent Asser Rig and his wife. The altar is thought to be
original, and above it there is a crucifix by Claus Berg. The font is
Romanesque. There is a 1.7m-long runestone in the churchyard, with
the inscription 'Sasser raised the stone and made the bridge'. (There
is in fact a bridge known as Sasser's Bridge crossing the river S of
Fjenneslev!)

   Now continue to (7km) **Ringsted** (17,000 inhab.; Tourist Information:
Sankt Bendtsgade 10), another of the historic towns in this part of
Sjælland.

Now a modern city, Ringsted is closely associated with the history of Denmark in
the Middle Ages. However, its history goes much further back, to the times when
it was a major centre of the pagan religion, corresponding in its cultic significance
for the people of Sjælland to Odense for Fyn and Viborg for Jutland. It has been
surmised that the oldest church here was built on the site of the pagan shrine, as
has happened elsewhere. It is here that the present Sankt Bendts Kirke stands.
   Thanks to its central geographical position, Ringsted maintained its importance
throughout the Middle Ages; coins were minted here in the 11C, and its
significance is underlined by the fact that when King Knud Lavard was murdered
in 1131, his body was brought to Ringsted for burial. He was proclaimed a Saint
and officially canonised in 1161, and at his shrine a monastery was built in the
mid-12C. Valdemar I was closely associated with Ringsted, and lived here for a

time. He designated the church the site for royal burials, and c 20 members of the medieval royal family are buried here.

Ringsted, too, was the scene of many important political meetings in the Middle Ages. It was given a royal charter in 1441. It was not, however, of great significance as a trade centre, and it was not until the advent of the railway in the mid-19C that Ringsted emerged as a geographically well-positioned trade and business centre, a position it has maintained ever since.

The central feature of medieval Ringsted is without doubt **Sankt Bendts Kirke**, the old monastic church originally known as Sankt Knuds Kirke, one of the oldest and most impressive brick-built churches in Denmark. It dates back to c 1160, when it replaced the earlier and more modest church in which Knud Lavard was originally buried, and was completed at the beginning of the 13C. It suffered from a fire in 1241 and was rebuilt with a splendid vaulted ceiling, the new building being consecrated in 1268 by the Bishop of Winchester, in whose own Cathedral both Hardeknud and Knud (Canute) the Great were buried. It is in the shape of a cross, with five apses in the E end and four chapels on the E side of the transept. The tower is from the 16C.

Over the centuries the church suffered from neglect, and the present elegant building is the result of a restoration from 1900–08. It contains many frescoes, including some particularly impressive ones in the central vaulting, with portraits of St. Knud and King Erik Plovpenning, Knud IV, the Virgin and St. Catherine, and memorial friezes to Danish kings and queens as well as the coats of arms of some 100 members of the nobility. The auricular altar is from 1699, the altar crucifix from 1650 and the font from c 1150. The splendid pulpit, similar to the royal pew in Roskilde Cathedral, is from c 1600. Of the 20 royal tombs, mention should be made especially of those of Knud Lavard, Valdemar I and Valdemar II.

The much-loved Queen Dagmar was also buried here in 1212, as was her less loved successor Queen Bengerd (1221). Here, too, lie Erik Plovpenning and Erik Menved. The graves of Queen Dagmar and Queen Bengerd have been despoiled, but in that of Queen Dagmar was found a small Byzantine reliquary in the form of a crucifix, now on display in the National Museum and known as the Dagmar Cross. All these tombs, and many more from the Middle Ages, are to be seen in what is one of the main royal churches in Denmark.

Ringsted has few other remains from bygone ages. However, there is a further relic of the Middle Ages on the Market Square (*Torvet*) in the form of three flat stones, traditionally thought to have been the site of the medieval *thing*—the public assembly. These are the only ones extant in Denmark. One of them is adorned with a 19C graffito—a games board inscribed by English soldiers garrisoned there during the occupation of Sjælland in 1807. The statue of Valdemar I on the Market Square is from 1937, the work of Johannes Bjerg. Of other older buildings there is the old posting house, Postgården, from 1795, an imposing building which is now a bank, and the Mahler houses, close to Sankt Bendts Kirke and dating from the late 18C. Nearby is the *Agricultural Museum*, illustrating 200 years of Danish agriculture. On the corner of Kongensgade and Køgevej you will find the restored *Ringsted Mill*.

EXCURSION FROM RINGSTED TO HARALDSTED Take the 215 NW from Ringsted and turn right after 7km to **Haraldsted**, from where there is a minor road leading E to the chapel on the edge of the forest. Haraldsted is where St. Knud Lavard was murdered in 1131 by his cousin Magnus in an effort to remove a rival contender for the throne. A sacred spring is said to have appeared on the spot where the deed was done. A chapel was erected close by, and the foundations are still visible. A 4m-high wooden cross was erected here in 1902.

In Haraldsted itself there is a stone standing on the site of the house in which Knud Lavard had spent the previous night, and close by there is the church in which he was originally buried, containing a great deal of medieval furniture in addition to frescoes in the chancel. On 26 June each year Roman Catholics walk in procession from Ringsted to commemorate the burial of Knud Lavard.

Continuing your route you leave Ringsted on the A14 N, turning left after 10km to drive through *Jystrup* to the mansion of *Skjoldenæsholm* (4km). Built in 1766, this is now a conference centre. It stands near the site of Valdemar IV's Skjoldenæs castle; nothing remains of this original castle, though the mound on which it was built can still be seen. Close by is the large-scale tramcar museum, **Sporvejsmuseet Skjoldenæsholm**, with some 30 tramcars from Copenhagen, Århus and Basel, all in working condition and running on two tracks. In addition there are exhibitions and models (limited opening May–Oct).

Back on the A14 it is now only 20km NE to *Roskilde (39,800 inhab.; Tourist Information: Fondens Bro 3), which received its charter in 1268. Of all the historical towns in this part of Denmark, it must surely be the most important. Indeed, it could be argued that it is the most famous of Danish cities outside Copenhagen. The present-day fame is doubtless based on the magnificent Cathedral with its many royal associations, but its importance goes far back in history.

Roskilde was admirably sited to play an important part, being on the major land route across Sjælland, and with a deep fjord giving easy access to open waters. Certainly the name is known from the time of Harald Bluetooth, but it was Knud the Great who first saw its potential, and he created a bishopric there in 1020, making generous gifts to it to establish its churches and other ecclesiastical buildings. In 1370 the diocese owned 2600 farms in Sjælland, and by the Reformation a quarter of all the farms on the island as well as 30 large estates belonged to it.

The Reformation was catastrophic for Roskilde, which owed its status almost entirely to its ecclesiastical significance. Most of the churches were demolished, and the stones and bricks were used elsewhere—in Copenhagen, at Kronborg, on estates throughout Sjælland. Many of the art treasures in the Cathedral were destroyed, and the chancel containing Queen Margrethe's sarcophagus was closed off for a century and a half. Things began to change though towards the end of the 16C when James VI of Scotland visited Roskilde to discuss questions of dogma with the famous theologian Niels Hemmingsen, who had been dismissed from Copenhagen and exiled to Roskilde as a crypto-Calvinist. Roskilde now became the home of several Renaissance artists and craftsmen, whose work is still well known in Danish churches.

The 17C Swedish wars brought great suffering to the city, and there was a terrible visitation of the plague in 1711, followed by serious fires between 1731 and 1735, some the work of an arsonist (who was caught and executed). Consequently, there are no 17C houses left and few from the first half of the 18C, though the main outline of the old city was retained in the rebuilding.

As elsewhere, the advent of the railways in the 19C brought renewed growth, and Roskilde benefited by becoming an important rail junction. Nowadays, the ease of communication with Copenhagen has added to this; only 30 minutes away by rail, Roskilde has acquired many of the characteristics of a commuter town.

Duke Knud Lavard was born here in 1096, and the 16C hymn-writer Hans Christensen Steen in 1544. Roskilde has also been the birthplace of many other important figures in the history of Danish culture.

It is the glorious *CATHEDRAL, the fourth to be built on this site, that gives Roskilde its special significance for Denmark. The E section was completed by the mid-13C, and the entire structure was in place by 1282. The N tower is from the late 15C.

The overall plan of this magnificent brick-built Cathedral was new for its time and remains impressive to this day. It consists of a lofty nave

0 metres   20

E

1   Christian IX's chapel
2   St Bridget's chapel
3   St Andrew's chapel
4   Christian IV's chapel
5   Oluf Mortensen's porch
6   The Chapter House
7   Frederik V's chapel
8   Christian I's chapel
9   The Clock
10 Queen Margrethe's sarcophagus
11 The open octagonal chapel

ROSKILDE CATHEDRAL

*The Christian IV chapel in Roskilde Cathedral. The
painting shows the king with his eye bandaged after
being wounded in battle. Photo: Lennard*

with a broad aisle on either side and ending in a great apse, though
the original plan for a transept with three aisles was never carried out.
The N and S aisles are lined with a series of chapels which are mainly
the burial places of Danish royalty. Over 20 kings are buried here and
15 of their queens, as well as many of their immediate families.

Pride of place goes to Queen Margrethe I, who lies behind the high
altar in a magnificent marble *sarcophagus surmounted by a figure of
her as a young woman. Immediately N of the great W door—the main
entrance—you will pass St. Sigfred's chapel, from 1405, and beyond
that—on the N side—*Christian IX's chapel, built between 1917 and
1924 and the burial place of 20C Danish royalty.

Moving towards the E, you pass St. Bridget's and St. Andrew's
chapels before reaching the bombastic *Christian IV's chapel, built
between 1614 and 1640 partly under the supervision of Christian IV
himself, and protected by ornate wrought-iron gates, the work of
Casper Fincke. It is the most Gothic of all the chapels, which are
otherwise predominantly Renaissance in style. The central feature is
the surprisingly modest black sarcophagus surmounted by the king's
sword, and surrounded by other royal sarcophagae. Notable, too, are
the 19C frescoes, depicting scenes from the life of Christian IV and the
bronze statue of the king by Thorvaldsen.

Continue E past Oluf Mortensen's porch at the start of the apse (perhaps better appreciated from the outside); then behind the altar around the apse, where you come to the Absalon Arch. This once linked the Cathedral with the Bishop's Palace and, subsequently, with the royal palace designed by Laurids de Thurah in 1736. It now functions partly as a museum and partly as the diocesan offices.

On the opposite side of the nave from Oluf Mortensen's porch stands the Chapter House, now the sacristy, dating back to the early 13C. Then, now moving W, you will come to *Frederik V's chapel, directly opposite that of Christian IV, and in striking contrast to it. Built in 1774 and completed by the neo-classical architect C.F. Hansen in 1820, it is dazzlingly light, a total contrast to the sombre splendour of Christian IV's chapel. Although the chapel contains numerous royal sarcophagi, the centre piece is the neo-classical sarcophagus of Frederik V by Wiedewelt, surmounted by an ornate pillar on which there is a profile of the King.

Further W again comes *Christian I's chapel from 1459, containing the sarcophagi of Christian I and Queen Dorothea; here, too, is the monumental tomb of Frederik II, and the chapel is richly decorated with frescoes. Another feature of this chapel is the *Royal Column on which many crowned heads have had their heights measured and marked. Adjoining this chapel is the SW porch, the present main entrance.

The last of the chapels is *outside* near the NW corner of the Cathedral, where an open octagonal *chapel contains the tomb of Frederik IX (d. 1972), who expressed the wish not to be buried within the Cathedral itself. This chapel was designed by Inger and Johannes Exner.

The central feature of the nave is, naturally, the high *altar, an ornate triptych from c 1560, made in Antwerp and considered one of the most splendid of its kind. Although in Renaissance style, it is composed in the manner of the older Gothic triptychs, with four main panels and four smaller ones, depicting scenes from the Bible in reliefs which are almost free-standing figures. There are known to have been at least 70 altars in the cathedral at one time, but little remains of them, no more than two figures from the 16C. The crucifix on the high altar is from c 1250. The choir stalls and lectern are richly carved Gothic work from the early 16C. In the nave, too, is Christian IV's pew, a richly carved and arcaded Renaissance work on two levels. The organ loft is from 1554, as is, in part, the organ itself. In the W end there is a famous *clock, from c 1500, including mechanical figures of St. George and the Dragon. Every hour on the hour, St. George's horse rears and tramples the dragon underfoot, at which the dragon issues a pitiful howl. Do time your visit so that you can watch this intriguing clock in action.

There are countless memorial plaques in the Cathedral, and 176 gravestones. Allow more than the odd half hour for your visit. Guided tours are arranged by the Tourist Information Office.

Immediately to the E of the Cathedral, and linked to it by the Absalon Arch from c 1200, is the *Palace* (Palæet), to the elegant design of Laurids de Thura, now partly a museum containing paintings and watercolours portraying Roskilde, together with a collection of 18C and 19C relics (open summer; limited opening winter). Among its uses has been that of the seat of one of the elected Regional Advisory Assemblies (Stænderforsamlinger) set up in the 1830s as a move towards parliamentary government in Denmark. The square, *Stændertorvet*, is so named in commemoration of this. Further E, in a

RINGSTED & KALUNDBORG

house from 1804 in Sankt Olsstræde, is *Roskilde Museum*. This contains a comprehensive collection illustrating the history of the Roskilde area from prehistoric times to the present century.

The statue of Roar and Helge on Stændertorvet illustrates the legend that the name of Roskilde stems from them and really means Roar's Spring. The square was the medieval market square, and here once stood the great Sankt Laurentius Church. Only its magnificent tower now remains, incorporated into the 19C town hall.

From Stændertorvet you can walk W down Skomagergade to Ringstedgade, where at No. 6 you will find a museum called *Brødrene Luetzhøfts Købmandsgård*, a proper old grocer's shop preserved in the style of the early 20C. It actually functions as a shop, and you can buy your goods there as they did in great-grandmother's time. Also in Ringstedgade, at No. 68, lies the *Håndværksmuseum*, a museum of old tools.

Retrace your steps as far as Jernbanegade, turn right, and take the 3rd road on the left, Fruegade, where you come to the other old church in Roskilde, *Vor Frue Kirke*. If Saxo is correct in dating it to 1073–88, this is the oldest church in Roskilde, and a find from 1060 in the churchyard nearby makes it seem that this might indeed be the case. However, in its present shape, the church stems rather from the mid 13C.

Older than this is the now unused *Sankt Ibs Kirke* N of the town centre, on Frederiksborgvej; only the nave remains standing, but it is from the beginning of the 12C.

If you leave Sankt Ibs Kirke along Sankt Ibsvej and continue into Havnevej you will soon come to what in medieval days was the separate village of *Sankt Jørgensbjerg* which grew up around a lepers' hospital. The area still has a village atmosphere, with many old fishermen's cottages and narrow streets, and here, in Kirkegade, stands the church of **Sankt Jørgensbjerg**. This singular church is very old, again one of the oldest in the country, dating back to c 1100, with a Romanesque nave and chancel to which have been added a Gothic tower and porch. Although built of stone, some of the architecture is reminiscent of 11C wooden stave churches. A drawing of a medieval ship has been carved into the E jamb of the door, together with a runic inscription. Other runic lettering is to be found in the chancel arch. None of the inscriptions has been interpreted. The N portal is believed to be the oldest extant piece of stone architecture in Denmark, with an unusual rounded relieving arch. As a church providing for a leper hospital, this church had special access and accommodation for the lepers, who were kept away from the rest of the congregation. Traces of this are still to be seen beneath the tower. The entire church was carefully restored between 1953 and 1955.

Being in this area, you are now quite close to one of the modern sights of Roskilde, the **Viking Ship Museum** down by the water. There is a path leading straight down to it from St. Jørgensbjerg, but there are also ample parking facilities on the site, if you prefer to take the car. The ships, once sunk in the fjord some 20km N of Roskilde in order to protect the approaches to the town, were salvaged in 1962, preserved and restored as necessary, and are now exhibited in this first-rate museum, which is well equipped with illustrations and regularly shows films in different languages. These ships are merchant ships, not those that carried Viking warriors; the largest, a sea-going vessel is 16.5m long and 4.6m wide. If you do spot Viking ships out on the fjord as well, they will be replicas, carefully reconstructed for experimental purposes.

EXCURSION FROM ROSKILDE TO LEDREBORG MANSION AND THE HISTORICAL VILLAGE OF LEJRE. Leave Roskilde along the A14 S and turn right into the 155 c 3km from the town centre. Immediately after this you must turn left, and now you will find yourself in a very special 7km-long straight avenue, leading up to the mansion of *Ledreborg. Dating back to the 17C, Ledreborg was redesigned and extended by Laurids de Thurah and J.C.Krieger in the 1740s, resulting in one of the most outstanding pieces of baroque architecture in Denmark. It is open to the public throughout July and on Sundays from mid-June and until the end of August. The park is open throughout the year.

Driving back towards the avenue you will come to a road pointing left to **Gammel Lejre** (1km), believed once to have been the seat of the ancient and more or less legendary kings of the area, the Skjoldungs, who are mentioned in the Anglo-Saxon 'Beowulf'. Much of the material on these kings is doubtless pure legend, and the 'royal farm' (Kongsgården) can scarcely have belonged to them, dating only from the 18C. Nevertheless the museum housed in it is well worth a visit, consisting of furniture and implements used by the farming family which lived in this house for 200 years. There is, too, in Lejre, a very large Viking stone ship, at 80m the largest known, as well as the remains of others. Excavations have revealed a Viking Age burial site. The large burial mound outside the village is from the Late Iron Age, the time of the legendary Skjoldungs. Lejre must have been something special, but it is not certain just how much truth can be attached to the legends. Whatever the case, Lejre today is a charming village, with many half-timbered cottages.

Just E of Roskilde there is access to the motorway 21 which will quickly take you through a mainly residential area to (35km) **Copenhagen** (Rtes 3, 4).

3 History of Copenhagen and a Brief Tour of Copenhagen by Car

COPENHAGEN (København) (1,200,000 inhab.; Tourist Information: H.C. Andersens Boulevard 22).

There was a village called *Havn* on the island now known as *Slotsholmen* as early as 1025, and archaeological evidence even points to there having been a Stone Age settlement here. In the 1160s King Valdemar I gave this village to Bishop Absalon of Roskilde as a gesture of gratitude for his political help. In 1167, in order to secure the population against attack from the sea, Absalon set about building a castle here, and it is from this event that Copenhagen's history dates. Not only did the castle afford security, but it also ensured that trade flourished. The name of Copenhagen still echoes this process, meaning in fact 'merchants' harbour'.

The earliest town grew up in the area between the shore and *Vestergade/Gammeltorv*. Copenhagen changed hands several times during the early Middle Ages, sometimes belonging to the king, sometimes to the Bishop of Roskilde, and for a time it was even in the hands of the Lübeckers, who saw its prosperity as a threat to themselves, and consequently razed it to the ground in 1368–69. By 1417, however, it was firmly in the hands of the Crown in the person of King Erik of Pomerania.

Throughout the early Middle Ages Danish kings moved from one part of the country to another, but by the 15C Copenhagen had become established as the capital of a united kingdom. It might seem surprising that this city far out on the E of the country should have achieved this, but it must be remembered that the southern part of present-day Sweden was then part of Denmark, and that Copenhagen thus occupied a fairly central position.

With its establishment as the administrative centre, Copenhagen grew in importance, and by 1479 the University was founded. In the 16C the city suffered from the political upheavals. It was twice besieged, the second time in connection with the Reformation movement. The Reformers won, to a large extent with the backing of the ordinary populace. Then, in 1588, King Christian IV came to the throne, and although his foreign policy was disastrous and almost led to national bankruptcy, his urge to create a splendid capital was never-ending. Copenhagen owes many of its finest buildings to him.

In the 17C Copenhagen was again besieged, this time by the Swedes, and the very existence of Denmark was at stake. The Copenhagen citizens defended the city bravely and brilliantly when the Swedes tried to storm it, for which King Frederik III rewarded them with a great deal of municipal freedom. He then received *his* reward in 1660 when the citizens of Copenhagen supported him in his struggle with the aristocracy. He won, and established the absolute monarchy.

By now Copenhagen was a sizeable city, with narrow streets and houses crowded close together. Hygiene was non-existent, and fire precautions were poor. In 1711 the plague broke out and about a third of the citizens died from it. In 1728 there was a disastrous fire that laid waste to the centre. Now, with the ambitions of the absolute monarch and a growing awareness of international architecture, Copenhagen was largely rebuilt, and some of the most elegant of its mansions and palaces made their appearance. In 1795 there was another great fire, and in 1807 the British fleet bombarded Copenhagen in an effort to bring Denmark into the Napoleonic Wars on the side of Britain. They failed. The centre was again rebuilt, this time largely on neo-classical lines, as is clearly seen in the area around the University, the Cathedral and Gammeltorv/Nytorv.

The ramparts were demolished in the 1850s, allowing concentrated building outside them. Great blocks of flats now appeared in the *Vesterbro*, *Nørrebro* and *Østerbro* areas, some of good quality, some little more than slums. The 20C has had the task of clearing the poorer ones up, and a good job has been made of it.

Broadly speaking, Copenhagen today consists of Copenhagen proper, Frederiksberg and a good deal of the island of Amager, to which the mainland is linked by a series of bridges.

Frederiksberg, just to the W of Copenhagen, has a history going back to the time of Absalon, when there was a village here called Solbjerg. By 1417 it was in the ownership of Erik of Pomerania, and it has since then traditionally been associated with the Crown—and always independent of Copenhagen. In the 17C Christian IV settled a number of Dutch smallholders from Amager (see below) along what is now Allégade in an attempt to improve local agriculture and horticulture. The experiment was a failure, but one result of it can still be seen in the Dutch character of Frederiksberg Church. When Frederik IV built a castle here in 1699, the area was given the name of Frederiksberg. By the end of the 18C it was becoming a place where the citizens of Copenhagen had their summer residences, and in 1857 Frederiksberg was given the status of an independent 'kommune', which it still retains.

Amager is the small island SE of Copenhagen, joined to the capital by a series of bridges, and in effect largely a Copenhagen suburb. It is the site of the new University campus, in Njalsgade, and, at Kastrup, of Copenhagen Airport. There is evidence of settlement here from as far back as the early Stone Age, and the fertility of the soil quickly established Amager as a source of agricultural products for Copenhagen. In 1521 Christian II—who had close links with Holland and considered Dutch market gardeners to be better than the Danes— brought a number of Dutch families to live and work here, settling them in *Søndre Magleby*. The colony grew and spread to other parts of the island, leaving clear traces on customs and dress.

In 1617 Christian IV decided to found a new town at the N tip of Amager; this became known as *Christianshavn*, and is to some extent inspired by Dutch town planning of that time, not least in the canals for which it is noted.

Amager is, of course, now totally assimilated into the rest of the country, but its curious history has resulted not only in the very special area called Christianshavn, but also some villages rather different in character from those otherwise found.

Like other old cities, Copenhagen had a central area which could not cope with modern traffic. However, the 19C demolition of the ramparts had left wide streets on what were then the outskirts. It has thus proved possible to keep much of the traffic away from the central area, which consequently is unusually well provided with pedestrian streets.

The other modern feature of Copenhagen is its notably well-organised integrated public transport system. Both the city itself and a very wide area around it are divided into zones, and within this zonal structure tickets are transferable at will between train and S-train to bus within given periods of time.

Quick tour of Copenhagen

There is much to see in Copenhagen, but like most cities, it presents problems for drivers partly because of the many one-way streets and partly because of parking problems. So, as a quick introduction to Denmark's capital city, we have designed a fairly quick and easy run around in your car, noting briefly the main places of interest and giving as much information as can reasonably be coped with on such a trip.

You start your tour in front of the pseudo-Byzantine Main Railway Station, **Hovedbanegården** from 1904–11, where there is a small car park.

With the station on your right, turn right into BERNSTOFFSGADE. You will then have the other entrance to the station on your right and on your left the side entrance to the famous **Tivoli Gardens** from 1853.

In about 250m you reach traffic lights, where you turn left into TIETGENSGADE. Here you continue with Tivoli on your left, and on your right, in c 200m, the side of the art gallery the **Ny Carlsberg Glyptotek**, usually simply known as **Glyptoteket**. You will catch a glimpse of the front façade of Glyptoteket at the crossing with H.C. ANDERSENS BOULEVARD 100m further on.—On Dantes Plads, just in front of the main entrance, stands the Dante Column, commemorating the 600th anniversary of Dante's death in 1921.—Take a quick glance right further down H.C. Andersens Boulevard and notice the **Lange-bro** lifting bridge from 1954, leading to the island of **Amager**.

Go straight on into STORMGADE, and continue over the next crossroads at **Vester Voldgade**. On your right, with the entrance from FREDERIKSHOLMS KANAL, you now have the **National Museum**.

A further 200m brings you, after the traffic lights, to a stretch of Copenhagen's canals, with **Frederiksholms Kanal** on your right. There is a small bridge 100m along this, **Marmorbroen** (The Marble Bridge), designed in 1739–45 by Eigtved on the orders of Christian VI. It gives access to a complex (in fact a tiny island) called **Slotsholmen**, which is the islet on which Bishop Absalon, the founder of Copenhagen, built his original castle. The imposing parliament building, *Christiansborg is part of this complex, and can clearly be seen. To your right, though partly out of sight behind Christiansborg, lie the Royal Arsenal Museum **Tøjhusmuseet**, housed in a building by Christian IV, the National Archives, **Rigsarkivet**, and the Royal Library, **Det kongelige Bibliotek**.

Meanwhile, you should drive straight on across the canal, where on your left you will have another canal, **Gammel Strand**, the most important Copenhagen quayside in the Middle Ages, and until recently an important fish quay. There was a fish market here until the 1950s, and there are still some excellent fish restaurants. (Note the statue of the fishwife at the far end.)—After c 150m you will have on your right **Thorvaldsens Museum**, looking for all the world like an Egyptian temple. The building was once the royal coach-house.

By now the street you are driving in is called VINDEBROGADE; continue along it, following the traffic right at the traffic lights, perhaps casting a quick glance left where you will see the **Højbro** bridge and beyond it the square, **Højbro Plads** leading to **Amagertorv** square and the main shopping street, **Strøget**.

As you round the bend you will have the façade of Christiansborg on your right. You are now going to turn left, so keep in the left-hand lane in order to cross the canal on the next bridge on your left. While the driver is concentrating on this, the passengers can look to the right and see the Stock Exchange, **Børsen**, built 1619–41 on the command of Christian IV, with its spire of intertwined dragons' tails. Beyond it is the **Knippelsbro** (1937), another lifting bridge leading to **Amager**, where the remarkable spire of Our Saviour's Church **Vor Frelsers Kirke** in Dutch baroque from 1682–96 can also be seen. The spire, with steps running around the outside and topped by a 3m figure of Christ, was designed by Laurids de Thurah in 1750.

The bridge you are now crossing is HOLMENS BRO, and you are in a street called HOLMENS KANAL. On your right you have the naval church, **Holmens Kirke**. Bear left with the main stream of traffic, passing the statue of **Niels Juel** unveiled in 1881 to commemorate the bicentenary of the Battle of Køge Bay. The National Bank, **National-banken**, from 1970, is now on your right.

After about 200m Holmens Kanal brings you to one of Copenhagen's most magnificent squares, KONGENS NYTORV. It was designed on the orders of Christian V, whose equestrian statue stands among the trees, and was intended to link the old town to the splendid new buildings being erected to the E of this area. On your left as you enter the square you will see one of Copenhagen's oldest and biggest department stores, **Magasin du Nord**, and on your right the Royal Theatre, **Det kongelige Teater**. The present building was built 1872–74 and modernised in the 1980s. As the traffic bears right at this point you will pass the front of the theatre; note the statues of Denmark's two great dramatists by the entrance, one of Adam Oehlenschläger, the other of Ludvig Holberg.

Having passed the Royal Theatre you will on your right—just before another canal—see the **Charlottenborg** art gallery. This building in Dutch baroque was built 1672–83 as the residence for the Viceroy of Norway, Ulrik Frederik Gyldenløve, son of Christian IV. It now houses the Danish Academy of Art.

Here you leave the Square, driving straight on into BREDGADE. But do note the area on your right, where you have another canal, NY-HAVN. It was dug 1671–73 and is lined with an array of 17C and 18C houses, and now an attractive street known for its cafés and restaurants. Note the anchor close to the road. Made in 1857 and taken from the 19C frigate 'Fyen', it lies there as a memorial to Danish seaman who died in World War II.

Bredgade is a very dignified road lined with neo-classical mansions. After 150m you pass **Sankt Annæ Plads** (St. Anne's Square) on your right, with a bronze equestrian statue of Christian X, and after that (No. 28) the rococo **Odd Fellow Palæ** built 1751–55 to a design by Nicolai Eigtved, and now a concert hall for chamber recitals.

About 450m down Bredgade you will come to traffic lights. On your left you will see the Marble Church, **Marmorkirken** or, to give it is proper name, **Frederikskirken**, again to a design by Nicolai Eigtved, continued after his death by Laurids de Thurah and Nicolas-Henri

Jardin and finally completed in 1894 by Ferdinand Meldahl.

Here you should turn right, into FREDERIKSGADE, which will lead you to the royal palaces of *Amalienborg, built around a square with the equestrian statue of Frederik V at the centre. Considered one of the finest pieces of European baroque architecture, these palaces are again to a design by Eigtved and were built between 1749 and 1760. The palace on the right nearest the harbour is the Queen's residence. You can drive straight on, right down to the water's edge, to see the new **Amaliehaven** park or just drive around the **Amalienborg** Square. But whichever you choose: return to the one-way-road **Bredgade**, and continue your trip, soon passing, on your left, the Russian Orthodox church, the **Alexander Newski Kirke** from 1883.

The next traffic lights along Bredgade are at FREDERICIAGADE, beyond which, on your left, you have the Eastern Regional Court and, on your right, at Bredgade 62 the Museum of Medical History, **Medicinsk Historisk Museum** in a building from 1785–87, originally the Academy of Surgery. On your right, too, you pass Denmark's principal Catholic church, **Sankt Ansgars Kirke**, designed by Gustav Friedrich Hetsch in 1842. A little further on the right lies the museum of decorative and applied arts, the **Kunstindustrimuseum**, in a building by Eigtved and Thurah from 1752–57, restored 1921–26 by Ivar Bentsen and Kaare Klint.

Where Bredgade ends at ESPLANADEN you bear right. The park on your left now is the **Churchill Park**. You will take the first road on your left, and as you do so you will have on your right the Resistance Museum, **Frihedsmuseet**, with exhibits from the Danish Resistance Movement of World War II. Behind the museum is the huge **Gefion Fountain**, designed by Anders Bundgård in 1909. Unfortunately you cannot see it from your car, but walk back to have a look at it, if you decide to try to park your car in this area. Also in the Churchill Park stands the English church, **St. Alban's Church**, built in typical English neo-Gothic in 1885–87.

Driving through the park you pass the Citadel, **Kastellet**, on your left. This is the site of a fortress built by Christian IV in 1629, and subsequently of a prison. Having passed the **Langeliniepavillon** restaurant, you will be driving very close to the waterfront, and here you are bound to find lots of people looking at the bronze statue of the Little Mermaid, **Den lille Havfrue**, by Edvard Eriksen, 1913. (Parking facilities are often reasonable a little further on.)

From the Little Mermaid you drive W, following the road and keeping the Citadel on your left, to FOLKE BERNADOTTES ALLÉ, where you again turn left. As you drive here you will still have the Citadel Park on your left and now also the railway on your right.

You will very soon come to a busy main road which on your left is called GRØNNINGEN, while on your right you have OSLO PLADS with **Østerport Station**. You should cross this road (there are traffic lights!), noting on your left a statue in memory of Carl Nielsen, 'Pan Playing the Flute', the work of the composer's wife, Anne Marie Carl Nielsen.

Once you have crossed the main road you are in ØSTER VOLDGADE, i.e. East Rampart Street, so called because it follows the old ramparts surrounding the city. On your right you can see the **Øster Anlæg** park, and on your left are the houses which Christian IV had built for his sailors between 1631 and 1639, **Nyboder**.

700m further on you cross SØLVGADE, on the corner of which you have Copenhagen's main art gallery, **Statens Museum for Kunst**. Behind it, in the same park, but not visible from this road is the smaller, but impressive **Hirschsprungs Samling** gallery.

Immediately after Sølvgade you pass, on your right, the museum of geology, **Geologisk Museum**, standing in the botanical gardens, **Botanisk Have**. On your left you have the **Kongens Have** park with Christian IV's sumptuous *Rosenborg Palace** from 1634.

A further 400m brings you to new traffic lights, at the crossing with GOTHERSGADE. Turn right here and drive along Gothersgade, with the **Botanical Museum** on your right. Cross FARIMAGSGADE and continue until you reach the Copenhagen Lakes (Søerne), about 500m in all, where you turn right into ØSTER SØGADE, catching a glimpse of the Queen Louise Bridge, **Dronning Louises Bro**, leading over the Lakes on your left as you turn. There has been a bridge across the Lakes here since 1562, and the present one dates from 1885–87.

Stretching from Gammel Kongevej in the W to Østerbrogade in the E, and crossed by several bridges, Copenhagen's three Lakes were originally reservoirs, as is the westerly Sankt Jørgens Sø still. They lie outside the old city, and are now a much-loved open space. The banks are lined with greensward and paths with benches, and where Gyldenløvesgade crosses them there is the idyllic **Søpavillon** restaurant, with lawns and gardens.

You are driving with part of the **Sortedams Sø** on your left, and, on your right, the Copenhagen Municipal Hospital, **Københavns Kommunehospital**, designed by Christian Hansen and built between 1859 and 1863 in neo-Byzantine style.

When you come to the next major crossing, easily recognisable by the **Fredensbro** bridge from 1904, you turn right into **Sølvgade** and across **Sølvtorvet**. You will now find you have the **Botanical Gardens** on your right and **Statens Museum for Kunst** on your left. On reaching the traffic lights, you turn right, into **Øster Voldgade**. You have been here before, and we have simply taken you along four sides of a square in order to show you the Lakes.

This time you drive across **Gothersgade**, coming to a very busy part of Copenhagen, NØRREPORT. This is the site of the medieval North Gate, and now the location of one of the busiest suburban S-train stations. As you approach the station you will find on your left the pedestrian street FREDERIKSBORGGADE leading to **Kultorvet** square, beyond which stands the Round Tower, **Rundetårn**, the 34.8m-high observatory tower built for Christian IV in 1642.

On passing **Nørreport Station** you should move into the left-hand lane, ready to turn (at the next traffic lights) into the rather narrow NØRREGADE. The church which can soon be seen on your right is **Sankt Petri Kirke**, one of Copenhagen's four medieval parish churches.

About 250m down Nørregade you pass the old buildings of the **University** on your left. The University has been here since it was founded by Christian I in 1479, and the building you are now passing dates from 1731. The main building, built 1831–36 to the design of Peder Malling, faces the Cathedral on your left. The Cathedral, **Vor Frue Kirke**, is a neo-classical building from 1811–29, designed by Christian Frederik Hansen, replacing the older building which had been destroyed by the British bombardment of Copenhagen in 1807.

Nørregade now continues to GAMMELTORV (Old Square), where you will see the magnificent Renaissance **Caritas** fountain, a gift to the citizens of Copenhagen from Christian IV in 1608, intended to provide them with fresh water. Immediately on reaching Gammeltorv you turn right, down VESTERGADE, but you should try to gain a quick impression of the lively scene on Gammeltorv, crossed by the pedestrian

street, **Strøget**, with **Nytorv** square beyond it, flanked by Christian
Frederik Hansen's neo-classical law courts, **Domhuset**.

After 200m Vestergade brings you to **VESTER VOLDGADE** (West
Rampart Street), where you turn left into RÅDHUSPLADSEN, Town Hall
Square. The vast Town Hall, **Rådhuset**, itself was built between 1892
and 1905, designed by Martin Nyrop. As you approach the Town Hall,
you will see just in front of you the statue of the horn-blowing Vikings,
Lurblæserne. They stand close to where the **Strøget** pedestrian shopping street meets the Town Hall Square.

Turn right in the middle of the Town Hall square, following the
traffic, and continue across the first traffic lights on **H.C. Andersens
Boulevard**. You are now on VESTERBROGADE and in 150m will, on
your left, pass the main entrance to **Tivoli**, built in 1889. In front of the
entrance a quick glance in the opposite direction will give you a
glimpse of the elegant roof of the old **Circus Building** from 1886 on
Axeltorv square.

Drive straight on past the next traffic lights, where you have the **SAS
headquarters** on your right. The road soon leads you over the main
railway line and passes **Frihedsstøtten** (The Liberty Column), a sandstone obelisk from 1792–97 commemorating the emancipation of the
peasantry. Immediately after this column you turn left and find yourself where you started, at the Main Railway Station.

4   Copenhagen on Foot or by Bus/S-Train

COPENHAGEN (København) (1,200,000 inhab., Tourist Information:
H.C. Andersens Boulevard 22).

In the following, Copenhagen, including Frederiksberg and
Christianshavn, is divided up into seven areas, for each of which we
have planned a walk taking you past the most important features.
Naturally, in a city the size of Copenhagen, not all attractions are so
close to the centre that they can be reached on foot. For those not
included in the walks, but easily reached by public transport, the bus
numbers or S-train routes are indicated.

WALK 1 (c 3km)

The walk starts and ends in front of the Main Railway Station, **Hovedbanegården**.

Main Sights: Tivoli, Rådhuset, Glyptoteket, National Museum.

The main railway station was built of brick in 1904–11 to a design by
Heinrich Wenck in pseudo-Byzantine style and is topped by a
pyramid-like roof. The main entrance facing the railway cutting N is
a Copenhagen landmark. The huge main hall is spacious and impressive, especially after being redesigned in the 1980s, and contains, in
addition to kiosks, snack bars and a cafeteria, banks, a post office, a
small supermarket, an office giving information on accommodation, a
baker and outstanding facilities for inter-railers.

Immediately in front of the main entrance you will find access roads
running alongside the railway track. These will lead you to (100m)
VESTERBROGADE, one of Copenhagen's main thoroughfares, a busy
shopping street with little of architectural interest. Here, you turn right,

in 100m crossing Bernstorffsgade and 100m further on coming to the main entrance to **Tivoli** on your right.

Tivoli, bounded by Vesterbrogade, Bernstorffsgade, Tietgensgade and H.C. Andersens Boulevard, was founded in 1853 by Georg Christensen and inspired by the London Vauxhall Gardens and the Vauxhall–Tivoli in Paris. The Government made the land available, left over from the old fortifications, and the Tivoli Lake is in fact part of the old moat. The 'Renaissance' main entrance, with its Corinthian columns and dome, is from 1889.

The site, which is not far short of 80,000 sq m, is part park, part pleasure gardens. There are tree-lined walks, illuminated in the evening, fountains and carefully laid-out gardens. And there are entertainments of all kinds, from the modern fairground to the Pantomime Theatre where classical pantomime, which can be traced back to the Italian *commedia dell'arte*, is still performed in the original manner. Built in 1874 in the style of a Chinese pavilion, the Pantomime Theatre is the oldest building in Tivoli. There is another 'Chinese' building, the Chinese Tower, while the Nimb restaurant is in 'Turkish' style. There is an open air stage for performances by acrobats and jugglers, the 'Tivoli Guard' marches around with its band, and there are musical performances of all kinds. A modern concert hall was opened in 1956, replacing the earlier one which was blown up in 1944. The gardens open before lunch, but in the afternoon they are rather quiet, an excellent pleasure park for children, and the adult entertainment does not really come into its own until the evening (open May–Sept).

Continue now for a further 200m to H.C. Andersens Boulevard, on the other side of which are Copenhagen's Town Hall Square and the Town Hall.

Rådhuspladsen (the Town Hall Square), cleared with the removal of the city ramparts in the 1850s, is, after Kongens Nytorv, the largest square in Copenhagen. It is also one of the busiest, surrounded on all sides by main arteries. Nevertheless, there is room for monuments, of which the statue by Anton Rosen of the Viking Lur Blowers is perhaps the most famous. Joakim Skovgaard's and Thorvald Bindesbøll's Dragon Fountain is also splendid. Note, on the top of the building on your left on the corner of the square, an enormous neon barometer topped by figures reflecting the weather—a girl carrying an umbrella when it is going to rain, and riding a bicycle when the sun is shining.

Rådhuset (The Town Hall), Copenhagen's sixth, stands some distance from the site of the earlier ones in Gammeltorv square. When the city ramparts were removed in the 1850s an open space was cleared and used as an exhibition park. It was then decided to build the new Town Hall here. The competition for the design was won by Martin Nyrop, and building commenced in 1892. The official opening was in 1905. The huge rectangular building with four wings enclosing a lofty covered courtyard (24m x 44m), is inspired partly by northern Italian architecture (very obvious in the courtyard), but to a very large extent must be seen as a piece of 19C National Romanticism, reflecting Danish medieval brick buildings. The tower is open to the public, and offers a magnificent view of Copenhagen.

In the Town Hall you will also find Jens Olsen's unique astronomical World Clock (access all year). Guided tours in English.

Turn right down H.C. ANDERSENS BOULEVARD to (50m) **Louis Tussauds Voksmuseum** (Louis Tussaud's Wax Museum), at No. 22, containing wax models of famous personalities in the Tussaud tradition. Here, too, is the **Holografisk Museum**, a permanent exhibition of international holography. Both are open all year.—And here you should note that the main Copenhagen Tourist Information Office is in the same complex.

The route now continues along H.C. Andersens Boulevard, with the Town Hall on your left, across TIETGENSGADE to (300m) the **Ny Carlsberg Glyptotek**, Dantes Plads 22.

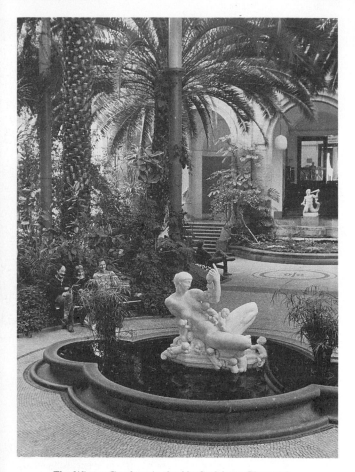

*The Winter Gardens in the Ny Carlsberg Glyptotek,
Copenhagen. In the foreground the Water Mother by
Kai Nielsen (1882–1924). Photo: Dieter Betz*

The ornate buildings date from between 1892 and 1906. Vilhelm Dahlerup's façade is inspired by Venetian architecture, and the interior is richly stuccoed. On entering, you will find the ground floor of this impressive museum mainly dedicated to sculpture, including works by Thorvaldsen, Herman Wilhelm Bissen and Jens Adolf Jerichau, but also a great deal of French sculpture, not least Rodin. The two upper floors are occupied by painting. The French Impressionists are particularly well represented, but there is also an outstanding collection of Danish art.

The second phase of building was by Hack Kampmann, in a more severe neo-classical style. This extension houses the largest collection of Etruscan art outside Italy, and in addition there is the famous collection of Egyptian, Mesopotamian and Greek art, much of it presented to the museum by the brewer Carl Jacobsen, son of the founder of the Carlsberg Breweries (open all year).

On Dantes Plads, just in front of Glyptoteket, there is the Dante Column, commemorating the 600th anniversary of Dante's death in 1921. It was presented

*The Bronze Age Trundholm Sun Chariot in the
National Museum. Here are the first spoke wheels in
Denmark, and the first sculpted horse.*

to Copenhagen by the City of Rome, and is now surmounted by a bronze statue
of Beatrice, executed by Einar Utzon-Frank. To the E of it there is a bronze plaque
with a relief of Dante by the Italian sculptor S.L. Andreotti.

Some 400m beyond the Glyptotek you can glimpse the **Langebro**
lifting bridge leading to the island of Amager. There has been a bridge
here since 1690, and the present one is from 1954.

After visiting the Glyptotek you should walk the few metres back to
Tietgensgade, cross H.C. Andersens Boulevard at the traffic lights and
continue past the next set of traffic lights at (100m) VESTER VOLD-
GADE. Continue in a straight line into STORMGADE, where on the left,
at No. 10, you will find the dignified **Holsteins Palæ**, a luxurious
mansion built 1683–87, the third storey being added in 1756. Once the
Natural History Museum, it is now the head office of an insurance
company. Opposite, flanked by a colonnade, is the **National Museum**.
The main entrance is not in Stormgade, but in FREDERIKSHOLMS
KANAL, the first turning on the right. (Opposite the entrance you will
see Christiansborg Palace and the Thorvaldsen Museum, which are
described in Walk 3.)

The core of Denmark's National Museum is Eigtved's **Prinsens Palæ**
from 1743–44, extended by further wings in Stormgade, Ny Vestergade and Vester Voldgade. Until 1807 such collections as there were,
were housed in various parts of Copenhagen. Then in 1807 the Prinsens Palæ was designated the Royal Museum for Nordic Antiquity,
being renamed the National Museum in 1892. The ethnographic

collection was moved here in 1845, the collection of antiquities in 1851, the Scandinavian antiquities in 1855. The Museum was radically extended in the 1930s and the collections were extensively redistributed in the 1980s.

The entire museum is divided into eight Departments, of which six are housed in this complex and open to the public: 1: Danish archaeology including the Viking Age; 2: Middle Ages to 1750; 3: 1750 to the Present; 4: Ethnographical Collections; 5: Egyptian, Classical and Middle East Collections; 6: Numismatics; (7: Open Air Museum—is in Lyngby, see below.); 8: Research Department (not open to the public).

This is a National Museum in the grand style, with a wealth of exhibits from all areas. The Viking Age is particularly well represented, with most of the major finds from Denmark exhibited according to the most modern principles. There are reconstructions of milieux and dress throughout, together with explanatory photographs and texts, many in English.—You must allow plenty of time to see this splendid museum.

Plans and descriptions in English are available in the entrance hall as well as guided tours in English July–Aug.

On leaving the National Museum you turn left and cross Stormgade into RÅHUSSTRÆDE. As you walk along here you should notice on your right the old houses in MAGSTRÆDE, a road from 1520 (the name really means something like Loo Lane). The oldest extant houses in this now quite idyllic street, Nos 17 and 19, are from the mid-17C. On your left you will find the small square VANDKUNSTEN, where in the 15C there was a watermill, driven by water from the neighbouring streams. Christian III constructed a pump here to supply water to Slotsholmen, the small island on which Christiansborg Palace stands, and in 1910 the fountain was erected, with water pouring from four lions' heads into a basin. The street sign 'Wand Konsten' on the corner is one of the oldest in Copenhagen, dating from c 1770.

The walk now continues along Rådhusstræde, but you may like first to walk left through Vandkunsten and along LØNGANGSSTRÆDE to take a look at (150m) **Vartov**.

Ultimately deriving from the old Holy Ghost Hospice, Vartov Hospital on the corner of Vester Voldgade and Løngangsstræde was built 1724–44. In the 19C it became a home for the elderly, with at one time provision for 450 people. In 1936 this home was moved to northern Copenhagen. The old buildings were restored in 1950 and now comprise various offices, including the central office of the Folk High Schools, private flats and a restaurant, in addition to which the Grundtvig Society has its offices here. Vartov is mainly known by the public, however, because of its church, as it was here that the great theologian and hymn-writer N.F.S. Grundtvig was pastor from 1839–72. Built in 1754–55 and painted grey, it has balconies on three sides. The pulpit is above the altar, framed in the Corinthian columns of the altarpiece from c 1725. There is a statue of Grundtvig, kneeling, in the courtyard, the work of Niels Skovgaard.

The walk continues now 150m along Rådhusstræde when you will come to BROLÆGGERSTRÆDE, which in the 17C was the centre of the brewing industry in Copenhagen. It was here that J.C. Jacobsen, the founder of the Carlsberg Breweries, was born in 1842, as a memorial plaque indicates. (The actual name Carlsberg derives from the name of J.C. Jacobsen's son, Carl.) The house is today the offices of the Carlsberg Foundation.

Rådhusstræde now opens up to a large open space which in fact consists of two squares, first NYTORV (New Square) and then GAMMEL-TORV (Old Square or Old Market Place).

Since the 14C Copenhagen's Town Hall had stood on the S side of Gammeltorv, and in the 17C Christian IV ordered the space S of it to be cleared in order to give the Town Hall a more dignified aspect. Thus Nytorv came into being. After the fire of 1795, when the Town Hall was destroyed, Gammeltorv and Nytorv were joined to form a single open square.

To the left as you enter **Nytorv** you will see the **Law Courts and Lock-up**. Built in 1805–15, they are among the buildings designed in neo-classical style by C.F. Hansen in his project for rebuilding the centre of Copenhagen after the fire of 1795 and the English bombardment of 1807. Some of the materials used came from the first Christiansborg and others from Hørsholm Castle (Rte 6).—Linked to the Lock-up by a bridge and facing Nytorv is the temple-like **Copenhagen City Court**, with a portal consisting of six Ionic columns. Note the inscription above the porch, the first words of the 1241 Jutland Law: 'With law the land shall be built'.

Gammeltorv to the N is indeed the old market place, dating back to the 12C, when Absalon founded Copenhagen. None of the really old buildings around it still survives, as Gammeltorv was razed during the great fire of 1728. On the other hand the only monument from Christian IV's time standing in a public square is to be found here. Erected 1609–10, the copper and gilt **Caritas Fountain** was the King's gift to the citizens of Copenhagen, intended both to embellish the city and to improve the supply of fresh water. Caritas is represented as a pregnant young woman holding one child in her arms and with a boy at her side, the whole surrounded by dolphins.

Nytorv and Gammeltorv are crossed by Copenhagen's most famous shopping street, best known as STRØGET. You should turn left into it. Lined like the rest of Strøget with a host of shops this western end is correctly called FREDERIKSBERGGADE, and will bring you in c 250m back to Rådhuspladsen.

Now cross the square diagonally to your right, and go over H.C. Andersens Boulevard into JERNBANEGADE, which will lead you to another square, AXELTORV, a small open space with seating and several sculptures. Here on one of the corners you will find the **Cirkusbygning**. Purpose built in 1885 and claiming to be the oldest circus building in the world, this has now served for circus entertainment of various kinds, plus other grandiose shows, for 100 years. Opposite, with its colourful, not to say gaudy, decorations, is the striking **Palads** theatre which houses altogether 19 cinemas.

Now go across Axeltorv, past the Vesterport S Train Station, across VESTER FARIMAGESGADE and into GAMMEL KONGEVEJ. Here, just at the end of the lakes, at No. 10 and c 400m in all from Axeltorv, you will find the **Tycho Brahe Planetarium**. Dating from 1989, it includes a space theatre and sophisticated equipment to give you the feeling of space travel (open all year).

The walk now goes across Gammel Kongevej and then left through the 100m-long Stenosgade, where, on the left, you will find one of the main Catholic churches in Denmark, Jesu Hjerte Kirke. On reaching Vesterbrogade you turn right and proceed for c 200m to a small square, VESTERBROTORV. Immediately after this, at Vesterbrogade 59, you will find **Københavns Bymuseum & Søren Kierkegaard Samling**, housed in a neo-classical mansion, from 1782–86. It became the Copenhagen City Museum in 1956, and offers a collection of relics from old buildings, tradesmen's signs, bicycles and street furniture to give an impression of what Copenhagen once looked like. These are supplemented with a collection of paintings and prints vividly illustrating the development of Copenhagen and the manner of life there over the centuries. There are models of Copenhagen in the late Middle Ages and in the time of Christian IV. The first of these large-scale models stands in front of the building in the summer. The Søren Kierkegaard

COPENHAGEN CENTRE
0 metres   600

M Metro Stations

collection was opened in 1960 (open all year).—ABSALONSGADE, running alongside the museum, has been maintained to give the appearance of an old street, with cobbles, gas lamps, benches and an old telephone kiosk, such as would have stood there between 1860 and 1940.

You now return along Vesterbrogade, where you will soon see **Frihedsstøtten** (The Freedom Column), standing in the middle of the road above the railway track. This sandstone obelisk, standing on a plinth of Norwegian marble and surrounded by four marble statues by different artists, commemorates the emancipation of the peasantry in 1788. It was designed by Nicolai Abildgaard and erected in 1797. Abildgaard was also responsible for the reliefs on the plinth.

The Main Railway Station is now on your right.

WALK 2 (c 2km)

The walk starts and ends on the Rådhuspladsen square.

Main Sights: Strøget, Rundetårn, the University, The Cathedral.

The walk starts at the E end of RÅDHUSPLADSEN close to the column with the figures of two Vikings blowing *lurs*, the ancient curved horns which have now become the symbol for Danish butter. With the column on your right you start to walk up FREDERIKSBERGGADE, the W end of the main shopping street, Strøget, which leads from Rådhuspladsen to Kongens Nytorv.

A good deal of what is known as *Den indre by*, 'the inner city' is now pedestrianised. *Strøget* is not the name of a single street, but means 'principal shopping street' and is the popular name for what is claimed to be the longest pedestrian street in the world. It links the two principal squares, Kongens Nytorv and Rådhuspladsen, and incorporates from the Rådhuspladsen end: Frederiksberggade, Nygade, Vimmelskaftet, Amagertorv and Østergade. It became pedestrianised in 1962 and crosses the other main pedestrian street, Købmagergade. Some of the side streets off Strøget have benefited from its exhilarating atmosphere and have been turned into fashionable shopping and café streets, for instance the area around Pistolstræde, behind Hotel d'Angleterre at Kongens Nytorv.

After 250m you will come to and cross GAMMELTORV/NYTORV (see Walk 1). Walk down Strøget as far as Vimmelskaftet 38, where you will find **Haandarbejdets Fremme**, the best-known shop for Danish embroidery, knitting, etc. A source of inspiration for the craftswoman.

The area you are in here is the oldest part of Copenhagen. On your right, after passing Gammeltorv/Nytorv you will find KNABROSTRÆDE and BADSTUESTRÆDE, where the butchers had their booths in 1377 before moving to Købmagergade around 1400. A public bath house was then erected here, from which it derived its name in the 17C. The next road on your right is HYSKENSTRÆDE, also one of the very oldest streets, referred to even in the 15C as being 'old'. The name means 'little house', and almost certainly refers to a public lavatory that is known to have been nearby in the 14C. The street's reputation improved with time, and in the 18C and 19C it had people of repute living here. It was badly damaged in the 1728 fire and widened in the rebuilding which took place afterwards.

Moving into the funnel-shaped part of Strøget, called AMAGERTORV you will, on the left, find **Helligåndskirken**, the Church of the Holy Ghost. A hospice existed on this site as early as 1296, and in 1474 was incorporated into an Augustinian monastery, which after the Reformation became a hospital. The present church was the S wing of this monastery. It was extended in 1582, when the tower was added; the spire is from 1594. The porch on the S side was the commission of Christian IV, incorporating a doorway originally intended for the Stock Exchange. In 1672 the King's Chancellor, Griffenfeld, built the round sepulchral chapel on the N side. The church was badly damaged in the 1728 fire, but by 1732 had been repaired and reconstructed, thereby losing most of its medieval character.

At the wider end of Amagertorv—the part that really is the square—you will pass some of the most distinguished of Copenhagen's shops, including Illums Bolighus (furniture and furnishings), and the main Danish Royal Porcelain shop in the magnificent Dutch Renaissance twin-gabled merchant's house (1616) at No. 6. For those interested in visiting the Royal Porcelain factory in Smallegade, Frederiksberg, free transport can be arranged from this shop by telephoning 31 86 48 48.—Opposite, at Amagertorv 9, is an old tobacconist's shop founded in 1864, which now houses the small Larsen's Pipe Museum.

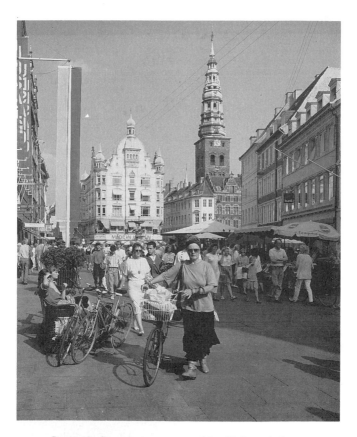

Strøget in Copenhagen, approaching Højbro plads, with Sankt Nikolai Kirke in the background. Photo: Ole Akhøj

There was a market square here on Amagertorv in the 15C, and in 1684 it was designated the market place where peasants from the island of Amager were to sell their wares. In 1795 it was joined to HØJBRO PLADS—the area leading down to the canal and through which you can see right down to Christiansborg Castle and Slotsholmen (Walk 3)—when this was established after the 1795 fire, replacing a number of narrow streets.—Højbro Plads itself contains some excellent examples of the neo-classical architecture of its time. Note especially the corner building, No. 21, with a façade of Corinthian pilasters above the present shop windows. The fine but somewhat romanticised equestrian statue opposite this building is of Bishop Absalon by Vilhelm Bissen. The fountain, **Storkespringvandet**, is from 1894.

Diagonally across Højbro Plads you will see the entrance to SANKT NICOLAI PLADS on which stands **Sankt Nicolai Kirke**, St. Nicholas' Church. The present church is from 1915–17, though there was one on this spot certainly as early as 1261, and probably rather earlier.

This is where the first Lutheran sermon was held in Denmark, and when the leading Reformer Hans Tavsen became parish priest here in 1529, it became the focal point of the Copenhagen Reformation movement. By the end of the 17C an imposing tower had been added, and St. Nicholas Church was the most splendid in Copenhagen after the Cathedral. It was almost totally destroyed in the 1795 fire, the tower being the only part of it left standing. After the Napoleonic Wars the ruined tower was actually used as a fire station, and St. Nicholas Square became a market place.
  In 1908–10 the tower was repaired and the spire, paid for by Carl Jacobsen, was added. The new church was then built between 1915 and 1917 to a design by H.C. Amberg. The intention was as far as possible to reconstruct the old church, of which there were detailed drawings. It was, however, not to be used as a church, and acted as a library until it was taken over in 1957 by the Church Army. The church is now used for travelling exhibitions, and there is a restaurant here, too.

At Amagertorv you leave Strøget and turn left into KØBMAGERGADE, another busy shopping street and, like Strøget, a pedestrian precinct. Købmagergade is thought to have been a main approach to the original Copenhagen as early as 1200. By the 15C it was the street in which the butchers had their booths, and the present name is in fact a distortion of the old 'Kiødmangergade', meaning, precisely, Butchers Street. It is a rather winding street with many ancient associations, in particular the Round Tower and Regensen. Many of the present buildings are from the 18C, and you will gain a better impression of what this street really represents in terms of architecture if you keep your eyes, not on the shop windows, but on the first floors and beyond.
  On the right, 200m up Købmagergade, you will find KLARE-BODERNE, which used to give access to a convent of nuns of the Order of St. Clare that had been established in this part of Copenhagen in the 15C. After the Reformation a royal mint was established on the site, giving rise to the nearby streetname of **Møntergade**. Of the present-day buildings it is Klareboderne 3, from 1731–34, that is of particular interest. Since 1787 it has been the home of Denmark's oldest publishing house, Gyldendal, and a plaque in the courtyard recalls that Søren Kierkegaard used to walk through daily on his way to school 1821–30.
  Directly opposite the spot where Klareboderne enters Købmagergade stands the Main Post Office, behind which, entered from VALKENDORFSGADE is the **Post- og Telegrafmuseum**, a museum illustrating the history of the Danish postal service. In addition to photographs and models, as well as old equipment, it contains a complete collection of Danish postage stamps (open all year).
  In a 19C warehouse at Valkendorfsgade 13 you will find the toy museum, **Legetøjsmuseum**, the ideal museum for children, with a splendid collection of over 25,000 items, including toys and dolls from former times and many countries. On the first floor there is a model

town and a model railway layout thought to comprise one of the biggest gauge 0 model railway collections in Europe. There is a also tiny children's cinema (open all year).

The next road to the left along Købmagergade is LØVSTRÆDE, a street with an idyllic name (Leaf Street, Foliage Street), where you would once have found a garden of the medieval Greyfriars Monastery. In the 19C the street had many literary associations. The author Meir Aron Goldschmidt lived in No. 8 in the 1840s. A short walk down Løvstræde and back again should really not be missed, as it will take you to the very intimate little square called GRÅBRØDRETORV at the other end with its cafés and restaurants.

This area was occupied by a Franciscan monastery in 1238, with its main wing in the present **Klosterstræde**. The monastery was demolished after the Reformation, though remains of the foundations are still to be seen in some of the buildings. Most of these are from the period of rebuilding after the fire of 1728, though those to the W are from a later rebuilding, after the English bombardment of 1807. In No. 3, Wessels Gård, there are two rooms to commemorate the 18C Dano-Norwegian poet Johan Herman Wessel, whose play 'Love without Stockings' is one of the classics of Scandinavian drama.

Walk back to Købmagergade and turn left. In c 200m you will reach **Rundetårn** (The Round Tower), with Trinitatis Kirke on your right and Regensen on your left. Built by Christian IV in 1642 as an observatory, the Round Tower now acts as the church tower to Trinitatis Kirke. A rather stubby cylinder decorated on the outside with pilaster strips, it is 34.8m high, with an outside diameter of 15m. A broad spiral ramp inside leads to the top, and it is documented that Tsar Peter rode to the top in 1716, followed by the Tsarina in a carriage drawn by six horses. Remember Hans Christian Andersen's 'The Tinderbox'? When the third dog has eyes as big as 'round towers', that is not what Andersen said. He said *the* Round Tower—and he meant this one. There is a splendid view of Copenhagen from the top (open all year).

Trinitatis Kirke (Trinity Church; 1637–57) was started by Christian IV and finished by Frederik III, and was intended as something approaching a University church. At the same time the upper floor was to be the University Library. The Round Tower was then added as an observatory. The roof and upper floor, including the Library, were badly damaged in the 1728 fire, and countless irreplaceable books and manuscripts were thus lost. On the other hand neither the church nor the tower was damaged in the 1795 fire or the 1807 bombardment. The present church is essentially 18C, with carved altarpiece and pulpit in rich ornamental baroque by Fridrich Ehbisch. A huge rococo clock from 1757 stands against the wall opposite the pulpit. The pews are from 1731, each with a carved shell on the bench end.—Of the many distinguished men buried here, mention must be made of the great Icelandic historian Arne Magnusson, while the most magnificent of the memorial tablets is that from 1698 on the N wall of the chancel to Field Marshal Hans Schack by Thomas Quellinus and Christian Nerger.

Regensen just opposite is the most famous of Copenhagen's old student residences. It was built 1618–28, also by Christian IV, and consists of four wings around an open square in the centre of which stands a lime tree. Regensen is still used for its original purpose, and the courtyard, entered from Store Kannikestræde, is open to the public.

A further 200m along Købmagergade brings you to KULTORVET square, which was established after the 1728 fire. Charcoal burners from North Sjælland used to come here to sell their products—hence

Copenhagen: Regensen student residences with the Round Tower in the background. Both are the work of Christian IV. Photo: Ellen Thoby

the name Kultorvet, 'Coal Market'. Now, however, it is a pedestrian area, with pavement cafés and fruit and flower stalls. One side of it is dominated by the building containing the main Copenhagen Municipal Library.

Beyond Kultorvet you can now see NØRREPORT, the site of one of Copenhagen's medieval gates, Nørreport (North Gate). Today Nørreport is one of the city's busiest S-train stations.

From Kultorvet, we suggest you retrace your steps the short way towards Regensen, turning right immediately before reaching it, down KRYSTALGADE, a street known to date back to 1492. The main interest here now is the **Synagogue**, standing just over half-way down on your right. It was built 1830–33 after the loss in the 1795 fire of the old Synagogue, to a design by Gustav Friedrich Hetsch. A basilica, it has its side to the street with windows and doors in what has been described as 'orientalised neo-classicism'. It was extended in 1885 and restored in 1958 by Henning Meyer.

Just beyond the Synagogue you reach NØRREGADE, where you turn left. You are now in the university area, with the side of the old University buildings on your left.

Copenhagen University was founded in 1479 and was originally housed in the Cathedral School. After occupying various buildings in the area, in 1731 it was installed in the purpose-built premises here on Nørregade now called Kommunitetsbygningen. The neo-classical 69m-long main building, facing S on to Frue Plads, was then erected to a design of Peder Malling in 1831–36 as part of the grandiose scheme for rebuilding the centre of Copenhagen. The entrance hall was decorated with frescoes (1844–53) of scenes from Greek mythology, the work of Constantin Hansen.

Adjoining the main University complex in Fiolstræde—a pedestrian precinct with many second-hand bookshops—is the University Library, built 1857–71 to a design by Johan Daniel Herholdt. At right angles to the main building, immediately behind the Cathedral, is the University Annex, formerly the Metropolitan School, by C.F. Hansen. However, this annex is no longer big enough, and the University is now largely housed on an entirely new campus on Amager.

Just before you reach the Cathedral Square, Vor Frue Plads, on your right you will see **Sankt Petri Kirke**. There has been a St. Peter's Church here on the corner of Nørregade and Sankt Pedersstræde at least since 1304. It burned down and was replaced on several occasions, but although it was badly damaged in the 1728 fire, the walls remained standing. Further damage was done in the 1807 bombardment, but the early 16C tower survived. Rebuilding was completed by 1816. More restoration work was carried out in the 1960s and 1970s, and in view of the many catastrophes and resultant rebuilding, it is remarkable that part of the 15C building can still be seen, facing Nørregade. The church has belonged to the German-speaking community in Copenhagen since 1586.

The interior is vaulted throughout and most of the furniture is 19C. There are, however, some older memorial tablets, one by Thomas Quellinus removed from the crypt in 1865, another by Johannes Wiedewelt in memory of his father, the sculptor Just Wiedewelt, also placed in the church in 1865. The vaulted sepulchral chapel contains many ornate tombs and memorials. There are other memorials, including one by Wiedewelt, in the churchyard to the N of the sepulchral chapel.

The University building faces on to VOR FRUE PLADS, where the main building is clearly Copenhagen Cathedral, **Vor Frue Kirke**. The Cathedral, formerly known as St. Mary's Church, is already mentioned at the end of the 12C, and was even then the most important in the city. There is evidence to indicate that it was founded somewhere between 1190 and 1200 by Peder Sunesøn, Absalon's successor as Bishop of Roskilde. The 1728 fire destroyed most of Gothic structure which had grown up on the spot, but the chancel survived until the 1807 English bombardment, when it was severely damaged.

C.F. Hansen was given the task of rebuilding it. He demolished the remains of the Gothic chancel, retaining only the walls of the side aisles and the tower, and produced a dignified neo-classical building fronted with an impressive main entrance behind Doric columns. The nave is flanked by arcading, rounded arches on square columns supporting balustrades. These in turn bear columns supporting the barrel vaulting of the roof. The light enters from between these columns. The figures of the Apostles standing in the nave are by Thorvaldsen, as is the famous figure of Christ constituting the altarpiece. The font, a kneeling angel bearing a shell, is also the work of Thorvaldsen and was presented to the cathedral by him. The cathedral underwent a complete restoration 1975–79.

Opposite the front façade you will find the Bishop's Palace, **Bispegården**. This dates from 1732, replacing a medieval palace destroyed by fire. It was restored by Martin Nyrop in 1896, and while it has brick walls facing the road, the courtyard is half-timbered and has an external gallery along one of the walls (not open to the public).

If you now continue along Nørregade, you will shortly come back to Gammeltorv. Here you turn right, along VESTERGADE, which you follow for 300m, reaching Rådhuspladsen, on the corner of which you will find the offices of one of Denmark's leading newspapers, 'Politiken'.

WALK 3 (c 1.5km)

The walk starts and ends in front of Christiansborg Palace and is limited to Slotsholmen—the island in the middle of Copenhagen, which besides Christiansborg is occupied by a host of historical buildings.

Main sights: Christiansborg Castle, Thorvaldsen's Museum, the Parliament building.

According to the medieval historian Saxo, Bishop Absalon, the founder of Copenhagen, established a castle on what is now called Slotsholmen (Castle Island) in 1167 as a defence against marauding pirates. Early 20C excavations have indeed uncovered the remains of this castle, which is portrayed on the oldest known Copenhagen Seal from 1296. As it was built for defence, so it courted attack, and both the Wends and the Lübeckers partly destroyed it in the 13C and 14C. Although originally in the ownership of the bishops, first Absalon and then the Bishops of Roskilde, King Erik of Pomerania took it into the Crown's possession and turned it in practice into the royal castle, which it remained until after the Reformation.

In the early 18C Frederik IV had the then antiquated castle modernised and extended. Later that same century Christian VI had it demolished and replaced with the first Christiansborg, a modern baroque palace partly designed by Eigtved and Thurah. The main wing looked on to a square ending at the Marble Bridge. This was the Royal Mews, looking much as it does today. The palace burned down in 1794. A second Christiansborg was then designed in neo-classical style by C.F. Hansen, whose aim was to reconstruct the entire centre of Copenhagen on neo-classical lines. That, too, burned down—in 1884. The third Christiansborg, the work of Thorvald Jørgensen, incorporates the only surviving parts of the earlier palaces, principally the Royal Mews of the first and the Chapel of the second. The foundation stone was laid in 1907, and the royal chambers were not finished until 1928. Unlike its predecessor, this palace has never been used as a royal residence, and it is now the home of the Danish Parliament.

This new Christiansborg palace observes the general plan of its predecessor, facing NE and overlooking *Christiansborg Slotsplads* (Christiansborg Palace Square) and, beyond that, the *Holmens Bro* bridge and *Holmens Kanal* leading to **Kongens Nytorv**. The style is neo-baroque, the 25m-high main façade clad in granite ashlars collected from 750 different Danish municipalities. The remaining façades are in Bornholm granite, except Prins Jørgens Gård between the main palace and the Chapel. This ensures a certain material continuity between the new and the old parts of the complex. The main palace complex is in the form of a square, with the rear wing opening on to the Mews, which in turn give on to the Marble Bridge and Frederik s-holms Kanal. The copper-roofed main wing is surmounted by a massive tower, ending in a grandiose crown. The weather vane is 104m above ground level.

Christiansborg is not generally open to the public, though there is access both to the Mews and to Prins Jørgens Gård. There are conducted tours with English-speaking guides through the royal reception rooms at certain times during the summer months. The Parliament is also open for conducted tours at limited times throughout the summer. More easily accessible are the palace ruins, which are open to the public from 9.30–14.00 most days, with access from the Slotsplads.

The equestrian statue of Frederik VII standing in front of Christiansborg is by

Herman Wilhelm Bissen and his son Vilhelm Bissen. Unveiled in 1873, it commemorates the signing under Frederik VII of the first Danish Constitution in 1849.

You should start your walk by going NW from the main entrance on Christiansborg Slotsplads, i.e. to your right as you face the palace. You will soon come to the entrance of Prins Jørgens Gård. You should, for the moment, go past this to visit the Palace Chapel, **Christiansborg Slotskirke**, which is immediately beyond the gateway.

Christiansborg Slotskirke, the Chapel from 1826, is the work of C.F. Hansen. It is in the neo-classical tradition, with the main entrance, to the NE, through a porch flanked by four Ionic columns. The rectangular building has a flat roof, with a shallow dome in the centre. The ceiling is vaulted, with the dome as its central feature. The altar, to the SW, is in a niche flanked by Corinthian pillars beyond which are figures of two Evangelists, the other two being in the W end. The royal balcony is above the entrance, and the organ is above this again.

On leaving the Chapel you should go back the 10m to the entrance to **Prins Jørgens Gård**, the great courtyard between the main palace of Christiansborg and the Chapel. The right wing is, of course, formed by the Chapel and, behind it, Thorvaldsen's Museum. To the left you can gain access to the Royal Reception Rooms in the Palace proper. They are reached by an imposing staircase, with statues by Jerichau and reliefs by Svend Rathsack. The impressive suite of rooms and halls includes the Fredensborg room, decorated with a painting of Christian IX and Queen Louise with their family in the garden of Fredensborg Palace, while the dignified Throne Room, with tapestry-covered walls, is dominated by two thrones designed by C.F. Hansen. The Christian IX room contains the famous painting of Christian IX crossing the border on a white horse to reclaim the lost lands of southern Jutland in 1920. The Danish Gallery, 40m long, is decorated with six huge allegorical paintings, while the Great Hall, **Riddersalen**, also 40m long, is resplendent with an intricate stuccoed ceiling, glorious candelabras and tapestries with motifs from the Scanian War. The patterned floor is made of black and white marble slabs.

On leaving the Royal Reception Rooms you continue through Prins Jørgens Gård, passing, at the end, the Supreme Court. On your right you will now be able to gain access to the **Thorvaldsen Museum** on Porthusgade.

When Denmark's great 19C sculptor Bertel Thorvaldsen presented his works to his native city in 1838, it was on condition that a suitable museum should be found. Frederik VI provided the site of the old royal coach house, and the architect Gottlieb Bindesbøll designed the present museum, incorporating some of the original walls. It is considered to be one of the finest of Copenhagen's neo-classical buildings, carefully matched with the Castle Chapel adjoining. The ochre exterior is partly decorated with murals, one being a portrayal of Thorvaldsen's return to Copenhagen. The five imposing portals are surmounted by a triumphal chariot designed by Herman Wilhelm Bissen, and the copper roof behind is crowned by a low dome. The major part of the collection is made up of completed works, models and sketches by Thorvaldsen himself, including many of the models for his major European monuments. In addition there is his collection of prints and sketches, his extensive library and his private collection of Classical sculptures, vases and bronzes.

On leaving the museum, you continue along Porthusgade as far as **Frederiksholms Kanal**, where you turn left. On your right you will now see the entrance to the National Museum. Some 50m on your left, you will find the entrance to the Royal Mews, via the Marble Bridge, **Marmorbroen** an elegant rococo bridge and one of Eigtved's finest works, completed in 1745. The name the Marble Bridge stems from its marble pavements. Note the elaborate symbolical decoration, which was carefully restored in the 1970s and early 1980s.

Ridebanen, the Royal Mews, remains from the first Christiansborg and was designed by the architect Elias David Häusser. The whole forms one of the finest pieces of Danish baroque architecture. Two pavilions by Eigtved from 1741 flank the entrance, which opens on to a wide courtyard. The N (left) wing houses the manège, while the low buildings behind colonnades on the right, contain, in addition to stabling, the **Karetmuseum**, a collection of royal coaches, and the Court Theatre. The oldest extant court theatre in the world, this is now the **Theatre Museum**, with a collection of paintings, drawings and photographs, posters, costumes and tickets, illustrating the history of the Danish theatre from the 18C to the present (open Wed, Fri, Sun, 14.00–16.00).—The equestrian statue of Christian IX by Anne Marie Carl Nielsen is from 1927.

From the Royal Mews you can gain access to **Rigsdagsgården**, the Parliament Courtyard, a large courtyard in front of the main entrance to the Parliament, the Folketing, housed in the S wing of Christiansborg Palace. This is the entrance for visitors to the Folketing.

The archway at the N end of this courtyard connects the Parliament building to the much older administration buildings on the other side. Closest to the archway is the three-storeyed **Gehejmearkivbygning** (State Archives Building) from 1715–20. It was taken into use in 1721, and in the course of the 18C the archives from Gottorp were removed here. After the loss of Norway in 1814 many of the Norwegian archives were added, and the collection was greatly increased as a result of political developments during the 19C. In 1889 it was given the name of **Rigsarkivet**, and in 1908 it was necessary to take over the adjoining building, the former Royal Library, built 1665–73 on the orders of Frederik III.

The present **Royal Library** is reached through a gateway diagonally opposite the Parliament steps, leading first to some delightful gardens containing a pond and a statue of Søren Kierkegaard by L. Hasselriis.

The Royal Library can be said to have been founded by Frederik III, who began the serious purchase of learned books in the 17C. It was, however, Christian V who moved the collection to the building commissioned by Frederik III. The present somewhat ponderous building in red brick is from 1898–1906 to the design of Hans J. Holm. The Entrance Hall, where there are extensive exhibits, is open all year round. The Reading Room is open to all for serious research but not for viewing.

Go back now to the Rigsdagsgård, and turn left. Through the archway 50m ahead you will come to TØJHUSGADE, where, on your left, you will find the Royal Arsenal Museum, **Tøjhusmuseum**, which is part of a complex established by Christian IV around a dock from which the Navy's ships took on supplies. The present museum is housed in the former Royal Arsenal from 1604. On two floors, it contains a vast collection of arms from pistols to heavy guns as well as uniforms and armour, many of great age (open all year).—The *Isted Lion*, a statue by Herman Wilhelm Bissen commemorating the Danish victory of Isted Heath in 1850, is in the courtyard.

If you now continue along Tøjhusgade you pass the Ministry of Education on your left. You should turn left at the end of the main wing, keeping the canal on your right, and walk to the end of the complex, where you will see the vast sweep of the roof of Christian IV's Brewery (1599–1605), one of the most impressive Copenhagen buildings of its time.

You are now on CHRISTIANS BRYGGE. Turn left again, and you will have the remaining old government buildings on your left, and the harbour on your right. You will pass the back of the Royal Library, and 50m beyond you will come to SLOTSHOLMSGADE. Turn into this. Here on your right you will see the Stock Exchange, **Børsen**, one of Copenhagen's finest Renaissance buildings, 127m long and 21m wide, built 1619–23 on the initiative of Christian IV and designed by Lorenz and Hans van Steenwinckel. In his eagerness for a grandiose building Christian IV had its original unadorned façade, facing Børsgade, decorated and the spire consisting of four intertwined dragons' tails erected in 1624–25. The E end was decorated in 1640, and the entire building was restored by Eigtved in 1745 (not open to the public).

At the end of Slotsholmsgade, on your left, adjoining the archway, you come to **Den Røde Kancellibygning**, the Chancellery Building, which was constructed by Frederik IV to house the 'Colleges', the forerunners of ministries (not open to the public).

Christiansborg Slotsplads is now immediately in front of you.

Walk 4 (c 2.5km)

The walk starts and finishes on Christiansborg Slotsplads.

Main sights: The Christianshavn area, Vor Frelsers Kirke, Holmens Kirke.

With Christiansborg behind you, you go right, along the main road, BØRSGADE, which runs past the Stock Exchange, **Børsen** (see Walk 3).

Beyond the Stock Exchange you come to one of Copenhagen's lifting bridges, the **Knippelsbro**. With the establishment of Christianshavn in 1617, Christian IV found it necessary to build this bridge to connect his new town with Slotsholmen and Copenhagen. Knippelsbro was then built 1618–20 and owes its name to a counsellor from Christianshavn called Hans Knip, who had the right to demand tolls from the passing ships. The present lifting bridge, from 1937, is the fourth to bear the name.

On the other side of the bridge, on the island of AMAGER, lies CHRISTIANSHAVN, which was established by Christian IV as a fortress-like town separate from Copenhagen. With one small exception, all its streets are straight and meet at a right angles and, unlike Copenhagen proper, Christianshavn has never been devastated by fire and has therefore retained much of its old character.

The main road here is TORVEGADE, and on your left, immediately after the bridge and on the corner of Torvegade and STRANDGADE, you will see the splendid modern **Foreign Ministry** building standing on an area known as Asiatisk Plads. However, you should not cross Torvegade to take a closer look, as you are going to turn right into the other half of Strandgade, noting—and perhaps visiting—the 17C café on the corner. Strandgade 6, **Tordenskjolds Gård**, a fine stone façade with a splendid half-timbered courtyard behind, houses the Danish Society of Authors, while No. 4 is the **Burmeister and Wain Museum** illustrating the history of the great shipbuilding firm. At the very end of this part of Strandgade you will find the rococo **Christianskirke**.

This very unusual church was designed by Eigtved only a year before his death and built between 1755 and 1759. It was originally intended for the German congregation in Christianshavn. In many ways it resembles a theatre, with a series of 'boxes' on three levels surrounding the altar. Directly opposite the altar is the royal 'box'. In keeping with the style of the Reformed Church, the altar is surmounted by the pulpit, which again is surmounted by the organ. N.F.S.

HELSINGOR   KLAMPENBORG

 M Ryparken   M Svanemøllen

ØSTERBRO

ØSTERBROGADE   STRAND   BOULEVARD   ØSTBANEGADE

M Nordhavn

NORD

HAVNEN

Frihavnen

Zoologisk
Mus

NØRRE ALLÉ   Faelledparken

ØRREBRO

TREBRØDADE

OULE
VARD

SØNDRNS ALLE   See large scale Central map

CHRISTIANSHAVN

NGEVEJ

ESTERBRO

SØNDER BLVD.   KALVEBOD BRYGGE   AMAGER   BOULEVARD   AMAGER BROGADE

Dybbølsbro M

Kobenhavns Universitat
(New Buildings)

VALBYGADE   Sydhavnen

N

Amager Faelled   SUNDBYVESTER

M Metro Stations

COPENHAGEN
GENERAL

0 kilometres   3

SJELLANDSBROEN   DRAGØR

Grundtvig was allowed to preach to his congregation here between 1832 and 1839.

You now return to the main road, Torvegade, and turn right, when you will come to a curious road consisting of a row of houses on either side of a canal, with the equally curious names of Overgaden neden Vandet and Overgaden oven Vandet (Upper Street Below the Water and Upper Street Above the Water). It is a street of particular charm, with old houses in various colours lining the canal where barges and all kinds of sailing ships are moored. Overgaden oven Vandet 10 is a small museum, **Brøstes Samling**, illustrating the history of Christians-havn. At its S end this road is crossed by STORE SØNDER-VOLDSTRÆDE, where, at No. 4, you will find **Det danske Filmmuseum**, the Danish Film Museum, containing in all some 13,000 films and huge numbers of photographs and posters, mainly connected with the Danish film industry. There are weekly film shows in the summer, but only for members of the museum.

Store Søndervoldstræde leads you to Dronningensgade. Turn left here and take the first street on your right, SOFIEGADE. The second street you come to is AMAGERGADE, where, at No. 11, you will find one of the most picturesque of all the half-timbered courtyards in Christianshavn, complete with outside gallery. Note, however, that this is a house in which people live—it is not a museum. Now continue along Amagergade to Torvegade and turn left, walking as far as the Dronningensgade crossing (the second street). Cross Torvegade here and continue straight ahead along Dronningensgade, and you will very quickly come to Vor Frelsers Kirke. **Vor Frelsers Kirke**, The Church of Our Saviour, is distinguished by its unusual tower, sur-mounted by a copper steeple, designed by Thurah, with a stairway of 150 steps encircling it on the outside. The height of this steeple, including the globe and surmounting figure, is 86.6m. Built 1682–96, to a design by Lambert van Haven, the church itself is in the style of Dutch baroque and shaped as a Greek cross. There are slender win-dows, rounded at the top, and separated by pilasters, and the main entrance is flanked by Corinthian columns. The altarpiece, ordered by Christian V from Nicodemus Tessin in 1694, is one of the most glorious pieces of baroque art in the country (open all year, with access to the tower, which is the highest vantage point with public access in Copen-hagen).

On leaving the church, we suggest you follow SANKT ANNÆ GADE down to the canal, where you again come to Overgaden oven Vandet. Turn right here and walk the 200m along the canal to reach Over-gaden oven Vandet 58, where the naval museum **Orlogsmuseum**, is housed in the dignified old naval hospital, **Søkvæsthuset** (1755). Here you will find 300 ships' models (the oldest from 1687) as well as a graphic history of Danish seafaring.—The author Johan Ludvig Heiberg and his wife Johanne Luise Heiberg, one of Denmark's greatest actresses, lived here in the 19C, and the trees in the garden are said to have been planted by Mrs Heiberg.

To get across the canal you will have to walk back to Sankt Annæ Gade again and then turn right. At the top of the road you reach Strandgade once more, where, overlooking the harbour, a row of old warehouses, now serving various purposes, has been modernised, while facing them there is a row of 17C merchants' houses. Turn left here and when you reach Torvegade you have completed your Chris-tianshavn circle.

Now cross the Knippelsbro bridge, but this time you should stay on the right-hand side of the road and turn right again just opposite the Stock Exchange. In the midst of a small patch of green on your left here you will find the naval church, **Holmens Kirke**, to which the entrance is reached 100m further on, from HOLMENS KANAL.

The tall gable of Holmens Kirke overlooking the canal is from an earlier 16C church and is Italian inspired, but the present building is otherwise from 1641, the time of Christian IV, and stands virtually as it then was, having avoided damage from fire and bombardment. The low vaulted ceiling in the nave has stucco decorations from the 1640s, while the brass rail dividing the nave from the chancel is from 1668. The auricular oak altarpiece is from 1661, with carved figures of the four Evangelists and reliefs of the Last Supper, Crucifixion, Burial of Christ and Ascension. The pulpit is also an outstanding piece of auricular work, supported on a figure of Moses and topped by a canopy in the form of a lantern.

Attached to the church, along the canal, there is a large sepulchral chapel from 1705–08, containing many sarcophagi. Pride of place goes to the naval heroes Niels Juel and Tordenskjold. The composer Niels Wilhelm Gade is also buried here, as are the architects C.F. Hansen and Gustav Friedrich Hetsch.

In the courtyard of the church there is a statue of Tordenskjold, the work of Herman Wilhelm Bissen, while a bronze statue of Niels Juel by T. Stein to commemorate the Battle of Køge Bay can be found in Holmens Kanal, 100m to the right of the main entrance.

However, on leaving the church you should now cross Holmens Kanal and follow it to the left till you reach VED STRANDEN, the road running alongside the canal, but on the opposite side of Christiansborg Palace. Keeping the canal on your left, walk as far as the bridge and you will now have the **Højbro Plads** square (Walk 2) on your right, and just in front of you the quay area called GAMMEL STRAND. As the name implies, this was part of the shoreline in the Middle Ages, and is thought to be the place where fishermen landed their catch. Until new laws prevented it in the 1950s, the Copenhagen fish market was here and consequently a long row of fish stalls, and those good old days are commemorated by the statue of the fishwife in her traditional dress now standing here. Many of the buildings facing Gammel Strand are 18C. Note particularly the sandstone porch of the old **Isenberghs Gård**, No. 48 (by Andreas Gercken). The fish restaurants are also to be recommended.

You can now cross the Højbro bridge over the canal and then the main road—and you are back at Christiansborg.

WALK 5 (c 3.5km)

The walk starts and ends in front of the Royal Theatre on Kongens Nytorv.

Main sights: Kongens Nytorv area, Amalienborg, Gefion Fountain, the Little Mermaid, the Marble Church.

Kongens Nytorv lies just outside the medieval East Gate and came to link medieval Copenhagen with the new districts being developed, first by Christian IV and then by Frederik III. It was, however, Christian V who set about converting what had been the site of the gallows into a square of great elegance, the virtual centre of modern Copenhagen. The exquisite buildings, many of which still survive, began to appear in the late 17C. At the centre of the square there is a park area, the main feature of which is the proud baroque equestrian statue of Christian V, from 1688, the work of the French sculptors Abraham César and Claude l'Amoureux. It commemorates Christian V as the real creator of Kongens Nytorv and is the oldest equestrian statue in Scandinavia. It must be admitted, however, that the present statue is a bronze copy by Einar Utzon Frank of the original in lead, which was in a state of decay by 1946.

Kongens Nytorv still has an air of distinction, partly the result of the open space, with its statue and trees in the centre, partly because of

Nyhavn, Copenhagen. Many of these old houses are now restaurants. Photo: Ole Akhøj

the associations of some of the buildings on it. At the side of the Royal Theatre there is one of Copenhagen's most famous department stores, Magasin du Nord. To the left of Magasin, at Holmens Kanal 2, is **Erichsens Palæ** which, built 1797–99 for one Erich Erichsen, was once the most magnificent neo-classical private building in Copenhagen, and the only one to have a façade facing Kongens Nytorv consisting of six Ionic columns. The architect was Caspar Frederik Harsdorff and the reliefs over the columns were the work of G.D. Gianelli. The building now houses one of Denmark's largest banks. This building is on the corner of VINGÅRDSSTRÆDE, where, at No. 6, now the Kong Hans Restaurant, there is a huge medieval vault. Beyond Magasin du Nord, ØSTERGADE, the eastern end of Strøget, issues, notable at this end for its fine shops, and beyond this again stands perhaps the most dignified of Copenhagen's old hotels, Hotel d'Angleterre. Then comes NY ADELGADE, which, for those interested in the history of the theatre, used to be called Lille Grønnegade and was the home of the first real theatre in Copenhagen, for which Ludvig Holberg wrote his first plays. There is nothing left of the theatre now, but the building has been splendidly restored to house the **Galerie Asbæk**, where some of Denmark's best contemporary artists exhibit their work on five floors. The gallery also contains a restaurant (closed in July).

Det Kongelige Teater, the Royal Theatre, has stood on the same spot in Kongens Nytorv since 1749. The original building, by Eigtved, was rebuilt 1773–74 by Caspar Frederik Harsdorff. This was in its turn replaced 1872–74 by the present building in Italian Renaissance style, designed by Vilhelm Dahlerup and Ove Petersen. In front of the entrance are statues of Ludvig Holberg (by Theobald Stein, on the right) and Adam Oehlenschläger (by Herman Wilhelm Bissen, on the left). To the left of the main theatre, in Tordenskjoldsgade, is the entrance to the smaller stage, **Nye Scene**, from 1929. A bridge connects the two.

You start this walk by going from the Royal Theatre in an anti-clock-wise direction, and following the traffic. You will first come to (100m) **Harsdorffs Hus**, an elegant neo-classical town house which was the work of Caspar Frederik Harsdorff, a former Professor of Perspective at the Academy of Art. The relief is in the gable is by Wiedewelt. Built 1779–80, the house influenced subsequent architectural taste in Co penhagen (not open to the public).

Immediately beyond Harsdorffs Hus comes the mansion of **Charlottenborg**, built 1672–83 by Ulrik Frederik Gyldenløve, the son of Frederik III. This is the first major example of Danish baroque architecture, and was partly built with material taken from *Kalø Castle* (Rte 8). There is a bust of Frederik V over the balcony above the entrance. The façade is of small dark brick with sandstone decorations while the central section of the roof and the lantern above are of copper. Since 1734 it has been the home of the Royal Academy for the Fine Arts, the first Principal of which was Eigtved. Now it also houses frequent art exhibitions. In the courtyard behind the main building there is a statue of Thorvaldsen by Einar Utzon-Frank.

Just beyond Charlottenborg you come to the end of NYHAVN.

Frederik III planned this canal, allowing ships to sail from the harbour right up to Kongens Nytorv and enabling merchants to build their houses directly along the wharves. It was completed in 1673. Hans Christian Andersen lived here at various times, in Nos 18, 20 and 67. Throughout the whole of the first half of the 20C the N side was a place of ill repute, but in the 1970s and 1980s a total transformation took place, and it is now a fashionable restaurant area, much frequented by locals as well as visitors to Copenhagen during summer months. Small ships are moored the length of the canal, adding to its atmosphere. The anchor standing at the Kongens Nytorv end is a memorial to Danish seaman lost during World War II; it bears the date of 1857 and once belonged to the 19C frigate 'Fyen'.—Nyhavn is one of the places from where you can take a boat trip round the Copenhagen canals and harbour.

From the Kongens Nytorv end of Nyhavn you take either STORE STRANDSTRÆDE or LILLE STRANDSTRÆDE to (150m) SANKT ANNÆ PLADS. You should cross the wide boulevard diagonally to the right into AMALIEGADE, which will take you to (300m) **Amalienborg Slots-plads**, Amalienborg Palace Square.

On the occasion of the 300th anniversary of the royal house of Oldenborg in 1748, Frederik V decided to found a new district for Copenhagen's most distinguished citizens, to be called Frederiksstad. The central feature was to be an octagonal piazza designed by Eigtved and containing four identical baroque palaces. These were to be financed privately by four wealthy owners, to whom the king gave the necessary land. Consequently the four palaces became known as the Brockdorff, Levetzau, Moltke and Schack Palaces. Apart from the period 1848–63, one or other of them has been the royal residence since the royal palace of Christiansborg burned down in 1794. Queen Margrethe lives in the Schack Palace, now known as Christian IX's Palace (none of the palaces is open to the public).

The square, with Italian mosaic cobbling from 1886, has at its centre one of Europe's finest neo-classical equestrian statues. The work of Jacques-François-Joseph Saly, it commemorates Frederik V, and was unveiled on Amalienborg Square in 1771.

When the Queen is in residence the ceremony of **Changing of the Guard** takes place on the Amalienborg square at 12.00 each day. The Guard leaves Rosenborg Palace at 11.30 and marches along Gothersgade, Nørrevold, Frederiksborggade, Købmagergade, Østergade, Kongens Nytorv, Bredgade, Sankt Annæ Plads and Amaliegade, returning via Frederiksgade, Store Kongensgade and Gothersgade.

While on Palace Square you should take the exit to the right, towards the harbour, to see the small **Amaliehaven** park, established in 1983 and sponsored by the huge shipping line A.P. Møller (Mærsk Line) to the design of the Belgian garden architect Jean Delogne and the Italian sculptor A. Pomadore.

Then return to the Palace Square and turn right, continuing along **Amaliegade**. As you walk along here, with tall 19C façades on either side, take the time to peer into some of the courtyards, especially on the left-hand side, where you will suddenly find yourself in 17C and 18C surroundings, showing clearly how the 19C built on to what was already there.

About 500m further on you cross ESPLANADEN and here, just to your left, is **Frihedsmuseet**, the museum of the Danish Resistance, containing a large collection of exhibits from the World War II Occupation (open all year).

Right in front of you, you will find the biggest public monument in Copenhagen, the **Gefion Fountain**. This most impressive fountain is from 1908 and the work of Anders Bundgård. It illustrates the legend of the goddess Gefion, who could take as much of Sweden as she could plough in a night. She transformed her sons into oxen and ploughed out the whole of Sjælland. (Much of Bundgård's other work is to be seen in the **Tingbæk Limestone Mines**—Rte 17.)

If you now continue N along the sea front, you will, in c 200m, come to **Den Lille Havfrue**, the famous Little Mermaid, sitting on a rock by the water's edge. This bronze statue, from 1913, is the work of Edvard Eriksen and the idea of erecting a statue inspired by Hans Christian Andersen's story came from Carl Jacobsen of the Carlsberg Breweries. The figure is modelled on the sculptor's own wife.

The area N of Esplanaden is normally known as the **Langelinje Park**. Covering some 20 hectares in all, it includes besides the Gefion Fountain and the Little Mermaid, the Citadel, the Liberation Museum and the English church. There are also other sculptures. Captain Ivar Huitfeldt and his crew, heroes of the Battle of Køge Bay, are commemorated here, as are the polar explorers Ludvig Mylius-Erichsen, N.P. Høeg and Jørgen Brønlund, and King Frederik IX.

Langelinje was always a favourite spot for outings for Copenhageners, not least the old romantic Langelinje Pavilion which, however, was sabotaged during World War II. The new Langelinje Pavilion, on the same site close to the Little Mermaid, from 1957, is in a totally different style, built to the design of Eva and Nils Koppel. From behind the glass façade you have a splendid view of the sea front and the many passing ships, and parking is seldom impossible.

Behind the Langelinje Pavilion lies **Kastellet** (The Citadel), the popular name for Frederik III's fortress *Citadellet Frederikshavn*. There were fortifications here under Christian IV, but the Citadel proper was built 1662–63 under Frederik III. From the S it is approached through a gateway called **Sjællandsporten** (The Sjælland Gate) bearing the date 1663, and directly opposite, to the N, there is **Norgesporten** (The Norway Gate). In typical baroque fashion, the blocks of old buildings, residences and storehouses are grouped symmetrically around the main street linking the two. The Dutch windmill is from 1847. The Citadel is no longer used as a barracks, but houses military offices and the Army Library.

The church, **Citadelkirken**, is from 1703–04. It is a small building with a saddle roof surmounted by a ridge turret. The original entrance, now bricked up, was through a porch flanked by four Doric columns in the long E façade. In 1728 the church was linked to the prison behind the W wall. The original large windows to the W were bricked up and replaced by 'peep-holes' through which prisoners could take part in services without being seen. Little remains of the original church furniture, except the carved altarpiece and two brass candlesticks. The organ loft is from 1756. (The Citadel is open all year round.)

When you are finished with the park, go back again towards Esplanaden. Here, in the S part of Langelinje, which has since World War II been known as the **Churchill Park**, you will pass the English **Saint Alban's Church**, built in typical English neo-Gothic of brick covered with flint between 1885 and 1887 to a design by A.W. Blomfield.

On reaching Esplanaden you should cross it and walk the few metres to the right, until you come to BREDGADE, a dignified thoroughfare running parallel with Amaliegade, and leading back to Kongens Nytorv. Some 100m down Bredgade you will find, on the left at No. 68, a rococo building from 1752 by Eigtved, flanked by two baroque pavilions by Thurah from 1757. This is the **Kunstindustrimuseum**, the Museum of Decorative and Applied Art. The complex originally constituted the Frederik's Hospital, which is the scene of part of the action in Hans Christian Andersen's 'Galoches of Fortune', but the hospital was closed in 1919, and the buildings were then turned into the present museum housing a collection of European and Oriental crafts. The main emphasis is on furniture, but there are special collections of porcelain, silver, textiles and book bindings. There are also collections of Chinese and Japanese work (open all year).

Just beyond the Kunstindustrimuseum is the principal Roman Catholic church in Denmark, **Sankt Ansgars Kirke**.

There was a chapel here as early as 1764, for the use of foreign embassy staff, but the present building dates from 1841–42. Although taken into use in 1842, it was not actually consecrated until 1865, on the thousandth anniversary of the death of St. Ansgar, who converted Denmark. The design is by Gustav Friedrich Hetsch and aims at maintaining the simplicity of early church architecture. The church itself stands a little back from the street, but with two pavilions—one a chapel, the other the side entrance—reaching the building line. When the church was built, Catholic churches were not allowed to ring bells, and so the belfry, standing behind the main building and invisible from the road, was not built until 1943.

Immediately beyond the church, at Bredgade 82, is the **Medicinskhistorisk Museum**, the Museum of Medical History. This neo-classical building was designed by Peter Meyn for the Academy of Surgery in 1785–87. The museum illustrates the history of medicine and dentistry, and the original auditorium with dissecting table, lit from above, is as when built (open for conducted tours Wed 11.00–15.00).

On the opposite side of Bredgade here, on the corner of FREDERICIA-GADE, you will see the imposing buildings of **Østre Landsret**, the Eastern Regional Law Courts. The elegant building in a mixture of Dutch and Italian styles facing Bredgade was built in 1701–02 by Frederik IV as a new opera house, and was used as a theatre between 1705 and 1708. The main building, in Fredericiagade 24, was the seat of the Danish Parliament from 1884 to 1918.

A little further down Bredgade you cannot fail to notice the golden onion domes of the Russian Orthodox Church, the **Alexander Newski Kirke**. It was built at the suggestion of the Russian Government 1881–83 to a design by the Russian architect David Grimm, in the style of 17C Moscow church buildings. The granite and brick façade, with a relief statue of Alexander Nevsky, is surmounted by three gilt onion domes, and the church itself, on the first floor, is reached by a marble staircase and decorated with Russian and Byzantine motifs.

On the opposite side of Bredgade, a little closer to Kongens Nytorv, at No. 54, you will see **Dehns Palæ**, a baroque mansion from 1755, designed by Johann Gottfried Rosenberg. It is now owned by Danmarks Apotekerforening (The Danish Pharmaceutical Association) (not open to the public).

You are now almost at FREDERIKSGADE, leading on the left to Amalienborg Palace, and on the right to **Marmorkirken**, the Marble Church.

Officially called Frederiks Kirke (Frederik's Church), this was originally intended as one of the centrepieces of the planned, but never completed, Frederiksstad district. The original drawings were by Eigtved, but after his death the work was continued by Nicolas-Henri Jardin. Because of the cost, the project was then shelved in 1770 and not taken up again until the financier Carl Frederik Tietgen undertook to complete it in 1874, this time with Ferdinand Meldahl as his architect. The finished church was then consecrated in 1894. The copper-covered dome (one of the largest in Europe) with an internal diameter of 30m is clearly inspired by St. Peter's in Rome and St. Paul's in London. The cylinder bearing the dome is encircled with arcading, and on the balustrade there are figures from the Bible and Danish church history. The interior consists of an enormous circular nave surrounded by arcading.

On leaving the Marble Church, continue along Bredgade, where after c 300m you will see on your left, at No. 28, **Odd Fellow Palæet**, another beautiful house from 1755, designed by Eigtved. Originally called the Berckentins Palæ, in the 1880s it was turned into a concert hall with 1500 seats, and in 1900 it was acquired by the Order of Oddfellows. It is still used as a concert hall.

A little further, and you cross Sankt Annæ Plads to the left, where, under the trees, you will see a statue of Christian X on horseback. The image of Christian X seems to be that of the equestrian king, as it was on horseback he crossed the German border in 1920 and it was on horseback, in his seventies, that he rode through all parts of Copenhagen during the Occupation to keep up Danish spirits, until a fall from the horse finally put a stop to it and confined him to a wheelchair until his death in 1947.

The church on the right-hand side of Sankt Annæ Plads is the baroque **Garnisons Kirke** built 1703–06, with a tower from 1886. Despite its name it is no longer a garrison church. Built of brick, the W front is divided by Tuscan pilasters supporting a gable. There is a small spire above. The seating inside is on two levels. The marble altar, from 1724, is by Just Wiedewelt and Didrik Gercken.—The composer J.P.E. Hartmann is buried here.

Opposite Sankt Annæ Plads, at Bredgade 11, you will find the **Georg Jensen Museum** with a splendid collection of silverware from 1904–40 by this famous company (open all year).—In the same building, antique and second-hand silver by Georg Jensen and A. Michelsen, and porcelain by Royal Porcelain and Bing & Grøndahl, are on sale. Bredgade is now famous for its antique dealers.

You are almost back in Kongens Nytorv now. On the corner of the square and Bredgade there is one more very imposing building to note: **Thotts Palæ**, which is now the French Embassy. It was built 1683–86 for Admiral Niels Juel, who died here in 1697. The original architect of the house is unknown, but we know that the modernisation of the façade was done by Nicolas-Henri Jardin in 1763–64, when the pilasters on the façade were crowned with Corinthian capitals, and the balustrade was added above the first floor.

You have now reached Kongens Nytorv, and the Royal Theatre is straight ahead.

WALK 6 (c 2.5km)

The walk starts and ends outside Østerport S-station in Oslo Plads. The suggested detours will add a further km to the walk. Østerport Station can easily be reached by S-train and is about 5 mins from the Central Station.

Main sights: Statens Museum for Kunst, Rosenborg.

Coming out of the S-train you would be wise to cross the busy OSLO PLADS road in front of the station by the subway so as to emerge on the western side of the road. Bear left, turn right into VESTER VOLDGADE (East Rampart Street) at the lights, and you should now be walking parallel with the railway track on your right. Note, in the triangular space ahead of you just before leaving Oslo Plads the statue of the flautist by Anne Marie Carl Nielsen, made in memory of her husband Carl Nielsen.

A few metres down Øster Voldgade you cannot fail to notice, on your left, the group of striking old houses, all painted ochre. These are known as **Nyboder**, and they were built when Christian IV decided to provide free housing for his sailors.

Originally there were 616 single-storeyed houses, but numbers were increased in the 18C, and then again reduced in the 19C. Of those still standing (and there are many) only the Museum, called **Nybodernes Mindestuer**, at Sankt Paulsgade 20, is left from the original buildings from c 1630, the remainder being from the later extensions. It is still a remarkable area, with clear, straight lines of houses and unadorned but pleasing architecture. The museum, which was founded in 1931, consists of rooms, furniture and objects showing a typical Nyboder house from the 19C. A bronze statue commemorating Christian IV as the founder, executed by Vilhelm Bissen in 1900, stands in the area, visible from Øster Voldgade.

On your right you will now have the remains of the ramparts and a park called **Østre Anlæg**, constructed on the ground cleared when the ramparts were removed. After about 800m you come to the crossing with SØLVGADE, where, on your right, you will find **Statens Museum for Kunst**, the National Art Gallery.

The building, by Vilhelm Dahlerup, is from 1895 and was originally intended as a home for the royal collection of paintings after the Christiansborg fire of 1884. The basic construction, on two floors, is two long wings connected by a short wing at either end. Apart from the removal of Dahlerup's grandiose entrance, the exterior is still unchanged, but the interior was partly redesigned in the 1960s. The very extensive collection covers West European art from Byzantine icons to contemporary work, with good representative collections of Dutch, Flemish and Italian paintings, the French Impressionists and an important collection of Matisse and early 20C French painting. The Danish collection is of particular importance, covering the entire development from the late 18C to the present day. Abildgaard, Jens Juel, Eckersberg, Købke and Lundbye are all well represented, and there is an entire room devoted to Hammershøi. The 20C is mirrored in the work of artists such as Harald Giersing, Asger Jorn and Per Kirkeby. There is a very large collection of copperplate engravings, including work by Dürer and Rembrandt (open all year).

Opposite Statens Museum for Kunst, on the other side of Sølvgade, lies the Geological Museum, **Geologisk Museum**, at Øster Voldgade 5–7. This museum of geology contains comprehensive collections of minerals, fossils and meteorites, with outstanding exhibits illustrating the geology of Denmark and Greenland (open all year).

If geology does not tempt you, then go diagonally across the traffic intersection to see **Rosenborg Have** (Rosenborg Gardens), which is the park—also known as **Kongens Have** (The King's Gardens)—covering some 12 hectares around Rosenborg Palace. Originally designed for Christian IV in 1606 when he started building Rosenborg, it is the oldest park in Copenhagen and since the 19C has been one of the capital's most popular parks. In the NE is the Hercules Pavilion from 1773, by Harsdorff, and there are numerous statues, including one of a horse and lion by Peter Husum from 1617. In the S end stand two columns once used in jousting tournaments, and here, too, you find 17 marble balls the size of cannon balls arranged on the lawn. As befits a park intended for a leisurely stroll, there is also a café for your refreshment.

Not only is a walk through Rosenborg Have a delight in itself, but it will also bring you to KRONPRINSESSEGADE, where, at No. 30, there is a small but very choice art gallery, **Davids Samling** (The David Collection). Housed in an unpretentious mansion from 1806–07 this is one of the finest collections of Oriental art in Scandinavia, founded in 1945 by C.L. David and presented by him to the State. The most important part of the collection consists of Persian art from the 8C to the 16C, and comprises both illuminated manuscripts and collections of glass, pottery, metal work and silks. There is also a collection of English furniture, Danish silver from the 17C and 18C and Danish porcelain (open all year).

While in Kronprinsessegade you should also note the curious booths lining Rosenborg Have known as **Meyns Pavilloner**. Kronprinsessegade was a new street built after the 1795 fire and the 'Pavilions', linked by elaborate wrought-iron railings, were a series of 16 individual small booths (4m x 4m x 4m) in neo-classical style built 1803–04 by Peter Meyn between the road and Rosenborg Park. They were intended as shops, but the experiment failed.

When you have seen all this, you should visit **Rosenborg** itself. The entrance to the castle is from Øster Voldgade, about 200m from Sølvgade, but it can be approached through the park from the S.

Christian IV's small palace of Rosenborg, built 1606–34, with its 45.5m-high square tower to the W and the two lower ones to the E, is one of the most famous buildings in Copenhagen. It is built of brick, with horizontal lines and other decorations of Gotland sandstone. There are elaborate gables at either end. On the W façade there is a lead bust of Christian IV and 12 busts brought to Denmark from Italy by Frederik IV. The copper roof is from 1712. Rosenborg was at first surrounded by a moat, part of which still remains.

Christian IV and Kirsten Munk had their rooms at opposite ends of the ground floor; these rooms still exist, and those of Christian IV are largely in their original state, particularly the oak-panelled *Winter Room*, with over 90 paintings in the panelling, and Christian IV's study with its oaken ceiling and Chinese lacquered panelling. Kirsten Munk's bedchamber was changed in the 1660s into a baroque chamber with stuccoed ceiling and marble decorations.

The rooms on the first floor are the result of rebuilding in the 18C, and the second floor contains the Great Hall, transformed by Christian V and decorated with tapestries. Frederik IV then had an opulent, barrel-vaulted stuccoed ceiling constructed, turning this room into one of the most impressive of all baroque rooms in Denmark. However, in 1917 the tapestries were removed for restoration and, as they were never returned, the room has consequently lost some of its former splendour. One of the special features now is the three silver lions standing in front of the throne.

In the course of time Rosenborg was used less and less for a residence, and the royal family began to house many of their treasures, including the crown jewels, here. Even in the 17C there are signs that outsiders to some extent were allowed access.

In 1849 Rosenborg was transferred to State ownership, and is now open to the public. The exhibits are arranged chronologically to give an impression of changing tastes and fashions from the time of its creator, Christian IV. It also contains exhibits from earlier times collected by successive monarchs, for instance Christian I's horn of silver gilt. Since 1922 the Crown Jewels have been on show in Christian V's Room. Clothes worn by kings and queens can also be seen, including the bloodstained tunic worn by Christian IV at the Battle of Kolberger Heide (1644).

This most interesting museum is virtually packed with people in the tourist season, but it is well worth joining the crowd. Guidebooks in English can be bought with the tickets.

On leaving Rosenborg you continue along Øster Voldgade to the crossing with GOTHERSGADE (c 250m), where, on your left you have the Guards' Drill Ground and, at No. 100, *Livgardens historiske Samlinger*. Housed in a 200-year-old barracks, this Royal Guards Museum exhibits an array of uniforms, weapons and documents pertaining to the Royal Guard over the past three centuries (open all year).

Opposite is the Reformed Church, **Reformert Kirke**. Despite the monopoly of the Lutheran church, immigrant Calvinists living in Copenhagen were given permission to hold services in 1685. In 1688–89 they built this church in Dutch baroque style, rectangular, with saddle roof and ridge turret, and with a façade decorated with pilasters.

Beside the church you will find ROSENBORGGADE, leading to ÅBENRÅ, where at No. 30 there is the **Musikhistorisk Museum**.

Founded in 1898 and since 1977 incorporating **Carl Claudius' Samling**, the Carl Claudius Collection of musical instruments from 1905, this museum is housed in a building from 1730. It contains a very large collection of instruments as well as a library and archives. Visitors are able to hear many of the musical instruments as they go through the collections. An extensive guide is available on entry (open 10.00–13.00 on Tue, Wed; 13.00–16.00 on Fri, Sat, Sun).

Now go back to the intersection of Gothersgade and Øster Voldgade. Here, on the northern corner, there is an entrance to **Botanisk Have**, the Botanical Gardens.

Before going in, however, you might like to go just a little further along Gothersgade and turn into RØMERSGADE, on the left, where you will find, at No. 22, the **Arbejdermuseum** (The Workers' Museum), founded in 1983 to illustrate the history of the working classes in Denmark. It contains a room in which you can eat and drink as people did in 1892!

And now, go to the extensive Botanical Gardens, where the collections of palms and cacti are of particular note. The present gardens were established between 1871 and 1874 on undulating land available on the demolition of the Copenhagen ramparts. The greenhouses (4000 sq m) were inspired by those in Kew Gardens in England and the Brussels Botanical Gardens. There are over 15,500 plant species in the gardens. The Museum building, on Gothersgade, is from 1875–76, and contains a large library and extensive collections, including 200,000 specimens of plants from Denmark and 160,000 from Greenland and the Faroe Islands. The general herbarium contains over a million specimens of flowering plants. The entire area is under the control of Copenhagen University, and as a guide to your tour you can hire a Walkman together with a tape in one of several languages.

You should leave the Botanical Gardens by the N exit, which will lead you, 200m to the right, to SØLVTORVET. Here, you cross Sølvgade and go into STOCKHOLMSGADE, where, 100m on the right, you will find another of Copenhagen's principal art galleries, the **Hirschsprung Samling**.

This gallery, founded by the cigar manufacturer Heinrich Hirschsprung, offers an exquisite, chronologically arranged collection of 19C Danish painting, including the early 19C Eckersberg, Købke, Bendz,

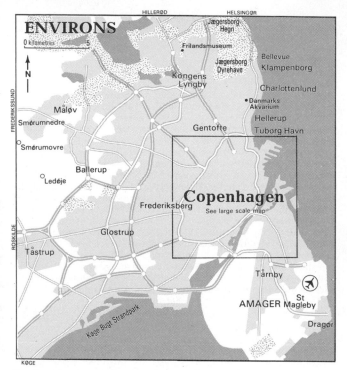

Roed, P.C. Skovgaard and Constantin Hansen, and the late 19C
Skagen painters Anna and Michael Ancher, Viggo Johansen and
Krøyer. The late 19C Realists and Naturalists Zahrtmann, Hammershøi and Ring are among others represented, as are the Fyn painters
Peter Hansen, Fritz Syberg and Johannes Larsen. The relief in the
tympanum is by Kai Nielsen. The purpose-built museum from 1908–11
designed in classical style by H.B. Storck is open afternoons all year.

On leaving the gallery you continue along Stockholmsgade which in
c 250m will bring you back to Oslo Plads, where you will see Østerport
Station diagonally to your right.

Walk 7 Frederiksberg (c 3.5km)

This walk begins at **Frederiksberg Rådhus** (Frederiksberg Town Hall).
You reach it by bus, taking either No. 1 (Frederiksberg.Ålstrupvej) or
No. 14 (Vanløse. Jydeholmen), both of which can be boarded on
Rådhuspladsen.

Main sights: Frederiksberg Have, Zoologisk Have.

Frederiksberg Town Hall, opened in 1953, stands at the junction of
GAMMEL KONGEVEJ, SMALLEGADE, FALKONER ALLÉ and ALLÉGADE.
It is brick built, in five storeys, with its main entrance facing Allégade.
Perhaps the most striking aspect is the 60m tower, with an observation
platform and the curious pavilion above. It is a clock tower, with faces
on each side, and contains a magnificent carillon of 48 bells which
plays different tunes at certain hours during the day.

At Smallegade 45, 600m behind the Town Hall, is the Royal Porcelain factory, the **Kongelige Porcelænsfabrik** (1775), which can be visited Tue and Thur, except late July and early August.

Return to Allégade now, turn right, and walk for 400m to the **Frederiksberg Runddel** roundabout, where FREDERIKSBERG ALLÉ, another main thoroughfare from central Copenhagen, emerges. Here you will find the main entrance into **Frederiksberg Have** park. But before walking into it, there are two places worth a visit at the roundabout: Frederiksberg Kirke and the Storm Petersen Museum.

The modest **Frederiksberg Kirke**, octagonal in shape and with a steep pyramidal roof, is built in the Dutch Protestant tradition and reflects the influence of the Dutch community in this area in the 17C and early 18C. It is the work of a Dutch architect, Felix Dusart. The roof is supported inside on eight pillars, and there is a gallery all round. The monograms of Christian VI and Queen Sophie Magdalene can be seen in the vaulting. As is usual in Dutch Protestant churches, the pulpit is above the altar. The altarpiece is by Eckersberg. To the N of the altar there is a memorial plaque to the 19C poet and dramatist, Adam Oehlenschläger, who is buried in the churchyard.

Just opposite the church to the left of the entrance to Frederiksberg Have is the **Storm Petersen Museum**, dedicated to the drawings, paintings and personalia of Denmark's most famous cartoonist and humorist. A particularly attractive feature is a collection of pipes which Storm Petersen had assembled throughout his life.

Now go through the gates to **Frederiksberg Have**, which, together with the adjoining **Søndermarken** S of Roskildevej, forms one of Copenhagen's major parks, the two together making up 64 hectares.

Frederiksberg Have was originally established close to Frederiksberg Palace (see below) by Frederik III in 1651 and redesigned around 1700 by Frederik IV. A century later Frederik VI developed it further, providing for canals, bridges, islands, and in general giving it the informal, relaxed feel which it has today. There is a Chinese pavilion (1798–1800), and a Swiss cottage to a design by Nicolai Abildgaard from 1800–01. The main entrance, from 1755, is by Thurah. Nearby stands a statue of Frederik VI by Herman Wilhelm Bissen.

You will inevitably want to savour the beauty and idyll of this park, which is these days so close to the centre of Copenhagen; and you might like to imagine the picture from the end of the 18C when the royal family was rowed around on the canals, while the local people stood on the bank applauding them. On your left (i.e. to the S) you will see **Frederiksberg Slot** (Frederiksberg Palace), standing impressive above open ground, and of which the original wing, an 'Italian villa', was built 1699–1703, overlooking the park, and still much as it was then. The two side wings were designed later, between 1733 and 1738, by Thurah and Elias David Häusser. The palace was long used as a royal residence, but since 1869 it has been Denmark's Military Academy.

You should now leave the park through the palace grounds where, in the E wing on the palace, you will see **Frederiksberg Slotskirke**. This is a small baroque chapel from 1710 by W.F. von Platen. A feature of the narrow nave is the Ionic columns on either side, while both the walls and the ceiling are elaborately stuccoed. On reaching ROSKILDE-VEJ turn right and 100m further on your right you will find the entrance to Copenhagen Zoo, **Zoologisk Have**.

Copenhagen Zoo was established here in 1859, and has since been steadily developed to contain some 2500 animals and birds, including the rather unusual okapi, and is run on the most modern principles: animals you can look at as well as animals you can play with. With its restaurants and its accessible tower it is said to be the most popular Copenhagen attraction after Tivoli (open all year). (If you want to visit the Zoo without seeing the other sights in Frederiksberg, you can take buses 28 or 41 from Rådhuspladsen.)

On leaving the Zoo, you should turn left into Roskildevej and walk back as far as Frederiksberg Palace. Here you cross the road and go into the park called **Søndermarken**. Just inside the entrance you will find a long avenue going off obliquely in a SE direction. Take it, and it will bring you out at the end of **Pileallé**. Just to the left of this exit, on the other side of Pileallé you will find RAHBEKS ALLÉ. No. 23 is the **Bakkehus Museum**. Hidden well away in a garden full of old trees, Bakkehuset (c 1764) does not look like a museum. It seems to be just another private home as it was under the ownership of the writer and critic Knud Lyhne Rahbek, when it became a focal point for the writers and artists of the Danish Golden Age period of Romanticism, many of whom actually lived there for a time. Now a museum, it is furnished as far as possible in the original style, often with the original furniture, in an attempt to preserve the atmosphere of the Rahbeks' home. There is even a coffee table with imitations of the cakes baked at that time! A room in Bakkehuset is dedicated to the leading 19C Romantic dramatist Adam Oehlenschläger and to the 18C poet and dramatist Johannes Ewald, in the opinion of many the greatest Danish poet ever (open all year).

From Bakkehuset you really ought to go back to Pileallé and finish your walk route with a little refreshment, for just to the left here, where Pileallé bends and becomes VALBY LANGGADE, you cannot—on looking down Ny Carlsbergvej—fail to see the entrance to the world-famous Carlsberg Breweries, Vilhelm Dahlerup's huge **Elephant Entrance**, with four giant elephants of Bornholm granite supporting the upper building, and the motto *Laboremus pro Patria* over the archway. The Breweries behind there are open for individual visits Mon–Fri at 9.00, 11.00 and 14.30, or, for groups, by arrangement, and a visit will also include the **Carlsberg Museum** (Valby Langgade 1), which illustrates the history of the Breweries and the work of the Carlsberg Fund. In the museum you will also find portraits of the Jacobsen family, antique statues and a staircase flanked by Thorvaldsen figures.

A walk back to the centre of Copenhagen is possible from here, making a short cut through Rahbeks Allé to Vesterbrogade and then proceeding along this busy shopping street for the rest of the way, but the distance is close on 3km, and you may prefer to take the bus, Nos 6 or 10.

SOME MORE COPENHAGEN SIGHTS

Not all the sights in Copenhagen can conveniently be grouped in walks, and some are a little too far out to reach easily on foot. The following list comprises some of these attractions, together with the way of reaching them by using public transport.

Danmarks Akvarium, Strandvejen 1, Charlottenlund. Situated in an area of parkland this modern aquarium is one of the largest in Europe and presents a well arranged collection of some 3000 fish from all over the world (open all year). The nearby **Skovriderkroen** is a well-known restaurant. Distance from Rådhuspladsen c 7km. (Bus 1 from Rådhuspladsen.)

Dragør is one of the villages on **Amager** founded by Dutch immigrants, and it has a rather different character from ordinary Danish villages. It is characterised by carefully preserved narrow cobbled streets, their sometimes thatched and half-timbered houses built close together near the harbour. This harbour is surprisingly big, and reflects the fact that in the 19C Dragør was the third largest port in Denmark after Copenhagen and Helsingør. But with the advent of bigger ships, that all stopped. There are several large old buildings near the harbour, including the old *Pilot's House*, with a small tower above the roof. The old warehouse from 1682 is now the **Dragør Museum** with an excellent local history collection, in addition to which there are re-creations of the interiors of old seamen's and fisherfolk's houses (open 1 May–30 Sept).—There are regular ferry sailings from Dragør to Limhamn in Sweden. Distance from Rådhuspladsen c 15km. (Bus 30, 33 from Rådhuspladsen.)

Frilandsmuseum, Kongevejen 100, Lyngby. This Open Air Museum is the 7th Department of the Danish National Museum and has nearly 100 old farms and houses of all sizes and in all styles, including furniture and implements, from the whole of Denmark. The buildings have all been dismantled and reconstructed in a large park. Most are filled with appropriate furniture and implements (open all year; times vary). Distance from Rådhuspladsen c 15km. (S-train to Jægersborg (Lines B or L towards Holte) and then change to the Lyngby–Nærum line, which will take you there through delightful countryside.)

Grundtvigskirken, På Bjerget. Designed by Peder Vilhelm Jensen-Klint, this huge church was built 1921–40 as a memorial to N.F.S. Grundtvig. It is based on the shape of a traditional Danish village church, but has the dimensions of a cathedral. There are variations on corbie steps both in the W façade and on the N and S walls, and there are flying buttresses around the apse. Much of the interior—the altar, font and pulpit—are designed by the architect's son, Kaare Klint. Distance from Rådhuspladsen c 7km. (Bus 10 from Hovedbanegården, 16 from Rådhuspladsen, 19 from Rådhuspladsen, 43 from Nørreport Station.)

Mindelunden i Ryvangen, Tuborgvej. This is a Memorial Park to Danish Resistance Fighters from World War II. Situated close to where captured members of the Resistance were executed, it was once the burial place of 198 of them. About 100 are still buried here, in identical graves. A statue, representing a mother with a dead son, the work of Axel Poulsen, is at the centre (open all year). Distance from Rådhuspladsen c 7km. (S-train to Hellerup Station.)

Ordrupgårdsamlingen, Vilvordevej 110, Charlottenlund. The Ordrupgård Gallery, developed from the private collection of Wilhelm Hansen and housed in a purpose-built gallery in landscaped gardens, offers a comprehensive collection of Danish 19C and 20C art (including Købke, Hammershøi and Ring). Housed in a separate gallery is a very extensive collection of French 19C and 20C paintings (Degas, Renoir, Pissaro, Cézanne, Gauguin and many others). Distance from Rådhuspladsen c 13km. (S-train to Klampenborg and then Bus 160.)

Store Magleby was the village in which the Dutch peasants were originally settled on Amager in 1521, and for two centuries it was predominantly Dutch. Church services were held only in Dutch or Low German. The church itself dates from 1611, with alterations from 1731. The pulpit is Renaissance (1614), and the pews and altarpiece are 19C neo-Gothic. The 18C half-timbered **Amagermuseum**, at Hovedgaden

4, has collections of local dress (very influenced by Dutch national costumes), paintings and interiors of cultural interest (open all year; times vary). Distance from Rådhuspladsen c 13km. (Bus 30, 33 from Rådhuspladsen.)

Tuborg Bryggerier, Strandvejen 54, Hellerup. The Tuborg Breweries, which have stood on this site since 1873, are open all year for individual visits Mon–Fri at 10.00, 12.30 and 14.30, and, by arrangement, for groups. Distance from Rådhuspladsen c 7km. (S Train to Svanemøllen and then Bus 1 or 21.)

Zoologisk Museum, Universitetsparken 15. This is a modern zoological museum, with a large number of models and exhibits of animal life. Children will love it (open all year). Distance from Rådhuspladsen c 3km. (Bus 24, 43, 84, 384 all from Nørreport Station.)

5   Copenhagen to Helsingør (Elsinore)

Total distance 47km. The route follows the 152 throughout.

From Central Copenhagen you should first make your way to Klampenborg, either by driving via Østerport and there following the Ringroad 02 and the 152 through Hellerup, or by joining the E47/E55 motorway and turning off at Junction 16 towards Klampenborg from where you follow the 152, Strandvejen N.

Now you are travelling into North Sjælland, the traditionally idyllic countryside N of Copenhagen, discovered and much loved by the Romantics in the 19C, as it had been by royalty before, and still the favourite area for day trips by Copenhageners on summer Sundays. It is nowadays increasingly a popular commuting belt, well served by first-class roads and the excellent integrated public transport system. As far as *Rungsted* you will find many large houses, built by affluent families seeking beautiful surroundings, but further out the smaller fishing villages have retained much of their character, though they, too, are now being taken over by families moving out of the city.
  The 19C was different from the 20C in that it was not particularly interested in the sea, and preferred rural rather than maritime idyll. Søren Kierkegaard certainly described Strandvejen as a track impossible to travel along for the sand. Nowadays travellers delight in the beaches, the light effects, the wide expanses of the Sound (Øresund) and the views of the Swedish coast to the right on driving N.

As you drive through *Klampenborg*, 11km N of Copenhagen, you pass the *Bellevue* beach, one of Copenhagen's favourites, where summer days see sun worshippers in their thousands sunbathing or swimming in the waters of the Sound. To your left you will find **Jægersborg Dyrehave**, the great deer park, once the domain of royalty, now a vast open space where people can roam at will, still catching frequent glimpses of the many deer on the hilly terrain. It is almost 3km across and, if you include the more northerly *Jægersborg Hegn*, stretches N for some 7km of unbroken open green land.

Jægersborg Dyrehave has been parkland of differing kinds since the Middle Ages, and is referred to in the 13C 'Valdemars Jordebog'. You enter the park through red-painted gates bearing the monograms of different kings. If you turn left off Strandvejen on to *Peter Lieps Vej* and continue along *Fortunvej*, you will come to the former home of one of Frederik VIII's gamekeepers, *Peter Lieps Hus*, now a popular café. Continue along Fortunvej, and you come to the site of what was once a sacred spring, *Kirsten Piils Kilde*. It was a place of pilgrimage in the 16C, and subsequently a fairground developed there. This gradually grew into the nearby *°**Dyrehavsbakken***, Copenhagen's first great amusement park, still said to be the biggest in North Europe. It has an older tradition than the 19C Tivoli, representing a more 'popular' form of entertainment, and today, alongside modern fairground entertainment, it has succeeded in preserving much of its original character. Perhaps a little noisier than Tivoli, it has a dynamism of its own, and is, in fact, very different. Dyrehavsbakken is signposted from Klampenborg and can be approached either from Fortunvej or from Dyrehavevej. Dyrehavevej will also bring you to *Galopbanen*, the Copenhagen Trotting Course.

On one of the highest points of Jægersborg Dyrehave stands the elegant rococo hunting lodge, **Eremitagen**, built in 1736 by Laurids de Thurah for Christian VI, and still in the possession of the Royal Family. The name, 'the hermitage', suggests the private nature of the original building, when it even contained a lift on which an entire dining table could be sent up to the royal apartments so the family could eat without the attentions of servants. The flat ground outside was, incidentally, the site of Denmark's first football match, in 1879.

Following the 152 N you will clearly see Eremitagen on your left, and beyond it the continuation of the park, Jægersborg Hegn. After 5km you pass through *Skodsborg*, and then (3km) *Vedbæk*, a small fishing village now equipped with an excellent marina. Continue for a further 4km and, on your left, just opposite the busy Rungsted yachting harbour, you will see **Rungstedlund**, the home and burial place of Karen Blixen. It is a house with a long history, and was originally an inn, part of which still survives. In 1773 another great Danish writer, Johannes Ewald (1743–81), lived there and wrote some of his finest poetry. A mound in the park close to Karen Blixen's grave is known as *Ewald's Mound*. Rungstedlund now houses the Karen Blixen Museum.

Just after Rungstedlund the 207 leads to *Hørsholm* (3km), once the site of a royal castle which was allowed to fall into disrepair in the 19C, and nothing now remains. In its former stables and barn, however, there is a museum, **Jagt- og Skovbrugsmuseum**, illustrating the history of hunting and forestry. In 1822 the important architect C.F. Hansen, who was responsible for redesigning much of central Copenhagen, built a church in his typical neo-classical style in the castle courtyard. This is now *Hørsholm Church*, containing an altarpiece by Thorvaldsen and a rococo font from the chapel of the now vanished castle. On Søndre Jagtvej you will find *Hørsholm Egnsmuseum*, with exhibits of local interest, particularly from the 18C and 19C.

Back on the 152 you continue N to (6km) *Nivå*, where, in the mansion of **Nivågård**, there is a very fine collection of Italian and 17C Dutch paintings (including Rembrandt and Ruisdael) and paintings from the 19C Danish Golden Age. 3km further N you reach *Sletten*, from where you can take a trip to the interesting island of *Ven*. This island is now Swedish, but it has a Danish history, being the site of the great 17C astronomer Tycho Brahe's famous observatory.

Yet another 2km, and you are in *Humlebæk*, where, on *Gammel Strandvej* (clearly signposted on the right of the 152) one of modern Denmark's most famous art galleries and artistic centres, *Louisiana*, is situated. Lying in delightful surroundings sloping down to the Sound, and surrounded by lawns dotted with sculptures by Jean Arp, Max Ernst, Calder and Henry Moore, it is an internationally renowned gallery of modern art, with a permanent collection and regular temporary major international exhibitions. There is a concert hall, and concerts and recitals are regular features.

Immediately S of Humlebæk is the *Niels W. Gade Museum*, commemorating the famous Romantic composer (Sat, Sun). Humlebæk is itself an old fishing village, and many of the old fishermen's houses still stand, giving their own charm to the beautiful surroundings. It is, too, the site of the mansion of *Krogerup* (1779), now Krogerup Folk High

School, situated on the road towards *Kvistgård* to the left of the 152.

Continue now to (9km) ***Helsingør** (Elsinore) (43,800 inhab.; Tourist Information: Havnepladsen 3), which is more than Hamlet's Castle.

Helsingør has a history going back to the beginning of the 13C, possibly earlier, and owes its growth and importance to its position on the narrowest part of the Sound, with the ferry connection with Sweden. It also had a strategic position, and when King Erik of Pomerania introduced Sound dues in the 15C, he set about building a castle to enforce them. At the same time he established Helsingør as an important ecclesiastical centre, helping to found no fewer than three monasteries in the town: Franciscan, Dominican and Carmelite. The present mansion of **Marienlyst** now occupies the ground on which the Franciscan monastery stood. The Dominican monastery became a hospital after the Reformation, but no longer exists, though remains were found in Fiolgade in 1936. The Carmelite monastery did better, and some of the buildings still stand, in particular the church, **Klosterkirken**.

In the 16C the town was destroyed by the Lübeckers, and it was twice visited by the plague. That same century Frederik II had the old castle dismantled and replaced by the present Kronborg (1574–83). This move, which was supplemented by the stationing of a barracks in the town, revived Helsingør. The 17C and 18C were a period of growth, lasting until the Napoleonic Wars, when Helsingør suffered badly. With the abolition of the Sound dues in 1857 it was hit yet again, as this meant that ships no longer all put in and brought trade. On the other hand, the opening of the railway in 1864, followed by the introduction of steam ferries to Sweden, brought new life to the town. The journey to Hälsingborg in Sweden takes 25 minutes.

*Kronborg Castle must remain the special attraction of Helsingør. It is situated on a promontory to the N, overlooking the harbour and the Sound. By the end of the rebuilding, the resplendent Renaissance edifice stood, as it does today, as four wings roofed with copper (hence the present green colour) around a magnificent central courtyard. It

Kronborg Castle, Frederik II's Renaissance castle, was largely destroyed by fire in 1629 but rebuilt in its present shape by Christian IV. Photo: J. Schytte

was badly damaged by fire in 1629, but rebuilt by Christian IV. After
the rather sombre approach to the castle, the first sight of the interior
is an experience, a glimpse of the inner courtyard through a rounded
archway flanked on either side by two Ionic columns with statues of
Neptune and Mercury in the niches between them. The archway is
surmounted by a bay window beneath which is a series of coats of
arms.

The courtyard is enormous and light, and it is from here that you
follow the set route through the rooms and halls. They vary from the
intimate to the splendid. In the N wing there is the king's chamber,
with its stuccoed window recesses, the painted panels in the ceilings
by Gerrit van Honthorst, and the alabaster and marble fireplace. In the
Small Hall (Lille Sal) there are seven of the tapestries ordered by
Frederik II, huge portraits of Danish kings. These, and the 104
others(!), were intended for the 63m-long Great Hall (Riddersalen)
with its floor of Gotland marble, but here, in a space made even more
vast by the total lack of furnishings, there are painted portraits instead.
Most sumptuous of all, perhaps, is the *Chapel (Slotskirken), entirely
furnished as it was at the time of Frederik II, with gloriously painted
and carved bench ends and royal balcony, not to mention the organ
from the time of Christian IV.

The castle now includes a museum—the **Handels- og Søfarts-
museum**—which illustrates Danish maritime history and Denmark's
colonial past, and beneath the castle the *casemates are partly open
for inspection. Here sits brooding the stone statue of Holger Danske,

the legendary hero who will come back to save Denmark in its hour of need.

Kronborg is not the only glory of Helsingør. The rest needs to be seen on foot. Start from the square in front of the station, and cross over to Strandgade with its old houses: *Stephan Hansens Gård* from 1760, *Claessens Palæ* from 1790 and *Mester Peiters Bod*, the old apothecary's shop. Now turn down any of the streets on your right to *Stengade*, where you will find more excellent examples of old buildings: *Odernes Gård* (No. 66) from 1459, the late Gothic houses at Nos 70, 72 and 74 from the 16C. No. 76 is a Renaissance house from 1579, while No. 64 is baroque, from 1739. There is a wealth of fine old houses in Helsingør. The whole of this quite compact district is distinguished by them, many of high architectural quality. Do not merely pass through. Take your time and savour what there is to see.

Now walk N along *Stengade* until you reach *Sankt Anna Gade* on your left. Here, on the corner of Sankt Anna Gade and Sankt Olai Gade you will find the Cathedral Church, **Sankt Olai Kirke**, easily recognised by its tall tower. Its history goes back to c 1200, but the present Gothic structure dates mainly from 1450; it has a broad lofty nave and chancel, both whitewashed, with massive Gothic arches on either side. The furniture is outstanding, mainly Renaissance and baroque. The auricular high altar from 1664 is by Lorentz Jørgensen and stands over 11m, with reliefs representing scenes and characters from the New Testament.

The exuberant rood screen from 1652–53, supported by 76 brass balusters, is by Claus Brahmeier of Hamburg and Jens Mortensen of Helsingør. The crucifix above it is Gothic, late 15C. The pulpit, from 1568, is one of the earliest Danish Renaissance works. Some of the bench ends are inscribed with coats of arms of the nobility or with that of Helsingør City, dated 1560. Of particular interest is the baptismal chapel, while an amusing detail (seen with 20C eyes!) is the black tablet on which parishioners were named if they had committed an ecclesiastical peccadillo.

It is now only a few steps further along Sankt Anna Gade to **Sankt Marie Kirke**. This is the S wing of the Carmelite monastery, which is the best preserved monastery in Denmark, standing much as it was when the monastery closed. St. Mary's Church, brick built, consists of a tall nave with side aisles, ending in both E and W with Gothic gables and windows; the light from these windows is the only direct light to the nave. The pointed arcades separating the side aisles stand on heavy square columns. On the N side of the nave the royal gallery bears the initials of Frederik III and Queen Sophie Amalie. There are late Gothic frescoes in the vaulting in the nave and on the wall of the S aisle. The baroque altarpiece is from 1637, the organ loft from 1630–40, the bench ends from 1700. The organ itself is from 1635. The composer Didrik Buxtehude was the organist here from 1660–68. The church is notable for a large number of gravestones and memorial plaques. Christian II's mistress, Dyveke, is said to be buried here.

The adjoining **Vor Frue Kloster** consists of the remainder of the Carmelite monastery, the whole of it surrounding the monastery cloisters. Immediately to the W stands the corbie-gabled **Carmelite House** (Karmeliterhuset), most of it dating from the early 16C, now, together with the Marienlyst (see below), forming the Helsingør City Museum, illustrating the history of Helsingør and the Sound dues.

Continue your walk now along Sankt Anna Gade and its curiously named continuation, Lappen (The Patch), to the beautiful park surrounding the elegant neo-classical mansion of **Marienlyst** (not to be confused with the well-known local restaurant by the same name!). Originally called *Lundegård*, it was designed by Nicolas-Henri Jardin in 1759 to the order of Adam Gottlob Moltke and bought by King Frederik V in 1760. On the death of the King it was taken over by Queen Juliane Marie, from whom it derives its name. The park was designed according to Romantic ideas and furnished with an artificial burial mound which was given the name of *Hamlet's Grave*, and it is still to be seen. It is, however, not one of the various places claiming to be the authentic burial place of the elusive prince. The science museum, *Danmarks Tekniske Museum* is 1km further W on Nordre Strandvej, the continuation of Lappen. Its exhibits illustrate scientific developments over the centuries, and include a room dedicated to H.C. Ørsted, the discoverer of electro-magneticism, a typewriter from 1867 and the first aeroplane to fly in Europe.

If you now return along Nordre Strandvej and turn left down *Strand-allé* (at the junction with Lappen) and follow this round into Strand-promenaden, you will come, on your right, to the *Øresunds Akvarium*, where you can see living specimens of the fish and marine animals from the Sound. Just opposite you will find **Grønnehave Station**, from where in the summer months you can travel by vintage railway to Gilleleje and back.

EXCURSION TO THE WEST OF HELSINGØR (total distance c 56km). The north coast of Sjælland is famous for its sandy beaches and clear water and is much loved by holidaymakers.

Take the 237 from Helsingør to (5km) *Hellebæk*, where the old **Hammer Mølle**, founded by Christian IV in 1597 and in its time copper mill, gun foundry and clothing mill, is now a working museum (open summer). Hellebæk is also notable for its workmen's cottages, the oldest dating from 1735.

Continue now to (7km) *Hornbæk*, with its popular beaches and sand dunes. 5km further finds you in another beautifully situated bathing resort, *Dronningmølle*. If you take the minor road S here towards Villingerød and turn left at Villingerød Church (2km), you will come to an area called *Rusland* (see Brother Rus, below), where the *Rudolf Tegner Museum and Sculpture Park* exhibits the work of the Symbolist sculptor and painter who himself founded the museum in 1937 (open summer).

From Dronningmølle it is otherwise no more than 3km to *Nakke-hoved*, with its 18C lighthouse (and inn), and a further 3km to *Gilleleje*, the northernmost fishing village on Sjælland, and now a much-visited tourist resort. Again, there is a magnificent beach, and daily fish auctions. This is the terminus of the vintage railway from Helsingør. The *Gilleleje Museum*, housed in the old school house, a fisherman's cottage and Nakkehoved lighthouse, boasts an excellent collection of exhibits illustrating local life over the centuries (open summer).

If you take the 227 S from Gilleleje and turn right after 4km, you will come to *Søborg* (2km) with the remarkably well-preserved ruins of the 12C castle which was the first brick-built castle in Scandinavia. The large—also brick built—Romanesque church here is contemporary with it; the tower is mid 13C. The original S door is still in use, while the N door has been bricked up, but is still visible. There are a few frescoes on the walls and columns in the nave. The altar is medieval, with an altarpiece from 1593 (originally in St. Mary's Church in Helsingør), the work of Hans de Brügge. The land around Søborg was once a lake—still called Søborg Sø. Draining began in the late 18C by means of the canal to Gilleleje, which still exists.

From Gilleleje the 251 S will take you to (8km) Græsted. Turn left here

to (4km) Kirke Esbønderup, where you will find a minor road leading
to (2.5km) *Esrum Kloster*, a Cistercian monastery, which was founded
by Archbishop Eskild around 1150. King Erik Menved's twin sons
were buried here, as was Valdemar IV's Queen, Helvig. Only the S
wing now remains, of which the W part is late 14C. This remaining
structure is part private residence, part store for the National Museum.
A Reformation polemic tells the story of how the Devil, under the name
of Brother Rus ('rus' means intoxication) set about seducing the monks
and did very well until he was finally unmasked and driven out.
Perhaps it is not too much to assume that it is his name that is attached
to the nearby *Rusland*—see above.

From Esrum Kloster drive S 1km to join the 205 E. On your right now
is *Esrum Sø*, the second biggest lake in Denmark—9km long—and one
of the deepest—21m. Drive along the 205 through *Horserød Hegn*
wood and past *Horserød Prison* (a camp for Russian prisoners of war
in World War I, an internment and later concentration camp during the
Nazi occupation in World War II, and now an ordinary prison) back to
(15km) Helsingør.

6 Helsingør to Copenhagen via Hillerød

Total distance 64km. E47/E55, 213 to (8km) *Gurre*.—Unclassified
road to (4km) *Tikøb*.—235, A6 to (18km) **Hillerød**.—201, A19 to
(34km) **Copenhagen** (Rtes 3, 4).

Leave **Helsingør** (Rte 5) S on the E47/E55, turning off at (6km) Junction
3 on to the 213 to (2km) *Gurre*. Just beyond the village, idyllically
situated on the S bank of *Gurre Sø* (lake) are the ruins of one of the
most famous of Danish medieval castles.

Gurre Castle was the favourite castle of Valdemar IV, whose mistress Tove,
according to legend, was murdered in a particularly nasty way by his Queen. She
invited Tove into the sauna, pushed her in first, locked the door and roasted her.
Valdemar was distraught and cursed God, for which he was condemned to hunt
the forest of Sjælland until Judgement Day. He is said to have uttered the words:
'Let God keep His Heaven, if only I can keep my Gurre.' This is the legend taken
over by the 19C poet Jens Peter Jacobsen, which, in German translation, forms
the text of Schönberg's 'Gurrelieder'. (Historically, Tove was actually the mistress
of Valdemar I, but that is another matter.)

The ruins now stand in places to a height of 5m, and indicate that the
castle originally consisted of a late 12C rectangular central tower
surrounded by a more or less square ring wall with a tower at each
corner. It is thought to have been demolished about the time of the
Reformation, and the materials in part used in the building of
Frederiksborg Castle (see below). Other material from it was used in
the 19C to build artisans' houses. Just E of the castle the foundations
of a 14C chapel are visible.

An unclassified road W takes you to (4km) *Tikøb*. The imposing late
12C Romanesque church here was given by King Hans to Esrum
Monastery (Rte 5) in 1489. Some of the original windows are visible,
and both the original doors, though the elegant S door is now walled
up. The round-arched windows in the E are from c 1200, as is the
porch, though this was later altered. The vaulting in the nave is 15C.
The splendid Renaissance pulpit is from the late 16C, and the baroque
altarpiece from 1723. A single bench end is dated 1597, but most are
modern.

From Tikøb you continue S on the 235 to the A6, where you turn right and follow this road to (9km) *Fredensborg Palace.

This magnificent baroque palace, started by Frederik IV in 1720 and given the name *Fredensborg* (meaning 'Peace Palace') to celebrate the end of the Great Northern War, stands in a large park sloping down to Esrum Lake. The complex consists of 28 buildings in all.

The central section of the palace, designed by Johan Cornelius Krieger, was built between 1720 and 1724, other parts following in succeeding years. The four side wings by Nicolai Eigtved are from 1753, and Laurids de Thurah was responsible for the palace steward's residence and the notably tall chimneys at the corners of the central cupola—necessarily built to this height in order to create sufficient draught. The white palace, with green copper roofs, is approached via an avenue leading to a circus surrounded to the left and right by two-storey buildings each forming three sides of an octagon. To the right of the palace are two lower wings, the knight marshall's residence and the domestic wing, known as 'Damehuset', and between them the chapel, all overlooking a green flanked by long, low buildings on two sides.

The interior of the palace is of a splendour befitting its surroundings. On entering you will come to the hall beneath the central cupola, the *Kuppelsal*, with its ornate stucco ceiling and its marble floor in black and white. The *Garden Room*, too, deserves special attention, having a magnificent stucco ceiling forming a framework around a painting by Henrik Krock representing Denmark and Norway asking the Olympic gods for peace. The rococo walls are decorated to match, with large-scale paintings of ancient Rome. Hendrik Krock is responsible for other splendid painted ceiling panels surrounded by intricate stucco work by the brothers Sturmberg. A total contrast is the strictly neo-classical 'Damegemakket' (Ladies' Chamber) from 1776.

The baroque Chapel, surmounted by a steep saddle roof topped by a ridge turret, is in the form of a cross with a gallery supported by Doric columns below and supporting Corinthian columns above. The pulpit, font and altarpiece are by Friedrich Ehbisch, and the painting in the central panel of the altarpiece is by Hendrik Krock.

Fredensborg was the setting for large gatherings of European royalty during the 19C, when Christian IX could claim to be the father-in-law of Europe. It is still the spring and autumn summer residence of the Royal Family, but in July the palace and the private garden, *Marmorhaven*, with statues by Johannes Wiedewelt, are open to the public, with conducted tours every half hour in the afternoons.

The wooded park, which is open to the public all year round, was designed by Nicolas-Henri Jardin in the 1760s. The sophisticated layout with vistas across Esrum lake provides for lime tree walks fanning out from the palace, and in particular a splendid avenue immediately behind it. A walk known as *Nordmandsdalen* presents a remarkable series of figures of Norwegian and Faroese peasants in national dress, commissioned by Frederik V.

From Fredensborg you continue S on the A6 towards (9km) Hillerød. As you approach the town you will, on your right, find a road (Rendelæggerbakken) leading straight to *Frederiksborg Castle.

Built on three islets in the Slotssø lake, this is surely the most famous historical castle in Denmark after Kronborg (see Rte 5). In 1577 the future Christian IV was born here, and as he grew up he decided to create of it a castle in the grand style. He succeeded in his ambition. In 1599 he started a lodge called 'Sparepenge' (Savings), in which he

Frederiksborg Castle, Hillerød. The present building in the Renaissance style dates back to Christian IV. Photo: John Sommer

lived while the old castle was demolished, and the new one built. The Royal Wing was finished by 1605, followed by the Chapel Wing in 1606. The exterior, symmetrically built in Dutch Renaisssance style, was more or less finished by 1611, with the exception of the Princess Wing, which was not completed until 1615. Work on the interior continued for many years, and a good deal of redesigning took place in the 18C. In 1859 the entire castle then went up in flames. Funded by J.C. Jacobsen, the wealthy brewer who founded the Carlsberg Breweries, it was then restored to something like its original state in order that it should become the **Museum of National History**, which it now is. The Chapel Wing (beneath which are the King's treasury and wine cellar) was the least damaged by the fire.

The resplendent *Chapel*, the setting for the coronations of the Danish Absolute Kings from 1671 to 1840, is one of the most magnificent parts of the present castle. Entered through a sumptuous Renaissance doorway, it is surmounted by intricate vaulting, while the richly decorated arcading on either side supports a gallery running right round. The ebony and silver pulpit and the flamboyant altarpiece, with a silver-gilt relief of the Crucifixion in the main panel, are the work of the Mores workshop in Hamburg, c 1606. The famous *Compenius organ* from 1610 is still in use, and there are recitals on Thursdays from 13.30 to 14.00. The carillon above the chapel plays a hymn melody every hour throughout the summer months.

The *Great Hall* is immediately above the Chapel, but the original was badly damaged during the fire, and this is a reconstruction—which, good as it is, lacks the splendour of the original carved panelling. That and the vaulted ground-floor dining room known as *Rosen*, were the first to be completely restored, as they were the ones about which most was known. *Christian IV's Chamber* is another room successfully restored, now containing large-scale paintings by Carl Bloch and Otto Bache portraying events from the life of Christian IV, while the *Audience Chamber* with its lofty stucco ceiling is much as it was in 1688.

As the Museum of National History, Frederiksborg now contains countless relics from the nation's past history, including both memorabilia, portraits, coats of arms and paintings depicting scenes of national importance. Added to this there is the outstanding collection of historical furniture which has been gathered from many sources over the past century. Some of the earlier exhibits reflect a 19C Romantic view of Danish history, while later additions to the collection reflect a more scholarly approach. The Chapel, still in its original state, was the place in which the Danish absolute kings were crowned, and since 1694 has been the Chapel of the Order of Knighthood. The Audience Chamber remains unchanged from the 17C, while the Great Hall was reconstructed c 1880. The ground floor in the Princess Wing is used for travelling exhibitions.

*Hillerød (25,500 inhab.; Tourist Information: Torvet 1) originated as a village near *Hillerødsholm*, gaining in importance when Frederik II came into possession of the estate in 1560. It thrived on the numerous visitors to the royal estate, and Frederik II made a vain attempt to establish it as a market town. It grew further under Christian IV, providing for the large numbers of workers and visitors. However, after suffering from a great fire in 1692 it was further reduced in status when the Court moved to *Fredensborg* in 1720. A certain amount of trade was now developed, until, in 1834, there was another catastrophic fire, followed by yet another a year later.

The result is that few of the old buildings in Hillerød have survived. The establishment of the Museum of National History in Frederiksborg, linked with the opening of the railway, has brought new growth, and Hillerød is now a busy, thriving town, an excellent shopping centre, catering for the large numbers of tourists attracted by *Frederiksborg*.

There are nevertheless a few older buildings still standing, for instance the old parsonage in *Kannikestræde*, the *Lowzowske Gård* from 1758 on the corner of Slotsgade and Møllestræde, and the *Batzke house* from 1720 on the edge of the Castle Park. The ethnographical museum, *Nordsjællands Folkemuseum*, is situated in Helsingørgade, containing both local historical collections and exhibits reflecting the history of North Sjælland's peasant culture.

EXCURSION FROM HILLERØD TO NEARBY GRIBSKOV FOREST AND NØDEBO. *Gribskov* forest lies just N of Hillerød and is reached by taking the A6 N and then either the 267 or the 227. (The latter will bring you direct to (6km) Nødebo on the W shore of *Esrum lake*, a spot of interest in itself, see below.)

Gribskov covers 56 sq km and encompasses several lakes. You can wander at will—but watch it: you can easily get lost! It was a place much loved by the philosopher Søren Kierkegaard, to whom there is a memorial stone at *Stjernen*, about 1.5km W of Nødebo, where he was fond of meditating. His wonderful lyrical description of Gribskov can be found in 'Stages on Life's Way'.

Nødebo is the village on the shore of Esrum Lake, just opposite Fredensborg. Its tiny stone-built Romanesque church (with a later and inappropriate ridge turret and belfry) was built by the monks of Esrum Monastery, and despite later additions has many original features left. There are frescoes from c 1425 and c 1460. Those in the chancel and nave are by the 'Big Nose Master', a series of anatomically impossible figures, many adorned with very large noses. Those beneath the tower are the work of the artistically far superior Union Master. The baroque pulpit from 1668 is by Esben Børresen. Nødebo also has a *dolls' museum* of an unusual kind: dolls in historical costumes, including figures representing Leonora Christina and Queen Victoria (open Easter and July).

EXCURSION TO ÆBELHOLT MONASTERY. Take the road W via *Tjæreby* to (6km) the junction with the A19, where the remains of the Augustinian *Æbelholt Monastery* from c 1230 can be found just opposite the junction. It became a place of pilgrimage for the old and infirm after the early Abbot Vilhelm was declared a Saint and after one of his teeth was reputed to work miraculous cures. Together with a garden of medicinal herbs, there is now a museum on the spot, exhibiting bones and skeletons illustrating illnesses prevalent in the Middle Ages. Little is left of the monastery except the buttresses and foundations of the chapel (open daily in summer; Sat, Sun at other times).

As you drive S from Hillerød on the 201, on the outskirts of the town you will see, on your left, a modern church, *Præstevang Kirke*, de-signed by Holger Jensen and built in 1962 to the pattern of the old Viking houses in Trelleborg (Rte 2).

After 13km the 201 will bring you to **Birkerød** (Tourist Information: Rådhuset).

Once a village, but now, no more then 20km away from Copen-hagen, largely a dormitory town, Birkerød stands in lovely wooded countryside, and there are still a few older buildings to be seen, harking back to former times. Among them the Romanesque church deserves special attention. Dating back to the 12C, this brick-built church contains a good collection of 16C frescoes, including one of the oldest portrayals of Judgement Day; you will also find there the chains worn by the local pastor when imprisoned by the Swedes in 1659. The late Gothic altarpiece from c 1475, with a central figure representing the Crucifixion, was probably made in Lübeck, and the auricular oak font is from c 1650. The Renaissance pulpit dates from c 1600. The important late 19C novelist Jakob Knudsen is buried here.

Just outside Birkerød, to the N, lies *Sjælsø* lake, where, in the woods, there is a restaurant called *Jægerhytten* (The Hunter's Lodge), said to be the spot where the English-born Queen Caroline Mathilde used to meet her court doctor and lover, Count Struensee, in 1770. She ended in exile, he on the scaffold.

4km S on the 201 lies **Holte**, another old village that is now an affluent Copenhagen dormitory. It is magnificently situated, sur-rounded by woods and on the shore of the idyllic *Furesø* lake.

Holte is mainly residential; there are few really old buildings among the rather fine turn-of-the-century villas, but *Gammel Holtegård*, a mansion built in 1757 by Laurids de Thurah for himself, stands on *Attemosevej*. To find this, you turn left at the traffic lights in the centre of the town and drive along Øverødvej towards Vedbæk. Attemosevej is then c 3km on the right. On Attemosevej, too, at No. 170, is a *museum*, containing prehistoric finds made in nearby Vedbæk. The central feature is 22 Stone Age Skeletons, many well-preserved, found in 1975, together with the ornaments and weapons found with them, all producing a vivid picture of the life of the hunters along the coast some 7000 years ago. If you follow Attemosevej S, it crosses Søllerød-vej, where, at No. 25, in the 300-year-old *Mothsgården*, there is a local history museum.

From Holte the road continues to (17km) **Copenhagen** (Rtes 3, 4).

7   Copenhagen to Århus

Total distance 98km plus ferry (3hrs). 156 to (30km) **Roskilde**.—155, A23 to (68km) **Kalundborg**.—Ferry to **Århus**.

The 156 from Copenhagen to Roskilde (Rte 2) offers only a few minor items of interest; however, from Roskilde to Kalundborg there are two suggested routes. The direct route (total distance 68km) is given first; see below for the alternative route via Dianalund.

DIRECT ROUTE FROM ROSKILDE TO KALUNDBORG (total distance 68km). Leave Roskilde on the A14 S and turn right after 3km into the 155 W, which will take you to (5km) *Kornerup*. Here there is one of the smallest churches in the country, with a Romanesque chancel and nave, Gothic porch, 18C porch and 19C belfry. The altarpiece, a triptych, is from c 1500, and the pulpit from 1590.

Continue another 15km and turn left into the A23. After 10km you come to the village of *Nørre Jernløse*. Here there is an interesting 12C Romanesque church with a wealth of decoration on the apse and chancel, and containing some exquisite frescoes from c 1500 representing Christ in mandorla, with Mary and John. There is a late Gothic antemensale, a baroque pulpit and Renaissance pews for the local aristocracy.

3km N of Nørre Jernløse lies the impressive three-winged Renaissance mansion of *Løvenborg*, built 1630, not open to the public, but clearly visible from the road. Surrounded by its moat, it rises from the surrounding marshy land in a grandiose vision, with Renaissance towers, steeples and gables, deservedly ranking among the finest of the mansions in Sjælland.

Back on the A23, you now drive 8km and turn right into *Mørkøv*, where there is one of the most richly decorated of Danish ˙churches. Virtually all the walls and vaulting are covered in a wealth of extremely well-preserved frescoes from c 1450, the work of a known artist, the Isefjord Master; their unusually light colours are the result of the techniques used when restoring them in the 1940s.

From Mørkøv you might like to drive SE on the 231 to the mansion of *Torbenfeld* (2km), the E wing of which was built in the 1570s. The impressive house, standing on a small island, is furnished with towers and spires; the S wing is a much altered medieval building, with cellars from c 1400, while the E wing was built in the 1570s. Two corner towers are from 1906 (not open to the public).—If you continue along this delightful road, in 3km you will pass another splendid mansion, *Kongsdal*, and, after yet another 2km, you will come to the beautifully restored church at **Undløse**, containing the Union Master's finest work in Denmark (most of this painter's work is in fact in Sweden).

Another small excursion from Mørkøv is to drive along a small road SW to *Skamstrup* (3km). Here is another church containing a wealth of frescoes, some from c 1350, some by the Isefjord Master, from c 1450; among the earlier ones is the oldest authentic—and quite detailed—painting of a ship in Denmark. It is seen in the legendary contest between St. Olav and King Harald III of Norway (who was killed by the English King Harold at Stamford Bridge).

From Mørkøv you follow the A23 to (6km) the idyllic village of *Jyderup*, where the small Romanesque church still stands in its entirety, though with later additions. Facing it is the fine half-timbered parsonage. Soon after Jyderup you will drive through the *Grevindeskov* forest, just to the S of which is *Skarresø* lake.

8km beyond Jyderup you reach the 155, where you might like to turn right to **Bregninge** (3km), where again there is a church with a large number of fine frescoes from three different periods. They include a frieze with pictures of the Creation from c 1300, a Wheel of Fortune (1400) and scenes from the life of St. Catherine from 1425. The altarpiece, too, from 1654, is a fine piece of baroque work originally sited in Dragsholm (Rte 8).

Return now to the A23, where after 2km you could visit the church in Viskinge before driving the last 10km to Kalundborg (see below). The frescoes (1425) in *Viskinge Church*, beautifully restored in 1965, are thought to be based on an altar painting in Wildungen in Westphalia. Of particular interest is the scene showing a serene face on a Christ weighed down under the burden of the cross He is bearing.

ALTERNATIVE ROUTE FROM ROSKILDE TO KALUNDBORD—VIA DIANALUND (total distance 83km). To take this more roundabout route, you leave Roskilde on the A14 S, turning right after 3km into the 155 W for

another 18km. Here you turn left to (3km) Tølløse. The road turns to
the right in the village; follow it to 1km Gammel Tølløse, where you
will find *Tølløsegård*. This has a history going back to 1370, the present
main building being an attempt from 1944 to recreate Peder Oxe's
Renaissance mansion from 1575. Continue now via (2km) Nørre Val-
lenderød to (4km) Ugerløse, then to (7km) Stenlille, turning right there
into the 255 towards (5km) Dianalund.

Immediately before reaching Dianalund you might turn left to Tersløse (2.5km),
where you will find **Tersløsegård**, once owned by the daughter of Esbern Snare
(see below), but most famous as the home of the 18C dramatist, essayist and
historian Ludvig Holberg. This is not a museum proper, but it contains three rooms
devoted to Holberg, restored to what is thought to have been their appearance
when the great writer lived there during the summers of 1745–53. The collection
comprises portraits of Holberg, illustrations, early editions and other memorabilia
(open Apr–Oct).

From Dianalund you now follow the 255 to (4km) Skellebjerg and from
there the 219 W to (4km) Ruds Vedby, with the mansion of *Vedbygård*,
dating back to the 14C. The present S wing is from c 1500 and the
imposing N wing from c 1540, while the W wing is partly 18C and
partly 19C. The great baroque poet Thomas Kingo was tutor to the
family here in 1659 (not open to the public).

The 219 now continues to (5km) *Sæby*, where the church contains
frescoes from three periods; those in the apse, in an Italianate style, are
from c 1150–75 and thus the oldest on Sjælland. Immediately N of the
village lies the large *Tissø* lake. To see the lake you should drive N
along the 219, which runs along its E side, passing on your right the
mansion of *Sæbygård*, where Thomas Kingo also taught the children
in his day, and which is the scene of one of his less devotional poems,
'Sæbygaards Koeklage' (The Lament of Sæbygård's Cows)—the object of their lament being the bull which has drowned in the local
pond.

From Sæby it is only 5km further along the 255 to *Gørlev* (Tourist
Information: Algade 47). As a small town, Gørlev has little intrinsic
interest, but it is nevertheless the home of the **Gørlev Stone**, one of the
most interesting of the Danish runestones. It now stands in the porch
of the Romanesque church, the inscription telling us that a certain
Thjodvi had the stone raised, after which it lists the entire runic
alphabet.

Leave Gørlev N on the A22 and drive 9km to *Svallerup*, where you
should turn right to (3km) *Ubby*. The church here is an exceptionally
fine late medieval building.

Built in brick by Esben Snare in 1179, it has an impressive nave lined with four
pillars on either side, all with trapezium capitals typical of the buildings attributed
to the Hvide family, supporting a series of Romanesque arches. The chancel is
also vaulted. The magnificent auricular altarpiece carved in unpainted oak by
Lorentz Jørgensen is from 1677. The carved Renaissance bench ends are from c
1600 and the pulpit from c 1620. There is a late Gothic crucifix, the work of the
Store-Fuglede Master.

This is an area rich in prehistoric monuments, but those in Ubby are
worthy of special attention. There is a dolmen chamber and six passage graves, two of which are double.

From Ubby you can follow the 219 back to (3km) the A22 and go on
to (2km) *Rørby*, where, in a church standing on a steep slope and
overlooking Kalundborg Fjord, there are 15C frescoes from the Union
Master's workshop (only discovered in 1981 and carefully conserved
by 1983) and a large Gothic triptych altarpiece from c 1500.

From Rørby it is only 5km along the main road to **Kalundborg** (15,500 inhab.; Tourist Information: Volden 12), which grew up around a castle and church founded c 1170 by Esbern Snare, the brother of Bishop Absalon. The oldest known charter is from 1485. Esbern Snare's castle, built as a defence against marauding pirates, was replaced with a much larger one further to the E by Valdemar IV, but his structure was virtually destroyed during the Swedish occupation of Sjælland 1658–60. All that is now left is the ruins of Esbern Snare's castle in the *Ruinpark* on Lindevej at the W end of the harbour, and those of Valdemar IV's on *Volden* closer to the centre of the town. The original church, on the other hand, still stands as one of the most unusual churches in Scandinavia.

The importance of Kalundborg at the time of Valdemar IV is signified by its role as a place of assembly for the nobility, and it was here that Valdemar signed his coronation charter in 1360. A Benedictine monastery was founded here in the 13C, but became a home farm for the castle after the Reformation, the buildings themselves being razed in the 18C. Kalundborg was an important centre during the Middle Ages, but its role was diminished in succeeding centuries. It regained its importance as a transit port for *Århus* in the 19C, more particularly with the building of the railway in 1874. Two big fires, one in 1901 and one in 1920, destroyed much of the old town, in particular the former, which burned down about a quarter of the buildings.
Despite these fires, however, Kalundborg has retained much of its old character. Particularly in the W part of the town there is a host of old streets and alleyways, and Kalundborg is the only Danish market town to possess four stone-built medieval buildings.

Esbern Snare's ***Vor Frue Kirke** (Our Lady's Church), built between 1170 and 1190, and now world famous, is the natural point of departure for a tour of the town. Its shape is unlike anything else in Denmark, reminiscent rather of Byzantine or Russian churches. Instead of the long nave and shorter transept, it is in the form of a Greek cross, with more or less equidistant arms. Each of the arms ends in a hefty octagonal tower surmounted with a spire, and an even higher spire towers over the crossing. This major tower, *St. Mary's Tower*, collapsed in 1827 due to insufficient foundations, and it has taken two major operations to restore it and the church interior to their original state.
The nave is square, and at the corners there are four granite pillars supporting the central tower. The four outer towers, named after SS. Anna, Gertrude, Maria Magdalene and Catherine, rest partly directly on the barrel vaulting of the four arms. In view of the grandeur of the exterior, the vaulted interior seems remarkably small. The altarpiece is an ornate, richly carved baroque piece by Lorentz Jørgensen, similar to those found in the churches at Køge (Rte 10) and Helsingør (Rte 5), with relief carvings of the Birth of Christ, the Last Supper, the Crucifixion, Resurrection and Ascension. The altar crucifix is from the 12C.
Just E of the church, in *Kirkestræde*, there is a row of old houses. Walk past these to *Torvet* (The Square), on the E side of which you will find the remains of Valdemar's castle, the tower known as *Folen* (The Foal). Immediately W of the Square is the neo-classical *Gyths Gård* (Gyth's House), where the Norwegian Nobel Prizewinner, the novelist Sigrid Undset, was born; there is a memorial plaque on the front. From the Square issue the two main streets of the medieval city, *Adelgade* and *Munkesøgade*. Adelgade 6 is the old Bishop's Palace, and presumably forms half of a four-winged residence; the W wing, with its imposing gable facing Adelgade, was used as a town hall from 1539 to 1854; after restoration in 1970 it has again been used for meetings of the town council. On the S side of Adelgade there is a row of half-timbered houses, one of which is early 17C.
Now walk past the churchyard, with its medieval mortuary chapel,

probably originally the house of one of the priests, to the complex of half-timbered houses known as *Lindegården* to the W of the church. The oldest of these buildings, forming the N wing on Adelgade, is from c 1650, the rest from c 1755 to 1786. Lindegården is now the *Kalundborg and District Museum*. This is a delightful museum, one room of which, the Rococo Room, is thought to be by the same team as was responsible for the *Lerchenborg mansion* (see below). In an area so rich in archaeological finds as this, there are obviously going to be excellent prehistoric exhibits. The Viking Age, too, is well represented, as are the Middle Ages, when Kalundborg was at its zenith. Other exhibits illustrate life in the 18C and 19C, and there are also reconstructions of rooms and a collection of peasant dress from the 19C (open daily in summer; limited opening in winter).—There is a *Local History Archive* at *Volden 12*, close to the Tourist Information Office; and to the W of Lindegården you will find the ruins of Esbern Snare's original castle.

Returning via Præstegade, you will pass the medieval tithe barn in the wall of the churchyard. Continue to Torvet now, cross it diagonally to your left and go down Volden to Lindegade and Kordilgade. In Lindegade you will find more half-timbered houses on the corner of Skibbrogade and also, at No. 4, a charming baroque house from 1763. In Kordilgade, now a pedestrian precinct, there is a fine half-timbered merchant house, *Ole Lunds Gård* (now an hotel and restaurant), as well as the baroque *Bryggergård* (The Brewer's House). The important 19C painter Johan Thomas Lundbye was born at Skibbrogade 8 (S of Kordilgade), and a plaque commemorates this.

On Kaalundparkvej, leading N from the Square, is *Kaalund Kloster* (Kaalund Convent), from 1751, originally the home farm of Kalundborg Castle, and now the seat of the local administration.

3km S of Kalundborg stands the great mansion of *Lerchenborg. This is one of the most perfect baroque mansions in Denmark, built 1743–53 by General Christian Lerche. The design is the general's own, but as he was a close friend of Laurids de Thurah and Nicolai Eigtved, the principal architects of his day, their influence can be guaranteed. Built on symmetrical principles, with a pointed gable over the main entrance and rounded gables at the end, the main wing, in white, comprises 17 windows on two floors overlooking a symmetrically laid-out French garden by Jean-Baptiste Descarrières de Longueville. The S wing and certain other rooms are open to the public, and a visit is a must.

The rooms, mainly rococo, are furnished in the appropriate styles with family portraits on the walls. The vaulted ceiling in the great hall is decorated with white stucco reliefs, setting off motifs from Ovid on the walls. On the top floor there is a collection of prehistoric relics found on the estate. The ubiquitous Hans Christian Andersen was a guest here in 1862, and there are Andersen memorabilia in some of the rooms.

A series of musical events is arranged here in August every year, and concerts are given in the great hall. There is a cafeteria at the entrance to the park, which is also open to the public (open pm late Jun to mid-Aug; closed Fri).

Close to Lerchenborg you will find the Asnæs Power Station (Asnæsværket), the largest in Denmark. Conducted tours are arranged on Tue and Thur in Aug, starting at 10.00 and taking c 2 hours. (Tickets obtainable from the Tourist Information Office in Kalundborg.)

Large and comfortable DSB ferries sail regularly and quickly from Kalundborg to **Århus** (Rte 14). From Kalundborg, too, you can take a ferry to the island of **Samsø**, which produces the first eagerly awaited new Danish potatoes in the springtime.

8   Århus to Roskilde via Ebeltoft

Total distance 134km plus ferry. A15 to (29km) Rønde.—A21 to (22km) **Ebeltoft**.—A21 to (4km) Ebeltoft Ferry Terminal.—Ferry to *Sjællands Odde* (1hr 40 mins).—A21 to (80km) **Roskilde**.

The direct route from Århus to Rønde takes you on the A15, allowing you occasional glimpses of the sea. At 16km you by-pass *Løgten*, where there is a six-sailed windmill, and a further 13km will see you in Rønde.—The more interesting route (36km) takes you inland, via the manor of Rosenholm.

Follow the A15 N, but only for 18km, to a point just beyond Løgten, where you turn left on the 587 to (1km) the 563, which then takes you to (3km) *Hornslet* (Tourist Information: Tingvej 16).

For centuries this area has been deeply influenced by the Rosen-krantz family, and they have left their mark on the imposing *church, approached through a decorative Renaissance gateway. The earliest known reference to a church here is from 1310, but there is believed to have been one on the spot since the 9C. The central part of the nave is still part of the Romanesque building. Extensions took place in the following century, when the porch was added. In 1560 the Romanesque chancel was demolished and the nave was extended E. Later additions were the elegant tower and the Rosenkrantz family's sepulchral chapel to the S.

There are some very old, but very fine, frescoes from c 1250 on the N wall; their motifs include a castle under attack and also, unique in Denmark, a scene from the legend of Parsifal. The altarpiece is from c 1525, and Claus Berg's centre panel from c 1530 is a splendid and imaginative depiction of Golgotha. It is flanked by English alabaster reliefs from c 1450.—Many members of the Rosenkrantz family are buried in the church, which consequently is provided with many ornate gravestones and memorials. A major restoration took place in 1963.

2km N of Hornslet stands the manor of ***Rosenholm**, the Rosen-krantz family seat and one of the most splendid and best-preserved of Danish Renaissance mansions. It was begun in 1559 by Jørgen Rosen-krantz, and has retained its outer appearance almost unaltered since 1600. There are four wings surrounded by a moat.

It is still the home of the Rosenkrantz family, but it is open from mid-Jun to mid-Aug. The furnishings belong to all the different periods during which it has been the family home and include large-scale French and Flemish tapestries and Spanish and Moorish furniture. The large gardens, with their avenues and walks, were designed in the 18C. The Renaissance pavilion from the end of the 16C, known as *Pirkentavl*, is said in fun to be known locally as the first Jutland university, owing to the private academy for the nobility once run there by the rather unorthodox 17C theologian Holger Rosenkrantz. There is a small museum in the cellar, filled with pottery and various objects retrieved from the moat.

Leave Rosenholm by the minor road just opposite the manor and drive to (2km) *Mørke*, where there is one of the largest medieval churches in Djursland (i.e. the peninsula NE of Århus), dating back to the 12C. The chancel and nave are both Romanesque, as is the very old granite font, and some particularly interesting features are the granite carvings on the S side; above the entrance there is a stone decorated with interlacing patterns like those found in Jelling (Rte 21), and there are two figures of dragons, one of them apparently eating a man lying beneath it.—The parsonage in Mørke is a beautiful half-timbered house.—The marshes, just to the W, are full of wildlife.

A road E will now take you to (5km) *Thorsager*, where, occupying a commanding position at the top of a steep hill, you will find the only round church in Jutland, thought to have been built by Valdemar II —though like that in Horne on Fyn it has suffered from 19C extensions and improvements.

From Thorsager another minor road leads S to (5km) *Rønde* (Tourist Information: Ceresvej 2).

From Rønde, there is a choice of routes to Ebeltoft—the direct route (19km) via the A21, or the alternative, coastal route (38km; see below).

DIRECT ROUTE FROM RØNDE TO EBELTOFT (total distance 19km). The direct route keeps you mainly on the A21. It is fairly fast, but the countryside you drive through is beautiful and varied, moorland and hills with fine views across the sea after passing through Egsmark.

Follow the A21 E from Rønde as far as (4km) Bjødstrup, where you should turn right down a minor road to (1km) **Møllerup**, a manor house with outbuildings dating back to 1681. The main wing was rebuilt in 1868 and the outbuildings are now partly used as a riding school, partly as a restaurant. The park is open to the public.

The original house is believed to have been built by Stig Andersen Hvide, the 13C folk hero Marsk Stig, who took part in the murder of King Erik Glipping in 1286. Marsk Stig's house was demolished when the new buildings were erected in 1681. Excavations in 1920 uncovered the foundations of the original house, which like the present one had three wings.

According to the medieval ballad, Marsk Stig was sent to fight for the king, whom he asked to take care of his wife while he was away. The king did so only too thoroughly, and when he returned, Marsk Stig was greeted by a sorrowful wife, Ingeborg, who told him what had happened and demanded revenge. Marsk Stig then murdered the king, announced the murder according to the custom of the day, and was outlawed for his pains. (The tiny island of Hjelm, where he spent the rest of his life, is some 4km off the mainland coast, and can be seen as you sail from Ebeltoft.) Møllerup is specifically mentioned in the ballad as the place where Marsk Stig returned to tell his wife of their fate.

Leaving Møllerup, following the same road E, after 1.5km you will meet the A21 again. Here you turn right and drive to (13km) Ebeltoft (see below).

ALTERNATIVE ROUTE FROM RØNDE TO EBELTOFT—THE COASTAL ROUTE (total distance 38km). This route takes you on a good unclassified road S from Rønde through wooded, hilly countryside to (2km) Kalø. On your right you will find the archetypal romantic ruined castle, King Erik Menved's **Kalø Slot** from 1314, outlined against the sea, standing isolated and inaccessible except on foot (open).

The castle stands on a tiny islet approached by a 500m-long medieval cobbled causeway with a drawbridge giving access to the square courtyard. The tower, 10m high and 12m square and with walls 3m thick, is now the best preserved part of the original complex, though there are remains of walls and some cellars. The original castle was dismantled on the orders of King Christoffer II, the brother of Erik Menved, but it was presumably rebuilt by Valdemar IV. In 1519 the future King of Sweden, Gustav Vasa, was held prisoner there by Christian II, but he escaped to lead Sweden in its breakaway from the union between the two countries. In 1672 Christian V gave the castle to his half-brother Ulrik Frederik Gyldenløve, the first husband of Marie Grubbe, who dismantled much of it and transported it to Copenhagen in order to build the palace of Charlottenborg (Rtes 3,4).

On the other side of the main road lies *Kalø Hovedgård*, the home farm originally belonging to the castle. The present half-timbered buildings are from the first half of the 18C. It is now used as a training school for hunters and as a biological research station.

From Kalø you drive S along the coastal road with magnificent views across Kalø Bay to (9km) *Knebel*, where there is a Romanesque/Gothic church restored by Axel Skov in 1956. The altarpiece was plundered from the Swedes some 300 years ago.

In Knebel, too, there is a memorial to the people of the Mols peninsula, the 'Molboer', the Danish equivalent of the English Wise Men of Gotham, about whose proverbial lack of intelligence many amusing stories have been told since the 18C. The water in the inlet here, Knebel Vig, is very deep, and afforded a safe harbour for medieval warships.

Just outside Knebel, on a road NE towards Agri, you will find the 4000-year-old *Postkær Stenhus*, one of the largest of Danish stone circles, consisting of 23 standing stones (some as high as 2m) enclosing a pentagonal chamber.

Leave Knebel on a minor road running S and then W along the coast of this varied and fascinating peninsula to (4km) *Tved*, where there is a mainly Romanesque church built largely of undressed boulders, which have been described as being 'of a strange barbaric beauty'. The walls in the W are extremely thick, suggesting that they were once meant as the foundations for a never-completed tower. It contains some well-preserved frescoes from the mid-16C, restored in 1942. The nearby parsonage is a beautiful half-timbered house and outbuildings.

If you drive a further 4km S from Knebel you will come to the imposing mansion of *Iisgård*, built in 1890, close to the mound upon which the original medieval mansion stood. You are in fact now at the tip of one of the forelands of the *Mols peninsula*, with views W towards Århus and SE to another of the forelands, Helgenæs. Like the entire Mols peninsula, the landscape here is undulating moorland, rising to almost 80m at its highest point.

Back in *Tved* the route takes you E to (4km) *Vistoft*, where the Romanesque/Gothic church was restored in 1942 by Axel Skov.

From Vistoft you can, if you wish, turn S and drive across the isthmus to the *Helgenæs* peninsula, again offering extensive views in virtually all directions. At the narrowest point of the isthmus there is a medieval wall, which a doubtful tradition maintains was built by Marsk Stig. Beyond it again there are some 19C entrenchments dating from the Dano-Prussian war of 1848.

Again, the terrain is very uneven, rising to 53m at *Høghøj* in the S. It is here that Saxo maintains that King Harald Bluetooth and his son Svend Forkbeard fought a bitter but inconclusive duel, and where King Harald was then murdered by his archer warrior Palnatoke in revenge for having been forced by the king to shoot an apple off his own son's head. It was in the waters off Helgenæs, too, that Magnus the Good defeated Svend Estridsen in 1044.

If you decide not to take a look at Helgenæs, from Vistoft you should drive E through Fuglsø and follow the glorious road right round *Ebeltoft Vig* (Bay) to (15km) Ebeltoft itself.

Driving along you will have views across the bay, and on your left is the *Mols Bjerge*, one of the more idiosyncratic areas of Denmark formed during the last Ice Age. Like other places called mountains in Denmark, they scarcely merit the name, but admittedly the terrain does rise to 120m just N of Fuglsø and, at *Agri Bavnehøj*, even to 137m—though this is too far from your present route to be seen. There are, meanwhile, several roads leading off the coastal road, and they will take you further into this moorland and woodland area, with its varied animal and plant life. There are excellent parking facilities. At all events, the Mols Bjerge are a wild moorland region, with gorse bushes everywhere; it is excellent walking country. A detailed plan of the area, showing marked paths, is available from tourist offices. Spend a little time here; the views can be quite stupendous.

***Ebeltoft** (4000 inhab.; Tourist Information: Torvet 9–11) lies on a natural, sheltered harbour, and this is presumably the reason for its having been established here in the Middle Ages.

Ebeltoft was granted a charter in 1301 by King Erik Menved, possibly as a sign of gratitude for its help against the outlaws living on the island of Hjelm nearby. Little is known of its medieval history, though there is a reference to the church there in 1458.

It suffered severely during the 17C wars with Sweden, and after some recovery of its shipping it lost most of its gains during the Great Northern War (1700–21) and went into a period of stagnation from which it was long in recovering. Attempts to build a new harbour were successful for a time, but it was not until the 19C that better times really came. The local mayor then borrowed church funds (without permission) to build a new harbour. The project was successful, though the mayor nevertheless lost his job over it.

Ebeltoft, the 'capital' of Mols, retains the atmosphere of an old market town. Photo: Lennard

Even in the 20C, however, growth in Ebeltoft has been modest in comparison with that in nearby Grenå, probably largely because the main railway system never reached Ebeltoft. Ironically, however, this lack of modern developments has led to Ebeltoft's special position as a tourist attraction offering a modern version of much that is traditional in a small Danish town, with cobbled narrow streets and a wealth of unspoiled old houses. And despite its apparent outlying position, it offers a car ferry terminal to Sjællands Odde and is thus a transit point for motorists wanting to travel between Jutland and Sjælland. Allow yourselves plenty of time to savour the charm of this now thriving Lilliput town.

Ebeltoft boasts the smallest town hall in the world, a single-storey half-timbered building topped by a small spire. It was built in 1576 and restored twice in the 18C and finally in 1909, when it was opened as the *Ebeltoft Folkemuseum*, mainly exhibiting furnishings and equipment from the locality, as well as archaeological and Siamese collections. The old lock-up lies beneath and is also open to the public.

If you walk down either Nedergade or Overgade, you will come to Kirkegade and *Ebeltoft Church*. It was referred to as a 'chapel' in 1458, but has since been extended. There are frescoes from 1521, discovered in 1919 and since restored.—The nearby old parsonage is now a doll museum, *Missers Dukkemuseum*, with a comprehensive collection of dolls and other old toys of many kinds (open summer).

In *Overgade* there is a large, well-preserved merchant's house, and there are others in *Adelgade*, one of them having an outside gallery in the courtyard. However, it is the general atmosphere of an old provincial town, with its many small houses, many now scheduled, which constitute the main attraction of Ebeltoft. You will perhaps not find many imposing houses, but you will move into a past age. And that is emphasised, if you happen to spend the night there, by the presence of town 'watchmen', who patrol the streets and at intervals sing out the old watchmen's rhymes telling the inhabitants what time it is and assuring them that all is well.

You will inevitably go down to the harbour, where you will find the frigate 'Jylland', launched in 1860. After many years of being left to rot, this fine old man-of-war is now restored to its former glory (open).

At Strandvejen 8 there is a *glass museum*, with a large collection of modern glass. A glassworks has been established at the side of it, and visitors can watch glass blowers demonstrate their skills (open summer).

ROUND TRIP TO THE AREA NORTH-EAST OF EBELTOFT (total distance c 26km). This short trip starts on a minor road NE to (3km) **Dråby**. This delightful, idyllic village with its charming thatched cottages has an unexpectedly large 13C church with buttresses to the N and S, popularly known as *Mols Cathedral*.

One assumes that Dråby was once a harbour, and that the church originally belonged to the nearby *Skærsø* estate. This, at least, would account for the size of the church. To the E there is an apse, and to the W a slender and graceful stilted tower. There are frescoes from the 15C and 16C, some by the Isefjord Master. The rather bombastic baroque altarpiece, with life-size figures of SS. Luke and John, is from c 1700. The church was restored in 1967–70 by Inger and Johannes Exner.

In Dråby, too, you will find the manor farm of *Lyngsbækgård*. The main house, in what is known as Jutland baroque, was built in 1784, and the principal half-timbered outbuildings, now protected, are two years younger.

You leave on a minor road N which will take you through (3km) Stubbe, along the S side of Stubbe Sø (lake), through Gravlev to (5km)

Hyllested, again an unspoiled village with narrow streets and thatched cottages.

Hyllested Church has a wealth of frescoes from c 1500, those in the nave by the Brarup Master. They were not discovered until 1967, and they have been conserved as near as possible to their original state. They represent both biblical scenes and grotesque fantasy figures. Outstanding is the Brarup Master's painting of the Creation.

E of Hyllested stands the late 16C manor house of *Rugård* (1km). With its two towers and its fortress-like appearance, Rugård is slightly forbidding. It must certainly have been forbidding to local people in the days of one of its owners, Jørgen Arnfeldt (d. 1717). He was a fanatical witch-hunter, who on the slightest excuse rounded up women he suspected of witchcraft, and had them 'tried' in the lake outside the house. If they floated, they were rejected by the waters and thus guilty—and so burned or tortured to death in the cellars as soon as they were dragged out. If they sank, they were innocent—but much good did that do them!

From Hyllested you drive W to (3km) Fuglslev, where you bear left after the church to (2km) Øksenmølle. Now turn left again into a road which takes you the W side of Stubbe Sø and back to (10km) Ebeltoft.

DIRECT ROUTE TO ROSKILDE. Ebeltoft *ferry terminal* (Færgehavn) is c 4km S of Ebeltoft. Here, apart from one of the shortest ferry routes between Jutland and Sjælland, you will find a large windmill park jutting out into the sea. And nearby is the holiday village, *Øer Maritime Ferieby*, with some 300 holiday cottages offering first-class accommodation and splendid facilities for 2400 visitors. The village has been built on an artificial saltwater lake which is entered via a lock.

The crossing to Odden on Sjælland takes only 1hr 40mins.

Odden Ferry Terminal is right at the tip of the narrow spit of land on the NW corner of Sjælland, known as *Sjællands Odde* (Sjælland Point). It is a low-lying area covered with weekend cottages, but otherwise with few salient features. On the other hand it has its historical significance.

7km along the A21 from the harbour, you will come to *Overby*, where you might want to make a short stop.

The waters around Odden were the site of a naval battle between the pride of the Danish navy, the 'Prins Christian Frederik', and a British naval squadron in 1808, when Denmark and Britain were on opposing sides during the Napoleonic Wars. It was a one-sided battle, which the Danish ship lost; it blew up and sank with the loss of 64 sailors and 129 wounded. The hero of the battle was a 25-year-old lieutenant, Peter Willemoes, who has become famous in Danish history.

In Overby the dead from the battle are buried in a common grave, and there are other memorials to the Battle of Sjælland Point. A model of the 'Prins Christian Frederik' hangs in the church, and the names of those killed are inscribed on oak panels. A memorial column by Thorvaldsen's pupil Vilhelm Bissen stands in the churchyard, inscribed with a poem by N.F.S. Grundtvig, whose father was pastor here from 1766–76.

The church itself has an early Gothic nave, with late Gothic extensions. Ironically, perhaps, three British airmen from World War II are also buried in the churchyard.

Now continue E along the A21 to (7km) Lumsås, from where you might make a DETOUR by turning off left to visit (10km) Nykøbing Sjælland and its surroundings.

Nykøbing (5200 inhab.; Tourist Information Algade 52) is full of tourists in summer, attracted by the wonderful beaches in the area, but it also has other things to offer. In Kirkestræde there is the *Museum*, with excellent collections of local historical interest; its gardens are themselves a museum, full of medicinal herbs (open summer).—2km S, near the coast road, you will find *Annebjerg*, where there is a museum exhibiting antique glass and Chinese porcelain (open summer).—A further 3km will bring you to *Sommerland Sjælland*, a large-scale pleasure park with all kinds of family entertainment.

Instead of driving back through Nykøbing, from Annebjerg you can head W, cross the 225 and drive to (5km) **Højby** to experience the impressive and high-lying church there for the sake of its magnificent Gothic frescoes. They are from c 1380 and of very high quality indeed, portraying Judgement Day, the voyage of St. Olaf, St. George and the Dragon, and the martyrdom of St. Stephen. The bench ends in the church are from 1555 and are splendidly carved, and the altarpiece is a triptych from c 1630. The pulpit is from 1656.

Now drive another 4km W and you are back on your main route again.

If you decide not to visit Nykøbing, you follow the A21 S from Lumsås, perhaps taking a look at the double passage grave known as the *Troldstuer* after 1km, on your left.—2km further S, also on your left, you will find a road leading off to *Stenstrup* (1km), where you might visit the excellent ethnological museum containing many of the archaeological finds from the area here which is unusually rich in prehistoric monuments (open summer).

Still following the A21 S you will soon find yourself in *Trundholm Mose* (Trundholm Marsh), an area full of burial mounds. It is here the famous Early Bronze Age Sun Chariot ('Solvognen') was discovered in 1902. Now one of the great treasures of the National Museum, this represents a horse (the earliest model of a horse found in Denmark) pulling a six-wheeled chariot on which stands a gold-plated bronze disc representing the Sun. The wheels are themselves of particular interest in being the earliest known example of spoked wheels in Denmark. The Sun Chariot is thought to be a model of a full-sized chariot of similar nature, and is a clear indication of sun worship in Bronze Age Denmark. It was presumably deliberately broken and sunk in the marsh as a sacrifice. The marsh had been drained by 1902, and the chariot was turned up by a plough.

10km S of Lumsås you will reach the 225, and here there is an opportunity for an interesting DETOUR, 17km out and 17km back again.

Leave the A21 and follow the 225 W which takes you along the coast through hilly countryside to *Høve* (8km), where there is a lively modern museum illustrating the development of this area over the ages. Continue now to **Fårevejle** (4km). Here there is a museum (open summer) showing the history of the stretch, known as the Lammefjord, which was drained at the end of the 19C by the construction of an embankment across the narrowest point of the fjord. Much of the fertile land thus uncovered is below sea level. The museum also contains exhibits associated with the Earl of Bothwell, the third husband of Mary Queen of Scots, who was imprisoned in the nearby Dragsholm Castle (see below), and who is buried in *Fårevejle Church*. A mummified body in the church is said to be his, though this is by no means certain.

To see *Dragsholm Castle*, you follow the 225 another 4km S, turning left 1km after you have passed the 231. Standing 1km away from the main road on what was once a narrow spit of land, the only link between Odsherred to the N and the remainder of Sjælland, it dates from 1250, and once belonged to the Bishop of Roskilde. After the Reformation the bishop was forcibly turned out, and the king put his own lieutenant in. Later, Dragsholm became a prison for State prisoners, of whom the most famous was the Earl of Bothwell. He died here. During the Swedish wars Dragsholm was badly damaged, but it was rebuilt at the end of the 17C and given more the character of a baroque palace, the appearance it now has. Today the castle is an hotel and restaurant, but some of the historic rooms, the cellars and the park are open to visitors on application.

11km after crossing the 225 the A21 brings you to the embankment across the *Lammefjord*. Old maps show that the Lammefjord used to stretch almost across to the west coast, virtually dividing Odsherred off as a separate island.

As part of the campaign to make up for the territory lost to Germany after the 1864 war the work of building the 2km-long embankment across the narrow part of the fjord was begun in 1873. This, together with a system of drainage canals, led by 1907 to the water level having dropped by 4.8m, and by 1943 by 7.5m, providing a huge cultivable area (5764 hectares), most of it of high quality soil. If you stop on the embankment and go to the top of the sea wall, you will gain some impression of what has been achieved.

4km after crossing the embankment, you will come to the small manor house of *Hagestedgård*. Former owners have doubtless been partly responsible for building the fair-sized Romanesque *Hagested Church* nearby. It still has Romanesque features, not least the many early 13C frescoes in the apse and chancel.

4km later you are on the outskirts of the village of *Tuse*, where there is a whitewashed church dating back to Romanesque times, though with many Gothic features. This church is particularly interesting for its very fine frescoes from the Isefjord Master's workshop, extending from the childhood of Christ to the Day of Judgement. The Three Kings are seen confronting three skeletons, while a girl churning butter is mocked by two devils. There is, too, a particularly graphic representation of other devils chasing people into Hell.

From Tuse you continue E, and in only 6km reach **Holbæk** (21,000 inhab.; Tourist Information: Nygade 8). This is one of the oldest towns in Sjælland, with charters going back at least until the end of the 13C, by which time it was the seat of a Dominican monastery. It probably grew up around a castle built by Valdemar II (the mound on which it stood is still visible to the W of the town, near the shore), and owed its original success to the fact that the small medieval ships could sail into its harbour without difficulty.

It maintained its position until the late 17C, but then suffered from the Swedish wars, and only began to make progress again with the increase in the corn trade in the late 18C. The 19C brought industry, and Holbæk's geographical position on the railway between Copenhagen and Kalundborg has maintained its economic strength.

One of the unusual aspects of Holbæk is the width of its main street, *Algade*, quite unusual in Danish provincial towns and giving it a rather special atmosphere. There are still a few old houses to be seen in Holbæk, the best preserved of which, in Klosterstræde, is now the Holbæk Museum (founded 1910), standing next to the elegant old Town Hall from 1844. In the museum courtyard an old house from 1660 has been rebuilt after being removed there from its original position close to the harbour.—In the courtyard of *Algade 28* there is another two-storeyed half-timbered house dating partly from the Renaissance and partly from 1719. Other more modest half-timbered houses, mainly from the 18C and early 19C, are still extant. Nothing remains of the Dominican monastery except the remains of the old S wing, which now form the parish hall of the 19C *Sankt Nicolai Kirke* which, unusually, stands N–S. The hall was partially rebuilt and used as a mortuary chapel, but it was restored in 1972–74 and put to its present use.

The *Museum** in Klosterstræde, which is part of a complex of old buildings dating from 1660 to 1667, contains no fewer than 51 exhibition rooms and as one of the best of Danish provincial museums, is well worth a visit, both for the very special atmosphere created by these old buildings, and for its excellent collections. There are re-creations of old rooms and shops and exhibits reflecting the development of the area from prehistoric times to the German Occupation. Of particular interest is the collection of pottery and silver.

A museum of a different kind is the *Zone Museum* in Skyttensvej 2, just to the W of the town centre. Zonen was the name of an ambulance, fire and rescue service which finally joined its former rival, Falck, to form the present Falck-Zonen, which operates all Danish emergency services, including ambulances. This museum is in the form of an emergency station from the 1930s and includes both vehicles and equipment (open school holidays).—Just S of the town, on the grounds of what used to be Holbæk Castle home farm, there is now a *nature school* in the midst of a varied forest area and animal reserves.

While in Holbæk, the church at **Tveje Merløse** 3km S on the A57 should really not be missed. It is one of the more unusual Danish village churches, dating from c 1125, and probably built by the same Asser Rig who built the church at Fjenneslev (Rte 2). The Romanesque character has been preserved, with windows with rounded arches, but the most notable feature is the twin towers, again reminiscent of Fjenneslev. Unlike Fjenneslev, however, this church is more or less in its original form, and is thus unique in Sjælland. There are frescoes from c 1200 in the apse, and the altarpiece is by Joakim Skovgaard.

We suggest that instead of taking the direct road from Holbæk to Roskilde, you follow an unclassified road E through Tjebberup and past *Eriksholm*, an elegant neo-classical mansion, built in 1788. It is not open to the public, but can be seen from the wooded countryside through which the road passes. At 8km you will cross Bramsnæs Bay on the *Munkholm Bridge*, opened in 1952.

On the far side, on the left, you will see the 18C *Langtved Færgekro* (Langtved Ferry Inn), echoing the time when it was necessary to be ferried across the straits here. It is a place with literary associations, both the mid-19C poet Christian Winther and the later 19C novelist Henrik Pontoppidan having been associated with it, while the surrounding area is scattered with burial mounds and kitchen middens.

It is worth stopping here, to admire the fine view and to walk through the forests with their prehistoric remains, while short drives in various directions will bring you to idyllic and unspoilt villages. Take, for instance, the 53 road N to (2km) Ejby and another 3km to *Kirke Hyllinge*, where the chancel arch in the church is decorated by the oldest known fresco on Sjælland. Drive 4km further N on the 53, turning right on a minor road past the mansion of Krabbesholm to (2.5km) *Gershøj*, with its healing spring. Here the road goes S through *Sæby* (with its idyllic parsonage) and then right along the coast through Lyndby, finally joining the A21/23 to (23km) Roskilde.

If you choose not to take this detour, but to continue along the road E after Bramsnæs Bay, you proceed past Ryegård Deer Park. At the far edge of the wood, some 3km beyond the bridge the road passes the late 19C mansion of *Ryegård*, with a history going back to 1350.

After another 4km you join the motorway to (13km) **Roskilde** (Rte 2).

9   Rødbyhavn to Ringsted

Total distance 112km. 153 to (18km) **Maribo**.—To (9km)
Sakskøbing.—(28km) **Vordingborg**.—A22, unclassified roads, 265 to
(32km) **Næstved**.—A14 to (25km) **Ringsted**.

Rødbyhavn, established when the old ferry port of Rødby found itself
5km from the coast with the draining of Rødby Fjord in the 1930s, is
the port of entry to Denmark on arriving from the German port of
Puttgarden. You are on the island of *Lolland*, one of the flattest parts
of Denmark (the highest point in South Lolland is only 22m). Some of
the island is below sea level, and there are 60km of dykes to keep out
the sea. It is an agricultural region famous for its beet crops. At the time
of the Valdemars the region was the target of raids by the Slavic
Wends, and some placenames (e.g. *Kramnitze*) still record their presence. In a later age, in the 19C and 20C, there was an influx of Polish
workers eager to take part in the beet harvests. They, too, have left
their mark.

You leave Rødbyhavn on the 153 and drive to (5km) **Rødby** (2600
inhab.; Tourist Information: Vestergade 1), where there is now little to
show that it was a thriving ferry harbour for centuries. Indeed, there is
little to indicate its age, as it suffered from a series of fires in the 18C,
that of 1774 leaving only five houses standing. A century later, in 1872,
Rødby suffered further devastation from catastrophic flooding. Apart
from a warehouse on the corner of *Østergade* and *Sædingevej*, there
is hardly anything from before the 19C, except the carefully restored
half-timbered *Willers Gård* in Vestergade, from 1729. In Vestergade,
too, there is the old excise booth from 1690. The elegant town hall is
from 1853.

Rødby experienced a period of growth in connection with the opening
of the direct route to Germany in 1963, and in 1981 it was able to
celebrate its 750th anniversary by erecting a fountain in the market
place symbolically representing wild geese resting on their way.

From Rødby there are two routes to Sakskøbing: the direct route (23km)
via Maribo, or the alternative route via Nysted (47km), which takes
you through charming countryside (see below).

DIRECT ROUTE TO SAKSKØBING VIA MARIBO (total distance 23km). Just
2km N of Rødby, on the 153, you drive through *Sædinge*, a village in
which the Brarup Master has been responsible for the frescoes in the
church. Then drive 2km N, to follow the 297 E to visit *Holeby* (3km),
where the area's first sugar beet factory was built. It still stands, though
it is now a paper mill. On Højbygårdvej you will find, too, a museum,
Polakkasernen, illustrating the work of the Polish girls who used to
come annually to take part in the beet harvest (limited opening,
summer). Beet harvesting may not sound particularly romantic, but it
must be appreciated that beet and the sugar produced from it have
had an inestimable significance for this part of Denmark.

Højbygård manor, which was the site of some of the earliest attempts
to produce beet sugar at the end of the 19C, stands 2km S of Holeby.
It dates back to c 1400, though the present buildings are from 1761.
Note the huge granary.

Back on the 153 you drive direct N to (9km) the beautiful and historical
town of **Maribo* (5468 inhab.; Tourist Information: Torvet 1A), situated
on the narrow neck of land linking two lakes, Nørresø and Søndersø,

around which there are now footpaths for those wanting a delightful walk.

Maribo has grown up around a Bridgettine convent founded in 1416 by King Erik of Pomerania at the wish of his mother, Queen Margrethe I. Queen Margrethe had herself been brought up by the daughter of St. Bridget of Sweden, and it had been her wish to create a Danish equivalent to Vadstena, the home of the Bridgettine Order. The religious centre was constructed according to a vision of St. Bridget, and was to provide a monastery to the S and a convent to the N. The monks and nuns were to be strictly segregated. The galleries used by the nuns to separate them from the monks and the congregation still exist in the church, which has had the status of Maribo Cathedral since 1809.

The convent was not closed at the Reformation, and the last Catholic nun did not die until the 1570s, after which the convent became a Lutheran 'adelig jomfrukloster', i.e. a religious house providing accommodation for the unmarried daughters of the nobility. These particular daughters frequently caused scandals, and the king had the establishment closed in 1624. The church belonging to it became the parish church of Maribo. The convent buildings continued in existence for some time, and Leonora Christina, the imprisoned daughter of Christian IV, after her release from Copenhagen Castle in 1685, was allowed to live in it until her death in 1698. She is now buried in the Cathedral, and her minute coffin is visible through a window in the crypt (lit by a clearly indicated switch nearby).

The ***Cathedral**, with a lofty main nave 60m long and two almost equally lofty aisles, was built 1410–70, and is unusual in that the choir is in the W, according to the wishes of St. Bridget. The vaulted roof is supported by a series of octagonal columns. The original tower was demolished in 1736, but the remainder of the Cathedral has retained much of its original character, not least thanks to a careful restoration carried out in the 1860s. A particular treasure is a late 14C painting representing St. Bridget herself. It is thought to be the oldest extant painting on canvas in Scandinavia, but has suffered greatly from the ravages of time and is kept in the dark. Permission to view can, however, be obtained. A few remains of the convent and monastery are to be seen to the S of the Cathedral. A further relic from Bridgettine days is the fact that the Cathedral bells are rung six times daily.

Outside the area associated with the Cathedral there are some well-preserved tiny old houses which are still in use, some dating back to the end of the 18C. On the town square, *Torvet*, there is the splendid *Quades Gård* from 1825, a town house with a dignified neo-classical façade. There, too, is the old town hall from the 1850s. Close by, in Jernbanegade 22, is *Lolland-Falsters Stiftsmuseum* (Diocesan Museum), with extensive historical and archaeological collections, not least a room dedicated to the story of the Polish beet pickers, who once were an annual feature of Lolland. It also contains a collection of 13C crucifixes.—Jernbanegade 24 houses the *Lolland-Falster Art Gallery* with an extensive collection of Danish art, including many major works, from 1750 to the present day.—At Meinckesvej 4, beautifully situated behind *Bangshave*, the park behind the Cathedral, there is an open air museum, *Frilandsmuseet i Maribo*, exhibiting farm buildings from Lolland-Falster (open summer).

The poet and dramatist Kaj Munk was born in a house on the market square. The actual house has given way to a supermarket, but there is a plaque in the wall commemorating him.—A statue to Kaj Munk stands to the right of the town hall.

A novel EXCURSION can be made from Maribo on the *Museumsbane*, a private railway, the oldest in Denmark, through 8km of idyllic scenery close to the Knuthenborg Safari Park (Rte 11) and nearby Bandholm (Rte 11) with its excellent yachting facilities.

3km E of Maribo in *Engestofte*, a Gothic church and a mansion are well worth a visit. The small church is surmounted by a ridge turret from 1660 and there is a N chapel from 1786, designed as a mortuary chapel and now used as a porch. The nave is in the shape of five sides of an octagon. The original lancet windows have been preserved on the NW wall, and the interior is covered by cross vaulting. There is an ornate triptych from c 1510, originally from Maribo Cathedral. The centre panel is dominated by the Virgin, crowned and carrying the child Jesus. She is surrounded by five angels, and flanked by two saints on either side. The main figures on the very beautiful side panels are those of St. Bridget and St. Clare.

Engestofte mansion has a history going back to 1393, but the present harmonious building in yellow and white is from 1805–07. Until 1967 the manor was in the ownership of the Wichfeld family, and in the church there is a memorial plaque to the Scottish-Irish wife of one of the last members of the family, Monica Wichfeld, (b. Massy-Beresford) who was active in the Danish Resistance movement and ended her days in a German prison in 1945.—In the woods nearby stands the half-timbered *Engestofte Hospital* from 1770; this was not a hospital in the modern sense, but rather a hospice, a home for the poor of the Engestofte estate.

From Maribo you follow the 153 and drive N to (9km) *Sakskøbing* (see below).

ALTERNATIVE ROUTE FROM RØDBY TO SAKSKØBING—VIA NYSTED (total distance 47km). You drive E from Rødby on an unclassified road to (4km) *Tågerup*, where the Romanesque/Gothic church on your left, in which the Romanesque window in the chancel has been reopened in modern times, has frescoes from three different periods—1425, 1450 and 1500. It is those by the Brarup Master in the vaulting of the nave that are of particular interest. In their portrayal of biblical scenes they show a striking realism: Adam is seen both in Paradise and, later, hard at work in the fields, while Eve is working with a distaff, surrounded by her children, one of them with a whip and top. A runestone bearing the inscription 'Åsten's sons raised this stone after their brother Spærle, Esbern Næb's skipper', lies outside the porch.

1km further brings you to *Lungholm manor*. Its history goes back to 1450, but the present imposing main wing is from 1857, standing between, unusually, two oblique side wings from 1639. It is now a large riding stable. It also offers a wolf park and museum, the only chance in Denmark to see wolves in (well-fenced-in) natural surroundings (open summer). The house itself is open for conducted tours.

Continue now through (2km) Errindlev, turning left after 1km to drive N past (2km) *Bremersvold manor* from 1802. 1km further N you will see on your left *Kærstrup*, a manor house standing behind a moat and with a history going back to the 12C. The present elegant building is from 1765, though it was considerably altered and spires added in 1836. The 297 is now a km further on, and here you turn right for after 9km later to follow the 283 to (14km) Nysted.

Surrounded by wooded countryside, **Nysted** (1500 inhab.; Tourist Information: Adelgade 65) is a delightful small coastal town, one of the smallest market towns in Denmark, with charters going back to 1409. As might be expected in a town of this kind, there are many old houses, often half-timbered, in streets which have kept much of their original character. In *Adelgade*, where many of the half-timbered houses are to be found, you will also discover a large, two-storeyed half-timbered warehouse. Where Adelgade enters *Torvet* the large early Gothic church (c 1300) stands, surmounted by an elegant lantern spire from 1649–50. At the N end of Ny Østergade the *old watertower* has now been transformed into an observation tower, offering magnificent views, and with exhibits on four floors as you go up (open Jun–Aug).

A main attraction in Nysted is Aalholm Castle with the **Aalholm Automobile Museum**, one of the biggest in Europe, with some 300 vintage cars exhibited in four large halls. The collection includes some very rare models, all carefully restored to pristine condition (open summer; limited opening winter). Here, too, a vintage railway train from 1850 will take you on a 20-minute ride through the park and along the coast.

Aalholm Castle itself (open summer) is first mentioned in 1329, though its origins probably go much further back. Valdemar IV is known to have stayed here, as did several later monarchs. The present imposing though rather forbidding building, said to be one of the oldest inhabited castles in Europe, certainly contains sections surviving from the 14C, though other parts reflect 19C alterations. Parts of it have been turned into a museum reflecting the way of life over the centuries and including not only elegantly furnished rooms and fine works of art, but also the old kitchen area. Or you might visit the cellar where King Kristoffer II was imprisoned in 1332. And do not forget the 'Secret', the early toilet conveniently placed over the moat.

Countess Amalie Raben of Aalholm was one of the great inspirations for the 19C poet Emil Aarestrup, who lived in Adelgade from 1827 to 1838 as the local doctor. It was to her he wrote some of his finest love poems. Others he wrote to his wife, with whom he had 12 children.

From Nysted an unclassified road leads N through (3km) *Kettinge*, where there is an old Dutch mill and a bird park (both open summer). From there the 297 takes you to (2km) Frejlev, from where you might like just to drive 4km further E to visit the delightful *Frejlev Skov*, the most southerly beech forest in Denmark, with many prehistoric monuments.

3km NE of Frejlev you will come to the mansion of *Fuglsang*, built in 1869 and now a 'refugium', an institution owned by the Danish church, and open to anyone wanting to spend a minimum of four days for study or retreat or, simply, holidays.

2km later take a minor road left to (2km) *Toreby*. The enormous church here, the biggest village church on the islands of Lolland and Falster, has a history which can be traced back to the early 11C, when there was a wooden church here. Then a stone apse was fixed, and extension after extension was built in the 13C, 14C and 15C, resulting in the present impressive building.

Now take the A9 W, arriving in 7km at the village of *Radsted*, where the large Romanesque/Gothic church has for centuries been associated with the owners of *Krenkerup*, which you will find 1.5km off the main road just opposite the church. This is an early 16C mansion which has retained most of its original character. The oldest part is the E end of the N wing, probably from c 1500, while the rest was added by the powerful Chancellor Mogens Gøye, who died in 1544. There were alterations to the exterior in the 19C. Krenkerup is not open to the public, but can clearly be seen from the W.

From Radsted it is only 3km to Sakskøbinq.

Sakskøbing (4750 inhab.; Tourist Information: Torvegade 4) is an old town surrounded by wooded countryside and standing by an ancient ford. Its position made it an important traffic centre in the Middle

Ages; now an important centre for the sugar beet industry and the site of a large modern sugar refinery. There is a pleasing market square with a bronze statue (1940) by Gottfred Eickhoff representing two Polish beet pickers, while in the park in front of the church there is a bronze statue by Lise Ring: 'Girl with Umbrella'.—The heavily rebuilt church dates back to the 13C and contains a pre-Reformation altar-piece and a finely carved pulpit from 1620.

Of the old buildings in Sakskøbing, one of the finest is the 18C *Wichmanns Gård* in Torvegade. Also in Torvegade, in what is now a bank, there is a memorial to one of Sakskøbing's most famous residents, the mid-19C poet Emil Aarestrup. He is remembered today for his elegant love poems, often humorous, and sometimes daringly erotic for the time.

On the S outskirts of the town, you will find an amusing *watertower*, in which the head-like shape of the upper portion has been exploited to provide a smiling face surmounted by a hat (open).—A road NW leads 4km to the mansion of *Orebygård*, its towers rising majestically above the fjord and clearly reminiscent of Frederiksborg Castle (Rte 6). The park is open to the public.

From Sakskøbing you drive NE along the 153, turning left after 2km to *Berritsgård* (1km), a dignified and well-preserved brick-built mansion from 1586, once the home of Arild Huitfeldt (1546–1609), Chancellor and the author of an important early history of Denmark. Adjoining the main house there is a huge barn from 1789. Note the avenue stretching in a straight line due N from the house to the *Guldborg Sound*, 7km away.—Now drive back to the main road, turn left and proceed to the (10km) Guldborg Sound, which you cross by the 170m-long bascule bridge built in 1933–34. You are now on the island of *Falster*.

2km after the bridge you might turn right to *Brarup* (2km), where the Romanesque/Gothic church displays a wealth of frescoes. Those in the apse and chancel are from c 1300; those in the nave, covering all the wall space, date from the end of the 14C and are by the Brarup Master, who has been given his name from this church. The altarpiece is late Gothic, c 1450.

1km W of the 153, in **Kippinge**, is likewise an impressive historical church, crowned with a lofty lantern spire from 1701. This was one of the most important Danish places of pilgrimage in the Middle Ages, said to possess a relic of the Holy Blood. Consequently, it has been richly endowed, and still has some splendid furniture which was restored to its original colouring in 1928. In the chancel there are frescoes from 1300–50. The exquisite auricular altarpiece was richly carved in 1633 by Jørgen Ringnis, who was also responsible for the auricular pulpit two years earlier. There are two Gothic crucifixes, one from 1350, the other from 1400.

After the Reformation faith in the relic continued for some time, but it is thought then to have been destroyed, and a triptych from the late 15C representing the crowning of the Virgin became an object of veneration instead. This in its turn gave way to a holy spring nearby, St. Søren's Well, to which people travelled from afar, and which still exists. The significance of this shrine is confirmed by the fact that Christian IV's wife, Kirstine Munk, visited it in 1642—and was scolded by the king for kneeling before the altar, praying, he said, for his early death.

Continue now N on the 153, after 8km crossing the old *Storstrømsbro* (Storstrøm Bridge—Storstrøm being the name of the waterway crossed at this point). When it was opened in 1937 this 3.2km-long bridge was the longest in Europe—and the second longest in the world. It still carries both road and railway, but the carriageway is no longer sufficient for all the motor traffic across the water here, and so in 1985 the new Farø Bridges (Rte 10) were opened 5km to the E, carrying the E47/E55 motorway. The bridge will bring you to (3km) **Vordingborg**

(9000 inhab.; Tourist Information: Glambæksvej 3), on the island of Sjælland.

Thanks to the castle which used to stand here, Vordingborg is one of Denmark's major historical towns, with charters going back to 1415 and possibly beyond. It is to be supposed that the town of Vordingborg grew up around the royal castle which was founded at the time of Valdemar I. The site was strategically important, ideally suited to expeditions against the Wends, and a natural spot for the ferry between Sjælland and Falster. It was not, however, a geographical position favouring rapid development, and Vordingborg's role during the Middle Ages seems to have been limited.

It was the castle that was important. Exactly when it was founded is uncertain, but it certainly existed under Valdemar I and, judging by piles driven into the fjord to prevent enemy ships sailing in, it was fortified long before this. Valdemar II extended it, as did Valdemar IV. Both Valdemar I and Valdemar II died here, and Valdemar IV was buried in the castle chapel until Queen Margrethe I had his body taken to Sorø monastery chapel. It was Valdemar IV who built the Goose Tower, which is the only part of the castle now standing intact.

The castle was the scene of meetings of the Danehof State Council, and it was here that the greatest of the Danish medieval laws, the Jutlandic Law, was signed by Valdemar II in 1241. The first phrase of this Law, 'With law the land shall be built', is known to every Dane and adorns the façade of the old Law Courts in Copenhagen.

Vordingborg remained a small town throughout the Middle Ages, still deriving its main importance from the castle, where both Frederik II and Christian IV were in residence for a time. In the 17C it was enfeoffed to Prince Jørgen, the younger brother of Christian V. Prince Jørgen then married Princess Anne, the future Queen Anne of England. In this connection it is interesting to note that the music known in England as Purcell's Trumpet Voluntary is in Denmark known as Prince Jørgen's March! In 1655 the town was struck by the plague, and in 1658–60 it was totally plundered by occupying Swedish troops. In the 18C it became a garrison town (as it still is), but it was seriously damaged by a series of fires. It was not until the mid-19C that real growth occurred, thanks to the advent of the railway with the resultant easier access and the potential for industrial development. This trend was further helped by the building of the Storstrøm Bridge.

Very little remains of older buildings in Vordingborg. The old chemist's shop in *Algade* is from 1826, and there are old houses in *Riddergade*, opposite. The important 19C novelist Meir Aron Goldschmidt was born in Algade 133 in 1816 and is commemorated by a plaque on his home. (His novel 'A Jew' is partly set in Vordingborg.) The former *Town Hall*, from 1845, standing in Algade, is also a dignified neo-classical building, now used as a courthouse and lock-up.

It must, however, be the extensive ruins of the **Castle** which are the main attraction. It was once an enormous complex, and the outer walls, of which several stretches are still to be seen, extended over a total of 650m; there were eight towers, of which the **Goose Tower** still stands (open summer).

In the castle complex you will find the **Sydsjællands Museum**, part of which is in what was once Prince Jørgen's Castle. The museum's exhibits cover the prehistory and history of this area, the oldest being a 12,000-year-old spear and arrow heads. There are naturally many exhibits connected with the history of the castle and with the town's military history, together with others of ethnographical interest—a reconstruction of a peasant's living room, a collection of costumes, a display of craft implements. There is also a room dedicated to Goldschmidt. Likewise in the castle complex is a botanical garden with over 300 medicinal and culinary herbs.

The large **Vor Frue Kirke** church is Gothic, mid-15C, though the chancel may be from c 1400. There is a fresco of the Crucifixion on the chancel arch; both this and others discovered in the vaulting over the chancel are the work of the Helligtrekonger ('Three Kings') Master responsible for the Christian I Chapel in Roskilde Cathedral. The magnificent rood screen is from the same workshop. The ornate altarpiece, depicting the Crucifixion, is by Abel Schrøder from 1641, and the rather unusual Renaissance pulpit is from 1601. In the S aisle there is a late Gothic altar with a relief of St. Anne. Most of the bench ends are from the 1930s, but there are six from the 1590s.

There are some fine mansions in the Vordingborg area. If you take the A22 N, after 1km you will find, on your left, a road leading towards *Rosenfeldt* (1km). Much of the complex was built 1776–78, of bricks taken from the ruins of Vordingborg Castle, but the main Renaissance-style building, giving on to a grass-covered octagon surrounded by lime trees, is from 1868–69.—Having seen this, you should go further E along the curious *Knudshoved Odde* (Knudshoved Spit). It juts 15km out into the sea. You can only drive half-way along it, to a car park, but then you can walk to the end if you wish, with the sea lapping the land to either side. There are numerous prehistoric remains on the Spit.

1km NE of Vordingborg, just S of the A59, you will find *Iselingen*, built in the style of an Italian villa by a Swiss businessman in 1802, a spire being added in 1920.

You leave Vordingborg by the A22, making a short detour into the village of *Kastrup*, only 3km N of the town, to see the Romanesque church there. It is built of unhewn boulders, unusually asymmetrical in shape, and with walls varying enormously in thickness. Standing on high ground and dedicated to St. Clement, the patron saint of seafarers, it has retained two of its original windows in the N wall and one in the S wall. The altarpiece is late Gothic, c 1500, and there is an early Gothic (c 1300) crucifix as well as a great deal of other early church furniture.

Now drive N another 4km to a minor road E pointing towards (3km) Sværdborg. We suggest you leave the main road here and go across country.

In *Sværdborg* there is yet another *church* with some unique and fascinating frescoes. There is a host of them in the vaulting, including a primitive baptism, taking place in a barrel, and with God's hand raised in blessing and the Holy Spirit in the form of a dove swooping down to the spot where the font once stood. However, the really special ones are a series of apocalyptic pictures depicting the end of the world, showing the seas rising, the trees covered in red dew, towns and houses destroyed and fire devouring the entire Earth.

Follow this minor road through (2km) Lundby, turning right on the main road and then at the Romanesque church left to drive to (2km) *Lundbygård*, a manor given by the king in 1660 to one Svend Poulsen, better known as 'Gøngehøvdingen', in recognition of his determined (and bloody) opposition to the Swedes during the 1657–60 occupation. The present neo-classical main building of Lundbygård is from 1815, restored 1910 and 1943. The E wing is now a *museum* containing prehistoric exhibits found in the area.

After a left turn the road will bring you N to (2km) the main 265, where you turn left again and proceed to (5km) *Mogenstrup*. Here a sacred spring, St. Magnus' (i.e. Mogens') Well was once the scene of midsummer fairs; the Romanesque church contains good frescoes from c 1425, signed 'Martinus bene fecit'. Originally, as is common in this area, there was only one window in each wall of the nave; these original windows are bricked up now and have been replaced by others, but their outlines are still visible.

The road now continues to (10km) *Næstved** (38,250 inhab.; Tourist Information: Købmagergade 20A).

VORDINGBORG & GAVNØ

Næstved certainly goes back to the 12C. At the mouth of the Suså river (the longest in Sjælland) and on the intersection of important roads from Ringsted and Slagelse, it was ideally placed for the development of a market town. Its earliest surviving charter is from 1426, but there were earlier ones. A monastery was founded here in c 1200 (on the site just outside the present town now occupied by *Herlufsholm School*), and Næstved was of sufficient consequence for medieval kings to visit it regularly and for important negotiations to take place here. The loss of the monastery at the Reformation was a blow to the town, as was the Swedish occupation between 1657 and 1659. A Danish garrison was subsequently established here, bringing some financial advantages, but the real improvement only came in the 19C with the growth in agriculture and the development of industry thanks to the advent of the railway running from Køge to Vordingborg. Further growth came after 1930 when the present harbour was established, and now Næstved is the biggest town on Sjælland after Copenhagen.

Næstved is a garrison town, and the Royal Guard Hussars parade through the streets every Wednesday morning. Wednesday and Saturday are market days, and on Saturdays in June and July there is musical entertainment in the pedestrian precincts.

Næstved has grown up around the main square, *Axeltorv*, and it is in this area that the largest concentration of old buildings is to be found.

There are two churches, Sankt Peders and Sankt Mortens. **Sankt Peders Kirke**, standing on the square by the same name, is a large, imposing Gothic building 56m long and 20m high. The tower is 35m. In the E wall of this tower and in the N arcade of the nave there are traces of an earlier Romanesque church, of which nothing else remains. Unlike any other church in Denmark, the chancel is in the form of seven sides of a decagon, with lofty pointed windows and buttresses. Among the frescoes there is one of Valdemar IV and his Queen, Helveg, kneeling before the Trinity, presumably done soon after the king's death in 1375. A late Romanesque crucifix hangs beneath this. The choir stalls are from c 1500, while the carved pulpit from 1671 is one of the major works of Lorentz Jørgensen, with reliefs of Adam and Eve. The bench ends in the closed pews are from 1580, the work of a local Master.

Sankt Mortens Kirke is also Gothic and brick-built, but much smaller. This, too, is built on the site of an earlier Romanesque church, of which remains can be seen. There are frescoes showing St. Martin of Tours, the patron saint of the church, but the main glory of this building is the exuberant 6m-high auricular altarpiece from 1664, the work of Abel Schrøder, the organist in this church for 42 years, showing reliefs of the Passion, the Last Supper, the Crucifixion and the Resurrection. The panels are divided by twisted columns. The pulpit, from 1602, is thought to be the work of Abel Schrøder's father. There are pews for the local nobility, dated 1598, and there are other bench ends from 1577.

On the N side of *Sankt Peders Kirkeplads* square you will find the medieval *Town Hall*, the only one of that time extant in Denmark, the oldest part being from the first half of the 15C. The ornate gable overlooks the road.—Next to it on the left there is a beautiful half-timbered house from 1606, and on the right is *Gøyernes Gård* (The Gøye House), in which are incorporated the remains of a stone-built house from the 16C.

On the S side of Sankt Peders Kirkeplads there is a row of medieval brick-built houses. The oldest of them, *Gottschalk's House* (No. 8) dates from c 1400, and its W extension is from 1500. To the E of it are seven houses from 1482, probably shopkeepers' and artisans' houses, now known as *Mogens Thuesens Stenboder* (Mogens Thuesen's Stone Houses); two of them now form part of **Næstved Museum** (limited opening). The row ends in the E with the old grammar school, in which the early philologist and folklorist Peder Syv lived from 1659–64 as headmaster. In Kompagnistræde, just to the E, there is the 15C guildhall, *Kompagnihuset*, the only extant medieval guildhall in the country. It has recently been restored, but is not open to the public.

None of these, however, is the oldest building in Næstved. That honour goes to the old hospital, the **Helligåndshus** (The Holy Ghost House) on Ringstedgade, which is mentioned for the first time in 1398. It is now also part of Næstved Museum and houses excellent exhibitions of local history and handicrafts as well as a splendid collection of old carvings.—A further house to be viewed is the half-timbered **Apostelhuset** (The Apostle House) in Riddergade, so called because there are reliefs from 1520 of Christ and the twelve Apostles in the mullions between the windows of the façade. The house was originally a guildhall. There are other half-timbered houses here and in Møllegade, Vinhusgade, Østergade and Ringstedgade.

In *Hjultorv* square you will find a tiny equestrian statue, reputedly the smallest in Denmark, standing opposite the courthouse. Conversely, there is an enormous statue of a troll near the *Munkebakken* hill, representing the legend that a great troll once set out to bury Næstved in sand, and dropped it all outside the town.

On the outskirts of the town, to the NW, on Herlufsholm Allé, you will find **Herlufsholm School**. When the Benedictine monastery was closed after the Reformation, the buildings came into the ownership of Admiral Herluf Trolle who, together with his wife Birgitte Gøye, left the buildings to a trust as a school. It has since become one of the most distinguished of Denmark's ancient boarding schools, the school Chapel is open to the public from May to Sept and contains the largest ivory *crucifix in Europe, from 1230.—Herluf Trolle and Birgitte Gøye lie in sarcophagi behind the altar, and the historian Arild Huitfeldt is also buried here.

One of Denmark's great houses, **Gavnø**, is just outside Næstved. It is reached by driving S on the A22 to the S outskirts and then turning right through Appenæs to Gavnø (3km).

As the name suggests, Gavnø was originally an island, but it is now connected to the mainland by an embankment. In 1398 Queen Margrethe I acquired it and founded a Dominican convent. Part of it still exists in the present chapel. After the Reformation the nuns were allowed to live here as before, but on their deaths the convent was secularised and adapted for use as a private mansion. It was further modified in the late 17C and finally in 1755–58 transformed into the magnificent rococo house of today—which nevertheless still bears traces of its medieval origins.

The house contains what is said to be the largest private art collection in Scandinavia—over 2000 paintings. Among them are the oldest extant portraits in Scandinavia, dating from the 15C and painted on wood. Of particular interest, too, is the sumptuous panelled chapel from 1401, which has been developed from the medieval convent chapel. The carved altarpiece is by Abel Schrøder, 1670, and the main panel is framed by 44 coats of arms; a further 16 coats of arms form the framework to the top panel. The pulpit, standing on a headless troll with his face on his stomach, is also from the Schrøder workshop. It was partially restored in 1913, when repairs were carried out to the bench ends, many of which are from 1576 and 1651–53. One rarity is a bridal pew from the late 16C.

A major tourist attraction in the spring is also the *Park with a host of tulips and other bulbs.—An attraction of a different kind is the fire engine museum, also in the Park. Both the Park and the house are open to the public from 1 May to 31 Aug.

A trip out from Næstved along the 265 W will, after 7km, bring you to a fork. Take the left fork and drive to the delightful Karrebæksminde, or across the tiny bridge to Enø, both places providing you with marvellous bathing beaches.

The area E of Næstved also has its attractions. Leave on the A54 and drive as far as (7km) Holme-Olstrup; following the road left you pass Holmegård (2km), a mansion from 1635. This house, which is privately owned, has given its name to the parish and to the world-famous **Holmegård Glassworks**, 2km further on (open). Here you can see glass-blowing as well as the techniques of modern glass production. There is also a glass museum here and a shop where you can find good bargains.—You can now return to Næstved via (1km) Fensmark, where there is church from the time of Valdemar I. The 19C poet Christian Winther (1796–1876) was born in the idyllic parsonage here, as is recorded on a stone.

Leave Næstved on the A14, driving N to (14km) Herlufmagle, where there is a Gothic church with modern frescoes, and on to (9km) Vetterslev, where another splendid altarpiece from 1671 by Abel Schrøder is to be seen, as well as an auricular pulpit from 1628. While here, you should drive 3km NW to the village of Vrangstrup, where you will find one of the smallest and most unusual churches in Denmark, from c 1200. This asymmetrical but charming building bears many traces of its Romanesque origins. On the N side it has changed little since it was built, while on the S side a late medieval porch surmounted by a thatched ridge turret has been added. This church, too, possesses an altarpiece and pulpit by Abel Schrøder, as well as bench ends from 1550. And there is a host of late Gothic frescoes in the vaulting.

Now return to the A14 and continue to (6km) **Ringsted** (Rte 2).

10   Copenhagen to Gedser

Total distance 155km. 151 to (38km) **Køge**.—(53km) **Udby**.—E47/E55 to (40km) **Nykøbing Falster**.—E55 to (24km) Gedser.

It is possible to cover all this route on the E55, but we suggest other and more interesting routes. The trip to Køge is not exciting. You can either take the motorway E20/E47/E55 and drive S to Junction 31, turning off there at Jersie Strand and joining the 151 S. Or you can take the 151 all the way from Copenhagen and drive through the suburbs and ribbon development all the way to (38km) Køge. If you take the 151, however, you will drive past the grandiose project from 1980: *Køge Bugt Strandpark* (Køge Bay Beach Park), 6km of 'improved' beaches, with artificial lakes and facilities for bathing and boating.

Køge (30,000 inhab.; Tourist Information: Vestergade 1).

Køge originated as a village at the mouth of the river and near a suitable ford, close to the present-day Gammel Køgegård. It was established in its present position during the 13C, where it thrived on herring fishing and trade with Germany. King Erik Menved gave Køge a charter in 1288, and throughout the Middle Ages Køge was an important trading centre. A large church, Sankt Nicolai Kirke, was built in the 14C. In 1484 King Hans established a Franciscan monastery which existed until 1531, when the buildings became a hospital. In 1633 there was a great fire, and the town suffered further from Swedish occupation during the 17C Swedish wars. It was also the scene of one of the great Danish naval battles, the Battle of Køge Bay (1677).

Unlike many other Danish towns, Køge was spared further major fires, and thus still has many of its older buildings—there are said to be more half-timbered houses here than in any other Danish town except Ribe (Rte 15). It experienced a new period of growth in the 19C with the advent of the railways, and it now has a direct S-train connection to the capital, as a result of which it has attracted a great number of commuters in addition to its natural population.

The broad market square, *Torvet*, with its statue of Frederik VII, is the obvious place to start a tour of the town. The medieval whipping post, where the local prostitutes—referred to as 'Køge Hens'—were punished, is no longer there, but many of the older buildings are. The *Town Hall* has a neo-classical façade from 1803, but behind it there are buildings going back to 1552, making this the oldest town hall in the country still in use as such. To the left of it stands the old lock-up, which has now been incorporated into the complex. In the courtyard behind there is a fountain from 1979.

The building next to it is made up of two merchant houses with courtyards, from 1610 and 1619. It now houses the **Køge Museum**, a splendid collection, distributed through 30 rooms, of local antiquities. There are furnished rooms illustrating the style and manner of living of the area, costumes, furniture both ornate and simple, implements, coaches, and old coins—including selections of two very large hoards of silver coins discovered in 1978 and 1987, one weighing 35kg and thus the largest find of silver ever made in Denmark. Both hoards were presumably hidden from the occupying Swedes in the 17C.—Another important archaeological feature is the *Strøby Egede Grave*, a find made on the coast just SE of Køge. The grave from 4000 BC contained the skeletons of three adults and five children, the greatest number yet found in a grave of that age.—A literary curiosity is a windowpane taken from the nearby inn, *Norske Løve*, on which Hans Christian Andersen scratched the words: 'O God, O God, in Køge'.—Out in the courtyard there is a butcher's booth from c 1500, moved there from the Square, where it was in use until 1914.

Opposite the museum in the wall of the present Unibank there is a plaque commemorating the 'Køge House Cross'—a supposed visitation by the Devil which resulted in the burning of several witches in 1612.

Nørregade is the pedestrian shopping area, and the original character of many of the buildings is hidden behind modern shop windows. It illustrates the good general principle that one should keep one's eye on the upper storeys, where there are still plenty of signs of the original half-timber construction. No. 29, a former school building, is an art gallery of an unusual kind, *Køge Skitsesamling*, with sketches and models by some of Denmark's best younger artists.

The E end of the great **Sankt Nicolai Kirke*, Køge's main church, overlooks Nørregade. The church stands on the site of an earlier brick-built church from the first quarter of the 14C, some of which is incorporated in the tower to the W. This tower was long an important landmark, and it was used by Christian V to watch the Battle of Køge Bay. The main nave, vaulted and flanked by Gothic arcading and vaulted aisles on either side, is from 1375–1400. In the 15C there were some 15 side altars, none of which has survived. The choir loft is unusual in being decorated with a mixture of Evangelists, Muses and symbols of the Arts and Senses.

Køge church is one of the most richly furnished in the country, and the pulpit and canopy by Hans Holst from 1634 are probably the finest example of 17C Danish carving. The carved baroque altarpiece from 1652 by Lorentz Jørgensen is also among this master's most outstanding works. The black marble and porphyry font is from 1613, holding a dish of Nuremberg silver from 1635. There are both Gothic and Renaissance bench ends, but the main impression is made by the 104 magnificent baroque pews from 1624.—Over 150 tombstones are found in the church, more than in any other Danish church except Roskilde Cathedral (Rte 2).

If you leave the church by the main entrance you will come to *Kirkestræde*, where just to your left in front of the Library you will find the oldest datable half-timbered house in Denmark, with the year 1527 over the doorway. It now houses the children's library. Walking back through Kirkestræde towards Torvet you will find a whole row of old houses, including No. 13, *Smedegården*, with two 16C benches outside.

Now cross Torvet diagonally to *Brogade*, where there are yet more old half-timbered buildings, most of them again carefully restored. No. 7 is *Jensens Gård*, with storehouses in the yard; it has been carefully restored to give an idea of a complex of merchants' warehouses. The art gallery *Køge Galleri* is now housed here. No. 17 is *Langkildes Gård*, where the largest silver hoard was found, and No. 19 is *Hugos*

Gård, a 17C half-timbered house with a cellar from c 1300, now a wine bar.

The last road leading from Torvet, *Vestergade*, also contains some impressive buildings, of which the two-storeyed *Richters Gård* from 1644, now a restaurant, is outstanding.

There are many more old merchants' houses in Køge, and most of the courtyards are open to the public. The Tourist Information Office here organises guided tours of them in summer.

Now continue along Vestergade and cross the ring road. Some 200m beyond, on the left, you will find an old avenue leading to the mansion of *Gammel Køgegård*. Here you can park your car and walk the 500m right up to the house, which is private, but has a park open Wednesday, Saturday and Sunday afternoons. Turn right in the courtyard, walk another five minutes W and you will reach the beautiful wooded, as well as geologically interesting area, **Køge Ås** (Køge Ridge) containing the enclosed graveyard, *Claras Kirkegård*, with the tomb of Nicolai Frederik Severin Grundtvig. He lies there with his second wife, Anna Marie, who was the sister of the then owner of Gammel Køgegård.

From Køge you have the choice of two major routes as far as **Nykøbing Falster**. The direct route (93km) is detailed first. For the alternative route (134km), via the island of Møn, see below.

DIRECT ROUTE FROM KØGE TO NYKØBING (total distance 93km). Leave Køge on the 151 S, until, in 15km, you reach a road to your right to (7km) *Haslev* (9700 inhab.; Tourist Information: Torvegade 9), an historically interesting town in that it owes its growth to the abandoning in 1862 of the old rules governing market towns, which effectively prevented expansion elsewhere. This, together with the coming of the railway, allowed Haslev to develop. It is known as an educational centre, having both a folk high school and a teacher training college, each connected with the evangelical wing of the Danish Church, 'Indre Mission'. This is decidedly 19C provincial Denmark, with only a couple of small half-timbered cottages to remind one of the time when Haslev was a village.—The *Museum* on Frederiksgade does, of course, contain exhibits from earlier days, the horse-drawn fire-engine and other exhibits reflecting its beginnings as a station town.

Haslev is an excellent centre from which to visit some of Denmark's more famous great houses. A minor road SE leads to ***Bregentved** (3km), the largest estate in Sjælland. There was a castle here in the days of Erik Menved, but the present white rococo buildings are relatively modern. The N wing is from 1650 and the S and E wings from 1886–91; the chapel is from 1735. The park is open to the public, but the house is private.—Note the long **Holte Avenue** of 551 lime trees, planted in 1751, established in honour of Frederik V by the then owner Adam Gottlob Moltke. Hans Christian Andersen was a frequent 19C visitor here, and it was here that he wrote the beginning of 'The Ugly Duckling', the introductory scene being inspired by Bregentved park. The final scene, however, in which the swan comes into its own, is the park of the other great house in the area, Gisselfeld.
***Gisselfeld**, with its red brick walls and corbie gables, stands 4km S of Haslev on the road to Vester Egede. Isolated on a tiny islet in the middle of a lake and approached by bridges on either side, it has a history going back to 1370. The present Renaissance castle was built between 1547 and 1575 by Christian III's seneschal Peder Oxe, who for a time was the virtual ruler of Denmark. The house is private, but the park with its beautiful lake and some 400 different tree and bush species is open to the public from Palm Sunday to October. The greenhouses, which are also open, contain many rare species.—In the old watchman's house there is a museum illustrating the history of Gisselfeld.
Just SW of Gisselfeld you will find *Hesede Skov* (Hesede Woods), an idyllic and charming forest area with a famous 19C restaurant, the Villa Galina.

Leave Haslev on the road SE to (8km) Olstrup, where you rejoin the 151, passing the Torup Sø and Ulse Sø lakes on the way. You are now 3km from the crossroads at Rønnede, a town which itself is of no particular interest, but lies close to several places worth a visit.

In *Kongsted*, 2km SE of the crossroads, there is a large late Gothic church with a splendid array of frescoes from c 1450 on the walls, and vaulting in the nave. Those in the vaulting illustrate the childhood and Passion of Christ, those on the walls consisting of figures of saints together with a number of coats of arms. It is from this church the fresco painter called the 'Kongsted Master' is given his name. The altarpiece is from 1600 and the Renaissance pulpit from 1619.

With the church on your left you can now drive on a minor road to the 154, turn right and immediately left to *Lystrup* (3km altogether), a mansion from 1579 in Dutch Renaissance style by the same architect as was responsible for Vallø Castle (see below).

Return now to Rønnede, cross the 151 and the motorway as far as Vester Egede (4km), where you turn left to go to *Sparresholm* (3km), a Renaissance mansion from 1609 consisting of a main wing and two short saddle-roofed side wings from about 1700. The *Sparresholm Vognsamling* (Sparresholm Carriage Museum) exhibits over a hundred horse-drawn carriages of many kinds dating back to the 17C, and is the only museum of its kind in Denmark (open summer for groups by arrangement only).

Rønnede Royal Privilege Inn, South Sjælland, is typical of many still extant from the early system of inns covering the whole country.
Photo: John Sommer

Now follow the 151 20km S. Here, just before the road dives under the motorway, on your left, lies the charming early 19C *Udby Kro*, one of the Royal Privilege Inns. These inns have a history going back to the 12C, when Erik Glipping decreed that a system of inns should be built every 40km on important roads. Until 1912 they were only for travellers, and local people were not allowed to use them. There are now 113 such inns left, of which Udby is an excellent example.

You will find **Udby** itself just W of the 151 after you have passed the motorway. This is a very special village, both because it is largely unspoiled and possesses a great deal of intrinsic charm, and also for its historical association with the great hymn-writer and educationalist Nicolai Frederik Severin Grundtvig, who was born in Udby parsonage

Udby Church, South Sjælland. The hymn-writer and educationalist N.F.S. Grundtvig was curate here between 1811 and 1813. The church is Romanesque, with frescoes from five different periods.
Photo: Lennard

in 1783. He spent his childhood here and returned in 1811 to be his father's curate until 1813. On a 38m mound to the W of the church there is a 2.5m-high memorial stone to him.—The parsonage, from c 1650, is still in use, but one of the four wings is the *Grundtvig Museum* (open pm Apr–Oct). The parsonage garden, a miniature park—and the subject of one of Grundtvig's best poems—is always accessible, but visitors are asked only to use the paths clearly indicated.

The Romanesque *church* consists of an apse, chancel and nave with Gothic vaulting. There are frescoes from five different periods: ranging from the late 13C to c 1578. The altarpiece from 1585 is by the prolific Sjælland master, Bertel Snedker of Vordingborg. The granite font is Romanesque and the pulpit early Renaissance from 1584.

From Udby we suggest you take the E47/E55 motorway S to (14km) the *Farø Bridges*, Farø being the name of a small island in the straits between the islands of Sjælland and Falster. The new bridges carrying the motorway were opened in 1985, and consist of a low-level bridge from Sjælland to Farø, immediately followed by a high-level bridge from Farø to Falster, a total of 3322m in length. The central section of the high-level bridge is supported by two enormous concrete pylons which can be seen from far away.

At 5km (Junction 43) you leave the motorway again, taking the 293 W to (5km) **Nørre Alslev**. Here in the church there is a most unusual and very famous late 14C fresco depicting a medieval chain dance, with a king and a bishop as well as lesser mortals holding hands and joining the dance. But the dance is led by—Death.

There are two other friezes like it in Denmark, one at Jungshoved near Præstø (see below), the other at Egtved (Rte 1). The theme is particularly associated with a frieze with the same motif in Lübeck in North Germany. Hence the Danish way of speaking of someone looking seriously ill: he looks like Death in Lübeck. The Nørre Alslev frescoes are the work of the 'Elmelunde Master' (see below) and is one of a large number of frescoes from four different periods in this church.

Now follow an unclassified road S for 5km and turn left into Eskilstrup (2km), the home of *Lolland-Falster's Tractor and Motor Museum* (open summer; limited opening winter). For those with literary interests it must be mentioned that, 5km further E, lies the village of *Torkilstrup* where in the idyllic parsonage, Bernhard Severin Ingemann was born.

From Eskilstrup you head S again and join the E55 as far as to (5km) Stubberup, from where you might take a minor road E to *Tingsted* (2km). In this Romanesque church there are again frescoes from 1475–1500 by the great 'Elmelunde Master', an artist of rare imagination and humour who here paints scenes from the life of Christ, but supplements them with the Wheel of Fortune and a little episode in which a Devil is spoiling the milk as it is being churned, the whole interspersed with intricate floral decorations.

Return to Stubberup, and drive S on the E55 to (5km) Nykøbing Falster (see below).

ALTERNATIVE ROUTE FROM KØGE TO NYKØBING FALSTER—VIA STEVNS PENINSULA AND THE ISLAND OF MØN (total distance 134km). You leave Køge on the 209 SW. After 4km you turn right and then 1km further left in a beautiful avenue of trees leading you to (3km) *Vallø Castle**. The history of the castle goes back to the time of Christoffer II, but the present dignified Renaissance building is from 1580–86, with later additions in 1651 and (by Laurids de Thurah) 1735–38. Since the 18C it has been an *Adelig Jomfrukloster*—a home for the daughters of the aristocracy—but wider access has been possible since 1976. There is no public access to the house, but the magnificent park is open throughout the year, as is the adjoining Deer Park, where suitable paths are clearly marked.

From Vallø Castle, we suggest you do not return via the long avenue, but take the road E to (1.5km) *Valløby* village. There is a church here dating back to Romanesque times, but it is mainly Gothic with elaborate Renaissance additions, of which the magnificent E gable is the most striking. It completes the new Renaissance chancel from 1590, one of the few in the country. Among the most impressive items are some pew ends from 1591, with intricate inlaid patterns and carved figures, surmounted by the coats of arms of Peder Bille and Birgitte Rosenkrantz.

On leaving Valløby you have the problem of getting across the *Tryggevælde river*, which virtually cuts off the *Stevns peninsula*. You will have to turn N on the 209, as though going back to Køge, turning right after 2km on the 261, initially a coastal road which will take you through *Strøby Egede*, an area dotted with weekend cottages to (6km) *Strøby*, which has a Romanesque chancel and nave with a Gothic extension from c 1500. It is built mainly of limestone ashlars taken from the huge limestone deposits at Stevns Klint (see below), and contains a series of 14C frescoes depicting the Passion. In the churchyard there is a memorial to the novelist Martin A. Hansen who spent his childhood here, and doubtless here acquired much of the sense of tradition and cultural history which marks his work.

1km SE of Strøby you turn left on the road to (3km) *Magleby*, where there is again a church of interest. The earliest part, the nave, is 13C, with a late Gothic chancel from c 1500. At the E end of the nave there is a 17C sepulchral chapel. The Renaissance altarpiece is from 1606, with paintings from 1610; the pulpit dates from 1614; the pews are late Renaissance. A medieval tithe barn is incorporated into the churchyard wall to the E.

From Magleby the minor road continues to (3km) the impressive **Gjorslev Castle**.

The first castle here was owned by Rane Jonsen, by tradition responsible for the murder of Erik Glipping, and executed in 1294. The present main wing was built c 1400 by Peder Lodehat, Queen Margrethe I's Chancellor, and Bishop of Roskilde.

It is one of the oldest inhabited buildings in Denmark today. The looming cruciform principal wing, dominated by a 30m-high tower, is unique among European castles. A Gothic hall in this wing is sometimes used for concerts. The N wing is from 1638, the S from 1843. The whole complex is encircled by a moat. Gjorslev remained in Church hands until the Reformation, since when it has been either in Crown or private ownership. The approach from the E, along Bredgade, is itself an experience. This wide road, cobbled apart from the central carriageway, is lined with half-timbered artisans' houses from the time of Frederik IV, and this scene must thus have remained almost unchanged since the early 18C. The 20 hectare park, containing many rare trees, is open to the public, but it can only be entered from the S. The castle itself is private.

NE of Gjorslev lies the delightful *Gjorslev Bøgeskov* (Gjorslev Beech Forest), a beautiful wooded area, with lakes and some 55 burial mounds, one of them 51m long, and with a magnificent view across Køge Bay. There is a restaurant here, too.

From Gjorslev you continue along a minor road through *Holtug* with its high-lying Romanesque/Gothic church, long used as a landmark, to (7km) **Store Heddinge** (3000 inhab.; Tourist Information: Hybenvænget 4).

Store Heddinge *church* is one of the most unusual in Denmark—though one wishes the restorers had left it alone. Built of limestone ashlars, it consists of a rectangular Romanesque chancel (probably inspired by Byzantine models) and a unique octagonal Romanesque nave (apparently inspired by Aachen Cathedral), with a Gothic W tower and porch. The chancel is well preserved, but the nave has been drastically altered. As a drawing by a 17C historian clearly shows, it was once much higher than at present, with eight columns supporting a central section, and a vaulted aisle around it, more in the style of the round churches of Bornholm. The chancel is equipped with a confusion of more or less hidden passages and rooms, probably reflecting the original intention that it should be suited for defence. The construction of the very substantial W tower seems to indicate the same purpose.

In spite of its modest size Store Heddinge is actually a market town, with a charter from 1441 (and probably earlier). Like other towns, it suffered fires and a Swedish occupation, but there are still enough older houses to have preserved something of its atmosphere. Fitting for such a small 'town', it can boast Denmark's shortest street, no more than 1.85m—but with a street name: *Trianglen* (The Triangle). It has also boasted five distilleries (at a time when the total population was 576!), of which one, at Algade 22, still stands, though it is no longer in use.

ROUND TRIP FROM STORE HEDDINGE TO STEVNS KLINT AND RØDVIG (total distance c 17km). Take an unclassified road SE through Højerup to (5km) the limestone cliffs of this area known as **Stevns Klint**. In places the cliffs offer a sheer drop of 40m to the sea. They stretch over some 15km, are full of fossils, and are completely different from anything else in Denmark. For centuries limestone has been quarried here, and many of the local buildings are made of it. However, only the soft chalk from the lower layers is now used—for blackboard chalk. The *Stevns Museum* illustrates the history of the area, with a geological section, exhibitions of implements used in the quarrying, local costumes and furniture—and relics from the Battle of Køge Bay. There are art exhibitions in the museum during the summer (open pm May–Oct).

Højerup Church, or what is left of it, is one of the products of the local limestone quarries. Now standing starkly outlined right on the brink of the cliffs, it dates back to c 1250, and according to legend moves 'a cock-stride' inland every Christmas Eve to avoid falling into the sea. The sea got it in the end, when the chancel fell over the cliff in 1928. The altarpiece was severely damaged by the collapse, but parts of it were saved and are on view in the remains of the building today. The pulpit from 1605 is still intact. The cliffs are now reinforced at this spot, and the church is safe—but not in use (open summer).— There is a memorial grove near the church, with statues of well-known local figures.

Now follow a small coastal road SW to (5km) *Rødvig*, a favoured tourist resort in the summer, with weekend cottages, good beaches and excellent yachting facilities. There is a small marine engine museum here, *Rødvig Skibsmotormuseum* (open Jun–Aug), with 80 fishing boat engines from between 1917 and 1970, all in working order. The *Rødvig Flint Kiln* (reconstructed, originally from 1870), once used to fire powdered flint for glazing porcelain, stands on Havneplads and is now a museum and viewing platform.

From Rødvig you take the 261 back to (7km) Store Heddinge again, possibly stopping after the first 2km in *Lille Heddinge*, where a ticket bought to the *Stevns Museum* (above) will—on application—grant you free entrance to both an old smithy here (on Broveshøjvej 19) as well as to a cavalry school, *Den gamle Rytterskole* on Stormarksvej 1, one of 240 cavalry schools established by Frederik IV in 1721. It is now a small museum and includes a collection of works and memorabilia of the painter Niels Larsen Stevns (1864–1941) (responsible for the murals in Viborg Cathedral, Rte 20). The limestone ashlar church in the village is part Romanesque, part Gothic, with an unusually lofty nave (8.5m). There were once two floors to the nave, the upper one being for storage and for keeping watch. It is assumed that this church formed part of the defences against the Wends. There is also a newly restored windmill.

From **Store Heddinge** you now continue W on the 154 for 12km to a crossroads where you have Karise on your right and Vemmetofte on your left.

Take a look first at *Karise* (3km), where there is yet another of the fortified

churches of the region. Traces of embrasures and parapets are still to be seen.
The building dates back to 1261. The brick-built chancel is again unusually high,
10m, suggesting that there were once two floors, while the nave is 6.9m. Despite
the different heights of the chancel, nave, tower and N porch (built of alternating
layers of brick and limestone), when seen from the N this church has a
harmonious effect, with its five corbie gables. To the S, however, the effect is
cancelled, thanks to the addition of the bombastic mausoleum chapel built by the
influential Moltke family and designed in neo-classical style by Jardin and
Harsdorff. It is dominated by the sarcophagus for Adam Gottlob Moltke, the
one-time owner of *Bregentved* castle and close friend of Frederik V. This is
surmounted by a medallion by Wiedewelt, who also designed the sarcophagus
containing Moltke's first wife. It is not the design of the chapel as such that jars,
but the fact that it is in such close proximity to a medieval church with which it
is totally out of proportion.

Return now to the 154, cross it and drive to *Vemmetofte Kloster* (3km), not a
convent in the ordinary sense, but another 'Adelig Jomfrukloster', a home for the
unmarried daughters of the aristocracy. Like Vallø Castle, it had its rules altered
in 1976, and is now a retirement home. Its history goes back to the Middle Ages,
but the present baroque house dates from 1715–24. It is not open to the public,
but there is access to the park.

Just beyond the estate lies the lovely wooded *Vemmetofte Strand*, ideal for
bathing. There is also a restaurant.

If you decided against both Karise and Vemmetofte you just follow the
154 for another 4km and then take the 209 to (5km) **Fakse**. The town
has a distinguished son: it is the birthplace of the great Viking warrior
Rollo who raided England and defeated King Athelstan, then
proceeded to conquer and found what is now known as Normandy. He
was given the title of Robert of Normandy before he died in 927.
William the Conqueror was one of his descendants. There is a
memorial stone to Rollo by the Town Hall.

To most Danes today, however, Fakse does not mean Rollo—it means
beer. *Faxe Brewery* is among the biggest in the country, and it is open
for visits (and tastes). The tiny thatched half-timbered house by the
entrance in *Torvegade* is the place where it all started. Also in Torvegade you will find *Fakse Geologiske/Kulturhistoriske Museum* with a
collection from this geologically exciting area, in addition to a local
historical collection (open summer; limited opening winter).

2km SE of the town centre lies *Fakse Kalkbrud*, the limestone
quarries, an impressive sight, 1km long by 500m wide—and up to 50m
deep. Limestone has been quarried here since the 13C and has provided materials for many buildings. Some of the chalk is so hard that
it has become known as Fakse marble, and has been used for facing
buildings. The quarry welcomes visitors.

Having seen the quarry you really ought to drive just 3km further SE
to the old village of *Fakse Ladeplads*, the harbour from which the local
limestone is loaded for export, as it has been since the Middle Ages.
There are huge silos at the water's edge, but there is also a modern
marina, for outsiders have learned to appreciate this seaside resort just
as much as the locals used to do.

On the road back to Fakse, you will in 4km come to *Blåbæk Møller*,
a picturesquely situated watermill and windmill, the former certainly
continuously functioning since 1664 (open on application).

2km NW of Fakse stands the mansion of *Jomfruens Egede*, made up
of two individual wings placed on either side of a small chapel. The S
wing has 16C remains, while the N is from 1636; both were restored
(i.e. redesigned) in 1797.

From Fakse it is easy, if you wish, to drive 6km W and join the faster
direct route at Rønnede, but we suggest you stick to this route, having
got this far, and with the splendid island of Møn so close at hand.

So follow the 209 S. In 9km you pass, on your right, the very old inn at *Vindbyholt*, one of the Royal Privilege Inns. The present building is from 1623, and has records of over 200 visits by royal guests on their way to and from the castles of Nykøbing and Vordingborg. 2km further on you will find a road on your right leading to the *rag oak* (Kludeegen) in *Leestrup Forest*. You will have to park your car in the small car park and walk into the forest to find this curious phenomenon. In old superstition this oak tree had healing powers. A sick person had, on the Thursday night after the new moon, to pass nine times through the divided trunk to be cured. In addition to that, anyone seeking a cure had to hang an article of clothing in the tree as a sacrifice. There are still rags hanging here, and there are signs that the ancient practice is still continued.

Another 9km sees you in **Præstø** (3200 inhab.; Tourist Information: Adelgade 91), a quiet market town with a charter from 1403, snuggling splendidly at the S of the **Præstø Fjord**, with views of virtually the whole of the fjord coastline. It has retained a great deal of natural charm, with a tiny fishing harbour, winding streets with mainly 19C houses, a cobbled market square with its neo-classical *Town Hall* from 1823, designed by C.F. Hansen.

There was a monastery here before the Reformation. The *church*, from 1470, is all that is left. It is large and impressive, with three corbie gables on the buttressed S wall. From the outside these look like three chapels, but inside they turn out to be part of a wide extension to the original nave. The present altar is modern, but the ornate auricular altarpiece from its predecessor hangs at the E end of the nave.—At Rødeledvej 1, the *old pottery* from 1898 is now a working museum.

On the coast immediate N of Præstø stands the mansion of ***Nysø**. The elegant baroque building from 1671–73 was something of a cultural centre in the 19C. The then owner, Holger Stampe, put a studio at the disposal of Bertel Thorvaldsen, who executed some of his most important works there. The great sculptor was, however, not the only visitor, and many of the most prominent figures of the Golden Age of Danish Romanticism were frequent guests, including, of course, Hans Christian Andersen. There is a *museum* in Nysø now, dedicated to Thorvaldsen (limited opening). There is also access to the park when the museum is open.

To the E of Præstø there is the *Jungshoved* peninsula. This is the area once more or less run by the famous hero Svend Poulsen, better known as Svend Gønge or 'Gøngehøvdingen', during the Swedish occupation of 1658–60. He was what today would be known as a successful guerrilla leader. At the S of this small peninsula stands *Jungshoved Church*, one of the three Danish churches with a fresco portraying the Dance of Death (cf. Nørre Alslev above). The church, from c 1225 and unusual in itself in having the tower on the N side, stands beside the mound on which there was once a medieval castle which by tradition played a part in Svend Poulsen's operations.

You leave Præstø on the 265 S to (15km) Kalvehave, where you cross the 1943 11-arched *Dronning Alexandrines Bro* (Queen Alexandrine's Bridge) to the island of ***Møn**. 10km along the A59 brings you to **Stege** (3800 inhab.; Tourist Information: Storegade 5), a small, idyllic, provincial market town with a charter dating back to the 13C, and with a charter from 1268. At the time of Valdemar I it was the site of a castle. Stege grew rich between the 13C and 16C, thanks to the herring fishing in the area, but it has since, apart from a period at the beginning of the 19C, stagnated—and thus kept its charm.

You will find here delightful cobbled streets and half-timbered artisans' houses as well as early 19C merchants' houses recalling this later period of affluence; one of these, *Empiregården* in Storegade, is now the *local museum* with exhibits from 7000 BC to the present day.—The adjoining *Mølleport*, the last of the town's three gate towers, still stands as the best-preserved town gateway in Denmark. Correspondingly, the medieval ramparts have also survived in good condition.

On the market square, *Torvet*, you will find a grand late 18C merchant's house, the *Kammerrådsgård*. There is a *dolls' museum* in Grønnegade 14, and in Havnevej 14 you will find *Dansk Brandværnsmuseum*, illustrating the history of the Danish fire brigades.

For a town so small, the Gothic *church* with a lofty and dignified nave from c 1525 is remarkably large, 60m long, and thus one of the biggest provincial churches in Denmark. The tower is characteristically built in alternating layers of red and limestone bricks.

Elmelunde Church, Møn, showing the elaborate frescoes by the late 15C Elmelunde Master.
Photo: Lennard

EXCURSION TO EAST MØN (total distance c 35km). This excursion is really a MUST! Follow the 287 E, the first stop being at (4km) *Keldby* (or *Kelbymagle*). The *church here is from the early 13C, and entering it is like going into a medieval art gallery. It is a large church, and the vaulting is simply covered in frescoes from four different periods, from 1275 to 1600. Some are the work of the Elmelunde Master. The altarpiece and pulpit are of a splendour to suit the murals; the late Gothic altarpiece from 1500, ornate and richly carved, with Christ in the central panel surrounded by four panels depicting His life, and with the twelve Apostles in the outer panels. The equally ornate Renaissance pulpit is from 1586.

Only 1.4km to the S there is in *Keldbylille* a late 18C four-winged thatched farm which was left to the National Museum in 1864 and has been preserved in its original state as a museum (open summer; limited opening winter).

4km E of Keldby in *Elmelunde*, is the *church that has given its name to the great medieval Master. Like Keldby, this church too is filled with the most glorious frescoes, many illustrating Bible stories like the slaughter of the Holy Innocents, others exhorting the priest to speak loud and clear! The Elmelunde Master has painted Christ in Majesty over the altar. As you admire these sublime frescoes, you might reflect on the fact that they were whitewashed over after the Reformation! Elmelunde Church, partly dating from c 1075 and thus one of the oldest stone-built churches in Denmark, received a new altarpiece and pulpit as a gift from Christian IV's daughter, Leonora Christine, in 1636. Both are still in place, proudly showing Christian IV's monogram.—Immediately E of the church there is a large Bronze Age burial mound, and it is assumed that the church was built on a heathen shrine, as so many of the older churches were.

You continue E, through (3km) *Borre* with a church from 1250 remarkable for its decorative brickwork, to (3km) *Magleby*.

From here there are three excursions. They are all quite short, and it would really be a pity to miss out any of them.

If you drive 3km N you will find the mansion of **Liselund**, thought by some to be the most perfect neo-classical house in Denmark, a delightful thatched mansion from 1772–95, surrounded by a romantic park containing several pavilions typical of the time—a Chinese pavilion, a Swiss pavilion and a Norwegian pavilion—all reflecting the late 18C fondness for the idyllic (guided tours May–Oct).

A short drive E through the woods, brings you to the majestic *Møns Klint (Møns Cliff), a 'wild and weatherbeaten shore', towering limestone cliffs rising at their highest point to 128m, and constantly changing their profile thanks to winter storms. Those of you who have been here before will now look in vain for the impressive rock formation known as *Sommerspiret* (The Summer Spire)—it collapsed into the sea in January 1988. The restaurant/hotel at Møns Klint is most beautifully situated.

Driving S from Magleby you will pass the *Klintholm manor*, approached by an imposing avenue, but not open to the public. In **Klintholm Havn**, 3km further, you have a busy little fishing harbour dating back to 1878. It has well known fish restaurants and a smokehouse where you can buy products on the spot.

Leave **Stege** on the 287 S and stop for a while at (7km) *Damsholte*, where the tiny rococo church from 1743 is unlike any other in Denmark. The nave is rectangular, with a five-sided extension at either end. It was the work of the age of pietism, and according to pietist custom the altar and pulpit are in one.

After another 5km you will come to a crossroads leading N to Tostenæs and S to Kokseby.

If you are interested in archaeological remains—and there are a great number around here—you should turn N to visit *Klekkende Høj (2km)*, a large burial mound with two entrances and, after a further 3km along the same road, *Kong Asgers Høj* (2km), a huge passage grave with an 8m passage leading to a 10m-long burial chamber. Take a torch with you.

Archaeologists will also be interested in a third important monument, this time 3km S of the crossroads, through Kokseby and *Fanefjord*. This is the longest burial mound in Denmark, surrounded by a stone circle made up of 145 enormous boulders.

Nearby *Fanefjord Church* is the third of the Elmelunde Master's churches, his finest work in the view of many. Fanefjord was once an important medieval harbour; the now isolated church, originally dedicated to St. Nicholas, dates from the late 13C, when there was a busy market town on the spot. It is filled with frescoes, those on the chancel arch from c 1350, the remaining exuberant array from c 1500 by the Elmelunde Master—colourful, imaginative, drastic: scenes from the Old and New Testaments, Christ as Judge of the world, figures of saints, grotesque figures of demons, and a wealth of floral decoration.

Return to the 287 from Fanefjord.

Your route now continues S and W to the small island of *Bogø*. Just S of Bogø town you take the ferry (half-hourly sailings) to Stubbekøbing on the island of Falster. (You can also, if you so wish, drive right across the island to (6km) the Farø bridges, and from there follow the direct route above.)

Stubbekøbing (2300 inhab.) is another small fishing port that was of strategic significance in the Middle Ages. It then grew with the herring fishing, but has since sunk into provincial idyll, with old half-timbered houses in quiet streets. The main street, Vestergade, contains several old buildings, for instance *Trojels Gård*, from 1708, once part of a merchant's house with courtyard. Others have been spoilt by the installation of modern shop windows, but the upper floors betray their true age.

It has been claimed that the dignified *church* is one of the most interesting buildings on Falster. The Romanesque nave is late 12C, the chancel from c 1250, the St. Anna Chapel on the N wall late Gothic. The main structure is limestone, though brick has been used in some of the arcading. There are frescoes from five different periods, ranging from 1250 to 1520. The altarpiece is High Renaissance, from 1616, and the rood screen four years younger. The auricular pulpit and canopy date from 1634.—On Nykøbingvej you will find a museum, *Motorcykelog Radiomuseum* (limited opening).

A short excursion from Stubbekøbing takes you along the 293 E to *Næsgård* (5km), Denmark's first agricultural college from 1849. From this spot a road N leads down to *Borrehuset*, where Marie Grubbe of Tjele (Rte 20) lived in her final years as a ferrywoman, rowing travellers across the Grønsund Straits to Møn. It was here Ludvig Holberg met her. There is nothing left of her house, but it is moving to stand here and think of the fate that was worked out on this spot.—Continue S on minor roads through *Korselitse Østerskov*, the longest stretch of coastal forest E of Storebælt to (6km) **Hesnæs**, a tiny fishing village with beautiful thatched cottages. They were architect designed in the late 19C and have all their walls insulated with straw on the outside.

Return to Stubbekøbing via (3km) *Moseby* with its idyllic parsonage from the 1770s and (2km) *Åstrup*, where the Elmelunde Master is again responsible for a wealth of frescoes, supplementing others from the 13C on the chancel arch.

From Stubbekøbing take the 271 S through Horreby to (19km) **Nykøbing Falster** (18,700 inhab.; Tourist Information: Østergade 2).

Nykøbing Falster, one of the three Danish towns by the name of Nykøbing, was given a charter by Valdemar II. It originated as a defence against the Wends, and a large castle was established here. In the 13C the king was often in residence, and here Valdemar IV signed a peace treaty (one of many) with the Hanseatic league in 1365. In 1419 a Franciscan monastery was founded, and since 1532 its chapel has been the parish church. The castle brought affluence and trade to the town, and this continued until the mid-17C, when Nykøbing went into decline. The castle was sold for demolition in 1767. Agricultural improvements in the 19C brought renewed prosperity, and this was accelerated after the establishment of the first bridge to Lolland in 1867, followed by the arrival of the railways, and finally the establishment of direct connections with Germany via Gedser to Warnemünde in 1903.

The buttressed late Gothic *church*, standing at the junction of Store Kirkestræde and Klosterstræde is the old Franciscan monastery church and at one time formed the S wing of the monastery, the W wing of which is also partially extant, now used as a parsonage. The tower, with its onion spire, is from 1766. The vaulted nave is whitewashed, emphasising the ornate carving of the Renaissance altarpiece presented by Frederik II's queen, Sophie of Mecklenburg, in 1618. There is an auricular pulpit, supported by a figure of Moses; it and its canopy are from 1640, the octagonal metal font from 1648. The most curious feature is Queen Sophie's genealogical table on the N wall of the chancel, with portraits of each ancestor painted in 1626 and surmounted with a carved top section from 1627. One of the numerous sepulchral tablets contains a well-preserved painting by Lucas Cranach the Elder, from c 1540.—In the gardens near the church there is a medicinal herb garden, laid out in 1969.

A few old buildings are scattered around the central part of the town, but do not give an overall impression. There is, for instance, a half-timbered house from 1580 in Langgade, and a richly decorated façade from c 1620 at the corner of Frisegade and Store Kirkestræde. Best known of the old houses is *Czarens hus* (The Tsar's House) on the corner of Langgade and Færgestræde—perhaps symbolically now facing a small square with Mogens Bøggild's delightful granite fountain representing a bear, from 1939. The carefully restored and maintained house from c 1700 was indeed used briefly by Peter the Great on his way to Copenhagen in 1716. A wooden plaque, written in German, commemorates this.—Czarens hus is now part restaurant, part the *Falsters Minde* museum (entrance in Langgade) with exhibits from a unique Viking shipyard S of Stubbekøbing and a model of Nykøbing Castle. Of this once splendid castle there are now only a few ruins left at the N end of Slotsgade.—The *Halskov Vænge Museum* in Parkvej provides an experience of life—and death—in the Bronze Age.

The TWO ROUTES merge in Nykøbing, and from here you follow the E55 S, soon passing on your right, *Hasselø Nor*, where there was a settlement of Dutch market gardeners in the early 17C. 7km S of Nykøbing you reach Væggerløse, where the newly restored *Stouby Mølle* from 1790 is the only post mill of this particular type in Denmark (limited opening).

Immediately S of Væggerløse you will see a road E to (3km) **Marielyst**, a seaside resort par excellence. It is in the centre of a 10km stretch of magnificent beaches, one of the best in Denmark, with all conceivable facilities for holiday-makers.

Following the E55 S from Væggerløse you pass through the *Bøtø Nor*, another area once cultivated by Dutch farmers. A small area of this low-lying land has not been entirely drained, and in it there is a 100 hectare bird sanctuary, the home or resting place of many rare birds, including cranes. 12km S you reach the gentle village of *Gedesby*, with its half-timbered thatched cottages and the ramparts of Valdemar II's castle of Gedesgård.

In 4km you reach **Gedser** (1200 inhab.), which owes its existence to the ferry connections to Germany. The first service was opened in 1903 to Warnemünde, and in 1951 this route was replaced as the main route to southern Europe by the Gedser-Grossenbrode connection. In 1963 the Gedser–Travemünde service opened. Although the services to Travemünde (3½hrs) and Warnemünde (2hrs) still exist, Gedser lost most of its traffic to Rødbyhavn (Rte 9) with the establishment of the more direct route to western Europe in 1963.—Places of interest in Gedser are the *Gedser Remise* railway museum in Stationsvej, with locomotives and passenger coaches from c 1900 onwards (open weekends Apr–Sept), and the *Geological Museum* in Skolegade (open all year). *Gedser Lighthouse* is also open for visitors in the summer.

11 Maribo to Odense via Svendborg

Total distance 105km—plus ferry. A9 to (34km) *Tårs* ferry harbour.—(Ferry Tårs–*Spodsbjerg* 45mins).—A9 to (9km) **Rudkøbing**.—(17km) **Svendborg**.—A9, A43 to (45km) **Odense**.

From Maribo to Tårs ferry harbour you have a choice of three routes: the direct route (34km, listed first), via Knuthenborg (45km), or via Nakskov (49km).

DIRECT ROUTE FROM MARIBO TO TÅRS FERRY HARBOUR (total distance 34km). Take the A9 W to (6km) Nørreballe, turning left here to Østofte (1km), where there is an interesting large church, partly dating back to the Romanesque period. Its brightly coloured and well-preserved frescoes contain some amusing motifs, one of them unique in Denmark: Eve being produced out of Adam's back. Elsewhere God is creating the animals, while at the Gate of Heaven the Archangel Michael is giving Adam the acorn from which will grow the tree providing the wood for the Cross.—Not far from the church you will find an old post mill.

A further 6km on the A9 you come to *Stokkemarke* where there is an impressive church with a late Romanesque nave and subsequent Gothic additions. The church tower is a particularly solid structure, with corbie gables on each side. The stained glass windows in the apse are by J.Th. Skovgaard.

Your next stop is in (9km) *Halsted*. The 12C church here once formed the N wing of a Benedictine convent founded by Jutta, the daughter of Erik Plovpenning. There are still some remains of the original building, e.g. a carved tympanum above the S door, while later features of note are some fine carvings on the 1636 pulpit and the entrance to a sepulchral chapel, from 1643.—Halsted convent was burned by the Lübeckers in 1510 and subsequently underwent radical alterations. There is nothing left of it now, and the site is occupied by a small mansion, *Halsted Kloster*, with a S wing from c 1590 and a neo-Gothic W wing from the 1840s. It is owned by the only family in Denmark to have a four-barrelled name: Krag-Juel-Vind-Frijs (park open summer).

Instead of now driving direct to (13km) Tårs, you might make the short DETOUR to visit the biggest town on Lolland, *Nakskov*. To do this you take an unclassified road W from Halsted leading direct to Nakskov (6km) (see below).

ALTERNATIVE ROUTE FROM MARIBO TO TÅRS—VIA KNUTHENBORG

(total distance 45km). Follow the A9 N out of Maribo to (3km) the 289. Here you should turn right and drive N to (5km) **Knuthenborg**, the site of an elegant mansion standing in a very large privately owned park, part of which is now the most comprehensive safari park in Denmark, crisscrossed by a full 16km of roads. It is approached through elaborate wrought-iron gates and offers not only a large stock of wild animals, but also a children's zoo, pony-riding and a model of the islands of Lolland/Falster (open summer).

From Knuthenborg it is only 1km to *Bandholm*, a small fishing village with picturesque old warehouses, and the terminus of the Maribo-Bandholm vintage railway.

Remain on the 289 NW for 12km towards Birket. Immediately before the village you will find a minor road going off left to *Lindet* (1km), where you will find Birket church. It is less the church that is of interest than the free-standing wooden bell-tower near the entrance to the churchyard. It dates from 1350 and is thought to be the oldest extant wooden building in the country.

Continue on the 289 for a further 3km, to a road leading S to *Pederstrup* (2km), a neo-classical mansion designed by C.F. Hansen. It has recently been restored and contains a museum commemorating the 18C land reformer Christian D.F. Reventlow. It moreover contains a collection of good sculptures. The park is open all year, the museum May to mid-Sept.

You should now return to the 289, turning off left again almost immediately to see *Kong Svends Høj* (King Svend's Tumulus), a huge passage grave, with a central chamber 12.3m long.—Another 10km on the 289 sees you in *Lille Løjtofte*.

Here there is a very small but almost totally unspoiled Romanesque church, the only later addition being the porch. Not only has this church retained its original appearance and atmosphere, but it also possesses a very special font, the work of the Majestas Master from the Swedish Baltic island of Gotland. It rests on a foot carved in the shape of four lions, and the outer facing is richly carved with reliefs of Christ in Majesty, the Annunciation, Mary's meeting with Elizabeth, The Birth of Christ, the Shepherds in the fields and the Three Kings.

1km beyond Lille Løjtofte you turn right and drive through Sandby to (10km) Tårs and your ferry.

ALTERNATIVE ROUTE FROM MARIBO TO TÅRS—VIA NAKSKOV (total distance 49km). Leave Maribo on the 153 SW, driving through (4km) Hillested and turning right after a further 1km on to a road to (3km) Øster Skørringe. Here you turn right on to the 275 and drive W past the mansion of Kristianssæde to (9km) Bjergeskov, where you should take the road S to (7km) *Dannemare*. Here there is a fine collection, *Galleri Præstegården*, of international modern art housed in the old parsonage, beside the church.—Now drive W from Dannemare, and in 2km you will see on your right the road to *Tillitse* (1km).

There is a small Romanesque church here, but the interesting feature is the runestone near the porch, with two inscriptions, one of them Christian: 'Eskil Sulkeson had this stone raised to himself. As long as the stone lives this memorial inscription, done by Eskil, shall stand. May Christ and St. Michael help his soul.'

Back on your route again you pass (3km) *Rudbjerggård*, a large half-timbered 17C mansion with an octagonal tower. In the course of its history it has belonged to two morganatic royal wives, Kirsten Munk and Countess Danner. 2km further on your left will give you a glimpse (if you want it), of *Sølvbjerg*, the site of the last public execution in Denmark in 1882. After another km you should follow a road leading right to (8km) Nakskov.

Nakskov (16,000 inhab.; Tourist Information: Axeltorv 6) is the largest town on Lolland, with a charter dating back to 1200. Formerly a shipbuilding town and ferry port, Nakskov has gone into decline since the shipyard was closed and the Langeland ferry transferred to Tårs. Like other parts of Lolland, Nakskov suffered at the hands of Lübeck in the 15C and 16C and was occupied by Swedish forces in 1659. However, the picturesque roads leading from the centre of the town to the harbour with its half-timbered warehouses (some dating back to 1600) point to a high level of trade and affluence in the past.

Standing on the corner of the market place, Axeltorv, is the elegant rococo Theisens gård from 1786. If you go into the courtyard you will find a series of renovated warehouses from the 18C, now used for meetings and other local activities. At the furthermost end of the complex, standing on the corner of Badstuestræde and Havnegade is a splendid half-timbered warehouse dating back to at least 1702. The long wing in Badstuestræde has been described as one of the most picturesque half-timbered buildings in the country. Axeltorv itself is unusual in being triangular, a shape going back to the Middle Ages.

To the N of it lies Nakskov Church, *Sankt Nikolai Kirke*. Mainly from the 16C, it still contains parts of the original Romanesque structure from the 13C. The elegant altarpiece is the work of Anders Mortensen, 1656, and the pulpit, from 1630, is by Jørgen Ringnis, as is the panelling beneath the tower. The great chest, with its five locks, is from 1573, while the tall spire dates from 1906.—In Tilegade nearby, E of Axeltorv, a working museum has been installed in *Den gamle Smedie* (The Old Smithy), where a blacksmith works, using tools some of which are 200 years old.—There is a statue in Axeltorv of King Christian X, placed there in 1952 in commemoration of the Liberation.

The Catholic church of Saint Francis is from 1921, built largely for Polish sugar workers in the sugar refinery which has long been one of the main sources of industry in the town.—The harbour area in Nakskov is characterised by a collection of charming old warehouses, outstanding among which is *Dronningens Pakhus* from 1590, the oldest building in the town.

On leaving Nakskov, you drive N through Branderslev to (5km) the A9. Here a left turn will quickly bring you to (6km) Tårs.

The ferry from **Tårs** sails (45 mins) to *Spodsbjerg*, a small village on the island of Langeland, from where the A9 takes you to (9km) Rudkøbing. The old main road is still in existence, and provides a more leisured and picturesque route.

Rudkøbing (4700 inhab.; Tourist Information: Bystrædet 3) is the principal town on the island and was once an important trade centre, which received its charter in 1287. The town centre has maintained much of its old aspect, with decorative old-fashioned cobbled streets, an impressive church—possibly partly dating back to 1105, but mainly from the 16C and 17C—a windmill placed high above the town, and numerous old fishermen's houses which have been thoroughly restored. One, in Brogade, was converted into a tiny Catholic church in 1925, to serve the many Poles who used to come to work in the sugar beet fields.

Other characteristic features are the numerous old merchants' houses, half-timbered, with impressive steps leading to sometimes quite ornate main entrances. Outstanding among them are *Den bayske*

Gård in Østergade, now a private house, and the *Old Chemist's Shop* (open summer) in Brogade, dating from 1856.

This was the birthplace of the Ørsted brothers—Hans Christian (1777–1851), the discoverer of electromagnetism, the founder of modern science in Denmark, and a leading influence on the Danish literary Romantic movement, and Anders Sandøe (1778–1860), an influential jurist and statesman in his day.

The shop, which houses a collection of old furniture and equipment, and the garden behind it, containing a chestnut tree said to date from the beginning of the 18C, is now part of the Langeland Museum.— Hans Christian Ørsted is commemorated by a statue by Bissen on the picturesque *Gåsetorv* square, while Anders Sandøe Ørsted has his statue by J.C. Berg in the *Ørstedpark*.

The *Langeland Museum* in Jens Winthersvej offers a large collection of relics from the island. Langeland is rich in archaeological sites, and it is thus natural that over half of the museum collection should be of archaeological interest. The exhibits are arranged chronologically, covering the Stone Age and Viking Age in particular detail, the latter exhibits reflecting the discovery of rich Viking graves in the area.

Rudkøbing is well equipped for the tourist trade, and has much to offer in the way of cafés, restaurants and street entertainment. Sightseeing walks are arranged on Thur in the summer. Apart from its road connection to Fyn, Rudkøbing also provides a ferry connection to Marstal on the island of Ærø (Rte 12) and to the tiny island of Strynø, no more than 3km x 2km, with its small population of close-knit islanders.

EXCURSION FROM RUDKØBING TO NORTH LANGELAND. As its name suggests, *Langeland* is long and narrow, and it would be a pity to leave it without exploring some of the charming villages.

The 305 road runs N–S through the whole island. Drive first towards the N, to (10km) the village of **Tranekær**, dominated by its splendid castle, which can be traced back to the 13C. Since 1672 it has been the residence of the Ahlefeldt family. Resulting from several alterations and restorations, the present building consists of two wings linked by an octagonal tower surmounted by a spire. There is a public pathway through the park, giving clear views of the castle which is otherwise not open to the public.

Perhaps the most famous member of the Ahlefeldt family was Count Frederik, still known as the General. He attempted to create in Tranekær something approaching a South German duchy, and the relationship between the castle and the surrounding village—a relationship unique in Denmark—reflects clearly the feudal nature of this attempt. The old stables are now a restaurant (*Café Herskabsstalden*), and are situated opposite the private theatre which the General had constructed near the entrance to the castle. Even the poultry did well, and the old henhouse, topped by a tower used as a dovecot, is now a small *art gallery*.

Other buildings of note in this idyllic village are the inn (*Tranekær Gæstgivergård*), dating from the 18C, and, immediately S of it, the musicians' houses, two long, half-timbered houses intended to house the General's musicians and players. The rather uninspiring church dates back to c 1450, but was completely rebuilt in 1886. Most of the Ahlefeldt family are buried there. Normally closed, the church is open for two hours daily in the summer.

Opposite the castle there is a sculpture park, *Galaksen* (The Galaxy), the work of the modern sculptor Jan Axel Starup. It consists of 27 boulders, the largest weighing ten tonnes, arranged in a spiral and bearing inscriptions and symbols.—1km N of the Castle lies *Slots-*

A rural scene in Langeland, archetypal idyllic
Denmark. Photo: Ole Akhøj

møllen (The Castle Mill), a well-preserved windmill, completely restored in 1985 (open summer).

Of the many mansions on Langeland, one of the most famous is
Egeløkke, situated 1km W of the main road to Lohals 5km N of
Tranekær (park occasionally open; house private). This is the mansion
where the young Grundtvig was appointed tutor, only to fall in love
with the mistress of the house, Constance Leth, one result of which
was his first religious awakening. A visit to the churchyard in *Bøstrup*
(immediately W of the main road just before you turn off to Egeløkke)
will give a sight of Constance Leth's grave.

2km N a minor road leads W to *Dageløkke* (1.5km), a holiday centre
providing swimming pool, yachting harbour and children's play-
ground, and 6km further N you pass the 400-year-old mansion of
Steensgaard before reaching (3km) *Lohals*, the northernmost village
on Langeland, which has a small harbour with yachting facilities and
a ferry connection to Korsør on Sjælland. It is also a fishing port. A
popular site for weekend cottages, this area has first-rate bathing
facilities; you can hire boats and bicycles, and fishing trips can be
arranged in the Langeland Belt which is famous for its cod fishing.

EXCURSION FROM RUDKØBING TO SOUTH LANGELAND. Take the 305
S from Rudkøbing as far as (9km) Lindelse. Here you turn left and bear
left again at the village of Hennetved (1.5km) to reach the mansion of
Skovsgaard (1.5km), now owned by Danmarks Naturfond (the equivalent to the National Trust). The mansion itself is not open to the
public, but the park and shore are, and *Langelands Museum* has an
exhibition of horse-drawn carriages from the late 19C and early 20C

here (open summer). The farming on the estate is now based entirely on ecological principles.

4km S of Lindelse you will come to the village of Humble with its long dolmen known as *King Humble's Grave*, probably the best known of all the prehistoric monuments on Langeland. There are parking facilities outside the impressive, partly Romanesque Humble church; follow the road for about 100m before turning into a path leading through a farmyard to the dolmen itself, well preserved and positioned high above the surrounding countryside. It measures 55m x 9m and is surrounded by 77 large stones. It is to be assumed that 'King Humble' was mythological.

Returning to the main road, you should drive through the village and then fork right to Ristinge (5km) to see the long dolmen at *Ristinge Nor* (clearly marked to the right of the road) and the dolmen chamber at *Ristinge Klint*. This latter is reached by following the beach at Ristinge along the cliff face from where there is a path leading up to the dolmen. The beach at Ristinge is one of the finest of the many in Langeland, with sand stretching for several kilometres and ideal bathing waters.

The 305 S from Rudkøbing leads ultimately to the lively port of *Bagenkop* (28km), from where there are regular ferry connections to Kiel (2½hrs). Also, there are plentiful signs of traditional and modern fishing, and a well-equipped yachting harbour.

Returning to the main route, the A9 from **Rudkøbing** runs across a bridge to the flat island of Siø and then by causeway to the wooded and hilly island of Tåsinge. It skirts Tvede Skov forest on the right, and keeps close to the coast. In Lundby, 10km from Rudkøbing, you will find a road to your left leading to *Landet* (1km) where the famous romantic couple, the Swedish Count Sixten Sparre and his beloved tightrope dancer Elvira Madigan, lie buried. When she left him in 1889, the Count followed her to Denmark and shot her before committing suicide himself. Of older date are the many fine Romanesque granite sculptures in the church.

In (3km) *Bregninge* there is one of the churches most frequently visited by tourists, a heavily restored Romanesque church from the tower of which there are wonderful views over the whole of the archipelago to the S of Fyn. It was once said to be possible to see 65 church towers, 20 mansions and 30 windmills from here. Bregninge also houses a small museum illustrating life on the island in a bygone age.—Just outside the village an old windmill has been adapted and turned into an excellent café/restaurant, also with splendid views.

On the S outskirts of Bregninge there is a road to the right leading to Valdemars Slot (Valdemar's Castle) (3km). The wooded road first passes the remnants of an old fortification, *Kærstrup Voldsted* (Kærstrup Ramparts) and then one of the most famous trees in Denmark, the *Ambrosiuseg* (Ambrosius Oak), so named because the 18C poet Ambrosius Stub, who was a tutor in Valdemars Slot, is said to have been fond of sitting under its branches to write his poetry. The tree is thought to be between 400 and 500 years old, and the 20m-high trunk has a girth of 7m.

***Valdemars Slot** itself was built by Christian IV between 1639 and 1644, and was intended for his son, Count Valdemar Christian, who, however, was killed in battle in 1656. It was a mansion truly worthy of a king's son, designed by Hans van Steenwinckel, the architect responsible for Rosenborg Palace in Copenhagen, and bigger than Rosenborg. The original building, badly damaged in the wars against

Sweden (1657–60), was later presented to the naval hero Niels Juel for his part in the wars. In 1678 he began a reconstruction in the baroque style of the day, and it is this magnificent building which now stands on the original site.

One of the largest privately owned mansions in Denmark, it is open to the public, and great efforts have been made in the 21 rooms to which access is given to preserve the appearance of a house in use, even to the extent of lighted candles on some of the tables. The style of the rooms varies from the royal apartments through the great hall and the chapel to the servants' quarters. There are also many important historical relics, not least among which is Niels Juel's own sea chest. The house itself looks out on to a park and an artificial lake surrounded by 18C outbuildings and a pavilion overlooking the sea. In summer, light refreshments are served in this, while there is a bistro in the N wing. The crypt under the chapel houses a restaurant.

Instead of returning straight to the main road, you could continue N and drive through (1km) *Troense*, an old shipping village characterised by its old half-timbered cottages. There is a small maritime museum (*Søfartsmuseum*) here with relics of the China trade for which Tåsinge was once a centre. From the harbour there is a clear view of the island of Thurø, now linked to Fyn by a bridge. The road leads via Eskær back to the A9.

N of Bregninge the A9 crosses a bridge opened in 1962 linking Tåsinge and Fyn and leads you straight into (4km) Svendborg.

Svendborg (25,000 inhab.; Tourist Information: Møllergade 20), the second largest city on the island of Fyn, was founded in the 13C, the earliest record of the name dating from 1229. It was granted a charter in 1253. Built on high ground overlooking the islands of Tåsinge and Thurø, it commands splendid views of the South Fyn coast and archipelago. It has a good, sheltered natural harbour, and this contributed to its growth in the Middle Ages, when trade with the Baltic and the Hanseatic League flourished, to become one of the most important market towns in Denmark. It suffered from the many wars in the Middle Ages, and was burned down on more than one occasion. After a period of peace, Svendborg again suffered under the 17C wars against Sweden, being occupied by the Swedes for 18 months and partly destroyed. The Napoleonic Wars also saw foreign troops there, this time French and Spanish, but since then Svendborg has grown steadily, to become a centre for trade and communication with the islands off the south coast of Fyn.

The old part of the town has maintained its character, with steep streets and many impressive old houses. Of particular interest are *Hulgade* and *Bagergade*. The area is dominated by one of Svendborg's principal churches, **Vor Frue Kirke** (Our Lady's Church). It was originally built between 1253 and 1279, and still bears traces of its early Romanesque character, though alterations in the late Middle Ages have resulted in a predominantly Gothic structure. The spire dates from 1768. The interior is well-proportioned and spacious, giving a sense of light and harmony. The pulpit bears the dates 1597 and 1599, though the carved figures were added in the course of a radical restoration in 1884. The simple altar is from around 1600, but the altarpiece is the work of the important 19C painter Eckersberg. The 27 bell carillon in the tower plays hymns four times daily.

Vor Frue Kirke stands on the highest point in Svendborg (originally the site of the castle), and overlooks the market square with its town hall, theatre and the elegant *Wiggers Gård*, a half-timbered building built in 1939. Although now principally a car park, the square is, for several days in August every year, the site of a re-creation of a typical 19C market.

Vor Frue Kirke is not, however, the oldest church in Svendborg. That honour goes to **Sankt Nicolaj Kirke** in Gerritsgade nearby. It dates back in part to the mid 13C, and thanks to a sensitive restoration in the 1890s is now largely returned to its original form. The granite font is late Romanesque, and the Renaissance pulpit is from 1585. The altarpiece from 1894 is the work of Joachim Skovgaard.

N of Vor Frue Kirke runs *Fruestræde*, an unspoilt old street in which the poet and hagiographer Johannes Jørgensen lived as a child, and to which he returned in his old age after spending many years in Assisi. Part of the house (No. 15) has been turned into a memorial museum (*Johannes Jørgensen Mindestuer*) and is open to the public on Tue. No. 3 is *Anne Hvides Gård*, the oldest dwelling house in Svendborg, built in the 1560s, and now part of the Svendborg and District Museum. However, the main part of this museum is in Viebæltegård, on Grubbemøllevej 13, where in addition to static exhibits there is a goldsmith's workshop.

The elevated part of the town is ringed by a road called Dronningemaen, on which (No. 30) is situated *Svendborg Zoologiske Museum*, with zoological collections tracing the development of animal life over the last 13,000 years (open summer; limited opening winter).

Beyond Dronningemaen is a hill called *Ovinehøj*, in fact the old site of execution. From here there are views over the town and the surrounding countryside and Sound. To the E of the town, on another hill, is *Svendborg Navigation School*. It stands close to the site of the medieval *Ørkild Castle*, long in the possession of the bishops of Odense, and burned down during the Count's War at the time of the Reformation. There is little to see of the castle now, though there are a few traces in the Caroline Amalielund park, where a further attraction is an open air theatre.

A walk E from Svendborg, along the coast, brings you to the wooded area encompassing the old Christiansminde Hotel, recalling an elegant past age, with views across the harbour and Sound, and of the bridge linking Tåsinge and Fyn. A great bonfire is lit here every year on Midsummer's Eve. The sculptor Kai Nielsen was born in Svendborg, and several of his bronzes are to be found in the town.

From Svendborg the A9 continues towards Odense through a wooded and at first fairly flat landscape. After 16km you will come to the village of *Kværndrup*, where, situated on a hill there is an originally Romanesque church unusually with the tower in the E. Among the many tombstones in this church is that of Frands Brockenhuus, who had the nearby castle of *Egeskov (open summer, Rte 14) built in the 1550s.

A further 5km towards Odense will bring you to the village of *Ringe*. Here, too, there is an interesting church, originally Romanesque, but with Renaissance additions, and this time with its tower on the S side. The S chapel, designed by Harsdorff and Wiedewelt, contains the tombs of General H.H. Eickstedt (d. 1801, one of the conspirators who betrayed Struensee) and his family. Ringe Museum contains a good collection illustrating village life in mid-Fyn from prehistoric times, but with the emphasis on the 18C and 19C (open summer).

A short journey E on the 323 here will take you to *Ryslinge* (3km), the site of the first Grundtvigian folk high school, founded in 1850. Apart from its early medieval church in which a feature is the Romanesque granite sculptures, the village also contains the Nazareth Church, a *valgmenighedskirke* (free church) built in 1866 for the Grundtvigian pastor Vilhelm Birkedal, who had been dismissed from his post as a pastor in the Lutheran state church, and whom his parishioners were reluctant to lose. It is the first such church to be built in Denmark. To the S of it stands a memorial statue of Birkedal.

5km N of Ringe you will find a road off to the right to *Sønder Højrup* (1km), where there is an art gallery: *Lindeskov Hansens Kunstsamlinger* (open summer).

At (3km) *Årslev* we suggest that you leave the A9 and turn left to (4km) *Nørre Lyndelse*, where you can visit the childhood home of the composer Carl Nielsen (1865–1931). The house (described by the composer in his autobiography 'My Childhood in Funen') is now a museum illustrating Nielsen's life, and with particular emphasis on his childhood. His wife, Anne Marie Carl Nielsen, was a sculptress, and a beautiful statue by her in memory of her husband and portraying him as a boy playing the flute, stands to the W of the village.

From Nørre Lyndelse you can follow the A43 to (12km) **Odense** (Rte 1), passing on your way *Bramstrup*, the manor dating back to 1689 where the boy Carl Nielsen worked as a cowherd and goose herd.

12 Rudkøbing to Middelfart via Ærø

Total distance 102km. Ferry crossing to **Marstal** (1hr).—Unclassified roads to (12km) **Ærøskøbing**.—(16km) *Sæby*.—Ferry to **Fåborg** (1hr).—329 to (36km) **Assens**.—313, unclassified road to (38km) **Middelfart**.

From *Rudkøbing* (Rte 11) you take the ferry to Marstal on the unspoilt island of *Ærø*, which for centuries belonged first to the Margrave of Brandenburg and then the dukes of Holstein and Schleswig, being left as an integral part of Denmark after the 1864 war which otherwise detached the duchies from the kingdom.

Small as it now seems, **Marstal** (2700 inhab.; Tourist Information: Kirkestræde 29) is a town rich in seafaring history. It has been said that there is not a sailor anywhere who has not heard of Marstal, and in terms of tonnage it was once the largest port in Denmark. The harbour is not entirely natural, and the mole is supposed to have been constructed in a somewhat unusual manner: the sea used to freeze over during the winter, and when the ice was thick enough, huge boulders were dragged out on to it and carefully arranged so that, when the thaw came, the boulders fell into position on the sea bed.

Marstal reached its peak of affluence in the 18C, the age of mercantilism, and the seafarers who formed its inhabitants have put their stamp on the town's appearance. With the advent of the steamship, the town lost its importance, but it has in recent years made a comeback with coaster traffic. There are also plenty of square-rigged sailing ships to be seen there in addition to countless small yachts, and there is a small modern shipyard. Most of the narrow streets, many named after Danish heroes, slope down to the harbour. The houses in them, mostly from around 1800, are tiny and stand on minute plots, an arrangement stemming from the system of taxation in operation at the time. Some are built of brick, others are half-timbered.

There is a splendid *church in Marstal, built in 1738 on high ground so as to be seen from the sea, and full of hints of the seafaring nature of the town, not least in the shape of six ships' models hanging from the roof, while the organ loft is called *the bridge*. The altar candlesticks had their first home in a temple in Peking. The altarpiece (1881) by Carl Rasmussen shows Christ calming the waters, and the figures portrayed are those of sailors well known in Marstal at the time. One interesting, perhaps unique, feature is the existence of two fonts; one dating from c 1150 and made of granite, used to be reserved for children born in wedlock, the other, in black stone, being for the less fortunate. The present clock is the work of Jens Olsen, famous for his world clock in Copenhagen City Hall.—The churchyard, too, reveals a seafaring tradition and contains a famous gravestone with the inscription: 'Here lies Christen Hansen at anchor with his wife; he will not weigh until summoned to God's throne.'—There are two museums in Marstal, the *Skipperhus* in Teglgade (open July) and the *Maritime Museum* in Prinsensgade, both of them rich in seafaring exhibits.

From Marstal follow an unclassified road W for 8km and branch right there to (4km) ***Ærøskøbing** (1200 inhab.; Tourist Information: Torvet). Even at first sight Ærøskøbing is quite remarkable. It received its charter in 1398, and is the only town in Denmark to be scheduled a conservation area in its entirety, much of it being virtually as it was in the 17C. Altogether 36 houses are Class A listed. In place of the minute sailors' houses in Marstal, here there are splendid dwellings, often half-timbered, with bow windows, gables and impressive steps and doorways, redolent of the wealth of the town in the 17C before Marstal began to usurp its place in the 18C.

The two oldest houses are in Søndergade: *Kjøbinghus* (now a café) from 1645, and *Priors Hus* from 1690. The general 17C charm can be experienced by a walk along the narrow, cobbled streets from the *Gaasetorv* square along *Søndergade*, passing through the main square, **Torvet**, with its two wooden pumps and the old grammar school, then right into *Vestergade* and right again down *Gyden*, left into *Brogade*, right into *Nørregade* and back to *Gaasetorv*.—The street lamps are now electric, but they have retained their original shapes.

Free guided walks, with an English-speaking guide, are arranged on Wed mornings by the Tourist Information Office.

There are three museums, the main ethnographical collection being in *Ærø Museum* in Brogade (open summer). In the *Museumsgård* in Smedegade there is a collection of bottle ships and carvings. Then there is the beautiful half-timbered *Hammerichs Hus* containing a valuable collection of china and porcelain. This was the gift of the sculptor Gunnar Hammerich, who also gave Ærøskøbing the 150 plaster casts of his works which are now housed in the *G. Hammerichs Skulptur-samling* in the cellar of the Town Hall. The present, whitewashed copper-spired church, the second or third on this site, is quite modest in size, and was built 1756–58 (restored 1950); it contains a medieval font (13C) and 17C pulpit.

Ærøskøbing was the birthplace of Anders Arrebo (1587–1637), the father of Danish prosody and the author of a large-scale epic poem entitled 'Hexaemeron'; there is a bust of him in the park near the harbour.

There is both a youth hostel and a camping and holiday ground in the town, and bicycles can be hired for a modest charge—an ideal way of experiencing the relatively traffic-free roads and the none-too-hilly terrain.

From Ærøskøbing there is a ferry connection (1¼hrs) to Svendborg (Rte 11), a delightful sail through the archipelago, passing between the islands of Drejø on the left and Hjortø on the right.

You leave on the unclassified road leading towards Søby. Turn right on reaching the main road from Marstal to Søby, and you will almost immediately come to the village of (5km) *Tranderup*. Here there is an unusual, rather intimate *church*, with a tower surmounted by a wooden superstructure in French Empire style built in 1832 and designed by C.F. Hansen, the architect responsible for the Copenhagen Cathedral. The Romanesque church houses a pre-Reformation altar, and above the chancel arch there are early 16C frescoes, one portraying the Virgin and Child, the other a bishop. The chancel is built at an angle from the nave.

Without noticeably leaving Tranderup you suddenly find yourself in (1km) *Vindeballe*, and from here you could just take a quick trip W to some chalk cliffs, *Vodrup Klint* (2km), which give views across the Als peninsula.

The fields closest to the sea have sunk well below the level of the surrounding land, producing a curious terraced formation. There are steps and paths giving access to the shoreline, where it is possible to walk undisturbed for kilometres. A walk sufficiently far S (4km) will bring you to one of the largest windmill farms in Denmark. Ærø is well placed to make use of wind power; some 10 per cent of the electricity here is already so produced, and there are plans to make the island totally independent of electricity produced by traditional methods.

A further 3km on the main road brings you to the delightful village of **Bregninge**, where there are views across the sea on both sides of the island. Here, too, is a very fine church, lying in a secluded position in a large churchyard to the left of the road and of particular interest in that it houses an unexpectedly ornate altarpiece, carved c 1530 by Claus Berg. It is a triptych, the centre panel portraying the Crucifixion, and the two side panels representing the Apostles and a group of saints. There are early 16C frescoes including, behind the altar, a representation of Christ the Judge of the World, while opposite the pulpit there is the head of a jester. A bell rope once came out of his mouth, and the hole, worn askew, is still there.

Another 1km N will bring you to *Søbygård Voldsted* on the right. These 12C earthen ramparts built by Valdemar I as a defence against the Wends lie beside a large farm (privately owned) partly dating from the 16C. It is possible to catch a glimpse of the farm as you walk along a path leading beyond the ramparts and on to the *Vester Mølle* windmill at the top of the hill. This was in use until 1980 and is well preserved—but can only be seen from the outside. The view from it is magnificent.

Søby is only 500m away now, a small but lively town which is the home of a sizeable fishing fleet, a shipyard and a dry dock. The streets were once quite broad and winding, and in places (e.g. in Nørregade and Søbakkevej) small houses have been built 'in the ditch', on tiny roadside plots of land made available to the less well-off workers. Søby church dates from 1745, and has an altarpiece (1870) by Jørgen Roed.—Beyond the town it is possible to walk to the tip of the narrow strip of land leading to *Næbbet* (The Beak), an area with good bathing, fine views and teeming bird life.

There are ferry connections from Søby to Mommark on the island of Als (Rte 14), and to Fåborg on Fyn, each journey taking about an hour. On the latter route there is a view of the tiny islands of Avernakø on the right and Lyø on the left. If, on your trip across Ærø, you have fallen for its unspoilt charm, **Fåborg** (7000 inhab.; Tourist Information: Havnegade 2) will provide a gentle transition to mainland life.

Fåborg is one of the coastal towns established in southern Denmark after the final defeat of the Wends in the 12C. It is first mentioned in 1229 in a document written by Valdemar II, and it received its charter in 1251. The castle built here was destroyed during the Count's War, and it was really only in the 19C, with increased trade, that Fåborg flourished in earnest, becoming a centre for the corn and meat trade with Norway, England and the Duchies. It was badly hit with the loss of the Duchies in 1864, but by then its character as the home of well-to-do merchants was established, and much of that character still exists today.

There are, however, still signs of earlier times. The 15C *Vesterport*, at the end of Vestergade, is the old gateway to the town, carefully restored in 1917. It has a rounded archway and is surmounted by corbie steps to a height of some 10m. In *Lille Tårngade*, close to the market square, there is a 19m-high bell-tower with carillon from the second half of the 15C. Close by there are a number of late 18C half-timbered houses.

The main square, *Torvet*, is the highest point in the town—7m above sea level—and there you will find the Town Hall (1840) and a fountain in bronze by the Svendborg sculptor Kai Nielsen, the impressive *Ymerbrønd*, portraying the giant Ymir drinking milk from the cow Audhumla as it licks the boulder from which was to emerge a man, Burir, whose grandsons were to be the first three gods of Norse mythology, Odin, Vili and Ve. The square is at the centre of the oldest part of the town, which stretches from *Holkegade* in the W to *Jomfru-lågen* in the E. Together with many small half-timbered houses there are two fine 18C merchants' houses in Holkegade, one of which, *Den gamle gård, Holkegade 1, is now a museum housing furniture and other exhibits relating to Fyn. In Vestergade there is the well-preserved *Voigtske gård*, now partly a furniture and clothing shop, the home of the Voigt family with whose daughter, Riborg, the young Hans Christian Andersen fell in love.

The present parish church is *Helligåndskirken* (The Church of the Holy Ghost), a large late 15C Gothic structure once forming part of the Holy Ghost Monastery, traces of which can still be seen on the N wall. The nave is divided into three, giving on to a narrower and lower chancel. The altarpiece, portraying Christ in Emmaus, is the work of Vilhelm Marstrand (1858), and was gived to the church by L.P. Voigt on the occasion of his golden wedding.

The *Fåborg Museum for Fynsk Malerkunst, (Fåborg Gallery of Fyn Painting), Grønnegade 75, was founded in 1910 and now ranks among the leading art collections in Denmark, far more comprehensive than Carl Petersen's tiny neo-classical entrance might suggest. The building is small, consisting of two main rooms and a number of side rooms in which there is a collection of paintings and sculptures by artists associated with Fyn. The original granite sculpture for the Ymerbrønd is here, as are other works by Kai Nielsen, and there are paintings by Johannes Larsen, Poul Christiansen, Anna Syberg, Fritz Syberg, Peter Hansen, Jens Birkholm and others less well known. These are not minor works of art, but paintings of international stature, occasionally on classical themes, but mainly representing the Fyn landscape and rural life.

In addition to the Ærø ferry, there are others from Fåborg to the small islands of Bjørnø, Avernakø and Lyø, as well as a car ferry to Gelting in Germany.

An interesting brief excursion from Fåborg is to the *Kaleko Water Mill Museum* on Prices Havevej about 2km from the town. You drive E on the A44 and on the outskirts of Fåborg turn left towards Diernæs. The Mill is then c 1km ahead on your right. There is thought to have been a mill here since the mid 15C, and the present one is from the 17C. The idea is to give visitors a glimpse of a miller's life in past centuries.

Leave Fåborg on the 329 NW and drive to (5km) *Millinge*, where, in
an old half-timbered grocer's shop at Assensvej 279, there is a *museum*
of toys ranging from an 18C Italian doll to 20C model cars. 1km further
you will find *Stensgaard*, a splendid half-timbered mansion mainly
from the 16C, but partly going right back to the 14C. It is now an hotel.

Continue to (3km) *Faldsled*, where there is a good inn, and 4km later
you pass on your left the mansion of *Damsbo*. It dates from 1656, and
consists of two parallel single-storeyed wings with ornate gables at
either end, and joined by a high wall. In (2km) *Jordløse* there is a
church dating back to Romanesque times, but mainly built in the late
Middle Ages. The principal item of interest is a carved late Gothic
altarpiece from c 1515, the work of Claus Berg's Odense workshop,
representing the crowning of the Virgin. The nearby parsonage is a
delightful half-timbered house with outbuildings around a courtyard.
Originally built in 1734, it was badly damaged by fire in 1981, but has
since been restored.

The road now continues to (5km) *Hårby*, from where you have a
choice of routes to Assens, the direct route (16km), or the alternative
route via Gummerup (25km, see below).

DIRECT ROUTE FROM HÅRBY TO ASSENS (total distance 16km). From
Hårby you take the 323 W. After 5km you will find a minor road on
your left to *Dreslette* (2km). The church here dates back to
Romanesque times, and there are a few Romanesque traces left. At the
end of the 18C it was 'modernised', and the huge three-storeyed tower
was added. There are 111 steps to the top, but there are breathtaking
views when you reach it. Return to the main road and continue to
(5km) Ebberup, which itself has nothing of interest to offer, but you
should turn S here to *Hagenskov* (2km), otherwise known as
Frederiksgave, a magnificent neo-classical mansion from 1774–76,
designed by Georg Erdmann Rosenberg, a pupil of Nicolas-Henri
Jardin.—600m SE of the present house you can see the mound on
which the medieval Hagenskov stood.

1km further S you will find in *Å* the very beautiful botanical gardens,
De 7 Haver, displaying trees, shrubs and plants from seven European
countries and boasting specialised collections, for instance of old-
fashioned roses and rhododendrons.

Return now to Ebberup and follow the 323 for c 3km. Here you will
find the *Kærum Church* on your right. It is to be assumed that the
entire church was once decorated with frescoes in an elaborate—and
unique—pattern of branches, leaves and flowers, many of which have
survived.

From Kærum the 323 takes you straight into (3km) Assens (see below).

ALTERNATIVE ROUTE FROM HÅRBY TO ASSENS—VIA GUMMERUP (total
distance 25km). Leave Hårby on the 329 N to (4km) Gummerup, where
you will find the four-winged **Landmålergård** (The Surveyor's House),
one of the finest half-timbered houses in an area full of them. It was
bought in 1930 by the Vestfyn Hjemstavnsforening (West Fyn Regional
Association) and is now open as a museum illustrating rural life in
former times in this part of Fyn (open summer).

Gummerup has another distinction in being the birthplace of the poet Ambrosius
Stub, the first lyric poet, properly speaking, in Denmark. There is a memorial
stone to him in the village.

From Gummerup you drive further on the 329 to (2km) Glamsbjerg,
where you take the 168 W past (6km) *Øksnebjerg*, easily recognisable

by the Dutch windmill from 1859. This was the scene of a bloody battle during the Count's War in 1535, when Christian III's ruthless commander, Johan Rantzau, confronted the Lübeck army seeking to restore the hapless Christian II to the throne. Rantzau won, and slaughtered 3000 peasants supporting the other side. There is a memorial here to the peasants killed on this occasion.

Continue now past (1km) *Øksnebjerg Mill* to (13km) Assens.

Assens (6000 inhab.; Tourist Information: Østergade 57) is known as far back as 1231, though the date of its first charter is uncertain. After the Battle of Øksnebjerg Rantzau's troops sacked Assens, before proceeding to mete out the same treatment to other towns on Fyn. In 1658 Assens suffered Swedish occupation. It is now a quiet, small port, used mainly for fishing and yachting (there is a marina with room for 600 yachts), and with a ferry to the small island of Bågø. The main source of income is a sugar factory.

The town centre and the harbour have retained much of their old-fashioned character. Near the harbour there is a statue of one of Denmark's great naval heroes, Peter Willemoes (1783–1808), who was born here. He stands on a plinth, and is surrounded by a cobbled area in the shape of the *Prins Christian Frederik*, the ship on which he was killed in battle off Sjællands Odde (Rte 8). Just in front of the statue is a small hut, a *cooking house*, built in the days of sailing ships to provide sailors with hot food, for they were forbidden to have fires on their wooden ships while in harbour.

The birthplace of Peter Willemoes is one of the most spendid houses in the town, situated on the main street, *Østergade 36*. Built in 1675, it is now a museum with a special emphasis on maritime exhibits. Also in Østergade stands the striking *Town Hall* dating back to 1781, though the façade in Renaissance style is the result of radical rebuilding in 1891 and 1917. In the same street there is a statue of Klaus Berntsen, who was Prime Minister from 1910–13, representing Assens in the Danish parliament for 40 years. Still in Østergade, there is a plaque on No. 23 commemorating the sculptor Jens Adolf Jerichau who was born here.

Close to the Peter Willemoes house stands the church, **Vor Frue Kirke**, after St. Knud's Church in Odense the longest in Fyn, and characterised by the lofty, light impression it imparts. The oldest parts, the Holevad Chapel and the base of the steeple, date back to 1295, though the building was not completed until 1488 and is thus mainly Gothic in character. The steeple stands 48m high, and is the only octagonal steeple in Denmark apart from Kalundborg (Rte 7). There is a gravestone from c 1200 by the wall between the chapels. Close to the font, dating from 1910, stands a marble angel by Jerichau, and a large painting by Dankvart Drejer, 'Christ appearing to the Apostles and the Three Mary's', adorns the S wall.

There is a Catholic church in Nørregade, Vor Frelsers Kirke (Our Saviour's Church), run by Redemptorists. Built in 1927, it is in a pleasing, simple style. Signs of earlier affluence are found in several merchant houses. There is an ethnographical museum in *Mands Samling*, Damgade 26, and a museum of silver, glass and antiques in *Fabrikant Ernsts Samlinger*, Østergade 57.

There are good bathing beaches close to the town, and further excellent opportunities for bathing on the coast both N and S. The Tourist Information Office can arrange for fishing excursions in Lillebælt.

For the DIRECT ROUTE from Assens to Middelfart, the 313 N, winding
through wooded countryside, brings you to (5km) *Holevad*, where the
old schoolhouse is now a café, with old furniture and antiques. From
here the 313 continues N and after 22km you will come to an unclassified road leading W to (11km) Middelfart (see below).

For the more interesting, coastal ALTERNATIVE ROUTE follow the 313
N to (7km) Salbrovad, turning left here to (9km) **Wedellsborg**, the
largest estate in Fyn. The large whitewashed mansion dates in part
from the 14C, though it is mostly from the 15C and 16C. It can be seen
from the large park, to which there is public access.
    Now take a minor road from Wedellsborg N through Eskør to (7km)
Tybrind. This is the area of a major Bronze Age find, and two of the
best-preserved *lur* (Bronze Age horns) ever discovered were unearthed
nearby. The road forks in Tybrind and you take the left fork, proceeding
through Rud and Føns to (6km) *Ronæs*, where there is a museum of
Asiatic antiquities and Chinese and Tibetan costumes. 1 km further you
turn left again and remain on coastal roads to (5km) Gamborg, from
where there is only another km to a main road taking you (left) direct
to (7km) Middelfart.

Middelfart (12,000 inhab.; Tourist Information: Havnegade 10) was
historically the site of a ferry between Fyn and Jutland—and it retained that function until the first bridge was built across Lillebælt in
1935. It is mentioned in the early 13C King Valdemar's Landbook and
in the Knytlingesaga, and received its charter in 1496. As a ferry site,
Middelfart has had its share of famous historical personages on their
travels, not least Christian II, who spent a month here in 1523 after the
Jutlandic nobility had renounced their allegiance to him, and it
suffered both under the Count's War and the 1658 war against
Sweden.
    Middelfart has never been one of the richer towns on Fyn, and this
is seen in the modest nature of many of the older buildings, though the
charm of the half-timbered houses is ever present. There are some
larger ones, however, one of which, *Brogade 8*, dates from c 1600 and
is now a folk museum. *St. Nicolas' Church*, over 40m long, with corbie
gables, mainly late Gothic, though with a Romanesque chancel,
stands on Algade, on a hill overlooking the harbour. The richly
adorned auricular altarpiece is from c 1650, and the predella contains
a painting by Eckersberg from 1842. The bench ends are mid 17C, and
two of them bear the insignia of Christian IV. The marble font in the
form of an angel dates from 1845 and is the work of Thorvaldsen's
pupil H.W. Bissen.—There is a large collection of gravestones in the
church, several dating from the mid 16C.
    Middelfart is exactly half-way between the two bridges spanning
Lillebælt. Immediately W of the old bridge stands the mansion of
Hindsgavl, dating back to c 1200 (remains of the original ramparts can
be seen), but now a neo-classical building from 1784. The main house
is now used as a conference centre. The park, with views across the
sound and to the tiny island of Fænø, is open to the public.

13 Tønder to Kolding

Total distance 81km. A11/A25, A25 to (15km)
Løgumkloster.—(18km) *Toftlund*.—(48km) ***Kolding**.

You leave ***Tønder** (Rte 15) on the A11/A25, driving N for c 6km. Turn right on the A25, and follow it for c 9km until you meet the 401. Here you should divert by turning right and going to Løgumkloster (2km).

Løgumkloster (3000 inhab.; Tourist Information: Østergade 2A), is a large village with wide streets and greenswards and many 18C houses. It contains the remains of a Cistercian monastery founded in 1173. Building on the *church began in 1190 and was completed more or less in its present form by 1325. The oldest extant part is the present N door, while the chancel and impressive corbie gable are high Gothic. Note in particular the splendid E end, with its intricate windows and gabling. The monastery was suppressed after the Reformation, in 1548, though the buildings were left standing for some time. A section of the W wall can still be seen, and on the E wing the chapterhouse and dormitory have been restored.

The chancel is large in relation to the nave, reflecting the fact that the clergy sat there, while the nave was reserved for the lay brothers. One notable architectural feature is the lack of vaulting at the intersection of the nave and transept, giving it the appearance of a cupola. There are, as is customary in a Cistercian monastery, few decorations in the spacious and beautiful church, but in the chancel there are some interesting misericords from c 1500. There is also a 14C reliquary in the wall, with space for 16 relics. An elaborate antependium from 1325 is now in the National Museum in Copenhagen. In the crypt there is an exhibition illustrating the history of the monastery and of the Cistercian order in general.

Immediately adjoining the W wall of the church is a building known as *Slottet* (The Castle), now used as a training centre for the clergy. It was built as a hunting lodge in 1614 by Duke Johann Adolph of Gottorp, and has subsequently been used for various purposes. The bishop and poet Hans Adolf Brorson lived here for a time, and it is said that it was here he was converted to his pietist views.

An attempt has been made in the present century to re-create something of the spiritual calm with which Løgumkloster was formerly associated, and in 1959–61 a *Refugium* or Retreat Centre was built and opened. It is connected to the church by a covered walkway and is open to people of all religious persuasions seeking a respite from everyday life.

On the opposite side of the river there is now a folk high school, and close by a modern bell-tower, *Frederik IX Klokkespil*, with a carillon of 49 bells on which aspiring carilloneurs are trained. It can be heard six times a day.—A museum called *Holmen* contains exhibits reflecting medieval church life and modern church art (open Easter–October). In front of it there is a statue by Alice Buchhave of a Cistercian monk.

The annual fair in August, *Kloster Mærken*, is the largest in Scandinavia. Originally called St. Bartholomew's Fair (Bettemøs Mærken), it starts on the third Saturday in August, close to St. Bartholomew's Day, the 25th. There is a statue of three jugglers on the town square commemorating this event.

A more sombre commemoration is found in the cemetery immediately S of the town, where there is a memorial to 70 Russian, Belgian and French prisoners of war who were held here during World War I (when this was German territory), and who died during a typhoid epidemic. The memorial was placed there by their fellow prisoners.

From Løgumkloster you drive NW to (2km) *Løgumgårde*, where the old parish church of *Nørre Løgum Kirke* is situated. This consists of a Romanesque chancel and nave, with Gothic extensions, including a late 14C tower. The auricular pulpit is from c 1630 and the (much adapted) altarpiece from 1400. The entire church is decorated with frescoes by the Lily Master.

You then drive N, through (4km) *Nørre Løgum* village, turning off left after a further 5km to (3km) *Arrild*. Here you will find an impressive church with a Romanesque nave and Gothic tower. The beamed roof is richly decorated with acanthus leaves. The altar has a painted Gothic antependium and is surmounted by an elaborate triptych from c 1475. Much of the remaining furniture is also of early date, not least the carved bench ends from c 1550.

In Arrild, too, there is a modern holiday village, consisting of some 400 holiday homes, many of them available for letting. Information on these can be had in Toftlund Tourist Information Centre.

7km further N on the A25 you arrive at *Toftlund* (Tourist Information: Søndergade 5), a small town, centrally placed, with excellent road connections to Tønder, Ribe, Haderslev, Åbenrå and Flensborg, and giving easy access to the beautiful countryside—woodland and moorland—in this part of South Jutland.

The *church here is an unusual shape, the nave on the S side being lined with three gables which for all the world look like the gables of houses facing the road, such as are seen in Tønder and other towns in South Jutland. The pitched roofs on these gables are intended to harmonise with that surmounting the much older tower. They represent extensions from 1912 to 1913 to this otherwise Romanesque/Gothic church.

The nearby *Tislund Church* is the oldest in South Jutland. To reach this you take a road E from the N outskirts of Toftlund towards *Bevtoft*, turning left after c 3km. The small church is entirely Romanesque with the exception of a porch from 1852. There are four original Romanesque windows, of which one, in the N side, has not been bricked up. Note the small, rounded chancel arch, unchanged since it was built. There is a reliquary in the medieval altar. The altarpiece is an early 16C triptych with simple but skilfully carved figures, and the granite font is Romanesque. The pulpit is from c 1575, unfortunately 'modernised' c 1700, when the original carving was planed off to make way for some second-rate paintings of the four Evangelists.

9km N of Toftlund the A25 runs through *Gabøl*, from where it is worth driving the extra 8km W along the A47 to *Gram* (Tourist Information: Torvegade 13), where **Gram Mansion** is a fine sight. Standing on a bend by the main road, it was built c 1500 to replace a castle dating back to 1231 which stood some 3km further NW. Surrounded by woodland, and fronted by the castle pond, it now houses the *Central Southern Jutland Museum*, with archaeological and geological collections connected with the area. Perhaps most surprising is the six-million-year-old skeleton of a whale discovered in a claypit nearby.—On the opposite side of the main road, you will find the *South Jutland Fire Service Museum* (open summer).

From *Gabøl* you drive further N on the A25 through delightful varied countryside to (13km) *Jels* (Tourist Information: Den gamle Mølle). Here there is a thoroughly restored windmill (open summer), and here, too, in the woodland down by one of the three local lakes, there are some impressive ramparts dating from Viking times, *Jels Voldsted*.

There is also an open air stage where there is so-called Viking entertainment in July.

The road now runs NE to (11km) *Vamdrup*. This small town, now virtually unknown, was once the Danish border station for the main European railway lines to Scandinavia. It was built by the English when the Danish railways were expanding rapidly, and the English presence is still to be seen in some of the architecture. The old railway station is now a *museum* illustrating the history of the railways. In Vamdrup, too, is the source of the *Kongeå*, the river once forming part of the border between Denmark proper and the South Jutland duchies.

From Vamdrup the road continues NE to (5km) *Hjarup*, where there is a 17C half-timbered former parsonage. 5km further on the road meets the E45, which you can join if you wish to go N or E without going in to Kolding. Otherwise you drive a further 5km to ***KOLDING** (42,000 inhab.; Tourist Information: Helligkorsgade 18), which is Denmark's seventh-largest city.

Kolding is first mentioned in the 13C *King Valdemar II's Jordebog* (a kind of Domesday Book) and has a charter from 1321 (though this was probably not its first); it was an important commercial centre in the Middle Ages because of its position as a junction N–S and E–W and its proximity to the German-speaking lands to the S, and it still has a busy harbour, the most important in the country for the export of cattle.

In the Middle Ages the castle, *Koldinghus*, which King Erik Glipping saw as 'a gateway and key to the realm' was a place where the Court met, and many members of the nobility subsequently had mansions there or in the immediate neighbourhood. As a consequence, Kolding was the scene of more than one dramatic event. It was there that in 1365 Valdemar Atterdag was reconciled with the sons of the hated Count Gert of Holstein, who at one time ruled all Jutland, and who in 1340 held Kolding in pawn. In 1411 Erik of Pomerania concluded a peace treaty here with Duchess Elizabeth of Schleswig. Later, the ubiquitous Christian II met his uncle Duke Frederik (later King Frederik I) here in 1522, and Kolding was the site of an abortive attempt in 1534 to put an end to the Count's War. Skipper Klement, the peasants' leader during the Count's War, was for imprisoned for a time in the fortress of Koldinghus.

A period of decline ensued in the 17C continuing until the mid 19C when the harbour facilities were greatly improved; later the advent of the railways brought new significance and new trade. In the 1848–50 war against Holstein, Kolding was at first the site of the Danish military headquarters, but was for a time occupied by enemy troops.

*Koldinghus, standing on high ground overlooking the surrounding countryside and fjord, is the only royal fortress now surviving in Jutland, and several kings have been closely associated with it.

Koldinghus was the birthplace in 1545 of Duke Hans the Younger, the first ancestor of the present Danish Royal House, and the following year of his younger sister, Dorothea, an ancestor of the present British House of Hannover. Christian II included it in a list of three castles (the others being Ribe and Skanderborg) which were to be maintained. Frederik II lived here as a boy, Christian IV is said to have written his first Latin essay here, and Frederik IV met his future mistress and subsequently queen here when he sought refuge against the plague in 1711. It was the favourite residence of Christian III, and he died there on New Year's Day 1559.

It is not known exactly when the first Koldinghus was built, but historical sources claim that it was founded in 1284 by Duke Abel as 'a defence or border fortress' after his brother, Erik Plovpenning, had burned down parts of Kolding. It is, however, certain that Erik Glipping helped rebuild the castle in 1268. Christoffer of Bavaria built the N Wing in 1447, and Christian I added the W Wing in 1470. Christian II was responsible for the S Wing, with its royal apartments, and for the E Wing. Christian IV, the king who provided Denmark with many fine buildings and an enormous national debt, built the Chapel and the great tower on which he placed four 2.25m-high sandstone figures: Hannibal, Hector, Scipio and Hercules. High above the surrounding countryside, and each facing his own

ODENSE

KOLDING
0 metres   300

Geografisk Have

point of the compass, these figures, with the three Scandinavian crowns on their
shields, symbolised Christian's dream of a united Scandinavia—under himself.
Only Hercules survives, and he faces S.

Koldinghus has suffered from fire and damage on many occasions. The N and
W Wings burned down in 1533; there was another fire in 1597; and yet others in
1627 and 1644. In 1658 Polish troops stormed the castle, which at the time was
in the possession of the Swedes. The greatest catastrophe, however, came in 1808
during the Napoleonic Wars. Spanish troops stationed in the castle accidentally
set fire to it and it was almost completely razed to the ground. Christian IV's great
tower collapsed and took much of the vaulting of the Chapel with it. The decision
to rebuild Koldinghus after the 1808 fire was not taken until 1867, the National
Museum being given responsibility in 1890. The task was completed in 1989, and
the castle, looking much as it did in the Middle Ages, is now open to the public.

Adjoining the castle is the well-preserved and charming old part of the
town, largely reserved for pedestrians. Here, at Axeltorv 2, is *Borchs
Gård*, a large, three-storeyed house said to have the most elaborately
decorated gabled façade in Denmark. It was built in 1595 by an
apothecary, Herman Reiminck, whose initials are worked into the
decorations in the lintel over the front door. There are acanthus leaves
and angels' heads, and at the top of the gable there is a huge rosette.—
The oldest surviving house in Kolding, *Helligkorsgade 18*, bears the
date 1589 and was the home of a shoemaker; it is again three-storeyed,
a typical Renaissance half-timbered house, restored in 1915. Together
with the house next door, *Morten Eriksens Gård*, with an inscription
stating that it was rebuilt in 1632, it gives some impression of what
Kolding must have looked like when houses of this kind and size were
commonplace.

The principal church in Kolding, *Sankt Nicolai Kirke*, standing on Kirketorvet, was founded in the mid 13C, though after a thorough restoration in the 1880s there is now little left of the original building. Nevertheless, it still contains a splendidly carved and imposing Renaissance altarpiece and pulpit dating from 1589 and 1591. Claus Lauritzen's sandstone font, in the same style, is from 1619.

The 19C National Romantic poet Carl Ploug (1813–94) was born in Kolding. He is commemorated with a statue, and there is a plaque on the spot where his house used to stand. There is a certain irony in the fact that Carl Ploug's doggedly nationalistic ideas were those largely responsible for the Danish defeat at the hands of the Prussians in 1864. On *Jernbanepladsen* there is also a statue to the Liberal politician Chresten Berg (1829–91).

The *Trapholt Art Gallery* opened in 1988 as one of the largest galleries in Denmark. Situated in a beautiful position overlooking the Kolding Fjord, it specialises in Danish art and handicrafts from the present century and incorporates all the most modern museum principles.

Geografisk Have is a botanical garden, with a fine collection of trees and plants from all over the world, including a rose garden with 125 different varieties, a scent garden and the largest bamboo grove in Europe.

Kolding boasts one of Denmark's largest marinas, situated at the mouth of the harbour. It is possible to hire boats, and there are sailing trips on the fjord on Wednesdays and Sundays in the summer.

14 Tønder to Nyborg via Sønderborg

Total distance 137km, plus ferry. A8 throughout.—(37km) *Kruså*.—(28km) **Sønderborg**.—(16km) *Fynshav*.—Ferry to *Bøjden* on Fyn (50 mins).—(11km) **Fåborg**.—(45km) **Nyborg**.

This route at first runs close to the 63km-long border between Denmark and Germany. The border has not always lain here; after the 1864 war it was much further to the N, but a plebiscite was held in the area in 1920 to decide on a final border between the two countries; voting took place parish by parish, and the present line follows the local wishes then expressed. Even after World War II, no changes were made to the 1920 border, which over the years has become less and less formal. For much of its length it follows the courses of rivers, but elsewhere you will find villages where it runs straight down the middle of a street, or farms with fields on either side of it. In theory you still need a passport to cross it, but in practice you are unlikely to be asked for one if you decide to go and have a drink in a German inn on the opposite side of the street.

There *is* a border, then, and it is both political and cultural, but there are equally areas of cultural affinity. One of these is the work of the great Expressionist painter Emil Nolde (1867–1956), who was born in the now Danish village of Nolde; but he was a German-speaker and by the art world has always been considered as belonging to German Expressionism. There are plenty of signs of his presence on the Danish side of the border, but the magnificent **Nolde Museum** is in Seebüll, just S of the border in Germany.

From ***Tønder** (Rte 15) you take the A8 E to (14km) *Burkal*, where there is a Romanesque church from the first half of the 13C, one of the most richly decorated in South Jutland.

The outstanding feature is the glorious 17C painted ceiling over the nave, which was revealed during restoration work in 1943. Against a blue and blue-grey background there are 13 medallions representing Christ and the Apostles, accompanied by 26 others representing the arts, virtues and seasons. The altarpiece is a rare piece of Renaissance work from 1622, the centrepiece containing reliefs instead of the more usual paintings; the pulpit and canopy, typical of this area, are from the same period. The crucifixion group fixed in the chancel arch is much earlier, from 1500–25.

In Burkal you will also find the large Grøndal farm with a barn built in the Holstein style—brick walls, whitewashed, surmounted by a sweeping thatched hipped roof, rounded over the doorways.

Before continuing you might also like to drive 2km S to *Rens*, where there is a large old watermill.

From Burkal you take the A8 to (11km) *Tinglev*. There is little of architectural interest here, but Tinglev is the focus of German cultural life in the region. Between 1920 and the period after World War II, great efforts were made by the minorities of both countries to maintain and support their cultures, and Tinglev provides plenty of evidence for this, with German schools and nursery schools, German-language newspapers, and German-language political organisations. For many years nationalist feelings on both sides ran very high indeed, but now things are different, and tolerance reigns—though no one in this area can be unaware that two cultures meet here.

The A8 continues SE through (10km) Fårhus where you turn right towards *Frøslev*, a place which has played a role in modern history.

Frøslev was the site of a concentration and internment camp during World War II, and many of the 13,000 or so Danes held here were further despatched to concentration camps in Germany itself. After the war the name was changed to Fårhus Camp, and Danish collaborators were housed here to await trial. Now it has been thoroughly restored and is the home of several *museums: The National Museum has exhibits here, as have the Danish Civil Defence and Red Cross Organisation. Some of the accommodation has been left as it was when used as an internment camp, and there are also exhibits to show what life was like in South Jutland during the Occupation (closed Dec–Jan).—A UN museum is at present being prepared, to illustrate the work of the 36,000 Danish soldiers who have served under the UN flag since 1948.

From Frøslev it is only 2km E to *Bov*, N of Padborg. Again there are memories of wars here. On 9 April 1848 Danish troops fought and won a battle at Bov against Schleswig-Holstein troops, and there are graves in the churchyard to remind visitors of this event and of the 1848 war in general. Both N and S of the present border there are countless places with memories of border conflicts over the ages (often in the form of war memorials and soldiers' graves), ranging from the Dannevirke fortifications (now S of the border) to a memorial in *Padborg* to the three border guards shot on duty at the time of the invasion in 1940. *Bov Museum*, housed in a building from 1528, contains excellent local collections covering the history of the *Military Road* (Rte 21) and displaying uniforms from the various wars affecting the region.

A further Danish relic now S of the border is Christian IV's Copper Mill (Danish Kobbermølle, German Kupfermühlle), just S of Kruså, where much of the finest 17C and 18C Danish copper was produced. The mill itself has gone, but the houses which Christian IV built for his workers still stand, in much the same style as Nyboder in Copenhagen.

From Bov you should drive NE 2km to the Danish frontier town of Kruså, and from there you can stay on the A8 right to (11km) Rinkenæs. However, we suggest you leave the A8 1km after Kruså towards *Kollund*, and cover this short distance along the slightly longer coastal road instead.

This *road, which provides outstanding views of the Flensborg Fjord and the

German coast and town of Glücksburg opposite, has been called the most beautiful coastal road in Denmark. Certainly Hans Christian Andersen subscribed to the view: 'The countryside around the Flensborg Fjord is without doubt one of the most picturesque parts of Schleswig; there are great forests, hills almost as big as mountains, and the ever-varying scenery of the winding fjord and the many quiet freshwater lakes.'

On the way you will pass through (4km) *Kollund* with its church from 1971, built in traditional Danish village style. A further 3km brings you to *Sønderhav*, with a view of the tiny *Okseøer* islands where tradition has it that Queen Margrethe I died of the plague in 1412. From Sønderhav it is a further beautiful 5km to *Rinkenæs*.

In *Rinkenæs* there are two churches, of which the older, standing on high ground, but without a tower, is Romanesque, with a 16C porch. It still contains some, but not all, of its original furniture—two statues of saints from the original altarpiece, the Virgin and Child, and twelve figures of the Apostles. The pulpit is from 1606. There are many old gravestones, including that of the first soldier to fall in the war of 1848. Some of the remaining furniture—a crucifix from the chancel arch and some late Gothic candlesticks—have been transferred to the new church, built in 1928–32 in traditional village church style. The carvings on the pulpit were begun by the sculptor Otto Bülow, but he was murdered by Occupation forces in 1943, and the work was completed by others.

From the outskirts of Rinkenæs it is well worth taking a walk along the fjord on the old *Gendarmsti*, the path once used by patrolling frontier guards.

Now continue to (2km) *Alnor*, where you should leave your main route, turn left and drive to Gråsten (2km) for a short DETOUR.

As you approach Gråsten (Tourist Information: Ahlefeldtvej 4), there is a view across the Nybøl Nor (Nybøl Cove) on your right, and then, on your left the Slotssø, Palace Lake. After passing this you turn left on to the 481, and immediately on your left again you will arrive at what you have really come to see, **Gråsten Palace**. This three-winged structure dates from 1759 when it was built to replace the earlier palace, much of which was destroyed by fire in 1757. It was redesigned in 1842 and given in 1935 to the then Crown Prince and his wife, and it is still the summer residence of the Queen Mother, Queen Ingrid. When Queen Ingrid is not in residence there is public access to the courtyard, castle and exuberant baroque *Chapel, which, with an altarpiece stretching from floor to ceiling and much as when originally consecrated in 1700, is now used as a parish church. When the Queen is in residence, there is a ceremony of changing the guard on Fridays at 12.00. The deer park is normally open to the public.

Hans Christian Andersen visited the castle in 1845 as the guest of Duke Christian August of Augustenborg, and it was here he wrote his story 'The Little Match Girl'. Here, too, the memories of a frontier area are preserved, in that there is a memorial outside the castle grounds to the colonel who, single-handed, offered resistance to the Gestapo in 1944 when they came to arrest him—and after a three-hour-long battle paid with his life.

During the third weekend in July each year, Gråsten has a festival of tilting in the ring, and during the last week of August there is a large-scale fair and market in the town. Throughout the summer pleasure boats sail on the fjord and you can enjoy the beautiful landscape from the water.—W of Gråsten lies one of Denmark's finest beech forests. It is open to the public, and there are countless paths for a walk in idyllic surroundings.

Leaving Alnor you should take the A8 E across the Egernsund narrows to (5km) *Broager* (Tourist Information: Storegade 23), the main town on the undulating **Broagerland** peninsula dotted with small woodlands, crisscrossed with hedges, with steep cliffs overlooking the fjord to the E, and with long stretches of excellent beaches from which to bathe.

From far afield you can see **Broager Church**, with its twin towers, an

unusual sight in Denmark. Legend has it that these towers, surmounted by decorated tiled spires, were built in memory of Siamese
twin sisters who were joined at the hip. (And 19C excavations did
actually unearth the skeletons of such twins.) So tall are the towers that
during the 1864 war the Prussians used one of them as a look-out post
to direct gun fire at the Dybbøl fortifications further E. In 1923 restorations uncovered frescoes from both the 13C and 16C, including Christ
in Majesty in the apse and, in the N transept, a series depicting in
graphic detail the martyrdom of St. George. Clearly connected with
these is the splendid (though restored) life-size figure of St. George on
horseback slaying the dragon, standing in the tower.

To the E of the church is a free-standing wooden belfry of a type
commonly found in this area. Topped with an octagonal spire, it dates
from 1650, and is the largest in the country.—Nearby there is a memorial
mound surrounded by stones bearing the names of the 190 members
of the parish, then German citizens, who were killed in World War I.
Of older date are both Danish and German graves from the two
Dano-Prussian wars.

A minor road SW of Broager will bring you to *Brunsnæs* (3km), with a clear view
across the Flensborg Fjord to the German side about 2km away. Due E of Broager
you come to the very hilly *Broager Mark*, an area ending in the high cliffs on the
E coast, overlooking Sønderborg.

If you take the A8 E from Broager and then turn right into the 481, you
will come to (4km) **Dybbøl**. If any place in this part of Denmark signifies
national feeling *vis-à-vis* German culture, it must surely be this.

There were battles here during the first Dano-Prussian war of 1848, and then the
area was fortified in 1857 with extensive 'earthworks to serve as a second line
of defence in the event of the Dannevirke fortifications falling in a future war. On
the night of 5 February 1864, during the second Dano-Prussian war, Dannevirke
did indeed fall, but the Dybbøl fortifications were not yet complete, and after a
violent bombardment lasting 34 days, they, too, were taken, an event which in
practice brought the war to an end and put the entire area under German rule
until 1920. After the war the Prussians completed the fortifications, and most of
those now on view were in fact built by them, not the Danes.

Dybbøl has come to symbolise Danish defeat and Danish national aspirations,
and the particular symbol of these is the **Dybbøl Mill**, standing on high ground,
and offering panoramic views of the entire fortified area. Originally built on this
spot in 1744 or 1745, the windmill has been burned down three times, twice as a
result of the wars, and once by accident in 1935. The entire area is full of war
graves, of both Danes and Prussians, one of the most touching being of two Danish
soldiers buried in a private front garden beside the road at nearby *Bøffelkobbel*.

The area around Dybbøl has figured in patriotic poetry and in fiction, nowhere
more poignantly than in the novel 'Tina' by Herman Bang, where the mood of
the Danes during the battle near Dannevirke is graphically portrayed. There is
now a museum (open summer) with exhibits from the wars and the 1920
reunification of the area with Denmark, and the area immediately surrounding
Dybbøl Mill is a national memorial park. From an earlier period there is the
Romanesque church from c 1250, with a crucifix over the chancel arch from c
1200. On the hill at Dybbøl you will also find the huge red granite erratic boulder,
the *Dybbøl Stone*, 8.8m long, 6.7m wide and 2.7m high.

From Dybbøl it is only 3km along the 481, crossing the elegant high
bridge built in 1980 to span the narrow Als Sound, to Sønderborg, the
principal town on Als, the seventh largest of the Danish islands.

The island of *Als* is c 34km long from NW to SE, with a curved E coast lined with
dunes and fine beaches, while the west coast is indented and irregular, approaching to within 120m of Jutland at *Als Sound* with its deep and sometimes
fast-flowing water. The countryside is wooded and varied—and very beautiful.
The roads are good and allow you to experience this rather special island at your
leisure. And while you do so, you should remember that the present idyll covers

over a past which has been marked by violence extending back to the Wends
and the Vikings.

Sønderborg (25,300 inhab.; Tourist Information: Rådhustorvet 7),
meaning 'Southern Castle', has grown up around a royal castle dating
back to the 12C, probably founded by Valdemar I (Valdemar the
Great) as a defence against the Wends, and later becoming a residence both voluntary and involuntary for Danish kings when in the S
of the country. It was here that Christian II spent 17 years of his life,
from 1532 to 1549, after the safe conduct promised him had been
broken by the nobility. As imprisonments go, his was probably rather
comfortable.

If there is a scarcity of old buildings in Sønderborg, with the exception of the area around Havbogade, it is for once not because of fires,
but because it was severely damaged by Prussian artillery during the
1864 war. However, the **Castle**, now a museum, stands, massive and
impressive, on a tiny headland jutting out into the S entrance to the
Als Sound. It forms an irregular rectangle, with a 10m-high tower built
into the NW corner, and shows traces of rebuilding in the 14C. The
character of the castle changed in the period 1550–70, when it was
transformed into a Renaissance palace with no military potential.
During the 17C Swedish wars, however, it fell into disrepair, and it was
then reconstructed in the 18C in baroque style. In the 19C it was again
severely damaged, serving for a time as a military hospital and then as
a Prussian barracks. The 20C has seen a gradual restoration, first in
the 1930s, then in the 1950s and 1960s. The chapel, often called the
Queen Dorothea Chapel after the Queen who was responsible for
much of the 16C rebuilding, was restored in 1954–55 and reflects the
new church style deriving from the Reformation, with the pulpit occupying a central position.

As the largest provincial *museum in Denmark, the castle now has
extensive collections illustrating the history of the castle and the
surrounding area; it also contains a fine art collection including works
by C.A. Lorentsen, C.A. Jensen and C.W. Eckersberg, who is sometimes called the father of Danish painting. Naturally, the Dano-
Prussian wars of the 19C are well represented, as are the two world
wars and the reunification of this area with Denmark in 1920. Of
curiosity interest are the decrees issued by the self-styled President of
Als when, in 1918, as part of a naval mutiny in North Germany, a
disgruntled sailor by the name of Bruno Topff proclaimed Als a repub-
lic. His presidency lasted for three days.

There are the remains of one other very old building in Sønderborg,
though in the course of the 17C, 19C and 20C it has been extensively
rebuilt. Even the name was changed in 1957 from St. George's Church
to St. Mary's Church, *Mariekirken*. Nevertheless, there is some old
furniture left, the altarpiece being from 1618, the font from 1600, and
the carved pulpit (the work of Master Hinrich Ringerinck of Flensborg)
from 1599. On the N wall there is a cupboard from the 15C. The other
church in Sønderborg, built in 1957 and designed by Kåre and Esben
Klint, the architects responsible for the Grundtvig church in Copenhagen, is modern Gothic, an adaptation of the traditional corbie-gable
village style.

The medieval tradition of tilting has been maintained in South
Jutland, and a four-day-long festival of tilting is held in Sønderborg
each summer, beginning on the second Saturday in July, preceded by
a solemn procession of those taking part.

From Sønderborg the main road goes NE to (3km) Ulkebøl, where it rejoins the A8. *Ulkebøl* itself is now virtually a suburb of Sønderborg, with a good deal of industry and the airport. Here, too, however, in what was once a separate village, stands the Romanesque *church which was formerly the principal church for Sønderborg, extended and rebuilt in 1787 to exhibit some of the architectural features of the Augustenborg Palace Chapel (see below). There is an ornate triptych from c 1525, carved in Antwerp, and, above the altar, a late Romanesque crucifixion group from c 1250. The tower is remarkable in being as broad as the nave.

From Ulkebøl the A8 continues to (5km) **Augustenborg** (Tourist Information: Storegade 28) on the island of Als. Strictly speaking, *Als*, does not form part of southern Jutland, but is a separate entity, once the domain of the Dukes of Augustenborg. It was a Duke of Augustenborg who built the first *Augustenborg Palace* in 1660, while a successor replaced it between 1770 and 1776 with the present three-winged mansion, the biggest and most imposing in this part of Denmark, dignified, totally symmetrical, slightly severe in its splendour. It has had a mixed fate, having been a military hospital and a barracks—and is now a mental hospital. The park is open to the public: note the memorial plaque near the tree under which Hans Christian Andersen used to sit. The splendid baroque chapel is used as a parish church, with rich, ornate decorations in white and gold.

EXCURSION TO NORTH ALS FROM AUGUSTENBORG. From Augustenborg you take a minor road N to (3km) *Ketting*, where, standing on high ground overlooking the delightful village, there is yet another church with an unusually broad tower, dating back to the early 13C. The original chancel and nave, which were slightly older, were pulled down and replaced in 1773. The altarpiece is from 1743, but parts of two earlier altarpieces from c 1450 and 1500 can also be seen in the chancel and on the N wall, while there is a crucifix from c 1300 above the chancel arch. The large parsonage from 1802 is a little E of the village, approached by an avenue of elms and chestnuts. There is a bishop's palace (Bispegård) in Ketting, for this was the seat of a bishop from 1819, when Als and Ærø (Rte 12) formed a diocese, until 1864, when Als became part of the diocese of Schleswig.

An unclassified road now leads N to (2.5km) *Egen*, another charming and idyllic village. Here you will find the largest (75m long) thatched church stable in Denmark, with stabling for 34 horses to rest while their owners are in church. The church itself, originally dedicated to St. Martin, goes back to the 13C. The chancel and nave are Romanesque, the remainder later. There is a free-standing medieval bell-tower in the churchyard, erected on top of an ancient burial mound.

A further 9km NW will bring you to *Oksbøl*, where there is another church with a Romanesque nave and chancel, and a massive Gothic tower surmounted by a tiny 18C lantern. The 15C altarpiece was put back in the church in 1957 after spending many years in museums.

Continue N from Oksbøl to (2km) *Nordborg* (Tourist Information: Storegade 16–18), where the old village has been extended to the SE and now adjoins the modern *Langesø*, built for the workers in the Danfoss factory only 4km away (see below). Nevertheless, Nordborg has its charm, and to the N lies *Nordborg Castle*, dating back to the 11C, and in its way forming a North Als parallel to Sønderborg Castle. And like Sønderborg, Nordborg has been used as a prison, for Bishop Valdemar of Schleswig, and for Erik Glipping (when he was 12 years old!). The original castle has been destroyed, and the present building dates from 1909. It is now a college, and the grounds are open to the public in summer.

From Nordborg the 405 goes SE to (3km) *Havnbjerg*, where there is a Romanesque church containing remains of Romanesque and Gothic frescoes. The altar painting is by Eckersberg. Here, too, there is a splendidly restored thatched Dutch windmill from 1835 (open), together with a dwelling house and outbuildings of unusual type. The 405 now continues to (1km) *Danfoss*, the home of the Danfoss factory—refrigerators, thermostats, central heating—which was the brainchild of a local inhabitant in the 1930s and since the 1950s has grown to employ over 6000 people.

Hjortspring, 2km further along the road, is where in 1920 a 4C ship, surrounded by weapons, was found in a bog where it is assumed to have been put as a sacrifice. It is now in the National Museum in Copenhagen.

From Hjortspring you return to (12km) Augustenborg.

EXCURSION TO SOUTH ALS FROM AUGUSTENBORG. This in effect a rather longer alternative to the main route (below) from Augustenborg to the ferry harbour at Fynshav, but it also gives you an impression of the beautiful scenery of South Als.

Leave Augustenborg on a minor road S to (3km) *Kirke Hørup*, where there is a Romanesque/Gothic church with a free-standing medieval bell-tower, partly rebuilt in 1689. Part of the altarpiece is from 1425. In Kirke Hørup, turning left on to the 427, you travel via Skovby and across the Drejet embankment to *Sønderby* (17km), where there are panoramic views across the Flensborg Fjord. Here, too, is *Kegnæs church*, built 1615–16 by Duke Hans, with a porch from 1695, on the outside of which there is an original sundial. The altarpiece is from 1450, possibly transferred from Sønderborg, which received a new altarpiece in 1618; the chancel arch crucifixion group is from c 1500.

You will now have to return to Skovby by the same route, and from here you then take a minor road N to (2km) *Lysabild*, where there is a medieval pilgrims' church containing a chapel dedicated to the Holy Blood. There are also frescoes from 1425 depicting the Crucifixion. As part of the foundations to the N wall a Bronze Age cresset stone has been used and is still visible. W of the churchyard lies the parsonage, from 1826, with a magnificent example of a Holstein type barn, from 1783.

From Lysabild you drive N to (2.5km) a crossroads. If you turn right here you will come to (2km) *Mommark*, where you can take the ferry to Søby on the delightful island of Ærø (Rte 12). Otherwise, you continue N through *Blommeskobbel*, with its prehistoric remains, to (8km) Fynshav ferry harbour.

Returning to the main route, on leaving **Augustenborg**, you continue along the A8 for c 5km until you come to a road on your left pointing N to Hundslev. Take this road and drive as far as *Notmark* (1km), where, standing in a beautiful churchyard, there is a fine church, with a Romanesque chancel and nave, and a late Romanesque tower of impressive proportions, finished with gables to the N and S. The nave has a beamed roof, while above the chancel there is vaulting bearing frescoes of coats of arms. A processional crucifix above the altar is from c 1525. Nearby there is a thatched stable in which parishioners could keep their horses while at church. The parsonage, clearly visible from the road, is from 1688, a delightful thatched half-timbered house with patterned brickwork, thoroughly restored in 1952. It is the only Danish parsonage originally having dwelling house, stables and barn all under one roof. And huge this hipped roof is, with its two broad gables.

Return now by the same road, and cross the A8 to go only as far as **Asserballe** (1km) where the Romanesque church stands on high ground. It affords panoramic views from its relatively high tower. However, despite several pieces of old furniture, it is particularly for its literary associations you should see this church and the nearby parsonage. It was in the idyllic *parsonage here that the novelist Herman Bang was born in 1857, and it is this house in which much of the action in his autobiographical novel 'The White House' is set. Asserballe is similarly the setting of Bang's novel 'Tina', with its moving portrayal of the Danish defeat at the hands of the Prussians in the 1864 war—though it has to be admitted that Bang was no longer in Asserballe when these events took place.

Go back again to the A8 and drive E to (4km) *Fynshav*, where you take the ferry to Bøjden on the island of Fyn (50 mins). Here you follow the A8 E to (6km) **Horne**.

Horne boasts one of the seven round churches in Denmark, and the only one on Fyn. The trouble is that the original round church has been extended to comprise the usual chancel, nave and tower, though it is still clearly distinguishable, 17m in diameter and much like those on Bornholm (Rte 25). There have been two floors in the original circular part, and there are arrow slits placed high in the 2m-thick walls, indicating that the upper floor was at one time used for defence. The original Romanesque chancel has been replaced by a long Gothic nave of the same height as the rotunda. The vaulting is late Gothic throughout. The grey, blue and gold furniture is early 19C, and the painting over the altar is by Eckersberg. The marble font used at present is by Bertel Thorvaldsen, while there is another Romanesque granite font near the NW pillar in the round church. The crucifix above the chancel arch is from 1525. One of the impressive features in the church is the *balcony directly facing the pulpit. It was built for use by the Bille-Brahe family, the owners of the nearby mansion of Hvedholm; their imposing neo-classical chapel can be seen in the churchyard outside. Hvedholm itself, rebuilt in the late 19C, lies to the right of the road c 1km further E, and is now a rest home.

4km further on, the A8 brings you to the N outskirts of Fåborg (Rte 12). Do not just pass through this old town. It is well worth a visit.

From Fåborg there are two suggested routes to Nyborg and the nearby ferry harbour of Knudshoved. The direct route to Nyborg (total distance 51km), listed first, goes straight across Fyn, the alternative follows its S coastline.

DIRECT ROUTE FROM FÅBORG TO NYBORG (total distance 51lm). Leave Fåborg by the A8 NE, skirting the delightful wooded hills of *Svanninge Bakker* to (8km) Korinth.

In the village of *Gerup*, 1km W of Korinth, the old school from 1784 has been turned into a *school museum*, open Saturday afternoons.—N of Korinth on the E side of the beautiful **Arreskov Lake**, the biggest lake on Fyn, you will find the 16C Renaissance *Arreskov mansion*, where visits to the park and the house can be arranged.

2km further along the A8 you will reach the great mansion of *Brahetrolleborg*. This was originally a Cistercian monastery from 1172, called Holmekloster, and the 13C church constituting the present N wing is the only remaining part of the early buildings. Other parts date from the 15C, and alterations and extensions were also carried out in the 16C, 17C and 19C. A thorough restoration in 1985 uncovered remains of the original monastery. After the Reformation the complex was taken over by the Crown and the name was changed, first to Rantzausholm and then, in 1667, to Brahetrolleborg. In the 18C the estate was turned into a model of social and agricultural progress. The park is open to the public.

From Brahetrolleborg you continue along the A8 for 9km, where, on your left, you reach ***Egeskov**. This is an absolute must. It is one of the best preserved and most romantic of all Denmark's Renaissance castles, standing in the middle of a lake on a foundation of oak piles and huge boulders. With its twin pointed towers and ornate gabled walls it is the archetypal fairy-tale castle. The surrounding park, also among the best kept in the country, dates from the 18C and is divided into sections representing gardens in different traditions. It is famous for its hedges, and it contains one of the few mazes in Denmark. The house itself has undergone several restorations, most recently in the 1970s and 1980s, and one of the most impressive features is the great *hall, now regularly used for concerts. The grounds also house a *museum* of veteran cars, aeroplanes, motorcycles and horse-drawn carriages. Egeskov is open to the public from May to September.

*Egeskov Castle, mid-Fyn, is one of the finest
Renaissance castles in Denmark.*

2km beyond Egeskov you reach Kværndrup (Rte 11), from where you might take an unclassified road E in the direction of Gudbjerg as far as *Mullerup* (7km), an estate with a history going back to 1474, situated in idyllic surroundings in the midst of a series of lakes and canals. The present building is from 1887 and now serves as a centre for the sale of antiques.

Otherwise leave Kværndrup to the NE and follow the A8 to (7km) *Gislev*, where there are some fascinating early 16C frescoes in the church. Done in an unsophisticated style, they represent scenes from the life of Christ, and it has been suggested that the way in which Mary is shown worshipping the Child may indicate the influence of Brigittine visions. These frescoes are all in the vaulting, and there are remains of others, portraying Gethsemane, on the N wall.

From Gislev you can drive straight on to (6km) Ørbæk. However, we suggest you take a slightly less direct route.

Turn left in the middle of Gislev on to a minor road leading N to the mansion of *Lykkesholm* (2km), dating from the 1780s, and, like so many of the mansions in this area, associated with visits by Hans Christian Andersen. It is not open to the public, but clearly visible from the road to the N.—Continue to (1km) Ellested and turn right into the 323. Ørbæk is now only 4km away, but just before reaching the village you will find a track to your left leading to *Lindeskovdysse*, the Lindeskov Dolmen. Surrounded by 126 large stones, this is the longest long dolmen in Denmark. Drive on now to Ørbæk.

In the Romanesque church in *Ørbæk* there is again a wealth of colourful frescoes from c 1500, the work of a local artist known as the Clog Master. The baroque altarpiece is late 17C, incorporating figures from a late Gothic triptych; the pulpit dates from c 1592.—Just 1km S of Ørbæk stands the mansion of *Ørbæklunde*. It is visible from the road, and you can get closer to it on foot, but not in your car. It is unusual in being one of the last fortified houses to be built in Denmark (1560–93). The spire is from 1593, and the side wing was added in 1660 (no public admission).

From Ørbæk the A8 continues to (7km) *Vindinge*, where the church possesses a large and famous crucifix by Claus Berg from the 1520s.

Now you can drive into (4km) **Nyborg** (see below).

ALTERNATIVE ROUTE FROM FÅBORG TO NYBORG—VIA SVENDBORG (total distance 60km). Leave Fåborg on the A44 driving E. In (16km) *Vester Skerninge* there is a Romanesque church with an altarpiece by Eckersberg (1817). 2km further on you come to *Ollerup* where you will pass its famous High School for Gymnastics, which is clearly visible from the road, an impressive set of buildings dating from between 1920 and 1939.

You really ought to allow yourself a short DETOUR here. Turn N near Ollerup church on to a small road leading towards Egebjerg, simply to experience the most impressive scenery in South Fyn, the *Egebjerg Bakker* hills some 3km away.

Immediately after the Ollerup High School you pass *Hvidkilde Lake*. Here you will find a car park from which there are marked walks through the beautiful park of *Hvidkilde House*. 1.5km further, on your left, you pass Sørup Lake before arriving in **Svendborg** (Rte 11).

From Svendborg you continue NE on the 163 to (7km) *Skårup*. The church here dates back to 1319, and some of the original Romanesque features are still visible amidst the Gothic extensions. In the church-yard there is a Gothic tithe barn which was once used to house the poor of the parish. The altarpiece, which was restored in 1929, is an elaborate Gothic carving from c 1470. The pulpit is mid 17C. The nave and chancel have vaulted ceilings, but that in the late Gothic tower is flat; it is said that the pastor used to keep his beer on the floor above it. The E frame of the S door of the church reveals a primitive Romanesque carving of a ship.

2km further N, in Vejstrup, you will find *Vejstrupgård*, a small mansion from 1754, in the grounds of which there is *Vejstrup Watermill*, the biggest two-wheeled watermill in Denmark, built in the 1830s. From Vejstrup it is only 7km to Hesselager, our next stop on the main route. However, if you don't mind a little meandering, we can take you past a few more mansions and another church before then.

3km N of Vejstrup on the left you come to a road leading to Gudme. Take this, and immediately after leaving the main road, on your left, there is the mansion of *Broholm*, with a history dating back to 1326, though the present buildings are from 1642, the square tower having been added in 1895. The principal wing is on a small islet in the middle of a lake. The courtyard is open to the public.

Continue to (2km) *Gudme*, where there is a church of particular note. You will immediately notice the enormously wide late Gothic tower, much bigger than is to be expected on a church of this size, and somehow out of keeping with the corbie steps at the W end and over the S door from 1603. All the vaults inside are decorated with fresco ornamentation, and there is another large fresco on one of the walls illustrating the legend of St. George. A date above the chancel arch indicates that they are from 1488. The altarpiece is a simple carving from the end of the 15C, and there are two late Gothic choir stalls, thought to be from Claus Berg's workshop.

Return now to the 163 via Broholm, turn right, and almost immediately left again on to a minor road leading to (4km) *Lundeborg*, a tiny fishing village with views across the water to the island of Langeland. There used to be ferries from here to Langeland, but the Svendborg-sund Bridge has put an end to that. However, the village is well worth visiting. There are paths along the coast in each direction, and the bathing is good. If you need a nice inn at this stage, it is here too.

On returning from Lundeborg, in 1.5km you come to a crossroads. Turn right here. This road will take you in the direction of Hesselager, and in particular past (2km) **Hesselagergård**, one of the oldest and most impressive mansions in Denmark. Hesselagergård is first mentioned in 1446, and the present building, dating from 1538, was erected on the orders of the great Chancellor Johan Friis (1494–1570). It is visible from the road, with an unusual rounded Venetian *gable thought to have been built to the orders of Johan Friis himself after he had seen similar structures in Germany. It is a splendid piece of Renaissance architecture. The interior contains many elements from an earlier age, for instance a huge fresco and other unusual pictures, and in the cellar the remains of a dungeon—but the house is not open to the public.

2km further on lies Hesselager village.

The rather atypical *Hesselager* *church repeats the rounded gables of Hesselagergård mansion (see above). On the orders of Johan Friis they were added to the original Romanesque church in 1550. There are some frescoes in the church, including an illustration of the fable of the fox and the stork (which, here, is a crane), and the coats of arms of members of the Friis family. Among the numerous gravestones and memorials in the chapel, there is one ordered in 1557 by Johan Friis in memory of himself and his family. It portrays a very realistic figure of Death holding the coat of arms of the Friis family.—To the N there is a well-preserved tithe barn, half of which served as a school around 1600, later to be used as a poor law institution.

If you follow a minor road E of Hesselager church for 2km you will find the *Hesselager Stone*, otherwise known as **Dammestenen** (The Damme Stone), a granite boulder thought to weigh about 1000 tonnes. It is 12m high and 46m in circumference. Legend has it that a witch threw the stone at the church in Hesselager, but missed. In practice it was brought here by ice from Norway during the Ice Age and is the largest erratic boulder in Denmark.

From Hesselager, take the 163 and continue N for about 2km to Langå, where you can turn left past the church to *Rygård mansion* (2km). There is access to an area close to the house, but not to the house itself, which can only be glimpsed through trees. Rygård was built just before Hesselagergård (c 1530), but looks much more the sombre medieval castle, with water on two sides, it stands on piles driven into the marshy ground of a tiny island.

After the medieval aspect of Rygård and the early Renaissance air about Hesselagergård, the time has now come to see the neo-classical façade of *Glorup*. To find this you return to Langå, drive 1km N and turn left towards Svindinge immediately on leaving the village. Glorup is about 1km down this road.

There has been a mansion here since 1599, but the present neo-classical building dates from 1765. It is not open to the public, but there is access to the park on Thursday afternoons and all day Sunday. This *park is itself well worth a visit, the work of the French garden architect Nicolas-Henri Jardin, containing areas in the French and the English styles. There is a 'temple' from the 1870s, containing a statue of Andromeda by Johannes Wiedewelt—possibly originally intended for Moltke's Palace, part of the royal Amalienborg palace in Copenhagen (Rte 4).

Glorup was one of the many mansions on Fyn which Hans Christian Andersen was particularly fond of visiting. He went there for the first time in 1839 and returned no fewer than 24 times over the next 30 years.

Back on the 163, drive N for a further 4km and turn off to (2km) Frørup, where you will find *Østfyns Landbrugsmuseum*, the East Fyn Agricultural Museum, an extensive collection of old agricultural implements. There is a garden attached, where you can eat sandwiches or buy a cup of coffee.—From Frørup you can continue N along a quiet road to (5km) Kogsbølle, turning right there to *Stevnshøj*, a vantage point 65m above sea level, with a splendid view across Nyborg and Knudshoved. From here, too, you can see Holckenhavn, the last call before Nyborg, reached by continuing to the 163 and turning left.

Holckenhavn, the largest private mansion in Denmark, was originally called Kogsbølle; it came into the possession of the Ulfeldt family and was then called Ulfeldtsholm until Christian IV's mother-in-law Ellen Marsvin acquired it and changed its name to Ellenborg. It was given the name Holckenhavn by its new owner, Eiler Holck, in 1672. Two wings of the present house were built in the 1580s, the principal and secondary towers in 1596 and the remainder in the 1630s. It was thoroughly restored between 1904 and 1910 with the intention of giving it back the appearance it had when Ellen Marsvin was in charge. She it was who was responsible for the unusually ornate chapel in which the carvings are said to have taken the artist seven years to complete. The house is not open to the public, but there is access to the park for limited periods on Tues and Sat afternoons.

From Holckenhavn you drive across the narrow Holckenhavn Fjord to (2km) Nyborg, continuing past the harbour and on to (5km) Knudshoved (Rte 2) if you so wish.

Nyborg (15,500 inhab.; Tourist Information: Torvet 9) with a charter from 1292 is a major provincial port, of particular importance for its ferry connections with Sjælland. These used to go from the centre of the town, but most are now centred on *Knudshoved*, the ferry terminal on the spit of land stretching 3km to the E. The ferry crossing takes about one hour.

The town grew up around **Nyborg Castle*, which was founded in 1170 by Knud Prislavsen, a nephew of Valdemar I.

It was one of a system of castles built along Storebælt as defences against the Wends. However, with its central position Nyborg soon became the meeting place for the Danehof and the Rigsråd assemblies and thus the capital of Denmark, until Copenhagen took over this function in 1413. Prior to this many official and royal documents were issued in Nyborg. Here, too, many events of national significance occurred: Erik Glipping signed his stern charter here in 1282; five years later, his murderers, Marsk Stig and Rane Jonsen, were outlawed here; in 1326 South Jutland was here enfeoffed to Count Gert of Holstein.

The original castle was surrounded by water and a brick ring wall. The keep was built into the E wing, while opposite, built into the W wing, was the dwelling house, the Palatium, where various kings and their retinues lived. Christian II was born here.

A period of decline began in the 17C. A great storm in 1620 wrought havoc, and during the war against Sweden 1658–60 such damage was done to the castle that it was no longer suitable as a royal residence. All attempts to maintain the building ceased, and in 1670 one of the towers was taken down. In 1702 a visiting French diplomat described it as 'an old castle falling in ruins, without tiles, and with several cracks in the walls'. In 1722 most of the castle was demolished, and some of the materials were used in building Odense Castle. Only the royal apartments and the keep were left standing, and the keep was reduced in size in 1822.

In 1849 the State took over the castle, and by the beginning of the present century its historical significance was becoming appreciated. In 1914 the National Museum was voted funds to begin the work of reconstruction, at the same time as carrying out archaeological excavations on the site. The old W wing was very largely restored to the appearance it had at the time of Christian III. This wing is now open to the public from March to October, sparsely furnished as it would have been then, though the furniture itself is mainly somewhat later. It is even possible to hire the old Great Hall and the old Danehof Hall for private formal receptions and dinners, and thus—against suitable payment—to entertain one's guests in the oldest royal castle in Scandinavia.

The main church in Nyborg, *Vor Frue Kirke* on Gammel Torv, was radically rebuilt in the 19C, but the W end of the nave is thought to have been built in 1389 on the orders of Queen Margrethe I, and the E end to be from 1428. The nave is separated from the aisles by arcading, and the pillars here clearly indicate the different period in which the two sections were built. The sturdy tower is from 1581, and the spire from 1588–89. Much of the furniture, including the altarpiece, is 19C, but there is a 1649 wrought-iron grating in the S side by Christian IV's artist craftsman, Caspar Fincke. In the S chapel there are two fonts, one, Romanesque, of granite, the other, Renaissance, of wood. The pulpit is a richly carved work by Anders Mortensen from Odense, dated 1653.

Of other old buildings in Nyborg, mention must be made of a medieval stone-built house, the *Korsbrødregård* just S of the church, on the corner of Adelgade and Korsbrødregade. The oldest part is from the early 15C, the remainder early 17C. Likewise in Korsbrødregade, the old parsonage also dates back to the 15C, but it was also extended and rebuilt in the 17C. It has been restored in the 20C.—There are various half-timbered houses, of which *Mads Lerckes Gård*, Slotsgade 11, is undoubtedly the most impressive today. Built in 1601 by Mads Lercke, with side wings added in 1637 and 1643, this house of 30 rooms is now a local history museum, particularly interesting for its reconstruction of an affluent burgher's home from the mid 18C (open Mar–Oct). It stands next to another of Nyborg's grand houses, *Dronningegården*, from 1760.

Nyborg suffered from a serious fire in 1797, and much of the subsequent rebuilding was in neo-classical style. Many of the dignified new buildings still stand in *Torvet*, *Kongegade* and *Nørregade*. A particularly fine, but slightly later, example is found at Korsgade 4.

A good stretch of the old ramparts to the N and W of the castle still exist, and they now form a public park. In particular there are good views from the section called Dronningens Bastion. The town gateway from 1666 has also survived.

15 Tønder to Ringkøbing

Total distance 160km. A11 to (46km) **Ribe**.—(46km) *Varde*.—(43km) *Skjern*.—A28, A15 to (25km) **Ringkøbing**.

If you approach Denmark by car from Germany, one of the likely points of entry is the crossing N of the German town of Süderlügum on the German highway 199, which in Denmark then becomes the A11 and takes you to Tønder. Other border crossings on the E coast will also almost inevitably take you there.

You are now in the area of Denmark known as *Sønderjylland*, southern Jutland, which as a border region has in times past seen more than its share of wars, from the 13C to the 19C. The excruciatingly complicated problems of the region stem from the fact that the two former duchies of Schleswig (Danish: Slesvig) and Holstein (Danish: Holsten) each had a different relationship to the Kingdom of Denmark, to which they were both nevertheless linked, and whereas Schleswig was predominantly Danish speaking, Holstein was predominantly German. When, in the 19C, national sentiments emerged, it turned out to be impossible to satisfy all parties, and war was the result. After the 1864 defeat of Denmark by Prussia, southern Jutland became part of Germany, which it remained until 1920, when a parish-by-parish plebiscite determined the present border.

*Tønder (8200 inhab.; Tourist Information: Østergade 2A) is only some 3km N of the border, and stands at the S edge of the area known as *Marsken* (The Marshland). This is the almost totally flat region bordering the North Sea, much of it below or just at sea level, protected by dykes like those in Holland. So not only has the region known wars, but it has in the course of time been subjected to natural catastrophes in the form of flooding. On one occasion in the 14C, some 30 churches are said to have been washed away, while thousands of the local inhabitants perished. Little wonder that laws were introduced compelling those owning land to help build dykes. These and the system of drainage canals saved the land, but in the course of the resultant transformation, Tønder, which had once been a harbour and of great importance for the export of cattle, found itself surrounded by dry land in the 16C. It still has a ship in its coat of arms.

Tønder is first mentioned in 1130, and it was granted a charter as a market town in 1243. When it lost its harbour facilities it turned to other means of making a livelihood, and by the 18C lacemaking was the region's principal occupation. By the end of the century it provided work for some 12,000 people, many of them working in their own homes. Fortunes were made by the lace merchants, as is apparent from the opulence of some of the early houses still standing in Tønder. Gold and silver smiths added to the wealth.

A walk through some of the old streets with their characteristic end-facing gables will quickly reveal the affluence of a former age.

Look, for instance, at the entrances to the 17C and 18C houses in *Østergade* or *Vestergade*, with their intricate carved portals in sandstone, impressive flights of steps, and sandstone lions guarding the entrance. And the doors themselves, with their exquisite rococo decorations. To top it all there is the *Amtmandspalæ* (The Sheriff's Palace) from 1768 in Jomfrustigen. Even the more modest houses, often with bow windows, speak of more than modest means. Standing on the town square is the oldest house in Tønder, the *Old Town Hall* from 1520, restored in 1987.

There was once a castle in Tønder, but it has now disappeared without trace. However, the old gatehouse is still there, and together with an adjoining further building from the 1920s it now forms the **Tønder Museum** with, among much else, a collection of old Dutch tiles reflecting the life of the area in the days when the export of cattle established a close link with Holland. Reciprocal trade brought the tiles to Tønder, and it was common practice to tile the interior walls of houses. The museum also contains a truly impressive collection of local lace and silver-work.—The old lock-up has been incorporated into it, as has the old whipping post in the shape of a man, the 'Kagmand', the only one left in Denmark.

Sønderjyllands Kunstmuseum is housed in the same building. Originally founded on Danish art presented by Danish artists to celebrate the return of southern Jutland in 1920, this gallery has grown over the years to include the work of both well-known and lesser-known Danish artists as well as others from northern Germany and Holland.

The principal church in Tønder, **Kristkirken** with its 47.5m octagonal spire, its Renaissance and baroque furniture reflects, like the dwelling houses, the wealth of a past age. It was built 1591–92 to replace the earlier St. Nicholas' church which was now too small. Nevertheless, this earlier church must also have had considerable character, and remains of it are still to be seen in the marble font (1350) and some of the carved bench ends, while the Renaissance pulpit from 1586 also stems from it. The baroque altarpiece is from 1695, and the splendid choir loft with its 18 scenes from the Bible dates from 1623. A further striking feature of the church is the 14—often bombastic—memorial tablets dating from between the 15C and 17C, lining the nave.

Near the S wall there is a bust of Hans Adolf Brorson, who was pastor in Tønder from 1729–37 before becoming Bishop of Ribe. However, this pietist pastor and bishop was also a poet, one of the greatest of Denmark's hymn-writers, and it is for this he is remembered. The Danish hymn book has on more than one occasion been referred to as 'the best anthology of Danish poetry'. Even prior to the Reformation there were hymns of note in Danish, but the post-Reformation Lutheran church has fostered a large number, many of the highest literary value.

Danish poetry would be able to enjoy considerable distinction even if it had not produced more than the poetry of Brorson, Kingo and Grundtvig, all of whom are most noted as writers of hymns and all of whom became bishops. Thomas Kingo, who was the earliest of them, was the great baroque poet. Brorson, a few years his junior, was the rococo poet, the man who saw God's greatness even in the smallest things in creation. He endured much suffering in his life, with the early loss of his wife and the mental illness of his son, and some of his hymns betray a longing for death, though others are more optimistic. In particular his later work showed an impressive command of verse form and linguistic inventiveness.

EXCURSION FROM TØNDER TO MØGELTØNDER AND HØJER DYKE (total distance c 26km). It is not only Tønder itself and its famous son that give this area a special interest. There is also Højer, 12km away on the west coast, and on the way there Møgeltønder and Gallehus.

You start your excursion by taking the 419 W, turning right after 3km to reach the tiny village of **Gallehus** (1km). There is not immediately very much to see here, only a few houses around a green on which there are two standing stones. Yet it was the place of two of the most important archaeological finds in Danish history, and because of them and their subsequent fate, the ultimate inspiration to one of the finest poems of the Romantic Age, 'The Golden Horns'.

The story must be told: in 1639 a young lacemaker, Kirsten Svensdatter, was walking through a field in Gallehus, when she stumbled on something lying just under the surface of the ground. She picked it up and found it to be a golden horn 75.8cm long and weighing just over 3kg. In 1734 a young farm labourer, Erik Lassen, walking nearby, stumbled over another one, rather shorter. The runic inscription and the ornamentation on the two horns suggests that they were made some time in the 5C. Christian IV actually used the first as a drinking horn, but in time both were put on display in the Royal Museum in Copenhagen. There, an enterprising goldsmith, Niels Heidenreich, decided he could put them to better use. He stole them and melted them down. Unfortunately for him, he was caught and spent the next 38 years in prison. Fortunately for us, drawings were made by Ole Worm, and on the basis of these it has been possible to reconstruct the horns, reproductions of which are now on view in the National Museum in Copenhagen.

A few doors from Niels Heidenreich in Copenhagen lived the budding young poet Adam Oehlenschläger, who just at this time became fired with the ideas of German Romanticism. He wrote his first major poem, 'The Golden Horns', in a verse form much like that of the old Eddic poetry and in expression a programme piece of Romanticism: the horns were the gifts of the gods to the innocent whom they had chosen—but they were put on display by unimaginative scholars with no sense of the real significance of the divine gift—and so the gods took them back. If there is any poem known by all Danes, it will be this.—To come back to Gallehus: the two inscribed standing stones mark the spots where the horns were unearthed.

Return to the 419, cross it and drive to (3km) **Møgeltønder**. There is little else here than a castle, a church and a very beautiful main street. But all this makes it worth visiting. The main street, *Slotsgade*, is lined on both sides by carefully tended old thatched houses once used by the castle staff. Many have the bow windows common in the Schleswig area. Both the footpaths and the road are cobbled, and between them is a row of lime trees on either side of the road.

As its name suggests, Slotsgade leads to the castle, *Schackenborg*. Built in 1664–67, this was extended and 'modernised' in the 18C, though the two side wings have retained much of their original character. It was the last fortified castle to be built in Denmark, and it still bears traces of its fortifications, not least in the form of several cannon. It replaced the older *Møgeltønderhus*, which was given to Hans Schack in recognition of his victory over the Swedes at Copenhagen and Nyborg in the 17C Swedish wars, and has remained in the possession of the same family since.

The •church, which has been closely associated with the castle, is large and impressive, with special pews (from 1691–92) reserved for the owners of Schackenborg. The nave and chancel are Romanesque, and to them have been added a Gothic transept and W tower. Parts of the E end are from c 1200. You will find this church particularly striking for the great number of frescoes it contains. Those in the chancel date from c 1550, while others over the chancel arch are from c 1275. Others again are considerably later—some even from the 19C when the older frescoes were subjected to a thorough and somewhat heavy-handed restoration. There is a splendid late Gothic altarpiece from c 1500, a late Romanesque granite font and a baroque pulpit (1694). The organ, from 1679, is one of the oldest in Denmark, and a special wooden vault has been constructed above it to make room for the pipes.—A reminder that this area was once part of Germany is found in the churchyard, where there is a memorial to soldiers killed in World War I while fighting on the German side.—*Kniplehusets*

Museum, at Sønderbyvej 1, is a museum of lace and lace-making from the 18C to the end of the 19C, demonstrating not only the products, but the methods used in lace-making (open summer; limited opening winter).

From Møgeltønder you will automatically continue on the 419 to (7km) *Højer* (Tourist Information: Højer Mølle), an unspoiled village of narrow streets and thatched houses and farms, many of them scheduled, the centre of the system of sluices used to control the water level in the Marshland. Like many of the churches in this region, that in Højer seems to huddle up to withstand the elements, sombre and tough. The old windmill is now a *museum demonstrating the battle against the threat from the North Sea (open Apr–Oct).

The system of *sluices, some from 1861, now supplemented by a new system from 1981, is most impressive, as is the double system of dykes, the new, outer one, running from Emmerslev, N of Højer, to the embankment connecting the German mainland to the island of Sylt. Take a look at the sluices and the museum (open Apr–Oct) in Slusevej, Margrethe-Kog just S of Højer. Nearby you will find the unusual farm called *Hohenwarte*, built in the 1860s as a replica of the University of Kiel and now a plant research station.

Back in Højer you join the 419 again and drive back to Tønder.

Returning to the main route, drive N from **Tønder** on the A11 to (11km) *Bredebro* (Tourist Information: Storegade 13), which, as the name implies, is the bridge over the river at Brede. Here there is an impressive and carefully restored church, originally from the 13C, but extended in 1772. The tower is from 1400 and the spire from 1694. A reminder of more modern times is the fact that the tower was struck by a shell in 1940, and that the shell is still there!

A touching memorial here remembers a sailor, Jørgen Martensen, who was taken prisoner by Turkish pirates in 1678. The local population collected money for a ransom, but the poor chap died before it was handed over—and so the money went to a memorial instead.

From Bredebro the A11 continues N to (12km) Skærbæk. However, if you are not short of time, we suggest you take this alternative and much more interesting route.

Leave the A11 at Bredebro and drive W on an unclassified road through (9km) Randerup, the birthplace of Brorson, there turning left to (6km) *Ballum*, a coastal village with many old houses. It is quite a modest place, but to those who have read their Karen Blixen it will be of interest, for it is from here that the story 'Sorrow Acre' (from 'Winter Tales') emanates. There is even a gravestone in the churchyard said to be that of the unfortunate mother, and locals might show you the field in which she harvested the rye. Believe it all if you like.

Drive N on the 419, after 5km passing on your right all that remains of *Misthusum*, a village that was washed almost completely away in a great storm in 1634. There is little left except a single house built from the ruins, and now a tiny museum of local history. 2km further brings you to the 10km-long embankment leading to Rømø.

*Rømø (Tourist Information: Havnebyvej 30, Tvismark) is a kind of tourist paradise, and the numbers of visitors in the summer reflect this. There is a broad shoreline, with excellent nude bathing facilities if you want them. The beach facing the North Sea is unbelievably wide: even where it is narrowest there is over 1km to the water at high tide. There is a rich animal life here, including many seals, and every conceivable sports facility.

Traditionally, Rømø has been an old-fashioned seafaring island with
scarcely any roads, and it was only in the 1960s, with the building of
the embankment, that this came to an end. The inhabitants try to
maintain some of their old customs, not least that of wearing national
dress on festive occasions. Yet untouched by modern life as it was until
a late stage, there are signs of plenty in the old houses on the island,
outstanding among which is what is now the museum, **Kommandør-
gården**, an impressive, solid house on suitably high ground, built in
1744 and restored by the National Museum in 1951. (A ticket to this
museum also gives you access to Toftum gamle Skole (Toftum Old
School), the oldest and smallest school in Denmark, in use from 1784
to 1874.) Like many houses in the area, the inside walls of Komman-
dørgården are clad in Dutch tiles, and there are richly carved beams
and decorations.

The island's wealth came from its seafaring tradition, particularly in
the 18C, and its whaler captains ('kommandører') have left their mark
on it both in the fine houses they built and, not least, in the splendid
gravestones which they ordered for themselves and their families—
and for which they tended to write their own inscriptions. Take a look
at the churchyard; it is unusual. The church is medieval in origin, but
was extended during the affluent 18C. It is a relatively large building,
though it is not without a certain intimate charm. Model ships hang
from the ceiling, and carved plants decorate the pews.

On returning to the mainland you stay on the 175 until, at 4km it
crosses the A11 just N of Skærbæk.

In *Skærbæk*, a former merchant's residence now houses a museum
with a comprehensive collection illustrating everyday life in southern
Jutland (limited opening all year).

On leaving the village you take the A11 N to (5km) **Brøns**, where
there is a church with a magnificent painted ceiling and beams decorated with floral patterns; the pews are painted bright blue and
equipped with carved bench ends, all overlooked by pale but beautifully preserved frescoes from the time of the Reformation. They are a
graphic presentation of the debate of the day, with the Pope, prelates
and high-ranking laymen gathered around what looks like a letter of
indulgence, while a group of (smaller) ordinary people are clearly
arguing with a monk. Meanwhile, this is a church of some size, the
early parts dating from c 1250. In addition to a large Romanesque font,
there is a tabernacle from c 1300 in the chancel and a late 15C crucifix
over the chancel arch.

The road to Ribe will now lead you through (5km) *Rejsby*, where the
late Romanesque church has an unusual octagonal spire and a painted
wooden ceiling. A further 5km brings you to *Hviding*, which was´once
on the coast and furnished with a harbour. There is a theory that this
was the original site of Ribe, and certainly Hviding was a rival to it in
the 12C. The large church in the nearby *Gammel Hviding* here reflects
this early status and has an unusual late Gothic altarpiece portraying
a host of figures surrounded by a rosary.

Just N of Hviding you will see a road to the left leading to Vester
Vedsted (3km), from where you can see, and possibly reach, the tiny
island of Mandø (7km). The Wadden Sea here is so shallow that there
is a special bus service to Mandø at low tide—but do not try to walk or
drive across yourself, as you are likely to stray from the road—which
disappears at high tide in any case.

Because of its isolation, **Mandø** has maintained much of its old character as a
fishing and seafaring community with a great deal of bird life, and Mandø village

is no more than a cluster of houses, a church, a school and inn (with accommo-dation). There are some small museums, though. *Mandøhuset* (The Mandø House), a skipper's house from c 1830, offers exhibits illustrating early 19C life on the island (open May–Oct). At Midtvej 3 there is an ornithological museum (open Apr–Nov), while the windmill, Mandø Mølle, on Søndre Strandvej, has been restored and opened to the public. The tiny church, once described as '17 paces from the altar to the door', dates from 1727, with a porch added in 1792. The painter Joakim Skovgaard did an altarpiece which stood in the church from 1890 to 1895, when it was removed because the wet salt air was ruining it, and the present altarpiece is a copy of it. The reindeer antlers serving as coat racks were found in the sea W of Mandø and are thought to be 10,000 years old.

Returning to the main route, on the A11, you have only got another 5km to drive before you arrive in ****RIBE** (8000 inhab.; Tourist Infor-mation: Torvet 3-5), one of the finest medieval cities in Denmark.

Ribe has a long history. It is first mentioned c 860 when St. Ansgar, who started the conversion of Denmark, was given permission to build his second church here (the first was in the now vanished Hedeby further south). From this it must be assumed that even at that time Ribe was a town of some importance, probably as a trade route to England and southern Europe. Certainly, archaeologists have uncovered over 60,000 artefacts from the Viking Age and before just outside the town. In 948 Ribe was given its first bishop, thus gaining yet more in importance, both as an ecclesiastical centre and as an increasingly busy trade centre. Its significance is further underlined by the fact that coins were minted here as early as the reign of King Knud (Canute) the Great.

Valdemar II gave the town considerable privileges and tax dispensations, and these were renewed by succeeding monarchs, the earliest of them dated 1242, the latest 1766. In 1127 King Erik held his son's wedding here, and accounts talk of an inordinately busy harbour and thriving trade at that time. By 1200, Ribe was the most important trade and transit centre in Denmark, with close links with many of the major trading cities in Europe. Towards the end of the Middle Ages, with the advent of better sailing ships capable of rounding Skagen, Ribe's international importance as a transit harbour began to diminish. Nevertheless, it was one of the first towns in Denmark to own a printing press, and the first printed edition of the Jutlandic Law of 1241 was done in Ribe in 1504. At the time of the Reformation there were some 20 guilds in the town.

With the completion of the cathedral, a Cathedral Chapter was established in 1145, and Ribe possessed, in the course of time, a large convent and three monasteries as well as some smaller religious houses and hospitals. There were six churches in addition to the cathedral and the chapels in the convents and monasteries.

At the beginning of the 12C, Riberhus Castle was built to the W of the town, and this became the setting for many royal occasions. In particular there is a tradition that the Valdemars were particularly fond of Ribe, and the much-loved Queen Dagmar, the wife of Valdemar II, died here in 1212 (though she was buried in Ringsted). The cathedral chimes play the melody of the ballad of Queen Dagmar on the hour at 12.00 and 15.00. Riberhus is named in Christian II's charter as one of the three Jutlandic castles which should be maintained. Nevertheless, by the time of Christian IV it was in disrepair; it was demolished by the end of the 17C, and now the only trace of it is the mound on which it was built and the remains of the moat surrounding it.

Ribe as a whole was not enthusiastic about the Reformation, and indeed the Reformation with the resultant suppression of the religious establishments helped reduce its wealth and influence. Its trade also suffered through the emergence of other trading centres, not least Copenhagen. Another negative factor was the fact that Ribe's harbour was on a river, not on the coast, which limited the size of the ships able to use it. Most of the goods taken to and from Ribe by sea were carried by lighter between the city and the harbour, some 7km downstream. The position deteriorated yet more when the river silted up in the 18C. Whereas many other towns in Denmark experienced a new period of growth in the 19C, this did not happen in Ribe. The loss to Germany of southern Jutland robbed it of a natural hinterland, and the emergence of Esbjerg as a major export port towards the end of the 19C affected it yet more.

In the Middle Ages Ribe had a reputation for being strict in the application of its laws, and it is certain that at least 12 women were burned as witches between 1572 and 1652. There is in *Sønderportsgade* a memorial to one Maren Splid, burnt for witchcraft on 9 November 1641 'between the gallows hills near Ribe'. The

RIBE

0 metres   200

N

RINGVEJEN

Ribe Å

SANKT PEDERS GADE

SALTGADE

SEMINARIEVEJ

PLANTAGEVEJ

NØRREMARKSVEJ

ROSEN ALLE

SANKT LAURENTII GADE

KORSBRODREGADE

GRØNNEGADE

PUKE STRÆDE

OVERDAMMEN

MELLEM DAMMEN

NEDERDAMMEN

Kunstmuseum

Quedens
Gård

SANKT NICOLAJ GADE

GIORTZ

TANGEVEJ

SKOVGADE

NYGADE

GRYDERGADE

SØNDERPORTSGADE

SVEGADE

TORVET   Cathedral
         Mus

PORT BROBORGADE

STENBODERNE

STOCKENS
PLADS

SANKT
CATHRINE
PLADS

DAGMARSGADE

Hans Tavsens
House

KLOSTERGADE

HUNDEGADE

St.Catherine's

HOLMEVEJ

GRÅBRØDREGADE

GRAVSGADE

KIRKEGÅRDS ALLE

H.A.BRORSONS VEJ

RINGVEJEN

TØNDERVEJ

DAMVEJ

HAJLUND VEJ

DAMVEJ

TØNDER

HADERSLEVVEJ

strictness of the regime in the town is reflected in the story of a woman whose son had been condemned to death by the Viborg Court, and who, on seeing him hanging in the gallows there, sighed: 'Aye, my son, but be thankful you were not tried by the Ribe court!'

Many famous names are associated with Ribe: the great post-Reformation bishop Peder Palladius was born here in 1503, and the poet Anders Bording in 1619. The Reformer Hans Tavsen spent the last ten years of his life here, and here, too, lived the 17C humanist Anders Sørensen Vedel from 1581 to his death in 1616. Hans Adolf Brorson ended his days as Bishop of Ribe, and close to where he lived, the poet Ambrosius Stub died in poverty in 1758. The two probably never met. Stub was overlooked in his old age, and he has his parallel in the 20C composer Rued Langgaard, who spent the last 12 years of his life as cathedral organist here. Langgaard was not really accepted as a composer in his day, and it is only now that his genius is being acknowledged.

The ***Cathedral**, with a floor level about 1.5m below the present-day square on which it stands, must remain the most prominent building in Ribe. It dominates the town, and its lofty 13C tower can be seen from miles around, high above the outline of the medieval buildings. In fact, this 48.6m tower was probably once even taller, but it partly collapsed in 1594, and the present shape was adopted when it was rebuilt in 1610. The other tower, the St. Mary's Tower, is from 1896, when it was erected to replace an earlier tower which had collapsed in the 18C.

Consecrated in 1125, this glorious Romanesque cathedral is in the form of a basilica with a nave flanked by two aisles on either side, the only such church in Denmark. Originally, it was built with a single aisle on either side of the nave, plus a transept and chancel. At the intersection between this original transept and nave there is a great dome 21.3m high, unique in Scandinavia. The two outer aisles, which largely hide the original ground plan, were added after a fire in 1402. Thanks to the combination of breadth and height brought about by the six arches and then the twin aisles and further colonnades on either side of the nave, this massive cathedral strikes the visitor as being peculiarly spacious and light.

There are three doors to the church, the most interesting being the one known as the Cat's Head Door on the S side, so called because the lion's head in the door handle was once thought to be that of a cat. This huge door is set in a splendid portal with two columns on either side and horseshoe-shaped arches above enclosing a carved tympanum representing Christ being taken down from the Cross, one of the most important pieces of Danish medieval sculpture. The whole is surmounted by a triangular gable with figures of Christ and the Virgin surrounded by angels.

There is a good deal of the medieval church furniture and decorations left in the cathedral, including some frescoes—though these have been damaged by the elements in the course of time. Now, in the midst of this magnificent Romanesque church, there is a modern altar, behind which some modern frescoes, mosaics and stained glass windows have been added, done by Carl-Henning Pedersen between 1983 and 1987. Some people are enthusiastic. Others are not. *De gustibus non est disputandum*.

Quite apart from the cathedral, the *centre of Ribe has been scrupulously maintained to keep its medieval atmosphere as far as possible, with narrow winding cobbled streets and half-timbered houses, most of which are still inhabited. Close to the E end of the cathedral, on the Square itself, is *Weis' Stue*, a tiny inn from 1600 with a carefully preserved 18C interior with beamed wooden ceilings, and walls either panelled or covered with Dutch tiles, all filled with period furniture. At the other end of the Square is the town's old school, *Katedralskolen*, dating as a grammar school from the 16C, but with a history going much further back. Some of Denmark's most famous names went to school here.—Nearby, also in *Skolegade*, are the remains of the old 16C Bishop's Palace, where Hans Tavsen spent his last years. There is now an archaeological museum on this spot.

Many half-timbered buildings as there are in Ribe, they are not the only houses of interest; there are some very old brick-built dwellings, including the 16C Tårnborg in *Puggaardsgade* (in which the 16C humanist Anders Sørensen Vedel lived). Puggaard itself, in *Gravsgade*, is a brick-built house from c 1400, at one time a residence for the canons of the cathedral. On the corner of Stenbogade and Sønderportsgade with its entrance from Stöckensplads square stands the oldest extant town hall in Denmark, dating from 1496. It was in this

1 St Mary's Tower
2 The Cat's Head Door
3 Altar table from 1988
4 Frescoes: stained glass windows
  and mosaics from 1983-87
5 Tombstone of King Kristoffer I (1259)
  believed to be the oldest royal
  tombstone in Scandinavia
6 The West Portal from 1225, Bronze
  doors by Anne Marie Carl Nielsen (1904)

RIBE CATHEDRAL

house that the poet Anders Bording was born in 1619, and it became the town hall in 1709.

Further along Dagmarsgade you come to *Sankt Catherinæ Plads*, the site of *°St. Catherine's Church* and monastery, one of Denmark's best-preserved monastic churches. The Dominican monastery was founded in 1228, but the present church, the third to be built on this site, is from 1433 and apart from the cathedral is the only one of the old churches to survive. It is some 46m long, 21.5m wide, and consists of a nave and two aisles, but without a distinct chancel. The tower is from 1618, but it had to be reduced in height. The font is medieval, the richly carved pulpit from 1591, and the altarpiece from 1650. The old cloisters also survive, and can be reached through the church.

A walk along Sortebrødregade will now bring you to *°Quedens Gård* on the corner of Overdammen. (A ticket also gives you access to the *Town Hall Museum* on Von Stöckens Plads and *Hans Tavsens House* on Torvet 17.) This is a splendid merchant's residence originally from 1580, built around a courtyard; the dwelling house is from the end of the 18C. It is now a museum, and the interior seeks to re-create rooms from the 16C to the 19C. A walk further on, down the narrow cobbled and pavement-less *Fiskergade*, will show you one of the lovely old streets, with alleyways leading off from it.

The old harbour is no longer used for serious purposes, but there are facilities for private yachts and launches. There are some old Wadden Sea ships on display, and there is also a post showing the water levels during various floods—the greatest being the famous flood of 1634 which destroyed Misthusum (see above).

In Skt Nikolajgade there is an art gallery (*Kunstmuseum*) exhibiting a wide range of Danish art.

Leaving Ribe, you will drive 7km N on the A11/A24 to just S of Gredstedbro, from where you can, if you wish, follow the A11/A24 and later the A24 to (21km) Esbjerg (Rte 1). If you prefer to go straight to (31km) Varde, which is our next real stop, you also follow the A11/A24, but you must be sure to stay on the A11, when the A24 c 5km later forks left for Esbjerg. We suggest however, you leave the A11/A24 altogether, turning right into Gredstedbro, just before you reach the town. If you do this, you have the chance of seeing two interesting churches before you are back on track again 7km ahead.

3km W of Gredstedbro, reached by a minor road is the first one, the rather fine Romanesque church at *Vilslev*. Here there are some well-preserved frescoes from c 1225, one of which, above the chancel arch, portrays a beautiful young Abel lifting his lamb up towards God. You will also find a stone showing the height reached by the floods in the storm of 1634.

From Gredstedbro you take the unclassified road N towards Bramming. At (4km) Sejstrup you should turn left to (1km) *Hunderup* to take a look at the church, in which there is a totally unexpected splendid marble sarcophagus, the work of the Flemish sculptor Cornelis Floris, who was responsible for the tomb of Christian III in Roskilde Cathedral (Rte 2). The tomb here is that of one of the owners of the nearby mansion of Kærgård, Niels Lange and his wife.

Proceed now W through Hunderup and rejoin the A11 2km ahead, turning right for (25km) Varde.

Varde (11,500 inhab.; Tourist Information: Torvet 5) once enjoyed a strategic position in an otherwise marshy area as a firm crossing of the large Varde Å river, which in the early Middle Ages formed a trade route. There was a royal castle here, Vardehus, and this, too, contributed to Varde's significance. In 1439 the local peasants stormed and burned down the castle and then took refuge in Varde itself. In return, the king's troops burned down Varde. Varde's earliest known charter is from 1442, though one must assume there were earlier ones, not least because the town boasts the oldest civic coat of arms in Denmark.

However, despite its long history, Varde has little in the way of old buildings, most of which have suffered in many disastrous fires. Even after the establishment of its great rival, Esbjerg, Varde continued to grow, partly because of the advent of the railway line. It is now a busy market town serving a thriving hinterland, and as a result of the demands placed on it, the old centre has been completely rebuilt, leaving little to remind one of the past except the general layout of the streets around the old square, *Torvet*.

Varde church on the W side of Torvet square was built around 1150, but suffered from the fires which ravaged the town. It was twice rebuilt in the 18C and then extended in 1812. The latest restoration was by Kaare Klint and Rolf Graae in 1965. The bombastic Renaissance altarpiece is from 1616, with 18C paintings in the panels.

There *are* some old buildings in Varde, first and foremost the elegant *Kampmannske gård* from 1781 on the corner of Storegade and Kræmmergade. It was built after the great fire of 1777, as is recalled in the inscription over the doorway: *ex cinere redivivus anno 1781*. There are several more modest older houses, usually of a single storey, built in dark brick; *Sillasens Hus* on Torvet is a good example of these.

Close to the Arnbjerg Park to the E of the town centre there is a delightful model of old Varde, *Minibyen*; the miniature town houses are built of brick and roofed with tiles, all one-tenth of normal size.—In the Arnbjerg Park there is an open air theatre, a memorial to those killed during the World War II Occupation, and a 'geographical garden'. Here, too, is *Varde Museum*, with excellent archaeological and ethnographical collections, including textiles, silver and 'jydepotter', the curiously shaped black clay pots associated with this area. They have a very old history indeed, and were fashioned without the use of a potter's wheel. They were then fired over a low flame, which produced a black finish. Nowadays they are tourist wares, but here you will see the genuine thing.

Further to the E of the town there is the pleasure park of *Varde Sommerland*; pay the entrance fee, and everything is free inside.

From Varde to Ringkøbing you have the choice of two routes, the direct one (68km) taking you across country, and the longer and more scenic (87km) along the North Sea coast. The direct route is described first.

DIRECT ROUTE FROM VARDE TO RINGKØBING (total distance 68km). Although the A11 N leads straight from Varde to *Skjern*, our suggested direct route is via the A12 and is only slightly longer. Leave Varde on the A12/487 NE to (10km) *Nørholm*. The mansion is not open to the public, but a narrow road just before the house leading right to *Nørholm Hede* skirts the gardens, and you can catch a glimpse of it from there. Nørholm Hede (Nørholm Heath) is a large expanse of moorland which, experimentally, has been left undisturbed so that studies of the flora and fauna of unspoiled moorland can be carried out, and a brief look at this area is well worth while. On returning to the A12/487 proceed N, after 1km taking the A12 fork to (11km) *Hjedding*.

One of the most important facets of Danish rural life for the past century or so has been the co-operative movement. Inspired by the co-operative movement in

England, farmers joined forces at the end of the 19C to provide co-operative facilities instead of being dependent on their own efforts or on the private dairies, etc. which tended to be in the hands of the large landowners. First came co-operative dairies, but then came slaughterhouses and other large ventures. Hjedding is the site of Denmark's first co-operative dairy, and fittingly it is now a *Dairy Museum* containing all the original equipment from 1882.

A further 2km brings you to *Ølgod*, where, thanks to the discovery of 171 old coins under the floor during restoration work, the original Romanesque church can be traced back to the 12C. The font indicates that it was dedicated to St. Laurentius. The tower and porch are Gothic additions.

Now follow the unclassified road past the church through Tarm (4100 inhab.; Tourist Information: Stationsvej 1) to (19km) Skjern.

You are now driving in an area that was once right off the beaten track, known as *darkest Jutland*, and it has thus developed its own local pride and its own local customs. It is an area where, perhaps because of the difficult conditions, Christianity flourished in a particularly demanding form, as is now borne out by the many churches in the area. As we shall see in a moment, it is a form of Christianity that has had far-reaching international reverberations.

Skjern (6400 inhab.; Tourist Information: Banegårdspladsen) was no more than a village before the railway came to it in 1875, and it now has the honour of being the most recent town in Denmark to be given a charter as a market town—in 1958. Not surprisingly, then, the oldest building, a watertower, dates only from 1875. In the adjoining buildings there is now a museum illustrating the development of the area. Another old building, the windmill, from 1882, is now a scheduled monument (open summer). The impressive Skjern Church contains Romanesque remains, but has been extensively rebuilt and extended. The richly carved altarpiece is from 1610–20.

What you do have, however, in this area, is excellent *fishing. Skjern Å* is one of the biggest of Denmark's rather modest rivers, and near Skjern it is joined by several tributaries. These, together with associated lakes within a radius of some 15km, have been carefully developed for fishing—for trout, perch, pike and, near Borris (9km W), salmon. Licences for this area can be obtained at any of the tourist information offices in the area. Fishing on the fjords and along the coast is free.

EXCURSION FROM SKJERN TO SÆDDING (total distance 20km, mainly on unclassified roads). The A11 takes you N through a landscape dotted with burial mounds to (7km) *Hanning*, where the well-preserved Romanesque church has been newly restored. A partly decipherable runestone has been used as the lintel over a walled-up door in the S wall.

In Hanning you turn right, following a minor road to (3km) *Sædding*, the place which Søren Kierkegaard in 1840 described as 'the poorest parish in the moorland region of Jutland'. Yet today it has been described as the nearest you can get in Denmark to a place of pilgrimage.

This is the village in which Søren Kierkegaard's father was born, and where, at the age of 12, he stood on a mound and cursed God—an event which he never forgot, which moulded him for the rest of his life, and which came to be of fundamental importance to Søren Kierkegaard, too. The modest Romanesque church, with no tower, consists of chancel and nave, with a later porch. There are commemorative tablets to the Kierkegaard family on the walls inside; the ship hanging from the roof, from 1939, is called the *Regine*—clearly a reference to Søren Kierkegaard's unfortunate fiancée, Regine Olsen. Kierkegaard certainly visited this church, and his brother, who became Bishop of Ålborg, preached in it. The father worshipped in it as a child, and the strict evangelical Christianity

preached in it has reverberated to this day under the influence of his philosopher
son. The family home no longer exists, but there is a stone to indicate the place
where it once stood.

From Sædding you drive S to (4km) *Sønder Årup*, rejoining the A11
and returning to (6km) Skjern.

The main route continues now along the A28, and you first pass through
the *Dejbjerg Plantation*, which offers relief from the predominantly
moorland landscape. In the middle of the plantation, 6km N of Skjern,
you come to a crossroads.

If you turn left here, you will come to *Dejbjerg* (2km), where the church has some
unusual features. Romanesque with Gothic extensions, it has a chancel arch
decorated with carved intertwined serpents and vines. The splendidly
ornamented pulpit is from c 1600, and there are elaborate benches for the pastor,
the parish clerk and the nobility. In the tower you can see some rather less
distinguished but very special benches. They were once provided for the use of
the gypsies and social outcasts who frequented the area, and who were excluded
from using the same pews as the rest of the local population.

Eight British airmen, shot down in World War II, are buried in the churchyard
here.—In a field S of the church a stone commemorates the finding in 1881–83 of
the Bronze Age Dejbjerg carriages, now reassembled in the National Museum in
Copenhagen.

If, however, you are more attracted by mills than by churches, you
follow the minor road right at the A28 crossroads, and after 1.5km you
will come to the beautiful **Bundsbæk Mølle** (Bundsbæk Mill), a restored watermill now forming part of the museum complex of the area.

7km later on the A28 you can turn off again right at Højmark to visit
Sønder Lem church (1km), where the ship hanging from the ceiling
was made by English prisoners of war held in Ringkøbing in 1808
during the Napoleonic Wars. There is a striking number of prehistoric
burial mounds around Sønder Lem, some 45 in all, many of which can
be seen from the church tower.

Another 4km N will take you to the A15 which you then follow W to
(8km) Ringkøbing (see below).

ALTERNATIVE ROUTE FROM VARDE TO RINGKØBING—THE COASTAL
ROUTE (total distance 87km). This less direct, but much more varied
and interesting route will take you through a completely different, and
quite distinctive, part of Jutland, much of it on the narrow neck of land
between Ringkøbing Fjord and the North Sea.

You leave Varde on the 181 W, turning off left after 4km into the 431
and driving to (4km) *Janderup*. Here, just S of the main road and
overlooking Varde river, stands the magnificent **Janderup Church**, a
Romanesque building from c 1200.

The 16C vaulting is covered with frescoes, this time not of a figura-
tive nature, but exclusively of fleur-de-lis designs. It is a style found in
several churches in this area, and is ascribed to a painter known as
Liljemesteren, the Lily Master. The altarpiece (1645) is the work of a
local master. It is elaborately carved and richly coloured, and surmounted with a figure of Christ in glory. Also richly carved is the pulpit
from c1600. Above the chancel arch hangs a crucifix from c 1300, and
nearby there are other medieval figures, the most splendid of which is
a statue of the Virgin and Child from 1503, representing Mary as
Queen of Heaven with the powers temporal and spiritual kneeling
beside her.—A particularly interesting feature is the old oaken
entrance door. It was removed when a new door was fixed in 1979–81.
However, as it is believed to be the original door the decision was

taken to save it. It now hangs just inside the new door, and can be swung open for inspection.

A further 3km along this road brings you to *Billum*, where there is another fine Romanesque church built of tufa. The lofty nave is less ornate than that in Janderup, but the apse is of special interest for its blind arcades. The apparently Romanesque windows are thought to be of later date. The altarpiece and pulpit are early 17C, the font Romanesque. The benches are old, probably 16C, and there are several medieval statues on the walls.

The road now continues towards (3km) Oksbøl—though you will have to leave the main road if you want to go into the village, which the 431 by-passes. **Oksbøl** (2800 inhab.; Tourist Information: Vestergade 27) has a particular treasure in its church, called **Ål Church** and situated in the N part of the village. The original Romanesque church, dedicated to St. Nicholas, the patron saint of seafarers, was built in the first half of the 12C, though it was later extended. There are, nevertheless, still many original Romanesque features—windows, both doors, and the original chancel arch. The profusion of frescoes is contemporary with the oldest part of the building, and it is believed that there were once friezes along the walls of both the nave and the chancel. Best preserved now is a frieze portraying a battle between knights on horseback, which has been compared with the Bayeux Tapestry, with which it is of course roughly contemporary. Stylised indeed, but it gives a vivid impression of the dress, armour, coats of arms—and brutality—of armed combat at the time. There is nothing to indicate whether it refers to a specific battle. There are other frescoes depicting the life of St. Nicholas, and there is a painted Romanesque lion over each door.

The wooden crucifix on the altar is an exact copy of the original crucifix from the early 12C. It is particularly interesting in that it demonstrates how crucifixes at that time portrayed Christ not as suffering, but as triumphant. The pulpit, with its carved figures of Christ and the four Evangelists, is baroque, and there are modern stained glass windows.

Oksbøl *is* only a village, and by the end of World War II it counted fewer than 1000 inhabitants. However, by that time it had become host to the biggest refugee camp in Denmark. With its 38,000 German refugees, the *Oksbøl Camp*, adjoining the village, formed for a time the sixth largest town in Denmark, with an area of 4 sq km and a circumference of some 8km. It was run by its own 'local authority' of refugees headed by an elected German mayor. There was a courthouse here, cinemas, theatre, churches and hospital, even a railway station. Little is now left of this enormous camp, from which the last refugees departed in 1948, though the present Oksbøl youth hostel is situated in what was the camp hospital.

There is, meanwhile, a museum here at Kirkegade 1, *Blåvandshuk Egnsmuseum*, with exhibits and a film illustrating life in the camp. The museum also contains exhibits illustrating the history of the area from prehistoric times to the mid 20C, including the Occupation (open summer; limited opening winter).—There is a large army camp in Oksbøl, where the *Pansermuseum*, containing an assortment of tanks and armoured personnel carriers, is open to the public from 15 June to 15 August.

EXCURSION FROM OKSBØL TO BLÅVANDSHUK PENINSULA. Before continuing N to Ringkøbing, you might make an excursion S to visit a very idiosyncratic area known as *Blåvandshuk*, the most westerly part of Denmark, and a peninsula giving access to 40km of unbroken sand and sand dunes. To do this you take the 431 from Oksbøl S to *Blåvand Kro* (Blåvand Inn) (17km). You are here in a village called *Oksby*, where you will also find the *Blåvand Museum* in the thatched and half-timbered former school, providing a graphic illustration of the difficult living conditions in this area in times past. Another indication of the same is in the other museum, *Blåvand Redningsbådsmuseum* (Blåvand Lifeboat Museum), at Fyrvej 25. On the most westerly point you will find the lighthouse, from 1900, where there is limited access to the top.

S of here is the sandy area known as *Skallingen*, reached by driving along a narrow road E and S—and then walking. In driving there you will go through *Ho*, where there is a large sheep market on the last Saturday in August.

On returning along the 431 to Oksbøl you might wish, after 13km, to turn left to (7km) the very fine bathing beach at *Vejers Strand*.

From Oksbøl you should take the road diagonally opposite Ål Church, Præstegårdsvej, towards Børsmose, and drive through Ål Plantage. About 1km along this road, on the left, you will find a last, poignant, reminder of the great refugee camp in the form of the *German Refugee Cemetery*, where some 1400 refugees are buried. It is now tended by the German War Graves Commission, although the majority of those buried there are, in fact, civilians.

Now move on towards (5km) Børsmose.

This drive will take you first through a wooded area, and then out into a quite remarkable and desolate moorland which has been subjected to continuous sand drift. Even so, oak trees have managed to establish themselves and survive—in the most peculiar shapes. The road in fact passes through a military area, the presence of which has paradoxically allowed a rich animal and bird life to develop in the area, and kept the ubiquitous summer cottages away.

At Børsmose you turn N and continue for 8km along a minor road to join the 465. If you turn left here, you will come to (1.5km) another delightful beach **Henne Strand** (1.5km). If you turn right instead and just continue with your route, you will quickly find yourself in (1km) *Henne Kirkeby*.

Here, on high ground overlooking the Filsø lake (which used to be much larger), there is one of the Romanesque churches characteristic of the region, built in the second half of the 12C by the Bishop of Ribe, who also owned Hennegård close by. The original church was extended in Gothic times, and can boast of a good deal of furniture from that period—an early 16C tabernacle fixed in a magnificently carved large altarpiece from c 1600, two side altars, one of them surmounted by a beautiful figure of the Virgin and Child. The pulpit, richly carved, is from 1573, the canopy from 1625. The church bell bears the date 1444.

Now turn left on to a minor road leading to (8km) Nørre Nebel, there joining the 181 NW. You follow this road for c 6km to a road on your right pointing to *Tipperne*.

Tipperne, probably meaning 'the tufts', is a miniature peninsula jutting out into the Ringkøbing Fjord—to all intents and purposes an inland lake with access to the sea; it consists of marshland and sand deposits, and is now an outstanding bird sanctuary, the home or resting place of countless sea birds, both sedentary and migratory. There is a small museum here and also an observation tower. The area immediately before Tipperne, *Værnengene*, is meadowland, similarly with a rich bird life, which can be observed from the road. Tipperne is state owned, Værnengene in private ownership, but both are protected areas.

There is public access to Værnengene daily from 1 Apr–31 Dec, 09.00–18.00;

Tipperne on Sun from 1 Apr–31 Aug, 05.00–10.00, and from 1 Sept–31 Mar, 10.00–12.00.

It should be noted that the whole of the Ringkøbing Fjord is a protected area, and that, although there are ample facilities for yachting and windsurfing on this very suitable stretch of water, they are not allowed anywhere near Tipperne. There are other parts, too, with restrictions. Tourist information centres will provide you with charts showing where, and where not, yachting and windsurfing are permitted.

Now follow the 181 and drive through *Nymindegab* to the area known as **Holmsland Klit**. This is a Nordic holiday paradise if ever there was one.

Not only do you find here some of the most impressive of Danish sand dunes, but the beaches stretch the entire 35km of this neck of land which at its maximum is 2.5km wide; the sand is white, the sea is clean and, except where marked, safe. Or you can hire a pony and ride along the sea edge. There are plenty of car-parking facilities. As you drive up, you cannot but be aware of the presence of the North Sea on your left, though you will only catch the occasional glimpse. On your right, however, you will have views across the Ringkøbing Fjord. There are, inevitably, cafés, cafeterias and camping grounds in the area, but there is room for them all. There are, too, some magnificent old farms, amazingly big for an area where life in the past has been hard indeed.

A drive of 15km will bring you to *(Nørre) Havrvig*, where there is an isolated church standing on high ground overlooking Ringkøbing Fjord. It is not old, and it is not architecturally splendid, but the churchyard is interesting, partly for the railings around the graves—a custom in this area—and partly because of the graves of several named Allied airmen shot down during World War II.

One more km and you come to **Abelines Gård** (Abeline's Farm), one of the largest and best-preserved of the many thatched farms on Holmsland Klit.

This really impressive farm was built in 1871—significantly, by a receiver of wrecks—and is today owned by a trust aimed at preserving West Jutlandic historic buildings. It is open to visitors in the summer and, almost unchanged since it was a family home, provides an impression of the furniture and daily life of West Jutland in the past. Note that there is no real bedroom—the beds are all in alcoves, in the old Scandinavian tradition. Yet this house was lived in until 1954! (open mid-June to early Sept—with café facilities).

Continue now N along the 181 to (6km) *Hvide Sande* (Tourist Information: Troldbjergvej 4). This busy town is new, having grown up with the establishment of access from Ringkøbing Fjord to the North Sea in 1931. Now all deep sea fishing from this area is based on Hvide Sande, which has become one of Denmark's major fishing ports. The machinery regulating the flow of water between the North Sea and the fjord is an impressive sight in itself.

About 5km N of Hvide Sande, on high ground, you will find *Nørre Lyngvig* lighthouse, originally built in 1906. It stands 36m high (53m above sea level in all), and there are 225 steps leading to the top from where you have panoramic views. At the bottom, while you are regaining your breath, there is a miniature museum illustrating local wild life (open Easter–Nov).

From Nørre Lyngvig it is 8km to *Søndervig*, another holiday home area and bathing resort. Here you turn right to join the A15, and after 7km you will be close **Gammelsogn Kirke**.

While the churches on Holmsland Klit have been relatively new, this is an old one. It is a Romanesque building with late Gothic tower and porch, standing behind a wall of huge boulders on the shore of the fjord. On the N side the Romanesque windows are still to be seen, but on the S side they were replaced by larger windows in 1880. The pyramidal spire is from the 18C. There is nothing opulent about this church, and it bears traces of having stood in a poor part of the country. It has, however, been the principal church in the area, to which the inhabitants of the Holmsland Klit used to sail or row on Sundays.— There are paths along the shore of the fjord leading both to Søndervig and Ringkøbing.

Back on the road, **Ringkøbing** (8400 inhab.; Tourist Information: Torvet) is a mere 2km away, across the Vonå river linking Ringkøbing Fjord with Stadil Fjord to the N.

Ringkøbing is one of Denmark's older market towns, with a charter from 1443. Excavations indicate that it was founded as a port in the mid 13C, and the central area is still built around the old town—of which, however, the church is the only building remaining. Fishing and the cattle trade led to considerable affluence in the 16C and 17C. However, in the 18C the entrance to the Ringkøbing Fjord at Nymindegab was partly closed by sand, making access difficult, and Ringkøbing's residual importance as a port then ended with the opening of the railway line in the 19C.
    The 19C had, meanwhile, been a time of prosperity, and the town's aspect is one of 19C brick houses with hipped roofs and white-painted cornices. It is a style typical of the architecture of the west coast of Jutland, and efforts have been made in recent years to ensure that these buildings are not superseded by 20C styles. Modern industry has come to Ringkøbing in the form of a shipyard and a factory for agricultural machinery.

One of Ringkøbing's oldest buildings, the former mayor's residence from 1807, stands on the main square, *Torvet*, close to the elegant old town hall, built in 1849. Nearby is the Hotel Ringkøbing, with parts dating back to the 16C. On Torvet, too, stands the rather modest, buttressed church, the oldest parts of which are from the early 15C, while the tower is some 200 years later, with gabling added in 1866. Notice that this tower is broader at the top than at the base. The somewhat low nave is cross-vaulted; the pulpit is late 16C. There is a sundial from 1728 on the W buttress.

To gain an impression of the older part of town, you should take a walk through the streets near the square, between Nørregade and Søndergade. Here you will find an array of mainly single-storey houses typical of West Jutland, and built at the turn of the 19C. The new town hall, near the harbour, is from 1969–70.—*Ringkøbing Museum*, Konge-vej 1, contains excellent archaeological and historical collections, including exhibits from the Mylius-Erichsen expedition to NE Greenland in 1906–08 (open summer; limited opening winter). Mylius-Erichsen spent part of his childhood in Ringkøbing, and there is a statue of him in front of the museum.

EXCURSION FROM RINGKØBING TO VEDERSØ (total distance c 51km). This trip will take you further along the North Sea coast, to several more of the best churches of the area, and to Vedersø with its reminiscences of the dramatist and priest, Kaj Munk.

You leave Ringkøbing on the A15, driving W for 5km and turning into a road on your right leading to (1km) *Kloster*, where you will find Nysogn Kirke. This name, meaning 'New Parish Church', indicates that it is the younger of the two churches in this area, the other being Gammelsogn (Old Parish). However, Nysogn Church is not exactly modern, being late Romanesque/early Gothic in style, of considerable dimensions and beautifully proportioned. The large crucifix over the altar is from c 1500, though it has been extensively restored.

From Kloster you drive W along a minor road to join the 181 at (4km)

Hovvig. This will take you N along the North Sea dunes (very close to the sea), with views across the *Vest Stadil Fjord* on your right. Here, as on Holmsland Klit, there are thatched farms, two of the best preserved being (5km) *Strandgården* and, 4km further on, *Bankgården*. Both are now protected buildings. Strandgården, an elegant building from 1875, is now a museum illustrating life in this part of the country, with a good collection of old agricultural and fishing equipment. The rich bird life of the area is also illustrated, and the museum contains a collection of first editions of the author Kaj Munk, who lived in nearby Vedersø (open summer).

Vedersø itself is 4km E of the 181, the road leading to it being about 4km N of Bankgården. The relatively modest Romanesque/Gothic church here is built of granite ashlars, but has little architectural significance. The interest inevitably centres on the fact that it was here that Kaj Munk was pastor from 1924 to his murder in 1944. He is buried in the churchyard.

Kaj Munk was in some ways a curious anomaly, in that he was originally quite positive in his views on the Italian dictator Mussolini. He soon had doubts about Hitler, but his patriotic fervour was not fully revealed until Hitler occupied Denmark. He then fearlessly opposed the occupying forces in his writing as well as in his preaching, and in 1944 he was one night taken from his home by the Gestapo, shot, and dumped by the roadside near Silkeborg.

From Vedersø you should continue S to (5km) *Stadil Kirkeby*, where the *church is one of the most splendid in this part of Jutland. It is richly decorated, perhaps reflecting the fact that it once belonged to the canons of Ribe Cathedral. However, the church is dominated by the golden altar, the sister piece to that in *Sahl Church* (Rte 18).

There are indications that these so-called golden altars were quite common in the 12C and 13C; seven have survived, five of them being in the National Museum, those in Stadil and Sahl still being in the churches for which they were intended. Legend has it that the altars in Stadil and Sahl once formed the head and foot of the bed belonging to an English prince who gave them to the churches as a thanks offering for safe deliverance from a storm at sea. In practice, they are highly sophisticated expressions of medieval faith.

At all events, this altar is believed to date from the period when the church itself was built, i.e. c 1200. It is made from wood covered with copper and then gold leaf, and was once the antemensale, being later installed in an ornate Renaissance altarpiece. It represents Christ enthroned, surrounded by 14 panels illustrating His childhood together with figures of the Apostles, and studded with quartz crystals.

The pulpit and organ loft in the church are Renaissance work, as are the pews, including those reserved for the local lord of the manor. A Romanesque piscina from the chancel has been repositioned in the tower. The entrance door is thought to be original, which makes it one of the oldest church doors in Denmark.

4km NE of Stadil lies *Tim Kirkeby*, where there is another interesting church, even if it cannot compare with Stadil. Situated in an isolated position, it has Romanesque, Gothic and Renaissance features, none of which has the sumptuous carving so often found. The elegant altarpiece, containing four Corinthian columns, is from c 1590. The side panels contain original paintings, the centre panel a later crucifixion scene. The altar itself is fronted with glazed tiling from 1957 depicting scenes from the life of Christ, the work of Jais Nielsen, who is also responsible for the stained glass windows in the tower.

You now drive 3km E to join the A28/A16, and you follow the A16 through Hee (Rte 20) back to (12km) Ringkøbing.

16 Kruså to Århus

Total distance 178km. 170 throughout.—(23km) **Åbenrå**.—(24km)
Haderslev.—(28km) **Kolding**.—(30km) **Vejle**.—(26km)
Horsens.—(26km) **Skanderborg**.—(22km) **Århus**.

If you approach Denmark on the motorway from Flensburg, you will
enter through the crossing post at Kruså. From here it is possible very
quickly to join the main E45 offering you a fast route to *Århus*.
However, the route along the old main road, now designated the 170,
is more interesting.

You immediately drive N along the 170 through Søgård village to
(11km) *Søgård* house. Just before the house you will find yourself
between two lakes, a large one on your left, a small one on your right.

The 170 here is actually built on the old ramparts of what was once the biggest
castle in Schleswig—Søgård (Lake House). Its quite dramatic history goes back
to 1357, and has been determined by the border conflicts over many centuries;
in 1643–44 it was totally destroyed. It was not rebuilt until the mid 19C, and the
present simple but elegant building—now a military barracks—dates from
1858–60. It was from here that a force of 32 men was sent on 9 April 1940 to
confront the German army when it invaded Denmark. Seven of the Danes were
killed before the entire force was overrun. There is a memorial to them, a
sandstone obelisk, at the entrance to the barracks.

Just N of Søgård you might turn left on the 481 and drive to *Kliplev* (3.5km) to
visit the former pilgrim church of St. Salvator, one of several places of pilgrimage
on the old Military Road (Hærvejen) (more about this road in Rte 22). Kliplev was
also the site of a major horse and cattle market, and while the pilgrims no longer
come, the market still exists. Nevertheless, the pilgrims' church is still there, built
in stages between 1400 and the Reformation, but apparently never quite built to
the planned size because the Reformation interrupted the increase in size.

The Chapel of St. Salvator is on the N side of the large nave, and many members
of the Ahlefeldt family, the former owners of Søgård, are buried here. There are
frescoes from c 1600, and in the churchyard there stands an excellent example
of the free-standing medieval bell-towers commonly found in this part of the
country. Here, too, there is a wooden frame from a grave dated 1550, the oldest
in Denmark. The porch is from 1775, and a sundial from that year is fixed in the
wall. In an outbuilding near the church there is a hearse from c 1800.

Now follow the 170 and drive to (12km) **Åbenrå** (15,500 inhab.; Tourist
Information: H.P. Hanssensgade 5), lying in wooded countryside and
idyllically situated at the head of the Åbenrå Fjord.

Åbenrå is the largest port in South Jutland, and it has grown around the excellent
harbour facilities. It has a charter going back to 1335, but is much older, probably
from the 12C. Like so many other towns in the area, Åbenrå has suffered badly
from the border conflicts. After the 1864 Danish defeat, it became the centre of
Danish national movements in the area. Then, with the return of the area to
Denmark in 1920, it was soon a centre for the German minority in North Schleswig.
There is still plenty to point to its position between the two cultures. On the one
hand it has a modern German grammar school, built in 1964, while on the other
it is the seat of the South Jutland Regional Library and the South Jutland Regional
Archive. The *Folkehjem* to the N of the town betokens the efforts of the Danish
population to maintain their own culture while under German rule.

Near the town centre stands *Brundlund Castle*, now the residence of
the Sheriff of Åbenrå and Sønderborg. It was largely rebuilt 1805–07
by C.F. Hansen. His design for Brundlund Castle reflects the austere
lines of his Copenhagen work, and seeks to maintain, as he put it: 'the
Gothic shape, which is so well suited to the beautiful romantic surroundings'. The original castle, parts of which still survive, was built
by Queen Margrethe I in 1411. It was here in 1945 that the Swedish
Count Folke Bernadotte successfully negotiated the return of Danish

and Norwegian prisoners from Nazi concentration camps.—Some 75m N of the castle you will find the castle watermill, an almost square building with a steep-pitched roof, dating back to the mid 16C. It was restored in 1952.

Brundlund Castle is not C.F. Hansen's only work in Åbenrå. He also designed the neo-classical *Town Hall* on the main square, Store Torv. The main hall is decorated with a large collection of portraits of Danish kings and queens.

Åbenrå's principal church stands just N of the old town centre and dates back in part to c 1250; the nave, transept and apses are largely original. The sacristy is late Gothic. However, the church was subjected to a major restoration in the 1880s, followed by another by Kåre Klint in the 1950s. The superb Renaissance pulpit is from 1565, and the grandiose baroque altarpiece from 1642. The Romanesque font is decorated with sculptured animals and other ornamentation.

Åbenrå Museum, founded in 1887, is situated in H.P. Hanssensgade, and contains collections relating to the archaeology and history of South Jutland and to the history of navigation and shipbuilding. There is a large collection of bottle ships and another of Danish paintings. Among the more famous exhibits is the Bronze Age skeleton, the *Nybøl Man*.

A good deal of the old town has been preserved despite several fires in the 17C and 18C. As in Tønder (Rte 15) the old houses are built close together, with gables facing the road. Most of them are modest in size, and the main area concerned is close to the church. In particular *Vægterpladsen* can provide the atmosphere of a bygone age. There are a few larger houses, including the splendid *Postmaster's House from 1755 at Søndergade 20, without doubt the most imposing house in the town. Other houses of distinction are also to be found in Slotsgade and Fiskergade. The late 18C Slotsgade 31, with hipped roof and ornate door, was formerly the mayor's residence.

The countryside immediately around Åbenrå is very beautiful indeed, as is the coastline. There is ample scope for walking and cycling in this ancient borderland, where relics of the past appear quite unexpectedly. Down by the fjord you will find the 4500-year-old burial chamber known as *Myrpold*. That there are good yachting and swimming facilities goes almost without saying. The annual local festival of tilting at the ring takes place here on the first weekend in July.

EXCURSION TO VARNÆS CHURCH. While in the Åbenrå area you should take the opportunity of driving the 12km E on an unclassified road to *Varnæs* to see a rather fine, but heavily restored, Romanesque/Gothic church with a magnificent 15C late Gothic altarpiece displaying an array of carved figures and scenes. A 14C censer hangs in the chancel arch. Like other churches in the region, this has no tower, but there is a free-standing medieval bell-tower in the churchyard. Inside it there are two iron collars once used for punishing malefactors.

From Åbenrå you now drive N on the 170 for 4km, when you will come to a road E to *Løjt Kirkeby* (2km). In the sizeable *church here you will find the biggest and most ornate altarpiece in South Jutland, dating back to 1520, the work of Claus Berg. This altarpiece is richly gilded and in addition to the twelve apostles has, as its centrepiece, a crucifixion scene with crowds of people, 45 in all, around the crosses. There are two representations of the martyrdom of St. Erasmus, and one of the figures has been identified as that of St. Ansgar, the monk who brought Christianity to Denmark.

The church is Romanesque, and contains frescoes from c 1520 which unusually have never been covered over, possibly because they are decorative rather than representational. There is a gilded crucifix from the early 15C, a pulpit from 1577, and a perspective painting from 1750: viewed from the right it shows the Crucifixion, from the left the Resurrection.

Now drive N 6km to *Knivsbjerg*, the highest point (97km) in South Jutland. Here a bombastic tower, the Bismarck Tower, was constructed in 1901 by the Germans to commemorate the incorporation of the area into Germany in 1864, but it was destroyed again by bombs planted in 1945. Knivsbjerg has, however, remained a focal point for the German minority, who hold rallies here, and there is a memorial to ethnic Germans who fell in World War II.

The road continues now to (14km) **Haderslev** (19,500 inhab.; Tourist Information: Apotekergade 1), standing at the head of the narrow Haderslev Fjord and straddling the river connecting this to Haderslev Dam, the biggest lake in South Jutland.

Haderslev received its charter in 1292. It appears to have come into being in the 12C at the junction of roads from Kolding and Ribe, developing into a thriving trade centre in the Middle Ages. The large Benedictine church became a collegiate church under Schleswig Cathedral. The other major building was the castle of Haderslevhus, first mentioned in 1326, in which Christian I signed his Charter. It was here that Christian II proclaimed the first Lutheran church law.

Haderslev was once even a royal residence: Frederik II spent a time here, and Christian IV celebrated his wedding and had several of his children baptised here.

Much of the town was destroyed by fire in 1627, an event which heralded a period of decline lasting throughout the 17C and 18C, despite continuing trade with Norway. In 1864 the town was taken over by the Prussians, and remained in German hands until 1920, by which time trade in the area had improved, and with it Haderslev's prosperity. This prosperity continued after the return to Denmark in 1920.

Haderslevhus Castle is no more, and *Haderslev Cathedral, also known as St. Mary's Cathedral, standing on the highest ground, is thus the dominant building, its mighty walls visible from far around as they tower over the surrounding buildings. The transept is from c 1250, the nave from c 1260, the soaring chancel, the most splendid Gothic chancel in Denmark, being added in c 1420; the remainder is of later date. There are signs in some of the ashlars used in the building that they must have formed part of an earlier granite church from c 1100. The final shape given to the church in the 13C was of a nave with an aisle on either side, these aisles being narrower than the nave, but of the same height. The vaulting is some of the loftiest in Scandinavia.

The original cathedral was partly destroyed by fire in 1627, but later restorations have aimed at re-creating it in its original form. The windows in the chancel are strikingly tall. The crucifix behind the altar is late 13C, and the figures of Joseph and Mary beside it are from 1425 and 1450. The pulpit and canopy from 1636. The unusual bronze font was cast in Flensburg in 1485; it stands on four legs fashioned in the shape of the four evangelists.

The restored Sieseby *organ, which can be seen to the left of the nave, is of particular interest. It is said that Lutheranism was preached for the first time in this cathedral, in 1525, and certainly Danish Lutheranism was partly fashioned in a synod held here.

However, the Cathedral is not the oldest church in Haderslev. That honour goes to *St. Severin's*, or Old Haderslev Church, in the W of the town, close to Haderslev Dam; unfortunately, its original Romanesque character has been altered over the centuries, not least through restorations in 1912. There are old frescoes as well as a striking modern one of the Apocalypse on the apse, painted in 1952 by Hjalte Skovgaard. The Romanesque font is decorated with carvings of animals and human heads.

In 1984 Haderslev was chosen as the 'town of the year' in recognition of the careful restoration of its old houses. These are particularly centred on the area near the Cathedral. Immediately W of the Cathedral, in Apotekergade, there are remains of medieval vaulted cellars, but most of the half-timbered houses in the area are of rather later date. The former Duke Hans Hospital, in Sønderbro, dates back to 1569. Slotsgade 20 is a house dating back to 1580, though with 17C additions. This fascinating building now houses the comprehensive *Ehlers Collection* of pottery (open summer; limited opening winter).

In the monastery churchyard in Præstegade you will find memorials to the dead from both sides in the Schleswig-Holstein wars and those who fought on the German side in World War I. Here, too, are buried many of those who were most politically active during the breakaway period in the 19C.

Haderslev Museum (open all year) is in Dalgade, a little E of the town centre. Archaeological exhibits account for a large proportion of the museum's collections, but there are sections devoted to local history and ethnography, and there is a re-creation of a 19C home. Among the exhibits is a copy of the clothes in which the early Bronze Age Skrydstrup Girl was dressed. (This remarkably well-preserved woman, now in the National Museum, was found in 1935 in an oak coffin in a burial mound at *Skrydstrup* to the W of Haderslev.)

The archaeological collections are all housed in a modern building opposite which there is a fine open air museum. Here you will find a large barn from 1620, once part of Øsby parsonage, now containing a collection of agricultural implements. There are also two 17C half-timbered houses, duly furnished, and a windmill.—*Den slesviske Vognsamling* (The Schleswig Carriage Museum) is just S of the museum, in Sejlstensgyde, opposite the yachting harbour. It contains some 40 different horse-drawn carriages and carts. The building housing them is itself a splendid relic from the past, built in the 18C as a riding school for the Holstein Lancers (open mid-Jun to mid-Aug).

The Haderslev area is well equipped for sports and outdoor activities of all kinds. Concerts are regularly given in the Cathedral and other churches in the district.

EXCURSION TO THE EAST OF HADERSLEV (total distance c 35km). This trip takes you through the area immediately S of Haderslev Fjord. You leave Haderslev on an unclassified road E to (3km) *Starup*, where you will find a remarkable 11C church built of calcareous tufa and showing English influence in its architecture. The nave, chancel and apse are original and have undergone very little alteration, but the side aisles are inferior 20C reconstructions. On either side of the nave there is Romanesque arcading surmounted by Romanesque windows beneath a beamed roof. During work on the church in 1919 the remains of frescoes were discovered. These were used as a basis for the reproduction frescoes which are now a striking—and unfortunate—feature.

From Starup you drive SE through Hejsager to (7km) *Halk Church*, with corbie steps in the W and over the porch and N-facing chapel. Unusually, the tower is in the E, above the elongated chancel. However, it is not only the architecture which is of interest, but also the furniture. The large and impressive bronze font is from 1491, made in the same foundry as those in Haderslev and Århus Cathedrals. A Gothic Virgin and Child is however much older, from c 1275, and there is a crucifixion group from the same time. The centre section of the colourful altarpiece is likewise Gothic, though the side panels are baroque. Also there is a number of Gothic altarpieces from former side altars, one of them portraying St. George slaying the dragon. On the vaulting opposite the pulpit (from 1559) hang two pieces of armour and a sword, said by legend to have belonged to a cadet who murdered a local farmer one Good Friday—and who is now supposed to haunt the church at Easter.

Halk is very close to the coast, and here, at *Halk Hoved*, you will find an impressive 26m-high cliff. The stretch SE of this is a favoured beach for bathing and sunbathing. And for countless holiday cottages.

Now drive back to Hejsager and on to (10km) *Årøsund*. Here, too, there are magnificent beaches, and you can take the hourly ferry to the tiny islet of *Årø*, only ten minutes away. There are only 200 inhabitants here, and this charming island has been left largely untouched by modern developments, though there is a camping ground here. There is plentiful bird life, too.

You will return to (15km) Haderslev through *Øsby*, where there is another large church dating back to Romanesque times, but mainly Gothic in its architecture. An interesting feature here is that it has no windows in its N wall. Another is that it contains one of the oldest Renaissance pulpits in Denmark, from 1559. On the W side there is a charnel house from c 1510, the only extant medieval charnel house in the country. The parsonage, standing nearby, is an imposing residence from 1765, brick-built and whitewashed.

The 170 will take you from Haderslev direct N to (11km) the very unusual small town of Christiansfeld. However, we suggest a slightly longer indirect route to guide you past a couple of interesting churches and a mansion on your way there.

You leave Haderslev driving E on an unclassified road towards Fjelstrup, and c 3km from the town centre, at Neder Åstrup, you turn right on to a minor road leading to (2km) Over Åstrup. Almost immediately, on your left, you will see the elegant small mansion of *Åstrup-gård*, built c 1780. A further 500m brings you to **Åstrup Church**, also on the left. This has a unique, very elaborately carved panelled ceiling from 1675 above the unspoiled Romanesque nave. The grandiose altarpiece from 1638 is similarly ornate and contains a central picture of the Last Supper. The pulpit, also in Renaissance style, is from 1621. On the S wall there is a splendid crucifix from c 1525.

Continue along this relatively high ground overlooking the fjord, turn left in Over Åstrup, and then right when you reach the Fjelstrup road to (6km) *Fjelstrup*, where there is a late Romanesque church (c 1200) with Gothic additions. Over the walled-up S door there is a tympanum with relief carvings of the crucified Christ between Mary and St. John. From Fjelstrup there is then a straight road to (6km) ***Christiansfeld** (2500 inhab.; Tourist Information: Kongensgade 5), passing close to *Tyrstrup*, where the Moravian Brethren (see below) first established themselves.

Christiansfeld is the home of the Danish Moravian Brethren, the *Herrnhuter*, and their presence has marked the village since their arrival in 1773. Although reduced now to a couple of hundred members, they have managed to maintain the centre of the village as they originally planned it. They first bought up the farm of Tyrstrupgård just outside present-day Christiansfeld, and in 1777 this was followed by the gift of another, Farvervrågård, to which they gave the name of Christinero. As their movement gained in strength, so, too, their influence grew in the area, and Christiansfeld became its centre.

The village received its name after Christian VII, who invited the Brethren to settle in Denmark, knowing them for their skills and reliability both as craftsmen and tradesmen. In a Denmark which at the time was rigorously Lutheran, they were given virtually full control of their own affairs, including church and school, and they were exempted from military service. For ten years they were also exempt from taxes and duties—much to the annoyance of merchants in Haderslev.

Christiansfeld was designed according to quite specific principles, built in the shape of a cross with the church at the centre and with straight intersecting roads starting from it. These roads were—and still are—lined with lime trees. The individual houses were also built to a pattern established elsewhere by the Brethren. There were large communal houses for the unmarried men, for unmarried women, and for married couples.

The central section of the *church, known as the Hall, dates from 1776–77, the side wings from 1795–97 and, with the exception of the ridge turret constructed in 1897, it is virtually as it was originally designed. It is built of yellow Flensburg brick, without decoration except that every fifth row of bricks stands c 5cm further forward than the rest, thus breaking the otherwise gaunt façade. The interior is similarly without decoration of any kind, with long benches facing a podium behind which there is a reproduction of Thorvaldsen's statue of Christ. The floor is made of untreated deal. Men and women enter through different doors.

The *cemetery, to the E of the town, is quite different from normal cemeteries. It is known as *God's Acre*, and the graves, each marked by an identical gravestone, are carefully arranged in sectors divided by paths in the form of a cross. There are no family graves; men are buried to the W of the main path, women to the E. All the graves, some 2000 in all, are numbered. A notable feature is the lime trees marking the different sections; they are the originals, planted in 1773 and 1774.

The old *communal houses still stand, one for the men (the Brethren) on the corner of Storegade and Kongensgade, one for the women (the Sisters) on Nørregade, and one for the widows on Birkevej (now the Brethren Museum—open summer). They are all built of the same brick as the Hall. So, too, are the individual, mainly single-storeyed, houses. The Brethren own an hotel, built in 1773, and it was in this that the ceasefire between Denmark and Prussia was signed in 1864.

For all their strict manner of life, the Brethren put a great effort into their skills, not least in the manufacture of honey cakes, for which the town is still famous. Stop and have a taste!

Leaving Christiansfeld on the 170 N you will at (2.5km), near *Frederikshøj*, cross the pre-1920 border. There are still markers to be seen. If you are interested in experiencing some of the atmosphere of the old border region, you should make a DETOUR detour here, instead of heading straight towards (11km) ***Kolding** (Rte 13).

Leave the 170 a few km ahead in Taps, turning right on a minor road through Åstorp to (4km) Sjølund. From here you follow an unclassified road N towards Sønder Bjert, but only as far as (3km) Skamling in order to visit the nearby **Skamlingsbanken** (Skamling Hill). Standing high above the surrounding countryside, and with a view across the straits to Fyn, this hill was the meeting place for Danish nationalists from the middle of the 19C. The first rally to be held here was in 1843, when some 6000 people met to assert their patriotic sentiments. The following years they were addressed by some of the most famous of Danish national figures. In 1863 a 16m-high obelisque was raised at the top of the hill. In 1945 about 100,000 Danes gathered here to celebrate the Liberation. Today Skamlingsbanken is a national monument rather than a significant meeting place.—From here the road takes you direct to (12km) Kolding.

There is a ring road around Kolding, so you can by-pass it if you wish—though, if this is your only visit to the region, you are well advised to experience this most interesting town, described in Rte 13.

N of Kolding the 170 continues. Follow it to c 15km from Kolding, when you will find a minor road W leading to *Øster Starup* (3km).

The relatively unspoiled Romanesque church in Øster Starup is famous for the splendid relief carvings around the two doors. At the E side of the bricked-up N door there is an almost free-standing figure of a lion killing a man, a violent scene in which the symbolism is thought to be that of a man tied to his fate and entirely in the power of the lion. There is a similar figure on the SW corner of the nave, and a beaked monster will be seen at the NE corner. The triumph over this evil is represented to the right of the S door: here, too, there is a lion, but it is balanced by the figure of the Archangel Michael slaying the dragon. On the font there are reliefs of the Tree of Life and symbols representing Christ. These Romanesque carvings are quite unusual, and well worth the short detour.

Now continue to (12km) **Vejle** (Rte 21), which is a beautiful little town in lovely countryside. If you are not coming this way again, do consider a short trip to the historic **Jelling** 11km NW (also described in Rte 21), before you continue NE.

There are two good routes from Vejle to Horsens: either direct (26km) or via the coast (63km). Your main road continues, but pending the completion of the motorway you will find it is renumbered for a short distance as the E45.

For the DIRECT ROUTE, drive along the E45 NE to (8km) Bredal, where you turn right on to an unclassified road to (1.5km) *Engum*. The rather modest church here, thoroughly restored in 1977, is filled with impressive, bombastic rococo furniture—pulpit, altarpiece, organ loft, benches, all from c 1760. The chancel arch is flanked by two angels with flaming swords, and there are Romanesque frescoes in the arch and in the chancel.

Another 18km will see you in Horsens (see below).

ALTERNATIVE ROUTE FROM VEJLE TO HORSENS—THE COASTAL ROUTE (total distance 63km). This more leisurely route takes you along the beautiful Vejle Fjord to the ferry port of Juelsminde and from there to Horsens. On the way you will pass close to several mansions, none of which, however, is among the most outstanding in Denmark; nor are they open to the public, though in some cases there is access to the park. You will, however, also pass through *Glud* with its fine open air museum.

You take the E45 NE for 6km, turning off right on the A23 to (6km) *Daugård*, where next to the Romanesque church you will find the small mansion of Williamsborg, from 1774. Continue towards Juelsminde. In 2km you will discover a minor road off right leading to *Rohden* (1km), a mansion built in 1898; the road goes through the grounds.

A further 3km along the A23 comes Stouby, from where we suggest you follow minor roads S through the woods right down to the coast, eventually reaching (4km) *Rosenvold*.

Built in 1586, Rosenvold is the most interesting of the mansions on this route, looking much as it originally did. For a time it was owned by Ellen Marsvin, the mother-in-law of Christian IV, and it was a favoured residence of her daughter, Kirstine Munk, Christian IV's morganatic wife, after Christian had rejected her.

Continue past Rosenvold and rejoin the A23 after some 5km at Smedskær.

Before driving further eastwards, however, you should cross the A23 and drive N to *Over Vrigsted* (2km). The church here is quite unusual, almost all of it dating from the beginning of the 12C, with remarkably few alterations. Some frescoes representing two heads were uncovered here in 1959; dating from between 1125 and 1150, they are thought to be the oldest surviving fresco paintings in Denmark. Now you return to the A23 and turn left.

After 4km you might turn right and drive to *Barritskov* (1.5km); the mansion here is mainly from 1916, replacing the former 16C building. The ruins of the earlier house can be seen from the entrance to the park.

Now return to the A23 and continue to (8km) *Juelsminde*, a ferry port with connections to Kalundborg (Rte 7). There is little of interest in Juelsminde, apart from the huge anchor from the frigate 'Jylland'— which itself is in Ebeltoft (Rte 8)—though the wooded surroundings and coastline are beautiful.

In Juelsminde you turn N and follow the 459 for 5km to Hosby, where on the E outskirts of the town you will find the pleasing mansion of *Palsgård*, built c 1500 but radically rebuilt 1804–06. The park is open to the public.

Back on the 459 you continue N to (7km) Glud, where there is a small open air museum, **Den gamle Landsby** (The Old Village), containing one of the oldest dated houses in Denmark (1662) together with other houses, many from the 17C and 18C, which have been reassembled here. Most are complete with historical implements and tools (open summer).

From Glud you take the 459 NW to (13km) **Horsens** (46,750 inhab.; Tourist Information: Det gamle Rådhus), passing at (7km) *Boller Castle* on your right. This castle, built variously between 1550 and 1759, was also a much-loved residence of Kirstine Munk, who died here in 1648. It now serves as a home for the aged.

Horsens has a history going back to the 12C and a charter from 1442. Lying in a fertile area, close to the fjord, it has had a less varied history of progress and poverty than many other Danish towns. Horsens has tended always to be relatively prosperous, though there was a lengthy period of stagnation in the 17C and 18C and, like so many other Danish towns, Horsens suffered badly during the 17C Swedish wars. It suffered, too, during the 1940–45 Occupation, when there was a good deal of Resistance activity in the town, followed by punitive action on the part of the occupying forces.

One curious feature of Horsens' history, however, is the presence there in the late 18C of exiles from the Russian royal family. They lived in the magnificent baroque mansion called Lichtenbergs Palæ—now Jørgensens Hotel—in which a Russian Orthodox chapel was established.

Søndergade, the main street, is unusually wide. It contains several 18C buildings, but was given its present appearance in the late 19C. It was at this period that the old Town Hall, now housing the town archive and the Tourist Information Office, was built in Renaissance style. Helms Apotek (Pharmacy) dates from 1736, and Jørgensens Hotel from c 1744. Several of the rooms here have been maintained in their original form. The only half-timbered house in the street is *Monbergs Gård*, from 1772.

Other early houses, albeit of a more modest kind, are found in the streets off. Many old buildings have in fact been pulled down, but there is still a respectable sprinkling left, sufficient to give an impression of what Horsens was once like. In *Smedegade* you will find several old merchants' houses; the biggest of them, No. 71, has been turned into modern shops, but every effort has been made to preserve its original character.

Probably the most unusual of Horsens' houses is *Claus Cortsens Gård* from 1718, a magnificent three-storeyed half-timbered structure surmounted by an onion-shaped dome. It was originally situated in Søndergade, next to Helms Apotek, but has been moved to the E of the town, and now stands on Sundvej, a little beyond *Horsens Museum*, which now is the home of many of the more interesting features from buildings demolished over the years. There are in addition archaeological collections and collections of silver, pottery and furniture associated with a now-vanished Horsens (open summer).

Behind the museum, on Carolinelundsvej, stands the art gallery, *Lunden*, with a large collection of paintings and graphics by Mogens Zieler as well as collections of classical and modern Danish art.—A museum of an entirely different kind is the *Arbejder-, Håndværker- og Industrimuseum* (Museum for Crafts and Industry), reached by going down Ny Havnegade, opposite Horsens Museum, and turning right into Stjernholmsgade. This museum, the only one of its kind in Denmark, is housed in the former power station from 1906, and contains exhibits demonstrating the industrial development of Denmark, and its effect on the way of life (open Jun–Sept).

As might be expected in a town of this kind, there are some interesting old churches. First, on the Square (Torvet), there is *Vor Frelsers Kirke* (Our Saviour's Church), built in the 13C, possibly by Valdemar II, though the onion-shaped dome above the tower is 18C. It is a large basilica, high to the vaulted ceiling, with brick interior as well as exterior. The pulpit and canopy, from 1663–70, with carvings of scenes from the Passion, are ascribed to Peder Jensen Kolding, and are considered among the finest of their kind in Denmark. Note, too, the imposing W door.

At the other end of Borgergade, which leads from the Square, you will find the other old church, **Klosterkirken** (The Monastery Church). This is the only remaining part of the former Franciscan Monastery, and was the subject of rebuilding in the 18C. However, nine of the monks' carved choir stalls are still there, with carved figures of SS. Erasmus and Gertrude on the gabling at the ends. Nor are these the only items of furnishing of interest: the altarpiece is late medieval, a crucifixion scene in the centre panel, with side panels containing the figures of the twelve Apostles and four saints, including St. Francis. An ornate carved rood screen stands at the entrance to the chancel, surmounted by a late Gothic crucifix, and there is a carved and gilded font screen from 1716 in the N aisle. The Lichtenberg sepulchral chapel is situated in the S aisle.

On approaching Horsens from Vejle, you will in the S end of the town have passed a church of an entirely different kind, *Sønderbro Church*, a strikingly modern structure designed by Paul Nieport—perhaps a little in the style of Le Corbusier.

Horsens has one world-famous son: Vitus Bering, the great explorer who gave his name to the Bering Sea and Bering Strait off the coast of Alaska. His name appears in Horsens in one street name and in the Vitus Bering Park near the railway station. There is a memorial plaque in the park flanked by two guns from the ship on which Bering sailed for the last time in 1741. They were a gift to Horsens by Nikita Khrushchev when he visited Denmark in 1957.

Horsens Fjord is a yachtsman's paradise, with many hospitable small harbours, tiny islands, and a delightful coastline—which also invites walking.—To the left of the 453 W of Horsens you will find in a well laid-out park *Bygholm*, a three-winged mansion from 1775, but with a history going back to the 14C. It is now a hotel.

There are again two routes to choose from between Horsens and Århus:

the route via Skanderborg (48km), described first, or the alternative route (47km), via Odder.

HORSENS TO ÅRHUS VIA SKANDERBORG (total distance 48km). From Horsens you take the 170 N straight to (26km) **Skanderborg** (11,250 inhab.; Tourist Information: Bibliotekstorvet 2). The latter part of your journey will be through increasingly hilly and wooded countryside, and 5km from Skanderborg you will come to Skanderborg Lake. You are here on the fringe of the Silkeborg–Skanderborg lake district.

Skanderborg was the site of a royal castle in the early Middle Ages, and there are many references to it in the medieval ballads. According to these, Valdemar II was here when in 1212 he heard that Queen Dagmar lay ill in Ribe, and it was here Marsk Stig came to renounce allegiance to King Erik Glipping and subsequently to announce that he was responsible for his murder in 1286. It was during a siege of this castle that Niels Ebbesen, another of Denmark's great medieval heroes, was killed in 1340. Frederik II (1534–88) extended the castle and in 1583 decided to found a market town around the castle. It never became a centre for trade, but there is now a certain amount of industry here, and the town is one of the centres for the tourist industry in this particularly attractive part of Jutland. As Crown Prince, Christian IV spent a good deal of time in Skanderborg, and here his sister, later to marry James VI of Scotland and I of England, was born. By the 17C, however, there was little use for a great fortified castle and it gradually fell into disrepair. It was sold in 1767 and demolished soon afterwards. With the exception of the chapel, which was retained as Skanderborg parish church, there is now nothing left of it although we know what it was like from contemporary drawings and etchings.

The castle *Chapel was built in 1570 by Frederik II as a chapel royal, and much of the resplendent carved panelling is still to be seen—the bench ends with the royal coat of arms and royal motto carved into them, and the pulpit. The chapel was carefully restored in the original style 1944–48. The crypt beneath, originally the castle wine cellar, was restored for use as a chapel in 1969. It is not open, but admission can be gained on application to the verger.

A little to the N stands **Skanderup Church**, dating back to c 1050. Although there have been later additions (including a tower with an onion-shaped dome from 1741), most of the original Romanesque structure is intact. In particular the apse is unusual; it is shaped like a horseshoe and has seven sections of exterior arcading into which open three circular windows. Apart from roof renewals, it is thought to have stood unaltered since it was built and is the only example of this design in Denmark. However, this is not the only very old feature remaining in the church. There are frescoes from c 1170, again with motifs such as the crucifixion of St. Peter and the death of Simon Magus which are unique in Scandinavian churches. There is a dramatic battle scene, too, which is earlier than others of a similar nature. The baroque pulpit and altarpiece from 1650 with ornate auricular carvings are probably by Peder Jensen Kolding.

The old part of Skanderborg is largely made up of modest half-timbered houses, often with a courtyard behind. A number of these still stand, especially in Borgergade and Adelgade, just N of the Castle Church. In Adelgade you will find *Skanderborg Museum*, in a building from 1888 overlooking the Lille Sø lake. It is particularly concerned with local history, but also has some interesting prehistoric exhibits.— To the W of the Castle Church lies the *Skanderborg Deer Park* on a headland jutting out into Skanderborg Lake, a delightful large wooded area with marked paths. There is an open air theatre, a kiosk for refreshments and a lakeside bathing area.

From Skanderborg you take the 170 N through (8km) *Hørning*, a delightful village with a pond in wooded surroundings and the charming *Bodilmølle*, a knife factory from 1740. The 170 then continues to (14km) Århus (see below).

ALTERNATIVE ROUTE FROM HORSENS TO ÅRHUS—VIA ODDER (total distance 47km). To drive by this route, which takes you through a varied landscape, you leave Horsens E on the 451. After about 5km, however, at Stensballe, you should turn off left and visit *Vær Church* (1km).

This DETOUR is less for the sake of the church itself than to see the grave of one of the great figures of 17C Denmark, Griffenfeld (1635–99). Born Peder Schumacher, this brilliant man rose to the highest post as Chancellor for the new absolute monarch Frederik III, and he was responsible for establishing Absolutism in law in 1665. He was ennobled for his work. By 1676, however, he was accused of treason and sentenced to death. After mounting the scaffold he was given a royal pardon and condemned to life imprisonment, first in Copenhagen, later in Trondheim, where he died. His remains were brought to Vær, and he now lies in a black coffin in a sepulchral chapel at the foot of the church tower.

About 1km on the other side of the 451 at Stensballe lies *Stensballegård*, a baroque mansion built in the 1690s by Frederik Krag, the son-in-law of Griffenfeld. It is visible from outside the park, but is not open to the public.

Continue on the 451 to (17km) Ørting, perhaps turning off right c 1km before Ørting to visit the church in *Falling* (1km), which is large and contains an altarpiece from 1635 by Peder Jensen Kolding. Particularly striking is the very large gateway leading into the churchyard.— From Ørting, too, a small road leads to *Hov*, where there is a ferry terminal serving the islands of Samsø and Tunø.

5km N of Ørting you arrive at *Odder* (8700 inhab.; Tourist Information: Banegårdsplads 3), one of the largest towns in Denmark without a charter, though its history certainly goes as far back as the 14C. It is a small road and railway junction with a good deal of light industry. There are few old buildings, but a large church stands in the centre of the town. The apse, chancel and nave are Romanesque, the remainder Gothic. This was once the home of one of Denmark's *golden altars*, but it has been removed and is now in the National Museum. There is nevertheless a beautifully carved altarpiece by Peder Jensen Kolding from 1645. The impressive archway leading into the churchyard is similar to that in Falling.

Odder *museum*, in an old watermill, has a good local ethnographical collection. Also one illustrating the history of the hunting rifle (open pm).—The old mansion of *Rathlousdal* to the W of Odder was demolished in the 1950s, but the park (with an old bear pit) is still there.

From Odder the 451 continues through (8km) Malling. 5km further on you turn right to *Moesgård* (1.5km) where the old half-timbered mill is now a restaurant. **Moesgård House** from 1780–84 has since 1970 been a prehistoric museum, giving a graphic presentation of the development of Denmark from the Stone Age to the Viking Age. Among the most important exhibits is the *Grauballe Man*, the well-preserved body found in a bog near the village of Grauballe in 1952. There are also ethnographical collections from Greenland and Afghanistan.—In the park outside there is what is called a 'prehistoric path', leading to reconstructions of prehistoric houses and barrows of various kinds (open May–Sept).

It is now only 7km to **ÅRHUS** (193,500 inhab.; Tourist Information: Rådhuset).

Århus is Denmark's second city. It appears to have originated no later than the beginning of the 10C, and by 948 it had a bishop; its coat of arms is known from

*Århus: 'The Old Town'. A reconstruction of an old
Danish town, consisting exclusively of original
buildings re-erected to form an open-air museum.
Photo: John Sommer*

c 1250, and its earliest known charter is from 1441. In addition to a great deal of industry and commerce, it has all the other marks of a major city—a university (founded 1928), music conservatory, business high school, and virtually every kind of educational establishment one can think of. There is a fine theatre, orchestra, concert hall as well as the biggest provincial library in the country. And a host of museums, including the Old Town, one of Denmark's two major open air museums.

Århus harbour is large indeed, providing a major ferry terminal, not only for domestic routes, but also for routes to Sweden.—Tirstrup Airport, 35km to the NE, serves the city, mainly with domestic flights, but with a small number of international connections (e.g. to London).

There is a theory that the original town was centred on the area around Vor Frue Kirke (Our Lady's Church), and it is beneath this church that the remains of the original episcopal church from the 10C have been discovered. The present cathedral was started in the final years of the 12C, bringing with it the increased trade that automatically came with a major ecclesiastical centre, even if medieval Århus could not compete with Viborg (Rte 20). Nevertheless, Århus underwent a period of rapid development in the Middle Ages, not least because of its harbour facilities, though it declined when its role as an ecclesiastical centre came to an end with the 1536 Reformation. Nevertheless, its geographical position allowed it to recover, and after a period of stagnation in the 17C it started to grow again from about 1750. It suffered severely from the blockades in the Napoleonic Wars, but later in the 19C, with the advent of the railways and the steamship, trade increased greatly, and Århus established itself as a major centre in Jutland, a development which continued throughout the 20C, until today it stands as a major city by any standard.

Århus is a busy city, and can best be seen and appreciated on foot. The main railway station (built 1926–29) is as good a place as any to start a walk. You should bear diagonally right and go down *Ryesgade* and *Søndergade*, the main shopping streets. Søndergade is now a rather brash pedestrian precinct, but as you walk down them you might give a thought to what these streets were like until the 1960s, when tramcars thundered down them, very close to the pavement on the right-hand side. You will soon come to the *Roman Catholic church* on your left in Ryesgade, built 1879–80 in neo-Gothic style. After crossing the bridge over Åboulevarden you will find on *Clemenstorv* (Clement's Square) the large Unibank on your left. In the basement of this building there is the *Vikingemuseum* illustrating the history of Århus in Viking times. Almost opposite you now come to *Bispetorv* (Bishop's Square) with its equestrian statue of Christian X, and you will be facing Århus Theatre from 1898–1900, with a scene from Holberg adorning its façade.

On the opposite side of Bispetorvet stands **Århus Cathedral**, originally dedicated to St. Clement. With a nave 93m long, this is the longest church in Denmark and certainly one of the most resplendent. The first church was built here in the 11C, and this, the third to stand on the spot, incorporates elements of the 13C Romanesque church. It dates from the 15C and apart from the Romanesque remains is predominently late Gothic.

The best-preserved Romanesque remains are the four chapels off the chancel, all of which have retained their original vaulting. The Gothic nave is the same width as the chancel, with lofty cross vaulting dating from 1477–87, and there is an aisle on either side. The pillars supporting the vaulting at the W end, which are based on the older church, are square, while the new ones at the E are octagonal. An impression of lightness and elegance is given by the tall, broad windows in the arcading on the N and S sides.

The cathedral boasts a wealth of frescoes, by five different masters, from the end of the 15C. They vary in content from decorative designs, coats of arms and Danish fables to the martyrdom of St. Christina, and, in the transept vaulting, a glorious representation of Christ as the Judge of the World, dated 1480. On the wall of the N aisle there are figures of St. Anthony and St. Barbara, and on one of the pillars on the S side Christ, crowned with thorns, is appearing to Pope Gregory. The Virgin enthroned is seen on one of the columns to the N. There is a St. George, and a picture of the Day of Judgement, and many more.—For anyone interested in Danish frescoes, this is a must, quite different in character from the frescoes in the village churches. Some of them have clearly surmounted side altars in times past, but the side altars have disappeared.

The *High Altar*, however, is still there, one of the glories of Danish churches. The altarpiece is one of the biggest and most elaborate in the country. The main section is the work of the Lübeck master Bernt Notke, presented to the church in 1479 by Bishop Jens Iversen. The centre panel contains three large-scale figures, of St. Anna with St. John the Baptist on the right and St. Clement on the left. The side panels contain figures of the twelve Apostles. The whole is surmounted by a baldachin put there in 1514 by Bishop Niels Clausen,

Fresco: St George and the Dragon

High Altar

Fresco: All-Souls picture

Romanesque chapel

Modern organ

Fresco: St Michael, the Weigher of Souls

pulpit

E

font

Original organ

Diocesan Convention room

ÅRHUS CATHEDRAL

representing the Assumption of the Virgin. The great silver candle-sticks on the altar are from 1706.

The bronze font from 1481 rests on figures of the four Evangelists, and is richly decorated with figures and inscriptions. The large crucifix hanging on the N transept wall is from the same period. The pulpit is a magnificent Renaissance work from 1588 with carved reliefs of biblical motifs. There is moreover a large number of, often ornate, memorial tablets, as well as intricate wrought-iron gates to some of the chapels and to the chancel. These include works by Thomas Quellinus and Caspar Fincke. The tombstones here go as far back as 1100.

After leaving the cathedral, you should take a look at the old part of Århus to the N of the cathedral, walking through Mejlgade, Rosens-gade, Graven, Pustervig and Klostergade. These streets were allowed to fall into disrepair until the 1970s, since when they have been renovated and restored to something like their old state. Many of the ground floors are now small boutiques. At Domkirkeplads 5 there is an unusual museum, *Kvindemuset*, dedicated to the history of women and their lives. The same building houses a museum presenting the Occupation as experienced in Århus (open Sat, Sun).

In this area you will also find Lille Torv square, beyond which is *Vestergade*, the site of the other very old Århus church, *Vor Frue Kirke*. This was built by King Erik Ejegod at the end of the 11C, and is the oldest building in Århus. Originally the episcopal church, it later became the chapel of the Dominican monastery, the buildings of which, now called Århus Hospital, still stand to the N and W of Vor Frue Kirke. The church has five sections of arcading on either side of the nave, of which the two easternmost form the chancel and are the oldest part of the building; the nave is from c 1400, while the S aisle and the tower are late medieval. There are frescoes from 1300 to 1350 in the chancel, and from the 16C in the S aisle. The ornate altarpiece from 1520 is by Claus Berg.—During excavations in the 1950s an old *crypt* was discovered; this has now been completely restored for liturgical use and is open to the public. It dates from c 1060, is built of calcareous tufa, and is the oldest-known vaulted room in Scandinavia.

Now walk along Vestergade to Thorvaldsensgade; turn right and go as far as Vesterbrogade. Cross it, and you will find the entrance to the famous open air museum *Den gamle By* (The Old Town). Despite its name, this is not an old part of Århus, but a reconstruction of an old town, incorporating almost 70 half-timbered houses transported here from different parts of Denmark, reassembled and arranged to form a very charming and authentic-looking village. There are houses and buildings of many varied kinds, including the mayor's residence standing on the market place. Many of the houses are themselves open for inspection, and are equipped with furniture and household implements suited to their age. The museum is open all year, though times of opening vary according to season. You are, however, at any time able to walk through the streets, even if the individual houses are closed.—Beyond The Old Town are the botanical gardens, *Botanisk Have*, which have a large collection of plants and trees of interest to specialist and layman alike. There is an *open air theatre* in this park.

Retrace your steps now, and continue along Thorvaldsensgade and Vester Allé, passing the Business Archives on your left as you walk up the hill. At the top of this hill you should turn right into Frederiks Allé; in a park on your right you will then see the concert hall, *Musikhuset*, the impressive complex built in 1982 as the home of the Århus Sym-phony Orchestra, The Danish National Opera and the Århus Festival.

ÅRHUS

0 metres   400

N

RANDERS · GRENÅ

NORDRE RINGGADE
TRØJBORGVEJ
TRØJBORGVEJ

DRONN MARGRETHESV

SKOVVEJEN

Statsbiblioteket
Museum of Classical Archaeology
University
Park
City Hospital

Jysk Medicinhistorisk Museum

LANGELANDSGADE

KASERNE

NØRRE BLVD
VENNELYST BLVD
NØRREBROGADE
ØSTBOULEVARDEN
VIBE GADE SVEJ

HOEGH GULDBERGS GADE

Århus Kunstmuseum

Station

NY MUNKEGADE

SJÆLLANDSGADE
HJELMENSG
NØRREGADE
KNUDRISGADE
NØRREPORT
MEJLGADE
KYSTVEJEN

SAMSØGADE
THUNØGADE
NØRREGADE
PARADISG
STUDSGADE

GRØNNEGADE
LOLLANDSGADE

Botanisk Have

NØRRE
ALLÉ

MUNKEGADE
GULDSMED GADE
BORGPORTEN
GRAVEN
MEJLGADE

SØ JROGADE
TEGLVÆRKSGADE

KLOSTERGADE
ROSENSGADE

LANGELANDSGADE

Vor Frue Kirke

Den Gamle By

VESTERBROGADE
VESTERGADE
VESTER ALLÉ
GRØNNEGADE
VESTERGADE

LILLE TORV
VESTERGADE

Kvindemuseum
Århus Cathedral

Vikingemuseum
CLEMENTS TORV
BISPETORV

VIBORG

THORVALDSENSGADE

ÅBOULEVARDEN
ÅBOULEVARDEN
FISKERGADE

Ferry Terminal

CARL BLOCHS GADE
LUNDINGSGADE
SKOVGAARDSGADE
MARSTRANDSGADE

VESTER ALLÉ

CHRISTIANSGADE
FREDERIKS GADE
SØNDERGADE
ØSTERGADE
EUROPAPLADS

SØNDRE ALLÉ
FREDENSGADE
DYNKARKEN
MINDET

RÅDHUS PLADSEN
Town Hall
SØNDER ALLÉ

Musikhuset

EGGERSGADE
SØNNERSGADE

VALDEMARSGADE

VESTER ALLÉ
PARK ALLÉ

FREDERIKS ALLÉ

i

Roman Catholic Ch.
RYESGADE

BANEGÅRDS PLADSEN
Railway Station
SPANIEN

BANEGÅRDSGADE

MP BRUUNS GADE

JAEGERGÅRDSGADE

FREDENS ALLÉ

JAEGERGÅRDSGADE
OLE RØMERS GADE
SANKT PAULS GADE

MARSELISBORG ALLÉ
SLAGTEHUSVEJ
STRANDVEJEN

SKANDERBORG & Marselisborg Palace
MOESGÅRD

Now make your way back along Frederiks Allé, to *Rådhuspladsen*, the Town Hall Square, with the famous *Grisebrønd*, the beautifully fashioned figure of a pig and its young, one of which relieves itself at regular intervals. Here, too, of course, is the main entrance to the *Town Hall*, from 1941, one of the best-known examples of Scandinavian architecture of its time, with its striking and unusual tower. Parts of the Town Hall are open for guided tours. You can go to the top of the tower at 12.00 and 14.00 on weekdays in the summer. But all the year round, at 12.00 you can hear the splendid striking clock and its chimes.—Now turn right into *Park Allé*, and you will soon be back at the railway station.

There is more to see in Århus. This time a car will be useful, but not absolutely necessary. You should make for Nørreport and drive/walk up Nørrebrogade. You will then, just beyond Sabroes Plads square, come to *Århus Kunstmuseum* (Århus Art Gallery), with an outstanding collection of Danish painting and sculpture from the past 300 years. Foreign artists are also well represented.—If you continue along Nørrebrogade, where you have the city hospital, Århus Kommune-hospital, on your right, you will, on your left find *Jysk Medicinhistorisk Museum*, with a comprehensive collection of exhibits illustrating the history of medicine (open Wed pm).

Continuing across Meyers Allé, you come to the *University Park*, with the main university buildings, dating back to 1928. The campus has been carefully designed to give an impression of space and relaxed beauty, and the halls of residence are placed in pleasing groups. There is a natural history museum in this park.

Turn left at Nordre Ringgade, passing by the main University buildings (which house a *Museum of Classical Archaeology*), and at the next main crossing, with Langelandsgade, you will find the main University Library, *Statsbiblioteket*. If you now turn down Langelandsgade, you will return to the centre of the city.

3km S of the town centre you will find, standing in a great park, the royal residence of *Marselisborg Palace* (built 1899–1902). The park is open to the public when the Royal Family are not in residence. Beyond it is the arboretum, *Forstbotanisk Have*.—In the same area, on *Christian Filtenborgs Plads* square, there is a museum, *Det danske Brandværns Museum*, containing over 80 fire engines from many different times (open summer), and from here again it is not far to the pleasure park *Tivoli Friheden*.

Århus **ferry terminal** is about 1 km from the railway station, well signposted. From here there are six daily ferries to **Kalundborg** (Rte 7) (sailing time 3hrs), where you will find excellent roads or fast railway connections to **Copenhagen** (Rtes 3, 4).

17   Århus to Ålborg

A.   Via Hobro

Total distance 108km. E45 to (36km) **Randers**.—(27km) **Hobro**.—(46km) **Ålborg**.

The main E45 N from **Århus** (Rte 16) is a good straight road, clearly marked.

After c 13km, you might turn off right to *Todbjerg* (3km), where there is a church combining the old and the new in an artistic and tasteful fashion. The nave and chancel are Romanesque, built of granite ashlars; the chancel arch and both doors have sculptured decorations, and there are decorated tympana over both doors. On the N wall there are some late 12C frescoes. The late baroque altarpiece contains paintings done in 1979 by Sven Havsteen-Mikkelsen. The church also contains a rococo pulpit, and a large painting from 1725 over the chancel arch. In the medieval church chest a 14C parchment letter (one of very few found in Denmark) and some 13C and 14C coins were discovered in 1905.

Return to the E45 and drive to (23km) **Randers** (56,000 inhab.; Tourist Information: Erik Menveds Plads 1), the sixth-largest town in Denmark.

Its history goes back certainly to the 11C, when coins were minted here, while in 1086 it is mentioned as the place in which the rebels opposing St. Knud were to meet. After the murder of the Holstein Count Gert by Niels Ebbesen, it was the bridge across the Gudenå river at Randers which was the escape route used by Niels Ebbesen and his men. Randers was then at the centre of a Jutlandic revolt against Valdemar Atterdag when he tried to raise taxes. The oldest charter known for Randers is from 1302, issued in Viborg by Erik Menved, but it is assumed there were earlier ones.

In the Middle Ages Randers was an important trade centre in the hands of the Lübeckers, thanks to its position at the mouth of the river. Three convents or monasteries were established here—first the Benedictine Vor Frue Kloster in the second half of the 12C, a Greyfriars Monastery in 1236, and then, in 1417, a Holy Ghost Monastery, to which St. Martin's Church was later attached. There were three other churches in the Middle Ages.

There was a rampart around Randers in the 15C, and after the Reformation the Greyfriars Monastery was given a less spiritual mission and transformed into Randers Castle. In the 16C the town suffered two great fires and was largely destroyed. This catastrophe was followed by the plague in 1602 and the usual series of occupations and sackings in the 17C wars against Sweden. It fared little better in the 19C wars against Prussia and Holstein, during both of which it was occupied. Meanwhile, maritime trade increased, and Randers had a large fleet of freighters by the end of the century. Heavy industry came to the town, not least in the shape of the railway's rolling stock works.

The only one of the medieval churches to have survived in any form is *Sankt Mortens Kirke* (St. Martin's Church) on Kirketorvet. Even this is not one of Randers' very early churches, the chancel apparently dating from c 1494 and replacing the original medieval structure. The nave and the St. Hans Chapel on the S wall seem to be slightly later. The transept arch collapsed in 1632 and was rebuilt in 1634, the new arch bearing the insignias of Christian IV and Queen Anna Cathrine. The tower was added in 1795–96. The lofty nave with pointed vaulting borne on octagonal pillars, separating it from the aisles, is light and spacious.

Of particular interest is the ornate W door, from 1700. It was formerly only used to allow the passage of coffins into the church, and the carved panels reflect this. The richly carved altarpiece is from 1765. The 1686 pulpit, a magnificent piece of baroque carving, is thought to be the work of Laurids Jensen from Essenbæk and harmonises with other outstanding baroque carvings, not least the organ loft. The font is from 1695. The model ship in the nave is dated 1632 and is the oldest known church ship in Denmark.

Nearby is the imposing *Helligåndshuset* (The Holy Ghost House), once part of the monastery of that name. It is one of the remaining medieval buildings in the town, built c 1500 and standing in the middle of the town on Erik Menveds Plads. It is on two floors plus cellar, with corbie steps at either end. After the Reformation it was sold to a noble family, but has since served as a school (Steen Steensen Blicher was both pupil and teacher here) and offices; it now houses the Tourist Information Office.—Yet Helligåndshuset is not the oldest brick-built house in Randers. That honour goes to the three-storeyed *Paaskesønnernes Gård*, from 1468, on the old Town Hall Square, *Rådhustorvet*.

One end of Helligåndshuset, at which there is a statue by Ane Brügger of *The Woman with Eggs*, looks out on *Houmeden*, a lively pedestrian shopping street containing some attractive half-timbered houses from a slightly later period in Randers' history. After Ribe, Randers is said to have more extant half-timbered houses than any other town in Jutland. Oldest of them is *Nygade 4*, a house from 1550, restored in 1985.

It is interesting to note that Nygade with the adjoining Rosengade formed the old Jewish quarter of Randers. There was a thriving Jewish community here in the 19C, a fact which is still echoed in the existence of a synagogue and a Jewish cemetery dating back to 1807.

Another splendid half-timbered house stands on the corner of Nørregade and Lille Voldgade, and Storegade can also boast some fine specimens. Half-timbered houses, carefully tended, are the hallmark, too, of another principal shopping street, *Brødregade*, which is known to have been there since 1468. One of the most elegant of them is now the *Toy Museum*, with a unique collection of toys and dolls from the turn of the present century.

The shopping centre known as *Slotscentret*, on the other hand, is unashamedly modern. On Saturdays in the summer there are entertainments of various kinds here, and during the Randers Week festivities in mid-August, street entertainments are increased and extended.

Many of Randers' medieval buildings have been lost, but the town can claim three fine modern churches: *Sankt Clemenskirke* from 1963, by Inger Exner, Johannes Exner and Knud Erik Larsen, which was awarded an architecture prize, incorporating rooms suitable for use other than for church services, with textile decorations, an altar of Norwegian marble, and a pulpit of stainless steel; the square *Sankt Andreas Kirke* from 1971, designed by Holger Jensen, deriving its light through windows in the roof; *Johanneskirken* from 1978, with concave walls and a separate bell-tower, and decorations by Herluf Tarp.

There is a flourishing cultural life in Randers, which has its own symphony orchestra. It performs in a new concert hall and theatre complex constructed in the old power station now known as *Værket* (The Works). In addition there are two major museums in the town, the Art Gallery *Randers Kunstmuseum* and the Museum of Cultural History *Kulturhistorisk Museum*. Both are now housed in a purpose-built gallery from 1969, known as **Kulturhuset** (The House of Culture), standing in Stemansgade.

The ground floor is taken up by the Library, while the History Museum is on the first floor, offering artefacts old and new, and showing, too, a re-creation of rooms from the turn of the present century. There are also some etchings by Rembrandt and Adriaen van Ostade. The Art Gallery is on the second floor, with a collection of Danish painting from the late 18C to the present day, including paintings by Hammershøj and Købke.

There is ample provision in Randers for sporting activities, and canoes can be hired by Randers Bridge.

EXCURSION ALONG RANDERS FJORD (total distance 58km). If you want to experience the beautiful Randers Fjord landscape you should leave Randers on an unclassified road NE towards Harridslev, very soon turning right and driving through the village of Albæk to (12km) *Støvringgård*, a mansion dating back to the 16C, with the existing buildings from the early 17C; they are now used as residences for unmarried ladies of a certain rank. The great hall and chapel (unchanged since the 17C) are usually open to the public in the afternoon.

Proceed now to (2km) *Mellerup*. The small church, which has retained many of its Romanesque characteristics including an original chancel arch, possesses a particularly interesting early Gothic crucifix, beautifully restored in 1944.

The route continues NW to (4km) *Tvede*, which is also worth visiting for the sake of its Romanesque church. It stands on high ground, and has some richly carved furniture from the late 16C—including ordinary pews and more elaborate ones for the gentry, and an intricately carved pulpit and altarpiece, both from 1594. An hourglass is fixed to the pulpit to remind the pastor to keep his sermon within reasonable limits.

Continue N past Gjessinggård on your right to (4km) *Øster Tørslev*. The church here is late 19C, but it was constructed of material from its Romanesque predecessor, of which it bears clear signs. A special feature is a crucifix from c 1250, in which the Cross is fitted into a carved arch.

A further 4km brings you to *Råby*, where there is a church with a most unusual collection of frescoes. These date from 1511 and represent on the one hand the more customary Apostles and Saints (e.g. St. Gertrude), and on the other a collection of fantastic figures including centaurs and mermaids, and in one case verging on the pornographic. (There is a suggestion that it was the intention to render these fearful figures harmless by painting them in a holy place.)

The road continues NE, and you should take a minor road to (5km) *Sødring*. Here you will find the small mansion of *Sødringholm*, built 1752, but with a history going back to the 13C.—The small 15C church in Sødring is pure Gothic. Some elegant frescoes from 1491 were discovered in the vaulting in 1902, done by an artist who has become known as the Sødring Master, one of whose characteristics is the rather feminine character of the male faces he painted.

You have now reached the mouth of the fjord and return to (27km) Randers.

Returning to the main route, drive N from **Randers** on the E45. In 8km you will reach **Råsted**. Again there is a church to see, and once more a church redolent with history, the main interest being the well-preserved 12C frescoes in the chancel and nave and over the transept arch, the most extensive well-preserved Romanesque frescoes in the country.

The S wall is decorated with a large-scale, detailed and realistic painting of the Crucifixion. Over the transept arch sits Christ enthroned, giving the Keys to St. Peter and a book to St. Paul, while the other Apostles look on. The arch also contains references to other scenes from the Bible and seems to symbolise the entire story of the Redemption. Then the chancel, which is elaborately decorated throughout, provides a much fuller and more tangible account of the Redemption, with the Holy Innocents being slaughtered by medieval knights, the whole being arranged with a beautiful sense of artistry and symmetry.

Drive for another 10km through gently undulating country, and you will come to *Handest*, which is the terminus of the Mariager–Handest vintage railway line running 17km between Handest and Mariager. At the Mariager end there is a large collection of rolling stock as well as three steam engines (from 1909, 1928 and 1949), diesel engines and diesel railcars, all lovingly restored and maintained. In the summer some trains go as far as Randers instead of stopping at Handest.

The E45 now takes you to (9km) Hobro (Rte 20) and then to (15km) Rold, where there is a large *Circus Museum* (open summer). It contains costumes, equipment and photographs of the Cirkus Miehe together with the Cirkus Miehe's riding school, a circus caravan and lorry.

A road off right in Rold will take you through Arden to the small mansion of *Villestrup* (10km), where the large baroque park is open to the public in the summer months. It dates from 1750 and has recently been totally renovated. Villestrup House itself is a stately home built in 1538 and is not open to the public. If you go another 1km E you reach *Astrup*, where there is an imposing church. This was originally Romanesque, but the first owner of Villestrup, Axel Juul, had it rebuilt in 1542 and transformed into what in effect is the first Renaissance church in Denmark. The octagonal tower and copper spire are unusual.

Return to Rold, cross the E45 and drive to the mansion of *Nørlund* (5km). The original Nørlund, first mentioned in 1414, was a fortified tower owned by a robber (the forest of Rold Skov was a good place for robbery of one sort or another—even into the 19C!). This robber band became too active, and Queen Margrethe I brought cannon in and destroyed the tower—and hanged its inmates. The present Nørlund, the third, was built between 1581 and 1597 by Ludvig Munk, who married Ellen Marsvin in 1589; their daughter Kirstine Munk, subsequently Christian IV's morganatic wife, was born here in 1598.

You should now follow the E45 N into *Rold Skov*, the largest forest in Denmark, covering an area of some 80 sq km—certainly enough to get lost in if you start walking. The most convenient place to leave your car is 8km N of Rold village, where there are ample parking facilities near the road leading off to Skørping.

We suggest that you get a local map before venturing too far afield. This is a forest rich in wild life, with numerous lakes (some of them suitable for bathing) and many burial mounds indicating that people have lived there for many centuries. There are lots of streams in Rold Skov as well as the three largest natural springs in Denmark. The water from them maintains a constant temperature, resulting in flora and fauna different from what is found elsewhere in the country. There are both red deer and roe deer, foxes, badgers, martens, squirrels, and even the odd wild boar. Birds of prey are relatively common, but there is a vast array of other birds, from the nightjar to the thrush and from the heron to the kingfisher. And for those interested in insects, there is a host to choose from. As for flowers and plants, they are legion, and Rold Skov is the only place in Denmark where the Lady's Slipper orchid is found.

Within a short walking distance from where you are parked you will find *Rebild* and **Rebild Bakker** (Rebild Hills).

This area has always been associated with Danish-Americans. After the large-scale emigration from Denmark to the United States at the end of the 19C, many first and second generation Danish-Americans went to great lengths to maintain their links with the 'old country'. In 1912 a group of them collected sufficient funds to buy some 100 hectares of land in Rebild Bakker, making a present of this area to the Danish people, on condition that it should remain in its natural state and be open to everyone, and that Danish-Americans should be able to hold their own celebrations there. The area has since been extended to cover a further 100 hectares. Now, every year on American Independence Day, 4 July, Danish-Americans and their Danish relatives gather to celebrate.

The park contains a replica of the house in which Abraham Lincoln was born; this is a museum of pioneering times in the USA, and there is a prairie schooner to add to the atmosphere (open daily Jun–Aug, weekends May and Sept). There is also a museum dedicated to old folk instruments and their music. However, irrespective of all these overtones, Rebild Bakker is an area of outstanding beauty, a clearing in the great forest, a terrain covered with heather and scrub, a jewel in what many would refer to as one of the most beautiful areas of Denmark.

On the opposite side of the E45 from where you have parked are the *Tingbæk Limestone Mines* (open summer). Limestone is no longer quarried here, and the old workings have been turned into one of the most idiosyncratic art galleries in Denmark, with sculptures and plaster casts by Anders Bundgaard, Carl Johan Bonnesen and Anton Laier. Bundgaard's most famous work is of course the Gefion Fountain in Copenhagen (of which there is a smaller version here), but he was also responsible for sculptures outside Copenhagen Town Hall and Christiansborg Palace, and for the Cimbrian Bull in Ålborg.

Your next stop on the E45 could be in (2km) *Gravlev*. Apart from possibly visiting Anders Bundgaards grave here, there might be one more memorial for you to see before leaving this area: the *Airmen's Stone* near Årestrup. The easiest way to find Årestrup is to turn left off the E45 at Gravlev and drive 5km S. You will see the stone just to the E of the village. It was placed there and inscribed in memory of the crew of a Liberator bomber shot down on this spot during World War II. All eleven on board were killed. Part of the memorial consists of one of the propellors from the crashed aircraft. The airmen were buried in a common grave at the time, but they were then reburied in Årestrup churchyard, where their graves can now be seen.

Continue now on the E45 to (4km) Støvring, where you turn right to the rather unusual village of *Volsted* (5km).

Once more, a church is the attraction, and at first sight you might wonder why. It is a small Romanesque building, without a tower, indeed at a distance without any striking features, more the sort of church found in the poorer areas of West Jutland than in this affluent region. Even inside, there appears to be little of interest. Yet at the entrance to the porch there *is* something, the very thing you have come to see—the 'signature' of the man who built it. It is the work of a 12C sculptor/architect called Goti, who is known to have been responsible for various churches in Jutland, and whose style can be sensed in sculptures in yet other churches. The porch itself is of later date, certainly not his work, but the sculpted ashlars from an earlier door have been incorporated into this, representing a lion at the top, the Temptation on the left and a bishop on the right. There are furthermore an Agnus Dei and other figures, while the name of Goti is actually inscribed on a stone in the porch.

Driving N you again have a choice. The E45 will take you direct to (18km) Ålborg (see below), and Exit 27 or 26 will take you right to the centre. You could, however, leave the motorway 7km N of Støvring, turning on the 180 towards Svenstrup for a short DETOUR.

Follow the 180 for another 7km and join the 187 W through Frejlev (4km). 4km further, on your right, you will find one of Denmark's major long barrows, now known as **Troldkirken** (The Troll Church). The central feature is a hexagonal burial chamber c 55m long, and it is surrounded by a circle of 47 large stones, some of those at the S end standing as much as 2.5m high. Placed high on a hillside, the Troll Church is an impressive monument, and there is an equally impressive view from it. In an area rich in burial mounds, this is the outstanding one.

You now continue to the next village, *Sønderholm* (1km), where there is a Romanesque church with Gothic extensions and later additions. One of the notable features is the large number of Renaissance frescoes, including 32 coats of arms, perhaps reflecting the fact that a sign of true nobility was the claim to coats of arms stretching back over 16 generations. The altarpiece and pulpit are both 16C. Among the many graves is that of Christence Kruckow, who was beheaded in 1621 for witchcraft.

7km further on lies *Nibe* (3500 inhab.; Tourist Information: Torvet) which has a charter dating back to 1727, though it is little more than a large village with a small amount of light industry. Its streets are narrow and winding, and most of the houses are modest single-storey structures—modest but by no means unattractive. Indeed, Nibe is one of those small fjord towns which have a very special idyllic charm of their own, and even without impressive architecture or historical relics, it is worth visiting in order to have a feel of a former age. In the 16C Nibe was an affluent fishing village, but the herring left, and those times are long past—though the coat of arms still contains three herrings.

The modest church, originally dedicated to the Breton St. Jodocus, is from c1450 and appears once to have been a place of pilgrimage. There is a richly carved altarpiece from 1704 and a pulpit from 1706. The Romanesque font may well stem from an earlier church on this site.—Nibe is unusual in having—in a small park on Kildevej—an active spring providing 1400 hectolitres of water a day.

You should now return to the 180 which will take you straight into the centre of (20km) **ÅLBORG** (114,000 inhab.; Tourist Information: Østerå-gade 8), the fourth largest city in Denmark.

Ålborg was first mentioned during the reign of Hardeknud (Hardecanute) (1018–42) (the son of Knud the Great), who was King of Denmark from 1035–42 and King of England from 1040–42. Thanks to its position, it grew quickly as a trading centre for other towns on the Limfjord, and it grew rich on the herring fishing and trade links with Norway.

The earliest known charter is from 1340, but it is believed that there were earlier ones. The first municipal law was granted by Valdemar II in 1342. The Benedictine Convent of Our Lady was founded as early as 1116, while the Greyfriars' Monastery is mentioned in 1268, and the Holy Ghost Monastery was founded in 1451. There are references to the city's having been fortified in the Middle Ages, but no remains of either moat or mound are now to be seen. By 1310 there was a castle in the S part of the town and King Hans died there in 1513. However, during the Count's War the castle was so badly damaged that it had to be abandoned. In 1915, during the building of the new police station in Rantzausgade, parts of the foundations of this early castle were found.

Ålborg suffered two disastrous fires, one in 1501 and one in 1530, but the major catastrophe was during the Count's War, when Skipper Klement took the town, only to be driven out by the merciless Johan Rantzau in 1534, after which the town was plundered by Rantzau's troops and all fortifications demolished. However, profits from the herring fishing quickly put Ålborg on its feet again, and the early 17C was a period of affluence, from which many of the splendid houses stem. Nevertheless, during the 17C wars, Ålborg changed hands on various occasions and was once more plundered and heavily taxed, and in 1663 it suffered another great fire. There followed a period of varying fortunes, and it was only in the latter part of the 19C that the city really began to flourish once more with the advent of the railways and the modernisation of the harbour. These developments brought the industries which are today associated with Ålborg: cement, shipbuilding, building materials, iron and steel, and—akvavit (i.e. snaps). 'Let's have an Ålborg' is at least one very common way of suggesting a glass of this Danish national drink.

In 1970 Ålborg was officially united with *Nørresundby*, which until then had been Ålborg's sister town on the N bank of the Limfjord, linked to Ålborg by bridge and tunnel. Together, the harbours of Ålborg and Nørresundby constitute the largest provincial harbour complex in Denmark. Just to the E of the city is the Greenland Dock, now the port for all sea-borne freight between Denmark and Greenland.

Present-day Ålborg has its own university and symphony orchestra as well as the second largest zoo in Scandinavia and several first-rate museums.

There is a good choice of car parks in the centre of Ålborg though you may have to look around for space. Perhaps that on Strandvejen, down by the Limfjord, will be the easiest to find; it is close to the castle, and it is here you might start your exploration of this fascinating city.

The present *Ålborghus* Castle was built on the orders of Christian III between 1539 and 1555. Although this was a royal palace, it was little used by royalty. Only two wings remain today, of which the E wing is in more or less its original shape, a compact half-timbered building. The wall of the N wing facing the courtyard is likewise of half-timbered construction, though slightly higher, and to a different design. It is now the official residence of the chief administrative officer of the county and houses the county administration. The courtyard is open to the public during daylight hours, and there is access to the old dungeons and underground passages.

W of the Castle, at Østerågade 25, is *Jørgen Olufsens Gård*, one of the fine 17C merchants' houses. Elegant as it is, it is put in the shade by another house in Østerågade: *Jens Bang's House* at No. 9, from 1623–24, which is generally acknowledged to be the finest merchant's house in Denmark. It is five storeys high, and is equipped with three impressive gables overlooking Østerågade and one overlooking Adelgade. At first-floor level on the front there is an octagonal bay, topped by a copper roof with a statue of Flora at the apex. There is a famous wine cellar, *Duus' Vinkælder*, beneath the house, open now as it has been for the past 300 years. The chemist's shop, Svaneapoteket, which is at ground-floor level in this building, has been there since 1651—owned by the same family throughout.

Nearby, in Gammel Torv, stands an elegant baroque building, the former *City Hall*, built between 1757 and 1762. On a gable above the front entrance there is the Danish coat of arms and Frederik V's motto 'Prudentia et Constantia'.—Round the corner, in Algade, there is the ***Budolfi Cathedral**, named after the English St. Botolph. The oldest parts of this elegant building date from 1100, but most of it is from 1400. It consists of a nave with an aisle on either side, the nave continuing straight into the chancel. The W tower was rebuilt in 1663 after one of the great fires, and the baroque spire was added in 1780. As befits a church of this size and dignity, there is a splendid baroque *altarpiece from 1689 and a pulpit from 1692, both made in the workshop of Lauritz Jensen from Randers. Both are massive and richly carved. The font is of marble. There are also frescoes from the beginning of the 16C, and among the paintings there is a portrait of the English-born Queen Caroline Mathilde (1751–75), the sister of George III. A special feature of the church is the carillon, which plays on the hour during the day.

The other principal church in Ålborg is *Vor Frue Kirke* (Our Lady's Church), which you reach by crossing Østerågade again, and walk down Algade. Vor Frue Kirke is then on your right. This was originally the church attached to the Convent of Our Lady, and was probably the main church in Ålborg in the 16C and 17C—even being referred to as the Cathedral in several documents. In its original form it stems from the second half of the 12C, and the Norwegian King Sigurd Slembe was buried there in 1140. The present building, consisting of a nave and two aisles, is the result of very extensive rebuilding in 1878. Even this church suffered from a fire in 1902, which destroyed most of the 17C altarpiece, and the present one is a 20C product. The metal font, on the other hand, is from 1619, and the carved pulpit from 1581. One relic from the first church is found at the W door, which is set in sculpted 12C ashlars saved from the original N door.

Retrace your steps now, walk past Budolfi church, turn right at Gravensgade and then right again at Adelgade; you will now find, on C.W. Obelsplads, the remains of the Holy Ghost Monastery, **Helligåndsklostret** from 1431, claimed to be the best preserved monastery in Scandinavia. The present W wing is original, while the N and E wings are 16C. The chancel of the chapel is from 1681, and the whole was subjected to a 19C restoration in 1847–48. There are frescoes from c 1500. Also known as Ålborg Hospital, this has been called Denmark's oldest charitable institution, and to this day it provides 26 homes for the elderly. Parties are conducted through it at 14.00 Mondays to Fridays in the summer season, and it is well worth a visit.

In general, you should wander through the old streets in this part of the city and savour the atmosphere of the remaining half-timbered buildings, or discover the narrow lanes like Latinergyden beside the monastery. In Hjelmerstald, Søndergade, Nørregade and Fjordgade some of the remaining old houses have been carefully restored.

Ålborg, however, is not only old buildings and statues, but it provides a host of entertainment possibilities. The famous *Jomfru Ane Gade* (quite close to Helligåndsklostret) is almost entirely dedicated to restaurants, cafés and clubs, and is one of a number of pedestrian streets in the centre.—E of the central area there is entertainment of a different character in Ålborg's *Tivoliland*. Here you will find all sorts of amusements including a 'Boomerang Ride' as well as more conventional fairground treats, restaurants, a park area, 'China Town', and musical entertainment. On a smaller scale, this is Ålborg's very effective answer to Copenhagen's Tivoli.

Vesterbro is the main artery in the city, and here you will find Anders Bundgaard's statue of the *Cimbrian Bull*, from 1937, the symbol of Himmerland drive and expansion, relating to the fact that the Cimbrians emanated from this area of Denmark known as Himmerland. There is a much gentler statue too: Gerhard Henning's 'Goosegirl', from 1937. Yet another contrast is Erik Heide's 'The Animal' in the courtyard of the *Medborgerhus* (Civic Centre) on Nytorv.

Further S on Vesterbro, on your left you will come to *Ålborghallen*, the Ålborg Hall on *Europa Plads*, a cultural centre opened in 1953 with theatre, concert hall, exhibition and conference facilities as well as a restaurant and bowling alley.—The Ålborg Hall stands on the edge of the *Kildepark*, a beautiful small park containing a large number of classical statues, including Thorvaldsen's 'Three Graces' and Anne Marie Carl Nielsen's 'Child of Bacchus'.—A little further on, on the opposite side of Vesterbro which here becomes *Hobrovej*, you cannot miss the *Ålborg Tower*, an observation tower rising to 105m above sea level and offering panoramic views of the city and the surrounding area.

In the same area as the tower, in *Mølleparken*, lies *Ålborg Zoo*, where there is a large collection of animals and birds, many in enclosures offering them a good deal of freedom.

Ålborg has an excellent selection of museums, chief of which must surely be *Nordjyllands Kunstmuseum*, also very close to the Ålborg Tower, but entered from Kong Christians Allé to the N. Designed by the Finnish architects Elissa and Alvar Aalto and their French colleague Jean-Jacques Baruel, this is one of the most successful of Danish museums. It specialises in 20C Danish and international art, modernist art, especially the COBRA and Fluxus groups, as well as extensive collections of contemporary paintings, and is the venue for many visiting exhibitions.

Further S, on Riihimäkivej just off Hobrovej, is *Danmarks Tekniske Museum*, the Science Museum. As the name suggests, it is a museum dedicated to the history of science, and there are both permanent and visiting exhibitions. There is special emphasis on instruments concerned with communication, from early typewriters to modern television, and from the abacus to the computer. There are various gadgets at which you can try your hand.

Another museum is *Ålborgs Historiske Museum* (The Ålborg Historical Museum), in Algade, with a large collection of exhibits ranging from the Stone Age to the 19C. Of the reconstructions of old rooms, the Ålborg Room is of particular interest. The doors, panelled walls and magnificent ceilings were taken from one of the old merchant houses demolished in 1866, so there is a completely authentic appearance. The furniture, too, is of the right age, though it was not taken from the original room.

The local history archives are in Peder Barkesgade 5, close to Vor Frue Kirke, and in the same building there are the Emigration Archives, containing material on Danish emigrants (open summer, limited opening winter).

B. Via Hadsund

Total distance 126km. E45—(52km) **Randers**.—507 to (31km) *Hadsund.*—**Ålborg**.

Drive N from Århus on the E45 for 24km, then turn right to (5km) *Voldum*. There is a rather splendid 17C church here, with a Gothic porch. The furniture is ornate baroque, the carved altarpiece being a work of one of Peder Jensen Kolding's pupils. The pulpit from c 1600 is supported on a figure of Moses. The pew for the local aristocracy on the N side is particularly elaborate.

The church stands at a crossroads. Turn left here and drive N for a further 2km, and you will come to the large, three-winged mansion of **Clausholm**, a fine example of baroque art. Dating from the end of the 17C, it stands in an elegant park in the Italian style, with avenues of lime trees and some magnificent fountains. Concerts are given in the sumptuous chapel, where there is an organ thought to be from 1601. Clausholm is open to the public in the summer months, and there is a cafeteria in the cellar—where a collection of antique stoves is on display.

You now continue N to (2km) Årslev, there turning right to (4km) **Hørning**, where there is yet another and extremely interesting *church. It is quite small, consisting of a Romanesque chancel and nave built of granite ashlars. Vaulting was added in the Middle Ages, as was the transept; the tower, with an octagonal lantern standing 32m high, is early 18C. At the end of the 17C elaborate stucco decorations were added to the vaulting in the nave and chancel, giving the entire church an atmosphere at once intimate and opulent. The baroque altarpiece is mid 17C, as are the wrought-iron font and the richly carved pulpit.

Although the present appearance of this church is fascinating in itself, however it stands as a token of the continuity of religious practice. During restoration work in 1886–88, an oak beam from c 1050 was discovered; it bears carvings in much the same style as the Jelling Stone (Rte 21)—a leaf decoration on one side, and a carved serpent on the other, still showing the remains of the original yellow and red paint.

During further restoration work in 1964 excavations uncovered evidence that a wooden church had formerly stood on this same spot. At a lower level still the excavations uncovered a burial mound from c 1000, in which there was an undisturbed burial chamber containing the skeletal remains of a woman beside whom was positioned a table—the oldest known such in Denmark—and a decorated bronze dish. The chamber in which she was buried is similar in shape to that in the northernmost burial mound in Jelling. These old relics have been taken over by the National Museum, where they are now on display.

From Hørning you drive 1km NE to the A21. Turn left and continue to (14km) **Randers** (see above).

The distance from Randers to Hadsund is served by two good routes: (31km) is described first; for the alternative route via Mariager (35km) see below.

RANDERS TO HADSUND VIA HALD (total distance 31km). Leave Randers on the 507 N, driving to (12km) *Hald*, where, in the Romanesque church, you will find an *altarpiece from 1500 that was once in St. Martin's Church in Randers. It stretches across virtually the whole of the chancel and completely dominates the little church by dint of its size and its splendour. The central panel represents the Holy Trinity flanked by the Virgin and St. Martin, while the two wings represent the twelve Apostles and the four Fathers of the Church. Some late Gothic frescoes were uncovered in 1899 on the chancel arch, and more were found in 1924 in the vaulted roof of the chancel.

Continue to (4km) *Gjerlev*, where the church has an altarpiece by Skovgård. Before reaching (15km) *Hadsund* (see below) a DETOUR can be made, turning off towards *Havndal* 7km N of Gjerlev.

Here you will first drive past the 17C mansion of Trudsholm before reaching one of the sights you have come to see, *Lyshøj Mølle* (4km). This mill, from 1894, has been thoroughly restored and is in working order (open summer).—A minor road now continues to *Udbyneder* (1km), where in the Romanesque/Gothic church you will find a large number of fine frescoes from 1515–20 depicting the Day of Judgement and various saints and coats of arms, one of the best works by the Søndring Master.—A further 3km along this road will bring you to the mansion of *Overgård*, one of the most imposing in this part of Jutland, dating from the end of the 16C, and still retaining much of its original Renaissance character. Overgård is not open to the public, but there are sometimes concerts there in the summer.

Drive back now to the 507 and cross into (8km) Hadsund (see below) by the new (1978) bridge across the Mariager Fjord.

ALTERNATIVE ROUTE FROM RANDERS TO HADSUND—VIA MARIAGER (total distance 35km). From Randers you drive N on a good but unclassified road towards Mariager. After 9km you should turn right to *Spentrup* (2km), where there is yet another church to visit, this time one with literary associations.

Spentrup Church is not one of the largest, but it still retains much of its original Romanesque character, not least an interesting fresco from c 1200. This represents two female figures, one blindfolded and holding a lance which has transfixed a lamb, while the other has a chalice into which the blood from the lamb is running. The blindfolded figure represents Jewry, unable to see the truth, and in its blindness doing to death the Lamb of God, while the other figure represents the Church, sighted and redeemed by the Blood of Christ.

The real interest in this church, however, is the fact that the important 19C poet and short story writer Steen Steensen Blicher was pastor here from 1825 and lies buried in the churchyard. A large boulder decorated with a lyre and a laurel wreath stands on the grave in memory of him. (There is more about this very important 19C figure in Rtes 20 and 23, which will be concerned with a number of places with which Blicher is especially associated.)—In *Malvines Hus*, Stationsvej 47, here in Spentrup, you will meanwhile find a museum containing Blicher's works and a large number of his personal effects (limited opening summer).

Blicher was born in Vium in Jutland and quickly grew aware of the beauty of the then Jutlandic heath and the fascination of the stories, legends and people associated with it. In 1824 he published a short novel entitled 'The Diary of a Parish Clerk', which has established itself as one of the classical works of Danish literature. One of his finest short stories, 'Late Awakening', is a fictitious account of the occasion in Spentrup when he discovered that his wife was unfaithful to him. He was severely criticised by his contemporaries for publishing a story which was too open and dealt with subjects best left alone.

Back on the main road you drive N through a beautifully hilly and wooded area to (14km) **Mariager** (2100 inhab.; Tourist Information: Torvet 4), one of Denmark's smallest market towns, with a charter dating from 1592.

Mariager grew up around the Bridgettine convent which was founded there in

1410, when it was no more than a tiny hamlet. The convent was given the right to establish a harbour, and this brought trade to the locality, even though only small boats could enter it. Neverthelesss, local bricks and lime were loaded in Mariager in considerable quantities, mainly for domestic use, though some were exported to Germany. The town's dependence on the convent and the trade created by visitors and pilgrims meant, however, that it went into decline after the Reformation, more particularly after 1588, when the former convent lost its new position as a residence for unmarried daughters of the aristocracy.

Mariager suffered serious fires in 1573 and 1583, and the importance of the limestone quarry diminished. A further blow was the re-routing of the main road between Randers and Ålborg over Hadsund rather than Mariager, as it had traditionally been. Nor did Mariager benefit from the advent of the railways to the extent that many had hoped, and it has remained a small, idyllic town situated on a very beautiful fjord. In recent years a great deal has been done to maintain this image, and to make the most of Mariager's charm for the growing tourist industry of the region.

In view of its former dependence on the Bridgettine convent, it is not surprising that Mariager should be dominated by the **convent church** standing on a wooded hillside overlooking the yachting harbour. Nevertheless, what is now left is only a small part of the original building from 1460–80. The present cruciform church has a transept with wings roughly the same size as the nave and chancel. The N, S and W wings formed part of the original convent church, but the E wing is modern, dating from rebuilding in 1933. In its present shape it is some 43.5m long including the tower, though excavations have shown that it was at one time 75.7m. There was a danger of collapse

This dual representation of Christ is in the Convent Church at Mariager. Photo: Kirsten Nijkamp

in the 18C, and consequently the size of the original convent church was greatly reduced. The chancel was drastically lowered, but this was corrected in the rebuilding work carried out in 1931–33.

The present carved oak altarpiece is from the 17C, and the pulpit from 1724. More interesting is the pre-Reformation *Grave of Christ, a wooden coffin containing a life-size figure of Christ, formerly used in Holy Week rituals. You have to open the door to the room and switch on the light yourself—and the effect is quite startling.—There is another life-size figure of Christ as the man of sorrow behind the main altar.

Among the many tombstones is that of Stygge Krumpen (c 1480–1581), the last Catholic Bishop of Børglum and of his brother Otte Krumpen (c 1485–1569), who led Christian II's campaign against Sweden in 1520. Stygge Krumpen's tombstone—said to be a true likeness—stands in the church, but the Bishop's body is now buried in the churchyard. The only other remaining building of the original convent is the N wing, which stands close to the church and is used as a court registry.

Of other buildings in Mariager, mention should be made of the 18C merchant house, **Den gamle Købmandsgård** in Kirkegade 2, a beautiful building which is now a most interesting museum and art gallery with a good local historical collection and a model of the old convent and church (open summer). Close by is the old Post House, a half-timbered building from the 18C, which for a time was used as a parsonage and is now an hotel and restaurant containing furnishing from the 17C.—The old apothecary's house is built on a 15C basement foundation and stands on the site of a former guest house belonging to the Convent. The 1850 fire engine house is also still standing, and the old brewery from 1876 has recently been restored.

Near the central area is Munkholm Park, in which there is a sacred well, St. Helen's Well.—The vintage railway line between Mariager and Handest has its terminus here. Trains run on Sundays in June, July and August, and additionally on Tuesdays and Thursdays in July.—There are bathing facilities at the harbour.

A short walk along the Hadsund Road will bring you to *Hohøj*, a hillock which has been the setting for many conventions and meetings, and where there is a fine view across the fjord and countryside.

From Mariager you drive on the 555 alongside the fjord straight to (12km) *Hadsund* (4400 inhab.; Tourist Information: Rutebilkiosken, Jernbanegade 4) which is little more than a village and owes its existence purely to its position as a suitable place at which to cross the Mariager Fjord. Historically, it was a ford, and as late as 1840 there were only seven inhabitants. In 1860 a small transit harbour was established here, and a steamship route was opened between Hadsund and Copenhagen. The advent of the railways brought more growth, and a bridge was built over the Mariager Fjord in 1904. In addition to the harbour facilities, there is now some light industry.

Hadsunds Egns Museum has a good collection illustrating life in the area over the past 300 years (open summer; limited opening winter).—Hadsund was the birthplace of the 20C novelist Hans Kirk.

Between Hadsund and Ålborg there is again a choice of routes: the direct route (43km) comes first; the alternative route (62km) via the coast follows below.

DIRECT ROUTE FROM HADSUND TO ÅLBORG (total distance 43km). The 507 is a straight road through undulating countryside. After 7km you arrive at a crossroads, indicating Korup on the right and Astrup on the left.

Take the left turning and drive to *Astrup* (6km), where there is a rather splendid church, one of the earliest Danish Renaissance churches, from 1542. It consists of a chancel and nave, separated by a very wide chancel arch, an elegant porch, and a tall octagonal tower in the W. The 1634 carved altarpiece, depicting the Last Supper, was made in Ålborg. The granite font is Romanesque, with reliefs of a man's head flanked by two lions, and a heavily armed man in battle with a dragon.—Continue W for a further 1km to see the imposing late Gothic mansion of *Villestrup* from 1538–42. The splendid 5-hectare baroque park, for which loam was brought from the surrounding countryside, was established around 1750 in the style of French and Italian parks, and has been open to the public since 1988 (open at varying times during the summer).

Back on the 507 you drive 16km N, where you should turn off right to Komdrup (4km) and Sønder Kongerslev (a further 2km), both of which have churches of interest.

The small church in *Komdrup* is Romanesque, from c 1200. The original N door is still in use, while the S door has been bricked up. No original windows have survived, and the church was the subject of rebuilding in 1884. The altarpiece is late Gothic, probably the work of one of Claus Berg's pupils. A triptych, in the centre panel are figures of God the Father, Christ, Mary with the Child, and John the Baptist, and twelve Saints in the side panels.

Take the road SE from the church to *Sønder Kongerslev*, where there is another interesting small Romanesque church. The octagonal Renaissance tower is one of only two of this shape in Denmark, the other being in Astrup. Like the nave and chancel, this tower is built of granite ashlars at the base but it changes to bricks at the top and ends in a pyramidal roof. There is an altarpiece from 1597 and a beautifully carved pulpit from the same time.

The 16C mansion of *Kongstedlund*, which has been associated with this church, lies c 1.5km SE. From high ground here, looking E, you have a view of the unreclaimed, and now protected, marshland Lille Vildmose.

Back on the 507 you drive past one of the biggest and most interesting mansions in North Jutland, **Lindenborg**. It has a history going back to the 14C, when it probably originated in connection with a ferry across the Lindenborg Å river, on which it stands.

The present buildings, situated on a mound and surrounded by a moat, date from 1583–1616, much of the original building having been destroyed during the Count's War. There are three wings, of which the S wing from 1583 is considered to be one of the most interesting Renaissance buildings in Jutland, possibly designed by the same architect as designed Kronborg Castle in Helsingør (Rte 5). One special feature is the octagonal tower containing a spiral staircase, which overlooks the courtyard. On the S side there are two round towers at the corners, and the façade is broken by two projections shaped as four of the six sides of a hexagon. Lindenborg is not open to the public.

From Lindenborg you drive a further 4km, to *Gunderup*, where there is a large church (34.8m long) of unusual design, sometimes referred to as 'Himmerland Cathedral'. The nave and chancel are Romanesque. The Romanesque N door still survives, as do two of the original N windows. The Romanesque font is of granite and in it are carved a human head and two animals with intertwined tails. There are two runestones in the porch; one of them was found by a burial mound and is of particular interest. The inscription on it reads: 'Toke raised this stone and made this memorial to his stepfather Abe, a stout yeoman farmer, and Tove his mother. Both lie in this mound. Abe left his possessions to Toke.' There is a very similar inscription on rune-stones found in the church in Sønder Vissing (Rte 23). As the Sønder Vissing stones show, Toke was the grandson of king Gorm the Old, who is remembered on the runestone in Jelling (Rte 21).

After a further 9km N on the 507 you take a road left leading to (6km) **Ålborg** (see above).

ALTERNATIVE ROUTE FROM HADSUND TO ÅLBORG VIA THE COAST (total distance 62km). Leave Hadsund on the 541 E to (12km) Als, calling first at (3km) **Visborg**, where the 16C church has an unusually large array of Renaissance furniture: an altarpiece from 1600, still containing an original painting, a pulpit in the same style, carved benches in the chancel, other pews from the 16C and 17C, an elegant wrought-iron altar rail from 1600, and above the sacristy door a painting of the Seefeld family, mother, father and eleven children, who then owned the mansion of Visborggård nearby. A memorial stone to them stands at the side of the altar. It was in fact Jakob Seefeld—who died in 1599 and was buried in this church—who was responsible for the building. The Seefeld family grave is in the churchyard.

Close by the church is the mansion of *Visborggård*, a huge house surrounded by a broad moat and looking more like a castle, the S wing of which dates back to 1575–76. Of the original seven towers only two remain to flank the imposing façade with its magnificent sandstone gateway. It was Jakob Seefeld who had it built—or rebuilt—in the grand Renaissance style after an older castle had been burned down by Skipper Klement's followers.

Visborggård is now a home for the mentally sick and not open to the public. There is, however, public access to the park, where there is a memorial of special significance to the Danes. When, in 1920, southern Jutland was returned to Denmark, King Christian X marked the occasion by riding over the border on a white horse. That horse had come from Visborggård, and it is now buried there in a marked grave.

Soon after leaving Visborg, you will drive out of the undulating terrain and come to a flat expanse of land, which will extend most of the way along this coastal road. You will soon reach *Als*, where there is a regional museum in the form of a typical Himmerland farmhouse from the mid 19C, with contemporary furniture and farm implements from the area.

The 541 will now take you N along the coast through a flat landscape to (5km) *Øster Hurup*, a fishing village with excellent bathing facilities and a recreation park set in magnificent scenery.

On your way N you will now pass *Lille Vildmose* on your left. This is an area of 55 sq km of drained marshland, largely now under cultivation, but much of the S part is kept in its natural state and is not open to the public. In the centre of Lille Vildmose lies Tofte Lake, a bird sanctuary, to which there is also no admittance, though you can drive up to an observation platform from which you can follow the bird life.

12km further N brings you to *Dokkedal*, another fishing village which has become a bathing resort. It has a very fine beach, safe for children, and is well equipped with car parks, toilets, etc.—*Mulbjerge*, just N, is excellent for flying kites.

6 more kilometres and you are in Egense, where you turn W on to the 595. Just after entering this road you will come to a large house called Egense Kloster (Convent), formerly belonging to Mariager

Convent, though there has never really been a convent here (no public admittance).

Drive 9km W on the 595 to a road leading left to **Sejlflod** (2km). This is the only place in Denmark actually to have a *pyramid (open). Standing 8m high, this is a copy of the Egyptian Cheops pyramid and was built by a psychologist who believed that special healing powers could be attributed to it.

Rather older are the extensive prehistoric remains centred on *Toíthøj*, a burial mound just to the W of the village. Artefacts and graves from as far back as 3500 BC have been found there, leading to the suggestion that Sejlflod is actually the oldest settlement in Denmark. It is moreover situated in extremely varied and interesting terrain, surrounded by hills, heathland and, over the drained marshes, in close proximity to the sea.

Back again on the 595 you come to (5km) *Klarup*, where there is a charming small Romanesque church with a Gothic tower. Most of the furniture is from the 18C, and there are several rococo paintings reflecting the influence of the pietists of that time. There is a wrought iron door from c 1700 and a wrought-iron altar rail from the same period.

Just beyond Klarup, on the right, lies *Klarupgård*, a splendid, low-built half-timbered house from the 18C, ultimately with a history going back to the time of Erik Menved. From Klarup you drive straight into (13km) **Ålborg** (see above) by crossing the E45 and continuing on over the railway line. You then take the second road right (Hobrovej), which will take you straight into the centre.

If you wish to go N without visiting Ålborg, you simply take the E45 on the outskirts of the city.

18   Århus to Thisted

Total distance 165km. A26 to (67km) **Viborg**.—(37km)
Skive.—(30km) *Nykøbing Mors*.—(31km) **Thisted**.

From **Århus** (Rte 16) the A26 takes you through undulating country-side to (23km) *Voldby*, where there is a splendid auricular altarpiece by Claus Berg portraying the martyrdom of 10,000 knights. The pulpit is contemporary with it.—A narrow road N just before the church will take you to *Frijsenborg* (4km), the majestic 19C neo-Renaissance mansion at the centre of one of the largest estates in Denmark.

7km further on you come to a road leading S to *Gjern* (3km).

Here there is a motorcar museum, *Jysk Automobil Museum*, displaying some 135 cars, lorries and motorcycles of 65 different makes, all painstakingly restored. The oldest car is a Belgian Vivinus from 1900, and the motorcycles come from countries as diverse as the US, Denmark, Sweden, England and Germany (open summer).

Gjern's other claim to fame is that the artist Erik Raadal was born here and used the village as the motif for most of his work, thus producing the most comprehensive picture in art of any village in Denmark. There is also a new Lake Uplands Holiday and Course Centre offering accommodation for 110 on seven farms.—Nearby flows the Gudenå river, and the old towpath along its banks offers the opportunity of splendid walks.

Returning to the A26, you can now continue to (4.5km) Fårvang, where you might turn left and drive S to *Tvilum* (5km).

Standing alone here in idyllic surroundings, close to the Gudenå river, is a church which once formed the N wing of an Augustinian monastery from the early 13C, and where there is now a copy of the first complete Danish translation of the Bible, from 1550, known as Christian III's Bible. The church is small and unadorned, with a simple dignity of its own. There is a Romanesque font and a carved late medieval altarpiece.

A further 4.5km on the A26 will bring you to *Kongensbro*, where a famous old inn stands at the crossroads, a favourite haunt of anglers. Drive on through (6km) Ans, with the 13km-long *Tange Sø* on your right.

This lake was created in 1920 when the biggest hydro electric power station in Denmark was built in Tange, just to the N. If you turn right immediately after the lake you will come to *Tange* (4.5km), where part of the power station is a well equipped and very popular electricity museum (open summer).

Otherwise you drive straight on to (22km) **Viborg** (Rte 20). If you do not want to visit the fine old capital of Jutland, you can remain on the A26, which is clearly marked on the ring road, and drive straight to (30km) Skive (see below). This direct route has little of interest, however, so at (10km) *Fiskbæk* we suggest you leave the A26, driving N for a time along the W side of the *Hjarbæk Fjord*.

The unclassified road you should follow turns off right just after you have passed the high-lying church, and will first take you past the little inlet where Canute is said to have gathered his fleet to sail to England. A further 12km along this road, will bring you to *Ørslev Kloster*.

Like so many other monasteries and convents, Ørslev Kloster was turned into a private residence after the Reformation, though, as elsewhere in Denmark, the nuns were allowed to remain in the convent until their death—the last lived for 60 years after the Reformation was proclaimed. It remained in private hands until 1964, when it became a study centre for Kulturhistorisk Museumsforening (The Cultural History Museums Association); since 1969 it has been a place of retreat for writers and artists.

Standing surrounded by trees on raised ground, the whole complex has meanwhile retained much of its original ponderous dignity. The large church, the N wing of the complex, is part of the original building from c 1200, with Romanesque apse, chancel and nave in the general style of village churches of the time, though a good deal larger. The tower is Gothic, though it underwent considerable alteration in the 18C. Among the objects of interest in the church is a memorial to the Faroese patriot (and pirate) Magnus Heinesen, who was a friend of the then owner. He was beheaded in Copenhagen in 1589, and a year later, when the execution was declared to have been a mistake(!), permission was given for his body to be taken to Ørslev and buried.

From Ørslev Kloster you return to the 579, which you will just have crossed, turn right there and drive along this road and later the A26 to (14km) **Skive** (19,500 inhab.; Tourist Information: Østerbro 22), which received its charter in 1231. The town lies at the neck of the Skive Fjord, where Karup Å river enters it. Skive's history goes as far back as AD 1000, but it has suffered from fires on several occasions, and there are few really old buildings left. However, just outside the town, on the shore of the fjord, stands the 16C mansion of *Krabbesholm*, a large dignified brick building which is now a folk high school. Outstanding among its rooms is the great hall, furnished with a series of large-scale frescoes. The other principal historical building in Skive is the old church, *Fruekirke*.

Fruekirke has a history going back to 1304, and stands in an almost Italianate churchyard. The chancel and nave are Romanesque, but there are Gothic additions. By the 19C the church was becoming too small for Skive, and there were plans to demolish it. It was then discovered that beneath the whitewash there was an elaborate collection of frescoes, and it was decided to restore them and maintain the church. There are some 50 figures from the Bible and church history, surrounded by a flowered pattern, and there is an astounding wealth of colour and invention in a church which has retained much of its Romanesque character. The altarpiece is from 1600 and the altar candles from 1650. One of the candelabras is 17C, while the other two are copies.

In Havnevej, between Ågade and the railway line, stands *Skive Museum*, where in addition to antiquities and Denmark's largest collection of amber (11,000 pieces) there is a good art collection and a Greenland Room containing a large number of Greenlandic exhibits. Another building of particular interest is *Gammel Skivehus* on the corner of Østertorv and Søndre Boulevard. Today an hotel, it is on the site of an 11C castle, and incorporates a splendid early 18C half-timbered wing which is open to the public and contains a collection of relics from the earlier Skivehus Castle.

Skive is a good centre for excursions.

EXCURSION FROM SKIVE TO SPØTTRUP CASTLE, LIHME CHURCH AND LEM CHURCH (total distance c 44km). Leave Skive to the W on the 573

Spøttrup Castle, near Skive, is one of the best preserved of Danish medieval castles.
Photo: John Sommer

and drive straight to (20km) ***Spøttrup**, said to be the most perfectly preserved medieval castle in Scandinavia. It is unusual to begin with in that it stands empty, with public admission to all parts; unusual, too, in its compact, forbidding aspect, as it stands on low unwooded ground, unadorned, isolated and surrounded by a moat behind high ramparts, approached through a stern gateway across a narrow bridge—clearly intended to be a castle capable of being defended. And defended it was when Skipper Klement's followers attacked it during the Count's War in 1534. The original building of three wings is from c 1500, the fourth wing being late 16C (open May–Sept).—In the adjoining park there is a reconstructed medieval herb garden with some 300 different herbs; there is also a rose garden—and, very conveniently close by, a restaurant.

Follow the road N turning left at the first crossroads. This minor road will take along the coast to (8km) *Lihme* (or *Lime*), where there is a large and architecturally interesting church, one of the oldest in Denmark, built probably around 1100 and reconstructed c 100 years later. The tower in the W exhibits an arched frieze decorated with carved heads. The apse is enclosed on the outside by half columns, and at the E corners of the chancel, just below the roof, there are jutting figures of animals carved in the ashlars, reminiscent of the figures often found jutting out of the wooden stave churches of Norway. Inside, in the chancel, there are frescoes from 1507, in which the tracery is possibly Irish-inspired, but the most interesting feature is doubtless the stone font with its beautiful symbolical frieze depicting stags, knights and dragons, which has not so far been finally interpreted.

From Lihme a further 3km E on the 189 will bring you to *Lem*. Here, too, there is a church of some renown. The combination of Romanesque apse, chancel and nave, and a Gothic tower is not unusual, but the carvings on the Romanesque granite ashlars are, and they are remarkably well preserved. On the apse, too, there are many carved figures, both in the ashlars and in arches formed by the half columns. A further 15 ashlars elsewhere in the walls show carved figures. There are late 16C frescoes in the chapel.

From *Lem* it is 15km on the 189 back to *Skive*.

EXCURSION FROM SKIVE TO THE ISLAND OF FUR (total distance c 57km). The tour starts on the 551 N from Skive, following the road along the fjord for 12km, when you turn right to *Jenle* (1km) near the coast. From 1907 this was the home, and is now the burial place, of the Jutlandic poet and novelist, Jeppe Aakjær. In poems of great lyrical intensity and showing a deep love for the ordinary Jutlandic peasant struggling for his existence, and in novels remarkable for their revelations of the brutality of 19C rural life, Aakjær established himself as a leading literary figure at the turn of the 20C. Jenle (the name means 'isolated' in Jutlandic dialect) is now in State ownership, and the house, very much as when Aakjær lived there, is open to the public in the summer, giving a lively impression of the poet's writing and work for cultural and political progress, not least in the form of great rallies held in the grounds.

Return to the 551 and drive N to (3km) *Grinderslevkloster* where the church once formed part of an Augustinian monastery founded c 1150. It is part Romanesque, part Gothic, with an apse surrounded by half columns surmounted by carved heads. The prior's door on the S side is flanked by carved ashlars in the form of a lion and a dragon, and surmounted by a tympanum with a cross carved inside a frieze. Mid 16C frescoes by the Torum Master include a Madonna and Child, in which the realistically portrayed child Jesus is reaching for a pear, the traditional symbol for the mother's breast.

The Torum Master takes his name from the village of *Torum*, 6km further N. Here he is thought to have been responsible for most of the extensive and well-preserved frescoes in the church. Discovered in 1952, they cover both walls and vaulting with motifs from the Bible as well as several figures, including SS. Paul and Christopher. The Romanesque granite font is decorated with 16 carved figures.

Another 4km sees you at the narrow *Fur Sound* separating the mainland from the tiny island of **Fur**. There is normally a ferry connection every 30 mins, and the crossing takes 5 mins. Fur is one of the areas in Denmark (the others are on Mors) famous for deposits of mo-clay, also known as diatomaceous earth or kieselguhr, and made up of the skeletons of microscopic algae mixed with clay. The substance is both light (it will float) and tough, and it is used largely for insulation. These are the only known deposits of mo-clay in the world; they are 60m deep in places, and the countless fossilised plants, fish and insects in them provide a paradise for anyone interested in biology or geology. Some of the best fossils are found in the museum (open Apr–Oct) in *Nederby*, 2km N of the Sound.

You return to (29km) Skive on the 551.

EXCURSION FROM SKIVE TO HJERL HEDE AND TO THE CHURCHES AT SAHL AND EJSING (total distance c 49km). From Skive you take the A34 S to (6km) *Estvad* with its Romanesque church and tower from c 1470. The magnificent carved Gothic altarpiece, a triptych, is from 1502, and the church possesses a Romanesque chalice and censer. There are some late Romanesque frescoes from c 1225 as well, restored in 1893.

Now follow the A34 S for 7km. Here you come to a crossroads, and if you turn right you will in a further 6km arrive at Sevel. (To make a short cut driving across the *Hjelm Hede* heath as far as Søgård is an experience, but you need a good map to find the old track, and a good car to drive along it!)

Just before reaching Sevel you will see *Stubberkloster* convent signposted to the left. You can only cover some of the distance by car, but it is well worth the trouble to walk the rest, for the landscape around here has a grandiose rugged beauty of its own. There is not much left of the 13C Benedictine convent down by the side of Stubbergårdsø lake, but the ruins are scheduled, and there are well-preserved remains of cellar vaulting inside the present building.—In more recent times, this area has provided the inspiration for one of Denmark's best-known women writers, Marie Bregendahl, who was married to Jeppe Aakjær from 1893 to 1900.

In *Sevel* itself there is again a delightful church, standing on high ground, with sweeping views from its well-kept churchyard— strangers to the village have even been known to express the wish to be buried there for the sake of the view! The chancel and E part of the nave are Romanesque, the remainder Gothic. Traces of the former men's entrance are clearly seen on the S wall, and of the women's entrance on the N wall, but neither corresponds to the present entrance through a porch from 1765. The pulpit is from 1605, while the gallery is slightly older. The tower contains not only an impressive church bell, but also a carillon, which plays three different hymn tunes morning, noon and evening, and which was given to the church in 1938 by one Andreas Gade, the great-uncle of one of the present authors.

From Sevel it is only 4km to **•Den gamle Landsby Museum** at *Hjerl*

Hede. This is one of Denmark's most famous and extensive open air museums, a reconstructed village comprising over 40 buildings brought from all over Jutland, and illustrating the development of Danish village life from 1500–1900—a grocer's shop, a smithy, a school, workshops of different kinds, a Romanesque church with murals, a windmill, and several farmsteads. The 'village' is open from April to November, but in July each year not only does it show off its buildings, but large numbers of people dress in the appropriate costumes, demonstrate their skills and trades, and bring everything to life. At the same time there is a reconstruction of a Stone Age settlement—also with volunteers suitably dressed.

When you have seen the village, you should not miss a walk out on to the broad heath. It is protected, and gives an excellent impression of what virtually the whole of Jutland was like 150 years ago. It is well worth walking as far as the long and curiously shaped *Flyndersø* lake, the largest moorland lake in Denmark. It resembles the Stubbergårdsø, but is considerably larger and has steeper banks. Both originated at the end of the Ice Age, when the retreating ice left behind vast accumulations here. On melting, these formed so-called kettle-holes which then filled with water.

You should now drive to (3km) **Sahl**, again to see a church, but once more with something very special. Sahl Church contains the best preserved of one of what are known as Denmark's *golden altars. The church itself is quite large, Romanesque from c 1150. The pews are closed, with carved bench ends. It used to be the custom for men and women to sit on their own sides of the church, and it is interesting to note here that the benches for men on the S side are higher and sturdier than those for women on the N side.

Meanwhile, it is the altarpiece which is bound to attract your attention. It now stands as a single unit, but it once consisted of an antemensale, standing in front of the altar, and a predella, standing on the altar itself. It all consists of an oak base covered with chased copper which in its turn is gilded. The whole is covered with biblical figures, scenes from the life of Christ, and Christian symbols, and the effect is quite remarkable. There is a very similar altar in Stadil (Rte 15).

Now drive 3km W to the 189, where you turn right after 2km and then left to **Ejsing** (2km). Yet again, it is a church you should visit, and yet again it is a large one with special features. The chancel and nave are Romanesque, and there are sizeable late medieval extensions including an aisle with columns and vaulting. The blue-painted pews and bench ends from c 1760 are decorated with pietist symbols. The pew for the local squire is rococo in style, the glorious oak pulpit and canopy baroque (and said originally to have been intended for Viborg Cathedral), the sculpted font Romanesque (the oldest piece in the church). There are excellent frescoes (including a very obviously male Adam) from c 1500 in the chancel, behind the altar and in the S chapel—where there is a pompous memorial stone to Axel Rosenkrantz and his wife.

It is, however, in the sacristy that you find the most unusual features. Here, there is a Lutheran confessional from the 17C, and here, too, through a large trapdoor in the floor, you might (on request) see the mummified remains of a fully robed 18C pastor and his wife, lying on beds of hops in open coffins.

Leaving Ejsing, you rejoin the 189 N and drive back to (18km) Skive.

Returning to the main route, from **Skive** you drive N along the A26 to (25km) Sallingsund. The region you have been crossing is called

*The golden altar in Sahl Church, near Skive. One of
a small number of such altars showing a high degree
of craftsmanship, and full of subtle symbolism.
Photo: John Sommer*

Salling, and on the other side of the sound lies the Limfjord island of
Mors.

This island is similar in shape to Jutland itself, and legend has it that when God
was making Jutland He first made this as a model; however, as the model ended
up being so beautiful God could not bring Himself to destroy it, and so He placed
it in the middle of the Limfjord.

Mors is now connected to the mainland by bridges. Some 24,000 people live here in 17 villages and the sole town of *Nykøbing*. For the tourist there are plentiful facilities for hiking, cycling, fishing, sailing, and there is a full range of overnight accommodation.

After crossing the elegant 1730m-long Sallingsund Bridge, you will very soon find signs pointing left to *Jesperhus Blomsterpark* (Jesperhus Flower Park) (1km), a favourite place for excursions. The park, in the wooded, undulating countryside of Legind Bjerge (mountains!), covers some six hectares and boasts of half a million summer flowers in beautiful surroundings, with fountains, lakes, aquarium and aviary. It also claims to have the 'largest and longest waterfall' in Denmark— though this is surely an example of Danish humour. It does, however, have plenty of amusements for children (open mid-May to mid-Sept).

Back on the A26 you almost immediately turn off right to (3km) *Nykøbing Mors* (9500 inhab.; Tourist Information (summer): Havnen 4). The town is locally only called Nykøbing, but as there are three major towns in Denmark called Nykøbing, their location is often added to the name. Though only small, the town has nevertheless had a charter since 1299, and today has a small amount of light industry, not least a plant processing the oysters for which the Limfjord is famous. The oldest and without doubt the most beautiful building in the town is the former *Dueholm Monastery*, approached via Vestergade and Dueholmgade.

The monastery formerly belonged to the Order of St. John of Jerusalem, and was established by the Bishop of Børglum in 1371. The present 16m-long W end of the main building is from 1450, while the remainder of the main building together with the side wing was added after the Reformation, when the monastery went into private ownership. The monastery now houses *Mors historiske Museum* (The Mors Historical Museum), which proclaims itself to be an 'old-fashioned' museum in which many exhibits are displayed in an apparently disorganised fashion so that visitors can indulge in voyages of discovery.

Indoors there are collections of paintings of Mors, local historical finds, furniture, pottery and glass, while in the loft, with its original roofing construction, there is a collection of ploughs, a reconstruction of the interior of a peasant house and, in the E end, a reconstruction of a small church with old local church furniture. The side wing contains the archaeological collection, and the garden exhibits some reassembled Bronze Age graves from Mors. Also various ancient stone pieces from early churches can be found here.

On Rådhustorvet (Town Hall Square) there is a foundry museum— the *Støberimuseum*—housing a collection of products from the old Mors Foundry and, in addition, some old Norwegian and German stoves (open Jun–Aug).

Nykøbing church is neo-Gothic, from 1891, and contains some misericords, presumably from Dueholm Monastery, and a fresco by J.T. Skovgaard.

The Dano-Norwegian novelist Aksel Sandemose (1899–1965) was born here, and there is a memorial plaque on his childhood home in Ferkenstræde. It was good of Nykøbing to put it there, as Sandemose's portrayal of his home town, under the name of Jante, is anything but flattering.

EXCURSION FROM NYKØBING TO WEST MORS (total distance c 24km). Take the 545 road W for 17km to Hvidbjerg, turning left after the church on a minor road to *Glomstrup mansion* (3km). Glomstrup, from 1797, but with a history going back to 1376, is now a museum, supplemented by an open air museum of 14 various buildings on a

2500 sq m site (open Jul). They house collections of 18C and 19C furniture and tools in their contemporary settings. There is a childrens' museum, too.

Return to the 545 and drive on to (4km) *Karby* where there is an unusual, newly restored and splendidly appointed church, part Romanesque and part Gothic, with, in the sacristy, some 17C frescoes which still exhibit medieval qualities. There is a Romanesque granite font, a pulpit from 1600, an auricular altarpiece from 1690, and two richly decorated pews for the local nobility.

You now return on the 545 to (20km) Nykøbing.

EXCURSION FROM NYKØBING TO NORTH MORS (total distance c 50km). Leave Nykøbing on the 581, driving 24km N to *Feggesund* sound. The last 2km are driven on a very narrow spit of land, with views of Thy to your left and straight ahead, and of the small island of Livø and the mainland coast near the town of Løgstør (both Rte 23) on your right.

This is a wild, desolate area to which many legends are connected. It seems likely that this was one of the places where the Vikings collected their ships before sailing out into the North Sea (as was then possible via Thisted). Legend also tells of one King Fegge who became jealous of his brother, Horvendil, murdered him and then married his wife. Following ancient Scandinavian tradition it then fell to Horvendil's son to avenge him. And the son's name was—Hamlet! Fegge is said to be buried here, and a stone has been raised in memory of all this.

If you wish to go straight from here to Thy and Thisted. There is a ferry sailing every half hour, the journey takes five minutes, and Thisted is then 20km away (Rte 21). However, there are other things to see in this N area of Mors. On your way back to Nykøbing you should turn off right at 5km (in Hesselbjerg) to visit the mo-clay deposits and the *Mo-clay Museum* (1.5km) on Skarrehagevej 8.

Back on the 581 you drive a further 3km S and then turn right again on to a minor road leading to (2km) *Nørre Dråby*, passing a small archaeological and geological museum within the first km. From Nørre Dråby you should follow a coastal road S along splendid beaches to (5km) Flade, where, at the nearby *Salgjerhøj* you will find the highest point on Mors, offering a magnificent panorama of the island, the fjord and the countryside all round. It is claimed that on a clear day you can see 34 church towers from here.—3km further W *Hanklit*, a mo-clay cliff, rises vertically 60m above the Limfjord, a sight of great majesty, and now a protected area.

From Flade you return to (13km) Nykøbing.

From **Nykøbing**, the last part of Rte 18 follows the A26 NW. 21km ahead you come to the 381m-long *Vilsund Bridge*, built in 1939 as one of the several bridge projects introduced to counter the unemployment of the great Depression. On arriving on the mainland region of Thy across the sound, you drive N along the coast to (10km) **Thisted** (Rte 22).

19 Thisted to Ålborg via Skagen

Total distance 307km. A11 to (43km) *Fjerritslev*.—(29km) *Åbybro*.—A55 (25km) *Løkken*.—(27km) **Hjørring**.—(16km)

Hirtshals.—E39, 597, A40 N to (47km) **Skagen**.—A40 S to (41km)
Frederikshavn.—E45 to (12km) **Sæby**.—E45, unclassified roads, 559
to (33km) *Dronninglund*.—559, E39 to (34km) **Nørresundby** (for
Ålborg).

From Thisted, take the A11 as far as (25km) *Øsløs*, where you will find
a small museum in the house where the novelist Johan Skjoldborg was
born. Skjoldborg has no international reputation, but he was known in
his day as one of a group of writers fighting for better conditions for
the developing rural proletariat.

The direct route from here to (18km) Fjerritslev (see below) is via the
A11, passing at 4km *Bygholm Vejle*, an area famous for its teeming
bird life, especially in the migration season—6000 hectares are designated a bird sanctuary.

A more interesting ALTERNATIVE ROUTE however, is as follows.

In Øsløs leave the main road, turning left on to a minor road N to
(3km) *Højstrup* where there is a Viking burial ground. This consists of
about 25 small burial mounds, some partially preserved ship burials,
and some 75 standing stones. Continue N along this road through
Tømmerby to (4km) *Tømmerby Kirke*.

One of the largest churches in the region, this originally consisted of
a Romanesque apse, chancel and nave built of granite ashlars. In the
late Middle Ages a brick tower and porch were added. The ashlars
forming the outer wall of the apse contain numerous sculpted human
and animal figures, and above the N door there is the figure of a
dragon carved in the tympanum. The altar consists of a massive stone
slab containing a reliquary (now empty) and supported by four octagonal granite pillars. The altarpiece is from c 1600, while the pulpit,
probably the work of the same local artist, seems to be inspired by that
in Thisted. The church contains two Romanesque gravestones, one
from c 1200.

From Tømmerby church you drive W to (1km) Frøstrup, where you
reach a main road and turn right for Fjerritslev.

Art lovers will want to make a slight DETOUR first. Instead of turning right on the
main road, turn left, drive for 3km and then turn left again towards *Langvad* (1km)
where there is a delightful art gallery, *Kirsten Kjærs Museum* exhibiting 200
paintings and 100 sketches by Kirsten Kjær, who was born nearby in 1893.

Driving N from Frøstrup, you should make a DETOUR after 4km to see
the special North Sea coastline around here. Turn left to **Bulbjerg**
(3km), which is a 47m-high moraine-covered limestone formation
ending in a sheer cliff overlooking the coast, reached by a winding
path, and giving extensive views. There is a shelter, with illustrations
explaining the countryside around. *Skarreklit*, or what is left of it, a few
hundred metres further on, is on the actual coast. This limestone
pillar used to stand about 100m from the shore, the last relic of the former
coastline and a landmark famous for its jagged outline; in September
1978 it collapsed in a ferocious storm.

You should now return to the main road, turn left, and follow it to
(16km) *Fjerritslev* (Tourist Information: Østergade 20). As a town
Fjerritslev has little to offer apart from its busy shops, and a local
brewery which is now a museum illustrating the history of brewing
(limited opening mid-Jun to Aug). However, it is within reach of some
of the most beautiful stretches of the North Sea coast, and that is why
there are two routes covering the distance from Fjerritslev to Åbybro.
The direct route largely follows the A11 throughout; see below for the
alternative North Sea route.

DIRECT ROUTE FROM FJERRITSLEV TO ÅBYRO. From Fjerritslev you drive E along the A11. At (13km) Svenstrup a minor road leads right to *Kokkedal* (3km), a 16C mansion standing on high ground and surrounded by a moat, one of the few medieval palaces fully open to the public. It is now an hotel and restaurant, with an art gallery and a splendid hall used for concerts and meetings.

2km further ahead on the A11 you reach Brovst, where *Landsbymuseet* (The Village Museum) in the 18C N wing of *Bratskov mansion* is a working museum, including a smithy and a school room from about the turn of the century. The 16C main wing is also open to the public.

5km S of Brovst lies another mansion, *Oksholm* from c 1470, which was once part of a Benedictine convent called *Øland Kloster*. The convent chapel now forms the N wing of the mansion and is used as a parish church. There is a balcony for the nuns, presumably formerly with access from the former E wing. The late Gothic altarpiece representing the Virgin and eight figures of saints, is of particular interest, as is a 6m-high pre-Reformation tabernacle. The house itself is not open to the public. Nearby is the carefully restored *Oksholm Mill*.

From Brovst you drive another 8km E along the A11. Here you reach a minor road right signposted **Gjøl** (9km). Admittedly it is a fairly long detour, but the village has got something rather special to offer.

***Gjøl Church**, with its unusually long Romanesque nave, is famous for its stone engravings, many by the 12C master Goti, who is responsible for stone carvings in other Jutland churches, too. Here, on the S door in Gjøl, he has even left a portrait of himself, sitting chipping away at the stone with his pick hammer. Nearby, he has carved his own name and those of his helpers. They have depicted the Fall, Mary with the Infant Jesus watched over by an angel, a bishop, a lamb carrying a cross, and two lions held apart by a cross. Master Goti has included himself in the scene depicting the Fall, sitting just behind Adam, and in almost exactly the same position as Adam.

This particular relief classes Gjøl Church as a 'Paradise Church', the only one in Scandinavia. Other churches with the same motif are known from Gorki in Russia and in France, and the symbolism signifies that in entering this church one is going back to the springs of life. The church also contains frescoes from the 1530s representing the Tree of Jesse, the sacrifice of Isaac and Jacob's ladder. The altarpiece is a richly carved late Gothic work from c 1520, possibly the work of Hans Brüggemann, with a centre panel representing the Adoration of the Magi.

Back on your main route again you follow the A11 through the village of Birkelse to (6km) Åbybro, passing the elegant 16C manor house of Birkelse on your right.

ALTERNATIVE ROUTE FROM FJERRITSLEV TO ÅBYBRO—THE NORTH SEA ROUTE (total distance 35km). This route, which follows unclassified roads, will be particularly attractive to those who like walking. It first takes you from Fjerritslev NE along a country road to (8km) *Hjortdal*, where there is a small, relatively unspoiled 12C church. Its tower is remarkably squat, and it is said that the taller one preceding it was demolished during the Napoleonic Wars, when Denmark was at war with England, so as not to act as a landmark for the enemy. Immediately beyond the church the road goes left, right down to the shore at (2km) **Slettestrand**, where you may find fishing boats landing their catch on the sand and have the opportunity to buy the freshest plaice imaginable. You should park your car and walk W along a beautiful shore overlooked by *Svinkløv Plantage*, a plantation of pine and spruce, which like most plantations is open to the public. 3km ahead you will have your reward in the shape of a nice hotel, most conveniently placed overlooking the sea.

There is also a really excellent art gallery here, *Lien Kunstcenter*, with visiting exhibitions of a high quality.

Now drive E between the sea and the extensive wooded bank

known as *Lien* (The Brae) until, 3km further on your right, you reach
a farm called Fosdalgård. Here again, you should park your car and
take a delightful walk, this time up the narrow, densely vegetated
Fosdal valley to *Lerup* (2km), where there is a church and a sacred
spring called Vor Frue Kilde (Our Lady's Spring), from which water
still flows. This used to be a place of pilgrimage. The 12C church in
Lerup contains some 16C decorative frescoes and a carved 17C altarpiece. The Romanesque font is interesting for the primitive outline
figures engraved on it.

The Lien area is almost mountainous in character, and many artists
have chosen to live here, often offering their products for sale to
passers-by.

You now drive a further 6km N, turning right here at a T-junction to
(16km) Åbybro.

Returning to the main route, from **Åbybro** you take the A55 N turning
briefly left off the main road at c 4km to follow a parallel road through
Kås. Immediately N of this village you will find (3km) **Jetsmark
Church**, dating back to c 1100 and containing some of Jutland's most
famous frescoes.

The nave, chancel and apse are Romanesque, the tower late medieval. The frescoes, which cover all the vaulting, are from 1474. Against
a background of stars in the chancel there are the symbols of the four
Evangelists, prophets and Fathers of the Church, and in the nave there
are New Testament scenes and portraits of saints. The figures represented are, of course, in medieval dress, and the liveliness of the
proceedings is best indicated by a painting above the pulpit representing the murder of the Holy Innocents, in which one woman is
robustly wielding a club in defence of her child. The porch contains a
runic stone from the Viking Age. You now continue N and rejoin the
A55.

3km later you should make a DETOUR turning left on to the 559 to
the favoured seaside resort of **Blokhus** (6km) (Tourist Information:
Aalborgvej 17), with wide, firm sands stretching for many km. The
whole of the west coast of Jutland offers splendid beaches for bathing,
but this is one of the best, the ideal place for a family holiday by the
sea, and without the over-commercialisation associated with many
seaside resorts—though there is plenty of entertainment, from bridge
drives to horse racing, and open air sports from football to surfing. It is
an area rich in summer cottages, many of which can be rented.

From Blokhus you return to the A55 and drive 5km N and through
the village of Saltum. Here, at a crossroads, stands the monumental
Saltum Church dating from c 1150 with an impressive, broad tower,
famous for its frescoes from 1525; these include the Tree of Jesse
amidst an arabesque-like pattern of leaves, together with many
directly amusing motifs. Unlike many medieval frescoes, these have
never been completely whitewashed over. There is also much interesting furniture in the church, not least the richly carved hexagonal pulpit
from the end of the 16C, while on the N wall there are several
medieval carved figures.

2km W of Saltum lies *Fårup Sommerland*, an entertainment centre
with amusements of many kinds including horse riding for the young,
and a miniature railway. Everything is free once you have bought your
admission ticket, which lasts all day.

Totally free is the *Saltum Beach* (4km W), another splendid bathing
area.

From Saltum you drive N to (10km) *Løkken* (Tourist Information:

Vrenstedvej 6), if anything an even more popular resort than Blokhus, likewise with glorious beaches and excellent holiday facilities, including sports hall, swimming baths and tennis courts. *Løkken Museum*, in an old skipper's house from 1850, has a local history collection (open May–Sept).

On leaving Løkken on the A55 you drive NE for c 2km, turning right on an unclassified road to *Børglumkloster monastery (4km), a place with a long and turbulent history.

Børglum was originally a royal residence, and it was here that St. Knud was staying when the Vendsyssel rebellion, which was to lead to his death in Odense, was instigated. By 1139 there was a Bishop of Børglum. It is not known exactly when the Premonstratensian monastery here was founded, but it was certainly in existence by 1205. The Bishop of Vendsyssel chose Børglum as his residence, and Børglum then became in effect the Cathedral of Vendsyssel, replacing Vestervig (Rte 22). With the passage of time the monastery gathered great wealth, and the bishops gradually became powerful men in the realm. Not all of them, however, were men of humility: one, Bishop Tyge, expelled the monks and fortified the monastery in defiance of the king; but most infamous were Niels Stygge Rosenkrantz and Stygge Krumpen, who stand as symbols of the corruption in the Church in Denmark before the Reformation.

After the Reformation the monastery was secularised and the buildings fell into disrepair. At the beginning of the 18C a local farmer, later ennobled under the name of Frederik Kjærskjold, began to restore the buildings. On his death the task was continued by his wife and finished c 1750 by his daughter and her second husband, the highly gifted architect Laurids de Thurah, who designed many of the most important 18C buildings in Copenhagen. It was doubtless he who was mainly responsible for the impressive mansion we know as Børglumkloster today.

The present buildings largely preserve the aspect of the medieval monastery, consisting of four unadorned wings around a courtyard. The magnificent *church, 39m x 20m, forms part of the N wing of Børglumkloster and is thought originally to date back to c 1220. It consists of a lofty vaulted nave with an aisle on either side, mainly late Gothic, but with remains of the original Romanesque building. In one of the pillars there is a man's head carved into the ashlar. Most of the furniture is rococo—the pulpit, the enclosed pews, the altar rail. On the N wall stand two important tombstones, those of Bishop Jep Friis and Bishop Niels Stygge Rosenkrantz. One of Frederik Kjærskjold's achievements was to restore the church, which he did in the grand style, in 1734 providing it with a huge altarpiece 12m high and almost as wide, all backed by painted drapery creating the impression of black velvet.

There is admission to part of the castle, the courtyard and the church from Whitsun to the end of August.

Now drive N on the A55 for 5km and turn left towards (8km) Lønstrup. On your way there you will pass minor roads leading off left to Rubjerg Knude and, later, Mårup church.

Rubjerg Knude is a 74m-high cliff. The former lighthouse there is now a museum (open May–Oct), demonstrating the effects of sand drift. The trip there is itself an experience, for this is an area profoundly marked by sand drift. The astounding effect of this process is clearly demonstrated in the museum—and, if more be needed, by the abandoned Rubjerg church, only part of which has survived.

Mårup Church is another abandoned Romanesque church in desolate surroundings; however, there is still some furniture left, including a carved altar. Many of the graves in the churchyard are surrounded by fences to prevent the flowers on them from blowing away, and at the W end of the church there is an anchor from an English man-of-war, 'The Crescent', that was stranded here during the Napoleonic Wars, in 1808: 226 members of a crew of 300 are buried in the churchyard.

From Lønstrup you move E again, soon passing a very high-lying church on your left. This is *Vennebjerg Church*, situated higher than any other in this county of Vendsyssel, a clear landmark which can be seen from afar, and for this purpose the N side is always painted white.

A further 12km brings you to **Hjørring** (24,000 inhab.; Tourist Information: Akseltorv 5), which received its charter in 1243, growing during the Middle Ages into a flourishing and relatively large town with three churches standing quite close together, all of which, unusually, have survived. A period of decline followed the Reformation, but new life came at the end of the 18C, and Hjørring has continued to flourish. The main commercial activities are now situated to the E of the town proper, and no effort has been spared to preserve the atmosphere of the older parts of the town.

A particular feature is Hjørring's keen interest in the arts; since the 1960s it has accumulated a unique collection of modern Danish sculpture which is distributed in key positions throughout the town with the intention of introducing art into everyday life. A pamphlet available from the Tourist Information Office lists 52 localities with almost 100 sculptures, some of them of considerable size.

Most impressive perhaps is *Springvandspladsen* (The Fountain Square), with its water organ amidst sculptural decorations by Bjørn Nørgaard. This is off Søndergade in the centre of town.—Go further E into Østergade, and on the right you will find Seidelinsgade. Here is the art gallery, *Hjørring Kunstmuseum*, containing some splendid frescoes by Niels Larsen Stevns, depicting the history of North Jutland; in addition there is a good collection of North Jutland art.—Returning to Østergade and to Søndergade, you come to Skolegade, where, on the right in Museumsgade running between Skolegade and the old square Akseltorv, you will find the local history museum, *Vendsyssel Historiske Museum*, established in 1889 in three old school buildings and the rather splendid house in which the rural deans once lived. In addition to old statues from pre-Reformation churches, it contains prehistoric as well as medieval exhibits, while from more recent times there is old agricultural equipment, an old grocer's shop and a dentist's surgery from the turn of the present century.

The three old churches in Hjørring, all from the 13C, are well worth a visit. The oldest is *Sankt Olai*, dedicated to the Norwegian King and Saint, Olaf, and standing on the site of an older wooden church, remains of which were found in the 1960s. It is built of granite ashlars, and has no tower. *St. Catherine's Church* is the largest of the three, but it has been so thoroughly rebuilt that most of its early character has gone. The present transept is in fact based on the original nave, the present nave being a later addition. The large auricular altarpiece is from 1651. Architecturally rather better preserved is the brick-built Romanesque *Sankt Hans Kirke*, in which both the nave and chancel are nevertheless late Gothic. This church contains some fine frescoes.

Hjørring was the birthplace of the late 19C dramatist and novelist Henri Nathansen and the 20C novelist Knuth Becker, both of whom are commemorated by plaques.

From the outskirts of Hjørring the A55 takes you N to (9km) *Tornby*, where there is a Romanesque church containing a small but ornate late Gothic altarpiece from c 1525. There is a runic inscription on the N wall. When it was first interpreted in 1913 it was thought to say that the writer of the runes had one Whitsun morning enjoyed Joan in the church. Alas, nothing so exciting. Later scholarship has shown that it was not Joan, but *tone*, i.e. music, that gave Thorstein such pleasure.

Unusually, the ship hanging in this church is a lightship. Around
Tornby there is a large nature reserve.

After a further 3km you might turn right to visit *Horne* (2km), where
a stone burial chamber from the Older Bronze Age can be seen to the
W of the Romanesque church. An inscription on the pulpit from 1589
contains a quotation from Luther: 'A good priest must do these three
things—enter the pulpit, say something, and descend again.'

Returning to the A55 you go on to (4km) *Hirtshals* (7000 inhab.;
Tourist Information: Vestergade 32), the third of the major ports on the
west coast of Jutland. With its harbour completed in 1930, Hirtshals is
now an important centre for the fishing industry, with ferry connections to Norway. For the tourist, the main attraction must be the
Nordsømuseum (North Sea Museum); indoors there is an aquarium
containing some 70 species of North Sea fish, while outside there is a
pool with seals and dolphins, and with many exhibits reflecting the
fishing industry of the region.

Hirtshals Museum at Sophus Thomsensgade 6 is housed in a fisherman's house from 1880, and is furnished to show the living conditions
of a fisherman and his family at the beginning of the 20C. It also
contains a section illustrating the history of the local bitter *snaps*.

From Hirtshals take the E39 SE, turning off left after 4km on the 597
to (14km) *Tversted* (Tourist Information: Østervej 10). Instead of just
passing straight through Tversted, you could turn right in the village
and drive to *Bindslev* (4km), where the church has a most unusual 13C
fresco of the Madonna and Child; there is clearly Byzantine influence
at work here, and it has been suggested that the fresco was inspired
by an illuminated book.

Leaving Tversted on the 597 E you pass a large eagle reservation
(*Tuen Ørnereservat*) (open mid-June to mid-Sept), before at 15km you
reach the A40. Here you turn left and drive to (6km) Hulsig where you
turn left again to visit Råbjerg Mile and Kandestederne (4km).

Go for a walk in **Råbjerg Mile**, a wild area of sand and sand dunes, so vast and
so untouched that at times you could imagine yourself in the Sahara. You will
find nothing like it anywhere else in Denmark. Nearby *Kandestederne* is again
a well-known holiday area. You can in fact drive as far as this on the broad sandy
beach all the way from Tversted!

Driving N again on the A40 you should turn off right after a further
9km. Here you will come to yet another example of the effects of sand
drift in the church buried in the sand, **Den Tilsandede Kirke**. Built in
the 14C, this church was originally Skagen Church, dedicated to St.
Laurentius, the patron saint of seafarers, and was the longest church
in Vendsyssel. Then, around 1600, sand drift began to affect the area,
threatening the church itself by the end of the 18C. For 20 years people
dug their way into it every Sunday, but by 1795 it was abandoned by
royal decree. The furniture and church fittings were sold, and the nave
was used as a quarry, only the tower remaining intact, used as a
landmark for shipping. It still stands, and is now a favourite spot for
tourists.

You now return to the A40, turn right, and are soon in (3km)
**Skagen (12,000 inhab.; Tourist Information: Sankt Laurentiivej 18),
the most northerly town in Denmark, situated on the narrow spit of
land dividing the waters of the *Kattegat* from the *Skagerrak*. You can
drive almost to the tip, *Grenen*, walking the last stretch to see where
the waters of the two meet, and feeling almost surrounded by water.
In so doing you cannot fail to notice the intensity of the light reflected
from the sea on all sides. You can, if you wish, stand in the sea, with

one foot in the Kattegat and one in the Skagerrak—but **you must not try to bathe at this spot**. The currents are extremely dangerous. If you want to bathe, choose some of the other excellent beaches nearby.

Skagen was granted a charter in 1413. It was an important shipping and fishing centre, and in the 16C it was actually bigger than Copenhagen. However, sand drift occurred, Skagen suffered under the various 17C wars and went into serious decline, and by the beginning of the 19C it was in a miserable state, with no doctor, no lighting, scarcely any roads. A road constructed in the 1850s was buried in sand. However, life returned in the second half of the 19C, and then came the event that really put Skagen on the map again—its discovery by a group of Danish artists, who saw the artistic possibilities of an old-fashioned community, and who appreciated the intensity of the light on the landscape. Skagen now became a focal point of Danish art, and a school of 'Skagen painters' arose, ably supported by many writers, too. Names such as Michael and Anna Ancher, P.S. Krøyer, Viggo Johansen and Laurits Tuxen are inextricably associated with Skagen. Some settled there, others visited regularly. And they attracted painters from Norway and Sweden, too. The poet particularly associated with the group, and himself an able painter, is Holger Drachmann, whose poems inspired by the sea are in the same spirit as the paintings of his fellows.

Apart from the general charm and exhilaration of the place, it is the work of these artists which makes Skagen an absolute must. *Skagen Museum** contains some 1000 paintings, sketches and sculptures, some of them on a very large scale, which together constitute the very essence of Danish art. They are all housed in a splendidly planned gallery where it is possible to view even the largest paintings from the distance from which they have the best effect (open summer; limited opening winter).—Close by is *Brøndums Hotel*, a favourite haunt of the artists, and a place with memories of them. Today we can be thankful that the artists had a tendency to pay their hotel bills in kind!

A different impression of these same artists in their daily lives, however, is to be found in *Michael & Anna Ancher's House**, two minutes away from the Skagen Museum and not to be missed either. The Anchers lived there from 1884, and it was this delightful, low-ceilinged house that became one of the meeting places of the Skagen artists. After the death of her parents, their daughter Helga, also a painter, lived there until her death in 1964. The house has since been carefully restored, and great efforts have been made to re-create the atmosphere of the artists' home; their furniture is there, their piano, their china, their artists' equipment. There is even an unfinished sketch on an easel. The walls are covered with paintings and sketches. One almost feels that the artists themselves could appear at any moment (open summer; limited opening winter).

A little further away, in Hans Baghsvej, lies *Drachmann's House*, where the poet and painter lived from 1902 until his death in 1908. In 1911 it was opened to the public, and is filled with paintings by Holger Drachmann himself and his contemporaries (open Jun to mid-Sept). So closely bound was Drachmann to Skagen that he chose to be buried here, and his tomb, designed by Krøyer, stands in the dunes at the very N of the peninsula.

Although Skagen is particularly associated with the art of the turn of the century, modern artists, too, have flocked here, and their work is to be seen in *Grenen Museum* at the northernmost tip of the land (open May–Sept).

A museum of a slightly more usual kind is *Skagen Fortidsminder*, in

P.K. Nielsensvej. This open air museum consists of eight buildings which have been moved here from the vicinity—a poor fisherman's home from the mid 19C alongside that of a more affluent fisherman, both furnished in the appropriate style. There is a lifeboat station, a windmill, a memorial hall, and a fishery museum containing many exhibits of local interest (open Mar–Nov).

When you have savoured the art of Skagen and seen how the fisherfolk lived in a former age, you should not only wander around the idyllic streets and harbour with its countless fishing boats, but you should try the fish in one of the numerous small fish restaurants around the harbour. Modest on the outside, they are almost without exception very fashionable inside and justly deserve their reputation as some of Denmark's finest fish restaurants. *Gammel Skagen* on the W outskirts of Skagen has some very nice restaurants too.

It is scarcely surprising that Skagen should be about the most popular holiday resort in Denmark.

You leave Skagen again by the A40, passing Ålbæk and *Råbjerg Mose*, an area of marshland and heath. 34km S of Skagen you should turn left to visit *Strandby* (2km). Strandby itself is a fairly ordinary small coastal town, but it contains a most unusual modern church, from 1966, the work of the architect Jacob Blegvad. Apart from the bell-tower and the office building to the W of the church, there is not a straight wall in sight. Instead, the lines are those of a ship, with a great, sweeping tiled roof, and the comparison with Le Corbusier's chapel in Ronchamps is inevitable.—From the shore near Strandby you can glimpse the tiny *Hirsholmene* islands, only the largest of which is inhabited—by some 20 people.

Return to the A40 and drive the remaining 7km S to **Frederikshavn** (25,500 inhab.; Tourist Information: Brotorvet 1), which was not given a charter until 1818, but today is the largest city N of the Limfjord, the terminal of the main railway line from Copenhagen (there is a private railway taking you on to Skagen), and a ferry port serving several towns in both Norway and Sweden, in addition to the Kattegat island of Læsø. There is a shipyard here and a good deal of industry, in addition to the fishing industry. It is a city bustling with life, and with a clear international—especially inter-Scandinavian—atmosphere. On the other hand, there are relatively few old buildings apart from the early 19C fishermen's houses at Fiskerklyngen, standing cheek by jowl in narrow lanes, and the old *Gunpowder Tower*, now a military museum (open Apr–Oct). The main church, *Frederikshavn Kirke*, a colossus from the late 19C, has an altarpiece by the Skagen painter Michael Ancher; the Town Hall is from 1977, pleasing but not out-standing. Close by is the *Kulturhus*, containing a museum with a good collection of exlibris, and travelling exhibitions of modern art.

There is, however, something special very close to Frederikshavn. In the W outskirts of the town, 1km S of the 585, lies the exquisite small mansion of **Bangsbo**. Although its history can be traced back to the 15C, the present buildings date from the 18C, thoroughly restored 100 years later by the then owner, Johan Knudsen. Knudsen, together with his brother, started a literary periodical in Copenhagen, and thus came into contact with many of the leading literary figures of his day, in particular becoming a close friend of the novelist Herman Bang. Bang spent much time in Bangsbo and even went so far as to express the vain wish that he might be buried there. When Johan Knudsen retired from Copenhagen, he turned Bangsbo into a cultural centre. Anne Marie Carl Nielsen designed the garden, and the architect Thorvald

Bindesbøll the entrance porch, over which Johan Knudsen's initials are to be seen. His guests here included some of the most famous (and, in the eyes of some contemporaries, infamous) names in Scandinavian culture from the end of the 19C.

Bangsbo is now a *museum owned by Frederikshavn. Along with local and literary exhibits the main building contains Europe's largest collection of hair decorations (an amazing sight). The outbuildings have exhibits of an entirely different kind. One contains an excellent museum of the World War II Occupation of Denmark—uniforms, weapons, vehicles, proclamations, all chronologically arranged to give an impression of developments over the years. Another is dedicated to shipping and includes a glorious collection of figureheads. And by no means least among the attractions at Bangsbo is a remarkably well-preserved merchant vessel from the 12C—the *Ellingå ship*.

Adjoining Bangsbo there is an extensive deer park to which there is free admission.

Some 2km further W on the 585 will bring you to *Cloostårnet* (The Cloos Tower), an observation tower built in 1962, standing 160m above sea level. It affords panoramic views of the whole of Vendsyssel. On the opposite side of the road here you will find *Flade* church, dating back to the early 13C, but with modern frescoes from 1958.

You leave Frederikshavn on the E45 and drive S along the coast to (12km) **Sæby** (8000 inhab.; Tourist Information: Krystaltorvet 1). If Frederikshavn bears the stamp of modern times, Sæby clearly reflects its long history, an enchanting small town idyllically situated on low-lying ground mainly to the S of a stream, Sæby Å, and close to a gently wooded area quite unlike the otherwise stern countryside of Vend-syssel.

In the Middle Ages Sæby (meaning the town by the sea) belonged to the Børglum Monastery, as did the nearby Sæbygård mansion (see below). The river provided a natural though unreliable harbour, through which the monastery transported goods. In the late 15C a Carmelite monastery was established, dedicated to the Virgin, and the town became known for a time as Mariested. The church belonging to it still stands, but the remaining buidings have disappeared. To this day the Virgin and Child form the town's coat of arms. Even after the Reformation, Sæby flourished, until Frederikshavn took over the lead, and for a time Sæby went into decline. By the 19C, however, it was on its way up again. Nevertheless, it has not grown into a large town, and although there is some light industry, Sæby has maintained its unspoiled character.

The artists and writers who frequented Skagen also found Sæby. Holger Drachmann stayed at Clasen's hotel in Algade, as did Herman Bang—and Bang based one of his most wicked novels on his observations there. The novelist Gustav Wied was there for a time, and Ibsen was a visitor in 1877; it was probably there that he wrote his 'Lady from the Sea'.

Algade is the original main street, leading to the imposing church deriving from the Carmelite monastery. Most of the houses are of historical interest. They include the old courthouse (No. 7) and the former Clasen's Hotel (No. 3) which is now a home for the elderly. Here, too, is a former town hall as well as an old home for the poor, established in 1723 and bearing the name Rhuuses Hospital. The old Town Hall, which today serves as the police station, is from 1847, but it is predated by an even older one, from the early 18C, in Strandgade, at the E end of Algade. Facing it is what was once the hospital; it has stood here since 1565, but was rebuilt in 1675 and today constitutes one of the oldest buildings in the town. It has now been turned into accommodation for pensioners. On the corner of Algade and Sønder-gade stands the 17C *Konsul Ørums Gård*, now *Sæby Museum*; it

*Detail of a church mural in Sæby, North-East
Jutland. The devil is taking the soul of the dead
man, while the lover is comforting the widow.
Photo: Kurt Bering*

contains local history exhibits and reconstructions of an old shop and
a schoolroom from c 1920.

At the E end of Algade is *Klostertorvet* with the *church dedicated
to the Virgin. It is a remarkably narrow building (8m) in relation to its
length (54m), really consisting of an extension of the small church
standing here before the establishment of the Carmelite monastery.
The Carmelites lengthened it without widening it. One of the features
is the murals uncovered during restorations in 1905–06. On the N wall
of the original part of the nave there are biblical motifs and several
coats of arms, from c 1465; in the three E severies (bays of vaults) there
are later representations of the story of Joachim and Anna and of the
Day of Judgement—these include a famous grotesque representation
of a devil taking away the soul of a dead man, while his grieving wife
is already giving in to the charms of a new lover; in the vaulting of the
S chapel there is a later mural, a design from c 1520, consisting of
leaves around the coats of arms of the last two bishops of Børglum.

The altarpiece, a triptych, is from c 1520 with a carved centre panel
representing the Virgin and Child standing on the Tree of Jesse; the
side panels are paintings of the shepherds and the Magi worshipping
the Child. In the chancel there are 20 misericords from c 1500, two of
them with elaborately carved bench ends, and there are many other
pieces from both before and after the Reformation. Of particular
interest is an unusual wooden font from 1645 in the S transept. The

*Voergård, North Jutland. This east wing is from
1586–91, outstanding for its harmonious design, and
for the elaborate portal in the centre.
Photo: John Sommer*

splendid Renaissance pulpit and canopy are dated 1577, and were
restored in 1906.

W of the town centre lies Sæbygård wood and further on Sæbygård
mansion. Both can be reached on foot by following the stream, or you
can drive if you prefer. The woods—largely a conservation area—
cover 120 hectares and consist mainly of beech. They are high-lying
and have to be approached via a steep slope which denotes the
coastline of 14,000 years ago.

The original *Sæbygård mansion* belonged to Børglum Monastery,
but the present house, surrounded by a broad moat, dates from 1576.
The octagonal spire over the main entrance is from 1861. There are
four wings, of which the main one, to the N, is still in use as a private
dwelling. Sæbygård houses extensive collections of paintings and
porcelain, and the great hall with its beamed ceiling is particularly
impressive. The mansion is open for conducted tours every day in the
main season, and arrangements can be made for groups at other times
through Sæby Museum.

On leaving Sæby you turn S following the E45 for 14km. Here a road
leads left to (2km) ***Voergård**, an impressive and ornate Renaissance
palace surrounded by a broad moat.

Again, this is a building once owned by Børglum Monastery, and it was Bishop Stygge Krumpen who built the N wing. The remainder was built by 1591. The house is first mentioned in 1481, but it is not known when the first house was built. It still stands, however, as part of the N wing within the courtyard. Voergård is in private ownership, but there are conducted tours of the main wing throughout the summer months. It is not strictly speaking a museum. Consequently, in the setting of a glorious house you will find paintings by, among many others, Raphael, Frans Hals, Rubens, Corot and Goya; splendid furniture from the time of Louis XV and Louis XVI of France; a collection of Sèvres porcelain, along with the porcelain used by Louis XVI and Marie Antoinette during their imprisonment, counterbalanced by that used by Napoleon during his 100 days; there is Spanish furniture, Flemish tapestry, and a Chinese room. This is a home of great splendour, and one of the most comprehensive private collections open to the public view in Denmark today (limited opening from Easter to beginning of Sept).

After the Reformation Voergård was owned by the Crown, but in 1578 it came into the hands of one Karen Krabbe, who gave it to her daughter Ingeborg Skeel. It was she who was responsible for building the E wing, and so impressed was King Frederik II that in 1588 he presented her with the ornamental portal, which according to tradition was originally intended for Frederiksborg Castle (Rte 6). After Ingeborg Skeel's death in 1604 Voergård fell into neglect, and it was severely damaged during the 17C wars. Despite some restoration work in the 18C, it was not until the palace came into the ownership of Peder Brønnum-Scavenius and subsequently of Erik Scavenius that it was restored to its present state. In 1955 it was bought by the Papal Count E. Oberbech-Clausen, who was responsible for increasing the collection of art treasures in the house, and who decreed that the art and antique collection and the main wing should be opened to the public on his death. The N wing, on the other hand, is reserved for the Order of St. John of Malta, for which a Chapel has been established.

1km further down the road lies *Voer Kirke*, the church built by the earlier owners of Voergård and used by them. It consists of a Romanesque nave extended by a Gothic chancel, tower and porch on the S side. However, beyond the porch, and fundamentally out of proportion to the structure as a whole, there is a huge square tower forming a sepulchral chapel from 1585. It contains an elaborate monument, from 1600, to Erik Banner and Ingeborg Skeel, the owners of Voergård.—Erik Scavenius, the controversial Danish Prime Minister during part of the World War II Occupation, lies buried in the churchyard here.

Driving E again, you turn right in the village of Præstbro and continue through Dronninglund to (14km) the 559. Here you make another right turn and drive on to (2km) the mansion of *Dronninglund Hovedgård*. A Benedictine convent was established here c 1268, thriving and growing until the nuns complained of bad treatment by Bishop Stygge Krumpen of Børglum. After the Reformation the convent became a private house. The present Dronninglund Hovedgård (conducted tours in the summer) is partly based on the convent buildings, as is particularly obvious in the E wing.

The adjoining *church is considered one of the best examples of Romanesque architecture in Vendsyssel. During restoration work in 1943 a large number of 16C murals was discovered, representing biblical motifs and knights; one depicts Alexander the Great on an elephant doing battle with a King Arthur on horseback. There is a very large Renaissance altarpiece from c 1600, a carved pulpit from 1580 surmounted by an auricular canopy, and a gallery for the owners of the house, from 1600.

A further 7km W on the 559 brings you to *Hjallerup*, in June the scene of Europe's biggest horse fair. This is an event which is now of diminishing importance, but the fair has a history going back many centuries.

12km beyond Hjallerup, still on the 559, you come to the E39. Here at the crossing you will find *Tylstrup Kro*, one of the historical Royal Privilege Inns, where you can still find everything from a cup of coffee to a well equipped room for the night. If you want something more elaborate, you can proceed a further 1.5km and turn left here to *Gammel Vrå Slot* (1km), an old mansion now serving as a luxury hotel while maintaining the atmosphere of the great house.

However, the main object of coming to Tylstrup is to turn S on the E39 in order to visit (5km) **Sulsted Church**. Hidden away 1km E of the main road, this contains some of the most impressive and famous murals in the country. If it is closed the key can be obtained from a house adjoining, and it is worth going to the slight trouble of getting it. The vaulted ceiling is sumptuously decorated with frescoes from 1548 depicting the life of Christ, with accompanying text, unusually, in Jutlandic dialect. Not only are they impressive in their array and variety, but they clearly demonstrate the dress of the time at which they were painted, and thus provide a fascinating social document. A further interesting feature is that they include a portrait of the Virgin as Queen of Heaven—yet they were painted *after* the Reformation. Most of the remaining church furniture is from c 1600. Steen Steensen Blicher's favourite daughter, Malvine Steensdatter, is buried in the churchyard.

You now return to the E39 and drive the remaining 10km to Nørresundby, passing Hammer Hills on your left. Here the main attraction, **Lindholm Høje**, a ridge to the W of the town, is one of Denmark's most important and extensive archaeological sites. It contains the remains of an extensive settlement dating back to between AD 600 and 1100; almost 700 Iron Age and Viking Age graves, including 150 ship settings, have been discovered here, all excavated 1952–58. Grave goods found during excavations are now housed in a purpose-built museum in Vendilavej, just W of the site. The site itself has been preserved in its excellent state thanks to the activities of sand drift, which seems to have taken place in the 10C, covering the earliest part of the town to a depth of 3–4m. Also W of the site, on Fr. Raschs Vej, there is a herb garden containing 250 medicinal herbs carefully arranged. Here, too, there is a half-timbered pipe-making house containing collections of pipes and textiles.

From Nørresundby you have a choice of routes S across the Limfjord to **Ålborg** (Rte 17) and beyond. There is the bridge from 1933, 635m long and 12.5m above the surface at its highest point, which will bring you into the centre of the city. Alternatively, you can follow the E45 and take the more recent, but less picturesque, 552m-long tunnel, 10m below the surface. If you do not intend to stop in Ålborg, this is clearly the route to take.

20   **Ringkøbing to Hobro**

Total distance 130km. A16 to (43km) **Holstebro**.—(51km) **Viborg**.—A16, 517, E45 to (36km) **Hobro**.

From **Ringkøbing** (Rte 15) the A16 leads N to (8km) *Hee*, a small village where there is a remarkably large church built of granite ashlars, one of the most interesting Romanesque churches in Jutland. The chancel, nave, vestibule and tower are all Romanesque (though the subject of

radical neo-Romanesque rebuilding in the 19C), while the two chapels
on the S side are of later date. Despite the efforts of the 19C, the W end
still has some splendid original features, and is at times reminiscent of
Ribe Cathedral. The late Renaissance altarpiece is from 1635, its three
sections being defined by white columns. Two heads jut out at the top
of the tower; according to one legend the church was built by a troll,
and the heads are those of him and his wife.

J.C. Christensen, the Danish Prime Minister who presided over the introduction
of democratic rule into Denmark in 1901, is buried in the churchyard. There is
also a memorial to him in the garden of his house in the main street.

Now follow the A16 to (17km) the A28, on which, after 1km, you will
find **Ulfborg Kirkeby** with an interesting Romanesque/Gothic church
with some unusual features. Even the exterior is striking, consisting
of a transept as high as the nave, with a gabled chapel beside it to the W,
and to the E a gabled porch beneath a substantial tower—certainly not
a poor church, but perhaps reflecting the austerity of the area in its
small windows and the general sense of compact strength. Inside, the
chapel and the transept are joined by a series of rounded arches. It is,
however, the pulpit, from c 1587, which immediately attracts attention,
projecting from a carved gallery stretching the width of the nave. It is
one of only two such left today, though the signs are that this construction was once fairly common. The painted panels in the gallery represent the 12 tribes of Israel. In the chapel there is an ornate, large-scale
sandstone and marble memorial to the State Councillor Preben
Gyldenstierne and his two wives.

Back on the A16 you now continue to (18km) Holstebro, driving
through countryside which bears the traces of the harsh weather West
Jutland has been subjected to. To the E of Ulfborg there is a wide
undulating tract of heathland, now a conservation area. It is inter-
sected by several streams, the vegetation is mainly heather and
juniper, the soil sandy. Few people live there, the villages are small,
their churches tiny and without towers. It is worth driving along some
of the narrow roads to gain a feeling of this quite unusual area and to
sense what West Jutland was once like.

Holstebro (29,000 inhab. Tourist Information: Brostræde 2) is first
mentioned in 1274 and has a charter from 1584, though it is thought
that there were earlier charters which were burnt in a fire in 1552. It is
situated at an intersection of major routes N–S and E–W, and straddles
the Storå river at the most convenient crossing place between two
areas of moraine hills.

As a market town Holstebro flourished in the 16C, with a large ox
market and with trade via Hjerting (near Esbjerg) with Holland. After
a period of decline in the 18C, it gradually recovered in the 19C,
largely thanks to the advent of the railways, and attracted a good deal
of industry. Since World War II it has been a garrison town. The A16
by-passes the town, and there is a further ring road quite close to the
town centre.

At the centre of this inner ring road lies *Store Torv* (Grand Square),
which has always been the focal point of the town. However, there are
no really old buildings left, as Holstebro suffered no fewer than 13 fires
in the space of 200 years, and what did not disappear on one occasion
vanished on the next. Even the main church, *Holstebro Kirke*, is only
from 1907, and is of little intrinsic architectural interest, though it does
contain some splendid church furniture, the best of which is the
exquisite carved Flanders altarpiece from around 1510, portraying
scenes from the life of the Virgin. Other treasures are the pulpit, the

candelabra and several memorial tablets. Nor should one forget the carillon of 48 bells.

A total contrast to this church is the *Nørrelands Kirke*, from 1969, designed by Inger and Johannes Exner and containing rooms and buildings intended to incorporate the church into the daily lives of the local inhabitants. It is in the shape of a cube, and receives its light mainly from slit windows in the roof. The pews are grouped in a fan-like pattern around the altar. The free-standing bell-tower consists of a belfry standing on narrow girders and reached by an open spiral staircase.

Like several other Jutland market towns, Holstebro has recently shown great interest in the arts. There are two art galleries: the *Holstebro Kunstmuseum* in Sønderbrogade contains collections of modern Danish and international art, while the *Jens Nielsen and Olivia Holm-Møller Gallery* in Nørrebrogade exhibits work both by these two artists and other contemporary Danish painters. In Sønderlandsgade there is a museum for miniature works of art (*Museum for Kleinkunst*), containing nothing larger than 10cm x 15cm.—Like other towns, too, Holstebro has made great efforts to embellish its streets, and there are numerous pleasing sculptures scattered around the town, outstanding among which must be a Giacometti in front of the old Town Hall in Nørregade.

Other museums include *Dragon- og Frihedsmuseum* on Kirkepladsen with exhibits from military history and the World War II Occupation (open summer; limited opening winter). For philatelists the attraction must be *Old Post Office* in Østergade (open Sat). Nevertheless, the major museum is *Holstebro Museum* in Museumsvej, with a large collection of artefacts from prehistoric, historical and modern times, and including a collection of silver and a reconstructed silversmith's workshop.

Holstebro has an experimental theatre, the Odin Theatre, and there is a second theatre in *Holstebro-Hallen*, where there is also a concert hall and exhibition and sports facilities.

EXCURSION FROM HOLSTEBRO TO THE NORTH SEA COAST AND LEMVIG (total distance c 138km). Leave Holstebro on the ring road, taking the A16 SW to (18km) the A28, where you turn N to (1km) *Ulfborg Kirkeby* (see above). Continue another 3km on the A28 and on your left you will find a striking archway, built in 1790, leading to the mansion of **Nørre Vosborg**, the oldest of the medieval fortified houses of West Jutland. It is thought that King Erik Menved once owned it. The original house was destroyed in a storm in 1532, and the present building from 1552 was a replacement for it (open summer). Hans Christian Andersen visited Nørre Vosborg in 1859 and there met Captain Marryat, the author of 'The Children of the New Forest'—but without any obvious meeting of minds.

The A28 continues N through Vemb village, E of which there is a bird sanctuary, to (11km) Bækmarksbro. Here you turn left, driving past (9km) *Bøvling Church* with its 18C onion-shaped spire, and 1km further on *Rysensten house* on your right. With a history going back to 1414, and once known as Bøvling Castle, the present Rysensten has a main wing dating largely from 1638–39.

7km N of Rysensten you arrive at Dybe, where you take a minor road W to (4km) the coastal village of *Ferring*, once a favourite resort of authors and artists, the most important being the Expressionist painter Jens Søndergaard, whose former summer cottage here is now a museum and well worth a visit (open summer; limited opening

winter). Ferring old church contains some unusual 12C frescoes which
were restored in 1987, and which seem to show English influence.

You can walk along the broad sands both N and S of Ferring and
gain an impression of the grandeur of this West Jutland coastal
scenery—though in the summer you will have to share the experience
with a lot of others. You might also gain an impression of the violence
of which the sea is capable here! All along the coast there are remains
of World War II coastal defences, and 2km S of Ferring there is the 26m
high *Bovbjerg lighthouse*, standing on a 46m-high moraine cliff.

Return to the 181, and turn N once more towards (c 18km) *Harboør*
which, with its 1950 inhabitants, is a sizeable fishing port, one of the
centres of the west coast fishing industry to this day, and one where
life in the past has been unusually demanding. According to one
source, the parish of Harboør has been subject to more flooding and
sand drift than any other except Agger immediately to the N. It is,
however, the harsh life of the fishermen one thinks of first and foremost. In 1893 it was the scene of one of the most famous tragedies in
19C Denmark, when 26 fishermen were drowned during a storm.
There is a memorial to them in the churchyard, which contains many
other reminders of tragic events, not least a memorial wall inscribed
with the names of all fishermen who have drowned here. Inside the
church the Renaissance altarpiece is fittingly equipped with a central
panel from 1910 showing Christ among the fishermen's families.

Before proceeding N, just take the road W from Harboør to *Langerhuse* (2km), where *Flyvholm Rescue Station*, from 1847 is now open as
a museum illustrating the work of the coastal rescue service. Over 700
stranded seamen have been saved by crews from here (open summer).

The drive N from Harboør to (10km) *Thyborøn* is along a narrow spit
of land, where you can see water on both sides. Thyborøn itself (Tourist
Information: Nordsøkaj 41) is a modern fishing port which has grown
up this century on the S side of the narrow Thyborøn Channel. The
harbour was constructed between 1914 and 1917. There is little of
architectural or cultural interest in Thyborøn, but there is the atmosphere of a genuine fishing port. On the square, *Torvet*, you will find
the anchor of a Russian frigate, the 'Alexander Nevsky', which sank
off Thyborøn in 1868. The son of Tsar Alexander II was on board, and
both he and virtually all the crew of 734 were brought ashore alive.
Only eight members of the crew died, of whom two are buried in the
churchyard in Harboør. On a totally different level, there is the attraction of the *Snail House*, a house covered with snail shells from all over
the world (open summer).

There are excellent bathing facilities in the neighbourhood of Thyborøn and Harboør, not least along the shore of the Channel, and
angling from the moles is permitted. A tiny ferry crosses the Channel
once an hour.

The time has come to turn S again on the 181, this time making for
Lemvig, joining the 513 after 18km. 3km after this you pass the small
Romanesque *Heldum Church* with some good frescoes and an altarpiece by the distinguished Jutlandic artist Niels Bjerre. The church
bell, now in a belfry outside the church, is from the 14C. From here it
is only 2km to *Lemvig* (7500 inhab.; Tourist Information: Toldbodgade
4) a town with privileges dating back to 1545, lying on low ground by
the Lem Bay, and surrounded by quite high terrain. It is mentioned as
early as 1234, but it has never been of great significance, a small
market town without any particular distinguishing features other than
its general charm. There is a harbour, and Lemvig once had some
importance as a fishing port, but it lost its position with the growth of

Thyborøn. Nevertheless, the idyllic setting and the charm of the area give Lemvig and its surroundings an undeniable attraction.

Now you should turn S down the A28, after 8km turning left into the 521, which on your left will take you past *Kronhede Plantage* and *Klosterhede Plantage*, together forming the biggest tree plantation in the country, back to (25km) Holstebro.

Returning to the main route, you leave **Holstebro** E on the A16, passing at (26km) the confluence of the Karup and Haderup rivers at *Hagebro*. This is an anglers' paradise, well provided with overnight accommodation, 5km further sees you in *Sjørup* and from here—weather being good—a short EXCURSION S from here is well worth doing.

Follow the 186 S for 5.5km and turn right here in the middle of nowhere into the area called **Kongenshus Mindepark**. Leave your car in the car park a little further on and have a brisk walk!

You are now in the midst of what used to be known as the *Alhede* (The Great Moorland), a desolate area which was populated in the late 18C by German settlers brought in from the Rhine and Main areas by the king in an attempt to cultivate the vast tracts of moorland covering Jutland. (Even as late as 1850 a third of all Jutland was moorland.) Each family was provided with primitive accommodation, two oxen, a cow, and implements to set about cultivating the infertile moorland. (*Karup*, nearby, is said to have the poorest soil in Denmark.) This they did, with great difficulty and at great expense, succeeding in cultivating first buckwheat, then rye and potatoes—for which they became known as 'Potato Germans'. They retained many of their German characteristics until the mid 19C, but have now become totally assimilated.

What is now called Kongenshus Mindepark (Kongenshus Memorial Park), covering 1200 hectares, is one of the first areas in which cultivation was attempted, in 1754. The king financed buildings here, but the original scheme was a failure—as was an attempt early in the 20C to introduce reindeer—and, ironically, the area is now a conservation area intended to preserve part of Jutland as the whole of the region once was, and to remember the many unknown men and women who spent their entire lives cultivating the moorland. The names of some 1200 others, high and low, are still known, and these have been engraved partly on the large boulders along the path in the Mindedal (Memorial Valley) and partly on the smaller stones forming a circle at the end of the valley. Take a walk along the path here and perhaps beyond. The heather is a splendid sight when in full flower, and there are many kinds of berries and a rich and varied bird life—including the rare black grouse.

There is an hotel in the area and a small museum illustrating the flora and fauna and showing a collection of household implements associated with the cultivation of the moorland (open mid-May to end Aug).

Back on the A16 after 3km you will reach the village of Daugbjerg. To your right you will see *Daugbjerg Dås* (Daugbjerg Hill), rising 71m above the surrounding countryside, and affording a grand view of the area for those who climb it. But if that does not attract you, you should turn left to visit the abandoned lime workings, *Daugbjerg Kalkgruber* in Dybdalsvej (open May–Aug) and, 2km beyond them, **Mønsted Kalkgruber** in Kalkværksvej at *Mønsted* (open May–Oct).

These workings, thought to date right back to the 10C, stretch underground for many km (those in Mønsted extend in all over 35km, in three galleries), and reach a depth of 70m in places. It is possible that the two complexes were once linked. There are conducted tours by torchlight in Daugbjerg, where all the lime was dug out and transported by hand, but in Mønsted, where industrial methods were used in more recent times, there is a clearly lit route to follow. So huge is part of the workings in Mønsted—and so good the acoustics—that concerts are held here on occasion.

Nowadays, the constant low temperature in the Mønsted mines (c 8°C) enables them to be used for the storage of large quantities of cheese. They also contain a museum dedicated to the bats which are often to be seen in the mines, and the old lime kilns, now disused, still stand. Lime from Mønsted was used in the building of Ribe Cathedral and Gottorp Castle.

The mines in their time proved a source for legend and superstition, and a gipsy woman caught here was burned as a witch on Daugbjerg Dås in 1602, accused of having eaten the hearts of six new-born children in order to become invisible: she only needed to eat a seventh in order to achieve her objective, but was, inevitably, caught in time. Blicher also set some of his most dramatic stories in the Daugbjerg mines.

From Mønsted there is only 15km to *Viborg (29,500 inhab.; Tourist Information: Nytorv 5), the old capital of Jutland.

Viborg is one of Denmark's really old cities, with a history going back to the 8C. The first element in its name, *vi*, suggests that it was once a sacred spot, and there is thought to have been a place of sacrifice close to where the present Cathedral stands. Viborg's charter as a market town dates from 1150. For centuries this was where the nobility elected and did homage to their king—from 1027 with the election of Hardeknud (Hardecanute) until 1665 when homage was done to Prince Christian, subsequently Christian V. King Erik Glipping was crowned here in 1259 and, after being assassinated in 1286, buried before the high altar of the Cathedral (though his tomb was almost entirely destroyed by fire in 1726).

Viborg was the site of one of Denmark's four regional assemblies, the seat of a bishop from 1065, the site of a stone-built cathedral from c 1130, the home of five monasteries and convents and ten other churches. It was in Viborg that Hans Tavsen launched the Reformation movement, and it was in Viborg that Skipper Klement, the leader of the peasantry during the Count's War, was hanged in 1536. The law courts were situated here, and when, in the 19C, Denmark made its first hesitant move towards popular government, one of the regional advisory assemblies was set up here.

Nevertheless, with the establishment of Absolute Monarchy in 1661 and the gradual concentration of power and administration in Copenhagen, Viborg's importance declined, a process which was enhanced by the city's lack of easy access to the sea. As in the case with other towns in Jutland, it underwent a period of growth in the 19C with improved communications and especially the arrival of the railway, and in the 20C it has experienced further expansion and seen the establishment of thriving industrial concerns. At the same time, much of the older part of the city remains, and it has retained the feel of an old cathedral city, combining this with the informal modernity which is a characteristic of so many Danish cities.

The old city was grouped around the *Cathedral, but it is useless to seek in this monumental building the features which make, for instance, the cathedral in Ribe so outstanding, for little remains of the original structure from 1130 apart from the crypt. The present building dates from 1876. The original granite building, one of the largest such buildings in Europe, was demolished in 1863. It had suffered a great deal of damage and decay—and reconstruction—over the years, and it was decided to replace it with a dignified neo-Romanesque building of grey granite, inspired like the cathedral in Lund in Sweden by Rhineland churches. It is severe in its design, but austerity is combined with a monumental grandeur, and all is now set off by the vast frescoes (1899–1906) by Joakim Skovgaard in the nave, chancel and transept, which add colour and warmth, and which are a major attraction for visitors.

The paintings on the walls of the nave depict scenes from the Old Testament, while the rather later oil paintings on the ceiling and dome represent scenes from the childhood of Christ and figures of the Prophets. The New Testament is represented in the transept, while the chancel and apse present Christ in glory. One of the qualities of these murals is Skovgaard's wish to paint in a Danish national spirit. Whether his great project is entirely successful is a moot point, and opinions are divided. Nevertheless, it should be experienced.

The nave, in which so many of these paintings are to be seen, is flanked by seven rounded arches on either side, surmounted by arcades, while the huge transept arches are similarly rounded. Most of

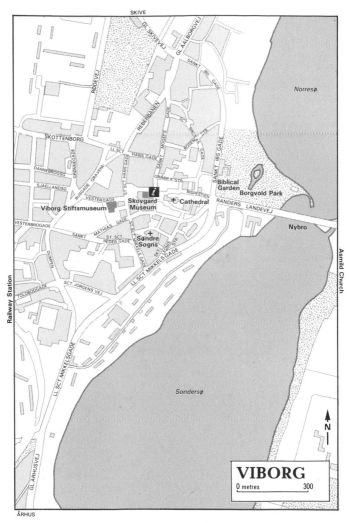

the furniture in the Cathedral is 19C, but there is a splendid 14C seven-branched candlestick standing almost 3m high and a late Gothic crucifix as well as several ancient gravestones and memorial tablets.

The Cathedral stands on high ground overlooking a pleasing square, and surrounded by streets with names betokening the ecclesiastical past of the city: *Gråbrødre Kirkestræde* (Greyfriars Church Street), *Bispestien* (Bishop's Walk), *Sortebrødrestræde* (Blackfriars Street)—and quite close by is the street with the curious forlorn name of *Navnløs* (Nameless). These are the streets to wander about in if you want to have at least some feel of what old Viborg was like. Close by are the pedestrian streets of Vestergade and Sankt Mathiasgade, busy as are all shopping precincts, but yet with a good deal of charm. In the middle of them, in Hjultorvet square, stands *Viborg Stiftsmuseum* (Viborg Diocesan Museum—formerly the Town Hall) with a collection of exhibits relating to the history of Viborg from prehistoric times to the present century. On Domkirkestræde, immediately S of the Cathedral, there is the *Skovgaard Museum*, with a collection of paintings by Skovgaard and others associated with him.

Leaving the Cathedral Square at the W end, close to the Skovgaard Museum, you should go down Sankt Mogensgade, cross Sankt Mathiasgade and go down Mageløs ('Matchless'), diagonally to your left. This will bring you to what is the oldest surviving church in Viborg, **Søndre Sogns Kirke**. It was once called Blackfriars Church, and until 1529 it was part of a Dominican monastery from the 13C. It is thought that the central part of the nave is actually from this original church. The remainder is later, not least the 23m high tower, from 1702. The ornate gilt altarpiece, standing well forward in the nave and leaving room for a confessional behind, is an early 16C triptych carved in the Netherlands, and brought to Viborg in 1728 from the chapel in Copenhagen Castle; it has been called 'the finest of Denmark's carved Flemish altars'. The pulpit is from 1728, in its over-rich decoration reflecting the pietist domination of Danish church life at this time, culminating when the pietist Christian VI came to the throne in 1730. The closed pews, too, are decorated in the pietist spirit, with over 200 paintings by Mogens Christian Thrane. In Sankt Leonisstræde at the end of Sortebrødre Kirkestræde you will find the 15C brick-built *Domprovstegård* (Dean's Residence) which in a varied career once served as a women's prison.

To the E of the Cathedral, skirted by Sankt Ibsgade and Randers Landevej (the A16), lies the charming *Borgvold Park*, leading down to the lake which once denoted the boundary of the city. On Sankt Ibsgade, too, you will find a *Biblical Garden* containing a unique collection of plants and trees associated with the Bible. Originally the result of a private initiative, it is now the responsibility of the City of Viborg. Viborg also houses comprehensive Local History Archives and the Public Records Office for North Jutland, both of which are open to the public.

On Randersvej, on the E side of the lakes the Heath Society (Hedeselskabet), which has been responsible for the cultivation—and now the preservation—of the Jutland heath, has its offices, with exhibits to which access is granted on application. Here, too, very close to the lakes stands *Asmild Church*, a very rare example of an 11C basilica, once forming the N wing of an Augustinian convent. The W part of the nave is part of the original structure. This was a very large church, with aisles on either side of the present nave, both with apses and probably both with square chancels. The low tower in the W is from c 1500. Much of the present richly decorated furniture, including the pulpit and canopy, the organ loft and the pews, is 18C, though the font is Romanesque. In the porch there is a runestone discovered in 1950.

EXCURSION FROM VIBORG TO HALD AND FINDERUP (total distance c 22km). This is a short trip through beautiful countryside to a site of historic interest. You leave on the A13 S and after 6km turn right on to the A12 to (2km) **Hald**, an estate with a history going back at least to the early 14C. The present house, *Hald Hovedgård*, is the fifth to bear the name. It overlooks a beautiful lake surrounded by wooded slopes, from the top of which there is a view of Viborg in the distance. It is easy to understand why the 19C novelist Meir Aron Goldschmidt called

Hald 'one of the most beautiful and most romantic places in the Kingdom of Denmark'.

The first Hald, usually called Brattingborg, is surrounded by still visible earthen mounds and a 20m-wide dry moat. In 1346 Hald was bought by Niels Bugge, one of the mightiest nobles in the land, who built a powerful castle to ensure his influence and safety. He was killed 13 years later, and his castle fell into disrepair. Nevertheless, remains of it (now known as Gammelhald—Old Hald) still stand close to the lake shore SW from the present building. In 1528 a third castle, surrounded by massive ramparts, was built nearby on a promontory jutting out into the lake E of the present Hald. A good deal of restoration has taken place in this century, in particular the reconstruction of the tower. A fourth, and subsequently a fifth, Hald were built in the 18C.

The present mansion is now used as a cultural centre. The converted barn contains an exhibition covering cultural history and natural history (open pm in summer).

If you now continue along the A12 for 2km and turn right, in a further 3km you will come to *Finderup*. This is the scene of the famous murder of King Erik Glipping in 1286. According to tradition he was murdered in a barn here, but there is little to see of this now. A house in which he is reputed to have stayed is undoubtedly not so old. However, a memorial has been placed on the most likely spot for the murder, just W of the church. From Finderup there is a minor road leading straight back to (9km) Viborg.

Returning to the main route, from **Viborg** the A16 leads E. After 10km you should turn off on the 517 NE to (6km) **Tjele**, a manor house with long historical associations. Indeed, Tjele claims to be the oldest manor in Denmark. Certainly, part of the present buildings date back to 1380, having survived the ravages of the Count's War, while the remainder was rebuilt in 1585.

Tjele is approached through a gateway near the church. The present offices and cafeteria are in a half-timbered house, formerly the stables dating from 1612, to your right. Here you can buy tickets for the conducted tour of part of the four-winged complex. *Sønderhuset* (The South House) is the oldest wing, perhaps the oldest extant secular building in Denmark, a strongly built two-storeyed house 10m x 17m with walls about a metre thick, a deep cellar, and an upper floor much resembling the hall in Nyborg Castle (Rte 14), large enough for concerts to be given in it (and the acoustics are good). The present elegant *dwelling house* (not open to the public) adjoins it. It dates from the late 16C, was originally half-timbered, but has now been partly reconstructed in brick. On the W side, facing the dwelling house, are the stables and outbuildings, while the courtyard is entered through a large gatehouse in the N, built slightly later than the dwelling house. Despite the different styles characterising the complex, it is spacious and pleasing, an idyllic and romantic remnant from the past.

The past, however, was not always idyllic. Inevitably, Tjele suffered under Skipper Klement, but it is not on account of this that it has its special place in history. In 1636 the estate was bought by one Erik Grubbe, whose daughter Marie Grubbe (1643–1718) has become famous in literature. In 1660 she was married to King Frederik III's son, Ulrik Frederik Gyldenløve, and went with him to Norway when he was appointed Viceroy. The marriage broke up in 1670, after which Marie Grubbe was married to a less exalted member of the nobility, Palle Dyre, and the couple settled in Tjele. By 1691, however, Marie Grubbe was again divorced, having embarked on an affair with a farm servant, with whom she then settled in Grønsund on the island of Falster (Rte 10). Here Ludvig Holberg came across her, by now a simple (and coarse) ferrywoman rowing passengers across the straits between the islands of Falster and Møn—while her husband was in prison. Her fate has been the subject of several books—by Steen Steensen Blicher, whose best novel, 'The Diary of a Parish Clerk' is inspired by her story, by Hans Christian Andersen ('The Story of Hen Grethe') and by Jens Peter Jacobsen, whose novel 'Marie Grubbe' is a bold and penetrating study of the psychological forces which made Marie Grubbe act as she did.

You should not leave Tjele without visiting the adjoining church. Parts of the original Romanesque structure remain, but the church was extended at the same time as additional buildings were put up for the manor in 1572, so the main part, including the tower, is now Gothic. The interior is relatively dark, but it is an impressive small church, with an atmosphere of its own, and containing a massive memorial in alabaster and marble to Geert Diderich Levetzau, who bought Tjele after the Grubbe family. This, like the enormous black baroque sarcophagus in the vestibule at the W end, is the work of Frederich Ehbisch, who was responsible for the stucco ceilings in Rosenborg in Copenhagen. Erik Grubbe is also buried here. The font is from the now vanished church in the nearby village of Foulum.

On leaving Tjele and moving N, on your left you will see the 8km-long *Tjele Langsø* (Tjele Long Lake). In 16km you join the E45, where you turn left and drive a further 4km to **Hobro** (9500 inhab.; Tourist Information: Adelgade 26), a small, old market town. Its earliest known charter is from 1560, but there were earlier ones going back to c 1300, and the town is certainly older still. It stands at the narrowest part of the Mariager Fjord and was thus a natural place first for a ferry, then for a bridge. In more recent times Hobro's geographical situation was enhanced by the creation of the harbour in 1834 and the advent of the main railway between North and South Jutland, which together helped create an industrial infrastructure. Nevertheless, Hobro's rural character is emphasised by its being the site of one of the biggest cattle markets in Denmark.

Centred on the fjord, Hobro now spreads up on to the surrounding higher ground. The story goes that at the end of the 19C, a gathering of young people in Zürich was discussing what was the most beautiful place they had seen. Most had been to the most famous places in Europe and spoke in glowing tones. Then a young Dane got up and said, in Jutland dialect: 'Ah, but have you been to Hobro? That is the loveliest place on earth.' You may or may not go all the way with him, but the dictum has stuck, and 'Haa do wot i Hobrow?' has become the motto of the town. Its position is certainly charming, as it snuggles around the fjord crossing, surrounded by hilly ground covered with woods and stretches of juniper.

Like so many other Danish towns, Hobro has been severely damaged by fire on several occasions, and thus there are few really old houses left. Nevertheless, there are still a couple in *Adelgade*—the old dyer's house (No. 44) and a fine patrician house with an outdoor staircase leading to a gallery overlooking the inner courtyard (No. 73). A long half-timbered house from 1774 in Vestergade is now **Hobro Museum**, containing an extensive collection of exhibits from the old Viking fortress of Fyrkat (see below), local silver, porcelain and archaeological finds from the area (open summer).

There are some other, less distinctive, older buildings down by the river. *Hobro Church*, built 1850–52 by the architect Michael Gottlieb Bindesbøll, who designed the Thorvaldsen Museum in Copenhagen, is quite unusual. It combines the neo-Gothic shape of the traditional Danish village church with the alternate horizontal rows of red and yellow brick usually associated with Byzantine style. Whether you like it, is a matter of taste. The local population must have found it daring, and in a restoration in 1871 Bindesbøll's bold interior decorations were removed and replaced by something less startling. The present mosaic altarpiece from 1952 is the work of Johan Thomas Skovgaard, based on a 1931 design by his father Joakim Skovgaard.

A visit to **Fyrkat** is a must. To reach it you leave the town via Vestergade and drive c 2km SW. Here lies the smallest of the four extant Viking fortresses erected towards the end of the 10C, possibly by Harald Bluetooth, all of them built in strict symmetry to the same pattern. The indications are that the original fortress was burned down at some time after it had been abandoned, and consequently only the outlines of the various buildings are now visible. The complex is enclosed inside a circular rampart 120m in diameter, with dry moats to the N and W, and consists of 16 28.4m-long houses with convex walls, arranged in groups of four around a square courtyard. Each house contained three rooms, providing living quarters for some 50 people. (Although Fyrkat was undoubtedly a fortress, it provided living accommodation for both women and children.) A smaller rectangular house stood at the centre of each courtyard.

To the NE of the complex, which was entered by four gates on the points of the compass, there is the burial ground containing some 30 graves which yielded rich grave finds in the excavations in the 1950s. Of particular interest is a woman's grave in which the corpse was laid in a carriage containing jewels and a chest of personal belongings. A quarter of Fyrkat has not yet been excavated, the decision having been made to leave it for future archaeologists. Just outside the complex itself stands a reconstruction of one of the houses. Remember that the principal treasures found in Fyrkat are on display in the museum in Hobro. In the nearby Fyrkat Møllegård there is a 225-year-old watermill. The fortress area and the watermill are open to the public from Easter to the end of August.

EXCURSION FROM HOBRO TO KLEJTRUP AND TO SNÆBUM (total distance c 29km). To take this short trip, with something for children and something for those interested in archaeology, you should drive W on the 579 for 11km and then turn left for 3km along a minor road to *Klejtrup*. Here at the S end of the lake there is a large-scale (50m x 100m) *Map of the World*, with land-masses built of boulders and earth in the shape of the continents, and with water from the lake representing the oceans. The main rivers are there, and the major mountain chains, and each country is marked with its own national flag. Close by on a promontory to the SW lies Klejtrup Voldsted, the ramparts of a now vanished castle, by legend said to have belonged to the medieval hero Niels Ebbesen, who slew the Holstein Count Gert and liberated Jutland from foreign rule. However, it is also attributed to other historical or legendary figures. What is certain is that it is early medieval.

Now drive N again, across the 579 to (6km) *Snæbum*, where there are three huge double passage graves dating back to c 3000 BC. One has been badly damaged, but the other two are among Denmark's best preserved passage graves. Nearby you will find 15 burial mounds, of which 13 are aligned on a slope to the SE of the village. Open all year round.

From Snæbum you return to (9km) Hobro.

21 Middelfart to Holstebro

Total distance 136km. 421 to (10km) **Fredericia**.—(25km)
Vejle.—A18 to (11km) **Jelling**.—(29km) *Brande*.—(26km)
Herning.—(35km) **Holstebro**.

From Middelfart (Rte 12), you will automatically cross **Lillebælt** (Rte 1)
via the old bridge and follow an unclassified road to (10km) **Fredericia**
(28,500 inhab.; Tourist Information: Axeltorv).

Fredericia is a city of historical importance, though it was not founded until 1650,
when Frederik III created it as a fortress. Seven years later it was overrun by the
Swedes, and all the Danish defenders were killed.
   Among pre-19C Danish cities the town planning of Fredericia is unique, in that
all the streets within the original fortifications run in parallel straight lines,
intersecting at right angles. Thanks to its strategic position and its function from
1679 as a garrison town, Fredericia suffered attack during the Dano-Prussian
wars of 1848 and 1864; it was besieged by Schleswig-Holstein troops from May
to July 1849, and in the 1864 war was actually taken and occupied by Austrian
troops. On 6 July each year the Battle of Fredericia, which broke the 1849 siege
at the cost of heavy Danish losses, is commemorated in the town.
   A harbour was opened at Fredericia in 1808, and has gradually been extended
until it now offers some 3000m of quays. Fredericia's position as a major railway
junction began to emerge in 1866, when the first railway line was opened. This
was followed by the opening of a ferry harbour in 1872 linking Fredericia with
Strib on Fyn. The opening of the first bridge over Lillebælt in 1935 brought
increased railway traffic.
   Until 1909 Fredericia remained a fortress, surrounded by the still-existing
ramparts which are the most extensive of their kind in northern Europe,
extending in all for 5.5km and now forming a green belt between the old town
and the modern developments which came post 1909. One of the old city
gateways, *Prinsens Port*, still stands, as do a powder magazine from 1675 and gun
positions from 1849.
   A particular feature of Fredericia's history is the right of religious freedom which
it received in 1674 and 1682. The first Jew was granted citizenship in 1679, and
by 1719 there was a sufficiently large Jewish community to warrant the establishment of a synagogue. A Catholic mission was established in 1674, and by 1686
a small wooden church had been consecrated. This was replaced by a permanent
building in 1767. Around 1720 large numbers of French Protestants (Huguenots)
settled in Fredericia, and consequently a Reformed Church was consecrated in
1736.

When permission to expand Fredericia was granted in 1908, one of the
first buildings to appear was the watertower which stands on the
ramparts and dominates the town to this day. Open to the public in the
summer, it offers a view of the ramparts and the older part of the town.
The ramparts themselves are covered with grass and bushes, but
efforts are now being made (especially near the watertower) to restore
parts of them to their original state.
   In a town with a history such as that of Fredericia, it is clear that there
will be national and military memorials to visit. Most famous of these
is Herman Vilhelm Bissen's 1858 bronze statue of the Danish Soldier,
'Landsoldaten', standing where Danmarksgade and Norgesgade
meet near the ramparts at Prinsens Port. The statue was financed
through voluntary contributions from the whole country.—More bombastic is Bissen's bust of General Bülow standing in a triumphal arch
near the town hall. This, too, was paid for by voluntary contributions,
as was that to General Olaf Rye standing on *Ryes Plads*.
   Two touching monuments are to be found in the cemetery of Trinitatis Kirke. One is to the 500 soldiers killed when the Swedes took the
town in 1657, the other, a monument by Bissen showing two soldiers
laying a dead comrade in the grave, marks the common grave of those

who fell in the 1849 Battle of Fredericia.—A memorial of an entirely different kind is that at Oldenborgs Bastion to Danish railway workers killed on duty.

Trinitatis Kirke is the principal church, dating from 1690. It contains eight impressive stained glass windows, an ornate baroque altar from 1692, and a Romanesque font, presumably moved there from a disused church in the abandoned village of Ullerup. The font is surmounted by a splendid canopy. The neo-classical *Michaelis Kirke*, in Vendersgade, was built in 1665–67, but the present building is a modern reconstruction after a fire in 1955. Both the Reformed Church from 1735 and the Catholic Church from 1767 still stand.

Fredericia boasts a great number of parks. One of the best is *Madsbyparken*, close to the railway station, containing a large play park for children—including an Indian encampment and a Stone Age hut for children to play in. There are pens with domestic animals, and a large artificial lake for rowing boats.

Fredericia Museum is in Jernbanegade and is centred on six half-timbered houses with relics not only from the military past, but also exhibits relating to the four religious persuasions associated with the town. There is a garden of herbs—including tobacco, which was introduced to Fredericia by the Huguenots.

In Riddergade 15 you will find a plaque in memory of the great 19C novelist Henrik Pontoppidan, born in this house in 1857. The son of a pastor, Pontoppidan broke with family tradition and became one of the leading representatives of the Modern Movement, in the eyes of many Denmark's most important novelist ever.

Leaving Fredericia, you continue N on the 421. At (6km) *Egeskov* you can turn off right to the beautiful area of *Trelde Næs*, unspoiled natural scenery, studded with half-timbered houses. The village of *Trelde* (2km) consists almost entirely of dwellings of this kind.

From Trelde Næs you proceed to (19km) Vejle, passing on your way near *Brejning* a remarkable twelve-sided church, designed by Mogens Koch and built between 1965 and 1976, and the delightful *Børkop watermill* (the motif of a 1962 postage stamp), now owned by the State and beautifully restored. It is used for cultural events and contains a restaurant.

Approaching the town, you will see the *Vejle Windmill* (1847) to the left of the road. Perched on high ground, it affords impressive views of both the town and the surrounding area (open summer).

Vejle (44,000 inhab.; Tourist Information: Den Smidtske Gård, Søndergade 14) lies in the midst of one of the hilliest and most idyllic parts of Denmark. The name means *ford*, and Vejle used to be just that. The E45 motorway now by-passes the town, carried across the fjord on yet another of the imposing bridges in this region; but until quite recently, all traffic N and S on the E side of Jutland had to go through Vejle's narrow, quite winding streets. Now the town has regained its old charm, and, with the surrounding tree-covered hills, it is unique in Denmark. Some would talk of its alpine qualities—though the height of the hills barely qualifies for that—others would say, with some justification, that it is the most beautifully situated town in Denmark. Moreover, it gives easy access to magnificent beaches, and offers countless opportunities for outdoor activities: bathing, riding, sailing, fishing and, not least, walking in the exquisite surroundings.

Vejle is first mentioned at the end of the 13C, receiving a charter in 1327. It did not play a large part in the events of the Middle Ages, but suffered badly during the 17C Swedish wars and, in 1659, from a visitation of the plague. Not until the 19C did Vejle really begin to show signs of life again, and it was only with the completion of the new harbour in 1827 that conditions in the town began to improve. During the Schleswig-Holstein wars Vejle was occupied on several occasions. The great leap came with the arrival of the railway in 1868, bringing in its wake the new and varied industries which still characterise the town.

Once you have crossed the Vejle river, you should make use of the good parking facilities and walk through the winding, hilly streets of the old town. Where the main road crosses Kirkegade/Havnegade, you will, on the left, find *Kirketorvet* square (parking). From here you could walk down Kirkegade to *Søndergade*, where you will find *Den Smidt-ske Gård*. This old merchant's house was restored in 1985 and now, in addition to housing the Tourist Information Office, forms part of *Vejle Kulturhistoriske Museum* (Vejle Museum of Cultural History). Here you will find an exhibition illustrating the history of Vejle. The section of the museum situated nearby in Flegborg 18 is mainly dedicated to local archaeology. Flegborg 16 is the art gallery, *Vejle Kunstmuseum*, with a permanent exhibition of paintings and sculptures.

Before continuing your journey, you might make an EXCURSION to *Grejsdal valley* (c 3km), a wooded idyll, a bird sanctuary of great beauty. To reach it, take the A18 and turn right on the outskirts of the town at the top of Gormsgade.

Between Vejle and Brande 40km further on, there are two routes, a fundamental choice between spectacular ancient monuments and the children's paradise of Legoland. The first route goes via Jelling; the alternative route (58km) via Billund.

FROM VEJLE TO BRANDE VIA JELLING (total distance 40km), Leave Vejle by the steep A18 road leading NW to (11km) *Jelling*, a spot inextricably related to early Danish kingship, and the site of the earliest known residence of a king of all Denmark. (Railway enthusiasts can travel by vintage railway from Vejle on Sun in Jul.)

Jelling village (Tourist Information: Gormsgade 4) itself is of modest interest—though the countryside you pass through on the way there is charming. The real attraction is the two enormous *·**Jelling Stones**, perhaps the most famous of all Scandinavian runestones. They stand immediately S of the present church, between two huge burial *·mounds measuring between 60m and 70m in diameter and standing 7–8m high—so vast that even the church is dwarfed by them, though it is by no means a small church for its time. The murals inside indicate that it has stood there since the 12C, when it replaced an earlier (probably 10C) wooden structure. Excavations in the 1940s and 1950s revealed traces of a yet earlier heathen temple beneath this wooden church. It appears, therefore, that the present church and churchyard occupy the central positions in what was once a heathen temple complex. A series of standing stones marks the outline of the temple.

The more northerly of the two mounds, known as Gorm's Mound, was excavated in vain as early as 1607, but farmers digging in it in 1820 came across a wooden burial chamber 6.8m x 2.6m x 1.5m. It contained a wooden coffin, but no corpse. There were clear signs that grave robbers had been there first. The S mound, Thyra's Mound, was excavated in 1861, but no burial chamber was found.

The two *runestones appear to be connected with these mounds. The smaller of them bears the inscription 'King Gorm made these runes in memory of Thyra his wife, the pride of Denmark'. The larger stone stands 2.43m high; on one side it is engraved with the figure of a lion, and on the other a figure of Christ. An inscription runs: 'King Harald had these runes made in memory of Gorm his father and Thyra his

*The runic stones in Jelling. The larger of the two is
the most magnificent runic stone in Denmark, and
the figure of Christ on it is one of the earliest known.
Photo: Lennard*

mother, Harald who conquered all Denmark and Norway and made
the Danes Christian.'

There is thus a theory that the heathen Gorm built the N mound for his wife Thyra
and raised the runestone in her memory, probably himself being buried in the
mound beside her. Harald Bluetooth was then responsible for the second,
Christian, stone, and it is likely that he had the bodies of his parents removed
and buried in the wooden church he had built on the site of the temple which
Gorm had erected in his day. The romantic idea was that he did this in order to
give his parents a Christian burial, but a modern theory is that he did it in order
to ensure his own right of inheritance.

Gorm is generally accepted to be the first Danish king, from whom the present
Danish royal family is descended. Thyra may have been an English princess,
though this is not certain. Tradition has it that she was responsible for the
construction of the Danevirke fortifications which once denoted the border
between Denmark and Germany.

There is a small museum providing further information on the site at
Hygumvej 36, close to the church.

From Jelling the A18 leads to (8km) *Givskud*, where to the left of the
main road there is a large modern zoo and safari park with over 100
different species of animals, including some tame animals for the
children (open mid-Apr to mid-Oct).

Just after the safari park you will find a road off right towards Nørre Kollemorten
and Øster Nykirke. The road will be marked as an historical monument with the

usual sign, and is referred to as *Hærvejen*. In southern and mid Jutland you may already have seen signs indicating *Hærvejen*, and you are likely to come across more. It means *Military Road*, but this is a name ascribed to it by a German cartographer in the 17C, and it gives a wrong impression of its use and its history. Also known at one time as *The Ox Road*, it is an ancient route following the ridge of high—and hence dry—ground in the centre of Jutland. It was used by travellers, vagabonds, pilgrims and drovers, between the Danevirke fortifications (now in Germany) and Viborg. It was not a single, well defined path, and sometimes divided into different strands. Stretches of it are now a road suitable for traffic, while other parts are still more in the nature of a track. It is a favourite route for cyclists and hikers, well equipped with camping facilities, ancient inns and youth hostels, and although it does pass through a few large villages and smaller towns, it will not take you through the major centres. It thus offers a quiet, idyllic route from N to S often affording panoramic views of the Jutlandic countryside, much of it dotted with burial mounds.

You might like to follow Hærvejen as far as *Øster Nykirke* (9km), where you will find, 130m above sea level, a Romanesque church with a Gothic tower and 19C porch. It stands just W of a medieval place of pilgrimage, a sacred spring, *Sankt Peders Kilde*, traces of which are still to be seen on the opposite side of the road.

From Givskud the A18 continues to (20km) *Brande* (see below).

ALTERNATIVE ROUTE FROM VEJLE TO BRANDE—VIA LEGOLAND (total distance 58km). Take the A28 W towards Billund. This brings you at 7km to *Skibet*, where there is a Romanesque church with Gothic extensions, largely rebuilt in the 18C, Romanesque tympanum, and a series of frescoes discovered in 1952. Of particular interest is the frieze stretching over five arcades depicting a unique row of knights on horseback. The significance of these riders is uncertain, though one seems to be a Knight Templar, and may well refer to the legend of the Holy Grail.

A further 8km along the A28 you can turn off to the right to see *Engelsholm* (1.5km), a mansion in the French-Italian Renaissance style, with domed towers which are echoed in the associated Nørup church on the opposite side of the lake, and clearly visible from the park. You can walk in the surrounding woods and even get right up to the house, now a Folk High School, but you cannot go inside.

Return now to the A28 and follow it to (13km) *Billund* (Tourist Information: Åstvej 1), from where you can visit **Legoland** (Rte 1).

From Billund you take the 176 N; this merges with the A30, takes you through Give to (18km) the A18, where you turn left and proceed to (12km) Brande.

Brande (6000 inhab.; Tourist Information: Torvegade 1). The town is associated with Ernesto Dalgas, who was famous for his efforts to cultivate the Jutland heath in the second half of the 19C. There is a memorial stone to him in a park opposite the church. Brande also made itself a name in the 1960s when a group of young artists was allowed to decorate 24 gable ends in very bright colours.

Beyond Brande the A18 leads to 12km *Arnborg*, where the simple, unadorned Romanesque church has a carved altarpiece from 1608. A further 2km ahead a narrow road leads off right to *Søby* (4km). Here you will find a *museum illustrating the development of the nearby lignite mines—to which there is public access. Lignite was mined here in great quantities during World War II, as Denmark could no longer obtain proper coal. Great numbers of unemployed (at one time as many as 5000) flocked here in great numbers to work the mines, living in primitive conditions; all is graphically presented to the visitor. This strange, desolate area covers some 100 hectares.

ARNBORG & BRANDE

Returning to the A18, you continue to (12km) **Herning** (29,500 inhab.; Tourist Information: Bredgade 2). From being a tiny, out-of-the-way moorland village, Herning has experienced rapid growth over the past hundred years, and was given a charter in 1913. It stands at the intersection of two main roads, the A18 N–S and the A15 E–W, and is now known for its progressive policies. Conveniently placed for modern transport, it has attracted a large amount of modern industry—clothing, carpets, furniture, printing, computers—and with the space available all has been arranged so as to give a sense of light and air, nothing at all of the traditional industrial atmosphere.

And industry is here closely associated with art. Herning prides itself on its artistic achievements, and they are in turn based on its industries. A far-sighted shirt manufacturer realised that by putting a minute surcharge (less than 1p) on his shirts, he could afford to invest in works by artists some of whom have subsequently achieved international fame—Robert Jacobsen, Sven Dalsgaard and Svend Wiig

Hansen. Carl-Henning Pedersen, who is responsible for the modern murals in Ribe Cathedral (Rte 15), provided the factory with a 200m-long frieze, and has since established his own gallery nearby. Even the hospital is filled with paintings, to give it an intimate feel far removed from the usual sterile atmosphere.

The interest in art is immediately obvious in the town, and a walk through the pedestrian precinct will demonstrate this to the full. The entire area is dotted with sculptures, most, but not all, by modern Danish artists. Others are scattered around the town, including a Henry Moore in front of the Congress Centre, *Herning Kongrescenter* in Østergade.

There are few old buildings in Herning, the oldest being the architecturally outstanding mansion of *Herningsholm*, on the A12 at Viborgvej 72, 2km N of the central area. Said to be the most important piece of secular architecture in central Jutland, this house from 1579 has been tastefully restored and converted into a museum for Steen Steensen Blicher. Blicher's stories are so totally identified with the Jutland heath that it is natural for a town which itself has been part of the heath to honour him in this way. In addition to original manuscripts and first editions of Blicher's works, the museum contains illustrations to his work, paintings of the moorland with which he was associated, and the only known painting for which Blicher himself sat. There is also a room illustrating the history of Herningsholm. The carillon plays at 11.00, 13.00 and 15.00 (open May–Oct).

Just S of the town centre you will find *Herning Museum* in Museumsgade. This is one of the first public museums to be opened in Denmark, dating from 1892, and is partly an open air museum, with buildings including a traditional moorland knitting room and illustrating the history of Jutland from prehistoric times. In Museumsgade, too, you will find *Danmarks Fotomuseum*, which, as the name implies, is a comprehensive museum of photography.

3km E of Herning on the A15, in *Birk*, lies *Herning Kunstmuseum* (Herning Art Gallery). This is the former shirt factory where it all began, and in addition to the impressive frieze by Carl-Henning Pedersen it contains a comprehensive collection of modern Danish and international art. Close by, in a building which is an architectural attraction in itself is the *Carl-Henning Pedersen og Else Alfelt Gallery*, which, as the name suggests, is dedicated to the work of these two artists.—Adjacent is a sculpture park in which modern Danish and international sculptors are represented.—Adjoining this again are the *Geometrical Gardens*, a park based on geometrical principles and designed by C.Th. Sørensen, who was also responsible for the layout of both the sculpture park and the Herning Kunstmuseum.

While in this area, you should take a minor road N from the A15 in neighbouring *Hammerum* to *Gjellerup Kirkeby* (2km) to see the oldest dated church in Denmark. A lintel over a now bricked-up S door bears the date 1140. The nave and chancel are both Romanesque, though there are inevitably Gothic additions. Inside, there is a beamed ceiling, an unusual chancel arch 5m high, and several interesting items of church furniture.

From Herning you continue along the A18 to (6km) *Tjørring*. Here, in what is now a dormitory of Herning, there is an idiosyncratic modern church from 1977 with a roof sweeping up to form a tower, the whole looking rather like a wigwam—though an aerial view shows it to be in the shape of a Maltese cross. Inside, of course, it is circular. It forms a complete contrast to the other, Romanesque, church in Tjørring. Drive on to (14km) *Avlum*, where there is a church with an unusually richly carved gallery, and then finally to (15km) **Holstebro** (Rte 20).

22 Holstebro to Thisted

Total distance 84km. A11 to (16km) *Struer.*—(32km) *Ydby.*—(36km) **Thisted**.

The direct route from Holstebro to Struer on the A11 is quick and easy, but has little else to offer. A longer route (33km), E of the direct route, is slightly more interesting.

So we suggest that you leave Holstebro on the 189 and drive NE for 8km, turning right here on to a minor road leading to *Borbjerg* (4km).

The Romanesque church here has a most unusual antemensale very reminiscent of the golden altar in Sahl (Rte 18), though the product of a slightly different technique. It dates from 1200, and is made of copper-covered carved oak richly gilded. In the centre is Christ enthroned, surrounded by the Evangelists, and there are 24 more panels representing scenes from the life of Christ. The altarpiece, too, is interesting, the oldest section being English, from c 1425, representing St. George slaying the Dragon.—On the opposite side of the lake from the church there is an old watermill, now a restaurant.

Driving N on the 189 again you pass, at 6km, *Rydhave*. The original Rydhave mansion dates back to the 14C and was once in the possession of the Rosenkrantz and Gyldenstjerne families (shades of Hamlet?). The present buildings are from the mid 16C, subsequently updated in 1656 and 1794, and are now used as a Youth High School. The adjoining woods, planted in the 19C, constitute the most westerly beech forest in Denmark.

Now follow the 189 to (3km) Vinderup, there turning left on to the 513 to drive along the low-lying coast to (12km) Struer.

Struer (11,200 inhab.; Tourist Information: Rådhuspladsen) is one of Denmark's most recent market towns, its charter dating back only to 1917. It has grown up from a few scattered farms along the coast; in 1589 it was merely the site of a ford. By 1600 there was a small harbour here. In the 19C, when exits to the North Sea were established, Struer developed into a lively port, and the advent of the railways also benefited it. As it is mainly a 19C development, Struer has little to offer in the way of old and architecturally interesting buildings, though it is not without the charm of a Danish provincial town. The excellent *Struer Museum*, at Søndergade 23, is housed in the oldest building in the town, and specialises in local cultural history from the last 500 years (open summer; limited opening winter). The old fire engine house in Bjerggade is now a museum demonstrating the history of a provincial fire brigade. Struer is also known as the home of Bang & Olufsen.

Take the A11 N now, driving across the bridge, perhaps turning off to the right after 2km to visit the 8km-long island of *Venø* (147 inhab.), which is reached by ferry (sailing time 2 mins). Venø claims to possess the smallest church in Denmark, no more than 9.8m x 4.2m plus a tiny porch.

Back on the A11 you now drive N towards the bridge at (8km) *Oddesund* sound. (W of the road just before you reach the sound there are splendid bathing and camping facilities in the beautiful area of

Toftum Bjerge.) The 472m-long Oddesund Bridge linking West Jutland
with Thy in North Jutland was opened in 1938.

The interest in this immediate neighbourhood is as much in the impressive
scenery as in buildings and towns. Almost any road will bring you breathtaking
views across the many sounds and fjords, with an archipelago ranging from tiny
islets to the largest island in the Limfjord, Mors. These are the waters where many
of the great Viking invasions of England were prepared, the place of departure
for the invading ships of the Knuds (Canutes).

9km N of the sound you by-pass the village of *Hvidbjerg*, just to the
right of the main road. It is one of three villages in the area all called
by the same name ('white-hill') because of the limestone in the
ground. The large church in Hvidbjerg contains some quite realistic
frescoes showing a farmer driving a team of two white horses, with a
castle in the background. A figure of Jonas being devoured by the
whale hangs in the N chapel. According to legend the Bishop of
Børglum was murdered here in 1260, an event depicted in Hans
Christian Andersen's 'The Bishop of Børglum and his Family'.

13km further N on the A11 you will arrive at *Ydby*.

The area around here has a special character because of the many Bronze Age
burial mounds—some 200—found in all directions. Some, of course, have been
more or less ploughed in, but many are clearly visible and now subject to
conservation orders. Some stand singly, but others are grouped together. Thus a
group of 35 lies in the immediate neighbourhood of the church, and one of similar
size in the Dover Plantation to the E. Slightly further to the S, in *Ydby Hede* heath,
you will find a group of over 50. There is also a well-preserved dolmen chamber.
On the Boddum peninsula, a couple of km further on, there are the remains of
another 80 burial mounds.

There are two possible routes from Ydby to Thisted. The direct route
(36km) is listed first; the alternative route is given below.

DIRECT ROUTE FROM YDBY TO THISTED (total distance 36km). Continue further along the A11 passing close to (5km) *Hurup* (Tourist
Information: Jernbanegade 2), the birthplace of the painter Jens
Søndergaard. Then carry on driving N to (2km) *Heltborg*, where there
is a beautifully restored old windmill. Yet another km, on the right,
there is a farm called *Østergård* where there is a burial mound containing a remarkably well-preserved passage grave, to which there is
public access. A stone-lined passage leads to the 6.5m-long burial
chamber giving on to a small chamber 2m x 2m.

6km further you reach *Villerslev*, where the outwardly rather modest
church contains a wealth of post-Reformation murals discovered in
1973.

Immediately beyond Villerslev we suggest you leave the A11 and
turn right on to an equally good coastal road leading through Skyum
to (7km) *Skyum Bjerge*, a beautiful stretch of coastline with a magnificent beach suitable for bathing. As you drive N along this road you
have the most splendid views across the Vilsund Sound, first of the
island of Mors, then (at 6km) of the Vilsund bridge, and beyond that
again the fjord with Thisted in the background.

Vilsund Sound is 8km long in all and as much as 1.5km wide. The bridge across
it was designed by Anker Engelund, who was also responsible for the old Lillebælt
Bridge (Rte 1) and the Storstrømsbro bridge (Rte 9), and was opened in 1939. It
was widened in 1976.

From Vilsund Bridge it is 10km to Thisted (see below).

ALTERNATIVE ROUTE FROM YDBY TO THISTED—VIA VESTERVIG AND

VORUPØR (total distance c 55km). From Ydby you drive W on the 527, passing at 4km *Ashøj* hill, the highest point (94m) in Thy, from which there are impressive views of the surrounding countryside.

4km further on, in **Vestervig**, you should visit the *Museum* (open school summer holidays) in the old Judge's House as well as the church. Not only does it contain a pictorial history of the church but it possesses a collection of materials illustrating the history of schooling in the area.

The famous *Vestervig Church* is the biggest village church in Denmark. Its size is impressive and is explained by the fact that there was a Bishop of Vestervig in the 12C. The present church once formed the N wing of an Augustinian monastery which was destroyed in the 17C. It is 54m long, consisting of a nave and two aisles, and retains something of its original Romanesque character despite much rebuilding in the 15C and subsequently. It was finally thoroughly restored in 1917–21. However, the main attraction for the tourist is undoubtedly the *churchyard, with its unusual number of Romanesque gravestones. One, near the N door, is of particular interest, the traditional grave of Liden Kirsten (Little Kirsten) and her lover Prince Buris, the two placed not side by side, but end to end. The gravestone, 3.4m long and 50cm wide, decorated with two crosses and a now almost entirely illegible inscription, is from c 1200. An examination of the grave in 1875 showed that it does indeed contain two bodies, those of a man and a woman, lying end to end. Tradition has it that they are those of Valdemar I's sister Kirsten, and Burislejf Sverkersøn, the half-brother of Queen Sophie. Attempts to interpret the inscription, however, seem to indicate that the bodies are those of a brother and a sister.

The ballad of 'Liden Kirsten' (for which there appears to be no historical foundation) tells the following story: Queen Sophie asks King Valdemar if his sister might marry her brother, Buris. The king scornfully rejects the suit, calling Buris a horse thief, and Sophie vows revenge. While Valdemar is away at the wars, Sophie encourages Buris to seduce Kirsten, and when he at first refuses, she cuts magic runes and thus casts a spell on him. He now does the deed, and Kirsten gives birth to a child on the very day on which King Valdemar returns. When Valdemar discovers what has happened, he whips Kirsten to death and has her buried in Vestervig. He then has Buris' eyes put out, his left foot and right hand chopped off, and his right arm broken, and then chains him outside the church of Vestervig, from where he can just reach the grave of the girl whom he has after all genuinely loved. The supposed burial end to end would be the final brutality representing hatred going beyond the grave, though the ballad says nothing of this. In recent years it has become the custom for local brides to place a bunch of flowers on 'Liden Kirsten's Grave'.

From Vestervig you should drive N up the 527/181 to (19km) *Stenbjerg*, there turning on to the 571 left to visit the lifeboat museum (2km) at Stenbjerg Kirkevej 53 right down on the North Sea coast (open summer).

Return now to the 181 and continue a further 4km to the small fishing village of *Nørre Vorupør*, where there is a North Sea Aquarium containing 20 large pools of North Sea fish (open summer).

From Nørre Vorupør you take the 539 E towards Thisted. On the W outskirts of (10km) *Hundborg* we suggest you take an unclassified road N just to visit **Jannerup Church** (2km).

Looking quite modest on the outside, the church here is richly decorated inside and shows signs of considerable wealth, presumably resulting from votive gifts from pilgrims to the holy spring of St. Andrew which was once nearby, and, it is thought, from shipwrecked sailors giving thanks for deliverance. It retained its special status after the Reformation, as is indicated by the superb furniture in it. This includes a magnificent carved altar presented to the church in 1648, the work of Peder Jensen Kolding. To the left of the altar there is an equally splendid carved confessional from 1688. The only slightly less elaborate parish clerk's seat to the right of the altar dates from 1693. The pulpit, from 1675, is decorated with ornate carvings, and the ceiling with allegorical paintings.

From Hundborg you continue NE to (7km) *Sjørring*. Here you will first see on your left *Sjørring Volde*, a 10C mound on which a royal castle once stood, and which is now sometimes used for open air perform-ances. On your right, opposite the mound, is the large Romanesque church from 1160. The N door, still in use, is flanked by a column on either side surmounted by a rounded arch; the S door is still more ornate, with two columns on either side, supporting two concentric arches. The altarpiece is from 1640, and the elaborately carved pulpit from 1639. The tower was built in 1929.

There are two famous Romanesque *bishops' graves* in the church-yard, dating back to the 13C. On one of them there is a carved figure of a bishop, presumably St. Nicholas of Myra. According to one legend it is the grave of a bishop from Børglum who was drowned in the North Sea. Another legend has it that it contains an English bishop who fled from the Black Death—and brought it with him.

From Sjørring it is only 7km to **Thisted** (12,500 inhab.; Tourist Infor-mation: Det Gamle Rådhus, Store Torv).

Thisted lies in an area which still shows ample traces of prehistoric and Viking settlement. Even its name indicates this, like that of its county, *Thy*, stemming from the name of the god Tyr.

The earliest known allusion to Thisted is from 1367, when it was referred to as a village of the same status as Hovsør. Hovsør, once used as a winter harbour by Thisted, is now a very small village, 10km along the coast to the E. Nevertheless, it was Thisted which grew, and by 1524 it was granted a charter giving its citizens the same rights as those in Viborg. It was the seat of a Lutheran bishop from 1542–48. Yet its situation on the Limfjord, with limited access to the open sea, and with Ålborg in a much more favourable situation, limited its possibilities of expansion. After a series of fires in the 17C, as well the sufferings brought about by the 17C wars, it was steadily reduced in size until the establishment of the harbour in 1840—and the subsequent advent of the railway system—led to steady growth. Before the harbour was built, ships had to be loaded and unloaded away from land, and the cargoes taken to and fro by lighter; and in winter this was not possible. With the establishment of the channel between Agger and Thyborøn in 1825, making the W part of the Limfjord accessible to ocean-going ships, a harbour suitable for year-round sailing had become a near necessity.

Thisted is a charming and lively town with well designed older buildings like the *Old Town Hall* (now housing the Tourist Information Office) contrasting strongly with its modern replacement from 1978, with its elegant exhibition facilities. Careful restoration work has been undertaken in the area around *Nytorv* square.

There is a sizeable 16C church, replacing an older Romanesque church, and incorporating some of the granite ashlars from it. Some of these are decorated with sculpted heads, animals or designs which are clearly visible. The church was tastefully restored in 1973 to produce an interior of great charm. The large altarpiece, a triptych from c 1520, has the Virgin and Child as its central figures with St. Paul and Mary Magdalene on either side; the twelve Apostles are represented in side panels. Beneath is a painting of the Last Supper. The pulpit is from 1594. The slender octagonal spire rises 44m above ground level and is a landmark seen from far around. There is a runestone in the S wall, with the name Thord Amdissøn clearly engraved in runic lettering.

The Thisted Museum, **Museet for Thy og Vester Hanherred**, contains a very large collection of Bronze Age finds from the surrounding area. The museum also has exhibits of local rural life, as well as the Jens

Peter Jacobsen room. Art lovers will find several of the Expressionist Jens Søndergaard's paintings exhibited in the *Thisted Library*.

Thisted is inevitably associated with the great 19C novelist and poet Jens Peter Jacobsen (1847–85). Jacobsen's production was small, consisting of his poetry, two novels and half a dozen novellas or short stories. Yet both as a stylist and as a pioneering naturalist his influence on literature, not only in Denmark and Scandinavia as a whole, but outside Scandinavia (especially in Germany), was enormous in its day. His poem 'Gurresange', telling the story of King Valdemar and his mistress Tove, forms the text for Schönberg's 'Gurrelieder', while the English composer Delius, whose links with Scandinavia were legion, not only set some of his poems to music, but he also used part of the novel 'Niels Lyhne' for the action of his opera 'Fennimore and Gerda'. Jacobsen's birthplace in *Skolestræde* is now a scheduled monument. Jacobsen was buried in Thisted, and his grave is marked on the otherwise grassed-over old churchyard opposite the church.

Thisted was the birthplace of Chresten Kold (1816–70), the driving force in the Grundtvigian high school movement.—And it was also the site of the first co-operative store in Denmark, founded by Pastor H.C. Sonne in 1866, inspired by the 1844 store in Rochdale, England.

Modern Thisted has a fine marina, and this beautiful stretch of the Limfjord affords splendid opportunities for sailing and windsurfing. There is an open air stage in the Christiansgave park, with regular summer entertainments. As for shopping, restaurants and dancing, there are plenty of facilities.

EXCURSION FROM THISTED TO THE NORTH SEA (total distance 45km). Leave Thisted on the A26 N, turning left into the 557 after 4km. After a further 12km you reach *Klitmøller*, a small fishing village with excellent facilities for bathing, windsurfing and fishing. In the 18C it was a thriving small port, but other towns have long since overtaken it. It is well provided with cafés and restaurants as well as overnight accommodation.

You now have a very fascinating drive N, close to the sea and with the 4000 hectares of the magnificent **Hanstholm Wild Life Reserve** on your right. After 10km you arrive at **Hanstholm** (2600 inhab.; Tourist Information: Bytorvet).

Although the presence of a church from c 1200 indicates that Hanstholm has been here for a long time, it is essentially a modern port, mainly built since World War II. The fishing harbour was officially opened in 1967 and has since been extended to take larger ships: you can now sail from here to Norway or to the Faroe Islands. There was a great deal of controversy as to whether a harbour in such an exposed position and so far from the main centres could be justified, but Hanstholm's success has vindicated those who believed in the project. The coastal region here was very heavily fortified during World War II, and there are plentiful signs of this still, including areas still designated as dangerous. One of the biggest gun emplacements, at the end of *Molevej*, is now a *museum graphically illustrating the history of Hanstholm during World War II. A second museum at the S end of *Tårnvej* is centred on the old lighthouse (both museums open in summer).

You now take the A26 S towards Thisted. On your way there, however, it is possible to visit yet another interesting church. At (12km) *Nors*, where the lake is said to contain some of the cleanest bathing water in Denmark, you could turn left to (3km) *Hillerslev*, where there is one of the biggest and most unusual churches in the region, consisting of a Romanesque apse, chancel and nave and late medieval tower. The apse is supported by impressive pillars, and the stone altar also rests on a squat pillar. Like so many of the North and West Jutlandic churches, it reflects toughness together with its elegant lines, and has nothing of the light and gracefulness of the churches in Fyn and Sjælland. West Jutlandic churches are built to withstand the elements, and have the quiet determination which is said to be a characteristic of the people here.

From Hillerslev you can drive direct to (10km) Thisted.

23   Horsens to Fjerritslev

Total distance 168km. **Horsens**.—A52 to (47km) **Silkeborg**.—(34km) **Viborg**.—533 to (71km) **Løgstør**.—533, A29 to (15km) *Fjerritslev*.

From Horsens to Silkeborg you have the choice of two routes. The direct route (45km) is given first; see below for the more scenic alternative route.

DIRECT ROUTE FROM HORSENS TO SILKEBORG (total distance 45km). Leave Horsens (Rte 16) on the A52 in a NW direction, driving to (7km) Lund, where you should not fail to make a short detour straight away, turning left on the 185 to **Tamdrup** (1km). Here, standing so high that it was formerly used as a landmark by shipping in the Horsens Fjord, there is one of the oldest (mid 11C) and most remarkable churches in Denmark. It is too large to have been intended as a village church, and is believed to have been built by a king or some powerful nobleman. Among the interesting features are the murals dating from c 1150 visible over the chancel arch, among the oldest in the country. They have not been radically restored, and are consequently somewhat pale, but an examination in 1973 revealed that the gradual deterioration over the centuries has uncovered the actual drawings made by the artist when planning his work, and they can just be discerned under the paint. Other murals in the chancel are later, from c 1500.

The church, originally a basilica, has been altered and extended in later times, but there are still clear Romanesque sections to be seen. The granite font is late Romanesque, the altarpiece and pulpit early 17C. There is meanwhile another particularly interesting piece in this church, though it is only a copy of the original. This is an elegantly embossed copper antemensale depicting the story of the monk (later Bishop) Poppo who successfully underwent the ordeal by fire and thereby brought about the conversion of King Harald Bluetooth. The original from c 1200, which probably formed a reliquary, was of beaten gold, and is now housed in the National Museum in Copenhagen. This, too, indicates the royal or dynastic connections which the church is thought once to have had.

Close by and clearly visible stands *Tamdrup Bisgård*, a splendid half-timbered house from c 1784.

You now return to the A52 and drive N through beautiful wooded, undulating and increasingly lakeland countryside to (40km) **Silkeborg** (see below), possibly turning left after 18km along the 453 to *Bryrup* (5km), from where a vintage railway runs to the neighbouring village of Vrads (limited opening summer).

ALTERNATIVE ROUTE FROM HORSENS TO SILKEBORG (total distance 53km). Leave Horsens to the N and join the 461 after c 6km. 5km further on you will pass the mansion of *Urup* on your right. The history of Urup goes back to the 15C, but the present building is from the late 16C, and was radically redesigned c 1810. A further 3km brings you to Østbirk. It is the church here that is of interest. The nave is late 13C Romanesque, with a late Gothic transept and tower, and a 16C chancel. The present S chapel, containing five stone sarcophagi, is all that is left of the transept, the corresponding N wing having been demolished in 1851. Historically, this N chapel is interesting in that it once contained the tomb of the 16C naval hero Peder Skram, who owned the mansion of Urup which you have just passed. He now lies buried in the churchyard, where there is a memorial to him. The ornate carved altarpiece was brought to the church from a nearby monastery; it is late Gothic, from c 1480; the central panel represents God and Christ standing between the Virgin and a bishop saint. The insides of the side panels each contains eight carved figures representing four Apostles and four Saints, while there are paintings of the Passion on the outsides. The unusually large font is Romanesque and is decorated with carved figures of lions, dragons and human beings. The elegant auricular pulpit is late 16C, possibly the work of the master who carved the pulpit in Århus Cathedral, with which it has some similarity.

EXCURSION FROM ØSTBIRK TO DENMARK'S HIGHEST POINTS (total distance 18km). If you want to visit the 5 sq km of moraine plateau from the last Ice Age, which contains the highest points in Denmark, at Østbirk you should follow the 409 to (4km) Yding, turning right there towards (4km) Ejer. On this last stretch you will pass the high *Yding Skovhøj* (Yding Forest Hill) on your left, and in general the area here is where the highest points in Danmark are. At 171m *Møllehøj* ('Mill Hill') is just the highest, with *Ejer Bavnehøj* ('Ejer Beacon Hill') near Ejer a mere 170.95m. Nevertheless, Ejer Bavnehøj remains the more famous and is picked out from a distance by the tower built at the top. The floor at the top of this tower is 183m, and to those who climb the 60 steps leading to it, it offers a staggering view on a fine day.

A further 6km from Østbirk on the 461 brings you to Voervadsbro, where you should turn left on the 453 to *Sønder Vissing* (4km).

There is another interesting church here. Again it has a Romanesque chancel and nave with a Gothic tower (16C), and there are some late 15C fresco decorations on the chancel arch, and a mural depicting St. George and the Dragon.
More interesting, however, is the Romanesque gravestone standing at the gateway, and two runestones, one placed under the organ in the church, the other in the porch. That in the church, which was discovered as part of the stone wall around the churchyard in 1836, is very large and has clear links with the great runestones at Jelling (Rte 21) in so far as the inscription indicates a family relationship: 'Tove, daughter of Mistive, the wife of Harald the Good, son of Gorm, had these runes carved in memory of her mother.' The other, which was once used as a threshold stone at the entrance to the churchyard, reads: 'Toke made these runes in memory of his father Abe, a wise man.' This same Toke raised a stone with a similar inscription in Gunderup (Rte 17).

From Voervadsbro the 461 takes you N past *Vissingkloster*, the site of a 13C Benedictine convent, to (6km) the **Gudenå Museum** (open Jun–Aug). Standing on the actual site of a Stone Age settlement, the museum represents the largest collection in the country of Stone Age hunting and fishing implements (some 30,000 in all) relating to the region, the culture known as the Gudenå Culture. A further 2km brings you to **Gammel Rye**, which lies in outstandingly beautiful and varied hilly countryside, with sudden changes of view and surprising vistas. At one time it must have been an extremely isolated area, and probably for this reason Gammel Rye (or Rye, as it used to be called) became a religious centre and a place of pilgrimage in the Middle Ages. The present church is one indication of this. Originally dedicated to St. Severin, it consists of a nave and chancel in one, to which a modern porch has been added. Sizeable as it is, however, it represents only a small part of what was once a huge church on this site, closely associated with the pilgrimages to St. Severin's Well in the woods immediately W of Gammel Rye; the site, dry now, can still be seen. After the Reformation, the very large church, with its 52m-long nave and 33m-long transept, fell into disrepair, and it was reduced in size in the 17C. The oldest part of the extant building is from the early 15C. The impressive carved altarpiece is from 1630. Among other old remains in the church are some 15C gravestones from Øm Kloster (see below) and an early 16C crucifix.

A relic of the past of an entirely different kind is the local *Træsko-museum* (Clog Museum). The area has been known for its clog-making, and this museum has preserved both the tools and the styles of a bygone age (limited opening summer).

One site to be visited in this area is the ruined monastery of **Øm Kloster** (open Apr–Oct), standing on an isthmus between the Gudensø and Mossø lakes, 4km SE of Gammel Rye, and reached on a good minor road.

This Cistercian monastery was founded by French monks with an English abbot in 1172; it was dedicated to the Virgin and originally called *cara insula*. The community had gone to great lengths to find a place where it could be in peace, though according to a 13C history of the monastery that peace scarcely extended to relations between the Øm community and the Bishop of Århus, within whose jurisdiction Øm lay. The later history, in so far as it is known, seems to have been less tempestuous. Øm Kloster together with the school it ran, was even allowed to survive for a time after the Reformation, not being secularised until 1560 when the buildings were converted into a royal residence called Emborg.

The buildings were subsequently used as a source of materials for other purposes, including the building of Skanderborg Castle, but their foundations can still be seen in their entirety, the only Danish Cistercian monastery to be so well preserved. In addition, the canals bringing water to the monks have also survived.

A small museum has been built within the complex to exhibit finds made on the site: keys, chessmen, swords, surgical instruments from the hospital. There is also a valuable collection of medieval skeletons and bones. Just note how perfect the monks' teeth were—though the bones show signs of battle wounds, rheumatism and syphilis. About 1000 graves have been discovered and excavated, and some of them are on show to visitors.

A herb garden such as that used by the monks, and containing some 60 different species, was laid out in 1925. There were in all 14 monasteries and convents in this area, but Øm was by far the biggest of them. At one time it owned no fewer that 380 farms of various sizes.

Just W of Gammel Rye the elevated wooded ridge known as *Rye Nørreskov* (Rye North Forest) sweeps down to the shores of Julsø lake, and here you will find the famous ***Himmelbjerget**. To visit it you turn on to the 461 just N of Gammel Rye and simply drive to the top! You can, of course, reach the top on foot, and this is really the preferable alternative. Although not so high as Ejer Bavnehøj, Himmelbjerget stands out considerably more on the terrain; it actually looks like a (small) mountain.

A tower has been built at the top to commemorate King Frederik VII,

who granted Denmark its first Constitution in 1849, and it is surrounded by smaller memorials to other historical events. One of these
commemorates a meeting of the Danish people led by Steen Steensen
Blicher, who was not only a major writer, but also for a time politically
active, trying to impart a feeling of political awareness to his a-political
fellow countrymen. Another, the women's oak tree, is to mark the
granting of votes to women in Denmark in 1915. Over the decades,
many political meetings have been held at the top of Himmelbjerget,
and indeed, meetings of various kinds are still held there.

The view from the top is splendid, giving a panorama of the lakes
and forests all round; to the West Silkeborg can be seen, and to the E
Århus. Many is the poetic description of one of the most intriguing and
idyllic areas in Denmark. When visiting Silkeborg in 1853 Hans Christian Andersen described it as 'countryside which reminds you of the
abundant woodlands of the Black Forest or the grandiose isolation of
the Scottish heath'.

The 445 W and the A52 will easily take you from Gammel Rye to
(18km) Silkeborg (see below), if you so wish. However, if you do not
mind the longer distance (25km) we suggest you take the 445 E
instead and reach Silkeborg from the E, having driven anti-clockwise
around the lakes.

Your first stop in this case will be at (4km) *Ry* (Tourist Information:
Skanderborgvej 16), a modern but quite delightful town which sprang
up in the late 19C with the advent of the railway. Its tiny harbour caters
for the lake pleasure boats, and there are ample facilities for yachts
and the many canoeists who frequent the area. Here, too, there is a
freshwater museum, the *Færskvandsmuseum*, with an aquarium containing the fish native to the lakes, and exhibition cases illustrating the
flora, fauna and geology of the region (open summer).

From Ry you leave the 445 and take the unclassified road N towards
Låsby. In 3km you reach Tulstrup, where you come to a crossroads. If
you are interested in church architecture, and if Øm Kloster has whetted
your appetite, you ought really to go right here to Nørre Vissing (4km),
there turning right again on the 457 to *Veng* (3km).

Veng was the site of the monastery used by the Cistercians before they went to
Øm. Previously, Veng monastery had been in the hands of the Benedictines. They
had built a magnificent church here, and it still stands. It is the oldest monastery
church in Denmark, very big, tall, and unique in design. It is thought to date from
between 1100 and 1125. Not only is there an apse at the E end of the chancel,
but the transepts are also provided with apses to the E. In style it has many features
reminiscent of E English church architecture, and it is assumed that an English
builder must have been responsible for it.

Back in Nørre Vissing you follow the 457 n to (4km) Låsby, where you
join the A15 W to (8km) *Linå*, where there is yet another large church.
The apse, chancel and nave are Romanesque with later extensions.
Both the original remarkably elaborate stone entrances, each flanked
by three columns on either side, are extant, though the original S door
has been moved to form the W door. Inside, there is a brick-built
medieval altar, while the altarpiece is dated 1616. The carved font is
Romanesque, and the simple pulpit is from c 1630. The church was
thoroughly restored in 1966.

Before continuing to Silkeborg, you might like to savour this charming
wooded area by driving the 3km S along a minor road to *Svejbæk* on
the shore of the Julsø lake—and while there you ought to sample the
famous Svejbæk eels. Here, too, is the *Hotel og Restaurant Museum
Silkeborg*, a splendid collection illustrating the development of the

*The Tollund Man. The body of this man, who was
hanged c 220 BC, was found in a bog at Tollund and
is now exhibited in Silkeborg Museum.
Photo: Barry Hicks*

hotel and restaurant trade, housed in the old Hotel Ludvigslyst; one of
the attractions is the opportunity to sample the food and drink enjoyed
at the turn of the century.—There are minor roads from Svejbæk to
Silkeborg through Sejs. Alternatively, you can return to Linå, from
where it is a mere 8km on the A15 to Silkeborg.

Silkeborg (34,000 inhab.; Tourist Information: Torvet 9) is not an old
town. It was founded in 1844 by one Michael Drewsen, who that year
was allowed to establish a paper mill on the lakeside. There is still a
paper mill in Silkeborg, which otherwise is known for its teacher
training colleges and its schools. It was granted a charter as a market
town in 1900. There is no point in looking for very old houses in the
straight, intersecting streets, though there are said to be the ruins of
an old castle by the lakeside near the Viborgbro (Viborg Bridge).

This it not to say there is no charm to Silkeborg, but it is essentially
19C charm, concentrated on the main square, Torvet, and the adjacent
area. On the square an outsize chessboard is laid out on the pavement,
and at times in the summer tourists can try their skills on it.—There are
several sculptures by well-known artists adorning the pedestrian area,
and many of the buildings can boast of artistic ornamentation.—
Virtually in the centre of the town, too, there is the wooded *Odden*
(Headland), jutting out into the Langsø lake, where a large-scale
fountain is illuminated at night in the summer.

Two officially designated bathing areas are marked out in the Almind
Sø, c 1km S of the town centre. Here, as in all the other bathing areas
in the district, the water is very clean indeed.—N of Silkeborg lies the
Deer Park, *Dyrehaven*, where, in a World War II German bunker, you

will find a museum containing exhibits from the Occupation.—The fine **Silkeborg Museum**, in Hovedgårdsvej, contains one of the most famous of all Danish museum exhibits, the *Tollund Man.

The Tollund Man was discovered in a bog near Silkeborg in 1950; his head, with remarkably clear facial features, was almost entirely preserved; and his body was sufficiently intact for it to have been 'reconstructed', and there he now lies in the position in which he must have been when thrown into the bog some 2200 years ago. A second, rather less well-preserved body, that of the Elling Woman, is nearby, and the two are surrounded, on the 1st floor of the museum, by a reconstruction of an Iron Age village, with a comprehensive collection of weapons, tools and clothing, and figures clothed in reconstructions of Iron Age dress. There are drawings and models to illustrate the way of life in the Iron Age and to describe the process of reconstructing the body of the Tollund Man, listing other finds of a similar nature in Danish bogs. Apart from this central feature, the museum contains a collection of local archaeological and historical exhibits.

Silkeborg's other major museum is the art gallery, **Silkeborg Kunstmuseum**, in Gudenåvej. If the Silkeborg Museum is centred on the Tollund Man, this revolves around a more modern, but scarcely less famous figure, the modernist painter Asger Jorn, who was born in Silkeborg in 1914. The gallery contains over 100 of Jorn's paintings, in addition to ceramics and tapestries. On top of that, it possesses some 5000 works by 156 other important artists, some going back to the 17C, but mainly from the 20C, all presented to the gallery by Jorn himself. In addition there are many other items acquired independently. All this has established Silkeborg Kunstmuseum, a purpose-built gallery from 1982, as a major Danish art gallery, not to be missed by anyone interested in the visual arts.

Silkeborg is very much associated with its beautiful lakeland, and a trip on the lakes should not be missed. Combine your stay here with a day trip to Himmel-bjerget on the old paddle steamer *Hjejlen*, which was launched as long ago as 1861 by Frederik VII and is still going strong—an institution in its own right.

From Silkeborg, you take the A52 N for 11km, where you will find a minor road W to *Vinderslev* (1.5km). Here there is a quite elaborate church with a Romanesque chancel and nave, and a late Gothic tower at the W. Built of ashlars, it is richly decorated. In particular it has two ornate (but bricked up) Romanesque portals in the N and S. The N portal is flanked by three columns on either side, with a figure variously thought to be Christ or St. Francis in the tympanum; that in the S has two columns on either side and figures of a lion and an eagle in the tympanum. The tower is of later date, but this, too, contains Romanesque reliefs of lions. The vaulting and walls are decorated with late 13C frescoes, the most important work of the so-called Vinderslev Master. They portray the Day of Judgement, Heaven, Hell, devils and figures both realistic and fantastic, including Death carrying a scythe, a woman playing cards, a man passing water, and a flock of geese hanging a fox. They were at one time whitewashed over. Some other, 16C, frescoes in the chancel are less drastic and have never been covered.—In the churchyard there are two small Romanesque granite crosses.

In Vinderslev, too, there is the 15C Vinderslevgård manor house, probably extensively rebuilt at a later date. According to legend it is the owner of this house, Karen Krabbe, who is seen playing cards in the church mural. The stake was her house. She lost.

5km further N you come to the Kjellerup-Torning crossroads. If you are interested in the author Steen Steensen Blicher, you should turn left here and drive to *Torning* (7km).

Blicher was the pastor in Torning from 1819 to 1825, and it is fitting that the old
half-timbered parsonage where he wrote his most famous novel, 'The Diary of a
Parish Clerk', should now be a *museum dedicated to a great writer who has
been so closely associated with this part of Jutland. This fittingly modest museum
gives an impression of life in the region in Blicher's day and earlier, as well as a
collection of Blicher memorabilia and an array of stuffed birds and animals from
the area. (Blicher was a great hunter.) The museum also houses the Kjellerup
local history archives (open summer; limited opening winter).

There are Blicher relics, too, in the church and the churchyard. The pulpit is
that from which he delivered his sermons, and his name figures among the list
of Torning pastors. Several of the models for Blicher's characters are buried in the
churchyard, and in particular one notices Mads Doss, the lad who looked after
the sheep on the moors. One of the exhibits in the museum is thought to be his
snaps bottle. There is a memorial to Blicher himself just outside the churchyard.

From Torning you can take the A13 straight to (18km) **Viborg** (Rte 20).
However, there are more places associated with Blicher in the area,
and if you want to see them, we suggest you rejoin the A26 just outside
Kjellerup.

4km N of the Kjellerup-Torning crossroads there is another crossroads
with *Sjørslev* (1.5km) signposted to the right. Here you will find
another church with Blicher associations. It used to be owned by one
Steen de Steensen, the uncle of Steen Steensen Blicher. The Steensen
family's coat of arms is painted on the ceiling, and the family tomb is
in a mound to the NW of the church. The Romanesque font is one of
the most elaborately carved fonts in Denmark, and there is an Arab
style mausoleum in the churchyard.

Return to the A52, cross it and drive 1km further to the manor house
of *Aunsbjerg*, once the home of Steen de Steensen, and a place where
the young Blicher spent much of his childhood. It is also the setting for
some of Blicher's best-known stories. The manor goes far back in
history, to 1340, but the present building stems from the mid 16C,
though it was largely rebuilt in 1872 and 1917.

A further 1km brings you to the large farmstead of *Liselund*, and
1km further on to *Vium*, where Blicher was born in 1782. His father
was pastor here, and Blicher was presumably baptised in the Romanesque font which is still in use in the church. The frescoes, restored in
1968, are from the 16C and 17C. The building in which Blicher was
born no longer exists, but there is a memorial to him in the wall of the
present parsonage.

From Vium you take a minor road NW, crossing the A13 to (4km)
Lysgård Museum, once the first stopping place on the Military Road
(Rte 21) on the way S from Viborg. You will now find a sign on a house
near the church, saying 'Æ Bindstouw' (The Knitting Room), suggesting that this house is the setting for Blicher's story of that name. In
point of fact the house in which he set his story has been pulled down,
though the foundations are genuine enough. At all events, the present
building still re-creates the wretched surroundings of Blicher's story
(open summer).

Return now to the A13, turn left and drive through the delightful and
varied *Dollerup Bakker* (Dollerup Hills) to (12km) **Viborg** (Rte 20)—a
town not to be missed.

To leave Viborg you join the 533 N. In 7km, after driving through
undulating, partly wooded countryside, you cross the low-lying
Skalsådal (Skals River Valley). The sheer breadth of the valley here is
an indication of the size of Skals Å river in the Ice Age, when it could

be compared with the major European rivers. Now little more than a stream, it enters the Hjarbæk Fjord, a branch of the Limfjord, about 1km to your left.

The road by-passes Skals village, keeping to low ground and taking you in a further 4km across the Simested Å river, which also flows into the fjord at this point. Just beyond the river, to your right, lies Låstrup.

Turn left here just to have a look at *Lynderupgård* (3km), a magnificent half-timbered manor house mainly from 1556, standing on a square mound and partly hidden by trees. There is a fountain in the shape of four heads in the courtyard, believed to be the oldest fountain in Denmark. Lynderupgård is not open to the public, but the sight of it is well worth the short drive from the main road.

The 533 now continues N to (15km) *Gedsted*. The Romanesque church here dates back to c 1150 and retains many of its original features. Both the N and S portals can be seen, though the S door has been walled up. There are late Gothic frescoes including, in the N chapel, one depicting the martyrdom of St. Erasmus. The Romanesque altar contains a reliquary with a relic of the 11,000 virgins. The carillon from 1757 plays every day at noon.

From Gedsted you can drive E along the 561 to **Ålestrup** (10km), where you will find the delightful Jutland Rose Gardens (*Den jydske Rosenpark*) on sloping ground beside the Simested Å river. There is a display of some 15,000 roses of 200 different species as well as an art exhibition in the pavilion (open Jun–Sept).— In addition, in Ålestrup you will find the only *Bicycle Museum* in Scandinavia, containing about 100 bicycles ranging from the very oldest to the near-contemporary. This collection is supplemented with an assortment of sewing machines and old radio receivers (open May–Nov).—Ålestrup lies virtually on two rivers and provides excellent fishing facilities.

Now follow the 533 N for 4km to the crossing with the 187, where you turn left and follow the 187 SW to (5km) *Hvalpsund*. Here you will find delightful views across the fjord, though Hvalpsund itself has little to offer.

In Hvalpsund, however, you should turn S on a minor road to **Hessel** (2km), where you will find a most interesting and very special agricultural museum (Hessel Landbrugsmuseum) in a large old farm, the last completely thatched major farm in Denmark—some 3000 sq m of thatch altogether.

The history of Hessel certainly goes back to the 14C, and the present buildings date largely from the 17C and early 18C. Not only is an extensive collection of old implements and machinery housed in the outbuildings, while several rooms demonstrate the conditions under which farmworkers once lived and worked, but the present intention is to run the entire farm as a 'museum project', cultivating the land with reproduction old implements and according to old methods, including the rotation method. It is hoped in this way to keep in being both plants and animals which would otherwise not survive modern methods. Ploughing is done by horses, not tractors. On the first Sunday in July there is what is called a 'horse day', when many of these old implements are demonstrated, and there are other days during the summer when an effort is made to recapture the manner of life of a bygone age.

The main building exhibits rural dress and crafts, and there is plenty of authentic furniture. There is usually a textile exhibition in the summer months (open summer).

From Hvalpsund you drive 6km NW to **Fovlum Church**, either direct along a minor road or by returning to the 533 and turning left there.

Fovlum church is unique—Romanesque almost entirely as when built. In the view of the mid-20C novelist Martin A. Hansen: 'Surely no nobler church has ever been built in this country.' The porch is 19C, and the S door has been walled up, but the remainder is unspoiled Romanesque demonstrating beautiful workmanship. The granite ashlars are splendidly hewn, and the columns at the two portals are beautifully fashioned. The original Romanesque rounded arches are still in place over the apse and the chancel, and there are original stone sculptures. You will have seen many originally Romanesque Danish churches which have been adapted or extended in the Gothic style. Here is one which has maintained its original character. A must.

From Fovlum you drive N on the 533 to (7km) *Strandby*. However, those particularly interested in literature might like to take the slightly longer route via Farsø, making the driving distance 14km instead.

To reach *Farsø* (Tourist Information: Søndergade 48) you leave Fovlum, seeking the 187, driving in all c 6km N.

Farsø was the birthplace of the authors Johannes V. Jensen (1873–1950) and Thit Jensen (1876–1957). Thit Jensen is known as a novelist, feminist and spiritualist; her more famous brother as a poet, essayist, novelist and short-story writer. He is remembered, too, as one of the great linguistic innovators of 20C Danish literature. He was awarded the Nobel Prize for Literature in 1944, and is particularly associated with stories centred on his native region of Himmerland, which in his childhood was one of the most backward and outlying parts of Denmark—uncultivated moorland with poor communications with the outside world. Here, as the son of the local vet, he came into contact with many of the more colourful figures of the region and has immortalised them in his stories. Thit Jensen used Himmerland as the setting for her large-scale historical novels.

  The modest house in which Johannes V. Jensen was born, Søndergade 48, is now the local Tourist Information Centre and houses a small museum dedicated to him and his sister. She has her own small museum at Torvet 1, containing her own furniture and her letters and notes. She is buried in the churchyard here, as is her father.—Johannes V. Jensen felt more akin to pagan Denmark, and it is fitting that a huge memorial stone, inscribed with one of his verses, has been placed close to a prehistoric burial mound just S of the village.

From Farsø you take a minor road left immediately N of the village to (8km) Strandby.

There is a large, well-preserved Romanesque church with a Renaissance altarpiece standing on high ground in *Strandby*, but the main interest must be centred on the *Strandby Museum*, some 2km N of the village. This contains a large collection of archaeological remains found in the area, and closely associated with the so-called Ertebølle Culture (open summer, on application).

Ertebølle itself can be reached by turning left off the 533 2km N of Strandby. Just S of the village is the site of a Stone Age settlement and its huge kitchen midden dating from 4600–4000 BC. Originally measuring 140m x 20m x 2m, this is thought to contain the remains of 20 million oysters. However, there are the remains of other fish, bones of many different animals, weapons and household implements. The skeleton of a seated human figure has also been found there, and there are sufficient individual human bones here to suggest cannibalism.

  When the kitchen midden was established, Ertebølle was on the coast; subsequently the sea rose and flooded it, removing most signs of the actual settlement; then the land rose again and the water receded, so there is now a short distance from Ertebølle to the coast.—There is relatively little for the layman to see on the actual site, but there is an informative small museum (open summer).

As you proceed N from Strandby, you drive through several tree plantations, some of them, like *Trend Skov*, of considerable size. Trend Skov belongs partly to the Queen, who owns a hunting lodge here (not visible from the road).

9km N of Strandby, still on the 533, you reach **Vitskøl Kloster**. This is the ruins of one of the largest of Denmark's medieval religious houses, a Cistercian monastery founded in 1158 by King Valdemar I as a thanks offering for having won the battle of Grathe Hede. Vitskøl was intended to become the biggest monastery in Scandinavia, and at one time it owned no fewer than 400 farms. The 50m x 40m church, of which a considerable portion has survived, is thought by some to have been as splendid as that in the mother foundation of Cîteaux, but it was already in a state of disrepair by the Reformation, and like many other major buildings it was used as a quarry. Vitskøl was allowed to continue after the Reformation, but by 1563 it secularised, and the school attached to it was closed (the ruins are open to visitors).—The original W wing forms the present main building, but is now used as a detention centre and is not open to the public.

The adjoining *gardens are particularly interesting. They comprise a copy of the monastery garden in St. Gallen with the 16 herbs ordained for each monastery, an apothecary's garden with a systematic arrangement of the herbs according to which part of the body they were intended to heal, a general herb garden, a garden with herbs suitable for making *snaps* and, now, a scented garden for the blind.

From Vitskøl the road continues N to (3km) *Ranum* with a large church built in 1909. The two massive towers were added in 1931. The outstanding feature of this church is the huge fresco on the E wall of the chancel, painted in 1921 by Niels Larsen-Stevns, and depicting the Second Coming, with Christ descending through the clouds over Ranum.—Niels Larsen-Stevns, who played a part in the Viborg Cathedral frescoes, is one of the best large-scale artists in 20C Denmark, and this is considered to be one of his finest works.

EXCURSION FROM RANUM TO THE LIVØ ISLAND. Turn left off the main road in Ranum, drive the 3km to Rønbjerg and there take a ferry to the tiny Limfjord island of **Livø**. The trip takes 20 minutes, and the ferry sails regularly during the summer months. You cannot take your car, and neither can you take a dog with you.

There is a camp site on Livø, and other kinds of overnight accommodation are also available (reservations on 98 67 63 62). A cafeteria and grocer's shop provide for your other needs. The island, which once belonged to Vitskøl Monastery, is rich in wild life (there is a seal sanctuary), and is of particular interest to geologists. A 6.3km route for walking around the island is clearly marked, and maps are available indicating the most interesting areas.

The direct road from Ranum leads you straight to (9km) Løgstør. At 5km you should however make a quick visit to *Lendrup Strand* beach (3km). Much of the coastline here, dotted with summer cottages, is suitable for bathing, but Lendrup Strand is one of the best stretches. Here, too, you will find the S end of the 4km-long *Frederik VII's Kanal*, which extends all the way to Løgstør and was constructed in the 1850s to avoid the constant difficulties of sailing out from Løgstør, caused by the sandbanks in Løgstør Shallows. Better channels have now been dug, and the canal, no longer needed, was closed off in 1913. It remains, however, as a relic of past initiative, and the old tow-paths provide a much-loved walk along the coast in delightful wooded surroundings.

Løgstør (4300 inhab.; Tourist Information: Sønderport 2A) has a history going back to the 11C, when it was connected with the Viking fortress of Aggersborg (see below). By 1514 it was a fishing village engaged in the then lucrative herring fishery. When the herring failed, Løgstør attempted to engage in the corn trade, but was stopped owing to protests from big brother Ålborg. It suffered two major fires in the mid 18C. In the 19C Løgstør benefited from improved conditions for agriculture and from the improvement in communications which led to the establishment of industrial enterprises. The Frederik VII Canal also contributed to its increasing prosperity.

Løgstør boasts of no imposing architecture, not even an old church (the present church with its lofty spire was consecrated in 1893), but situated at the foot of a gentle slope it is a delightful small town, full of atmosphere, and characterised by narrow streets, fishermen's houses and, inevitably, the harbour area stretching over 2km until it merges with the Frederik VII Canal. Here, the former canal manager's house, whitewashed and with corbie step gables, now forms the *Limfjord Museum* devoted to the fishing and shipping associated with the area. It contains old implements, models, drawings and photographs illustrating the old way of life, and there is a collection of restored fishing vessels (open summer). The canal is crossed by the original swing bridge, and there are both a marina and excellent facilities for fishing.

On the hill leading down to the town, Løgstør Bakke, stands the house in which Johan Skjoldborg, the novelist and poet who championed the cause of the Danish smallholders at the end of the 19C, lived from 1917 to his death in 1936. The house was given to Skjoldborg by the smallholders in recognition of his work on their behalf.

5km N of Løgstør the 533 joins the A29 and takes you to the *Aggersund Bridge* spanning the narrows which once provided Løgstør with much of its ferrying income. It is an elegant 210m-long structure dating from 1942; the central part can be raised to allow the passage of ships.

Immediately beyond the bridge you can turn left to drive down to the (1km) *Aggersborg* site. This was the largest of the four Danish viking fortresses, and probably the biggest in all Scandinavia, three times the size of the far better preserved Trelleborg in Sjælland. Unfortunately for us, however, it was destroyed in the rebellion against Knud II in 1086, and there is little for the layman to see apart from a small section of the ramparts. The site is just NE of the *Aggersborggård* farm, and excavations have shown that the fortress had a diameter of 285m, containing in all twelve groups of four halls. The whole complex was surrounded by a rampart with four entrances. In addition there was a large Viking village just outside, and many archaeological finds have been made here.

Aggersborggård farm itself is scheduled, a beautiful half-timbered buiding, with a S wing dating back to 1758. It stands on the site of a castle built by Knud II at the end of the 11C.

The novelist Jakob Knudsen, whose father was pastor in the nearby church from 1864, spent part of his childhood in Aggersborg. There is a memorial to him outside the parsonage, where there is also a plan showing what the whole complex is thought once to have looked like.

Return now to the A29 and drive straight to (9km) *Fjerritslev* (Rte 19).

24   Fjerritslev to Copenhagen

Total distance 217km plus ferry. A29 to (65km) **Hobro** (Rte 20).—E45 to (27km) **Randers** (Rte 17).—A16 to (55km) **Grenå.**—(Ferry Grenå–Hundested 2hr 15min).—A16 to (13km) **Frederiksværk.**—211 to (18km) **Frederikssund.**—207 to (7km) *Slangerup.*—A6, 211 to (42km) **Copenhagen** (Rtes 3, 4).

From *Fjerritslev* (Rte 19) the route goes S along the A29, across (9km) the Aggersund bridge (Rte 23), and into *Himmerland*, as this area is called. A further 7km brings you to *Skarp Salling*, where there is an unexpectedly large and splendid •church from c 1150.

Why this large-scale basilica should have been built in this place is a mystery. It is far too big for an ordinary village church, and yet there is nothing to indicate that it has had connections with any powerful figure of the realm. One legend has it that it is a thanks offering from three sisters who were saved from drowning. The entire church was restored at the end of the 19C, but it is thought to retain much of its original character, and certainly it has always been of this size. The nave and aisles all end in apses, while a notable feature is the massive arcading both between the nave and aisles and at the W end of the nave. This church is a paradise for students of perspective. The main apse is believed once to have had windows, but is now limited to a single one, while the outside is decorated with blind arcading. The stonework presents several examples of sculptured heads, lions, dragons and geometrical designs. Among the decorations on the Romanesque font there is, unusually, a sculpted child's hand holding a cross. There are two Romanesque gravestones in the churchyard.

Continue further along the A29 to (21km) *Års* (6300 inhab.; Tourist Information: Himmerlandsgade 103), a lively small town, which lies at the centre of a very beautiful and varied part of Denmark, ideal for walkers, cyclists and anglers, and well equipped to cater for tourists.

Års is proud to recall that the Cimbrians probably originated in this area. They were a prehistoric tribe that, probably because of climatic changes and resultant difficult conditions at home, moved S and ravaged much of southern Europe 2000 years ago. *Cim*brian and *Him*merland are thought to be the same word.

Like many other Danish towns, Års has installed works of art in its streets and public buildings. There are sculptures by Per Kirkeby, Knud Nellemose, Jørgen Haugen Sørensen and Yan fra Vendsyssel, and the local grammar school has a large oil painting by Per Kirkeby and a ceramic frieze by Poul Gernes. The *Himmerlands Kunstmuseum*, at Søndergade 44, contains a collection of paintings and watercolours by Jens Nielsen. At the same address you will find the *Vesthimmerlands Museum*, with the Gundestrup Cauldron replica (see below) as its main attraction, but also containing many local archaeological finds as well as items of more recent local history.

There is certainly plenty of evidence of early activity around Års. Several preserved bodies—murdered, sacrificed or executed—have been found in the marshes, while the Roman historian Tacitus has given a graphic description of life here—not always exactly a comfortable experience, if one is to judge by his account. A dozen or so Iron Age settlements are known in the area of Års, and they have yielded large numbers of archaeological finds.

In the marsh near *Gundestrup* c 3km E of Års, known as **Rævemosen** (i.e. Fox Marsh, so called because of the many foxes that used to live here), one of the great archaeological finds was made in 1891. A farmer digging peat came across what has now become known as the Gundestrup Cauldron, a superbly ornamented silver cauldron 72cm in diameter, 43cm high and weighing 8kg, decorated with a figure of the Celtic god Cernunnos, lines of soldiers on foot and on horseback, bullfights and, on the base, the figure of a bull. It is obviously not local work, and must have been brought to the area as war booty. What it was originally intended for is not certain—possibly as a receptacle for sacrificial blood either from bulls or humans. The original, broken in such a way as to suggest that it was itself sunk in the marsh as a sacrifice, is now in the National Museum in Copenhagen, but an exact replica is on view in the *Vesthimmerlands Museum* in Års. The place where the cauldron was found is marked by a boulder on which there is a deliberately simple, unadorned but subtle inscription by Johannes V Jensen: 'Her fandtes Gundestrupkarret'—'The Gundestrup Cauldron was (or: was found) here'.

There is also evidence in the area of much later settlements, not least the many burial mounds dotted around the landscape, some of them of considerable size. There are also several runestones, one of the largest being in the churchyard in Års. It stands on its own at the entrance to the church, but it is believed that it was once incorporated into a larger complex consisting of two mounds and a single-stone monument, all of which have now vanished. There are inscriptions on two of its surfaces; that on the front is quite straightforward: 'Asser raised this stone here in memory of his master Valtoke.' For that on the back more than one interpretation has been suggested—either: 'The stone shall long stand here, it shall avenge Valtoke', or 'The stone shall long stand here denoting Valtoke's cairn.'

Approximately 3km S of Års lies **Borremose**, the largest of the Iron Age settlements, possibly once a fortress rather than a village. Discovered in 1929, it is believed to date back to c 200 BC and thus to be the oldest fortified settlement in Denmark. The couple of dozen houses there were clearly surrounded by a double moat and rampart. They have been excavated, and the outlines of some of them, all lying E–W and with a fireplace in the W, are now visible.—There is a car park close to the A29, and there you will find a plan of the site.

On your way S from Borremose to (23km) Hobro (Rte 20), you should perhaps pause in **Stenild** to visit the church, which contains a large and splendidly carved Romanesque font.—Even if you decide to by-pass Hobro town itself, the archaeological site of nearby **Fyrkat** (also Rte 20) should tempt you to spend a little extra time in the region, which is really very attractive.

From Hobro the route continues on the E45 to (27km) Randers. This stretch is described, though in the reverse direction, in Rte 17, mentioning *Handest* with its vintage railway, and **Råsted Church** which you must visit to see its outstanding frescoes.

Having passed Råsted you will have to decide whether to visit the old town of **Randers** (Rte 17) or to by-pass it. If you opt for a visit, you must leave the E45 3km S of Råsted to join the 180—if not, you stay on the E45 as far as Exit 41, where you take the A16/A21 E. You are actually circling the town, so you have to cross several intersecting radial roads before you really feel out of the built-up area.

16km from Randers centre you come to *Fausing* where those interested in fonts should stop to visit the *church in which there is a most unusual one from c 1300, made of metal and supported by three male figures thought to represent the rivers of Paradise.

From Fausing there is a choice of no fewer than three routes to **Grenå** and the ferry. The direct route (total distance 39km via the A16), taking you through mid Djursland, is described first; the two alternative routes—exploring North Djursland, and S of the main route—are detailed below.

DIRECT ROUTE FROM FAUSING TO GRENÅ (total distance 39km). 3km beyond Fausing you come to *Gammel Estrup, one of the finest of Denmark's great houses. Standing in a partly wooded area, the present main building with its 2–3m-thick walls is from the 15C, though the history of Gammel Estrup can be traced back to c 1350. Since 1930

Gammel Estrup has housed the *Jutland Manor House Museum*, and contains a comprehensive collection of furniture and tapestries, much of it comprising the original furnishings in the house, and reflecting changing fashions over the centuries. In addition there is a chapel and, beneath the house, an alchemist's cellar. Each year in June the Randers City Orchestra gives a concert in the Great Hall. The magnificent formal gardens with their lime tree avenues, canals and orangery are open for you to walk in, and there is a cafeteria in the old stable.

The farm buildings have been turned into the *Danish Agricultural Museum** with a vast collection of 25,000 exhibits relating to the history of agriculture. A blacksmith is there working on his anvil, and children wanting to work off their energy by threshing with a flail in the old-fashioned manner have a unique opportunity.

The author Henrik Pontoppidan, who in 1885 had referred to Gammel Estrup as the 'pearl of Danish manor houses', used it as the setting for the mansion of Favsingholm in his third major novel, 'The Realm of the Dead'.

From Gammel Estrup it is only 2km along the A16 to *Auning*, where Jørgen Skeel, one of the owners of Gammel Estrup, was buried in 1695, and where in the church he is commemorated by a huge baroque marble monument by Thomas Quellinus. The bombastic sarcophagus, surmounted by a reclining figure of Skeel, stands before trumpet-blowing cherubs and heroic figures covering the entire rear wall of the sepulchral chapel. In addition to Jørgen Skeel's sarcophagus, the chapel contains 14 further sarcophagi. In complete contrast there are some frescoes from 1562.

The A16 continues direct E, first through undulating wooded terrain, which gradually gives way to moorland. At 10km you can turn right and drive 1km S to the large-scale *Djurs Sommerland* pleasure gardens. Much of the area is given over to water, offering rowing and canoeing opportunities, or a sail on a timber raft. There are also facilities for shooting, pony riding, go-carting, trampolining and countless other amusements. And there is a Science Centre in the complex. Once you have paid your admission, all activities are free.

A further 5km brings you to *Ramten*. Here you might make a brief DETOUR and drive S on a minor road to *Tøstrup* (3km), where a wealth of frescoes from 1582 was uncovered in 1984–86 during the restoration of the Romanesque church.

Back on the main road, in *Ørum*, 3km E of Ramten, there is a church in which the centre panel of the altarpiece contains a well-known painting by a major 19C Danish artist, Constantin Hansen, of the Women at the Grave.

From Ørum it is a further 16km to Grenå (see below).

ALTERNATIVE ROUTE FROM FAUSING TO GRENÅ—THE NORTH DJURS-LAND ROUTE (total distance 49km). The route takes you through some interesting villages and introduces you to the work of a notable 12C artist.

Turn left off the main road at *Fausing* and drive on the 547 to (4km) Allingåbro, there turning left on to the 531 to *Ørsted* (4km), where the imposing *church glories in some particularly fine stone carvings, including a chancel arch decorated with figures of Christ and the four Evangelists. It is the work of Horder, the outstanding 12C craftsman of Djursland, who is also responsible for the very elaborate decorations around the doorways.

Back in *Allingåbro* you will, in *Vejlby Church*, find more work by this
Master. Here again pride of place goes to the stone portals.

4km E of Allingåbro a DETOUR can be made S to *Gjesing* (5km), where
the name of the otherwise anonymous Master Horder was established
on the basis of a gravestone. Now in the National Museum, this 'Gjesing
Stone' bears the inscription 'Horderus', presumably the signature of
the artist himself.

E of Gjesing village you will find the manor house of *Løvenholm*, now used as a
residential college. The E wing of this forbidding house is the original main
building from 1576, while the S wing, built in the same style, is from 1642–43.
The NE tower is from the original building, but that on the SE corner is again a
later addition, from 1643. After falling into disrepair, the house was restored in
1783 and given a splendid new interior. A further restoration was undertaken in
1901. Løvenholm, which has retained its original appearance almost unaltered,
is approached from the N across an embankment and bridge and along an avenue
of lime trees planted in the 18C. The park is open to the public.

Return to the 547 and continue to (2km) *Vivild*, from where there is the
chance to see two more manor houses—from the outside. You can
leave the 547 and drive N to catch a glimpse of *Julianeholm* (1km) and
Hevringholm (2.5km further on), continuing perhaps to *Hevringholm
Strand* (Hevringholm Beach) (1km), to experience some splendid
sandy beaches and a typical Danish weekend cottage area.

Instead of now following the 547 road direct to (9km) *Fjellerup*, you
may like to experience the beautiful countryside around here a little
more by leaving Vivild E on the old road, past the church and Vivild
Huse towards Tustrup. After about 4km you come to a car park and a
signpost on your right directing you to an impressive Stone Age burial
ground containing a stone circle, three long barrows, a dolmen chamber, a passage grave with a 10m-long chamber, the foundations of a
Stone Age house (probably a place of worship) and 16 burial mounds.
From Tustrup you then continue to (5km) *Fjellerup*.

From Fjellerup you follow the 547 to (9km) *Glesborg*, where there is
a Romanesque church with 16C frescoes depicting Abraham prepar-
ing to sacrifice Isaac. The Renaissance altarpiece and pulpit are from
1618, the gifts of Jørgen Kaas, the owner of the mansion of Mejlgård
5km NW. *Bønnerup Strand*, 7km N, is another of the splendid beaches
in this part of the country.

The route now continues to (3km) *Kastbjerg*, where the rather
unusual Romanesque/Gothic church has buttressed walls. It was
severely damaged by lightning in 1950 and restored in the 1960s by
the architects Johannes and Inger Exner. The untraditional altarpiece,
or altar *arrangement*, by Poul Winther, is from 1975.

This area is dotted with several more churches of interest. Leave
Kastbjerg on a minor road NE to (4km) *Rimsø*. Here Master Horder has
produced yet another impressive surround to the walled-up N doorway of the *church; a column on either side with characteristic cable
ornamentation, flanked by four figures with haloes; those on the left
are clearly Christ and Mary, both seated. The tympanum represents a
carved lion. Inside the porch there is another carved stone, a corbel
representing six seated figures in arcading, again with cable
ornamentation. There is a runestone close to the church.

Nor is the church the only sight worth seeing here: the *parsonage,
from 1593, is a beautiful old building, thought to be the oldest parsonage extant in Denmark.

A minor road NE from Rimsø takes you to (2.5km) *Sostrup*, a large
manor house built between 1599 and 1606. In 1960 it was sold to the
Cistercian Order, who now use the main building partly as a convent

and retreat centre, and partly as holiday accommodation. There are holiday flats in the old stable buildings, a restaurant in the house and a modern chapel in one of the outbuildings. Note the magnificent main doorway from 1620.

Sostrup lies in the parish of *Gjerrild*, and you should drive the further 500m to see the village, which can boast of numerous half-timbered houses.

In *Sostrup Church* (in Gjerrild) there are some particularly interesting frescoes by the Brarup Master from c 1500, one depicting a horde of devils storming Heaven, and being repulsed by the Divine Hosts. In the vaulting in the nave other frescoes represent the Creation, including a merman and mermaid(!), and the Fall, after which we see Eve spinning and Adam ploughing. From a purely historical point of view this is of special interest, providing a picture of a very early wheel plough.

A road will now take you S through Veggerslev to (5km) Thorsø. Here you should turn left to *Voldby* (1.5km), again to see a church with some fine Gothic frescoes from the end of the 15C, discovered under whitewash in 1891. The most unusual picture here is of a huge man-of-war, filled with soldiers and flying the Danish flag. Others portray grotesque figures, some of which border on the obscene.

From Thorsø it is 7km to Grenå (see below).

ALTERNATIVE ROUTE FROM FAUSING TO GRENÅ THE SOUTHERN ROUTE (total distance 46km). Leave Fausing on the A16 E, passing *Gammel Estrup (see above). 7km ahead, just past Auning, you turn right towards (5km) *Pindstrup*. There is a modern church here, from 1969, with a large crucifix over the altar by the important modern sculptor Robert Jacobsen.

Continue through wooded, often steeply undulating terrain to the hamlet of (4km) **Marie Magdalene**, so called after the sizeable church built here between 1425 and 1458.

Made of red brick, with a whitewashed porch, it is one of Denmark's best-known churches. Frescoes by the Vinderslev Master were uncovered in the apse, chancel and nave in 1904, and these have since been restored: the Day of Judgement on the vaulting of the apse, intertwined plants in the vaulting of the chancel, more plants and geometrical patterns in the vaulting of the nave—together with an immodest woman receiving her just deserts. A devil is applying a firebrand to her naked posterior, and the flames are issuing from her mouth. When first discovered earlier this century, this was thought to be unsuitable for a church, and it was covered over again. A later generation thought differently. The ornate pulpit (provided with an hourglass!) and canopy are baroque, from c 1650, and the altarpiece is splendid rococo work from 1757.

A peculiar feature of the church is the presence of two rowan trees growing out of the mortar of the porch. Legend has it that they have been there since the porch was built; they are scarcely as old as that, though at least one of them is thought to have been there for 250–300 years. There are many local superstitions attached to these trees, as, being without contact with the earth, they are immune from evil. Consequently, wood from them has been used to provide protection from sickness and evil—and the trees still survive.

1km further brings you to the village of Ryomgård, where you will find the *Djursland Railway Museum*, exhibiting uniforms, photographs and equipment from the age of steam trains, together with a large model railway system (open Easter–Oct).

The landscape here begins to show signs of the huge *Kolindsund*, once open to the sea, then, due to land movement, an inland lake, and finally drained at the end of the 19C to provide arable land. The site of the 17C manor house of Gammel Ryomgård on your right was in fact once a headland jutting out into Kolindsund.

5km E of Ryomgård, just before Kolind, you turn left towards Grenå, to (9km) Fannerup, where you turn right to (2km) Fævejle. Here you turn left once more, driving through Allelev to (4km) Vejlby, the setting for the most famous miscarriage of justice in Denmark.

In the 17C there lived in Vejlby a pastor by the name of Søren Quist, who is thought to have been responsible for the renovation of the altarpiece, and whose son's initials are to be found on the back of it. In 1625 Søren Quist was found guilty of murdering his farmhand, and he was executed the following year. His son, also pastor in Vejlby, had the case re-examined, and it emerged that two of the witnesses had committed perjury—for which they were in turn executed in 1634. The case was never fully cleared up, however, and the rumour later arose that it was actually Søren Quist's wife who was the culprit.—Søren Quist is the main character in one of Steen Steensen Blicher's best and most moving stories, 'The Pastor of Vejlby'.

Vejlby can boast of a beautiful 18C farm, the Ladefoged Farm. It was used as the setting for the first film on Søren Quist, made in 1920, and has in recent years been completely restored. During the process a well-preserved Iron Age grave was found in the grounds.

The road now leads to (3km) Ålsø, where there is a stone in the church porch said to be from the grave of Søren Quist, who was buried here in 1626. 3km E of Ålsø, at the end of an idyllic minor road, on a mound in a lake, stands the mansion of Katholm, with a principal wing built between 1588 and 1591.

From Ålsø, you now drive to (6km) **Grenå** (14,000 inhab.; Tourist Information: Torvet 1), which to most people is just a ferry port with regular sailings to Hundested on Sjælland, and to the Swedish ports of Varberg, Hälsingborg and Halmstad. The ferry to the small island of Anholt also leaves from here.

A market town with a charter probably from c 1300, it has a long history behind it, and excavations have shown that it was built on the site of a Stone Age settlement. In the Middle Ages it occupied an important position as the river provided access to the then 20km-long inland lake of Kolindsund to the SW.

After a period of stagnation and decay, Grenå experienced growth in the 19C with the establishment of a new harbour. Later in the century, the railway came to Grenå, then better roads, and in 1934 a regular ferry service was established to Hundested. Grenå has since attracted a good deal of industry, particularly the chemical industry and textiles. And as in most Danish coastal towns there is a thriving fishing industry. The present harbour was opened in 1958.

Grenå suffered a disastrous fire in 1649, which destroyed many of the old buildings, not least the church on the main square, Torvet. It was subsequently rebuilt, but there is little left of the original structure. Much of the furniture dates from the period of rebuilding, including the carved pulpit from 1650. There used to be another church in Grenå, to the NW of the town, but this fell into disuse in the 16C and was then demolished. The foundations were rediscovered in 1893 and there is now public access to them from Tjørnebakken. Close by is the restored 19C windmill on Baunhøj, the highest point in the town.

Of older buildings in Grenå, one of the largest and most beautiful, an early 18C galleried merchant's house in Søndergade, has been turned into the Djursland Museum. It contains extensive collections of local antiquities, coins, weapons, textiles and post-17C pottery. There are exhibits dating back to c 10,000 BC, and a reconstructed grave from the 1C AD. On Wednesdays in the summer there are demonstrations of the various trades represented in the museum. In this same building you will find the *Danish Fisheries Museum*, with exhibits illustrating the history and development of the fishing industry, including models of fishing vessels (both museums open summer; limited opening winter).—In *Lillegade* there are two other delightful preserved half-timbered houses, both from the mid 18C; one of them, known as *Aftenstjernen* (The Evening Star) is now a café. There are other older houses in *Storegade*.

In 1988 Grenå opened its new yachting harbour, situated between the commercial harbour and the beach.

Anglers will find the canals leading to and across Kolindsund ideal for their sport. Licences are obtainable at the Tourist Information Office in Grenå.

From Grenå harbour there is a short and easy 2hr 15min sail by ferry to Hundested on Sjælland.

Hundested (7600 inhab.; Tourist Information: Nørregade 22) has a history going back to only c 1800, and not until c 1860 was the first attempt made to develop it as a fishing port. By 1886 the harbour was opened, and in 1916 the railway was taken there, enabling the establishment of the Hundested–Grenå ferry route.

There is a memorial in the town to Valdemar Poulsen, the inventor of wireless telegraphy. Art exhibitions are held in the tower of the town hall.—The bathing beaches nearby, both to the N towards the high cliffs near *Spodsbjerg* lighthouse, and the S towards *Lynæs* are splendid.

Spodsbjerg was for many years the home of the polar explorer Knud Rasmussen, and the thatched house in which he lived when not undertaking expeditions is now a *museum commemorating him.

From Hundested there are two good routes to Frederikssund. The main, though longer route (31km) is detailed first; for the alternative route (21km), see below.

MAIN ROUTE FROM HUNDESTED TO FREDERIKSSUND (total distance 31km). You leave Hundested on the A16 which will take you straight to (13km) **Frederiksværk** (11,800 inhab.; Tourist Information: Gjethus-gade 5).

Frederiksværk received its name in 1759, and is Denmark's oldest industrial town, founded in the early 18C by Frederik IV. It became the site of a major ordnance works and the place in which explosives were once manufactured for the armed forces, and, in modern times, a centre for the metal industry. It received a charter in 1907, and grew to its present size as a result of the building of the railway, first to Hillerød (Rte 6) and then to Hundested (see above). The advent of the railways also opened up the tourist industry which benefited from the unusually beautiful countryside in the N part of Sjælland.

There are few old buildings in Frederiksværk, though the pleasing *Hotel Frederiksværk* on the market square dates from c 1800. On the other hand the canal between the Roskilde Fjord and the Arresø lake (the biggest lake in Denmark), around which the town was originally built, is still there, providing stretches of great charm.

A fine bronze statue by Axel Poulsen of a foundry worker stands on the market square, commemorating the principal occupation of the town.—On the square, too, close to the canal, is the *Frederiksværk Bymuseum* (Frederiksværk Civic Museum) (open mid-Jun to mid-Aug; limited opening winter), housed in two half-timbered houses from c 1800. It contains archaeological and other exhibits from the area, especially a collection illustrating the industrial history of the town. The open air *Krudtværksmuseum* (Gunpowder Works Museum) (open Apr–Sept) is also situated by the canal in the middle of the town. The old ordnance foundry, 'Gjethuset', is now an art gallery. Alongside its industrial significance, Frederiksværk has indeed managed to preserve a good deal of charm.

E of Frederiksværk is the *Avderød* peninsula jutting out into the Arresø lake, its idyllic surroundings now a favourite holiday spot. This peninsula was formerly the site of *Dronningholm Kongeborg* (Dronningholm Royal Castle). This, once one of the largest of Danish medieval castles, was said to have been built by Valdemar II for Queen Dagmar. Ruins are all that now remain, but they have been restored as far as possible—and they provide a wonderful view across the Arresø lake. Relics from the castle are now exhibited in Frederiksværk Civic Museum.

Immediately E of Frederiksværk, reached by a path along the canal, stands the neo-classical mansion of *Arresødal*, built in 1782 by Johan Frederik Classen, who was responsible for much of the early development of Frederiksværk; it is now a conference centre. Classen lies in a bombastic sarcophagus by Wiedewelt in the 19C church at *Vinderød*, 1km N of Frederiksværk.

The Frederiksværk area is dotted with summer cottages, of which there are said to be some 6000, and the coast has ample facilities for bathing and sailing. If you take the 205 N from Frederiksværk you come to one of the most varied and beautiful areas of North Sjælland, *Tisvilde Hegn*, an area planted with trees to combat sand drift in the 17C, and now a place of wooded charm. It borders one of the longest stretches of beach in Sjælland, extending 12km from Liseleje in the S to Rågeleje in the N.

Leaving Frederiksværk S on the A16 you arrive at (4km) *Kregme*. Here, standing on high ground, the quite impressive Romanesque church can be seen from afar, and the view from it, across the lake on one side and the Roskilde Fjord on the other, is magnificent.

You now continue your route on the 211 S, until at 5km you come to a minor road leading E to Skævinge (6km). **Skævinge Church** is the outstanding church in this area. It is again frescoes which are the main feature, this time a quite unusual post-Reformation series covering the walls from floor to ceiling. The motifs include David and Goliath, but pride of place goes to a huge painting of Holger Danske, Holger the Dane, the legendary heroic figure said to be sleeping beneath Kronborg Castle (Rte 5), ready to return to help Denmark in its hour of need. Holger Danske, in 16C dress, is seen confronting his enemy the Sultan Bruher, and both are armed to the teeth. The frescoes are not the only things of interest: there are fine examples of 17C workmanship in the bench ends and pulpit, while the altarpiece portraying Doubting Thomas is by the important 19C artist C.W. Eckersberg.

From Skævinge you return to the 211 through the villages of Lille Havelse and Store Havelse and drive S to (8km) Frederikssund (see below).

ALTERNATIVE ROUTE FROM HUNDESTED TO FREDERIKSSUND—VIA JÆGERSPRIS (total distance 21km). Leave Hundested on the A16 and at (32km) Amager Ruse turn right to (2km) *Sølager*, where you take the ferry (5 mins) to Kulhuse. You are now in *Horns Herred*, a beautiful, idyllic peninsula littered with archaeological remains, and now a much favoured holiday area. As you drive S on the 207 on your left is the *Nordskov* forest containing oak trees said to be 1000 years old. From Kulhuse it is a mere 10km to the splendid palace of **·Jægerspris**, and the 207 goes right past it.

The history of the palace probably goes back to the 11C, though the first direct reference to it is from 1318, when King Erik Menved's four-month-old son was killed there in an accident. Valdemar IV bought it; Queen Margrethe I spent time there, and it has been in the ownership of many Danish queens. It was given to Crown Prince Frederik (later King Frederik V) on his marriage to the English Princess Louise in 1743. However, the most famous of the ladies associated with it is the morganatic wife of Frederik VII, Countess Danner. Countess Danner, a commoner born Louise Rasmussen, was never accepted in royal circles, and the couple spent a great deal of their time here. The Countess is at her own wish buried in an open burial mound in the grounds. Frederik VII left the palace to her, and in 1873 she established it as 'King Frederik VII's Foundation for Helpless and Deserted Young Ladies, More Especially Those of the Humble Classes', much in the style of the English Dr Barnardo's Homes.

The main wing of the palace, the pink baroque 17C S wing with 18C extensions, is in two storeys, with 12 windows in each floor and towers with onion-shaped steeples midway on each side of the main entrance. The oldest part of the palace, the N wing incorporating the late medieval house known as Abrahamstrup and a substantial heptagonal tower containing a winding staircase, built by Christian IV, can be seen in the background. While the S wing overlooks the main courtyard, in the centre of which there is a life-sized bronze statue of a stag by Thorvaldsen's pupil Adelgunde Vogt, the N wing looks out on a delightful green. There is an 18C extension to the N wing, while Christian VI had an E wing built in the 1730s in order to join the otherwise separate N and S wings. The royal chambers were then installed in this newly built section.

A considerable part of the palace is now open to the public (Apr–Oct) for conducted tours each hour. In the S wing a number of rooms, including the king's study, are still furnished as they were in the days of Frederik VII and Countess Danner. Other rooms display archaeological treasures found in the area by Frederik VII who was keen to examine the prehistoric sites there.—The park is open throughout the year, and is itself of interest, containing not only the open burial mound in which Countess Danner's sarcophagus can be seen, but also 54 statues by Wiedewelt commemorating important Danish figures from early times to the 19C.

Before continuing to Frederikssund, you should drive S on a minor road to *Dråby* (2km) to visit the Romanesque church in which there is a splendid series of frescoes from the 15C Isefjord Master's workshop, including biblical motifs and scenes from the life of St. Lawrence.

From Jægerspris it is only 6km to **Frederikssund** (14,000 inhab.; Tourist Information: Østergade 3), which is reached by the Crown Prince Frederik Bridge from 1935. Near the W end of the bridge there is a local museum (*Egnsmuseum*) in an architecturally interesting old ferryman's house.

Frederikssund grew up in the 17C around the ferry connection across the narrow strip of the Roskilde Fjord, linking the E side, North Sjælland, with the W, Horns Herred (County), and was granted a charter in 1809. It is now a centre for food manufacturing, in particular for the soft drinks industry. Its proximity to Copenhagen was underlined in 1989 when the Copenhagen suburban railways, the 'S' trains, were extended as far as Frederikssund.

The town is famous today for two things. It has come to be known as the 'Viking Town', and every summer at the end of June and beginning of July plays with Viking themes are performed on an open air stage on the area called *Kalvø* where the river enters the fjord. This former islet, like the entire area here, does indeed have Viking associations; it is just S of a Viking settlement and was the site of a meeting in 1157 to decide on the succession to the throne.

The other, very different, cultural attraction in Frederikssund is the **J.F. Willumsen Museum**. Willumsen, one of the most important 20C Danish artists, is most famous as a Symbolist painter and sculptor, though he was also a ceramic and graphic artist. Just before his death he presented Frederikssund with all those works of his which were in his possession, on condition that the town built a museum suitable for them. The resultant museum was opened in 1957, but Willumsen, who died in the South of France, where he had lived for many years, never saw it.

EXCURSION FROM FREDERIKSSUND TO HORNS HERRED (total distance 33km). This trip takes you through the middle part of Horns Herred, visiting churches, mansions, a bird sanctuary and a doll museum.

From Frederikssund you cross the strait by the bridge and drive SW on the A53 to (10km) *Krogstrup*. There is a Romanesque pilgrims' church here. The carved altarpiece is from 1633 and the late Renaissance pulpit from 1625.

Continue 2km W to the small mansion of *Svanholm*, now a collective farm run on ecological principles, and from here a long avenue leads S to (4km) Skibby.

Despite an uninteresting exterior, Skibby *church is special and rightly famous, not only for its frescoes (which are themselves very splendid), but because it was here that in 1650 a manuscript now known as the Skibby Chronicle was discovered bricked in behind the altar. Written in Latin, it is a history of Denmark from 1046 to 1534, with the main emphasis on the period immediately before the Reformation. Intensely pro-Catholic, this is clearly the work of the great Catholic spokesman of the time, the Carmelite monk from Helsingør, Paul Helgesen. How the manuscript came to be hidden in Skibby church is not known, but the fact that it finishes in the midst of a sentence has given rise to much speculation.

Meanwhile, this is the biggest church in the county, the Romanesque apse, chancel and nave with five mighty pillars dating back to the early 12C. Many of the Romanesque features have survived. A series of outstandingly good frescoes dating back to 1175–1200 was discovered in the apse in 1855. The central feature is a portrait of Christ in Majesty. Restoration work began in 1858, the first (and perhaps rather heavy-handed) restoration of Danish Romanesque frescoes ever. Another series from c 1350 is in the vaulting in the chancel.

You now take a minor road E to (2km) *Selsø* lake. It is thought that—as late as the end of the 17C—this was not a lake but an inlet on the Roskilde Fjord. Now it forms an important bird sanctuary, the home of large numbers of water birds both native and migratory. The road will take you around the lake, gradually turning N.

You will then come to (2km) *Selsø Church* and, 300m further away, **Selsø House**. Standing in an isolated position, the church was originally Romanesque, with a tall apse filling three quarters of a circle, a very short chancel and a broad and lofty nave. The tower and porch are Gothic. Excavations have shown that there was originally a round church on this site. Selsø House has a history going far back, and the estate was probably established by Bishop Absalon in the 1170s. There was certainly a mansion here in 1288, and the great well in the courtyard, the biggest medieval well in the country, is probably from that time. The present house is over 400 years old, though it was partly redesigned in 1734, when it lost its Renaissance character and received its present baroque façade.

The interior is largely unchanged from the 18C, and in particular there is a fine great hall, with 4m-high marbled panels and an exquisite stucco ceiling; the enormous mirrors have been compared with those in Versailles. Splendid French tapestries can be seen in some of the other rooms. The rather more modest servants' rooms are also still in existence. Ironically, much of this has been preserved because the house has not been lived in for over a century. Since 1973, however, restoration work has been carried out, and most of the house is now open to the public, including the vaulted cellar from 1565. There are exhibitions of old dresses, weapons and an enormous number of toy soldiers and warship models, while concerts of classical music are regular held in the great hall (open May–mid-Jun weekends; mid-Jun–mid-Aug daily; mid-Aug–end Sep weekends).—From the beach of the small Østskov woods, 3km E of Selsø, you will catch sight of the island of *Eskilsø*, where there are the remains of an Augustinian monastery. There is little left of it, and there is no regular connection to the island, but it is nevertheless of historical interest, in that according to an early manuscript the monks of Eskilsø danced the medieval chain dances at an annual festival there in 1165—one of the earliest references to this dance which was widespread throughout Scandinavia in the Middle Ages and beyond, and which is still danced in the Faroe Islands.

Leave Selsø House to the NE, where a minor road leads to (2km) *Østby*, with an art and handicraft centre housed in a former co-operative dairy. Another 3km N will bring you to *Skuldelev*. It was in the fjord E of Skuldelev that the Viking ships now exhibited in Roskilde (Rte 2) were found and excavated between 1957 and 1962. Skuldelev is also the site of an important medieval sacred well, known as St. Olaf's well, which still flows.—An attraction of a quite different kind is the dolls' museum, *Skuldelev Dukkemuseum*, containing upwards of 250 dolls, many from the 19C; there are also old dolls' prams and a good collection of tin soldiers (open summer).

Now stay on the minor road going N, and you will come to (4km) *Gerlev*, where in the Gerlev Park there is an extensive rose park containing 3000 old-fashioned pre-19C scented roses in addition to 2500 modern varieties. Here, too, there is *Den danske Træsamling*, a plantation containing all the trees native to Denmark. From Gerlev it is only a further 4km back to Frederikssund.

From Frederikssund you take the 207/E53 E to (7km) *Slangerup*, a very old town, once standing on the important road from Helsingør to Roskilde. King Erik Ejegod was born here, and in 1095 he had a church built here. It was the site, too, of the first convent in Denmark, established by Valdemar I, belonging to the Cistercian order.

Like other predominently ecclesiastical centres, Slangerup found its role diminished after the Reformation. At the same time its importance on the Helsingør–Roskilde route also decreased. Today nothing remains of the convent, and only the tower on the present church is left of the original parish church from 1411. On the other hand, this large and dignified early Renaissance building from 1588, Gothic rather than Renaissance in style, is one of the few large-scale churches of its day, clearly intended for a future which Slangerup never achieved. A memorial to King Erik Ejegod stands outside the church.

Close by there is another memorial, to Bishop Thomas Kingo, who was born here and returned as pastor from 1668 to 1677. Kingo, who later became Bishop of Odense, was one of the greatest of Danish poets, the outstanding baroque hymn-writer whose best work has surely seldom been surpassed by any writer of hymns in any language.

A more modern era is reflected in the new *Aircraft Museum*.

Now go S now on the A6 to (2km) *Jørlunde*, where there is another very old church, early Romanesque, probably built in the 12C by the Hvide family, the most powerful of the great medieval noble families, to which Bishop Absalon himself belonged. The interior has been radically restored. There are fine Romanesque frescoes of scenes from the life of Christ, dating from 1175–1200, in the chancel and nave. The large-scale gilded altar is from 1613.

Continue through (3km) *Ølstykke* and join the 211 after a further 2km. Turn left here to (3km) *Stenløse*. Here, too, there is a Romanesque church with Gothic transept and porch. The auricular altarpiece from 1663 is the work of Lorentz Jørgensen.

Veksø, 3km further along the 211, has the remains of a Romanesque church, though it suffered from 19C rebuilding which removed the Romanesque nave and replaced the original apse with a new one. There are nevertheless Romanesque features still to be seen together with a magnificent Renaissance pulpit and Renaissance carved bench ends.—Veksø can also boast a collection of sculptures by well-known sculptors in *Veksølund* in Kirkestræde. This is the largest gallery for modern sculpture in Denmark, some housed indoors, some on display in the extensive gardens (open Jun–Sept).

From Veksø the 211 will take you straight to (22km) **Copenhagen** (Rtes 3,4).

The area you are moving into now may seem just as uninteresting as any built-up area close to a city, but the ancient villages are also here with their beautiful churches. If you are interested in historical churches, here are three more which ought to be visited.

The first is quite close to the 211, on the left, in (5km) *Måløv*. The Roskilde Fjord once stretched as far as this, and there was a heathen temple here. Sven Estridsen then built his first church in the 11C on the site of the temple. It was dedicated to St. Ib, and the present building consists of Romanesque chancel and nave, with Gothic tower and porch. Many of the original features—rounded windows and doors—are still there, while the round chancel arch has been reconstructed to maintain the aspect of a church of great character. There are numerous frescoes, some from the early 13C on the chancel wall, representing the Virgin, a bishop saint, Christ in Majesty, David and Solomon, and others, all of high artistic quality. Other frescoes on the side walls date from c 1450 and are the work of the Isefjord Master. The pulpit and canopy are from c 1600.—St. Ib's Spring is nearby.

Now cross the 211 and drive through Smørumnedre to (3km) *Smørumovre*. Again the church is Romanesque with a Gothic tower and extension to the nave. There are two porches, one late Romanesque, the other Gothic. Of the original Romanesque windows, only one is still discernible. However, there are again some fine frescoes, from c 1500, illustrating the Day of Judgement, the Last Supper and the Passion, but these are offset by a series of humorous, not to say bawdy, scenes, thought possibly to be illustrating light entertainment in the pauses in medieval mystery plays.

Your next stop is at (3km) *Ledøje* which you reach by taking the road from Smørumovre church towards Ballerup, turning right after 1km. The medieval *church in Ledøje is unique in Denmark, though of a type not unknown in Central Europe. Built c 1225, it is on two floors and in effect contains two churches, the upper one being for the owner of a former manor house, the lower for the ordinary people. Both the chancel and the nave on both levels are almost square, with columns on the lower floor to support the upper one. There are frescoes in both churches—but they are all from the 19C.

From Ledøje you now return to the 211 via *Ballerup* (where there is yet another church full of frescoes), and **Copenhagen** (Rtes 3, 4) is then only 15km away.

25 Bornholm

Round Trip of Bornholm (total distance 98km). 159 from **Rønne** to (10km) *Hasle.*—(13km) **Allinge/Sandvig.**—158 to (16km) **Gudhjem.**—(16km) **Svaneke.**—Unclassified roads to (13km) *Neksø.*—A38 to (14km) *Åkirkeby.*—(16km) **Rønne.**

Bornholm, with a total area of only 600 sq km and far from the other Danish islands, 180km out in the Baltic, is the archetypal holiday island. It offers a variety of scenery, woodland, rocky coastlines, idyllic small towns, magnificent beaches (some would say the best in Europe), yachting and swimming opportunities, archaeological remains and a vast ruined fortress.

The island is known to have been inhabited by 3000 BC, and there are many signs of prehistoric settlement. Seven hundred Bronze Age burial mounds are known, and of these about a third still exist. Those which have been excavated have often yielded valuable material. Other grave finds are from the Iron Age, AD 400–800, which is an age that has not left many traces elsewhere in Denmark. There is also a large number of runic stones, mainly—unusually—from the early Middle Ages (1000–1100), and most of the inscriptions reflect early Christianity.
The first historical reference to Bornholm is from c 890 when an Anglo-Saxon skipper, Wulfstan, visited it and refered to it in his account as Burgundaland. According to Wulfstan's account—written for Alfred the Great—Bornholm had its own king at this time, but it subsequently came under Danish rule. Lying close to the North European mainland, it was often the object of attack by the Wends, and for this reason some of the churches were fortified and suitable for defence.
Situated close to the Swedish mainland, Bornholm was also the object of attentions from that direction, and it was for c 200 years in the hands of the Archbishops of Lund, who ran it as their private dominion giving charters to the market towns, and applying their own laws. For a time, Bornholm was also tasted the rule of Lübeck. Like the rest of Denmark, it was occupied by Nazi forces in 1940, and was the only part of Denmark to be liberated by Soviet troops in May 1945. The principal town, Rønne, suffered heavily from the preceding bombardment.
Bornholm, with its rugged, impressive scenery, is a rocky island, totally different from any other part of Denmark. Its former isolation from metropolitan Denmark has led to a fierce sense of local pride, many different traditions, and even an accent distinct from what you will hear elsewhere in the country.

Bornholm is a 7–8hr sail from Copenhagen. The trip to **Rønne** is by comfortable modern ferries with excellent facilities. Alternatively, there is an overland route, through Sweden, with a ferry from Ystad to Rønne. And if you travel without a car, it is now possible to go to Rønne by hydrofoil from Copenhagen in under 3hrs. By air the flight lasts less than an hour.

Rønne (15,000 inhab.; Tourist Information: Havnen), which received its charter in 1584, is the biggest town on Bornholm and the home of almost a third of the total population. Most of the town consists of single-family houses, many of them half-timbered. There are rows and rows of these charming and well-tended early 19C houses, often in idyllic cobbled streets showing few signs of modern times.

A tour of the town would naturally start at the church which though pleasing to the eye is not of particular architectural interest, having largely been rebuilt in 1915–18. In Østergade, immediately E of the church, you will find *Karnapgården*, the only remaining of several former large houses with bay windows. Turning into Søndergade, you cannot miss *Hovedvagten*, from 1743–44, with its overhanging roof supported on columns and its curious rounded gable. Søndergade 11 is another large half-timbered house with an unusual tower-like construction intended to allow the inhabitants to watch the arrival of ships.

Now go N along Søndergade, across Lille Torv and Store Torv (the main shopping area) along Store Torvegade, where the splendid Exsteens Gård stands, to Storegade with the old Sheriff's Residence from c 1800. Nearby is the Commander's Residence (Kommandantboligen) from 1846, a long building with a large dormer. Two streets S is Laksegade, where the fine *Erichsenske Gård* (No. 7) is now part of the *Bornholm Museum* (see below). A building of a completely different kind is the old citadel, *Kastellet*, from c 1650, looking for all the world like one of the round churches—and with walls 3.5m thick. Reached via Strandpromenaden, it stands to the S of the town and is now a *museum illustrating the defence of Bornholm over the centuries (open May–Oct).

Bornholms Museum (open summer; limited opening winter), in Sankt Mortensgade, is a regional museum specialising in Bornholm's prehistory and history. Among its prize possessions is part of a large find of Roman gold and silver coins discovered near *Vestermarie* together with another find of 8C gold pieces all stamped with human figures. Altogether some 2000 of these figures have been found on Bornholm. In addition to these early exhibits there is a splendid collection of paintings by Bornholm artists. Just as Skagen (Rte 19) attracted a group of outstanding artists at the end of the 19C, so, somewhat later, did Bornholm, and their products are well represented here.—The nearby *Brødrene Langes Mindestuer* contains re-creations of old interiors. *Erichsens Gård* likewise re-creates bygone interiors as well as exhibiting memorabilia connected with the 19C poet Holger Drachmann and his first wife, who was herself an Erichsen (open May–Sept).

The harbour in Rønne is unusually large for a town of this size, reflecting, perhaps, the variety of traffic to this outlying island. There is, naturally, a marina, and there are first-rate sheltered beaches of white sand, offering good bathing facilities, both to the N and S.

From Rønne you take the 159 N towards (10km) Hasle, turning right at 5km to look at *Nyker* (2km), where you will find *Nykirke*, one of the four round churches for which Bornholm is famous.

Nykirke was built of unhewn boulders in 1150, though the steep roof is probably 16C. It is the smallest of the four round churches, and it is on two floors only, the third, fortified floor never having been completed. Some primitive 14C frescoes can be seen on the walls and the central column, and two runestones stand in the porch. There is a free-standing half-timbered belfry in the churchyard, to which access is gained through a gateway of a type commonly found in Bornholm farms.

Return to the 159 and continue to (5km) *Hasle* (1800 inhab.; Tourist Information: Grønnegade 3), an idyllic little town. Do not be put off by the simplicity of the church here: it contains an *altarpiece of rare beauty.

There are various legends as to how this altarpiece came to be here—the favourite being that it was a thanks offering from a sailor saved from shipwreck—but it is at least certain that it was made in a Lübeck workshop around 1510. The central panel is a crucifixion group, and the side panels portray four scenes from the Passion. The lifelike figures are carved with great skill, and the carved foliage is intricate and beautiful.

Apart from this, Hasle has the charm of its half-timbered houses. On Strandgade there are the relics of a past age in the herring smoke-houses. Bornholm is famous for its smoked herrings, and the island is dotted with such smokehouses, many of which are no longer in use due to changing fishing patterns.

The 159 continues N towards *Allinge/Sandvig*, but you should turn off left after 5km on a minor road to visit *Jons Kapel* (1km). Despite its name, this is not a chapel, but a group of rocks on the coast, the home of rare rock plants. It is reached by a wooded path and 108 steps. Legend has it that a monk by the name of Jon lived here and preached to the local heathen population. Whatever the truth, this is a remarkable sight.

A further 7km sees you in *Allinge/Sandvig*, two towns which have now more or less merged into one (Tourist Information: Kirkegade 6, Allinge). There are many hotels here, for the whole area provides a great variety of attractions: sea, beaches, yachting, countryside walking, archaeological remains.—Then there is a group of rock carvings, the *Madsebakke Helleristninger*, the best of such groups on Bornholm, comprising outlines of ships, footmarks, Sun symbols and a series of hollow circles.—And there is the *Moseløkken* quarry. Quarrying has been a major industry on Bornholm, but few quarries now remain. At Moseløkken there is in addition to a working quarry a museum, *Moseløkken Stenbrudsudstilling*, illustrating the traditional methods used for quarrying and treating Bornholm granite (open May–Sept).

However, the outstanding feature is inevitably the castle of ***Hammershus** (open all year), possibly the biggest ruined fortress in North Europe, standing on a 74m-high cliff on the west coast. It can be approached either by turning left off the 159 3km before you reach Allinge, or by a minor road from Sandvig, skirting the northernmost point of Bornholm, Hammeren, and driving past the Hammersø Lake. There are ample parking facilities.

Little is known of the origins of Hammershus, but building is believed to have been started c 1255 as a result of the struggles between the Danish King and the Archbishops of Lund. The first direct mention is in connection with the murder of King Erik Glipping in 1286, when the outlawed assassins sought refuge here. Christian II ousted the Archbishop in 1522. Hammershus was leased to the Lübeckers, who extended and strengthened it before leaving Bornholm in 1576. However, strong as the fortress was, it was no longer sufficient to withstand modern artillery, and in 1645 it was taken by the Swedish Admiral Wrangel during the Torstenson War; the admiral only had four cannon at his disposal. It was later used as a state prison, and Christian IV's daughter Leonora Christina was held here for a year. In 1743 Hammershus ceased to be used as a garrison, and from that time it fell into disrepair until it was listed as a national monument in 1822.

The Mantle Tower and courtyard are the oldest parts surviving, standing high above the rest. There were five floors, the top one added by the Lübeckers. It was here that Leonora Christina was imprisoned. The entire complex has been surrounded by a great ring wall probably from the same period. Parts of it still stand, the section to the W being over 9m high. On the E side a length remains near the corner tower, Blommetårnet, which is the best preserved of all the buildings in the castle. The bridge giving access to the castle from the E is the only such bridge to have survived in Denmark, though the drawbridge itself has disappeared.

From Allinge you can take a ferry to the island of Christians (see below).

Leave Allinge on the coastal road, 158, SE to (5km) *Tejn*. This stretch of the coast was the first in N Bornholm to be favoured by tourists for its sandy coves and extensive beaches. At Tejn, the biggest fishing village on Bornholm (post mill from 1859), you turn right and take the steep road leading to (4km) *Olsker* to visit the tallest of the round churches, 112m above sea level, with panoramic views across the N coast of the island.

Originally dedicated to St. Olaf (hence the name), it was built on three floors about 1150, and it shows obvious signs of having been constructed for defence, with nine openings clearly intended for dropping boulders on attackers. There are signs, too, of a wooden watchman's gallery having been suspended outside the church at the top. The nave is, of course, round, but there is a small rectangular chancel plus apse, both of them original. The porch is a later addition, but its date is not known. The interior is vaulted, though there are indications of an original flat roof, and there is a half-dome above the apse.

Continue E now on the 158. After 2km you come to *Stammershalle*, where there is a group of Stone Age graves and three standing stones. A further 4km brings you to *Helligdomsklipperne* (Sanctuary Cliffs), a group of rocks on the coast, formerly a place of pilgrimage thanks to the healing qualities of the water from the sacred spring, the *Hellig-domskilde*, nearby. There is one tall obelisk-like rock and several deep caves on this spot.

5km further on lies **Gudhjem** (850 inhab.; Tourist Information: Ejnar Mikkelsensvej 28), a small and particularly picturesque fishing village on rising ground sloping up from the coast, with steep streets and the usual well-kept half-timbered houses. A centre for Baltic trade in prehistoric times, Gudhjem is now a busy herring port, and there is usually plenty to see in the harbour. Herring—known simply as Born-holmers—are prepared for smoking in the traditional manner. They are, of course, on sale straight from the smokehouses.

Gudhjem Museum, with a collection of local art, is housed in the old railway station, which is now scheduled (open May–Sept). The church in Gudhjem is 19C, but just behind it you will find the ruins of the 13C St. Anna's chapel, with frescoes preserved on the S wall.—The import-ant painter of the Bornholm School, Olaf Høst (1884–1966), is buried in the churchyard here.

FERRY-EXCURSION FROM GUDHJEM TO CHRISTIANSØ. Gudhjem is the principal port with regular sailings to the tiny *Ertholme* islands, 17km NE of Bornholm, two of which, **Christiansø** and *Frederiksø* are inhabited, while the third, *Græsholm*, is a bird sanctuary.
    Christiansø was fortified by Christian V, and the stone-lined streets still reflect their military past. The island played a role during the Napoleonic Wars, when it was used as a base for attacks on British ships in the area. The remains of the fortress, including the tower, can still be seen. Frederiksø, on the other hand, was once used as a state prison; here, too, the fortified tower still stands. Apart from their tourist attraction, the islands are a favourite spot for artists. There are no cars on them, and the total population is c 130. A museum, the *Christiansø Museum*, is housed in the small tower, Lille Tårn, in the Frederiksø fortress, and contains a good collection illustrating the way of life on the islands, with emphasis on its military past on the one hand and its fishing on the other (open May–Sept).

There are two equally interesting routes from Gudhjem to **Svaneke**:

the direct coastal route (16km) is described first; for the alternative route (20km) see below.

COASTAL ROUTE FROM GUDHJEM TO SVANEKE (total distance 16km). 1km S of Gudhjem on the 158, in an area much favoured by artists, comes *Melsted*, another tiny fishing village. Here, housed in the 17C half-timbered *Melstedgård* farm, you will find an agricultural museum illustrating the traditional agricultural methods of the island, with implements and interiors from the 19C (open mid-May to Oct).

3km further S comes a rock formation known as Himmerigsport (The Gate to Heaven), and a further 3km sees the desolate reef, *Randkløve Skær*, 50m long, with 16m-deep fissures. 4km further on lies the fishing village of *Bølshavn*. Before arriving at (3km) *Listed*, you will pass a standing stone of granite known as *Helligkvinde* (Holy Woman), just beside a ship burial. According to legend the standing stone represents a woman and the ship burial her nine children who were turned to stone when her husband tried to murder them. It used to be the custom to salute the Holy Woman on passing her. You are now 2km from Svaneke (see below).

ALTERNATIVE ROUTE FROM GUDHJEM TO SVANEKE—VIA ØSTERLARS AND ØSTERMARIE (total distance 20km). For this route you take a road S from *Gudhjem* to (5km) **Østerlars** to visit the biggest and best known of the round churches, like the others built about 1150.

In addition to an oval chancel and apse, the church consists of a round nave, three storeys high. The exterior looks different from that of the other churches thanks to some massive buttresses surrounding it, presumably from the 16C and 17C. Once more the walls clearly show that the church has been fortified. There are two porches, that on the N side a uniquely splendid piece of Romanesque work.

The 13m-wide interior is vaulted towards the hollow central pillar which stands on a series of six arcades. The font is beneath these arcades, and the walls of this central pillar are decorated with frescoes depicting the life of Christ, from 1350–1400. There is a free-standing belfry in the churchyard; three runestones at the porch.

A road SE will take you now to (6km) *Østermarie*. Here there is a very old church ruin standing next to the present neo-Romanesque church from 1891. One unusual feature of this old church is the parallel rows of barrel vaulting clearly seen in the extant E wall. There are four runestones in the church, and two Romanesque stone graves were found beside it in 1932.

From Østermarie the road goes E past *Louisenlund*, the largest group of standing stones on Bornholm, 51 in all, and the very popular and long established *Brændesgårdshaven* pleasure park, and then finally to (9km) Svaneke.

Svaneke (1100 inhab.; Tourist Information: Storegade 24) one of the smallest market towns in the country, with a charter going back to the 15C, has been a conservation area since 1967 and was in 1975 awarded a gold medal by the Council of Europe for efforts to preserve its historical character. The harbour, which cannot be used in bad weather, was blasted out of the rocks in the 19C. The town as a whole starts on level ground near the harbour, where the older and larger merchant houses are still situated, and then rises steeply in terraces on the slopes just inland. This has resulted in numerous stone steps leading to the higher parts of the town. The simple church, originally Gothic, was largely rebuilt in 1881. Two listed windmills, an old post mill and a later Dutch model, stand on a hill above the town.

The internationally known philologist and Classical scholar J.N. Madvig (1804–86) was born in Svaneke, and is commemorated in a small park in Storegade.

Svaneke is the third port from which you can take a ferry to Christiansø.

From Svaneke you follow the coastal road to (3km) Grisby, turning right there to (2km) *Ibskirke*, a church thought to date from the same period as the round churches. It consists of a Romanesque nave, chancel and apse largely as it was when built; particularly notable is the massive tower with *warehouse doors* opening out on the second and third floors, suggesting that it was used as a butter store in the Middle Ages, its thick walls acting as good insulation. The altarpiece (1846) is by Eckersberg, and there is a statue of the Virgin from c 1500 and a crucifix from c 1300.

Return to the 158 and drive to (7km) *Neksø* (4000 inhab.; Tourist Information: Aasen 4), the second largest town on Bornholm and known to have had a charter in 1451. It is cosily situated in a depression near the sea and sheltered by hills to the N and W. It was badly damaged in 1945 when Soviet ships bombarded it prior to the liberation, but careful restoration and rebuilding work has hidden this. As most other towns on Bornholm, Neksø is characterised by houses of modest proportions, many of them surrounded by dry-stone walls. Of larger houses mention must be made of the old sheriff's residence in Købmagergade. The modest church is late Gothic, but largely rebuilt in the 18C. The foundations of the tower are from the 16C, but the upper part, including the ridge turret, is from 1910.

The author Martin Andersen Nexø (1869–1954) spent six years of his childhood here, from 1877–83, and has described life here in his memoirs as well as, in fictitious form, in Book Two of his novel 'Pelle the Conqueror'.

2km NW of Neksø lies *Paradisbakkerne* (The Paradise Hills). Much of this wooded and hilly area is now protected as an area of outstanding natural beauty. One feature of the hills is the large number of erratic boulders, one of which, *Rokkestenen*, still can actually be rocked, despite its 30 tonnes. In these hills, too, you can find the remains of an old castle, Gamleborg. Clearly, this is an area for walking, and suitable paths are marked, one for a 1hr walk, one for 2hrs and one for 3hrs.

S of Neksø you will find wide flat beaches, a total contrast to the rocky shores of the N. This is a favourite holiday area with countless holiday cottages. At *Dueodde* (9km) is the southernmost point of Bornholm, characterised by sand drift, and with huge expanses of white sand and extensive dunes. The area is now protected, though there are both hotels and a camping ground there.

Your round trip of Bornholm now continues W along the A38. After 4km you reach *Bodilskirke*, called after the English St. Bottolph. As in Ibskirke church, the tower, broader than the nave, has been used as a store. Close by the church there is the large group of standing stones called *Gryet*.

10km further on you will be in Åkirkeby, passing at 5km a road leading S to *Pedersker* (5km), where there is a Romanesque church with the nave, chancel and apse largely as when built, except for window and door openings. The stubby tower is 16C and the porch a 19C addition.

Åkirkeby (2100 inhab.; Tourist Information: Jernbanegade 1) received its charter in 1346 from the Archbishop of Lund and in the Middle Ages was the most important town on the island. The regional council met there until 1776. Since then it has been overtaken by the coastal towns and is now little more than a large village.

Åkirkeby was also once the centre of Bornholm's ecclesiastical administration, and so it is not surprising that there should be a particularly impressive *church here. The oldest parts stem presumably from c 1150, and the tower, with a saddle roof, must have been completed c 1200. The thickness of its walls suggests that it was fortified. The fine late Romanesque porch is from the same time and is the oldest extant Romanesque porch on Bornholm. Note in particular the corbels with carved lions' heads at the top.

The altarpiece is from c 1600, and there is a late Gothic crucifix from c 1500. The Renaissance pulpit is from c 1610. Pride of place, however, goes to the magnificent late 12C Romanesque font of Gotland sandstone, decorated with eleven reliefs of scenes from the New Testament, each of which is explained by runic inscription. The foot of the font is decorated with intertwined plants and the heads of lions and rams. Two runestones stand in the porch.

EXCURSION FROM ÅKIRKEBY TO ALMINDINGEN. N of Åkirkeby lies *Almindingen* (The Common), a wooded area covering c 24 sq km and the third largest forest in Denmark, harking back to the days when all Bornholm was covered by trees. There are roads through this area, but to be savoured to the full it really requires that you walk. There are plenty of marked paths and recommended walks, and a map can be obtained from the Tourist Information offices.

Ekkodalen (Echo Valley) on the S edge contains rocks up to 20m above ground level, and other groups of rocks are also to be found in the forest. Near Ekkodalen there are the ruins of another castle called *Gummelborg* and close by, standing by the lovely *Borgesø* lake are the ruins of *Lilleborg* which despite its name is the second largest fortress on Bornholm. It dates from the 12C and was destroyed by fire. Just S of Lilleborg is the highest point in Bornholm, *Rytterknægten*, topped with a granite observation tower standing 184m above sea level, known as *Kongemindet*.

The A38 will now take you direct to (16km) Rønne, passing through *Nylars*, where you will find the fourth of the Bornholm round churches, dedicated to St. Nicholas. Three storeys high, it is the best preserved of them all, with the original defence installations still in place. Built before 1200, this church consists of a nave, oval chancel and apse, with a porch added in 1879. The vaulted nave is supported by a relatively slender column. The small NW window high in the barrel vaulting is the only Romanesque window in Bornholm preserved intact. There are frescoes from c 1250 depicting scenes from Genesis. Two runestones stand in the porch.

There is much more to be seen on Bornholm, smaller things too numerous to list. We suggest that you make good use of the tourist information offices if you are going to spend a holiday here.

INDEX

Æ, ø and å are positioned at the end of the alphabet. Note that å is sometimes written as aa, an old-fashioned form.

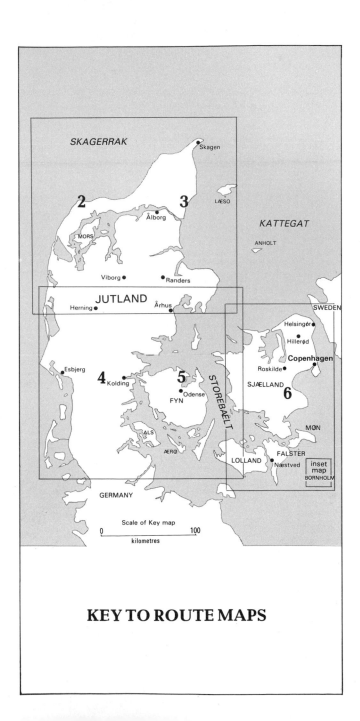

SKAGERRAK

Skagen

2　　**3**　LÆSØ

KATTEGAT

Ålborg

ANHOLT

MORS

Viborg ●　　● Randers

JUTLAND　Århus

Herning ●

SWEDEN

Helsingør ●

Hillerød ●

Copenhagen

Esbjerg ●

Roskilde ●

4 Kolding　**5**　SJÆLLAND

Odense　**6**

FYN

STOREBÆLT

ALS　　　　　MØN

ÆRØ

FALSTER

LOLLAND　Næstved　inset map

BORNHOLM

GERMANY

Scale of Key map

0　　　　　　　100

kilometres

KEY TO ROUTE MAPS

SKAGERRAK

Faroe Islands →

Blokhus

Hanstholm

Bulbjerg

Hjortdal

Lerup

Brovst

Svenstr

(19)

Klitmøller

(22)

Kirsten Kjaers Museum

Frøstrup

Tømmerby

Øsløs

Fjerritslev

(19)

(23)

Kokkedal

THY

Hillerslev

Nors

(19)

Aggersborg

Løgstør

Aggersund

Skarp Salling

Nørre Vorupør

Jannerup

Sjørring

Thisted

Hesselbjerg

Lendrup Strand

Ranum

(24)

Stenbjerg

Hundborg

(22)

Hanklit

Flade

Salgjerhøj

(18)

LIVØ

Vitskol Kloster

(23)

HIMMER

Villerslev

Skyum

MORS

Nykøbing

FUR

Nederby

Ertebølle

Strandby

Raevemosen

Borremose

År

(22)

Heltborg

Karby

(18)

Farsø

Vestervig

Hurup

Hvidbjerg

Glomstrup

Torum

Hvalpsund

Fovlum

Hessel

Gedsted

Ålestru

Thyborøn

(20)

Ydby

Grinderslevkloster

(18)

Jenle

Langerhuse

Limfjorden

Hvidbjerg

Spottrup

Lihme

Lem

Ørslev Kloster

Lynderupgard

(23)

Låstrup

Skals

Harboør

Heldum

Skive

Estvad

(18)

Hjarbæk Fjord

Ferring

Bøvbjerg Lighthouse

Lemvig

Oddesund

(22)

VENØ

Ejsing

Hjerl Hede

Den Gamle Landsby

Sevel

Fiskbæk

Viborg

(20)

Dybe

Rysensten

(20)

Bækmarksbro

Struer

Rydhave

(22)

Vinderup

Sahl

Stubberkloster

Sjørup

Daugbjerg

Mønsted

Finderup

Bøvling

Borbjerg

Hagebro

Kongenshus Mindepark

Hald

Lysgard

(18)

Nørre Vosborg

Vemb

Ulfborg Kirkeby

Holstebro

(20)

Alhede

Vium

Sjørslev

Kjellerup

Vederso

(20)

(21)

Avlum

Torning

JUTLAND (JYLLAND)

(23)

Vindersl

Silkeborg

Tim Kirkeby

Stadil Kirkeby

Hee

Tjørring

Herning

Julsø La

(15)

Hovvig

Kloster

Søby

Arnborg

(23)

Søndervig

Gammelsogn

Ringkøbing

(15)

Højmark

Sædding

Hanning

Bundsbæk Molle

Bryrup

Vo

Nørre Lyngvig

Hvide Sande

Dejbjerg

Ringobing

Havrvig

(15)

(21)

4

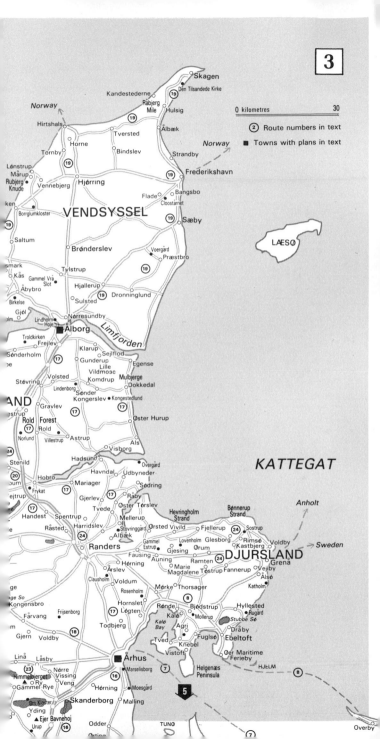

3

Skagen
Den Tilsandede Kirke
Kandestederne
Råbjerg
Mile
Hulsig

Norway

0 kilometres 30

② Route numbers in text
■ Towns with plans in text

Hirtshals
Tversted
Ålbæk
Tornby
Horne
Bindslev
Strandby
Norway
Lønstrup
Mårup
Frederikshavn
Rubjerg
Knude
Vennebjerg
Hjørring
Flade
Bangsbo
Cloostarnet
ken
Borrglumkloster
VENDSYSSEL
Sæby
Saltum
Brønderslev
Voergård
Præstbro
smark
Kås
Gammel Vrå
Slot
Tylstrup
Abybro
Hjallerup
Birkelse
Sulsted
Dronninglund
Gjøl
lm
Lindholm
Høje
Nørresundby
Troldkirken
■ Ålborg
Frejlev
Klarup
Sejlflod
Sønderholm
Gunderup
Egense
be
Lille
Vildmose
Komdrup
Støvring
Volsted
Mulbjerge
Lindenborg
Sønder
Dokkedal
Kongerslev • Kongestedlund
ND
Gravlev
estrup
Rold Forest
Øster Hurup
Rold ⑰
Rold
Astrup
Norlund
Villestrup
Als
Visborg
KATTEGAT
⑳ Stenild
Hadsund
Overgård
oum
Hobro
Havndal
Udbyneder
Anholt
ejtrup
Frykat
Mariager
Sødring
⑰ Handest
Spentrup
Gjerlev ⑰ Råby
Bønnerup
Strand
Hevringholm
Strand
→ *Sweden*
Tvede
Øster Torslev
e
Råsted
Harridslev
Mellerup
Ørsted Vivild
Fjellerup
⑳ Sostrup
Ol
Støvringgård
Glesborg
Rimsø
Kastbjerg
Voldby
DJURSLAND
Albæk
Gammel
Lovenholm
Ørum
Randers
Fausing
Estrup
Gjesing
⑳
Grena
ge
Hørning
Auning
Marie
Magdalene
Tøstrup Fannerup
Vejlby
ge Sø
Årslev
Clausholm
Voldum
Katholm
Kongensbro
Rosenholm
Mørke Thorsager
Fårvang
Frijsenborg
Hornslet
⑧
Hyllested
m
Todbjerg
Løgten
Rønde
Bjødstrup
Rugård
Gjern
Voldby
⑱
Kalø
Mollerup
Stubbe Sø
Lina
Låsby
Kalø
Bay
Agri
Dråby
⑳ Nørre
Tved
Fuglsø
Ebeltoft
Himmelbjerget
Vissing
Veng
Knebel
Øer Maritime
▲ Ry
■ Århus
Vistoft
Ferieby
HJELM
Gammel Rye
Marselisborg
Helgenæs
Peninsula
⑧
Yding
⑯
Hørning
Moesgård
▲ Ejer Bavnehøj
Skanderborg
Malling
5
Urup
⑯
Odder
TUNØ
Overby
Orting
⑦

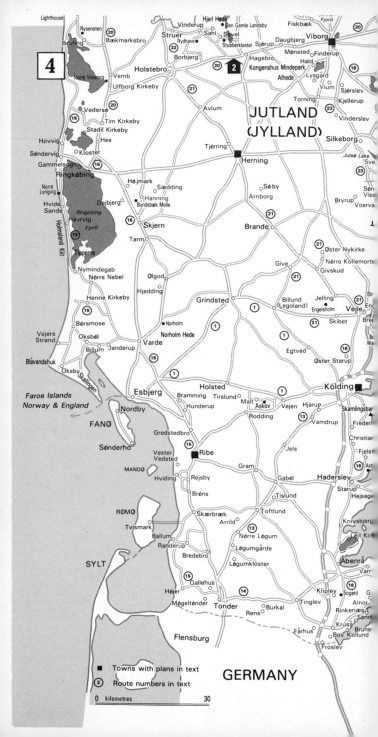

Towns with plans in text

② **Route numbers in text**

0   kilometres   30

GERMANY